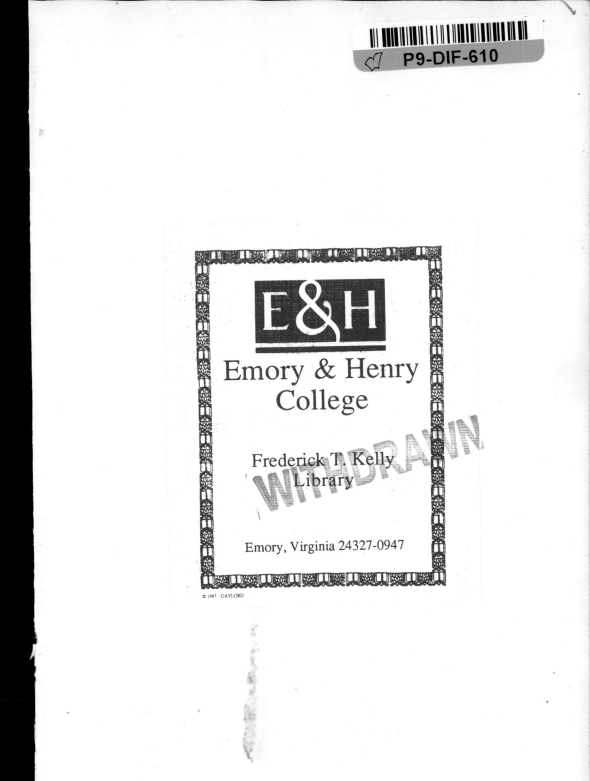

AMERICA'S WARS

and Military Excursions

AMERICA'S
WARS

and Military Excursions

★　　　★　　　★

EDWIN P. HOYT

McGraw-Hill Book Company

New York   St. Louis   San Francisco
Toronto   Hamburg   Mexico

1 2 3 4 5 6 7 8 9 D O C D O C 8 7

ISBN 0-07-030618-4

LIBRARY OF CONGRESS CATALOGING-IN-PUBLICATION DATA

Hoyt, Edwin P. (Edwin Palmer)
    America's wars and military excursions.
    1. United States—History, Military.   I. Title.
E181.H78   1987   973   86-27316
ISBN 0-07-030618-4

BOOK DESIGN BY PATRICE FODERO

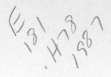
For My Wife

Contents

Introduction   ix

1. The Indians   1
2. The French   11
3. Rebellion   38
4. Revolution   55
5. War   68
6. Embarrassments of a New Nation   93
7. Troubles at Sea   101
8. Growing Pains   122
9. The War of 1812   135
10. Nice Little War   164
11. The Seminole War   172
12. Pirates, Yes; Indians, No   181
13. Westward Ho!   186
14. Beset North and South   191
15. The Mexican War   197
16. Assault on Japan   207
17. The Filibusters   219
18. The Ultimate National Tragedy   229

19. The End of the Trail   247
20. Coal and Colonies   260
21. Fomenting a Revolution   266
22. The Spanish-American War   277
23. "My Legation Is in Danger . . ."   291
24. Philippine Morass   297
25. Cuba Libre and Other Troubles   306
26. Bullets and Bananas   312
27. "The Pall of Negro Despotism"   318
28. Mexican Hat Dance   325
29. From the Mexican Border to Mobilization   330
30. The War in Europe   336
31. Forgotten Occupation   351
32. The Banana Wars   361
33. Trouble on the Yangtze   368
34. America's World War II Begins   378
35. Hitler First   383
36. The Invasion of Europe   389
37. Pacific Victory   400
38. Aftermath of War   409
39. The Berlin Blockade and What It Wrought   418
40. Aggression in Korea   424
41. Failure in Intelligence   435
42. The Long War   443
43. Vietnam Beginnings   448
44. Bay of Pigs   455
45. Wrong Time, Wrong Place, Wrong War   462
46. How to Win Every Battle and Lose a War   470
47. Reign of Terror   478
48. The Usual (Unusual) Crisis in Latin America   488
49. Space Ships and GI Shoes   496

Bibliography   502
Acknowledgments   507
Chapter Notes   509
Index   519

Introduction

This study of America's wars and military excursions is intended to give readers a sense of the continuity of the American military presence over four centuries. The book is proof of the old adage that wars and military excursions are extensions of political policy. For the most part wars represent a failure of politicians, whether it be by the Massachusetts Colony's refusal to treat with the Indians fairly, which was the beginning of the long period of Indian wars that did not end until the Wounded Knee massacre in 1890, or the concatenation of political errors that involved the United States in the war in Vietnam in the Eisenhower administration of the 1950s and then kept America bogged down for sixteen years.

Not all wars and military efforts could be so characterized, however. World War II in Europe was the direct result of Adolf Hitler's attempt to rule the Western world, and the West had no choice but to fight or be enslaved. In Asia and the Pacific, the war was the direct result of the Japanese militarists' aggressive designs on East Asia and the South Pacific. The only way that the United States could have prevented the attack on Pearl Harbor and the Philippines in 1941 would have been to become a co-conspirator with Japan in that nation's attempts to swallow up China. The claim has been made that President Franklin D. Roosevelt knew of the coming Japanese attack and concealed information from the army and the navy. This claim is not only specious, but it misses the whole point; when and where the Japanese attack was going to come was really immaterial. The important matter is that such an attack was inevitable after the United States cut off oil supplies to the Japanese. Japan, having no petroleum resources of her own, was dependent on the American and the Middle East oil fields, controlled largely by the Americans and the British. When these resources were cut off, Japan had only one recourse, to seize the oil fields in the Dutch East Indies and thus assure her tanks and ships a supply of fuel.

Sometimes America's wars were fought for noble purposes, sometimes for ignoble, sometimes for mixed reasons. An example of noble purpose is Abraham Lincoln's decision to court a war he knew would be inevitable by refusing to allow the Southern states to break up the American union in 1860. An example of ignoble purpose is the Mexican war, fought for territorial aggrandizement. An illustration of war fought for mixed purposes is the Spanish-American War: the vast majority of Americans believed they were fighting Spain to achieve independence for Cuba; the McKinley administration was fighting the war for territory. In the end McKinley did not get Cuba as expected, but did insist on taking over Guam, Puerto Rico, and the Philippine islands, which led the United States into a disastrous war against the Filipino people.

Sometimes, too, wars were begun for one purpose, which would be forgotten in the process, while the war would continue to be fought for quite another purpose. A prime example is the Korean War, which was never officially dignified by the United States government or the United Nations organization as a war, but was called a "police action." The term stems from the powers given (for the most part theoretically) to the UN to police the world. The Korean struggle began as a rueful American attempt to correct a political blunder; in 1950 Secretary of State Acheson announced in a major policy address that South Korea was not a part of the American zone of defense in the Pacific, and this led the North Koreans, with vigorous Soviet assent, to attack South Korea a few months later. The American response—reversing Secretary Acheson's announced stand and sending troops from Japan to try to stop the North Korean invasion of South Korea—was so widely acclaimed in the world that no difficulty was found in enlisting support from United Nations members, including the generally pacifist India, which sent a medical team to show its support. Under General Douglas MacArthur the American and other United Nations forces first made a determined stand against great odds, and then forged a brilliant victory over the North Koreans. Then, General MacArthur led America astray, moving on from repelling the North Korean attack to an attempt to destroy the North Korean government. If he had succeeded he wanted to move into Manchuria and take on the Chinese Communists as well. He met with Chiang Kai-shek on Taiwan, against the wishes of President Truman, to pursue that idea. Some of MacArthur's followers were ready to extend the war to the Soviet Union. This period marked a period of indecisiveness and a number of political blunders by the Truman administration which converted a laudable and largely disinterested effort to preserve the independence of South Korea into an attempt to further a particularly American foreign policy: anticommunism. After the United States forced the Chinese Communists into the war by failure to read their signals, the volte-face of most UN members gave an indication of how unacceptable the American policy had become.

The Chinese made equally serious blunders: when they overwhelmed the UN forces by sending nearly a million men into Korea, instead of contenting themselves with restoring the North Korean government and the 38th parallel division of the country, and set out to drive the United States out of Asia. The result of the two sets of blunders was a war that lasted two more years than it should have, with innumerable casualties and much suffering, and the ultimate resolution late in 1953 of a truce line that could have been achieved before the end of 1950.

America has suffered through three civil wars. Perhaps some people would quarrel with the idea that the French and Indian wars were "civil wars," but the fact was that the Indians owned the territory and their ownership was accepted by the early settlers, who bought land from the Indians. Many Indians dwelt among the whites in the settlements in the beginning. It was only later that the policy of separation became widespread.

The French and Indian wars began, really, with King Philip's War in Massachusetts in 1671. To be sure, there had been previous troubles with Indians. In Virginia the whole first colony had been wiped out by famine, pestilence, and Indian warfare in the sixteenth century. In 1636, racial antagonism had boiled over in Massachusetts with the murder of a New England trader named John Oldham. Colonial troops from Massachusetts and Connecticut decided to destroy the Pequot tribe, whose members lived between the Thames River and the present eastern boundary of Rhode Island, as well as on Long Island. On May 26, 1637, the English colonists ravaged the main Pequot village, at the site of what is now Stonington, Connecticut, and virtually exterminated the Pequots in the whole area.

King Philip's War, which began in 1671, was the result of the Indian realization that individual tribes could do nothing against the English. The tribal leaders believed they could unite and act together to drive the English out of North America. They were fifty years too late. Had they taken such a stand at the beginning of the seventeenth century, when the colonization was just beginning, their belligerence might have saved them. In those days some 800,000 Indians lived along the Atlantic shore, and the colonists would have been no match for them. The proprietors of most of the colonies might well have chosen to move their investment elsewhere.

The Indians lost King Philip's War, and the tribal remnants were thereafter driven steadily westward by the English expansion. Indian resentment became a ready tool for the French, who coveted all of North America as eagerly as did the English. In the wars that spread across the Atlantic from Europe, the French enlisted the Indians, particularly the Hurons, to harry the western boundaries of the English colonies. The French and Indian wars continued unabated from the last of the 1600s until the 1750s.

The French and Indian wars had two signal effects on the New England of the period. They instilled a hatred of Indians handed down to whites, generation upon generation, and they created a demand for defense expenditures that the colonists were at first unable, and later unwilling, to carry for themselves.

Unwillingly, particularly because of the expense of a whole succession of conflicts in Europe quite properly called the Hundred Years War, the British government felt that the colonists in America should pay their own defense expenditures. This feeling was enhanced by the colonists' growing sense of independence and the quarrel over taxation. London's answer, ultimately, was to move to control the American colonies more tightly if they wanted to be defended, and this answer led to enormous resentment in the colonies south of the Canadian border.

Thus the American Revolution was the result of a basic and growing misunderstanding among Englishmen. Yes, the Americans regarded themselves as Englishmen then, from 1578 when Sir Humphrey Gilbert received a royal patent for a colony in America and sailed to Virginia, until 1776 when the ties were finally broken by the American Declaration of Independence. With considerably more political sagacity than existed in London in the 1760s and 1770s, the American Revolution could have been prevented and the North American colonies would have remained loyal to England for as long as Australia and Canada did. But King George III was, in a phrase, a political idiot, and Parliament was filled with his toadies and men of ambition who wished to use the American colonies to relieve expenses at home. This policy was a complete departure from the policy of benign neglect that had changed the nature of the relationship between brothers on the two sides of the Atlantic and caused the Americans to grow extremely independent of the mother country.

In prosecution, the American Revolution was a peculiarly violent war, a civil war in every sense of the word, with brother pitted against brother and father against son. The British added two elements which made the war even more vicious: the Indians, who fought the colonists for vengeful reasons of their own, and the Hessians, those hired peasant boys from Germany, who knew nothing about the language, the customs, or the terrain of the country in which they fought, and were all the more savage for that. When the war ended, the Hessians went home to Europe and were largely forgotten by the Americans, but the Indians had nowhere to go, and successive generations of Indians paid dearly for the excesses of their forebears until the late nineteenth century when General William Tecumseh Sherman enunciated an American policy that had been building up for years: extermination.

World War I, as it related to the United States, was another sort of war altogether. Unlike the French, British, Italians, and Japanese, who split up the German empire at the end of the war, the Americans had no territorial ambitions to pursue. In 1914, sentiment in America about the European conflict was divided. Many people of German descent felt that the kaiser's government had right on its side. It would not be proper to say that the split was ever fifty-fifty, but it was certainly high enough to keep the United States out of the war for three years.

During those years no one attacked the United States, which pursued a policy of neutrality (even if the British got more benefit from it than the Germans). In spite of the propaganda campaign against "the vicious Hun" in Belgium and elsewhere, America's loyalties were divided. The major cause of American entry into the war was the German campaign of unrestricted submarine warfare, which brought about the sinking of the British liner *Lusitania* in 1915, with the loss of some American lives. Hardly a cause for a war, an outsider might say. But the German submarine campaign brought American emotions to a fever pitch. There were subsidiary causes, such as the "Zimmermann letter," a flagrant attempt by the German foreign office to utilize tensions between the United States and Mexico, but largely the American entry into World War I in 1917 was on ideological grounds. It was one of the few wars ever entered by any nation for such a reason. In other words, Americans were not fooling when they said they went to war to make the world "safe for democracy."

As far as military excursions are concerned, the reasons vary from the cupidity of William Walker, the filibuster of the 1850s, who set out to create an empire in South America, and thus sent the American navy into a whole series of military actions to stop it, to the Boxer Rebellion in China, which represented American participation in the nineteenth century's "gunboat diplomacy."

Some military excursions were for high purpose, some for low. The Caroline Affair of 1837, which very nearly brought war with Canada, was the result of a series of border incidents. The Veracruz Expedition of 1914 was a result of the totally misguided Latin American policy of Woodrow Wilson, who committed many blunders in that region and established precedents of interference with other nations that have lasted until the present time.

In a way there is as much to be learned about the American character from the minor military excursions of the United States as from the major wars. They were incurred for reasons ranging from generosity to the narrowest of self-interest. Throughout the military excursions, particularly in Latin America, runs a strain of political evangelism which is both naive and destructive to American self-interest. On the one hand the Carter administration finally abandoned the Monroe Doctrine as no longer applicable, and gave up the Panama Canal. On the other, the Reagan administration enunciated the basic principle of the Monroe Doctrine all over again, warning that the United States would not accept the incursion of the USSR into the Western Hemisphere. What should have been said was the "further" incursion of the USSR into the Western Hemisphere. But the American military presence in El Salvador and around Nicaragua tells its own story.

The essence of it all is that times change, and wars change, and military excursions take on different faces and even different meanings. Three American excursions of recent years have indicated a feeling of need to prop up American pride: the abortive Iran hostage rescue attempt, the Grenada avalanche, and the Gulf of Sidra affairs, in which the United States attempted to show Muammar Qaddafi that crime does not pay. One of the most interesting aspects of the Gulf of Sidra affairs was the failure of the American media to draw the parallels between the North African pirates of the 1980s and those of the early 1800s, the air attacks on Tripoli and Benghazi and the sea attacks by "Commodore Preble's Boys" on Tripoli, Algiers, Morocco, and Tunis that were called the Barbary Wars of 1801–1805. That media failure seems to be a result of a serious national problem: the failure of the American educational system to teach American youth the story of their own country.

One of the unfortunate losses of our modern society in its hurried ways is that of a sense of history. One of our historical magazines, frankly dedicated to entertainment, used to advertise a quotation from the late Winston Churchill to the effect that he who did not study history was doomed to repeat it. Like so many other things in American society, the quote was both a fake and a truism, since it was not invented by Winston Churchill but by an American advertising man. It is true nonetheless. This book is an attempt to show what happened in America's military affairs in the past, with an eye to possibly preventing some of the blunders in the future and offering the hope that United States military policy ought really to serve the nation's needs rather than the perceptions of the moment.

From the recital of the general trends of America's wars and military excursions, it is possible to draw a few conclusions. One of these is that victory does not always go to the great and most powerful, and that ideas are more powerful in war than other weapons.

In the French and Indian wars, the American colonists learned a great deal about fighting in a new way. They began sending their colonial troops out in the old English formations, with soldiers lined up shoulder to shoulder, firing and advancing, stopping, loading, advancing, firing, and then ending with a bayonet attack. Such tactics against the Indians were futile. The Indians hid behind rocks, and shot their arrows, and later their muskets, and still later their rifles. They picked off the colonial troops like flies. So the colonists learned, and adopted the moccasin and the deerskin legging, the knife and the use of terrain. When the English came to fight the revolution, they found themselves beset by these guerrillas. The same was true in the War of 1812. At sea the Americans invented a new sort of ship, the superheavy frigate, about thirty percent more powerful than the British frigate. This dichotomy of size and strength accounted for more American victories in the sea fights than the undeniable gallantry of the officers and men who manned the ships.

During the Civil War, both sides developed ironclad vessels to supersede the old sailing ships. The struggles between the *Merrimac* and the *Monitor* were not decisive, but they did prove that an ironclad had it all over the traditional wooden ship. Then, at sea, until the 1880s, development lagged as the naval officers tried to come to grips with new ways that meant scrapping the old traditions of fighting sail. In that formative period, while the Japanese and the Europeans pioneered the torpedo boat, America really did not have any military excursions to speak of. By the time of World War I the Germans and the British were out in front with the submarine and submarine torpedo as offensive weapons. The Germans had the really salient idea: to use the submarine to supplant the old surface raider concept which had been their mainstay for years. The problem with the submarine, of course, was that its use meant a new sort of warfare, assassination from the deep. The British were loath to accept this, and fought the idea until the brink of World War II. The Americans, seeing how the Germans had used their U-boats so effectively, embraced unrestricted submarine warfare as a concept on the day of the Pearl Harbor attack, and used it even more effectively than did the Germans for the rest of the war. One could even say that several of the American captains committed acts on the edge of atrocity in their shooting down of unarmed victims of ship sinkings as they struggled in the water or on rafts.

The aviation weapon, pioneered by the Nazis and the Soviets in the 1930s, also came of age in World War II. The Germans and the Japanese began the decimation of civilian populations by bombing. The Americans carried the process much further in the burning of Hamburg, and to its ultimate level in the firebombing of Japan's major cities. This firebombing was—and is—regarded by the Japanese as the greatest atrocity of the war.

The aircraft carriers dominated naval warfare in World War II. The Japanese made the most intelligent use of carriers at first, in groups, but the Americans soon learned the trick, and beat the Japanese at their own game.

The Korean War was fought with the weapons of World War II for the most part, although the helicopter was developed as an offensive weapon then. Use of the helicopter gunship, a most fearsome weapon, was perfected in the Vietnam War. But its effectiveness and the American strike tactics were largely vitiated by the proficiency of the Vietcong and the North Vietnamese at guerilla warfare.

Indeed, two military struggles of the twentieth century do much to reassure us that military supremacy in the end lies in the human spirit and not in the material resources at hand. In Vietnam, the people of the north were determined to win, and ultimately they defeated the most powerful nation on earth by wearing the population at home down to the bone. The same situation obtains in Afghanistan, where the Soviet Union is bogged down in a campaign reminiscent of Vietnam, wherein modern weapons have not sufficed to quell the spirit of an independent people.

If there are lessons to be learned from the history of America's wars, ultimately they pertain to the human spirit. As long as the people of America want to remain independent they will do so; only when it comes to the point that they will not fight to keep their freedom will they really be in danger.

CHAPTER 1

The Indians

It is ironic that when the Pilgrims came to New England in 1620 they were greeted as friends by the Indians, and yet one generation later that friendship had evaporated almost totally. One cannot blame the Indians, for they saw all around them the evidence of a way of life that was totally incompatible with their own. Indian culture was a cooperative, even socialistic system. The tribe was the prime unit, not the family or the individual. The Englishmen came with their individualism and butted immediately against the Indian system. When the Indians sold lands, many times they did not realize that they were divesting themselves forever, and they would not again be able to hunt, fish, or grow corn on those lands. The result was a dissatisfaction that turned, slowly, into Indian distrust of the white man.

And yet, can you blame the English entirely for the gap that developed between them and the Indians? In the beginning, at least, they paid whatever the Indians asked for the lands. In Plymouth and other communities they ran schools to educate the Indians. They offered the Indians their religion and they tried to transform them into Englishmen. Of course they failed and the gap grew wider than ever. But the schism was no wider in the American colonies than in the Spanish colonies to the south, or anywhere that Europeans settled.

*   *   *

One could say that a prime cause of the American Revolution of 1776 was the French and Indian wars. Parliament and the British Crown, which had

1

been protecting the American colonists for a hundred years, had grown tired of the expense of waging the French and Indian wars in the 1750s, and decided that the Americans should pay for their own defenses. In a nutshell, this was the background of the new system of taxes the London government tried to impose on the Americans. When that began, the Americans began moving away in spirit from the mother country. Life was not as simple as that in the colonies; it was so different from life in England that almost as soon as it began in the seventeenth century the new life begot different ideas among the colonists, particularly as to their responsibilities to England and the Crown's responsibilities to them. The matter of defense expenditure was, however, the major area of quarrel between the American colonies and King George III's government.

The question of defense came about because of the fierce competition among the European powers for North America. The English came to New England and Virginia. The Spanish came to Florida and the Southwest. The Dutch came to New York, the Swedes to New Jersey, and the French to Canada, down the Mississippi and to Louisiana. In the 1620s the European powers began bumping shoulders. The Dutch moved to the banks of the Delaware and up to Connecticut. The English expanded throughout New England.

In the south, even in these early days, there were troubles with the Indians. In Virginia Colony in March 1622, the Indians rose up and assassinated 347 English colonists, and threatened all the others in Virginia. Had it not been for the revelation of the plot by a Christianized Indian, perhaps the whole Virginia Colony would have been wiped out, as it had been once before.

The shock waves spread across all the English colonies. The English, particularly in New England, set great store by their efforts to convert the Indians to Christianity. That way, said the Puritans, lay the peace of the future. But the Indians in Virginia were showing an extreme reluctance to be converted and have their ways changed by foreigners.

Suddenly the English in New England realized that their situation was not that much different from Virginia's. Further, they blamed the Dutch and French for teaching the Indians how to use firearms and then supplying them with guns and powder and bullets in trade. In the three New England colonies of Plymouth, Massachusetts Bay, and Rhode Island, trade in weapons was strictly forbidden.

Until the 1650s there was enough room to accommodate the settlers and the Indians all with relatively little conflict. The Indians were either pushed away from the growing colonies or were surrounded by them, which led to the Pequot War of 1637, the first major struggle between the English and the Indians. The colonial victories virtually wiped out the Pequots in Connecticut, Rhode Island, and Long Island. That war also warned the

Dutch what to expect, and they prepared for trouble. So did the English colonists, who set up their first confederation. The colonies of Massachusetts, Plymouth, Connecticut, and New Haven formed the United Colonies of New England, a union whose principal purpose was common defense. Then the establishment of the Commonwealth in England, and the subsequent restoration of the monarchy, divided the colonists politically and prevented the New England confederation from amounting to much. But in the 1660s, when the Dutch were growing more aggressive and the French declared that New France (Canada) was now a French province with Quebec as its capital, the English in England and the English colonies took note. The wars of Europe were extended to the colonies. The 1660s and 1670s were notable for wars, English against the Dutch, and the French, who allied themselves in 1666 with the Indians, against the English. The colonists called for help from home and got it. But there was so much difficulty and there were so many different ideas among the colonists that the Crown wanted some assurances that it was supporting loyal subjects. In 1664 London sent four commissioners to the New England colonies to bring them together under royal rule.

This was also the year that the English sent expeditionary forces to conquer the Dutch colonies, which they did. With the exception of one brief period during the Third Anglo-Dutch War (1672), England now controlled the northeast and central American colonies, as well as those south to the Florida country.

At the same time as the European colonists were forced to become English or leave, the Indians were being pressed steadily westward. They did not go without a struggle. The most important of these struggles of the seventeenth century was King Philip's War.

For the previous twenty years, the Indians had been deprived of their lands by the whites. They had sold for fair prices, said the English. They had been cozened and cheated, said the Indians. There was truth in both claims. Even the English colonial historians lamented the practice of some colonists of "getting the Indians drunk on liquor and then cheating them." But the overriding truth was that the English were determined to expand their colonies westward, and the Indians saw that they were being pushed out of their tribal lands. They became ever more sullen and recalcitrant.

The case of King Philip and the Wampanoag tribe tells pretty much what was happening everywhere. Philip was the son of Massasoit, the chief who had welcomed the English colonists to Plymouth when they first arrived and had helped them so much to survive that first dreadful winter. How badly Indian-American relations had gone since then was indicated by the story of Philip. After his father died, Philip inherited the rule of the Wampanoags, and in the constant squabbling with the English, he drew around him three other tribes. The white demands on the Indians never ceased: they must give up this land and that, they must lay down their arms, they must submit to the white man's laws. In 1671, Philip signed a new set of agreements with the English, but even then his followers were planning a war by which they hoped to destroy the English colonies.

Philip's tribesmen were stockpiling arms and food and ammunition, which they smuggled down from the not-unwilling French in the north. They were angered at the trickery by which the English colonists took their land, tired of the enslavement of their tribesmen to white man's liquor, and sorry that they had ever befriended the whites.

There was little question in the minds of the Indians but that they were embarking on a most dangerous course. The sachem Passaconaway of the Merrimac region had recognized and warned of the dangers a decade earlier:

"I am now going the way of all flesh, or ready to die, and not likely to see you ever together any more," he told a gathering of his chiefs in 1660. "I will now leave this word of counsel with you: that you take heed how you quarrel with the English; for though you may do them much mischief, yet assuredly you will be destroyed and rooted off the earth if you do. I was as much an enemy of the English at their first coming to these parts as any one whatsoever, and did try all ways and means possible to have destroyed them, at least to have prevented them sitting down here, but I could no way effect it. Therefore I advise you never to contend with the English, nor make war with them."

Passaconaway's sons heard their father and did their best to stay out of conflict. But the pressures continued and grew worse as ever more colonists arrived to seek land.

King Philip's attack, planned for the spring of 1671, was delayed by heavy rain, and the English got wind of it. They seized his arms and hauled him into court at Taunton, there they forced Philip to sign a statement of submission to the colony of New Plymouth.

The English, of course, justified their every move. For one thing, Philip had rejected Christianity, and this was never forgotten or forgiven: ". . . in the year 1671 the Devil, who was a Murderer from the beginning, had to fill the heart of this savage miscreant with envy and malice . . . that he was ready to break into open war . . . pretending some petite injuries done to him in planting land . . ."

So Philip was forced to recant:

"I, having of late through my indifference and the naughtiness of my heart, broken my covenant with my friends by taking up arms with evil intent against them, and that groundlessly, I being now deeply sensible of my unfaithfulness and folly, do desire at this time solemnly to renew my covenant with my ancient friends." And thus, in words he could not possibly have appreciated, Philip was forced to give up his arms and pretend that he submitted to English rule.

By this time, the 1670s, the Indians had been forced to adopt the policy of the "forked tongue," saying what the English wanted, and nursing their grievances in private.

Philip waited and planned. By 1676 he expected to be able to put several thousand well-armed warriors into the field. But Philip's plans were disturbed by an English-educated Indian named John Sausaman, who was a school teacher at Natick. In the winter of 1675 Sausaman went to Namasket to go fishing, and while up in that country, which adjoined Philip's territory, Sausaman learned of Philip's plans. He hurried back to Natick and sent word to the governor of the colony. In a matter of days Philip knew all and sentenced Sausaman to death. Several warriors took John Sausaman to a great pond near Namasket, knocked him down, and pushed him under the ice to drown. They left his gun and hat on the ice and ran off, giving the impression that John Sausaman had fallen through the ice while hunting. But when friends found Sausaman a few days later and buried him, they noticed bruises on his head and reported all this to the English. The body was dug up, and the English said it was apparent that Sausaman had been murdered. Three of Philip's close supporters were caught, convicted, and hanged. Philip then began raising his armies and, growing ever more belligerent, began to kill cattle in the Swansea area (on the border of his lands) and to raid and rob English houses.

One day in January 1675, the Indians raided the community of Pawtuxet. The raid started with an ambush of Toleration Harris and a black servant, who were trapped by Indians lying in the brush beside the road. The Englishman and his servant were killed. The Indians then killed fifty cattle and eighty horses and burned fifty wagonloads of hay.

One day in the spring of 1675 an English settler shot a raiding Indian, bringing outright hostilities. The Indians retaliated by killing Englishmen. On June 24, at Swansea, several small pitched battles left eight Englishmen dead. When the English colonists found the bodies, the scalps were gone; they had been sent by Philip to the Narragansetts to show that Philip was in earnest. Now the alarm of war first sounded in Plymouth Colony.

The war did not go well for the Indians. By the end of July 1675, the English had pulled themselves together and driven Philip and his followers toward the Nipmuck country to the west.

The colonists raised military forces in Plymouth and Boston and marched out, soldier fashion, in columns down the roads. But the Indians did not march forth along the roads to meet them in battle. Instead they met the English by "skulking fight, creeping and crouching behind any bush, tree, rock or hill, sometimes one alone, two or three together, and then, as they see need, start up and run away, so fast, among the shrubs and rocks that no horse could catch them. But if they saw an opportunity they would fire at a man and run away, and sometimes run among the shrubs and not be seen." The English colonists stuck stubbornly to the roads and had very little chance to fire on the Indians, but they did take territory and drive Philip's people back.

At the end of June, the English advanced into the Mount Hope Peninsula, where they proved no match for the Indians in the swamps and forest land. So some of the English at least began to rethink their method of warfare. Captain Samuel Moseley of Boston was one of those who learned new methods. He employed Indian scouts who were enemies of the Wampanoags. He learned the art of fighting in the bush. And he became one of the most effective of the Indian fighters. Another was Captain Daniel Henchman.

In June 1675 the authorities in Boston learned that King Philip was holed up in the Mount Hope country, where he had killed several English colonists and left their bodies (minus scalps) on the road. When the word came, Captain Henchman's foot company was ready to march. It was late afternoon when they set out, and dark before they reached the Naponset River, twenty miles from Boston. It was a night of eclipse of the moon, and the men stopped to have a meal and wait for moonlight. As they sat on the ground, some morbid souls said they saw in the moon a black spot that looked like the scalp of an Indian. Others saw the shape of an Indian bow.

When the moon came out, Henchman marched his men again, this time to Woodcock's house, thirty miles from Boston. It was morning before they arrived. There they waited.

They were waiting for a company of volunteers under Captain Moseley.

Moseley's men arrived, and the augmented force prepared to find and fight the Indians. They all marched down to the Miles house, which was to be headquarters, located only a quarter of a mile from the bridge that passed over into King Philip's lands. A dozen of the colonists got eager and decided to go over the bridge and scout the Indians. On the far side they were fired upon by Philip's scouts. William Hammond was killed instantly by a bullet; Corporal Belcher, riding a horse, fell when the horse was shot from under him; and several others were wounded. The English fired back, but the Indians were already gone. The colonists picked up their dead and wounded and crossed back over the bridge. They returned to the guarded barricade—a perimeter it would be called in later days—established by Captain Moseley around the Miles house.

The next morning, the Indians attacked over the bridge, apparently not knowing that they faced two companies of colonial troops. Captain

Moseley staged a cavalry charge, drove the Indians back across the bridge, and pursued for more than a mile on the far side. The fighting was brisk. Twenty-year-old Ensign Savage carried the colors in the forefront of the charge. The Indians concentrated their fire on him and put a bullet through the brim of his hat, and another into his thigh. But he never wavered, and the men behind him drove the Indians into the swamp with the loss of several lives.

It began to rain. The charge had petered out on the edge of the swamp. Now, since no more troops came up from the camp, Captain Moseley was forced to withdraw.

At the camp they waited for reinforcements before going into the Mount Hope Peninsula and driving Philip down. Major Thomas Savage, the commander of the Massachusetts forces, was supposed to be coming up apace. But Major Savage was sixty-seven years old and a commander of the European school. In leisurely fashion he brought up his troops, a column of cavalry on each flank. They marched slowly, for they made many diversions. About a mile and a half out of Boston they found several newly burned houses and near one of them a Bible ripped up contemptuously by the Indians. Three miles down the road they came upon a collection of heads, scalps, and hands cut from English bodies and stuck up on poles. Major Savage ordered the column stopped while they buried the remains in Christian fashion and cursed the faithless Indians. Two miles farther they found a large group of wigwams, but no Indians, and then they came to a field of corn, and finally to Philip's own wigwam. All of these were destroyed. Eventually they reached the shore and marched along it. Captain Cudworth and one column turned down into Rhode Island. Major Savage continued but the storm grew so bad that he had to stop and bivouac the troops miserably in an open field.

Next morning, Major Savage missed his chance for greatness. He looked around, decided the Indians were gone, and retreated to Swansea.

That night he and other captains sent several companies out to the edge of the Mount Hope region. Captain Prentice divided his cavalry troop and patrolled, but when the men saw Indians burning a house and prepared to give chase, they found that their horses hampered them. There were too many fences, and the Indians got clean away. Lieutenant Oaks, who had the other half of the cavalry troop, had better luck. He and his men saw Indians and managed to kill four of them, including two of King Philip's senior staff, but they also lost a man, Trooper John Druce, who was shot in the bowels and died.

The troops all retreated to Swansea and reported that Philip's main company seemed to be in the neck of land at Pocasset, lying near Cape Cod. But this was not enough information for Major Savage, who again split his force, sending Captain Henchman and Captain Prentice to search the swamps. He kept Captain Moseley and Captain Page with their cavalry to protect his headquarters.

Moseley moved into the swamp, found Philip's camp, and thought he had the Indian leader trapped. He and his men managed to surprise some of Philip's men and very nearly captured the Indian headquarters camp. But late in the afternoon of the battle, Major Savage came up with the main body of colonial troops. He saw a number of English dead and wounded lying on the ground. It was growing dusk, and Englishmen did not fight at night. So, said Major Savage, it was time to sound the retreat. Thus King Philip escaped Captain Moseley, and worse, when the English did retreat, the Indians followed them out of the swamp, harrying them all the way and causing more casualties. The battle ended on July 4, 1675. The Indians had taken some casualties but they were in no sense defeated. English strategists had a lot to learn about fighting Indians.

At the end of July once again the English thought they had trapped Philip at Pocasset. But the Indian leader crossed to the north side of the Taunton River, passed Rehoboth, and entered the Narragansett country of southern Connecticut. The Narragansetts had already joined in Philip's war against the English.

On August 1 the English had the help of a band of Monehegen and Pequot Indians under Onecas, a son of Uncas, an English ally. These Indians had become Christians, hence their alliance with the colonists. Thus helped, the English force attacked Philip on August 1 twelve miles north of Providence, killed some of his staff, and forced the Indian leader to abandon many of his stores as he fled. But Philip again escaped a trap. He went into the Nipmuck country. The war now broadened.

Through the summer of 1675, the English war effort was seriously hampered by lack of supplies and ammunition. The colonies were not prepared for an emergency that would spread beyond Plymouth Colony's borders. Massachusetts, Rhode Island, and New York were all involved, but they were short of firearms. Massachusetts tried to buy five hundred muskets from New York, and so great was the need that Massachusetts finally began impressing all arms, including those found on ships coming into harbor.

All that summer the generalship of the colonial forces was in incompetent hands. The English forces that advanced into the field were likely to be riddled by the forest-wise Indians. On September 18, 1675, Captain Thomas Lathrop took his company into the forest. They were ambushed at a place called Bloody Brook, and sixty men were killed.

The English thought they had made an agreement with the Narragansett tribe to join with them to capture King Philip. But the Narragansetts, too, had learned to speak with forked tongues, and they did not honor their commitment. The end of the year came, and King Philip was still at large, harrying English colonists in Plymouth, Massachusetts Bay, and Rhode Island colonies. The three united colonies finally raised a militia army of 1,300 men and on December 11 attacked the Indians in the swamp country. The fighting was fierce, and the Indians retreated into the brush. The English, however, did not pursue, because of the bitter and untimely cold weather, which made it extremely difficult for them to care for their wounded.

So, having won the battle, they lost the campaign; the Indians evaporated from the scene, and the English militia was ultimately disbanded and the men returned to their homes. Here was one of the first illustrations of the difficulty of maintaining a militia force. Citizen soldiers could fight very valiantly, but they were incapable of sustaining a long campaign, particularly when there was no action—and so many chores left to be done at home.

A chance had been missed. Proof came in the winter of 1676 when a thousand Indians attacked in the Rhode Island woods. Captain Michael Pierce and seventy men were defending the Rehoboth area. They were surrounded, and most were killed. A few escaped. Two were captured and tortured. "Two of ye seventy they took alive; they tied to trees and ye Indian women whipped them almost to death, and then cut off some of their flesh and put therein hot embers after a most cruell barbarous manner. . . ."

This was not the first time that Indians had tortured captives—Indian warfare was known for its cruel savagery—but from such events the pattern of colonial attitudes toward the Indians was wrought. In half a century it had changed on both sides from friendship to a mutual contempt and hatred that was from this time on to control the relationship between Indians and whites.

That spring of 1676, the confident Indians attacked Providence and Pawtuxet. They killed a number of colonists, including women. This brought the English to retaliate against Indian women for the first time. As the Indians were congratulating themselves on their successes, they learned of the coming of a Connecticut colonial force. A group of Narragansett "tame" Indians, converted to Christianity forty years earlier, was led into battle by a son of the chief Uncas. The English captured the chief Canonchet, Uncas's son, and shot him. A new dimension was added to the Indian wars because the Narragansetts now began to enlist other tribes against the English.

In the campaign of the summer of 1676 the English set about destroying the Indian crops and stores of food. The aroused colonists, massed as militia, killed some five hundred Indians in the three colonies. The English played the game of divide and conquer well and Uncas and his people, and what was left of the Pequot tribe, had turned against the Narragansetts. The English now proved as fierce as the Indians:

Connecticut forces under the command of Major Talcott—some five or six hundred men, English and Indians, —very diligent, hardy, valiant men— hardened to hard duty and incensed by the barbarous inhumanity they have heard of and the evidence they have seen in the form of English bodies found in the woods, capture many Indians, and kill all they capture except some boys and girls. They so frighten the Indians that they hasten to surrender themselves to Massachusetts, Plymouth, or Rhode Island, where their lives are spared, excepting known notorious murderers.

King Philip fled into the swamp country, from which it would be difficult to extricate him. In August he was seen near Taunton, in Plymouth Colony. Captain Benjamin Church and a company of about forty militia did encounter the Indians and attacked them. More than a hundred of the demoralized Indians surrendered, but ten of them, including King Philip and a Narragansett chief named Quinnapin, escaped through the English line. They were tracked down in the Mount Hope country. Philip, friendly Indians informed the English, had cut off his hair. Quinnapin had been wounded. On August 12, 1676, Captain Church and Captain Peleg Sanford converged on the search area, each captain with forty men. They found Philip's camp. In the attack, Philip was shot through the heart by a "tame" Indian from Aquidnick Island, who cut off his head and hands and took them triumphantly home.

Thus ended King Philip's War. The English hoped now that they would have peace with the Indians of the New England area. But the fact was that the wars between the native Americans and the colonial interlopers were just beginning.

CHAPTER 2

The French

The French came closer than any others to creating a bond with the Indians, but this was because the French were mostly voyageurs, *hunters, trappers, and fishermen who shared the Indian ways. Only later, when French farmers settled Quebec and the Maritime Colonies, did tensions develop; finally, the Canadians treated their Indians in the same manner that their American cousins did.*

In the early years, the late seventeenth and early eighteenth centuries, the French were exploring the wide land that lay north and west of New England and New York. Samuel de Champlain found the lake that is named for him. Father Pierre Marquette traveled out to the Great Lakes and to the Mississippi River. The Marquis de LaSalle traveled down that river and established the first settlement at what is now New Orleans. From these travels they learned better than the English how enormous were the resources that lay to the west and south. Mobile was established by the French in 1710. New Orleans was established in 1718.

The conflict between French and English in North America was no more than an extension of the conflicts in Europe. In the seventeenth century France fought Spain and the Dutch. In 1689 the French, Germans, Swedes, and Spanish warred against the Netherlands and England. Thereafter France and England seemed either to be at war or on the verge of war most of the time. The first serious conflict to reach across the Atlantic was King William's War of 1689, about which some detail is given below. This war was actually the American phase of the War of the League of Augsburg, and it established the lineup of the Indians: Iroquois on the side of the English, Hurons on the side of the French. Those alliances would last all during the French and Indian wars, and would be one of the main reasons that the struggles that lasted until 1750 were given that particular name by the English settlers.

*   *   *

For hundreds of years the English and the French had been fighting each other. The Norman French had invaded England in the eleventh century and conquered the land, only to be more assimilated than assimilating. In the fourteenth and fifteenth centuries the English and French had fought the Hundred Years War. But the conflict, the roots of which were laid in the seventeenth century, and which was fought in America, as well as Europe, now was something different, exacerbated by the fact that by this time the English had changed a great deal. After the last gasp of Catholicism in England and the rise and fall of the House of Stuart in the seventeenth century, the English, unlike most of the rest of Europe, were to be Protestant, thanks to Henry VIII's fondness for women and his search for an heir. Another factor that was to determine the course of events in North America was a differing approach by France and by England to colonialism. The serious struggle between the two countries began in 1690, and was to last for seventy years.

The French claimed that their Breton fishermen visited the Newfoundland fishing banks in the earliest years of the sixteenth century, and probably they did. But it was Jacques Cartier, a Breton of Saint-Malo, who imprinted the name of France upon the New World, in a voyage that began in 1534, entered the Saint Lawrence River, and gave such names as Bay de Chaleur, Gaspé, and Belle Isle to the gazetteers. It was Cartier who founded Quebec City. More explorers followed, but they were just explorers with an eye to trade, not malcontents seeking a new society and a place to expand. True, during the last half of the sixteenth century the Huguenots had made two unsuccessful attempts to plant colonies in the New World (Brazil and Florida), but these were exceptions. Most of the French who came to North America came to make their fortunes, then return to the homeland to enjoy them. This attitude existed in England as well (the Anglo-Indians, for example) but it was not the guiding spirit behind the development of English North America, while it was the spirit in the settlement of French North America.

In 1609 Samuel Champlain, with two French assistants and a band of Algonquin Indians, set out to explore the Canadian hinterland, first to the Lake of the Iroquois, now called Lake Champlain. Here at Ticonderoga ("the place of meeting of waters") Champlain encountered the Mohawks, who objected particularly to the presence of the Algonquins in their territory. Champlain fired his arquebus, which contained four bullets. With that one shot he killed two Mohawk chiefs and wounded another. The Mohawks fled, but they did not forget. Champlain would live to be honored for many accomplishments; he was also the man who brought to France the eternal enmity of the Mohawks, later to be a boon to the English in the French and Indian wars.

The Jesuits, who in the sixteenth century were determined to Christianize the world, including China and Japan, sent a ship full of missionary priests to Port Royal on the Bay of Fundy. The English found them, captured the leaders, and took them to Virginia. But the French church persisted, and became a leading factor in the French colonization of Canada. Priests and soldiers, traders and relatively few farmers; that was the way of the French colony and it did not make for the fierce sense of possessiveness of the land that accompanied the English colonization in the south.

By 1689, the French were well-established in a military man's and trader's way, but they had never settled the question of the Iroquois, who regarded their five nations as the principal power in North America.

The French had enslaved some Indians and had taken them to Europe to work as galley slaves. Such behavior had its consequence; on the night of August 4, 1689, 1,400 Iroquois braves burst in on the village of Lachine near Montreal, and massacred the French inhabitants. France had already sent a strong man to settle the Indian problem, the Count de Frontenac. He was a tough seventy-year-old soldier, and he bore down on the Indians. The English called the Iroquois "brother." The French called the Indians "my children" and treated them accordingly. The Indians had plenty of discipline from the French but one problem arose: the Iroquois were not prepared to be treated as children.

Frontenac's purpose, ordained by the king of France, was to make war on the English and ultimately to seize all North America as a French colony. Louis XIV would send two warships to the waters off New York. Frontenac would send 1,600 troops to seize Albany and boat down the Hudson to seize New York next. The warships would then enter New York harbor and New York Colony would become French. The English Catholics could be expected to join the French and would be well treated. The Protestants would be killed or driven out into the wilderness where they belonged. With New York in French hands, New England was bound to follow. Soon North America would be French.

That was the thinking in the palace at Versailles.

To carry out this plan Frontenac had to deal with the Indians. The Hurons hated the Iroquois, so the Hurons were made friends of the French. They were to be used, and then? But that future was to be seen to later.

But around the campfires of the Iroquois there was another thought or two. The Iroquois regarded all North America as Iroquois territory. They were prepared to make some concessions to their brothers, the English.

The English, who had captured New Netherlands from the Dutch in 1664, had their own ideas on the subject. And so was set up the climate of belligerency in North America.

In the cold winter of 1689–90 three war parties of Frenchmen and Indians set out against the English colonies. One February night, one party assaulted the village of Schenectady. They battered down the doors of the houses. The Indians led the slaughter; some of the bluest blood of France stood by and watched the murders, and some of these nobles joined in to rape and kill the women and children, kill the men, and throw their bodies into the burning houses. They wrecked the little settlement and then set off northward, dragging along a handful of captives, mostly women. A brave blow had been struck against the English, and in Quebec and Montreal the heroes wrote home to France the tales of glory, forgetting to mention the gorier details. These tales were augmented by those from the similar war parties that had ravaged the borders of New Hampshire and Maine. The French felt that the "day of glory" was about to arrive.

But Louis XIV and Frontenac had failed to consider the bloodthirsty nature of an Englishman aroused. Down in Boston was Sir William Phips, a Boston carpenter who had grown rich and had been named the first royal governor of the Royal Colony of Massachusetts. One tends to think of royal governors as people like the Count de Frontenac, whose home turf, a château near Blois in France, boasted beautiful gardens, gold and silver plate, peacocks, and a private zoo. He dressed in silks and satins, flattered the ladies and expected to be flattered in turn, and always smelled of lavender water. Sir William often smelled of sweat and wood smoke. He had not learned to read and write until he was a grown man. He was so tough that he had quelled a mutiny aboard a ship of his by beating up the leader with his fists. Phips was an American. He prided himself as a "self-made man." His father had been a settler on the Kennebec River and had cast his lot with the New World. Sir William was second generation, said to be one of twenty-six children born of the same mother. He regarded himself as an Englishman, certainly, but an Englishman of a new breed. Royal governor or not, he once took his cane to Captain Short of the Royal Navy when the two disagreed on some minor point. Above all, Sir William was a Massachusetts patriot, and when the French assaulted his territory they took on a real bearcat.

Nor was Massachusetts wanting in fury against the French. The canny Iroquois were urging a joint English-Indian war to wipe out New France. New Yorkers liked the idea. So did New Englanders. The authorities in Boston had already decided that Quebec must be destroyed. The problem was that King Philip's War had emptied the treasuries of all the New England colonies, and they had not yet filled up again. Another problem: life in New England was a farm and business life, and there was not a good military commander in sight. William Bradstreet, head of the Massachusetts council of public safety, said they should ask London for help. The destruction of the French in Quebec would redound to the glory and profit of the Crown, so why should not king and parliament help out?

London was approached, and London said no. The Crown was busy with the war against the Irish. The American colonies must take care of themselves.

That decision brought a good deal of muttering in America, but there was nothing to be done about it. While awaiting the ship that brought the royal reply, the New Englanders had already set the wheels in motion for the fight. Cotton Mather and other evangelists (and there were plenty of them) were keeping the religious fires lit against the "damnable Catholics." The Massachusetts men put together a fleet of thirty-two vessels, the largest a ship in the West Indies trade, which carried forty-four guns. Volunteers were called, and when that was still not enough, a draft was made, a no-fooling draft that spared no household, one that took away two-thirds of the eligible men of such settlements as Gloucester.

Thus was an American tradition established: civic responsibility for the public defense, with no special privileges for rank. The New Englanders had already learned the price of freedom and safety. The citizens were paying for their warlike ambitions, but they were ready to pay; the French had gone too far.

Massachusetts still wanted a military commander, and Governor Phips was chosen for the job. The fleet sailed on August 9, with 2,200 men in the ships.

Meanwhile in New York, an overland expedition had been organized to attack Montreal. A combined force of New York and Connecticut militia started out. They made their way to the bank of Lake Champlain, and there they stopped. The leaders of Connecticut and New York could not agree on the next move. Further, the New York militia was split politically, a heritage from the recent upheavals of government in England. The colonists could not get behind one leader; everything went wrong. The birches would not peel properly to make canoes. The Iroquois tribesmen sensed the disorganization of the whites and lost confidence. A few cases of smallpox broke out, and the soldiers panicked. So the overland party collapsed after a single token foray into Canada, and the militiamen went home, deserting Admiral Phips and his naval force and making it almost certain that they must fail. Phips, of course, knew nothing of this desertion. The overland force was to be joined by an army of Iroquois, and the force was to be overwhelming.

Up in Canada, the Count de Frontenac had ceased to rejoice over the three murderous expeditions into the English colonies long enough to deal with some of his internal enemies. When he learned of the English plans, he began building fortifications at Quebec and at Montreal. When he learned of the retreat of the New York-Connecticut force, he moved to Quebec to face the naval danger.

The Massachusetts fleet showed up on October 16, 1690, rounding the island of Orleans and sailing into the basin at Quebec City. A junior officer was selected to take an impudent message to the French, demanding immediate surrender. The English envoy went ashore, blindfolded. The Count de Frontenac impressed him by appearing in full court kip. All the bright flowers of French aristocracy in Canada seemed to be there, in gold and silver lace, powdered wigs and plumes, ribbon, and conflicting perfumes (which the English said the French wore to hide their stink), but the display did not deter the officer from reading his message, which was a brisk demand for immediate surrender or else. Frontenac, said Admiral Phips, had an hour to decide. The envoy pointedly pulled out his watch and began to regard it with interest. It was 10:00 A.M.

Frontenac picked up the letter and threw it in the face of the envoy. Someone said the messenger should be hanged. The envoy turned pale when he heard Frontenac give the order for a gibbet to be erected. But Frontenac cooled down. He said the answer was no. No surrender, no hanging.

"I will answer only from the mouths of my cannon and with my musketry."

And so the Massachusetts officer was blindfolded again, led back over the barricades, and boarded the boat that had brought him ashore.

The trouble was that Admiral Phips was not really a military man. He had expected Frontenac to be so bedeviled by war on two fronts that he would give up. That failing, he was not sure what to do, so he made the mistake of doing nothing. The ships lay at anchor while endless meetings were held. A plan was devised to land on the shore below Quebec, cross around behind, and capture the town. It could have been done, but it had to be done in a hurry, and it was not—too many meetings, the sign of men trying to cover their tails. So Frontenac had time to call up more troops from Montreal and time for them to arrive, about a thousand strong. When Captain Ephraim Savage tried to bring a shipload of troops up to move behind the city, they were met by a hail of fire and never got to shore. Another landing was made the next day. The fleet opened fire on the fortress, and the fortress fired back. The end of the day was impasse, with the Massachusetts troops ashore, but the fortress intact, and the Massachusetts infantry still far from the objective.

Then, to add to his many other troubles, Admiral Phips learned that he was about to run out of ammunition. It was a shortage that would have been anticipated by a real military commander, but the colonists had to live and learn. The initial landing was drawn back. Another landing was made. It, too, failed to get behind and into Quebec City, and the fleet was almost impotent against the great fortress: its guns were too small and its supply of shot too limited. The admiral called a prayer meeting, and his advisers decided that God did not want them to take Quebec just then, so it was time to be homeward bound, before the ice began to pile up in the Saint Lawrence River. And they departed; the whole expedition had spent less than a week before it sailed away on October 23. The fleet straggled back into Boston in November, and the English colonists considered ruefully what they had learned: that the guidance of the Puritan God did not necessarily mean victory over the forces of the Devil up in Canada.

Frontenac, under the impression that his "victory" had been earned by superior French force of arms as well as superior religious belief and culture, spent the next seven years pursuing his French Majesty's wish that America be conquered. He did not do very well. In 1691 New York Colony sent Peter Schuyler up Lake Champlain to attack Canada and he did to the Canadian settlers what Frontenac's three war parties had done to the English, got almost to Montreal, but then had to turn back. So the reality was impasse again. Frontenac in 1696 made one last great move to destroy the Iroquois, journeyed south from Lake Ontario, and burned several Iroquois villages, but certainly did not conquer the Iroquois. He was seventy-eight years old; he had to be carried by the Indians across the portages between lakes and rivers. In 1697, a treaty (Ryswick) theoretically brought an end to the French-English wars in America, but actually it was meaningless. The war along the Canadian-American colonial frontiers continued unabated. War? It was a series of skirmishes, murderous raids for the most part, carried out by both sides, usually a small military force, with Indians, against a handful of farmers and their wives and children. The English outnumbered the French by twenty to one in the colonies, but the French outnumbered the English in fighting men, because most of the French were not family men, but *voyageurs,* hunters, and soldiers. And where the French had truly committed themselves to the land, as Charles LeMoyne of Montreal, a noble Frenchman who had come to Canada to settle, they were still French nobility, still thinking in terms of chateaux and vast land holdings, still soldiers. LeMoyne had ten sons and all of them were soldiers.

From Canada, the English seemed to offer easy pickings. They suffered from misgovernment by the officials sent from London. But they had the advantage of a fierce hold on the land they had occupied now for nearly a century. The vast majority of the English colonists were farmers, artisans, and smallholders. They were now Americans much more than the French were Canadians; had they all been whisked back to England at this point, they would not have known how to live. And the geographical and social

differences of the English colonies, Calvinism, Protestant (Plymouth), Roman
Catholic (Maryland), Quaker (Pennsylvania), and the mixed bag in between forced in time a certain tolerance, although there were many in-
stances of judicial murder by the authorities, such as Quakers hanged in
New England for practicing their religion. A unity was developing, caused
by facing common enemies: the French and the Frenchified Indians. The
French, dominated by the Roman Catholic church, had no such leavening
influences.

Around the turn of the eighteenth century the French in North America
presented a most fearsome aspect. Their depredations against the Iroquois
were so constant that finally the Iroquois sachems ceded their lands to
Queen Anne of England and sought the protection of the British Crown
as subjects of the queen.

The French depredations along the border were part of a deliberate
plan: the continuation of the Versailles plan to raise the frontier territory,
capture Boston, and move on from there to destroy New England. In the
summer of 1703 the French attacked the village of Wells on the border
with Maine. They had already done the same to half a dozen other small
places, but the destruction of Wells snapped something in the New England
mind. Then in February 1704, a young French nobleman named Hertel de
Rouville led a party of French and Indians to fall upon the sleeping village
of Deerfield, Massachusetts, where they killed a third of the inhabitants
and led a hundred and eleven men, women, and children into miserable
captivity. The wife of the Reverend John Williams, the Calvinist minister
of Deerfield was killed by a swooping blow from an Indian tomahawk.
The minister survived, escaped his captors, returned to New England, and
wrote the story of the Deerfield massacre. It was a best-seller in New
England and helped arouse the populace against the French and the Indians.

The English took most the worst of it in these years, but they did not
forget and their fury burned slow and sure. Their major problem in con-
testing the French was the lack of any central authority or plan, such as
the French very definitely had. The English of New York fought their war,
with their Iroquois allies, against the French and the Hurons of Montreal.
The English of New England saw as their enemy the French of Acadia.

Acadia, so long forgotten save by the romantic, was a French colony
including the modern Nova Scotia, New Brunswick, and the greater part
of Maine. The chief settlement, Port Royal, was located in the basin of
the Strait of Annapolis, not far from Cape Sable. The colonists were only
about a thousand in number. This was also the country of the Abenaki
Indians, the fiercest of France's converted Catholic allies in the war against
the English.

The ferocity of the Indians, the torture of the English prisoners, and the scores of atrocities wreaked upon the border settlers added each season to the score that the New Englanders wanted to settle with France. The community of Pemaquid had been destroyed by the French. Governor Phips had it restored as a fort. The fighting went on, the advantage almost always with the French.

In 1707 Samuel Vetch, a Scotsman, surveyed all this and announced that the French must be quelled. It would take the combined resources of the New England colonies and help from England. In 1708 Vetch went to England and found a sympathetic ministry in London, because the war with France (apparently interminable) was just then going very well. "Hit the French" was the policy. Vetch received promises from London, including one that he would be the first British governor of Canada.

Back in America, Vetch had promises of aid from the various colonies; Pennsylvania, New Jersey, Virginia, the outposts along the Mississippi, from virtually everyone who had in some way suffered from French depredations. Troops were to come from England by May 1709. New York would send a thousand men to attack by way of Lake Champlain. The New England militia and the British regular army men would go by sea to Quebec and finish this job once and for all. Only Pennsylvania, on Quaker religious grounds, and New Jersey finally refused to help; New Jersey because its governor said it had no quarrel with the French at the moment.

By early summer the New York force was in camp at the bottom of Lake Champlain, waiting. In Boston a number of English officers—a military mission in more modern terms—arrived to train the awkward American woodsmen in proper fighting techniques.

But the promised fleet from England did not arrive.

Late summer came. The crowded American camp near Lake Champlain was ravaged by pestilence. The camp began to wither away. Then came October, and an afterthought of a note from Whitehall that said the fleet promised to the Americans had been sent to Portugal instead.

There was anger in Boston, but anger would do no good. The colonists then conspired. They sent delegations from Massachusetts and New York to London to convince the ruling bodies that it was in their interest to support New England against France. Four Mohawk chiefs went along, as sort of sideshow, a media event, calculated to raise interest in North America. They arrived at just the right time, the winter of 1709–1710. The Duke of Marlborough had just won a series of victories over the French, and London was ebullient. The colonists were promised four frigates and 500 red-coated regular British soldiers to help them do the job.

In July 1710 this help from England arrived. It was the first real military assistance the colonists had ever received from their government and it changed their lives. They could now open their minds to visions of a vast nation of Englishmen on the American shore, without harassment from enemies. The Massachusetts government gave everything to the cause. The legislature enacted a law ordering compulsory military service for all able-bodied men. The soldiers sent by London were quartered on the people of Boston without so much as a by-your-leave.

It was all new and welcome, this attention from London: it proved that the government cared what happened to the Englishmen in this far corner of the world, beset by the vicious French. To man the colony's warships, sailors were impressed in the old British fashion. But except for some malcontents and some who were badly affected by the events, no one really worried about the impositions of the government. Public opinion was squarely behind the destruction of New France. The English had suffered too long to forget. It could not happen too soon.

In August all the preparations were made. Colonel Francis Nicholson, lately the lieutenant governor of New York Colony, was the military man in charge of the expedition. He had never had command of anything before, but he was bright. He had proposed a colonial federation to fight the French; Virginia, which at the end of the seventeenth century and beginning of the eighteenth was still not much worried about the French, had killed the issue with its objections. Sam Vetch was second in command. For once the colonies seemed united in purpose. New York, which had not done very well by its promises to this point, was impressed by the royal approval and backing of the plan. Rhode Island agreed to fight. Connecticut said it would send troops and even New Jersey finally agreed to put up £3,000.

On September 18, 1710, the force sailed away from Boston, bound for Port Royal, with flags flying and people cheering on the docks behind. It was an impressive fleet; three "fourth rate" frigates, two "fifth rates," twenty-six other military vessels, two hospital ships, and several supply ships. The landing force consisted of 400 Redcoats, and about 1,500 provincial troops trained under British officers.

A week later the attack began. The French soon saw that they were surrounded and outnumbered and outgunned, and surrendered the fort. The English marched in and promptly changed the name to Annapolis Royal. Samuel Vetch became the new governor.

And so Acadia was captured. It became Nova Scotia.

The taking of Acadia had cured the festering sore of the Massachusetts border with Canada. It had not done a great deal to resolve the problem of control of the North American continent. France was still strong in the north, and still bent on destroying the English colonies. The matter took an odd turn after the capture of Acadia. It was suggested to Louis XIV by his counselors that Massachusetts and New York should be encouraged to seek their total independence from England, by a promise from France to respect their independence as republics in America. Louis XIV—who detested Republics above all else! Out of this came another expedition, a much larger one, backed by London to capture Quebec City and Montreal.

Admiral Sir Hovendon Walker was chosen from Queen Anne's court to lead the new expedition against Quebec. Colonel Richardson would bring New York troops up the lake again and strike Montreal. But the major effort would come from the sea, from England itself, in a mighty fleet. To Boston in the summer of 1711 came seventy ships, led by nine men-of-war, 5,500 redcoat soldiers, and thousands of British sailors and marines of the Royal Navy, 12,000 men in all. It was the greatest British force that had ever graced the new continent with its presence, and certainly should have been adequate to take Quebec. Montreal would certainly then have fallen easily enough, England's trouble with the French would have been over, and the archives of American history would celebrate Sir Hovendon's name forevermore.

The admiral sailed with his armada on July 30, 1711. On August 22 the fleet was out of sight of land, in the gulf of Saint Lawrence above the island of Anticosti. A storm blew up. It was foggy. Admiral Walker lost his bearings. He was just off the north shore and thought he was off the south shore of the gulf. Late that night Captain Paddon of the flagship *Edgar* came to tell the admiral that land was in sight. The admiral did not have the good sense to ask what land, but assumed that it was the south shore. He ordered the fleet to head north—which sent it straight for the rocks of the rugged coast. Then the admiral went to bed.

He was awakened an hour later by a staff officer who said he must get up. The fleet was among the breakers. The officers could hear them.

The admiral said he knew what he was doing. And he turned over and went back to sleep.

The officer went away, but soon he was back, pummeling the admiral's door. The admiral said to go away, but the officer insisted. If the admiral did not do something soon the fleet would be lost, he said.

Grumbling against staff officers, the admiral hied himself from bed and appeared on deck in dressing gown and slippers.

The fog had lifted, the moon was out, and it shone down clearly on the rocks and breakers into which the fleet was heading.

"Captain Paddon, you may reverse course," said the admiral grandly.

The captain of the flagship did reverse course, and the flagship beat its way back against the onshore wind, sailed through the fleet, and was saved. But the fleet?

Some ships dropped anchor, which held, since the storm was abating. But, two supply ships, and eight transports laden with troops, were dashed onto the rocks and destroyed, and a thousand men lost their lives that night.

The loss was not overwhelming. The admiral had not lost a single warship. He still had 11,000 men with him and most of his supplies. But the disaster unnerved him and he turned around and headed homeward. Off the Massachusetts coast the colonial forces were dispatched back into Boston, and the admiral sailed for England. He got there safely, and the flagship *Edgar* put in at Spithead. The admiral went ashore, whereupon the flagship blew up. The explosion killed every man aboard.

In the 1720s troubles erupted in the southern American colonies between the English settlers and those from Spain. The Carolina colonies, which had begun with high hopes in 1629, had fallen on bad times, and early in the eighteenth century North Carolina and South Carolina were both surrendered by their proprietors to the Crown and became Crown colonies. In 1732 James Edward Oglethorpe was granted a charter to found the colony of Georgia, between the Savannah and Altamaha rivers, and came to America himself the next year. He began fortifying the southern frontier area, building forts on the islands offshore and at Augusta on the Savannah River. Oglethorpe made treaties with the Indians, notably the Creek tribe, the Cherokee, and the Chickasaw. With this backing he was free to drive the Spanish away from the borders of Georgia. In 1739 Britain declared war on Spain after a number of incidents in various parts of the Americas involving British and Spanish interests. This war was given the evocative name the War of Jenkins' Ear, because of an incident in which the Spanish cut the ear off a British merchant seaman named Thomas Jenkins. The war gave Oglethorpe the excuse he needed to go after the Spanish tooth and nail. He invaded Florida, and captured Fort Picolata and Fort San Francisco de Pupa. In May 1740 Oglethorpe began a siege of the Spanish city of Saint Augustine. He laid siege for three months, but then the Spanish brought up a superior force and he had to break off when the Spaniards threatened his siege from the rear. He retreated to Saint Simon's Island. The Spanish attacked him there, but he defeated them in the Battle of Bloody Swamp. The lasting importance of this backwoods war was the establishment in the minds of southern English Americans of their interests and claims over the Florida territory of the Spanish. Disputes and struggles would arise again and again in the next fifty years.

For thirty years after the abortive Walker expedition, the English and French colonies of North America maintained an "almost peace." France and England were not at war and did not go to war again until 1744. At that time, Prussia, Spain, and France allied themselves together against Britain and Austria, and the round of European wars began again.

Thirty years was a long time in the life of the colonies. The population of New England had grown to about 500,000, which made the American colonies a very profitable market. It was not, however, only one market but many, since there was no real cohesion among the colonies. What cohesion did exist was encouraged largely by the common fear of Indians and other enemies. As long as the French were not belligerent and stayed in Canada, the fear was not too great. But that changed in 1744 because of renewed ambitions of the government in Paris.

Geographically, the American colonies of 1744 were beset on three sides by foreign enemies. On the north were the French and their Huron allies. The French had also moved down the Mississippi Valley to New Orleans, and by 1700 had claimed an enormous chunk of territory which included most of the lands on the banks of the great river. They were busily exploring as far west as New Mexico. Natchez, Biloxi, Mobile—these were French settlements, and France coveted Michigan and every piece of land south of it along the chain of waterways. The whole Mississippi drainage system was claimed by France. As long as these claims were theoretical, they were of a piece with the English claims, such as that of Virginia, which claimed its north and south borders extended across the entire North American continent. Around 1700 nobody was moving any farther west than the Appalachian Mountains, so the claims were quiescent, but there was a definite, if generally unperceived, threat that the English colonies would be cut off at the Appalachians. To the south, the Spanish held Florida, another barrier against English colonial expansion farther than South Carolina. The English colonies were sometimes depicted by English mapmakers of the period as extending far to the west, a popular, but illusory conceit. There were far more French than English between the Appalachian Mountains and the Mississippi.

By 1740, however, the English movement into and past the Appalachians was a fact. Several stock companies were formed in Virginia to exploit the western lands. The conflict between the French and English then became inevitable. The Virginians, who had scoffed at the needs of the New Englanders earlier, now found themselves in the midst of the same troubles. Even the antimilitarist Pennsylvanians discovered that the French on their northern and western borders were determined to take land that Pennsylvania said was hers.

Warfare between France and England broke out again in Europe in 1744, and subsequently colored the relationships between the colonies once again. But this time the English colonies had twenty times the population of Canada. In 1745 the French attacked Annapolis, the old Acadia, which defended itself with help from Boston. The Massachusetts men prepared once more to go to war with the Canadians. Again the Massachusetts government asked for help from London, and got it, although a little late and a little reluctantly. Governor William Shirley had been ready to fight without it if necessary. On April 30, 1745, the combined New England and British forces arrived near Louisbourg, whence the attack on Acadia had come. A watcher on the shore counted ninety-six ships. The French government, unknowing, sent a single sixty-four-gun warship, the *Vigilant,* to confront an entire British squadron. After the *Vigilant* had lost eighty men, the French watched the defeat of their ship and their hopes. Louisbourg surrendered on June 17.

The Massachusetts men were delighted, and they determined that French Canada must cease to exist.

"*Delenda est* Canada," shouted Governor Shirley to the Massachusetts legislature. Another campaign was discussed, but London, which had promised much in the euphoria of Louisbourg's capture, reneged on its military commitment. No ships, no troops would be forthcoming.

The French sought to retake Louisbourg and sent a huge armada under Admiral le Duc d'Anvile. The fleet met disaster at sea, sickness and a terrible storm, and only a handful of the fleet's vessels ever saw France again. In the spring of 1747 the French launched another naval expedition to North America, under Admiral La Jonquiere. But the British Royal Navy ambushed the fleet in mid-Atlantic, captured the admiral, and destroyed the expedition.

In 1748, the French and English met to make peace, and the next move in the American-Canadian drama was dictated from Europe. As a part of a compromise in the settlement of the French-English war, England gave Cape Breton (Louisbourg) back to the French. So at the Peace of Aix-la-Chapelle, the interests of New England were subordinated to those of England proper, a matter that did not sit well in Boston and New York. What Massachusetts men had fought to conquer, London gave away as if bestowing a *petit cadeau* upon the French.

When the news of Aix-la-Chapelle reached the colonies, many a question about New England's future was raised in the taverns and in the legislatures—in the legislatures above all, for these colonists were by now self-governing men, and they would have their own way in America. This attitude inflamed the gentlemen of the Parliament on the Thames, who would have liked to have enforced the view that no colony had a right to make any laws that affected any other colony, and who did hold that all colonial laws were subject to the approval of Parliament.

London objected ever more strenuously to the independence of spirit of the American English, but they had set the course in motion a hundred years before. The comparison was there for all to see. Up north, where France had maintained total authority, sharing only with the church, there was no pushing and hauling among the settlers, who were French Canadians and did what their government willed. Down south, there were now thirteen colonies, each with its own systems and ideas. A great quarrel was brewing.

In 1749, despite the peace made at Aix-la-Chapelle, the French decided it was time for them to make capital of their claims to the Ohio and Mississippi river valleys, as far south as the Gulf of Mexico, and as far west as anyone could go, to the Pacific ocean. The English were to be shut out of the west.

"The Ohio," said the king of France, "is a French river. The lands bordering it are my lands. I will not endure the English on my land."

With that statement the king of France threw down the gauntlet that would mean war to the finish with England over North America.

A young Canadian, Celeron de Blainville, was chosen to lay the new claim. He launched his canoes on Lake Erie, made portage for seven days to Chautauqua Lake, and went down into the Allegheny River and thus to the Ohio. As the French traveled, they warned the Indians to have nothing to do with the English, because this was the French king's land, and they were the French king's "children." Let them not forget.

At several points along the Ohio River, Celeron buried leaden plates, each bearing an inscription announcing that he was taking possession of the lands in the name of the king of France. On trees along the route he nailed the arms of France stamped on sheets of tin. (Some of these lead plates and tin signs are still out there, hidden treasures in the land of the Ohio.)

Celeron went down the Ohio as far as the mouth of the Miami River, up that river, and by water and portage back to Lake Erie.

Following that expedition, France moved to take possession of the Mississippi and Ohio valleys. In 1753 Governor Duquesne of Canada sent a thousand men to build Fort Le Boeuf on the upper watershed of the Ohio River. The French moved into the Ohio Valley, constantly warning the Indians to have nothing to do with the English. The French were on the western border of lands claimed by Pennsylvania and Virginia, lands that the Virginians at least were getting ready to exploit.

Now into the scene came a young surveyor, a gentleman of the best sort from Virginia Colony, George Washington.

In the 1740s, young George Washington was surveying lands for Lord Fairfax, one of the largest landholders in Virginia. Fairfax owned a large amount of land in the Blue Ridge country and beyond the Alleghenies, according to royal patents. But, of course, these were English patents and not meaningful to the French.

In 1748, a number of prominent Virginians, including Lawrence Washington (George's elder brother), had organized the Ohio Company. If the company would erect a fort and settle a hundred families around it, said the government of Virginia, it would have a grant of 200,000 acres of land on the Ohio River. If that was accomplished in seven years, another 300,000 acres would be added to the grant.

Governor Robert Dinwiddie of Virginia encouraged the Ohio Company because he personally had a financial interest in the settlement of the western lands. He was also well aware of the implications of French movement on the other side of the Alleghenies. He decided to send an official mission to warn the French who were building forts and trading posts along the Ohio Valley that they were trespassing. He entrusted what anyone could see was a thankless and even dangerous mission to William Trent, a partner of Benjamin Franklin's in some enterprises. Trent did not get far. Some contemporaries said he succumbed to cowardice when he learned that the French were moving into the Ohio in large numbers. More likely he was overwhelmed by the futility of the mission.

As Governor Dinwiddie could see, there was not much time to spare. The governor turned to George Washington, the young brother of his friend Lawrence. George was only twenty-two years old, so entrusting a confidential mission to him was a sign of favor and approval. Of course, the mission did not call for particular military or political judgment.

So George Washington set off to the west to warn the French in the name of his governor and the king of England to vacate the Ohio Valley. Perhaps it was just as well that Dinwiddie had chosen a youth for the task, since, to anyone who knew the frontier, it was apparent that the French were serious in their claim, and that the next step would have to be a major confrontation.

Messenger Washington left Williamsburg on October 31, 1753, with a letter to the French commander. On November 14 he reached Will's Creek (now Cumberland) in the midst of a snowstorm. There he picked up guides and a work party and pushed on, reaching the Monongahela River on November 22. Here he learned that the French commander of the region had died suddenly and that the French forces had moved back to winter quarters on the upper Allegheny River. Washington thus had the wilderness area to himself. With his surveyor's eye he saw that the fork where the Monongahela met the Allegheny to form the Ohio River was precisely the right place for a fort to command the whole area and both rivers. From French deserters in the wilderness he learned the disposition of French forces along the Mississippi and in the Illinois country. He met a number of Indian leaders who had already objected to the French designs on territory they claimed as Indian lands. On November 30, Washington began traveling again, and a few days later he reached Venango, a settlement about sixty miles from Logstown, where the French colors were flying in front of a log house. The French received him cordially enough. At dinner they revealed that "it was their absolute design to take possession of the Ohio, and by God they would do it."

Being a little drunk, the French told Washington they knew the English could not possibly act quickly enough to stop the French investment of the Ohio. Washington was warned. On December 11 he reached Fort Le Boeuf on French Creek (Waterford, Pennsylvania). He delivered the governor's letter to Legardeur St. Pierre, the French commander, who neither spoke nor read English and so had to find an interpreter. Meanwhile, Washington measured the fort, counted the canoes and arms, and learned all he could about French dispositions and plans.

When the French answer came, it was of course, "Mind your own business. The Ohio is ours." So Washington headed back to Virginia. En route a Frenchified Indian tried to shoot him but missed. Later, Washington and a companion were thrown from a raft into the ice-filled Allegheny, but survived. Washington finally reached Williamsburg on January 16 and delivered the French answer to Governor Dinwiddie, who immediately published the correspondence. The English were warned.

Captain Trent was commissioned to build a fort at the Ohio-Allegheny fork. George Washington was commissioned a lieutenant colonel of the Virginia militia, and told to raise a force and take it to the new fort. Meanwhile reports (many of them grossly exaggerated) warned all the English colonies of the movement of the French. But what was not exaggerated was the fact that the French were recruiting colonists from Canada and Louisiana. Boston particularly was impressed and worried about that.

Seventeen fifty-four was the year of the Albany Congress, at which Benjamin Franklin and some other far-seeing men tried to bring the colonies together to face their common problems, with particular emphasis on the French and Indian questions. But Virginia would not even send a delegation, and the hope for colonial union failed. The best that could be said for the effort was that it raised the question of colonial interdependence and caused all thirteen colonies to consider the matter more or less seriously. In that sense, the Albany Congress could be called a forerunner of the later Continental Congresses.

In April 1754, Washington and about 200 soldiers left Alexandria for the west, on reports that the French were sending hundreds of soldiers into the Ohio River country. They were to reinforce Captain Trent with his fort at the Forks. But as they traveled they learned that a thousand French soldiers had descended on Trent and forced him to stop building. Trent was already on his way east.

Washington then decided that he would have to build a fort as close to the French as possible, and he chose a spot on Red Stone Creek where it met the Monongahela. On May 28, Washington's force encountered a French party. They fought. The French were defeated, and their dead were scalped by Washington's Indians, much to the fury of the French back up the river, who claimed that the French leader had been on a friendly mission to the English.

Washington moved to the place he had selected and there built Fort Necessity. Reinforcements came up. Supplies came too. The Virginians began building roads west. On July 3 the French attacked Fort Necessity. Washington had to retreat across the mountains to Virginia. The French had won the first round.

In a way, the New York Colony, always so close to the Duke of York and thus the Crown, reflected English thinking in the middle of the eighteenth century more than any other. When Virginians became upset about the depredations of the French on the Ohio Valley, New York chose to be supercilious. "It appears that the French have built a fort at a place called French Creek, at a considerable distance from the River Ohio which may, but does not by any evidence or information appear to us to be an invasion of any of His Majesty's colonies," said Lieutenant Governor Delancey of New York to the legislature on April 23, 1754.

But after Washington's defeat in the west, New York gave £5,000 for the common defense. Pennsylvania, which had earlier made light of the French and Indian problems, gave £6,000. New Jersey, without any territory exposed to the Indians and the French, refused to give anything.

Parliament from London urged diplomatic effort to make treaties with the Indians and thus pull the teeth of the French. When Virginia and Massachusetts and even Pennsylvania pleaded for arms and men, the prime minister, the Duke of Newcastle, was less than sympathetic. It was suggested to him that Annapolis must be defended.

The prime minister replied, "Annapolis. Annapolis. Oh, yes, Annapolis must be defended; to be sure, Annapolis must be defended. Where is Annapolis?"

When the king opened Parliament in the fall of 1754, he indicated the value he put upon the possessions that "constitute one great source of wealth." He was speaking of America primarily. Parliament responded by authorizing funds for two regiments of troops to be sent to Virginia. They were not, however, real regiments, but cadres of regiments, 500 men each: 1,000 redcoats to be augmented by 400 Virginia troops who would be enlisted to the colors. Major General Edward Braddock was put in charge of the 4th and 48th regiments. They sailed from Cork in January 1755.

The French responded with 3,000 troops and eighteen warships bound for Canada. Part of that fleet was waylaid by the British at sea, and the French-English wars began again in earnest.

General Braddock knew what he was about to do. Just before he left London he told a friend that she would never see him again: he was being sent with a handful of troops to do an impossible job in the wilderness.

The two English regiments arrived at Alexandria. Braddock went to Virginia and then to New England. A plan was devised to attack the French on four fronts. The two new British regiments were to take Fort Duquesne (Pittsburgh), at the Ohio's source. Two new colonial regiments were to take Niagara. A force of provincial militia was to seize Crown Point. And the New England regiments and ships were to take Beau Sejour and settle the matter of Acadia once and for all.

Braddock's army bogged down in the wilderness of the west. Sickness dogged the English soliders, who were not used to the climate. Braddock engaged the French, and the French beat him. Moreover, his presentiment proved true. They killed him.

In the west, then, the French had triumphed and the frontier was open to French expansion. More particularly, the frontier was open to French and Indian depredations, which became absolutely ferocious. The French regular soldiers in Canada were aghast at what their government allowed the Indians to do. But in Paris the counsel was to give the Indians free rein, they were necessary parts of the French war machine in North America, and they were, after all, only killing Englishmen and Englishwomen. So the French high command in Canada looked the other way at every sort of Indian bestiality. Life along the northern and western frontiers of the English colonies became ever more dangerous.

In 1755, the English captured Fort Beau Sejour. The Acadians were ordered to take an oath of allegiance to Britain. They hesitated, and the English—really the Massachusetts colonists—forced the issue. Colonel John Winslow, a Massachusetts man, forcibly evacuated all 6,000 residents of Acadia in November and December 1755. (The tragedy of displacement of a people was immortalized by Henry Wadsworth Longfellow, but not for nearly a hundred years, in his poem "Evangeline.") The Acadians were scattered all over Canada and the vast Louisiana territory until the end of the Seven Years War, when many of them returned to their old homes, having suffered the most severe hardships of any group in the New World.

In January 1756 the English attacked the French at Crownpoint in a battle that cost many lives but did not decide much. Having won the day, the colonists retreated, so the Crown Point expedition proved nothing.

The failure of the English and the colonists to win victories in the west and in New York increased the danger to that whole long frontier. As the French moved to open it, the Indians increased the murdering and looting along a line of settlements now 600 miles long. These settlements were small, and precarious, usually reached overland by trail, or by water. The cabins of the settlers were miles apart, easy prey for even a handful of Indians. Historian Francis Parkman described what happened on the frontier when an Indian party on the warpath came to the cabin of a settler in a little clearing in the woods:

The owner of the cabin was miles away, hunting in the woods for the wild turkey and venison which were the chief food of himself and his family til the soil could be tamed for the bearing of crops.

Towards night he returned and as he issued from the forest shadows he saw a column of blue smoke rising quietly in the still evening air. He ran to the spot, and there, among the smouldering logs of his dwelling, lay, scalped, and mangled, the dead bodies of his wife and children. A war-party had passed that way. Breathless, palpitating, his brain on fire, he rushed through the thickening night to carry the alarm to his nearest neighbor, three miles distant.

In the next few months that same scene was played out dozens, scores of times. Virginia and Pennsylvania and Maryland were unable to control their frontiers. The Indians already dispossessed of the lands of the eastern seaboard were wreaking vengeance for a thousand wrongs, and the settlers were the victims.

In 1755, then, it was apparent in Boston, New York, Williamsburg, and Paris that the state of hostilities between England and France would control conditions in the New World as well as the Old. This perspicacity did not extend to London, which was not nearly so interested in what was happening on the Ohio and in Canada as was Paris. On January 31, 1756, the king of France summoned the Marquis de Montcalm to Paris. Montcalm was instructed to lead a military force to Canada and take charge of operations there, to drive the English from North America. He sailed for Canada in April.

The English colonies were very much in disarray. William Shirley, governor of Massachusetts, had succeeded to the leadership of the military forces on the death of Braddock. He had proposed a general attack in the north. A council of war of the colonies was called, but achieved nothing. Pennsylvania and Virginia seemed unable to connect the French and Indians in Canada with the French and Indians on their own borders. Then, to add to the confusion in the colonies, Shirley was superseded in 1755; the Earl of Loudon was to be the new commander in chief in America. In fact, this change was positive and represented a broad shift in English colonial policy. Parliament had decided that the New World was to be defended.

Loudon came. Somehow a ragtag force of British regulars, trained colonials, colonial militia, scouts, traders, and Indians was put together and held together with bread and whiskey. The fighting in upstate New York continued; the French tried to cut communications between Oswego and Albany, and the English resisted. The English made forays against the Canadian borders, and the French resisted. French Indians massacred Englishmen and English Indians massacred French. The Indians had little to win but whatever they could loot for the moment. For this war was not being fought for the betterment of Indians, quite to the contrary. Both English and French commanders from the old countries complained about the stink, savagery, and sometimes cannibalism of the savages, and almost equally at the backwoodsmen they met on both sides as they pursued their war, white men, but unwashed, unlearned, their language often barely understandable to the gentlemen who came to lead the troops of both sides.

The worst of the warfare was going on in the mountains and waters of Lake George, where Rodgers' Rangers became famous for their Indian fighting.

However, the provincial legislatures and governors stewed over the defense measures to be taken, resenting every penny spent on the common defense and London's reluctance to pay all the costs. What they did not understand was the difficult situation in which Britain found itself in 1756: a new war with France, and unrest in India. The Sepoy Rebellion would erupt this year, bringing arson, rape, and murder of the British military and civil population in India. British men, women, and children would die in the "black hole of Calcutta." It would be many months before a punitive expedition would set British India to rights again. Had Parliament possessed all the good will in the world toward the American colonies, its resources would still have been scattered so thin by the needs of the Royal Navy and the eastern colonies that it would have had to depend on the American colonies to undertake a good share of their own defense. The colonists had grown so far away from the mother country that they barely had sympathy for the English troops sent to help them. In New York, the enlisted men from England were quartered in barracks, but the officers had to find lodgings for themselves. There were few enough inns, and they were very expensive. Loudon demanded that New York make provisions for his officers and was refused.

"God damn my blood," shouted the Earl of Loudon. "If you do not billet my officers upon free quarters this day, I'll order all the troops in North America here and billet them myself upon this city." True to his word, he began with Oliver DeLancey, brother of the late lieutenant governor. Six soldiers were sent to stay in Oliver DeLancey's big house. DeLancey objected, so Loudon sent six more. The New Yorkers then did what they should have done in the first place: raised the money to provide proper officers' quarters removed from the civil populace.

In Boston there was no objection to housing the troops: they were only too welcome. Boston housed them in Castle William and provided blankets, beds, cooking utensils, and other necessities.

In January 1756, Rodgers' Rangers had encountered a large French and Indian force on Lake Champlain and had taken refuge in Fort Ticonderoga, which controlled the waters of the north country. In March the French had launched a major drive against Fort Ticonderoga and Fort William Henry on Lake George.

In the summer of 1756 Montcalm captured Oswego along with 1,600 prisoners, so now the French had control of the Great Lakes region. The war was horrifying to those already involved in North America, and it was growing more so.

In July, Montcalm prepared to capture the whole north country. Eight thousand Frenchmen and Indians assembled at Ticonderoga. The French Indians by now had disintegrated into a lawless horde that stuck by their French masters largely because of the booty they hoped to amass. They no longer had any real tribal aspirations and they were ever more savage. It was their pleasure to kill every Englishmen they could, man, woman, or child, and in the most desperate possible manner. One night a Jesuit priest at Ticonderoga approached the fire of a war party which was squatting in the middle of the French camp. A number of bound English prisoners were huddled by the fire, watching in horror as the Indians ate their meat. The meat was the flesh of an English prisoner. More of the Englishman was boiling in a pot on the fire. The Jesuit protested and an Indian said:

"You have French taste. I have Indian. This is good meat for me."

The French camp commander had to shrug. If he tried to suppress the Indians' savagery, they would desert.

In August, Montcalm finally captured Fort William Henry, the most advanced of the English outposts. The terms of surrender provided for the soldiers and civilians to be escorted safely to Fort Edward, eighteen miles south. But as the English came out of the fort, the Indians attacked, and the French could do nothing to stop them. Fifty Englishmen were butchered, and their scalps and other parts of their bodies taken off by the Indians. Two hundred were taken off by the Indians as prisoners, to be tortured, raped, brutalized, murdered, and some of them eaten.

The Indians behaved with ever-increasing brutality. Captive women were forced to watch the murders of their own children and then eat the flesh of those children before they, too, died.

Even so, the Indians proved completely unreliable; they fought when they wished, and then they disappeared on their own business, so the French position after the defeat of the English garrison at Fort William Henry was not as promising as it appeared to be.

The whole north country was open to the French in the absence of any major English military force. Montcalm could easily have taken Albany and perhaps even New York, for on June 30 General Loudon was off on an abortive expedition against Louisbourg. But Montcalm's Indians had deserted him to disport themselves with their prisoners and enjoy their loot. Montcalm had no one to lug his cannon down to the Hudson River, so he retreated to Ticonderoga.

In 1757 the constant, horrifying pleas of the colonists were heard in Parliament, where William Pitt was made secretary of state for war in 1757 and prepared to move boldly in 1758. He decided that strong action must be taken in North America. He sent Lord Jeffrey Amherst to North America, along with General James Wolfe.

Ever more American colonial agents were coming from the colonies to London to plead various American causes, and one of them was the need for military assistance. Benjamin Franklin went to England in 1757 to argue for the taxation of the Penn estates to support colonial defenses. He and other colonial agents told the story of the North American colonies' troubles so effectively that Parliament was now thoroughly aroused to the danger of a French victory that would expand French power throughout the west and south to join with Louisiana, and pinch off the western expansion of the English colonies at the Alleghenies. More resources were allocated by England, but at the same time a demand was made by Pitt that the colonies raise 20,000 troops. The colonial governments were appalled at being called upon to spend so much for their common defense. How resentful they were depended on how immediate the threat seemed; New Jersey was more unwilling than Rhode Island, and North Carolina more unwilling than Pennsylvania. That year 15,000 men did make their appearance in the Albany area, but most of them were "summer soldiers." In the colonies, farmer soldiers would drift off at harvest time and by winter would almost all be gone home.

On July 5, 1757, the English attacked Fort Ticonderoga. They were strong, at least five times as powerful as the French defending force, but the French had prepared an unusual defense. They had cut down hundreds of trees in front of the fort. From inside their walls the French could fire at will upon the Englishmen as they crawled and climbed over the logs.

The result was a disaster for the English. Two thousand men succumbed to the guns and muskets of the fort, and the survivors panicked and ran halfway back to Albany, with no one in pursuit. Montcalm lost only 400 men in defense of the fort. The French had invented the "field of fire."

But the English persisted. In the fall of 1757 they took Fort Duquesne (Pittsburgh) and Fort Frontenac, which commanded Lake Ontario and the way west. Then they attacked Quebec.

The tables were now turned; the English had the major force in North America. Montcalm's regular French troops were down to about 3,000 men, nor could he get any help from Paris, because the French were suffering so greatly in the European war against England. The Duc de Belle Isle, the French minister of war, counseled Montcalm to have courage. He was planning a master stroke that would remove the pressure from Canada. France was going to invade England. In the winter of 1757–58 the French built hundreds of small craft in preparation for an attack on the English isles. But, like another cross-channel attack planned by Adolf Hitler in 1940, the invasion never came off. England's mastery of the sea in 1757 and 1758 had the same effect as her mastery of the air in the summer of 1940. The enemy could not gain control, so he backed away.

In Canada, Montcalm faced more difficulty. The governor of Canada, the Marquis de Vaudreuil, resented Montcalm's coming. Wherever possible, Vaudreuil and his men subverted Montcalm's orders pertaining to the defense of the colony. The result was a moral and physical weakening of the whole French colonial structure.

Then came the winter of 1758–59. A fleet of French ships arrived in Canada, but then the British navy moved, and France was cut off from her colony. Pitt had raised a large military force and was dispatching it to New England.

The center of British activity against the French moved to Halifax, Nova Scotia. This was an indication of the strength England had built up in Nova Scotia since the capture of Acadia. In May forty warships lay anchored in Halifax harbor, plus transports carrying 12,000 troops, of which 11,000 were British regular soldiers. This was the greatest military commitment England had yet made to the colonies. No longer was England putting them off with the advice that they really ought to defend themselves. Pitt was committed to the use of British troops to win this war.

After Louisbourg fell to General James Wolfe and a force of forty ships and 9,000 troops on July 26, 1758, Pitt prepared for more fighting to roust the French. Ten years earlier, even five years earlier, the English would have let such a victory suffice; but now, General Wolfe went back to England for consultations with Pitt while Lord Jeffrey Amherst remained in America, waiting and tidying up his army. Wolfe described what resources were necessary to win the day in North America. In the fall of 1758, he was ordered back to Halifax, starting February 17, 1759, with the greatest fleet ever sent to America—250 ships, 49 of them warships—and altogether about 30,000 more men to fight the French.

France could do nothing like that for Montcalm. Paris could not even send him 5,000 men. They sent him the sort of grandiose messages that always sound so much better in French than in translation. *(Courage, mon vieux! Le jour de gloire viendra! Nous attendons ta victoire!)*

Montcalm mounted the defense of Quebec with only five battalions of trained troops, supported by several thousand Canadians. General Wolfe landed on the lower side of the gorge at Montmorency and at the top of the island of Orleans. He put gun batteries at Point Levis across the Saint Lawrence from Quebec, and these battered the city every day, destroying the houses of the society district. But the Quebec fortress held, and when Wolfe made a frontal assault on the last day of July 1759, it failed.

Wolfe backed off and considered the matter. August passed. Winter was not far away and that would force the end of the campaign. He must take Quebec before snowfall.

The best chance for attack lay on the land side, for the fortress defense was weakest there. The plateau called the Plains of Abraham lay below it. But to get to the Plains of Abraham, the English would have to make a landing at the foot of a steep cliff and come up difficult trails, which could be made impassable if defended from above by the French. The shore was guarded well by French fortifications and cannon. A French regular battalion was camped on the Plains of Abraham.

On September 6, however, in the continuing struggle for command between Governor Vaudreuil and General Montcalm, Vaudreuil withdrew the French troops from the plains, and Wolfe saw his chance. The next day he made several feints at several other landings, pretending to attack. The French moved to meet the challenges. The English then withdrew.

On September 13 Wolfe launched his stroke. The English force embarked in small boats from warships lying above Quebec and came quietly down the river. French speakers among the English troops shouted loudly, pretending that these were French boats bringing supplies along the usual route, and 5,000 English soldiers got ashore unnoticed. They climbed the cliff and overpowered the guards, and the ships began bringing cannon to be dragged up the steep hill. All this while everything English that could fire on the river side of the fortress was firing away.

The English warships below the fortress maneuvered in the night, and boatloads of men could be seen, apparently moving for a frontal assault on the river side. To the defenders it appeared that the English were planning a major attack for dawn.

But as day dawned and Montcalm waited impatiently for reinforcements and provisions to come down the usual route above Quebec, he was informed that the English had invested the Plains of Abraham. He went to the edge of the city and saw for himself: thousands of redcoats on the plain.

Montcalm had already said that in case of such a development, his chance of salvation lay in immediate attack, and he ordered it. But Vaudreuil countermanded the order, so that some of the French troops did not attack. Montcalm interposed the 4,000 French under his control between Quebec and the English. His troops began to attack in the fashion of the day, which meant marching forward, stopping to fire a concerted volley of musket shots, swabbing, loading, priming, and marching forward again to fire another volley. The French, in the center of the line, moved forward, fired, stopped, reloaded, and moved forward again. The Canadians and the Indians on their flanks, forest fighters, lay down to reload.

The English did not fire at all. They had their orders from Wolfe. The English moved forward slowly in a thin red line until the French were only forty yards away. General Wolfe had ordered each man to load two balls in his musket and hold fire for one big volley. When only those forty yards separated the forces and the faces of the French were clearly visible, the English fired, and when the smoke cleared away, the French line was in tatters and Frenchmen, Canadians, and Indians were dying in ragged piles on the ground. Others were breaking and running back toward the city. The English then launched a bayonet charge. These were regular troops, and this was their métier. The Canadians and Indians panicked. The French regulars were overwhelmed. Wolfe and Montcalm were both mortally wounded, but the English had won their battle. Within a matter of hours, Governor Vaudreuil surrendered Quebec.

At the same time Lord Amherst was supposed to be moving on Montreal from Lake Champlain, but his progress was like that of a snail, so ridiculous that it occasioned a song from the Americans:

> *Lord Jeffrey Amherst was a soldier to the king*
> *And he came to the far country.*
> *To the Frenchmen and the Indians, he didn't do a thing,*
> *In the wilds of the far country.*

Amherst did not make Montreal that season.

Montreal held. At the beginning of 1760, Canada was still French. Paris still did not have any resources to send to help; London had plenty and Pitt was determined to use them. On April 27, 1760, General Levis attacked Quebec, but he did not capture the city. In May, a British fleet arrived at Montreal, and Levis retreated.

From this point on the French could only retreat and concentrate on Montreal. On September 7, the British split forces and converged on that city and Lord Amherst demanded immediate capitulation. There was really little recourse. Most of the French Indians had melted into the woods, the memory of those feasts of "long pig" now haunting them. On September 8, Governor Vaudreuil signed the surrender. All Canada was relinquished by France and became an English colony.

At the peace of Paris in 1763 France gave up all its territory east of the Mississippi River except the Louisiana area and New Orleans. Since the American southern colonies were still confined generally to the eastern coastal areas, Louisiana seemed a long way away. Off the Newfoundland shore, France was allowed to keep two tiny fishing islands, Saint Pierre and Miquelon. That was all.

The American colonists and the English did not forget the horrors visited on them by the Frenchmen's Indians. To the enormous chagrin of the French government and nobility, the English refused to give the French soldiers the usual honors of war bestowed on an honorable, defeated foe— keeping their weapons, parades, salutes, and other military courtesies. One of the cherished Western European myths that warfare was an act of gallantry had perished in this terrible struggle. (Despite any indications to the contrary, for instance, the "gentlemen's" air battles of World War I were strictly local aberrations.)

England was mightily pleased. She ruled the waves, and the sun never set on the British empire. The French having been conquered, the American colonies could now settle down and pay back to the Crown and the people of England some of the enormous expense that had been lavished on them in the past five years to defeat the common enemy. That was what London thought.

How wrong she was.

CHAPTER 3

Rebellion

There really never need have been an American Revolution. The late Ira G. Corn, Jr., student of history and notable as one of the owners of a copy of the Declaration of Independence, devoted several years to a study, as yet unpublished, which gave a cogent explanation of the real causes of the rebellion of the American colonies.

Taxation without representation, of course, was a slogan for the pamphleteers. But the fact was that the Americans by the 1770s would have been just as unhappy with taxation, even if they had been given all the representation in the British Parliament that they thought they needed. In fact, no Americans made any serious effort to get representation. They simply wanted to avoid taxation and British control of American business. The plain truth was that by 1770 the Americans had grown far away from the English.

The American colonies made some overtures to the Canadian colonies, hoping for a continental union, but the Canadians rebuffed them. At the same time, the government in London, having neglected the American colonies for a century, decided that its investment there was really excellent. The king and other colonial proprietors began bearing down for political and economic reasons. Lord Grenville was interested in revenue from the colonies, to be sure, but others in Parliament were more interested in political control, and King George III liked privately to consider the day when he might restore the absolute monarchy to England. It was a wild dream, but he was encouraged in his excesses by his courtiers and was not intelligent enough to see where the courtiers were leading him.

An important factor that encouraged the alienation from the Americans of English merchants and leaders was their perception of the Americans as willful and extremely selfish. It was true. The Americans expected England to pay the bills for American defense because American traders produced hundreds of thousands of pounds annually for the British official coffers, to say nothing of the profits of British merchants. The British, burdened by the cost of supporting an enormous navy and an equally expensive army, became annoyed with the American attitude.

The most sensible man on either side in the 1760s was Benjamin Franklin, the agent for several of the colonies in London. He went from town house to country mansion, to the London clubs, and even to Parliament, preaching the gospels of accommodation; but the fiery Boston patriots on the one hand and the arrogant Tory nobility on the other moved steadily toward the split. Without any more help than that, it was soon to come.

*   *   *

The end of French rule in Canada did not mean that the French were out of North America by a long way; they still controlled that enormous territory in the south and west called Louisiana. But at the moment the English had other preoccupations, and the French—as well as the Spanish in Florida—were more or less quiescent.

Since the beginning of the eighteenth century, the English government had struggled, although not always very energetically, with the problem of central authority in the colonies. No successful solution had been found. But with the end of the French and Indian War, England found herself with a possession in North America that was ten times the size of the original English possessions there. Thus new methods had to be found to govern the American colonies, and that included the new possessions in Canada.

The first problem of the English in the matter of securing internal peace in the American colonies was to settle affairs with the Indians. This was done by dividing the continent at the Appalachian Mountains. East of the Appalachians was English country; the colonies could expand there as they liked. West of the Appalachians was Indian country. The English colonists who had moved into the Ohio Valley were ordered to get out and move back east. Of course, they ignored the order.

In London Lord Grenville suggested the necessity of maintaining a standing army of 10,000 men in America.

As the Indian troubles died, the Americans had lost all interest in common defense and the maintenance of an army. What was the difference whether the Ohio Valley and the Mississippi were closed off by the French or by the London government in favor of the Indians? The English colonists could see none. Thus was a new sore to fester set up by an English Privy

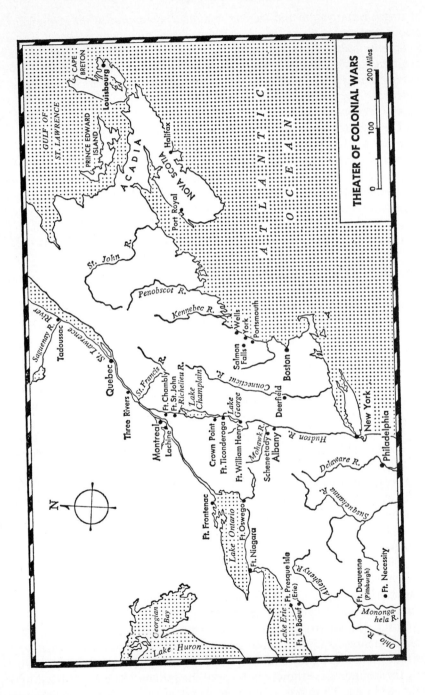

Council and king who had virtually no knowledge of the conditions in North America.

The Indian troubles had not ended completely. Within three months of the signing of the Treaty of Paris (February 1763), Chief Pontiac of the Ottawa Indians had plotted to seize Detroit by surprise attack. Foiled, he then went on the warpath, and within a month every English outpost west of Niagara was destroyed.

The colonists were furious and afraid. It was suggested to Lord Jeffrey Amherst that he use germ warfare: distribute the blankets of smallpox victims to the Indians, who were highly susceptible to the disease. Amherst liked the idea. Wiser heads prevailed, but only because colonists and British soldiers were also susceptible to the pox. Instead, the English resorted to a hunt-and-kill campaign by the soldiery. Soon Major General Thomas Gage succeeded Amherst, who was given leave to return to England. Gage's domain ran from Newfoundland to Florida and from Bermuda to the Mississippi River. Thus, in the military was established a central authority governing some aspects of colonial life and responsible to the Crown.

The immediate consequence of the French and Indian War and the conquest of Canada was a reaction in England: the colonies had cost the home government hundreds of thousands of pounds in defense. The British national debt had risen to £122,000,000 in 1763, and virtually none of it was being paid by the colonists.

An army was now established on the American shore, and it must be supported. Grenville estimated that a fair share of the cost for the colonies would be £200,000 a year.

The London government knew very little and cared very little about the costs to the colonists of the French and Indian troubles. Pennsylvania, for example, had spent £500,000. New England had spent much more. But at this point the colonies had insufficient representation in London to make their case, and by the time they got it, ideas and attitudes had settled into patterns. England came forth from the French wars with a people tired of heavy taxation. The colonies, suddenly discovered by London after years of neglect, offered a new source of taxes, and one that could not answer back in Parliament. The timing seemed ideal to solve many fiscal problems.

The first step toward the new parliamentary insistence on "colonial fiscal responsibility" was taken in Parliament in the spring of 1764 when Chancellor of the Exchequer George Grenville introduced legislation designed to raise money for the government by taxing the colonies. The bill was called the Sugar Act, though it dealt with sugar, molasses, textiles, coffee, indigo, Madeira and Canary wines—those standbys of the upper and middle classes—iron, hides, whale fins, raw silk, and other items. It banned the import into the American colonies of French wines and foreign rum. That meant the Americans could not buy directly from France or the French West Indies, but had to arrange for purchase of these goods, pay the cost and the import tax to England, and then another tax to export from England to America.

At the same time Parliament moved to straighten up its sloppy administration of the tax laws. For more than a hundred years, the English colonies in America had been regarded as a useful extension of the empire in the sense that they provided a place for shipment of criminals and ne'er-do-wells (Virginia) and the resolution of vexatious religious and social problems (Pennsylvania, New England, and Maryland). They also provided in the land grants a method for the king to pay off political and other debts to relatives and supporters.

But a new attention to the colonies had shown that they could, indeed, be an excellent source of revenue for the government, even without new taxes. The old taxes were not being paid, and sometimes, when they were paid to collectors for the Crown, the collectors did not turn in the money to London's representatives.

Every English port in America had its customs house, usually the most imposing building on the waterfront. But so lax had customs collection become that the Crown was getting only about £2,000 a year from all America, and that represented less than a quarter of the cost of paying the tax collectors.

Chancellor Grenville proposed to tighten up the laws and the practices. The center of tax collection was to be moved to Halifax, and in the future none but English money would be acceptable in the colonies. Several colonies had financed their military expenditures against the French and Indians by printing paper money which was nothing more nor less than an IOU. Parliament ordered the cessation of this process and outlawed the currency already printed.

Parliament's new fiscal measures came at a time when the American colonies, as well as England, were feeling the pinch of a postwar recession. American shipbuilders had been busy during the war with the French, providing small vessels. England bought most of its mast timber from New England. The trade in foodstuffs and hides and cotton had been great. Suddenly this fell off, English manufactured goods became more expensive, and foreign goods were largely prohibited except at impossible cost.

The net result of the Grenville attitude was a turnabout of English policy toward the colonies, and they recognized it immediately.

In every colony some protest was made. In Massachusetts the Boston town meeting showed the way. Samuel Adams served as chairman of the town meeting called to instruct the Boston members of the Massachusetts legislature in the attitude they were to take toward the new taxation.

"If our trade may be taxed, why not our lands and everything we possess or make use of?" Adams asked. "This we apprehend annihilates our charter rights to govern and tax ourselves. It strikes at our British privileges."

The report of the town meeting called on Massachusetts to resist the Sugar Act taxes and Grenville's general policies. From the point of view of the English, the man who led the Boston protest, Sam Adams, was a highly suspect character. He had failed in business, and had become for a time a tax collector for the Crown. Adams had collected the taxes, but he had never turned them over to the Crown. Consequently he was thousands of pounds in arrears with his tax collections. A prosecutor might take the position that this man was embezzling the Crown's funds. Small wonder, then, that Sam Adams had very strong views on taxation by the English central government. They grew stronger in the next few years, as he was pressed to pay up his arrears as tax collector. Stewart Beach in his 1965 biography of Sam Adams indicates that it would have been against the character of the public Adams to have embezzled, although some others believe he did. Perhaps. It seems obvious that one way or the other, the long battle (it lasted more than five years) on the tax issue must have affected Sam Adams very deeply.

But far more substantial citizens, with no possible stains on their escutcheons, felt the same. Sam Adams was a gadfly, a polemicist and publicist who had a knack for polarizing public sentiment, and then popularizing his cause. Richard Dana was a solid Boston citizen, and so was Nathaniel Bethune. These businessmen agreed that Sam Adams was to write the draft of the complaint to the legislature. Some 1,200 Boston citizens had been aroused sufficiently to attend the town meeting in Faneuil Hall that May 24, to applaud and then endorse the Adams protest.

What upset the Bostonians more than the Sugar Act was the new policy of London. The colonists suspected that the Crown and Parliament would now expect them to begin paying their own way. That meant they would have to pay the expenses of quartering the soldiers and pay the salaries of royal governors, judges, tax collectors, and other Crown officials. Since the colonists had not been doing so all these years, this idea was anathema to them now.

The rebellious mood grew all through the colonies month by month. The Massachusetts legislature helped speed the protest by authorizing a committee of correspondence to write to other colonial legislatures and promote a general protest against English government policy; in October the legislature petitioned London for repeal of the Sugar Act.

By 1765 every colony in America was objecting to the new attitude in London that the Americans were going to have to pay taxes in line with those of citizens at home in England. The American position was that there could be no comparison between the two ways of life, between the security of the English countryside and that of the frontier of the new continent.

This attitude that Americans were different would grow stronger every year.

Early in 1765, Chancellor Grenville and his advisers conceived of a stamp tax on American newspapers, pamphlets, lawyers' papers, licenses, all sorts of paper documents, even on playing cards. The money was to go into the royal treasury and be earmarked for defense of the colonies. The amount raised should be £60,000 per year. With the customs duties and the Sugar Act, Grenville hoped to secure from the colonies an additional £100,000 a year, or a third of what it was costing England to maintain the army in the colonies. The Stamp Act aroused every American who was suspicious of London, because it was the first direct tax ever imposed by Parliament on the Americans. When it was first mentioned in Parliament a number of "friends of the colonies" objected, but the majority of the members of the Commons saw it another way, and the measure passed by a five to one majority.

The word came to New England in May 1765, and within a few days everyone—tavernkeeper, lawyer, newspaper publisher, advertiser, ship's captain—the whole business community—found that they would be directly affected. The Massachusetts House of Representatives put out a call for an all-colony meeting to protest the tax. They tagged on another reason—a new treaty with the Iroquois Indians—but the real issue was the money matter.

Except for North Carolina, a newer colony, the Southern colonies were not moved to act. Virginia, South Carolina, Georgia, and Delaware did not respond. But New Hampshire, Connecticut, Rhode Island, Pennsylvania, and Maryland did send representatives. The Congress would not meet until October. Meanwhile the Boston merchants egged one another on. They signed a "nonimportation agreement" which meant they would not buy any more British goods until the Stamp Act was repealed.

The Stamp Act was passed by Parliament on March 22, 1765. Two days later the English army secured passage of an act that angered still another section of the colonists. General Thomas Gage was still having difficulty finding adequate housing for his men. So Parliament passed a law throwing the full responsibility for providing barracks and supplies on the American civil authorities.

The resentment against the one act fueled that against the other. In the Virginia legislature Patrick Henry got up and compared King George III to Julius Caesar, in his famous "give me liberty or give me death" speech, which was transmitted to England as the "treason" speech.

In Boston that summer, a group of men met under a great old elm in Hanover Square and named the tree the Liberty Tree. The tree was so large that it sheltered a score of men beneath its broad branches, and that is where the men met from time to time. They took the name the Sons of

Liberty. The organization had no roster and was semisecret. Their pledge was to colonial freedom; their method was violence. Swiftly the idea of a vigilante organization spread through the colonies until eventually the Sons of Liberty numbered several thousand men.

In Boston that summer the Sons of Liberty threatened a number of officials connected with the enforcement of the Stamp Act. On August 15, Andrew Oliver, the Boston stamp agent, was forced to resign in fear of his life. Eleven days later the Sons of Liberty invaded the house of Chief Justice Thomas Hutchinson of Massachusetts, and ransacked his library. The idea seems to have been to deprive the chief justice of the sources for his legal citations. They also invaded the admiralty court and burned its records, and robbed the house of the controller of the currency. This was certainly rebellion.

Another sort of rebellion was taking place in the West, where the British army's responsibility was to uphold the law: to prevent the Indians from coming east of the Appalachians and the settlers from moving west. They might as well have tried to stop the flow of rivers. Hundreds of Englishmen, Germans, and Scotch-Irish moved through the gaps in the mountains, seeking the lands of the West. If they did not own or buy land, they squatted. When the British army came to eject the settlers, the resentments grew.

Another of the laws passed to regulate America said that trade with the Indians had to be conducted at a military post. The law was impossible to enforce; if a trader was caught, he had to be sent east to the civil courts, and the military witnesses had to go, too.

Because of all this and because the revenues promised General Gage by the London government did not materialize, he wanted to move the bulk of his force in America from the West to the Eastern cities where troop management was much simpler. Also, as the Sons of Liberty and other riotous groups began breaking the laws, Gage was of a mind to use troops and bayonets for enforcement. At the moment, however, all was in flux, and the redcoats remained in the West with their impossible tasks, and the colonists rioted in the Eastern cities.

The government in London changed that summer of 1765. Grenville was succeeded as chancellor of the exchequer by Charles Townshend in the government of the Earl of Rockingham. In New York City that fall the Stamp Act Congress directed appeals to the king and Parliament. But the change of government meant a change of policy and early in 1766 the Stamp Act was repealed because Parliament saw what a terrible effect it had on British trade with America, down about twenty percent because of colonial resistance.

Parliament could be receptive to the demands of the colonists, but what was not very well understood in America was the new resolve in London that the colonies should remain British colonies of the Crown, subject to the government of the central authorities. The trouble was—and it was spreading like a cancer through the colonies in the 1760s—that the colonies had been neglected so long that the colonists had developed a powerful feeling of independence. Britain's sudden awakening to the problems of North America in the 1750s was very late. By 1766 General Gage had concluded that the drive for independence in the various American colonies was so strong that "it concerns Great Britain by a speedy and spirited conduct to show them that these provinces are British colonies, dependent on her, and that they are not independent states."

The original purpose of maintaining the standing army in America was common defense, but by 1766 the colonial governors, representing the Crown, were having such difficulty in enforcing the laws passed by Parliament to govern the American colonies that they were beginning to ask General Gage for Crown troops. To use colonial militia was extremely difficult, partly because the legislatures held power over the militia, and partly because public sentiment was against much of what the governors wanted.

General Gage sent troops to put down riots in New York Colony. He ordered troops to the assistance of the governor of Nova Scotia.

After the repeal of the Stamp Act in the fall of 1766, quarrels between the Tories and the Whigs in England created a deadlock in Parliament and relieved the pressure on the colonies to conform. But Charles Townshend, as chancellor of the exchequer, had the problem of raising money for government. When he announced that he would maintain the English land tax at four shillings to the pound, the landowners of England erupted: that was the wartime rate. When the country was at peace, as now, the rate should be three shillings to the pound. Grenville, now in opposition, led the fight against the four-shilling tax and won. The British government was then £500,000 short in its income for the coming year. Where to get it? From the colonies, said Townshend. And so a whole new set of taxes, the Townshend Acts, were levied on the colonies.

The result was a growing rebellion. Sam Adams and other publicists throughout the colonies began propagandizing their fellows with letters, broadsides, and pamphlets, all attacking the new taxes and the British government. One reaction was a new campaign among the colonists for "nonimportation"—the refusal to buy British-made goods. Meanwhile the new commissioners of customs had set up shop in the colonies and were finding it hard to collect import taxes. They asked London for naval or military power to back them up. The public response was to riot and burn the commissioners in effigy. Governor Bernard asked for military help. The fifty-gun warship *Romney* was sent down to Boston from Halifax, and her presence emboldened the commissioners to seize John Hancock's ship *Liberty* for smuggling and falsifying papers. That was followed by riots. The commissioners and their families took refuge aboard the *Romney*.

Meetings . . . conventions . . . riots . . . appeals . . . finally General Gage was asked to supply troops to be quartered in Boston to maintain order. With some reluctance, having learned of America's intransigeance and knowing that it was a precedent to bring troops into a major city, General Gage agreed and the 14th Regiment was ordered there at the end of August 1768 "to strengthen the hands of Government in the Province of Massachusetts Bay, enforce due obedience to the laws, and protect and support the Civil Magistrates in the preservation of the public peace and to the officers of the Revenue in the execution of their duty . . ."

The British army had come to troublesome Boston.

Parliament warned the Americans that it had the authority to legislate for the colonies in any way it wanted. The Townshend Acts, the seizure of the *Liberty,* the push by imperial authorities to force their will on the colonists, all contributed to the tensions, but the bringing of redcoats to be quartered in Boston changed the whole nature of the conflict. The colonists moved from a stage of insubordination and defiance toward open violent resistance to authority. At the end of September troopships arrived in Boston harbor from Halifax, and artillery units were landed in Boston town. A thousand British soldiers marched up from the port past the Town House, Queen Street to Tremont, and down to the Mall and the Common, fifes playing, drums beating. The people of Boston gathered to look, but there was no cheering. The troops were not regarded as men who had saved the colonies from the French. That was all long ago, and the troops should be back in England where they belonged, said the colonists. What the people of Boston were now seeing, according to their lights, was an occupation.

There was no immediate reaction by the people of Boston, except to look at the redcoats with suspicion. Parliament was suffering some serious reactions at home to its new policies. The Townshend Acts had triggered a new round of "nonimportation" activity in the colonies, and an enormous amount of rhetoric in the colonial legislatures on the general subject of taxation. Imports of British goods fell from £2 million to £1 million in just over a year. The Board of Trade was aroused—so were London merchants—and Parliament felt it all. The Townshend Acts, everybody agreed, had gone too far and annoyed too many people. The Quartering Act, making the colonies responsible for the housing and feeding of redcoats, was also regarded as an unnecessary evil, and it was soon withdrawn. But Lord Frederick North, the new prime minister of 1770, decided that the colonies must still be taught a lesson in principle. The Townshend Acts would be repealed—all but the tax on tea. That would be retained just to teach the Americans that Parliament was supreme.

The colonies responded grimly. In Boston, the citizens began making life difficult for the redcoats. Off duty they were shunned by most of the people. They were pushed and insulted and sometimes fights broke out. On duty in their red coats, they were also abused and reviled. A large number (forty in the first two weeks) deserted. A parade was held at Town House, and the commander announced a reward of ten guineas for information leading to the arrest of any deserter. The people ignored the money. A deserter was caught and flogged on Boston Common as an example of military discipline. Bostonians discovered they did not much like British military discipline—public lashings on the Common until the backs of the errant soldiers were laid bare to the bone by the cat-o'-nine-tails and the blood dripped down their legs. Lawyer John Adams was out of town when the redcoats came. He arrived back in town to discover that one of the regiments was exercised every day in Brattle Square, directly in front of his house.

Actually, the colonists were not nearly so mistreated as they claimed. John Adams took the defense of John Hancock in the case involving the seizure of the *Liberty* for smuggling (which she was obviously doing). He won the case with the plea that Hancock had been denied trial by jury. But that was not enough. The colonists had never had authority over them from the outside, and they could not stomach it now.

By 1770 emotions were winning the day in Boston. In Virginia, New York, and other colonies, the voices of dissent also grew louder. Parliament was angered and decided the colonies had to be punished. That attitude then crept into the legislative debates. The reports of the debates, reaching the colonies, triggered equally violent reactions there. Parliament said flatly that it had the right and responsibility to legislate over the colonies in behalf of all the English people. The colonists replied: "We will not submit to any taxes nor become slaves. We will take up arms and spend our last drop of blood before the King and Parliament shall impose on us."

These violent views did not represent everyone involved, by far. But by the fall of 1769 tempers were short and the little group of revolutionaries who were manipulating colonial public opinion were doing a good job.

The relationships between redcoats and citizens were helped to grow worse by Sam Adams and his friends. Governor Bernard and other officials wrote to Parliament, letters critical of various colonists. Colonial agents in London copied the letters and sent them back home. One day James Otis, Jr., a lawyer, politician, and Massachusetts patriot who still claimed complete loyalty to the Crown, picked up the *Boston Gazette* and saw that he was accused in one of these letters from Customs Commissioner John

Robinson of high treason. Otis became furious, went to the British Coffee House, a hangout of officials, found Robinson, bearded him, and said something insulting. Robinson came after Otis with a cane, a fight started, Robinson's British friends got into it, and Otis emerged badly beaten with a head wound that was caused by a British officer's sword. He sued for damages and his attorney was John Adams. They won, but the tension of the long affair drove Otis actually mad, and he had to be confined. He had meanwhile been elected to the legislature on the basis of this case. Ultimately Adams took his place.

So the colonial situation had grown so desperate that it drove men mad. The tension was growing in Virginia and in other colonies as well. Thomas Jefferson made his first appearance in the Virginia legislature that year (1769). Washington was there, and Patrick Henry and Richard Henry Lee. The governor closed down the Virginia legislature that year, and the Crown was not forgiven for it.

The colonists were driving west. In 1769 a Connecticut man explored that portion of the Mississippi valley directly west of Connecticut, for by the charter did not the Connecticut lands extend "indefinitely" to the west? Daniel Boone left his North Carolina home to go out and search for "the country of Kentucky" about which he had heard glorious claims. He found it, delighted in it, and moved his family there, in direct violation of Crown policy against colonial movement into Indian country. The Crown's Indian policy was already in shambles. The Americans were paying no attention to the land restrictions.

In the summer of 1770 Governor Bernard of Massachusetts was recalled by London, and on the day that he sailed away bells rang, cannon were fired on the wharf, the Liberty Tree was decorated with flags, and a bonfire was kindled on Fort Hill. The man appointed to succeed Bernard was Thomas Hutchinson, a native-born American, which ought to have augured well for the colony. But in an hour when the most active colonists were favoring minimal interference from London, Hutchinson proved to be the king's man all the way.

The soldiers and the working men of Boston did not get along at all well, at least partly because the soldiers liked to make a little extra money by working as laborers, particularly on the docks, in their off time. On March 2, 1770, a soldier went down to the docks, inquired about employment, was insulted by a civilian dockworker named Sam Gray, got into a fight, lost, and went back to his barracks for reinforcements. He brought several more soldiers back to the site, including Private Kilroy, a famous street fighter. The British soldiers fought the dockworkers again and lost. Their commander then complained to the governor. Nothing happened.

The weekend came and passed, relatively peacefully because it snowed. On Monday the weather cleared, and that evening soldiers and civilians went forth again, looking for trouble. Groups of soldiers roamed the streets with cutlasses and cudgels in hand, assaulting stray civilians.

At King Street, opposite the Customs House, a single redcoat was walking a guard post. Down by Faneuil Hall a mob was hanging around, and got into a fight with some soldiers—who were hustled off to their barracks by officers. Then the mob started out along the streets looking for trouble. They moved into King Street, spotted the sentry, and began pelting him with snowballs loaded with rocks. Private Hugh Montgomery, the sentry, shouted for the sergeant of the guard, and loaded his musket in the face of the threatening crowd. Up came the sergeant and six men, followed by Captain Preston, commander of the company. They stood with loaded guns, but Preston kept them from firing. The crowd grew bigger and noisier. Church bells were rung, and that brought more people to the scene.

A black man, Crispus Attucks, struck Private Montgomery, which made him drop his musket. He picked it up and shot Attucks dead. Private Kilroy, the street fighter, spotted his old adversary Sam Gray, the longshoreman, and shot him dead. Two other civilians were mortally wounded and several more slightly wounded.

Governor Hutchinson showed up and demanded some answers from Captain Preston. But the noise in the street was so great that he did not get them, and ultimately some people spirited Hutchinson away into the Town House to save him from the mob. He went onto the balcony and told the crowd to go home—that he was looking into the matter—and the crowd dispersed.

Hutchinson persuaded the colonel commanding the troops in Boston to move them into barracks; the colonel did.

Next day, the political implications began to become apparent. John Adams, Sam Adams, and others demanded that the British troops be removed from Boston. Governor Hutchinson said he had no such authority.

Impasse.

The Boston Massacre resulted in gaudy exaggerated funerals of the dead Attucks and Gray, who were transformed immediately from tough roustabouts into colonial heroes. The soldiers were tried for the shootings. The charge was murder. No counsel could be found. John Adams volunteered, and secured Preston's acquittal, because he had never ordered his men to fire. Soldiers Montgomery and Kilroy were convicted of manslaughter, and each was branded on the hand. Then they were returned to duty. The case was over. But not in the colonies. Boston, Massachusetts, and anyone elsewhere who was concerned with Britain's heavy hand on the colonies, would not forget the Boston Massacre.

For two years life seemed to quiet down. All the Townshend Acts but the tax on tea were indeed repealed. In the countryside the people of the colonies had grown tired of the conflict with England, and as England seemed to become more gentle, the colonists paid less attention to their foam-flecked revolutionaries. Surreptitiously at first, they began to buy British goods, and then the trickle became a current and a flood. In England the merchants rubbed their hands in satisfaction. It seemed that the troubles with the colonies were on the way to solution. Parliament, hanging onto the tea tax as a "matter of principle," indicated that no new taxes were even considered, and this pleased the American merchants. Only the politicians, the Crown governors, and the colonial legislatures continued to argue over the London government's *right* to tax the colonies. The theory did not interest businessmen.

What did interest the businessmen was avoiding taxes. The battle between the tax collector and the trader was never-ending. In June 1772, the customs schooner *Gaspee* ran aground near Providence, and a group of merchants attacked and burned the vessel. The commander, Lieutenant Dudington, was also wounded. In London, particularly because of the attack on a British officer, the government was furious and demanded an inquiry. They got it, but it was most unsatisfactory. Everyone of any importance in Massachusetts knew the names of the men involved, who had been led by merchant John Brown, but no one in the colony would testify against them. So the inquiry commission had to be disbanded, and no one was punished for an act of downright piracy.

After Lord North had announced that, "as a matter of principle," the tax on tea sent to the colonies would be retained, most colonists did what they could to avoid buying tea from England. They smuggled, they even quit drinking tea. And by 1773 this behavior pattern had helped a not-very-well East India Company reach the edge of bankruptcy. The company had already encountered enormous difficulties in India. The American boycott of tea had caused it to fill its London warehouses with tea. But the American boycott did not stop, and the directors of the company let the government know that the economic position was getting very serious. Parliament was faced with losing the £400,000 the company paid as a license fee in lieu of taxes.

The company wanted the right to send its tea to America without paying the export tax. That would enable the company to sell its tea cheaper than teas Americans were buying from French and other exporters. The company and the Americans asked that the much lower tax of three pennies per pound levied on Americans importing tea also be removed. Parliament rescinded the *export* tax, but not the other. Lord North said it was a matter of principle, to prove that Parliament had the right to tax the colonies. The East India Company was not too upset, for even with the three-penny tax, its tea could be sold cheapest in America. But they did not take into consideration the American attitude; the polemicists and publicists leaped upon this unfair situation, and renewed demands that all Americans avoid the English tea.

When the company got in touch with importers in America, it was warned that the business would not improve. But no one was listening in London.

So in the fall of 1773 consignments of tea were dispatched to the various American ports, sent by the East India Company to the merchants of its choosing, thus establishing a monopoly on the sale of English tea in the American market.

In Philadelphia, hardly a hotbed of rebellion in the past, the colonists met at the state house and passed eight resolutions against the British government's right to tax Americans. They called on the East India Company agents in Pennsylvania to resign, and they all did.

The same was true in South Carolina and in New York.

In Boston, as usual, the fine publicity machinery of Sam Adams and his friends gave a twist that was to make the Boston protest far more effective than the others.

On the night of November 1, the Boston merchants chosen by the East India Company to receive their tea were approached by the Sons of Liberty. A knock came at the door, and a written summons was passed to each: he was to appear at Liberty Tree at noon on the following Wednesday and publicly resign his commission as agent of the company. Two of the merchants chosen were sons of Governor Hutchinson. One was a nephew.

On the appointed day the merchants failed to show up at the Liberty Tree, so John Adams, John Hancock, and others appointed a committee which called on the tea merchants at the warehouse of Richard Clarke, a principal. All of the tea merchants were there. All refused the demand that they resign.

On November 5 John Hancock presided over a town meeting that adopted the Philadelphia antitax resolutions. Once again the Hutchinsons and other tea merchants refused to resign their East India Company commissions.

In New York demonstrations finally convinced the merchants to quit the arrangement rather than face violence. But in Boston, the governor's relatives persuaded the tea merchants to remain firm.

On November 17 came the word that the tea ships had sailed from England, bound for the various American ports. On November 18 the town meeting again entreated the Boston merchants to cease their efforts. Again the merchants refused, and this time the meeting broke up swiftly with no resolution at all. The matter had been passed into the hands of the Boston committee of correspondence—which meant Hancock, Adams, and radical friends. On November 22, the correspondence committees of Dorchester, Roxbury, Brookline, and Cambridge met with the Boston committee at Faneuil Hall and all agreed that the necessary action would be taken to stop the unloading of the tea. These groups represented the whole Boston area. In the next few days, town meetings in Cambridge, Charlestown, and other Boston suburbs affirmed the Philadelphia resolutions.

On Sunday, November 28, the ship *Dartmouth* appeared in Boston harbor. She carried 114 chests of East India Company tea. The committee of correspondence persuaded Quaker Rotch, the owner of the *Dartmouth*, to keep the *Dartmouth* outside until Tuesday. On Monday morning a mass meeting was called by the committees of correspondence of all the towns around. It was the largest meeting ever held and spilled over out of Faneuil Hall so that it had to be moved to the old South Meeting House.

It was the consensus of the meeting that if the merchants would not send the tea back, it would be thrown overboard from the ship, and they were so told.

On Tuesday morning the merchants replied that it was beyond their power to send the tea back. They tried to compromise, saying they would store the tea and not sell it, until they had new instructions from the East India Company. The answer was met with roars of disapproval.

That afternoon, Quaker Rotch suggested that the *Dartmouth* take the tea back to England. Other owners of ships that would be soon coming in with tea said the same. It seemed that the crisis had been resolved.

But Governor Hutchinson refused to let the *Dartmouth* sail. So the *Dartmouth* sat in the harbor. All the rest of the cargo was unloaded. Governor Hutchinson and the British authorities would not let the ships clear for England until the tea was unloaded. The colonists would not let them unload the tea. Two more tea ships arrived, and were directed to anchor at Griffin's Wharf, alongside the *Dartmouth*.

By December 9, the whole of New England was aroused; the committee of correspondence had done its job well. Public meetings reaffirmed the public decision: the tea must go back. Governor Hutchinson conferred with Admiral Montagu, the British naval commander. His two ships, the *Active* and the *Kingfisher,* were up for winter storage, but they were brought out and sent to guard the passages out of the harbor so no ships might leave without the governor's permission. Governor Hutchinson loaded the guns of the castle, to also bear on the harbor, and congratulated himself that he had solved the problem.

Angry public meetings on December 13 and December 14 incited action against the tea. At 10:00 A.M. on December 15 Quaker Rotch went to the customs house and again was told that he could not move his ships until they had unloaded the tea, and the tax had been paid. A large number of Bostonians were with him and heard the commissioners give their edict.

On December 16 Governor Hutchinson had gone to his country place in Milton. Rotch went to see him there, urged by committeemen to persuade the governor to overturn the commissioners and grant the release for the ship. A committee waited for him. He returned at quarter to six. It was already dark. He said the governor had refused him.

Sam Adams got up.

"This meeting can do nothing more to save the country," he said.

Was it a signal?

Outside, on the porch of the building, a war whoop went up. Looking out, the committeemen saw a crowd of fifty men done up in war paint with feathers in their hair and wearing blankets as the Indians did, each holding a hatchet in his hand.

Sam Adams and John Hancock raised a cheer and told the committeemen to come along. The party increased to about 200 men, with the "Indians" in the lead. They marched down to Griffin's Wharf, posted guards to see that they were not interrupted, and in the next three hours broke open the 340 chests of tea aboard the three ships, and dumped all 35,000 pounds of loose tea into the harbor.

Then everybody went home happily. The gentlemen of the committee of correspondence went to scratch their pens busily all night, writing to inform colonists elsewhere of what had happened. Next day the letters were on their way.

"All things were conducted with great order, decency, and perfect submission to government," announced the committee.

In Annapolis, when the tea arrived, colonists threw it into the sea. The same thing happened at Chestertown, Maryland, a port that in those days hoped to rival Baltimore.

"Perfect submission to government?"

That was not how it looked in London. Treason, defiance, rebellion, violence against king and Parliament, criminal conspiracy, were some of the charges made. No legal action followed the tea incidents in any colony, but thereafter the lines hardened on both sides. King and Parliament were determined that the colonies would submit to London's taxation; the colonists were determined that they would not. The tea tax was the symbol of the struggle: for £437 10s., the amount of the tax on that Boston tea, the government of England had just thrown away the American colonies.

CHAPTER 4

Revolution

The abortive plans of Parliament for taxation to bring the Americans into line failed more often than not. Rather than warning the economists of London to find another way to achieve their ends, the men in control of Parliament stiffened their necks and began insisting on the parliamentary power to tax all Englishmen everywhere, until the matter got completely out of hand, and the very word "taxation" brought cries of outrage on both sides of the Atlantic.

A dangerous state of affairs existed in North America after 1768, when the British cabinet opted to send troops to Boston to bring the colonists under control. Had Parliament known its colonists better, it would have known that no more unfriendly act could have been taken and that the reaction was bound to spread across the colonies.

*   *   *

By 1773 the publicists of rebellion had done a remarkable job of arousing the colonists of North America to the danger of losing the freedoms they had possessed from the beginning of colonization. They were not alone in worrying. Many Whigs in England were concerned because of the influence of cronies in the court on King George. The king had a proclivity for absolutism, and these toadies were encouraging him to try to assault the freedoms of Englishmen at home as well as abroad. All the more reason for the Americans to worry. Under the guidance of the committees of correspondence and the colonial legislatures, the colonists were made aware of the designs of the royal government. In fact, until about 1773 the major effort in behalf of freedom could not have been in the hands of more than 10,000 men of the two million people in the colonies. After the repeal of the Stamp Act, the average colonist, businessman, or farmer had wanted nothing more than to be let alone to pursue his interests. Had the London government shown the slightest signs of compromise, king and Parliament would have been met more than halfway.

It was not that nobody tried to avoid open conflict. Benjamin Franklin had been living in London since the middle of the 1760s as agent for Pennsylvania and other colonies. His time was spent testifying before parliamentary committees, talking to politicians, dining with men close to the Crown, all this aimed at explaining the American attitude to the English. The trouble was that British officials were also getting another sort of advice from such men as Thomas Hutchinson, the royal governor of Massachusetts. Hutchinson hated Samuel Adams and his cohorts of the committee of correspondence, and in private letters to English legislators and friends, called them traitors and urged Parliament to stand fast in its position relative to taxation.

In 1773 Franklin in London got hold of copies of these letters and sent them to Pennsylvania, where the committee of correspondence, in violation of Franklin's instructions, copied them and sent them around to other colonies. When Sam Adams got copies he read them before a secret session of the Massachusetts House of Representatives. Then he did worse—he had the letters printed—knowing how they would infuriate all concerned. The furor caused a duel in London and violence elsewhere. From that moment on, Governor Hutchinson was persona non grata to the dissident Massachusetts colonists.

And so were most officials of the royal government. One such was John Malcolm, a customs clerk whose job it was to watch over the unloading of vessels and see that no contraband was brought in and all taxes were declared. He was not popular with Massachusetts merchants and seamen. One day in January he got into a scuffle with some patriots, as the dissidents had come to call themselves, and ended up barricading himself in his house near North Square, with musket and sword, and taunting his enemies from his open window. A crowd gathered, and he continued his shouting. They brought ladders and a cart, came up and got him, stripped him, tarred and feathered him, and carted him around Boston, stopping at squares to beat him a little.

The tempo of dissent increased month by month. In 1774 king and Parliament decided to punish Boston for the Tea Party. The result was the Boston Port Bill, which closed Boston port until the East India Company should be compensated for its losses in the Tea Party. Two other laws of

Parliament, vigorously supported by King George III, virtually annulled the Massachusetts charter of government in favor of rule by the royal governor and his appointed council.

Had king or Parliament understood what they were doing, would they have continued the course? Probably. They *did* know what they were doing. Every effort was made by Americans in England and loyal Englishmen in Parliament to show the group in power that they were bringing about a rebellion of a totally different sort. But the king, being hardly an Englishman himself, had little understanding of the political processes, and his coterie egged him on to ever greater foolhardiness. The king and his counselors regarded the colonists as mutinous, and to them that meant intractable men who must be punished. They did not consider the alternative, that the miscreants would refuse to be punished and would instead break away from the British Empire. The thought was unthinkable. No one in power in London seemed able to see that each week the actions of the government were driving the colonies closer to revolution.

In America the new laws that came tumbling out of England were called the "Intolerable Acts," and colonial fury rose.

The first Intolerable Acts were followed by ever more punitive measures. A new Quartering Act, applicable to all colonies, said that the British army could quarter soldiers on any citizen without warning or agreement. Had king and council studied the record of the original quartering laws, which simply charged the colonies with the expense of maintaining the troops, they might have hesitated to thrust redcoats on the citizens of the colonies, particularly in view of the unsavory reputation the redcoats had gained with the people through quarrels and such affairs as the Boston Massacre. The new Quartering Act affected all thirteen colonies and the Canadians as well, but there was no problem in Canada, no resentment, and it was easy to see that the law had been enacted to punish the American and not the Canadian colonies.

By summer of 1774 Parliament and king had managed to convert a quarrel that was largely with Massachusetts, and to a lesser degree with New York and Virginia, into a general rebellious mood in all thirteen colonies, mostly by excesses in legislation. The committees of correspondence organized a Continental Congress to be held at Carpenters' Hall in Philadelphia on September 5.

Of all the colonies, New York was the most badly split on the questions of colonists' rights and responsibilities. King George III said that among the colonies, only Boston was more rebellious than New York, but he was wrong. Boston colonists were virtually united against king and Parliament by this time. New York's people were split almost down the middle.

By this time Boston was virtually an armed camp. General Gage was the new military governor of Massachusetts. He had been informed by the

English cabinet that if he saw fit, he might arrest any of the insolent colonists for violations of the law. If he felt it necessary he might order his troops to fire upon civilians. If he wished, he could arrest colonists and send them to another colony or to Britain for trial. King and Parliament had virtually established a military government in New England. One day, annoyed by many of the activities of the merchant John Hancock, General Gage revoked Hancock's commission as a leader of the Boston Cadets, a military training society. The cadets showed their rebellious mood by returning the king's flag and disbanding.

By this time, the mood in Massachusetts and other colonies was ugly. For years the colonists had maintained a store of muskets in Faneuil Hall. Quite legally, the colonies had militia, and the militia had stores of arms and powder; these had existed since the very first days of the colonies— at first as necessities in dealing with the Indians.

But in Massachusetts the presence of powder, muskets, and shot so close to the hands of the rebellious colonials made General Gage nervous. On September 1, 1774, Lieutenant Colonel Madison of the British army took 264 men up to Quarry Hill, a point of land between Medford and Cambridge, and there seized from the public magazine 250 barrels of powder and two field pieces.

This was but the most recent in a whole series of insults and injuries to the public institutions of the colonists, another sign that the British were now treating Massachusetts as occupied territory. That same day colonists began marching to meetings. The meetings were anything but riotous. Lieutenant Governor Oliver, who saw part of one of them, reported to General Gage that they were "ominously quiet." He warned Gage not to send any troops to try to stop the colonists from meeting. An erroneous report was circulated around Boston that six men had been killed by the redcoats. Colonists seized up their muskets and took them to the meetings. Officials warned Gage that if he sent men out even five miles, they probably would not come back alive, such was the temper of the colony that day.

General Gage was now writing back to England about his needs: "to reduce New England a very respectable force should take the field." He had five regiments at Boston and one more at the castle. He called down two more regiments from Quebec, and he sent ships to bring another from New York. He needed 20,000 more men, he told London. He made plans to raise a force of Canadians and Indians to fight in Massachusetts—he was prepared to bring the French and Indian War back all over again— more massacres, more rape and murder, scalping and cannibalism.

Throughout New England, colonists began to assemble, collect powder and shot and muskets from caches, and prepare for serious trouble. For years the women had gotten together for knitting bees, sewing bees, spinning bees. Now they gathered for cartridge-making bees and bullet-pouring parties.

The British complained that if they wanted bricklayers, suddenly there were none to be found in Boston. If they needed carpenters, all of them were declared to be employed. They had to send to Nova Scotia for skilled workmen. The reason was simple: most colonists had made a promise not to do *anything* to serve the British. In Worcester the male inhabitants from sixteen to seventy formed a militia, and agreed that a third of the members must always be ready to march. "In time of peace, prepare for war," they said. No man in the area, not even the poorest of the poor, would accept employment from the British army.

The English officers sent to Boston did not have much use for the people there. General Lord Percy, one of Gage's commanders, found them "full of fluff":

"The people in this part of the country are in general made up of rashness and timidity. Quick and violent in their determination, they are fearful in the execution of them (unless, indeed, they are certain of meeting little or no opposition, and then, like all cowards, they are cruel and tyrannical). To hear them talk, you might imagine that they would attack us and demolish us every night, and yet, when ever we appear, they are frightened out of their wits . . . "

The junior officers observed that Massachusetts men were not much: "The inhabitants of this province retain the religious and civil principles brought over by their forefathers. With the most austere show of devotion they are destitute of every principle of religion or common honesty, and are reckoned the most arrant cheats and hypocrites on the whole continent of America."

This young officer much preferred the women, whom he found easy to look at and easy of virtue. "Our camp has been as well supplied in that way since we have been on Boston Common as if our tents were pitched on Blackheath." As a whole, said he, the Americans were contemptible, and the thought that they might rebel was laughable.

So, to the British army, the Americans were cowards, scoundrels, and whores. Little wonder that there was trouble.

On August 6, General Gage had new word from London. Lord North had pushed through a law centering all executive power in Massachusetts in the hands of the royal governor. From London it was also suggested that Gage begin arresting such patriots as Samuel and John Adams and John Hancock.

The word of this new law was quick to get out, and Massachusetts townsmen began meeting once again. In the meetings the talk now turned to fighting.

And so came September and the Continental Congress, meeting in Philadelphia's Carpenters' Hall. Delegates appeared from each colony.

The Continental Congress of 1774 did not meet to discuss independence from England. Most of the delegates (Massachusetts's political arsonists excepted) wanted to resolve the problems between England and the colonies, but they wanted the resolution to be a return to the freedoms of the past. On October 8, the Congress resolved to support Massachusetts in its opposition to the Intolerable Acts.

When the Congress passed that resolution its members did not yet realize fully the obduracy of King George III, who would settle for nothing less than the capitulation of Massachusetts to the royal whim. Thus, right then, the American Revolution was made inevitable. All else that would come now—every attempt at conciliation—would be impossible.

A petition of grievances was drawn. The king would not even entertain it. The king had set his heart on revolutionizing the government of the colonies. He meant to restore royal power to rule. He could certainly never do that in England, but he expected to do it in America. The fools around George III assured him it could be done in America, and perhaps even in England.

Fortunately, although the men of the Congress did not understand the true nature of their king, they did take certain precautions in their session. They suggested that the people of Massachusetts form a government of their own, to collect taxes and hold them until the royal government became reasonable. They advised the people of all the colonies to arm and prepare for revolution. They proposed the strongest sanctions against Britain and British goods—no more trade with Ireland and England until matters were settled.

Back in New England, men prepared for war. The Massachusetts House of Representatives, defying a gubernatorial order forbidding its meeting anywhere, moved up to Salem for a session and appointed John Hancock to head a Committee of Public Safety, with power to call out the Massachusetts militia. Special groups of militia were organized. These (the "Minute Men") promised to be prepared for action in a minute.

The word got out on December 13 that General Gage planned to move troops up to garrison Fort William and Mary at Portsmouth, New Hampshire. Paul Revere rode there to warn the Portsmouth colonists, who took away the fort's cannon and powder before the redcoats could get there. On February 25, Gage's men set out to seize the military supplies stored by the militia at Salem. The colonists forestalled them, and moved the cannon. The redcoats arrived, there was a confrontation but no firing, and the British troops went back without the weapons. It had been a very near thing there on the bridge near the North Meetinghouse.

In the parliamentary elections of 1774 in England, the anti-American party won readily. (Bristol was the one place where America gained a new friend.) On November 18, letters arrived in London from General Gage assessing the American situation as it existed in September. If king and Parliament wanted to carry out all those new laws controlling Massachusetts, he said, they would have to conquer all the New England colonies, and even then, no one knew what attitude the other colonies would take. Gage proposed compromise.

The king snorted. No compromise.

"The New England governments," he said, "are now in a state of rebellion. Blows must decide whether they are to be subject to this country or to be independent."

At this point, Benjamin Franklin could not have agreed more. He had told friends on the eve of Parliament's opening that there now was no course for America but independence. In December, as Parliament debated what was to be done about America, King George decreed in council that export of arms to America was forbidden. As soon as the colonists heard, they began seizing every musket, gun, and bit of powder they could find.

On January 12, 1775, a cabinet meeting was held in London at which the grievances and propositions offered by the Continental Congress were rejected. All commerce with America was ordered stopped. The loyalists were to be protected, and all others were to be declared traitors and rebels, which meant they could be tried and executed if caught.

In the winter of 1775, the colonists were arming. Maryland established a militia, all the male inhabitants of the province forming into units of sixty-eight men each, under officers of their own choice. Ten thousand pounds was subscribed to support the militia. Urged by George Washington, Virginia colonists also moved to arm. Gunpowder plants were set up with subsidies from the counties.

That winter Gage had only 3,000 troops in Boston. Parliament sent him 2,400 more, along with six sloops of war and two frigates. The purpose, Parliament was told, was "less to act hostilely against the Americans than to encourage the friends of government."

Those honeyed words fooled almost no one on either side of the Atlantic.

There was sorrow in England.

"England," said Edmund Burke, "is like the archer that saw his own child in the hands of the adversary against whom he was going to draw his bow."

That would not stop England. The king would make sure of that.

The cabinet ignored General Gage's request for 20,000 men to bring the colonies to their knees, believing, instead, the reports trickling home from those arrogant redcoat officers that the Americans were nothing but a gang of rabble who would quit at the first whistle of a bullet over their shoulders.

The first thing to do, said Lord Dartmouth, secretary of state for the colonies, was to put all the rabble-rousers (like Sam Adams) in jail. The way to do that was to sneak up on them and arrest them all at once. In any event, "any efforts of the people, unprepared, to encounter with a regular force cannot be very formidable." That was the consensus in Parliament: the Americans would not fight, and so it was proper to intimidate them. On Thursday, February 9, most of Parliament's two houses went to the king's palace and presented a joint resolution, which Lord Rockingham said privately amounted to a declaration of war on the American colonies. George III would set about enforcing the laws, and "open the eyes of the deluded Americans."

That same day, in Massachusetts, the provincial congress appointed general officers to lead the Massachusetts troops. They were Artemas Ward and Seth Pomeroy, old soldiers from the French and Indian troubles.

General Gage's spies, who were everywhere, had bad news for their general. No matter where they went in New England, the people were talking of war. The Tories among them sniffed: the 5,000 British regulars could account for 50,000 of the rabble, they said. Gage also had bad news from London. The king had lost faith in him. That demand for 20,000 men had done it. The king now sought a new commander. His people approached Lord Jeffrey Amherst, who said he would take the post only if he had the 20,000 men to do the job. Nonsense, said Parliament; so William Howe was appointed new military governor and commander in chief of the army in America. Not that he wanted the post.

"Is it a proposition, or an order from the king?" he asked.

An order.

He accepted it, although his friends said he was a fool and he replied that he really did not want to go and fight against freedom. But he did. And with him went Henry Clinton, son of a former governor of New York Colony, and John Burgoyne, the bastard son of a nobleman. Burgoyne at least believed in his cause: "the Parliamentary right of Great Britain." Now British agents throughout Europe went to work to prevent the sale of arms to the Americans.

Massachusetts, now cut off from English goods, was quite properly seen from England as the center of the revolutionary movement. But nature took a hand. This winter of 1774–1775 was the most clement in years. And every colony did what it could to smuggle necessities to Boston.

In London, Parliament and king sought new ways to punish Massachusetts. A bill was passed depriving her of her fisheries; it would have been disastrous under other circumstances. Now it was just another piece of English tyranny.

Benjamin Franklin stayed on in London, hopeless but exuding hope. Samuel Johnson, the literary man and lexicographer, showed his innate hypocrisy by standing up for Parliament and king and becoming their propagandist. In March 1775, Franklin gave up, hurried to Portsmouth, and took ship for America. Had he remained another month, he probably would have been imprisoned. There was talk even as he left that he should be detained, as former Massachusetts governor Thomas Hutchinson suggested.

Americans prepared for war—not just colonial governments, and not just the organized colonies. In the Hampshire Grants, territory claimed by New Hampshire and New York, Ethan Allen organized the Green Mountain Boys, a regiment of woodsmen who belonged to no colony but were ready to fight England for land and freedom.

Everywhere, in New York, Virginia, Delaware, North Carolina, the colonists were prepared for war.

On Sunday, April 2, two ships arrived in Massachusetts, carrying the news that King George III and Parliament had pledged themselves to the punishment of America until the colonists yielded to royal authority and Parliament's right to tax them, the withdrawal of Massachusetts's fishing rights, and the decision to reinforce the army in America.

The Massachusetts Congress—the new colonists' legislative body—called an emergency meeting. It authorized formation of six companies of artillery and sent envoys to other colonies to urge them to strengthen their defenses.

The Massachusetts Congress adjourned on April 15. That day, General Gage secretly prepared an expedition to destroy the colonial stores of ammunition and supplies at Concord. But Sam Adams and John Hancock were warned, and the Committee of Public Safety moved the public stores. On April 18, General Gage sent a number of men into the communities around Boston, to stop travelers and intercept communications. On April 19, eight hundred redcoats, under Lieutenant Colonel Smith, crossed from the Boston Common to East Cambridge by boat. They said they would wade through the marshes and take the road through West Cambridge to Concord. As they left, a group of citizens were standing by, talking.

"They will miss their aim," said one.

General Percy, who was standing near, pricked up his ears.

"What aim?"

"Why the cannon at Concord," said the citizen, as if everyone would know that.

Percy hurried back to the fort, where he told Gage of the talk. Gage put out orders that all people were to be stopped everywhere in the Boston area.

Meanwhile, ahead of the troops were Paul Revere, heading for Charlestown to warn the men of Concord, and William Dawes, riding through Roxbury to Lexington on the same sort of mission.

Paul Revere had arranged with a friend to raise signals in the tower of the North Church: one lantern was to be raised if the troops were coming straight overland; two lanterns were to be raised if they were crossing the river. Five minutes before the guards along the Charles River were alerted to stop anyone moving, two of Revere's friends had rowed him across the Charles River past a man-of-war, and he had seen the two warning lanterns in the North Church steeple, streaming light toward the neighboring towns.

Across the Charles, a horse was waiting, and Paul Revere mounted. Just beyond Charlestown Neck he was stopped by two British officers on horseback, who asked who he was and where he was going. He answered inchoately, then suddenly turned into a swamp. One of the officers bogged down there. Revere escaped the second on the road to Medford. Hurrying through the town, he awakened the captain of the Minute Men and rode on, shouting as he went, "The redcoats are coming . . . "

The British troops were marching up the road when they heard the firing of muskets and the ringing of church bells. They had been discovered. Colonel Smith stopped and sent a messenger back to demand reinforcements.

Revere and Dawes rode on, met and joined company, and rode some more. They met Samuel Prescott and he joined up, calling out as they went to warn about the redcoats. At Lincoln they encountered a party of British officers who captured Revere and Dawes. Prescott leaped his horse over a stone wall, escaped, and galloped on toward Concord.

He arrived at about 2:00 A.M., rode to the meetinghouse, and began ringing the bell. Out came the Minute Men, young and old, muskets in hand, including William Emerson, the preacher, powderhorn slung over his shoulder.

The news spread swiftly. Lexington, a town of 700 people, was alive with armed volunteers. They assembled and the roll was called. A hundred and thirty men answered. Captain John Parker told them all to load their muskets with powder and ball, but not to fire first. Scouts were sent to find the British on the road. There was no sign of them, so the Minute Men dispersed, some to their houses, some to the tavern on the common. There they waited. The beat of a drum would call them to assemble. John Adams and John Hancock were there and would have joined the others at the tavern, but they were persuaded that they were targets and their efforts too valuable to risk, so they went down the road to Woburn.

The last stars were just winking out and false dawn settling in, when Major John Pitcairn of the Royal Marines came up the road, leading his men. The scouts down the road fired shots, warning the Minute Men. On the common, the drum beat.

Not 130, but fewer than 70 men now fell in, in two ranks, north of the meetinghouse.

Hearing the drum and the shots, Major Pitcairn stopped and waited for the other troops to come up. It was half an hour before sunrise when Pitcairn started out, on the double, with his marines, the grenadiers just behind them.

Major Pitcairn reined in his horse a hundred feet from the colonists on the common.

"Disperse, ye villains, ye rebels, disperse," he shouted. "Lay down your arms. Why don't you lay down your arms and disperse?"

The Minute Men stood, silent, not moving, as historian George Bancroft put it, "too few to resist, too brave to fly."

Major Pitcairn then fired his pistol at the Americans and shouted: "Fire."

The redcoats opened fire with a volley. Colonists fell like cornstalks. Jonas Parker was felled by a bullet. A redcoat then bayoneted him through the heart. Isaac Muzzey fell, and so did Robert Munroe. Jonathan Harrington was shot in the breast, ran toward his own house, and died on the threshhold, in the arms of his wife. Caleb Harrington was shot as he came out of the meetinghouse. Samuel Hadley and John Brown fled the green, but were pursued by grenadiers who killed them. Asahel Porter, who had been captured by the British on the march, tried to escape and was shot down.

Seven were killed, nine were wounded, and the rest ran for cover. The victorious redcoats formed up on the common, fired a volley into the air, gave three cheers for themselves, and then marched toward Concord.

There the Americans had assembled—about 200 strong—at the Liberty Pole on the hill. They saw the British coming, saw that they were four times their own number, and retreated, first beyond the Concord River by the North Bridge, and then up by a back road to high ground. There they waited.

It was 7:00 A.M. when the British marched into Concord, the light infantry on the hillside, and the grenadiers on the lower road. They stopped and began the search for stores. Three companies under Captain Laurie guarded the North Bridge. Three more companies moved up to the house of Colonel Barrett, leader of the militia, where arms were reported. But they found only some powder cartridges for cannon. Nothing else.

Up on the hill, men kept coming from other towns: Acton, Bedford, Westford, Littleton, Chelmsford. Soon there were 400 colonists on the hill.

Major Pitcairn led the search of Concord. In the yard of the tavern, he found two 24-pound guns, and these were spiked by his men. They found sixty barrels of flour and broke them up, 500 pounds of ball, which they dumped into the millpond. They burned the Liberty Pole and several gun carriages.

From the hill the Americans saw the redcoats on their bridge and the smoke from the fires. Colonel Barrett ordered the Americans to advance, but not to fire unless fired upon. Out stepped Captain Isaac Davis, the town schoolmaster of Acton, Major John Buttrick of Concord, and John Robinson of Westford. They led the way followed by the militiamen and the Minute Men, trailing arms. They came to the North Bridge. The British were already trying to pull up the planks to keep them from crossing. The Americans hurried up, the British fired, and Luther Blanchard and Jonas Brown were wounded. A volley came from the British and Isaac Davis fell dead. So did Abner Hosmer.

Major Buttrick jumped into the air shouting, "Fire, fellow soldiers, for god's sake, fire."

"Fire, fire, fire," went the call along the line. The Americans began firing. Several British soldiers fell. The others retreated toward the main body, leaving the Americans in possession of the bridge. One of the Americans, Amos Barrett, later recalled:

We then saw the whole body coming out of town. We then was ordered to lay behind a wall that run over a hill and when they got nigh enough, Major Buttrick said he would give the word "fire" but they did not come quite so near as he expected before they halted. The commanding officer ordered the whole battalion to halt, and officers to the front march. The officers [British] then marched to the front. There we lay behind the wall, about 200 of us, with our guns cocked, expecting every minute to have the word "fire." Our orders was if we fired to fire two or three times and then retreat. If we had fired, I believe we would have killed almost every officer there was in the front, but we had no orders to fire and there wasn't a gun fired.

They stayed about ten minutes and then marched back, we after them. After a while we found them a marching back towards Boston. We was soon after them. When they got about a mile and a half to a road that comes from Bedford and Billerica, they was waylaid and a great many killed. When I got there a great many lay dead and the roads was bloody.

The British retreated raggedly, losing men constantly to the pursuing Americans, who hid in the brush beside the road, fired, moved, and fired again. It was the old Indian tactic, now accepted by these frontiersmen. At about 2:00 P.M. Lord Percy came up on the road with a relief column of about 1,200 men with two field guns. Now the British had out in the field two-thirds of their available troops. Percy knew that more Americans were coming up all the time. He formed a hollow square around the rescued men, and after half an hour's rest, began the retreat to Boston. All the way they were harried by American marksmen. As the British retreated, they grew angrier at the harassment, and began burning houses and killing civilians inside them. The Americans followed, gaining courage, coming closer to fire on the enemy. It was only after sunset that the British escaped, across Charlestown Creek, and the battle ended.

The Americans lost 49 men killed and 34 wounded. Five men were missing. The British suffered 273 men killed, wounded, or missing.

And so the battles of Lexington and Concord ended on April 19, 1775. The Rebellion had come and gone. The Insurrection had been staged, and had not warned the British. The Revolution had happened, and there was no turning back. Now, it would be war.

CHAPTER 5

War

The American Revolution did not begin as an attempt by the colonists to break away from England. It was, in fact, an emotional confrontation between the beleaguered citizens of New England, particularly Boston, and the British troops who had been sent by a misguided London government to occupy Boston and force the people of Massachusetts to submit to the will of Parliament and the king.

The civil war—for that is how it was originally billed in the colonies—broke out at Lexington and Concord. It might have been stopped, but the viciousness with which the British troops tried to suppress the colonists militated against a political settlement. Even so, as late as the spring of 1776 the war could have been brought to an end if the London government had been willing to make any real compromises. By the time that government was willing to compromise, the summer of 1776, it was too late, and the colonists insisted that the independence of the American colonies was their main demand. It came down to a matter of weeks: Admiral Howe, entrusted by London with the task of treating with the Americans, was prepared to offer them almost anything short of independence. A year earlier, even six months earlier, it probably would have been workable. In August 1776 it was not. The commitment had been made and the colonists were not emotionally equipped to take it back.

Another year passed. It was 1777. London grew more fretful. The American rebellion was expensive, and politically embarrassing to the British government. Lord North would have liked a settlement, and he offered a new one, but not independence. Never that, said the king.

*   *   *

If the issue had ever been in doubt, by 1779 it was not. The Americans had enlisted the assistance of the French, who saw in the American rebellion an opportunity to strike a blow against their English enemies, and a new entree into the Western world. French support begot a grudging Spanish support, and that brought other interest in Europe, so that by scraping and scrimping the American colonies managed to keep their war effort together.

*   *   *

On the night of April 19, 1775, colonists kept on coming down toward Boston long after the sun had set and the redcoats had retreated under the guns of the British warships in the Charles. Needham sent 185 men, Danvers sent 131, and other towns sent as many as wanted to go. Cambridge was alive with musket-carrying militia that night, men who sat around fires and in the taverns, speaking of the atrocities of the British that day— for as they had retreated, the redcoats had bayoneted women and children and the old, anyone they found in the houses along their line of retreat, and they had looted the houses, then burned them. There was an element of hatred and vengeance in this treatment, something not discussed in the tactical treatises of General Gage's officers. In Cambridge that night, printers were already at work on newspapers and broadsides announcing the beginning of "the American Civil War."

April 20. The Cambridge area was literally alive with colonial militia. One watcher estimated that 20,000 colonists had made their way down toward Boston. But almost as soon as they arrived, they began heading back home. They had no food, no money, no organization. From Boston the summons went out to all the colonies, in one day to New York, in two days to Philadelphia, in three to Baltimore. It reached Mount Vernon and Williamsburg. It glided through the Dismal Swamp, whispered through the pines of South Carolina, and in a week all the colonies knew. The watchword: LIBERTY OR DEATH.

It was echoed from the Tidewater country to the Alleghenies, from the Gulf of Mexico to the Green Mountains. Massachusetts's first call was for arms and men to assemble at the headquarters at Cambridge, to mount a defense against General Gage's British Army of America.

On April 22, the Massachusetts Provincial Congress met at Concord and then adjourned to Watertown. One of the first acts was to establish an organized force. General Artemas Ward was chosen as commander. The army, said the Congress, was to be the Army of New England, and Massachusetts would enlist 13,600 men, who would serve until the last day of December.

Men began coming in from New Hampshire, Western Massachusetts, and Connecticut. Israel Putnam, a farmer of Pomfret, Connecticut, was building a fence with his hired men when the word of the massacre at Lexington came. He left the hired men and went out to arouse the militia of the nearby towns. When he returned he found that he had been elected a leader, and he headed for Cambridge, arriving in eighteen hours.

In New Haven, volunteer militia captain Benedict Arnold began marching his men toward Cambridge.

By April 23, Boston was surrounded and the British redcoats were prisoners in their barracks and fortresses. They had cut Boston off from the world. Now they were cut off from food supplies, and they began to suffer for it. They had scoffed that the Americans would not fight; Colonel Smith's column had barely escaped wholesale destruction, and that only because General Percy had come to rescue them. The army of General Gage was a defeated army.

But no one was fooled by that. The Americans knew of the power of Britain, which would soon be unleashed against them. Now it was a waiting game. The British gave safe conduct to the women and children and aged from Boston, and they came out, until Gage reversed himself, and kept hostages in the city.

What was to be done? Dr. Joseph Warren, chairman of the Committee of Public Safety, could not take much action. The Second Continental Congress had been called to sit in Philadelphia, and it would decide how the war would be prosecuted. But troops were hurrying to Cambridge, begging to be employed. Nathanael Greene arrived from Rhode Island with a brigade of 1,500 men. John Stark brought down a force from New Hampshire.

What was wanted by all these men of action was just that, action. The Massachusetts Provincial Congress authorized Benedict Arnold to take men against Fort Ticonderoga, and commissioned him a colonel. They did not know that Connecticut had already commissioned Ethan Allen and his Green Mountain boys to do the same job. Allen captured Fort Ticonderoga, and Benedict Arnold seethed with rage and jealousy.

A few hours after the capture of Ticonderoga, on May 10, 1775, the Second Continental Congress met at Philadelphia. Twelve colonies were officially represented; Lyman Hall of Georgia did not yet represent the whole colony. The Congress began sessions to establish the defense of the colonies. A petition to King George was prepared, but not many of the delegates had much faith in it, nor in England was there much faith now that what Parliament and king had put to wrong could ever be put to right.

On May 26, 1775, the 365-gun British frigate *Cerberus* arrived in Boston harbor, to deliver reinforcements, including the three generals Howe, Clinton, and Burgoyne. Howe had the great advantage for this high command of having fought at Louisbourg and Quebec, and he understood the frontier method of fighting. Indeed, he had been teaching a course in it to English troops just before his appointment as second in command of the army in America. Clinton had learned the general's trade in Germany, fighting for the Prince of Brunswick. Burgoyne was a man from the fast lane, gambler, womanizer, and politician (he had been elected to Parliament), but he was also a good soldier, as he had proved in the wars in Portugal.

On June 12 word came from London that General Gage as governor was to issue a proclamation imposing martial law and threatening the traitors of America with death. Any and everyone, however, would be forgiven if they laid down their arms immediately. Anyone and everyone, that is, except Samuel Adams and John Hancock.

The Americans snarled or laughed at the proclamation, so the generals planned an offensive. They would occupy the high ground of Dorchester and Charlestown above Boston, which would give them artillery command of the entire Boston area. But American spies brought the word to the Massachusetts Committee of Public Safety, and Dr. Warren ordered General Ward to stop it. Ward sent Colonel William Prescott with a thousand men and two field guns to Bunker Hill, the highest of the three hills on the Charlestown Peninsula. They marched on the night of June 16, carrying one day's rations and blankets. Colonel Prescott mistook his hills, and passed by Bunker Hill to camp on Breed's Hill, which was a tactical error. Breed's Hill was further down the narrow peninsula and could be evacuated only across that narrow neck of land. The enemy's warships could come up to rake the position, and it could be cut off by landing parties from the sea. There Prescott built a redoubt, including a six-foot parapet around a position forty yards square.

The Americans were digging away that night when General Clinton came out on reconnaissance, discovered what was going on, and recommended an immediate attack. General Gage ignored him. Next morning at dawn, the watch of HMS *Lively* spotted the impressive fortifications and opened fire. Clinton again that morning recommended an attack, by a force to land on the peninsula between Breed's Hill and the main American line. Gage again refused. He would make a frontal assault on Breed's Hill that afternoon at high tide with four regiments and an artillery company.

Although under fire from the British ships, at noon the Americans had completed their redoubt, which extended about half a mile along Breed's Hill on the harbor side.

That afternoon Colonel Prescott's force was reinforced by John Stark with the New Hampshire regiment, Israel Putnam with more troops, and Dr. Warren, who came up to fight as a volunteer soldier in the line.

Just before 3:00 P.M. General Howe took the troops against Breed's

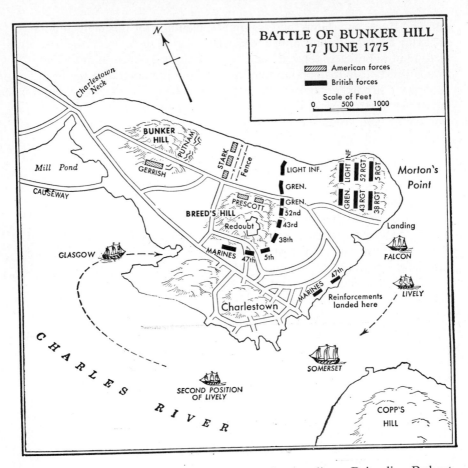

Hill, out in front of his light infantry and grenadiers. Brigadier Robert Pigott led another force, three regiments of army troops and Major Pitcairn's Royal Marines against the main line of the earthworks. What a show it was to be for Boston! People crowded the rooftops of the buildings to watch the fight. They saw Pigott's redcoats, heavily laden with packs and canisters, pushing through the thick grass at the shoreline and climbing the hill, stopping to fire volleys that thudded against the entrenchments and created huge clouds of smoke, but did no damage. The Americans did not fire.

At Concord, the officers of the American militia told their men to hold their fire. They knew that the American muskets were effective only at about sixty yards. So the Americans waited ("Don't fire boys, until you see the whites of their eyes") and the redcoats moved up the hill. At last, when it seemed the redcoats must dash forward and overwhelm the defenders, the American line opened up with an enormous volley. The redcoats fell by the dozen and huge holes opened in the line. They closed up, the Americans fired a second volley. This time the line disintegrated and the British staggered down the hill.

On the right, Howe's men had been trying to move along the shore to outflank the Americans, cross over and come up behind them, cutting them off from Charlestown. But Stark's men stopped that. They, too, waited. The British fired a volley, came on, fired another, and then, when the redcoats were fifty yards away, the Americans fired, and the destruction was enormous. Another volley and Howe's men retreated down the hill.

The British, furious at the watchers in Charlestown, and bent on eliminating a number of snipers on top of buildings there, set Charlestown afire and it began to burn, 500 buildings going up in smoke.

Brigadier Pigott attacked up Breed's Hill again, and again was driven back with heavy loss. Clinton came up with 500 redcoats who had been held in reserve. He found Pigott's force in complete disorder. Howe attacked again and suffered just as badly. All his staff were shot down, and whole companies were decimated save for three or four men.

Back on the beach, Howe and Pigott joined forces, aided by the 500 reinforcements. They concentrated on the earthworks on Breed's Hill.

Up behind the fortifications, the Americans were running out of ammunition. The British came up the hill, firing volleys, bayonets fixed. The Americans waited until the enemy was only twenty yards away, then let fly. The British front line crumbled. But it was the last American volley; there was no more ammunition, and the British stormed up and over the parapet, into the redoubt, bayonets flashing. Americans at the fence, thirty of them, stood and swung their muskets by the barrel at the British. One by one they were cut down, but in their defense they saved most of Prescott's men, who escaped through the smoke to Bunker Hill. Dr. Warren was killed by a shot through the head.

From high points along the hill, American sharpshooters slowed the British as they advanced on Charlestown Neck. The ships of the Royal Navy came in close to rake the narrow peninsula. Now the Americans suffered heavy losses in the escape back to the third eminence, Prospect Hill. The British advanced to Bunker Hill and entrenched. Neither force was in condition to attack. Beside them, Charlestown burned, and the occasional crack of a musket could be heard.

The day ended. The Americans lost 100 killed, 271 wounded, and 30 prisoner. The British had taken the position, so they won the victory. But was it victory! They had lost 228 killed, 826 wounded. The carnage among the officers who led their men was especially dreadful. The Americans had learned the lesson missed at Concord. Their muskets had been trained on the officers and very often found them. Royal Marine Major Pitcairn, who had shouted out so loud at Lexington, was one of those killed. The American smooth-bore musket ball, about the equivalent of .50 caliber, packed a tremendous force, and some of the Americans who had no musket balls had stuffed their muskets with bits of chain, nails, and other metal that made jagged, horrible wounds. A grenadier named John Randon was one of those hit, by a shot in the groin and another in the chest. They carried him back to Boston with the other wounded British soldiers, and he survived the night. But next morning the surgeon informed him that he had perhaps three hours to live and to make his peace with family and God. So Randon wrote a letter home, entrusting wife and family to the hands of God, promising to meet his wife in Heaven:

> The world recedes, it disappears
> Heaven opens on my eyes, my ears
> With sounds seraphic ring;
> Lend, lend your wings, I mount, I fly!
> Oh, Grave, where is thy victory?
> Oh, Death! Where is thy sting?*

More would I say, but life ebbs out apace, my tongue ceases to perform its office; bright angels stand round the gorey turf on which I lie, ready to escort me to the arms of my Jesus; bending saints reveal my shining crown, and beckon me away; yea, methinks my Jesus bids me come, Adieu! Adieu! Dear love . . .

Throughout the colonies, the reverberations of Lexington and Concord sounded. In June in Virginia, when the House of Burgesses met, some members appeared in hunting shirts, with woodsmen's axes by their sides, symbols of the militia. There was still talk of reconciliation, but such men as Thomas Jefferson, all in favor of reconciliation before, now spoke of it with a difference. The blood now shed meant that if Britain wanted reconciliation, she would have to give guarantees. But except for the outright loyalists among the Americans, Jefferson's was the most moderate of approaches to be found. The British had wanted war, they had started war, and now they had war. At Breed's Hill the British had won a victory. But what a victory! Any more such and Britain would not have enough troops left in America to fight.

The American tide was definitely running for general war. In Virginia, when Royal Governor Dunmore received a copy of General Gage's proclamation of rebellion, calling for the heads of Samuel Adams and John Hancock, the governor packed up and went aboard HMS *Fowey*, thus leaving Virginia to its people.

*Obviously original with Grenadier Randon, for he has misquoted 1 Corinthians 15, the source of the quotation.

The rapidity of development of the war situation indicated the colonial need for swift work to organize a military force, one acceptable to all the colonies. Virginia was the richest and most populous of all the colonies, so it would be extremely politic to appoint a Virginian. Dr. Warren, before he went to Breed's Hill, had cast his vote for George Washington of Virginia. Washington already had a distinguished career as soldier. He was now forty-three years old. He had begun his training as a midshipman aboard a Royal Navy frigate, but had to cut off his naval career to help his ailing elder brother manage family affairs. He had learned surveying and had gone into the Ohio country for Governor Dinwiddie on that famous military mission. He had fought the French and the Indians in the West. On June 15 the Continental Congress appointed George Washington as commander in chief of the colonial forces. So Americans now had a united government to which they listened, and a general. Now they must raise an army and prepare to carry on the long struggle for independence.

Major General Artemas Ward, commander of the Massachusetts force, was second in command of the new army. Third man was General Charles Lee. Horatio Gates was made a brigadier general. The new officers immediately went to join the American forces outside Boston, and there Washington took command under a giant elm in Cambridge, which would thereafter be celebrated as "the Washington elm."

Washington saw that the Massachusetts troops were better prepared than he, or anyone else for that matter, had expected. For the contemptuous British were singing a sarcastic ditty about the American fighting men:

The Yankey's Return from Camp

> Father and I went down to camp,
> Along with Captain Gooding,
> There we see the men and boys,
> As thick as hasty pudding.

CHORUS:

> Yankee Doodle, keep it up,
> Yankee Doodle, Dandy.
> Mind the music and the step,
> And with the girls be handy.

And so on, for fourteen verses, ending when the singer sees graves being dug:

> It fear'd me so I hook'd it off.
> Nor flop't, so I remember,

Nor turned about til I got home
Locked up in mother's chamber.

The tune was a catchy old British fife song, and it was not long before everyone in Massachusetts knew the new words. The British sang in derision. After Concord they had to find another tune, for the Americans took up this one, called it "Yankee Doodle Dandy," and it became the fight song of the American force in the war.

That summer of 1775 Washington was thinking about how best to assault the British. The Americans were woefully short of cannon. They had lost the field pieces at Breed's Hill. They had captured all the cannon of Fort Ticonderoga, but those would not win a war for them. The need was for guns and ammunition. Because of the need, the Americans remained quiescent all that year, and the British, bottled up in Boston, did so, too. By smuggling, the Americans acquired a supply of gunpowder and shot. Then came another problem. The enlistments of the New England men would end with year's end. Washington had to rush a campaign to enlist men for another year. By the end of the year, when some of the original Minute Men started home, Washington had a stable force.

General Gage was recalled to London for consultation, and sailed on October 10, instructing General Howe to hang on in Boston. He promised large reinforcements.

That winter of 1775–76 was a cold one for patriots and redcoats alike. The colonials brought in green wood from the forests and crouched over their sizzling fires. The British cut down the trees of Boston and tore down houses to burn. They got some supplies from Canada and some from the West Indies. So did the Americans.

In November a tiny American navy began to form, first with Massachusetts ships commissioned by Washington to raid the British supply lines. The first naval adventure had come just after Lexington and Concord. The British armed schooner *Margaretta* was lying in harbor at Machias, Maine, when a group of Americans decided to capture her. They set after her in a sloop that was loading lumber, armed with muskets, pitchforks, and axes. Trying to escape, the crew of the *Margaretta* let her jibe, the main boom swung around viciously and broke, and the *Margaretta* ran into Holmes Bay. Captain Moore, the skipper, raided a small merchantman in the harbor of a spar, made a new boom and headed out. The Americans began to catch up. The Americans started firing with their four light cannon and fourteen swivel guns. A shot from the lumber sloop killed the helmsman of the *Margaretta* and wounded everyone on the quarter deck. The sloop came up and grappled, the Americans rushed aboard with their knives, axes, and pitchforks, and hand-to-hand combat began. Captain Moore stood on the deck throwing hand grenades, until he was shot down. The Americans captured the *Margaretta*.

The Americans had set out spontaneously and there really was no commander of their sloop. After the battle, Jeremiah O'Brien was selected as captain. The guns and ammunition of the *Margaretta* were transferred to a larger sloop, and Captain O'Brien set out to sea. He captured two English cruisers, and took the prisoners into Watertown. Back at Cambridge the word came to Washington's headquarters. Jubilation! Jeremiah O'Brien was appointed a captain of the Massachusetts navy.

The British retaliated by ordering a landing at Falmouth and they stood off the town and bombarded it until they burned 400 buildings. But the colonists fought back and the British never did land.

All this had happened by the end of 1775 and several commissions had been given to New England captains. Captain John Manly in the schooner *Lee* captured the English brig *Nancy,* which carried munitions, including a large mortar which could be invaluable to a besieging army. Other American vessels commissioned by Washington captured several English transports loaded with supplies from Canada for the British in Boston. Captain Broughton was sent up to the Gulf of St. Lawrence with two ships.

In October two real warships, one a ship of ten guns and the other of fourteen guns, were ordered built. Then came orders for two more cruisers, one of twenty guns and the other of thirty-six guns. By the end of the year, Congress had authorized the building of a real navy:

Ship	Guns	Construction
Washington	32	Pennsylvania
Raleigh	32	New Hampshire
Hancock	32	Massachusetts
Randolph	32	Pennsylvania
Warren	32	Rhode Island
Virginia	28	Maryland
Trumbull	28	Connecticut
Effingham	28	Pennsylvania
Congress	28	New York
Providence	28	Rhode Island
Boston	24	Massachusetts
Delaware	24	Pennsylvania
Montgomery	24	New York

These were all small vessels, suitable to capture English merchant ships and to fight with the smaller English warships. There was no way the

Americans could then build a "ship of the line," one of those three-tiered monsters that had helped England dominate the seas. The Americans did not try. Their purpose was to harry and capture supplies. The ships would be gunned with nine- and twelve-pounders.

Three days before Christmas 1775, the Continental Congress created the navy. There was no admiral. Esek Hopkins was named commander in chief, but they called him commodore just as Washington was commander in chief of the Continental Army but they called him general. Hopkins's pay was $125 a month. Dudley Saltonstall, Abraham Whipple, Nicholas Biddle, and John B. Hopkins were captains. John Paul Jones was a lieutenant. By the end of December the congressional fleet was at sea: John Paul Jones hoisted a congressional ensign aboard the vessel *Alfred* on the last day of December. It was a pine tree, rattlesnake about to strike coiled at the foot, with the legend DON'T TREAD ON ME. As they were finished the vessels went out into Delaware Bay to work up for war cruises. The first assignment given the new commander in chief was to head south along the Virginia coast to stop the ravages of Lord Dunmore's British fleet. The first action was carried out by Commodore Hopkins with five ships. He put in at New Providence in the Bahamas and landed 300 marines. They captured the forts there, which yielded 100 badly needed cannon for the colonial forces. On the way home, in April 1776, the squadron encountered the twenty-gun frigate *Glasgow* and gave a good account of itself, forcing Captain Tyringham Howe to make an escape after a spirited fight. Twenty-three Americans were killed in this battle, and four Englishmen aboard the *Glasgow*. Three American ships were badly damaged, but even so when the squadron arrived in port the affair was greeted as a great "victory" by the Continental forces.

But Commodore Hopkins was not to enjoy it much. Hopkins was lucky because the large British squadron then stationed in Newport did not come out and wipe out the little American squadron. But Congress did not see it that way. The Congress was furious with him because he had not stopped the British in Virginia waters, and had not destroyed a British fleet. In October 1776, Hopkins was formally censured by the Congress, and in February 1777 he was fired. No other commander in chief was ever appointed to the Continental Navy.

In the early months of 1776 the war situation began to look better for the colonists. Colonel Henry Knox arrived in Cambridge with the cannon captured at Fort Ticonderoga. Washington placed them on Dorchester Heights. On March 3, General Howe was still considering the occupation of those hills, but he had done nothing. On March 4, General Howe awakened to find the ugly snouts of all those cannon looking down on Boston and his ships. What to do? He considered a frontal attack, and then remembered Breed's Hill. Dorchester Heights would be much more formidable. So General Howe evacuated Boston under the muzzles of the guns.

Washington said that Howe could leave Boston unmolested if he would not do any more damage to the city. So they agreed, and on March 17, Howe took his British troops and ships up to Halifax. With him went a thousand loyalists, "damned Tories" to the American patriots.

So the British Army of America spent the spring of 1776 in Nova Scotia.

The real British activity in America in the first half of 1776 was that of Lord Dunmore, who, having gone aboard HMS *Fowey,* had gathered a force together. Some were redcoats. Some were loyalists. Many were black slaves to whom Dunmore promised freedom in exchange for their fighting.

He began ravaging the Virginia coast. In January, his troops were defeated in battle at Great Bridge, south of Norfolk. He then burned Norfolk, but after that there was no place for him to go. He hung about the Chesapeake Bay for a few months, then secretly made arrangements to send the blacks to the West Indies—and back to slavery. He took his white soldiers off to join General Howe. The same sort of story could be told about affairs in North and South Carolina, where the colonists held off British attack under General Clinton.

In London, the British were preparing an unpleasant surprise for the American colonists. From many ideas advanced came a plan: occupy New York City, and then be prepared to move north or south, to cut the colonies in two. A second force from Canada could march south, and thus cut off New England.

And the plan was working with clocklike precision that June of 1776, as the colonists met in Philadelphia and decided on their Declaration of Independence from England. The declaration came on July 4, 1776. On July 5, the last contingent of British reinforcements embarked in England to come to America and try to make sure the declaration failed. From England came 370 transports, carrying 127,000 tons of war matériel and troops. From the south came General Clinton's army, somewhat mauled. From England came English and Hessian troops. On August 12 General Howe had 32,000 troops under his command. From Canada came 10,000 troops. General Howe's brother, Admiral Richard Howe, had 73 warships and 13,000 naval seamen. The British were now ready to crush the rebellious Americans and punish the leaders.

The Americans waited in New York. General Washington had brought the army down from Boston. They made such defenses as they could, putting a huge chain across the Hudson River near West Point, building Forts Washington and Lee to guard the Hudson. Troops were ferried across the East River to Long Island, where Brooklyn Heights overlooked lower Manhattan Island. The problem of defense was that Long Island was so enormous that there was no way the Americans could prevent Howe from landing his huge force and marching up, down, or across.

The British began landing on Long Island on August 22, 1776. In four days, Lord Howe put ashore an army twice as large as the one Washington could command even with the enlistment of a whole new flock of militia.

What now was Washington to do? He took an enormous gamble; he moved ten regiments from Manhattan to Long Island, under General Israel Putnam. On August 26 both sides were ready for battle. The Americans miscalculated and left their left flank unguarded at the Jamaica road, the British crashed through, and that day the Americans lost the battle, and 1,500 men. The rest fell back on Brooklyn. Fortunately the British did not press to capture Brooklyn. They could have.

From the British camp it now looked easy. Washington was trapped in Brooklyn. Admiral Howe need only sail into the East River, and cut the Americans off from Manhattan and the Bronx, and then General Howe's forces could mop them up. But Admiral Howe did not sail. Up came a storm that prevented him from entering the river, and Washington escaped across the bay.

Meanwhile, Admiral Howe was making one last effort to treat with the colonial political leaders, as he had been entrusted to do by London. Benjamin Franklin and John Adams met with him, but they insisted that the British now recognize the independence of the colonies, and Admiral Howe had no authority to do so. The meetings came to an end.

Midsummer had brought a new crisis to the Americans; the militia were farmers for the most part and it was time for them to be back in the fields preparing for the harvest. The militiamen began going home. In a week, three-quarters of the Connecticut militia had left New York. Massachusetts and New Hampshire men and upstate New Yorkers were not far behind.

The American army was driven up Manhattan Island to Harlem. Washington then moved up to White Plains, leaving 2,000 men to hold Fort Washington on the Hudson. Howe moved up to White Plains. Washington retreated to the Hudson, and crossed just before Howe captured Fort Washington. General Washington then retreated all the way to the Delaware River. He reached Trenton on December 3, 1776, and fled into Pennsylvania.

"The heart of the rebellion is now really broken," said Lord Howe's secretary. The British, who now had captured a whole colony, New Jersey, turned it over to the rape of the Hessians and redcoats. They plunged through the countryside, assaulting the women, murdering the men, killing children if they got in the way. John Hunt, speaker of the New Jersey Assembly, came home to children in hiding from the enemy troops. These Hessians, ashore in an unfamiliar land where they did not know the language or the customs, were nearly as savage as the Indians. They stole and they fought among themselves, and they put the finishing touches on the destruction of the old concept of the "gentlemanly war." The colonists who had come home to New Jersey for the harvest now organized themselves into fighting bands. They lay in the ditches beside the roads, and ambushed parties of Hessians and redcoats as they came along. There was no quarter given. The British had brought about the establishment of an underground and partisan movement that was to persist in every occupied colony until war's end.

Over in Pennsylvania, General Washington was now planning a fight. He knew that a strong detachment of Hessians was stationed at Trenton, another at Bordentown, and a third at Burlington, all close to the Delaware River. On Christmas night, 1776, Washington crossed the Delaware, marched to Trenton, drove out the Hessians, and attacked the main body, killing their colonel. Twenty-three officers and 888 men surrendered to the Americans. Washington then crossed the Delaware again, sent the prisoners to Philadelphia, and came back to take over Trenton.

The next attack was to be on Princeton. Lord Cornwallis, in command of the British in the north, marched to Trenton and attacked the Americans on January 2. The fighting was brisk, and lasted until late. That night the British slept; Washington left fires burning and silently withdrew his troops and marched to Princeton. They were met by the British 17th, 40th, and 55th Regiments. The fighting was very hard, and for a while it seemed the British would win; but Washington personally rode into the melee, and the British were forced back toward New Brunswick.

So the war was not over after all.

In 1777 the going was very hard for the Americans. The British held New York. The Americans lost battle after battle, yet there was one major factor working for them: the Americans could always find reinforcements in their countryside; the British could not. And even though the British won, because of their stylized fighting (march, volley, reload, march, volley, charge with bayonet), their victories were always expensive in terms of casualties.

In mid-June General Burgoyne arrived in Canada with about 7,000 troops, an enormous baggage train, and more than 130 pieces of artillery. He was planning to move down from the north and capture Albany, thus hoping to take New York out of the war. On June 30 his army reached Fort Ticonderoga and soon began moving south.

General Burgoyne attacked along Lake Champlain and threatened Albany. But General Philip Schuyler, the American commander in the north, began to lay waste to the countryside as he retreated. His men felled logs in the roads and destroyed the crops. General Burgoyne's army got stalled, and suffered from lack of supplies. Finally, Burgoyne's supply problems became serious and he could not move on. Again, the irregulars came into play, harrying the well-disciplined British army at every step. It was a hot sort of warfare, and it was very effective, for the Europeans were not equipped for fighting in heavy-wooded country. Their uniforms were heavy (the boots alone weighed twelve pounds). The Hessians waddled along in jackboots that came up their thighs, in tall hats that got stuck in the brush, and carrying heavy equipment at all times. The colonists, in deerskin or homespun and moccasins, carrying musket and a sack of ball and powder around their necks, looked from behind their trees and shot the gaudy soldiers down.

In August, Burgoyne's supply problems grew desperate. He learned that the Americans had a large store of supplies at Bennington, and he sent a column there to capture the supplies. American General John Stark was at Bennington with 2,600 men, most of them militia. But they were very angry men, aroused by reports of massacres conducted by Indians who had joined Burgoyne. The Americans attacked the British and defeated them. The British moved back to the protection of Burgoyne's army.

On September 13, Burgoyne crossed the Hudson River and began to move down the west side, toward Albany. Washington had not been very happy with the performance of General Schuyler, so he had replaced him with General Horatio Gates, who had then entrenched his troops at Bemis Heights, south of Saratoga. Burgoyne sent word to General Henry Clinton, the commander of British forces in New York City, and asked him to march north while Burgoyne marched south. Thus the Americans would be caught in a vise. On September 19, Burgoyne attacked Gates, hoping to outflank him on the left, but General Daniel Morgan stopped that ploy at the battle of Freeman's Farm. The British lost and retreated. General Clinton was coming north up the Hudson with a fleet, but he grew nervous and stopped at Kingston. He grew still more nervous up in these wilds with Americans all around him, and returned to New York for reinforcements, leaving Burgoyne out on a limb. On October 7 Burgoyne's supply problem was so serious he felt he had to attack immediately and he did. His forces seemed likely to take the American positions, until Benedict Arnold gathered around him a hundred men and stormed the British position, throwing the redcoats into a disorderly retreat. On October 8 Burgoyne retreated all the way to Saratoga.

Meanwhile General Gates was gathering men. The call for volunteers went out all over New England and men began to show up, until by October 10 Gates had three times as many men as Burgoyne had left. On October 13 he had Burgoyne surrounded, and the British general was nearly desperate for food and ammunition. He knew he could not fight again, so he asked for terms. The 5,700 men of his army laid down their arms and surrendered. The surrender terms to the British provided that Burgoyne's entire northern army would go home to England and never fight in America again in this war. Exit Gentleman Johnny Burgoyne, his reputation ruined.

That summer of 1777 General Howe had decided to capture Philadelphia, which should put a serious crimp in the morale of the Americans. On July 23 he embarked at New York with 15,000 troops in the Royal Navy's transports. The big convoy sailed down to the mouth of Chesapeake Bay and then up the bay to Head of Elk, where they arrived on August 25.

Washington, meanwhile, was well aware of the British plan. One of the strong points of Washington's command was his intelligence service, and his spies were extremely effective. He managed to round up 10,500 men, and proposed to make a stand to keep the British away from Philadelphia. He chose the eastern side of Brandywine Creek for his defense. General Howe came slowly and steadily up toward Philadelphia and on September 11 he attacked Washington at Brandywine. The British proposed to outflank the Americans with their superior force, and then to roll up the line. The attack in the middle by German General William von Knyphausen was largely a feint. The real strength was in Cornwallis's force that attacked General John Sullivan's Americans on the right flank. The Cornwallis troops did just what they were expected to do, and Sullivan's men began to panic. But General Nathanael Greene saved the day by stopping the British long enough for Sullivan's men to retreat in an orderly fashion. Still, the Americans were forced to move back toward Philadelphia, with the British in pursuit. The Americans lost a thousand men that day, the British half that number. The British then attacked General Anthony Wayne's rear guard, and routed them with a bayonet charge. The way was open to Philadelphia, which Lord Howe entered on September 26. The members of Congress, warned just in time, managed to escape to Wilmington, but it was a narrow squeak. The British had the American capital city under occupation, and the effect on American morale was serious. But Washington never faltered. Already he was planning a new strike against the enemy.

On October 3 the audacious Washington moved against Howe's main camp at Germantown. The attack began in the early hours of October 4, well before sunup. But in spite of Washington's excellent planning, his army let him down. Detachments got lost in the fog and failed to carry out their assignments. At one point American troops were firing on one another. Several units managed to penetrate into Germantown, but because others failed to support them they were forced to retreat. Again the Americans were defeated. Again General Greene saved the day with a brilliant rearguard action that let most of the American troops escape. Still, the Americans lost 700 men killed or wounded and 400 taken prisoner. The British losses, once more, were about half of Washington's. Within a matter of weeks, the whole Delaware River was cleared by the British and became a British waterway. General Washington moved back, and took up winter quarters at Valley Forge.

Seventeen seventy-eight. The Americans were holding off the British, although how long this could continue was problematical. Political troubles dogged the colonies, mostly concerned with the fierce feelings of each colonist for his own, but in their desperation they recognized the one salient fact, pointed out wryly by Benjamin Franklin during the Declaration of Independence days that now seemed so long ago:

"We must hang together, for if we do not, we shall certainly hang separately."

Lord North would very much have liked to get England out of the American mess. When he heard of the surrender of Burgoyne in December 1777, he prepared a new offer of reconciliation. But the French now intervened, giving the Americans an enormous lift by officially recognizing American independence. France and the new American Confederation signed treaties. That summer of 1778 France and England went to war, which meant the treaties would guarantee physical help for the beleaguered Americans. As for Americans at large: the country was "palpitating with joy at the alliance with France."

England sent a peace mission. Forget about the tea tax, they said. Forget all those coercive acts, and the prices on the heads of John and Sam Adams and John Hancock. Forget all that talk about Parliament's right to tax the colonies. Just come home, Americans.

So here, just three years after King George III said he would never be happy until the rebellious Americans were crushed, all that was changed in the minds of Parliament. Even the king had decided to be less demanding. He would now have settled just to see everybody in Boston back within the fold. But what had happened was not forgotten in America. There was no way back.

The Americans took Philadelphia. The peace commission went home to London, a complete failure. On the sea a handful of American captains raised hob with British trade and British supply lines. More than a hundred American privateers were out, commissioned by Congress and the colonies, slashing away wherever they could find a fat merchantman traveling alone. John Paul Jones was now a captain, his ship was the *Ranger,* and he was raiding the English where it hurt, off their own coasts. So cocky, so assured, he planned to rush in and kidnap the Earl of Selkirk, who lived on Solway Firth, but unluckily for Jones the earl was not at home that day. Still, Englishmen were getting the idea: despite the enormous sea power of Britain, the Americans could give them trouble on the sea as well as on the land. The Royal Navy was in somewhat the position of the American military in the 1980s, thoroughly equipped for a major war with a major power, but not equipped to stop will-o'-the-wisp guerillas who flitted about the seas in vessels no larger than a frigate.

In New Jersey, General Washington and General Howe faced each other like a pair of bulldogs, fighting here and there, but without conclusion. Over in Pennsylvania, the English and the Indians were up to the old tricks, massacring the settlers along the valleys. More rape, burnings, murder, kidnappings. On November 11, an English and Indian column hit Cherry Valley, New York, and some forty survivors of the fight surrendered, on condition that they would be treated as prisoners of war. The redcoats turned them over to the Indians, who massacred them all. The man in charge of the British western operation, Colonel Henry Hamilton, was called "the hair buyer" because of the prices he paid for American scalps.

The French came and brought a fleet of seventeen ships which helped draw English attention away from the Americans. Savannah fell to the English, who also burned Portsmouth and Norfolk. Burn, capture, capture, burn, kill, and be killed. Up and down the American eastern seaboard. No really decisive actions were fought.

Seventeen seventy-nine. As if the English did not have enough gnats nibbling at them, the Spanish now declared war on England in a sort of desultory way. Spain would not lend more than a pittance of money; the Spanish would not guarantee to fight for American independence. Their real interest was in jumping on the bandwagon and carving out a chunk of British territory for themselves. They were almost as much trouble to the Americans as allies as they were to the British as enemies.

But the war was not going so well for the Americans that they could be happy about it. In the summer of 1779 a committee of Congress again proposed terms for peace with Britain: independence was now the key. Independence had been declared, France had sealed the decision by promising to fight for the Americans until independence was won. The colonists could scarcely back out now even if some wanted to. Other matters had to be guarantee of American fishing rights in the waters common to the united colonies and Canada and the right to navigate the Mississippi. John Adams was named to negotiate a treaty if it could be done.

On the sea, John Paul Jones was a gadfly stinging the British here and there. He secured an old French ship, refurbished her, and called her the *Bonhomme Richard,* crammed forty-two guns aboard, and named her a frigate. He took on the British frigate *Serapis* and beat her.

The French navy did not come up with a decisive action. It was probably just as well, for the British, who had twice as large a navy, could have wiped out the French, as they had before. With American troops the French assaulted Savannah, and lost. Count Casimir Pulaski, who had come from Poland to fight for American independence, was killed.

Seventeen eighty. The war was going quite badly for the Americans. General Cornwallis was in Charleston, with 8,000 men, planning to take over the whole south. Washington's army headquarters at Morristown, New Jersey, was a dismal place. Soldiers were not getting paid, they were hungry and sometimes barefoot. Connecticut troops mutinied, but the mutiny was suppressed by Pennsylvania troops. At this time the one bright light was the help coming from France, including troops and weapons. In the south, General Cornwallis was moving, breaking up the American force at Camden, North Carolina, but finally being stopped by American sharp-shooters at the Battle of King's Mountain on the border between North and South Carolina. Cornwallis went back into South Carolina.

The long war brought many sorts of casualties. In September one of the most trusted American generals, Benedict Arnold, in a fit of pique because of envy of Washington, tried to surrender West Point to the British. This would have given them control of the central Hudson River. Arnold's British contact man, Major John André of the British army, was caught and hanged. Arnold switched sides, was rewarded with a commission as a British brigadier, and spent the rest of the war fighting against the Americans in Virginia and Connecticut. He also created a term "Benedict Arnold," which in the American language came to mean a peculiarly slimy sort of traitor.

Seventeen eighty-one. Back and forth. Back and forth. This period was notable in the field for very little; on the political scene it was marked by a striving for unity among the colonies. On the international scene it was marked by a growing dependence on France and a desperate search for funds with which to continue the rebellion.

One of the problems for the British was the widening of their war. The Netherlands came into it against England, not because of any alliance with the Americans, but for reasons of their own. But France was growing restless with the expense and length of the war (for that matter so were many Americans), and the expense was wearing everyone down. Franklin got a gift from the French of six million livres, and a loan of four million more. But it was not easy.

Military reputations flowed, and then peaked and ebbed. General Gates was defeated and lost his reputation. General Greene came up fast. Light-horse Harry Lee was a slashing star with his cavalry. In the winter of 1781 Colonel William Cunningham, under orders from British Colonel Balfour

at Charleston, led 150 white loyalists and blacks into the interior settlements of South Carolina, killing and raping. Finally they came to a house
that sheltered an American party of thirty-five men under Colonel Hayes.
After a fight the British force set fire to the American house. Those under
siege agreed to surrender if they were treated as prisoners of war. They
surrendered, marched out, and Colonel Hayes was immediately seized and
hanged from a tree limb. So was his second in command. Colonel Cunningham then personally killed several prisoners and told his men to join
the sport. One of them, a neighbor to those captured, walked up and down
the area, running his sword through the bodies of all his old neighbors,
particularly if they were not yet dead. One can imagine the hatreds that
were thereby engendered, racial and personal, that would last for generations. Anyone who really wants to understand American regional and
racial intolerances had best go back to the beginnings of the sixteenth and
seventeenth centuries and follow the details of the massacres and murders that are a part of American military history, through to modern
times.

In the southern campaign of 1781 General Greene won a victory, then
he retreated before Cornwallis. In March 1781, Greene "whupped" Cornwallis at Guilford. But the war went on. At Halifax, North Carolina,
Cornwallis's troops were let loose to commit more atrocities. This breach
of code was attributable to a growing British frustration in this war where
the Americans played the will-o'-the-wisp, and that most evasive man of
all, General George Washington, could never be pinned down. In the
spring of 1781 the atrocities continued. Lieutenant Colonel Brown, commander of a British unit in South Carolina, personally hanged thirteen
Americans, and delivered many patriots to the Cherokee Indians with the
Indian promise that they would torture the prisoners to death—which the
Indians did with great pleasure.

North and south, east and west, the various tribes of Indians were
involved, almost always encouraged by the British to war in their own
savage way. It was a phenomenon that would not be forgotten in America
for 150 years.

When General Benedict Arnold appeared in Virginia in the early part
of 1781, now as a British officer, General Washington wanted to get his
hands on the traitor. He sent one of his trusted staff officers, the French
Marquis de Lafayette, who had come to America to fight as a volunteer.
Lafayette took 1,200 men to catch Arnold. During the fighting and ne-
gotiating, Arnold wrote Lafayette a letter about exchanging prisoners which
the young Frenchman returned, refusing to correspond with a traitor. Arnold threatened to send all American prisoners to the West Indies, but
then Cornwallis arrived. He did not like Arnold much better than Lafayette

did, and he sent him off on some specious mission to New York to get rid of him.

So Cornwallis was in Virginia with 7,000 men, burning and laying waste to the countryside, and, of course, making the British ever more hated in the southern area of America. The Americans of that day computed that Cornwallis in his midsummer marchings up and down Virginia destroyed property to the value of £3 million.

After some sparring and fighting, Cornwallis moved his army to Yorktown on the first of August 1781.

As far back as the spring of 1781, Washington had been planning a truly brilliant move. The Count de Rochambeau had been sent by France to fight with the Americans, and he had brought an army of 5,000 men. To make best use of them, Washington had decided on a joint French-American attack on New York City. The battle would be joined by the French West Indian fleet too, under Admiral de Grasse. As late as July 5 this had still been the plan, and Washington's troops were camped near those of the French general above New York City. Then Washington received a letter from Admiral de Grasse in the West Indies, saying that de Grasse was leaving for America with his fleet and 3,000 more French troops, and would be in the Chesapeake Bay area, and ready for operations until October. Washington then changed his entire plan. The big battle with the British, he decided, would be fought in the South. Combining forces with Rochambeau, Washington marched south, made a feint at Staten Island, then continued on past and crossed over New Jersey, heading south for Virginia.

He managed to spend two days at Mount Vernon, his country home on the bank of the Potomac River, the first days he had spent there since the beginning of the war. Then he marched toward Yorktown, sending word to Admiral de Grasse.

On August 30 Admiral de Grasse arrived off Yorktown and immediately set up a naval blockade of the British garrison. His 3,000 troops then joined up with Lafayette's men, who had surrounded the garrison on the land side.

The next step was a naval battle. The British fleet under Admiral Thomas Graves arrived and Admiral de Grasse raised anchor and moved out to do battle. The French and English fleets fought a naval battle on September 5, but it was indecisive. For the next few days they maneuvered for position. Admiral Graves did not know it, but Admiral de Grasse was stalling; he knew that Count Barras with the French squadron at Newport was coming down to assist him. Count Barras appeared on September 10, and Admiral Graves, now outclassed, retreated to New York. The French now controlled the sea off Yorktown, and the land around the city was occupied by French and American troops.

Admiral de Grasse then sent several ships north to pick up General Washington's combined French-American army and bring them to Williamsburg. The voyage took ten days, and Washington's force arrived on September 24.

Washington now had an army of 16,800 men, about half of them French, plus the French navy. It was the strongest force he had been able to put together during the entire war.

On September 28, Washington began the siege of Yorktown. General Cornwallis abandoned his outer perimeter of fortifications two days later

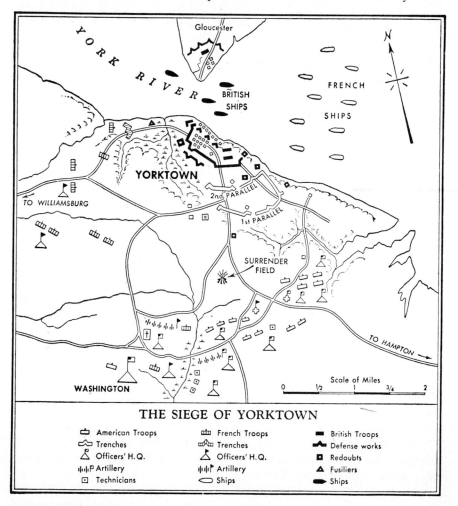

THE SIEGE OF YORKTOWN

American Troops	French Troops	British Troops
Trenches	Trenches	Defense works
Officers' H.Q.	Officers' H.Q.	Redoubts
Artillery	Artillery	Fusiliers
Technicians	Ships	Ships

to consolidate his strength on the inner line. Washington then brought up siege guns and trained them on the inner defenses of the British. No part of the British camp was safe from bombardment.

Still the British position was strong. Colonel Alexander Hamilton led an attack on the left flank of the British line, and captured two important redoubts, essential to the British defense. Cornwallis tried desperately to recapture the positions on October 16, but two fierce attacks failed. Cornwallis then saw his position as hopeless. He tried to escape with his troops across the York River, but a storm came up and put an end to the plan. The small boats he had at his disposal could not possibly operate in this weather.

Cornwallis then faced the inevitable. If he persisted in this position, his force could be overwhelmed at any moment. There was no way out. He sent an emissary to Washington's camp to begin negotiations for surrender.

One more incident was to convince Cornwallis that his position was indeed hopeless.

In the fighting at Yorktown, the French were on the left and they attacked:

Precisely as the signal was given, the French on the left . . . began their march in the deepest silence. At one hundred and twenty paces from the redoubt, they were challenged by a German sentry from the parapet; they pressed on at quick time, exposed to the fire of the enemy. The abatis and palisades, at twenty-five paces from the redoubt, being strong and well preserved, stopped them for some minutes and cost them many men. So as soon as the way was cleared by the brave carpenters, the storming party threw themselves into the ditch, broke through the fraises, and mounted the parapet. Foremost was Charles de Lameth, who had volunteered for the attack, and who was wounded in both knees by two different musket balls. The order being now given, the French leaped into the redoubt, and charged the enemy with the bayonet [named for Bayonne, France, where the weapon was invented]. At this moment the Count de Deux Ponts raised the cry of "Vive le Roi" which was repeated by all of his companions who were able to lift their voices. De Sireuil, a very young captain of yagers, who had been wounded twice before, was now wounded for the third time and mortally. Within six minutes the redoubt was mastered and manned, but in that short time nearly one hundred of the assailants were killed or wounded.

And thus, by the royal command of King Louis XVI did the regiment get the name of the Royal Auvergne; Oliver Wendell Holmes, the poet, later wrote a verse about them.

The battle ended that day, October 19, and the result was the surrender of a surrounded and beaten Cornwallis. The 7,000 British soldiers became prisoners of the Americans. Cornwallis sulked in his tent that day. Major General O'Hara marched the British army out to surrender to General George Washington. And the war on land was over.

No matter that the French had played their most important role in this last stage of the war, General Washington had won it, and none knew better than the French generals who had come to help him. Washington's great strength of character had upheld the American army through more than six long years of struggle, most of those years spent trying to raise forces and put together units capable of fighting. Washington had suffered wholesale desertions (such as the 1781 mutiny of the Pennsylvania division) and one defeat after another. During the early and middle years he seemed almost always to be on the retreat. But he was never caught, he was never defeated decisively. Always he rose from the field to move away, reorganize, and fight again. His courage and his military generalship were unquestioned and respected by nearly all who knew him. There were many ambitious generals in the American forces during the revolution, but not one who could have taken Washington's place, and had he died the whole military effort might well have come unraveled. Even in Congress, a most choleric and sometimes unruly body, the name of Washington invoked nothing but respect. More than any other figure he represented the American Revolution, and it is not hyperbole to call him the Father of His Country.

The French had played an enormously important role in the American Revolution, particularly in the last year. All this of course was gradually forgotten, and by the last quarter of the twentieth century, when France's and America's ways were anything but "twined," perhaps it would be useful to remember that several times in the past, Americans and French had been real friends and real allies.

The defeat of Cornwallis at Yorktown was the last straw for a discomfited and disgusted English government. The city of London petitioned the king to put an end to "this unnatural and unfortunate war." Only the king wanted to fight on—rather, he wanted his subjects to fight on.

"No difficulties can get me to consent to the getting of peace at the expense of a separation from America," said his noble majesty.

Washington went up to New York for the winter, to wait and see what the British were going to do next. Admiral de Grasse took his French fleet to the West Indies. In Philadelphia, Robert R. Livingston, the American Confederation's secretary for foreign affairs, wrote Benjamin Franklin, who was in Paris, the terms America insisted on if the British wanted peace. Parliament decided the British did indeed want peace, and called on the king to give it to them. The king was equivocal. Finally the king saw the handwriting on the wall.

So the House of Commons, which had brought the war to England, now removed the burden against the king's will. His mind, he said, "was truly torn to pieces," which might have been true in more ways than one. And finally, he shut up. "I was thoroughly resolved," he said, "not to open my mouth on any negotiation with America."

Thus the Americans achieved their independence, finally made official by treaty in 1782.

CHAPTER 6

Embarrassments of a New Nation

Finally, in 1781, the French fleet and French reinforcements sent to help Washington in the South had turned the tide for the Americans. The battle of Yorktown was not really decisive in the modern military sense. After it was won by the French and the Americans, Washington stood back and waited for the other shoe to drop so to speak. He did not know what the British would do next, and no indication had come that the British were so tired of the expense and difficulty of fighting a war across the Atlantic Ocean that they were ready to quit. It was several weeks before Washington really believed it, and he stood ready to continue the fight. So the war did not end in a rush of glory, but in the evaporation of the British will to send more troops and more ships to fight a never-ending struggle.

But it was not to be. The treaty was worked out, and then signed, and the French became a party to it. France was America's best friend in all the world.

But America in the 1780s found life as a new nation anything but easy. The trials of nationhood were many, and the structure of the American Confederation of independent states was ill-equipped to deal with the world. Working that out meant a rewriting of the basic document of American law, the development of the U.S. Constitution, and its original ten amendments.

There were problems with the Indians, which some states did not want to worry about. There were problems with the Barbary states of the Mediterranean, which saw in the new nation a source of tribute. There was, above all, a breach with France, occasioned by the French Revolution and the French execution of the man who had supervised France's generosity to

Americans, King Louis XVI. The Americans did not get along with the French revolutionaries, and relations soured very quickly. The result, as indicated, was something very near to war—America's first undeclared military excursion.

*   *   *

While the Americans were winning their freedom from England the world was scarcely watching. Halfway across the globe was the Ottoman Empire, whose Sultan Abdul Hamid I did not even know of the existence of the American colonies and could not have cared less about the matter. In the 1770s he was fighting the Russians for the Crimea. His empire extended from Gibraltar to India, and although the signs of disintegration were already showing, the Mediterranean was still a Turkish lake, guarded by the sultan's minions in Morocco, Tunis, Algiers, Cairo, and Tripoli. The little kings of these principalities paid allegiance and tribute to the Ottomans in what was then Constantinople but is now called Istanbul. If they failed, he would certainly send an expeditionary force to depose the offender and the ill-advised little king's head would most certainly roll, as heads had rolled in the past.

In their turns, the little kings of the principalities lorded it over their subjects and ruled the seas around them. Piracy was their business. Any nation without a strong navy either paid tribute to these minor despots, or found their shipping attacked and their sailors enslaved when they went into Algerine, Tunisian, Moroccan, or Tripolitan waters. In George Washington's time, the Americans had found it easier to pay tribute to the various deys, beys, and emperors than to establish a navy to protect American shipping.

Once the peace treaty with England was signed, the new American Confederation saw no further use for an army or a navy and took steps to disband them.

"Standing armies in time of peace are inconsistent with the principles of Republican government, dangerous to the liberties of a free people, and generally converted into destructive engines for establishing despotism." So said the Continental Congress when faced with the question of what to do about Washington's army. When some asked what was to be done with such military installations as West Point, the Congress begrudgingly provided for a very small force to guard what were obviously national installations. As of January 1784, the entire national army consisted of a regiment of infantry, numbering 527 men, and a battalion of artillery, numbering 138 men.

As for the navy, it was completely disbanded, the frigate *Alliance* being the last ship sold off in 1785. She was converted to become an "Indiaman" and went into the China trade.

The thirteen original colonies turned each to its own affairs and to the serious problems of working together under one flag as one nation. The process of revitalizing their agreement into what would become the Constitution of a United States of America began. But the Americans were not allowed the respite for which they hoped. Seeing that America was militarily weak, the smallest powers that had anything to gain from bullying America began to do just that. The first trouble abroad was with Algiers, one of the "Barbary" states of the North African coast, which had degenerated in the eclipse of Spanish power to become notorious for piracy. As soon as the dey of Algiers learned that ships that flew the American flag had no naval protection, he began preying on them. On July 25, 1785, the schooner *Maria* out of Boston was seized by a corsair vessel in the Atlantic, just outside the Straits of Gibraltar, and all the crew were carried into slavery. Five days later the Philadelphia ship *Dolphin* was captured. Her captain and crew also went into slavery. And because the Americans had no navy there was absolutely nothing to be done about it, except to negotiate from a point of complete weakness. The Algerians held twenty-one Americans prisoner, and demanded $3,000 a head for their ransom, an absolutely outrageous sum. Negotiations were carried out through third parties, but the years dragged on, the prisoners rotted in Algerian cells, and no progress was made. All that stopped the Algerians from further depredations against American shipping was a declaration of war against them by Portugal, and fighting which consumed all the corsairs' efforts for the next few years. The Americans set out to buy peace, concluding a treaty with Morocco which obliged the American government to make annual payments to the sultan. In effect, the United States was a vassal state.

At home in America, the problem did not get a great deal of attention. Eyes were turned to Philadelphia and New York; the Americans were building themselves a government, and in 1787 the Constitution was put together; in 1788 the ratifications were completed. The next year, 1789, the first session of the new U.S. Congress did turn its attention to the problems of defense, not because of the Barbary pirates, but because of Indian troubles on the American western and southern borders. On September 29, 1789, the U.S. Army was formed, with General Josiah Harman as commander of infantry and a major as chief of artillery. The total force numbered 846 men. They called themselves the 1st Regiment, U.S. Army. Soon they would be in action.

The Treaty of Paris, which ended the American Revolutionary War, gave the new American nation title to all the lands below the Great Lakes.

This land was called the Northwest Territory, and it was administered by the Americans with the understanding that ultimately the western territories would be carved into states. Colonists from the northeastern states moved into the northern part, which they called Ohio. Colonists from Pennsylvania, Virginia, and North Carolina moved along the Ohio Valley into the area called simply Territory Southwest of the River Ohio. The Indians had not been consulted in making this peace. The Miami Indians in the north and the Shawnee nation in the south never stopped their fighting. They went from fighting with the English and scourging the patriot settlers to fighting on their own, ambushing parties of settlers who came down the Ohio on flatboats, enslaving the women and children, killing the men. No community along the border was safe. One day in the section called Alabama a Shawnee raiding party struck a community that was large enough to have a school. One group of warriors surrounded the one-room schoolhouse, brandishing firebrands, and prepared to break in and assault the teacher and children. The teacher locked the door. That was all he could do; he had no weapon. The Indian warriors circled the log cabin. One Indian found a chink in the door, pushed through a musket, and shot the teacher dead as he led a last prayer of his pupils. The Indians then broke in and massacred the children.

Small wonder that the murdering was reciprocated. The Shawnee chief Cornstalk and his son were killed one day when on a visit to an American fort. Along the frontier came a new slogan:

"The only good Indian is a dead Indian."

That attitude controlled American feelings and behavior toward the Indians for more than a hundred years.

To try to bring peace, Arthur St. Clair, governor of the Northwest Territory, had called an assembly of all the Indian nations of the area in 1789, at Fort Harmar on the Muskingum River. There he had worked out boundaries for territory that would belong to the Delaware, Ottawa, Potawatomi, Sac, Wyandot, and Chippewa Indians. In exchange for ceding other territories, these Indians were given money, muskets, iron tools, and other compensation. At the moment they were happy enough. But another tribe, the Miami, had responded to the governor's call with a series of murderous raids on the flatboats coming down the Ohio. So serious did the danger grow that Governor St. Clair stopped all emigration south of Pittsburgh, and sought guidance from Philadelphia.

St. Clair's agents reported that the violence was undoubtedly stirred up by the British, and he cited chapter and verse. From the south, Congress had equally disturbing reports of Indian violence abetted by the Spanish. But Congress was not in a fighting mood. No was was wanted. And so the Ohio troubles were regarded as a "local" problem. Governor St. Clair turned to General Harmar to solve it.

In the summer of 1790 General Harmar called for militia from Virginia and Pennsylvania to augment his federal force, and established his head-quarters for a punitive expedition in a log fort at what is now Cincinnati. At the end of September, five battalions, mostly militia, set out to attack the towns of the Miami Indians. Harmar burned five towns. But the Indians retaliated: Little Turtle, war chief of the Miami, ambushed Captain John Armstrong and a party of thirty American soldiers at the Eel River. Captain Armstrong managed to hide in the reeds where he heard and saw the torture of his companions that went on all night long. Next day Armstrong rounded up the survivors. There were eight. From that point on, the regulars were not inclined to give mercy to any Indians they captured.

Little Turtle was a good general, and his Indians were better soldiers than the mixed bag of regulars and militia of the Americans. Late in September the Indians fought a force of 400 Americans at the Maumee River. The militiamen panicked and broke, and the Indians slaughtered them. A messenger was sent back to General Harmar's camp for help. But Harmar had lost confidence in the militia and in his own troops. So no help came. The defeat brought an end to the punitive campaign, and the murderous raids of the Miami Indians on the settlers grew worse than ever. These Western Indians, unfortunately for themselves and the settlers, did not have the understanding of the tide of history shown by King Philip's sachem Passaconaway a hundred years earlier when he warned his brethren against fighting the English, because no matter how many they killed, in the end the English would defeat them. As with Americans of the 1980s, history was not the long suit of the Western Indians.

Encouraged by the confusion created along the western American frontier, the English in Canada doubled their efforts to set the Indian nations aflame. The English supplied the Indians with weapons and encouraged them. All the confusion they could cause among the Americans was seen to strengthen the English hand in Canada, and as long as the Americans were afflicted with their growing pains of organizing a nation, not much was done about it. But in 1790 the new American government was established. The people of the states of New York, Pennsylvania, Virginia, the Carolinas, and Georgia had had enough reports of the murder and mistreatment of their people who were trying to settle the West. Until now, the Indians had been able to do much as they pleased. Now came a demand from the states with borders on the Northwest Territory for much stronger action.

Governor Arthur St. Clair, who had been both a British officer (Quebec) and an American general (Yorktown), was given command of the United States Army, which had now been expanded into two regiments, the 1st and 2nd. President Washington personally sent St. Clair off into the wilderness to fight Indians with one warning: "Beware of surprise."

St. Clair traveled west. On the Great Miami River he stopped to build Fort Hamilton. As was the custom, the Americans had their women with them, 200 of them, to tend to the needs of 1,400 men. St. Clair marched to the headwaters of the Wabash River, and on November 3 camped beside a small stream. Little Turtle's Indians struck them there, for St. Clair had forgotten Washington's warning and his pickets were weak. The Indians dashed into the camp, killing and scalping women as they stood at the campfires. In an hour half of St. Clair's army was lost, and he had three horses shot from under him. St. Clair found an opening in the Indian lines and fled, taking with him as many people as he could. The others, 900 men and 56 women, were massacred by the Indians.

General Richard Butler, the second in command, was killed slowly, then a renegade American named Simon Girty forced open the dead general's mouth and filled it with dirt. "Indian dirt," he said. Let the white man eat the Indian dirt of which he was so fond.

With two years of victory behind them, the Indians grew bolder than ever. The torturing grew worse, and more refined. The Indians liked to bring a captive up to earshot of some American stockaded settlement, and there burn him at the stake, slowly, so that his screams would terrify the Americans. The terrorism, however, aroused even a somnolent Congress to a realization that some serious action must be taken to stop, not just annoy, the Indians. The word *army* was still anathema, so they established four "Legions of the United States," each to be composed of 1,000 men. General Anthony Wayne, known as "Mad Anthony," was put in charge.

This army trained in 1792, while the politicians talked. A great conclave of British, Americans, and twenty-eight Indian nations was called for 1793 to bring peace. It failed.

When the Miami Indians saw Mad Anthony Wayne and his men in action, they nicknamed Wayne "Blacksnake," for a snake that looks ferocious but eats mice. In the fall of 1793 the Indians confirmed their diagnosis: they attacked a military convoy, routing the ninety-man escort and killing sixteen men. There was nothing to worry about from the Americans, they said. They did not see Mad Anthony Wayne take his troops to the place where Little Turtle had humbled General St. Clair, dig up the field guns the Indians had buried, and build a fort which he named Fort Recovery. They did not watch as Mad Anthony Wayne instructed his troops in the fine art of bayonet fighting, his favorite method of infantry attack. And so, the Indians felt quite secure when Mad Anthony Wayne embarked on his military expedition of 1794.

The British, having succored their redskins, now had shown why they took such interest in the welfare of the Indians. The British moved down into the territory that was American under the Treaty of Paris. They held

Detroit. They built Fort Miami on American land on the Maumee River. One Indian nation after another danced the war dance against the Americans. On the last day of June 1794, Little Turtle attacked Fort Recovery and captured many horses. But when he counted Indian noses the next day, he found that not only had his men failed to breach the barricades, but he had many casualties. Little Turtle, then, brought the one voice of caution to the Indian and British jubilation meetings. He had been wrong, he said. Blacksnake had the fangs of a rattler.

General Wayne assembled his force, his supplies, and waited. Up came 1,600 Kentucky riflemen under Major General Charles Scott, mounted men who could shoot. These were more than militia, and Wayne's infantrymen now knew what to do with the bayonet.

They marched out, the American Legion in blue uniforms with buttons buttoned as the general demanded. Wayne believed in field intelligence, so he had a network of spies ahead, and scouts who were in touch with the spies. And Mad Anthony knew his enemy Little Turtle, for one of Anthony's men was William Wells, an American who had been captured by the Indians when he was a boy, been brought up as an Indian brave, married Little Turtle's daughter, and knew a great deal about his father-in-law.

Little Turtle was camped at the confluence of the Au Glaise and Maumee rivers; around him was the country where the Indians grew their corn and squash. Wayne marched up there, and built a log fort on the Maumee. The Indians said they wanted to talk. Wayne talked, but he built Fort Deposit, as a place to leave heavy equipment.

Encouraged by the British, Little Turtle decided to ambush the Americans. On August 18 he was ready, with a thousand men in a field where scores of trees had been felled recently by a tornado. Across the plain was the Maumee River.

As Little Turtle waited for the Americans, he appointed Tecumseh, a young Shawnee, as his battle chief. But the Americans did not come, not for two days, and his Indians grew restless. Then, on August 20, out of Fort Deposit the Americans moved.

The fight began when Tecumseh fired his musket. The Indians shot and shot well. There was confusion in the American ranks. But then the long line of blue-clad infantry, rifles before them, the bayonets shining, moved slowly into the fallen timber. Some blue-clad men fell, but the others came on inexorably. Most of the Indians panicked and fled. The others were cut down. Finally the charge ended and the bayoneters became riflemen, firing at the retreating Indians and renegade whites. The Indians ran back to the British fort and there found the heavy wooden gates closed against them. They fled then. Mad Anthony Wayne spent the autumn laying waste to the Indian lands. They would have no great food supply for the winter.

In 1796 a new agreement with the British brought the evacuation of Detroit. The Americans negotiated with the Indians and secured 25,000 square miles of new territory by treaty, extending west to Ohio. The Indian boundary was Indiana.

Peace, it seemed had finally been established in the Northwest.

CHAPTER 7

Troubles at Sea

The little despots of the Barbary States of the Mediterranean found that America was an excellent source of revenue for them. They recognized the great truth of the early nineteenth century: that the United States was too weak and too deeply involved in its home affairs to stand up against anyone. It was easier to pay tribute than to build a navy. Even when a sort of navy was built, the American government preferred to pay rather than fight.

Out of this period came the halcyon days of the American navy, the period in which its "fighting sail" could be compared in derring-do and gallantry to the British Royal Navy. The stories of "Preble's Boys" mark the high-water point of American naval history of the nineteenth century.

*   *   *

In 1792 Captain John Paul Jones found himself in a strange position for a man of action, a hero of the revolution. He was appointed by the United States government to be agent for the liberation of the American captives from Algiers. What a thankless task it was! He had no navy to back him, nothing but a piece of paper appointing him consul to Algiers. Jones, who was in Paris, died before he could set sail for Africa, and another man was chosen.

Trouble with Algiers—except for the handful of survivors of the original 21 seamen enslaved by the corsairs—had been at a minimum for several years. The reason for this was the continuing war with Portugal: the Portuguese had stationed a naval force just outside Gibraltar, and any pirate ship that came out was set upon without ado. The Algerines stayed inside their own waters. But in 1793 the war with Portugal suddenly ended, and the Algerines were soon up to their old tricks. A squadron of Algerine vessels moved out into the Atlantic, and by October 1793 had captured another ten American vessels and taken another 105 prisoners to the slave cells. The dey of Algiers, in his contempt for the Americans, announced that if Minister Barclay, the man chosen to replace John Paul Jones, attempted to set foot in Algiers, the dey would make sure that he was killed.

Despots never seem to learn just how far they can go. With America, festering for years under the ignominies of a vassal relationship with the African pirates, this was too much. President Washington called a meeting of his cabinet and, after consulting with the members, on March 3, 1794, sent a message to Congress, giving all the history of the Algerine difficulties and recommending strong action. Three weeks later Congress presented him with a law authorizing the construction of six frigates of at least thirty-two guns each. Unfortunately there were still faint hearts in Congress, and men concerned more with budget than national power. The law was directed specifically against Algiers, and provided that if the difficulties with that nation be resolved, the building program be suspended.

So six keels were laid:

Ship	Guns	Construction site
Constitution	44	Boston
President	44	New York
United States	44	Philadelphia
Chesapeake	38	Portsmouth, Va.
Constellation	38	Baltimore
Congress	38	Portsmouth, N.H.

When the dey of Algiers learned of this building program, suddenly he changed his tune. A treaty was negotiated. It was an uneven treaty, with many of the same "vassal clauses" as those with Tripoli and Morocco, two other Turkish principalities on the coast of North Africa. The fact that it was signed by America indicates just how concerned the growing nation still was with domestic problems on the American continent. It was better to have peace at any price in the Mediterranean and not have to fight for it. The treaty provided for large annual payments to the Algerines if they did not attack American shipping.

But the attempt to stop the building of a navy was this time short-lived. The reason was difficulty with England and France. The English had continued to give America trouble on the high seas at the end of the revolution, particularly by their unpleasant habit of impressing seamen from ships they stopped and declaring that the seamen were British deserters. Sometimes this was true. Sometimes it was not. In 1790 and 1791, as Britain prepared for war with Spain and then with Russia, so many American seamen were impressed into British ships (sometimes whole crews) that the United States government appointed consuls in English ports, whose job was primarily to protect American seamen.

Then, trouble with France . . .

The Americans ended the war of revolution with the most kindly feelings toward their French benefactors, the government of Louis XVI. Then came the French Revolution.

The French Revolution had begun in 1789, and at first was regarded with enthusiasm by the Americans. Was not the Marquis de Lafayette chosen commander of the French National Guard? Did not France adopt a Declaration of the Rights of Man, and abolish the feudal system? But by 1792 the Jacobins had seized power and converted the revolution from a popular uprising against the excesses of the nobility to a radical political oligarchy. The next year America's friend, Louis XVI, was killed at the public guillotine and Napoleon Bonaparte entered the scene. The French and English were at war again.

In America sentiment soon divided. The French were old friends, but not these French. Paris expected that the Americans would join their struggle against England. In fact France behaved as though the Americans were junior allies. They had some reason: during the Revolutionary War the Americans and French had signed a mutual defense treaty. At first the followers of Thomas Jefferson worked for adherence to France, the followers of President Washington favored the English. But ever more Americans became disenchanted with French excesses, and the Americans decided that the United States would be neutral in the conflict between France and England. But the French privateers were already sailing into American ports. The French ship *Embuscade* captured the British merchantman *Grange* —*inside Delaware Bay.*

This sort of violation of American rights was much more visible to Americans than the outrages committed by the Barbary pirates thousands of miles away.

The French also stopped American ships, and were known to seize them. This behavior threatened American trade abroad and American ships, and caused a reluctant Congress, even though it had terminated the original frigate act, to reconsider in 1796 and begin the building of a real navy.

Three frigates, the *United States,* the *Constitution,* and the *Constellation,* were launched in 1797. The next year Congress appropriated nearly a

million dollars to build twenty smaller ships and authorized the establishment of a Department of the Navy. The first secretary was Benjamin
Stoddart.

By the spring of 1798, public opinion was so thoroughly aroused against
the French that Congress was pushed further. More vessels were authorized.

Having a navy to enforce its policies, the American government could
now deal with the French: Congress authorized the president to capture
all American vessels that had fallen into French hands, and any French
ships off the American coast that were suspected of depredations against
American shipping. The treaty with France was solemnly disavowed on
July 7, 1798, and Americans were authorized by Congress to begin making
war on French ships off the coast, although no declaration of war was ever
made.

Here was the precedent for President Lyndon Johnson's famous Tonkin
Gulf Incident and the Tonkin Resolution of 1964, which plunged the United
States deep into the Vietnam War.

The United States Marine Corps was established that summer of 1798,
and so quick were young men to enlist that immediately America was
prepared to go to war. The navy on paper as of July 1798 consisted of
thirty vessels, but actually, except for a handful of frigates and lesser ships,
the Americans had to depend on privateers, privately owned ships sailing
under "letters of marque" issued by the U.S. government, which authorized them to take prizes.

The first ship to go to war was the *Ganges,* built during the revolution,
converted to an Indiaman, and now converted back to a twenty-four-gun
warship. Second was the frigate *Constellation,* and third the twenty-gun
Delaware. Her captain, Lieutenant Stephen Decatur, was the first American to capture a French ship. In mid-June he was sailing for the Florida
coast when he sighted the French *Croyable.* He recognized her as a privateer that had captured several American merchant ships, and he forced
her to surrender and sent her under a prize crew into Delaware. She was
condemned as an enemy vessel on piratical business, and joined the American navy as USS *Retaliation,* since that is what she represented.

In July 1798, Captain John Barry took the forty-four-gun frigate *United
States* to sea. He was ordered up to the waters off Cape Cod, to join
Decatur's *Delaware* and the eighteen-gun *Herald,* and there to form a
squadron. That was America's first naval force. The second, which moved
out late in July, was built with four small brigs (ten to fourteen guns each),
sailing with the forty-four-gun frigate *Constitution.*

The warships kept coming. In August the *Constellation* and the *Baltimore* sailed down to Havana, and from under the noses of a handful of
French privateers that had been waiting outside Havana like sharks, spir-

ited home to America a convoy of sixty ships. It was the first convoy and a very successful one, a fact long forgotten by Admiral Ernest King and other American naval officers in the 1940s, when they scoffed at the British system of convoying ships to safety from submarine attack.

By the end of 1798 the American navy had twenty-four warships at sea, all it could afford at the moment. But the public did not think they were enough, and so a number of ships were being built in various ports *by public subscription* to be turned over to the navy. Patriotism in 1798 was a powerful force.

If the French were presumptuous and disregarding of American rights, so were the English. On November 16, 1798, an American convoy from Havana was sailing north under escort of the twenty-gun American sloop USS *Baltimore,* when they encountered a British squadron led by the ship of the line *Carnatick,* with seventy-four guns. The British commodore captured three of the merchant ships. The *Carnatick* stopped the *Baltimore* under force of arms, sent a boat to board her, and announced that the whole crew was being impressed into the British navy. Captain Phillips, not knowing what to do, consulted a "legal gentleman of some reputation" who happened to be aboard. The lawyer took the lofty position that American vessels were allowed by Congress to make war only on the French—not the British—and so he must submit. The British took off fifty-five members of the U.S. Navy crew, but later sent back fifty members. The British then sailed away with five impressed American sailors and three American ships. Captain Phillips of the *Baltimore* sailed back to Philadelphia, put the story before Congress, and was quickly dismissed from the naval service without trial. The reason, of course, was the feeling in the naval establishment that Captain Phillips had been guilty of cowardice. In the face of the enemy? That was a difficult legal matter, but not for the public. Americans were furious at British audacity. The cry "Free Trade and Sailor's Rights" that was to ring thunderously throughout the land ten years later began here.

But the people of America were way ahead of their government. No American demand was made for reparation. No particular fuss was raised; and thus the British were encouraged to a practice that became ever more obnoxious.

What the American people wanted was heroes, and they soon found one: William Bainbridge, lieutenant commandant of the twelve-gun sloop *Retaliation,* the old *Croyable,* captured from the French. In November 1798 Bainbridge was cruising off Guadeloupe with two other American warships, the twenty-gun *Montezuma* and the eighteen-gun *Norfolk.* They came up to a superior French squadron, which the senior officer of the American squadron took to be British. He sent Bainbridge in the *Retal-*

iation to reconnoiter them. Bainbridge closed up and discovered that the vessels were French, not English, but by that time a frigate was after him and opening fire, and then another frigate came up on the other side. With no chance of anything but annihilation, Bainbridge surrendered to the two frigates. And thus the French regained their *Croyable.*

Bainbridge and his crew were transferred to the forty-four-gun frigate *Volontaire* as prisoners. The second French frigate, the *Insurgente,* went off to chase the *Montezuma* and the *Norfolk,* and the *Retaliation-Croyable,* under a French prize crew, went along.

Captain Barreault of the *Insurgente* was confident of victory. The *Montezuma* was only a brig of 340 tons and the *Norfolk* a brig of 200 tons. Their guns were nine-pounders and six-pounders, scarcely capable of penetrating the hull of a forty-four gun frigate. The *Insurgente* was a very fast sailer and was overhauling the American vessels, as the crew of the *Volontaire* gathered on the forecastle to watch and cheer. But aboard the *Volontaire,* Captain St. Laurent, the French commodore, asked his prisoner, Commandant Bainbridge, just what armament the American ships carried.

"The *Montezuma* carries 28 twelves and the *Norfolk* 20 nines," lied Commandant Bainbridge.

Commodore St. Laurent was shaken. Those two vessels could give his frigate a bad time and might incapacitate her for further important duty. He called off the chase.

When Captain Barreault came back, puzzled, and asked why, the commodore told him. Barreault, who had seen the guns, said that Commandant Bainbridge's tale was anything but the truth. The Americans always called it a *ruse.* The French called it a *canaillerie,* a gross violation of one of the old civilities of the sea, where officers were supposed to tell the truth at all times, even to the enemy. But "time crumbles things," as Aristotle said. Here crumbled one gentlemanly rule of war.

The French bit their lips and did not murder Bainbridge on the spur of the moment. He and the crew of his ship were taken to the French colony of Guadeloupe as prisoners, and there the governor made what to Bainbridge seemed a slinky proposition. He and the crew would be restored to the *Retaliation* and she would be set free if Bainbridge would promise that Guadeloupe would not be molested by American ships. He refused to consider the matter. (He had no such authority, obviously.) The French were now growing concerned about several incidents of American defense of their shipping, and the governor decided he had best not court open declaration of war. So he freed the Americans and sent them back anyhow as a cartel, which meant a repatriation of prisoners of war. On arrival in America, Lieutenant Commandant Bainbridge went to Philadelphia to report.

Like Captain Phillips, Bainbridge had surrendered his ship to a *force majeure*. But the American authorities saw the cases quite differently. Phillips, they had said, had surrendered improperly.

If he had sent the British back to their ship of the line, and told them they would have to fight to get his men, and if then the ship of the line had opened fire, and he had surrendered, Phillips would probably have gotten off. It was the fact that he had surrendered without a shot being fired that had meant the difference. Such action was totally unacceptable as a precedent. The feeling persisted in the navy forever after. In 1968 the U.S. Naval Intelligence ship *Pueblo,* which had nothing but monkey business to keep it close in to the North Korean shore, was set upon by North Korean vessels, and her captain surrendered her. The crew was imprisoned but ultimately was released after much embarrassment to the United States. Captain Lloyd Butcher was never officially punished for giving up his ship, but his career in the navy was at an end.

So it would be. Bainbridge's actions were deemed flawless in the best of the young naval tradition. They *became* the tradition. He was commended for his presence of mind in lying, for his refusal to accept any deals with the French, promoted to master commandant, and given command of the *Norfolk,* which his "ruse" had saved. To the public, Bainbridge was the first real hero of the new navy.

By 1799 the United States Navy had grown; one squadron moved around Trinidad and Tobago, one covered the passage between Cuba and Santo Domingo, and one cruised off Havana.

These were the days of the great battles between individual ships of "fighting sail," and the American commanders were looking for battle and glory. On February 9, 1799, Commodore Thomas Truxton of the frigate *Constellation,* with four lesser ships of his squadron, was cruising near the island of Nevis, when the lookouts made out a ship to the south about fifteen miles away. Truxton ran down toward the stranger, which then ran up an American flag to match his. This was not meaningful, because warships often ran up whatever flag they wished, for various purposes. In this case the ship might be American, which Truxton firmly doubted, knowing virtually all of the American warships by sight. She might be an Englishman, pretending to be American to entice a French ship within fighting distance. She might be French, doing the same to an Englishman. Truxton ran up signal flags, asking in the American code, "Who are you?" The strange ship could not answer, and finally ran up the French ensign, and fired a shot, which meant she was ready to do battle if that was what Truxton wanted.

It was precisely what the commodore wanted, the first chance since the end of the revolution for an American warship to get alongside an enemy and fight.

The *Constellation* came down on the other, and she waited. The ships drew beam to beam and began firing. Soon the guns of each ship were riddling the canvas of the enemy, aiming to wreck her sailing capacity. The French were doing a better job, although the *Constellation* was better rigged. The French damaged the foretopmast near the lower cap, which made the foretopsail a liability. In command of the mast was Midshipman David Porter, who hailed the deck to ask what to do. He got no answer from officers too busy directing the guns and the ship, so he took it upon himself to cut the stoppers and lower the yard. It was precisely the right thing to do; he thus saved the topmast from falling, and the *Constellation* recovered her speed. Soon the Americans put in three raking broadsides, which hurt the enemy badly. The *Constellation* then moved around through her own smoke, so that the enemy could not see her, and suddenly appeared, with all guns of the starboard side ready to rake her enemy's stern. Then the enemy ship struck her colors.

When her captain was brought aboard the *Constellation,* he proved to be Captain Barreault and the ship the *Insurgente.* She was in bad shape. Seventy men had been killed or wounded. The *Constellation* had lost only her foretopmast and yard, three men wounded, and one dead, but not from enemy action. A seaman had flinched away from his gun on the gundeck early in the action and his lieutenant had followed ordinary procedure: pulled out his pistol and shot the man dead as an example to all others.

Lieutenant John Rodgers, the first lieutenant of the *Constellation,* was sent aboard the French frigate with Midshipman Porter and eleven men to supervise the removal of prisoners to the *Constellation.* But a storm blew up, and there they were, 13 Americans with 173 enemy sailors. Rodgers stood by with pistols while Midshipman Porter and the armed Americans chivied the Frenchmen down into the lower hold, secured all the firearms aboard, and posted armed sentries at every passageway. They had orders to shoot on sight anyone who appeared. For three days and three nights the Americans sailed the French frigate thus, until they brought her into Saint Kitts, where the *Constellation* was waiting for them.

That adventure won Lieutenant Rodgers his captaincy, and brought Truxton all the glory he wanted. Even Midshipman Porter had his share in a modest way. In the navy he was regarded as a comer.

The French had been treating Americans in Paris with a good deal of contempt, until the loss of the *Insurgente.* Immediately there was a change and Paris promised to deal with American representatives more favorably than they had recently. Fine, said the Americans, and continued to build up their navy until in 1800 it numbered thirty-five warships, ten of them frigates of thirty-two guns or more. These were not to be compared to the great ships of the line of the eighteenth century. In modern terms, the comparison would be like that of a missile frigate to the battleship *New Jersey*. The frigates could sail rings around a ship of the line, but woe to them if they got under the thirty or forty guns of a big ship's side. The war in the Americas was fought almost entirely with frigates and smaller vessels, partly because the big ships of the English and French navies were occupied in European waters, partly because the coastal American waters lent themselves to the use of these smaller vessels.

Not every American action was a victory, by far. On February 1, 1800, Commodore Truxton was out again in the *Constellation* off Guadeloupe, all alone. He saw a sail. It appeared to be a big English merchantman, but turned out to be a large French man of war, mounting fifty-two guns. The *Constellation* was rated at thirty-eight. But Truxton was appointed to put himself in harm's way, and he forged on. In the evening, after several hours of sailing, he caught up with the French warship.

The ships came up and exchanged broadsides, one, two, three times, and then fired freely as they drew away from each other. Altogether the fight lasted from about 8:00 P.M. until 1:00 A.M., when the French ship moved to draw away. Truxton was going to chase, but then the first lieutenant came up and informed him that the mainmast was about to collapse. All the shrouds were shot away. So Truxton took the men from the guns and had them try to put the mast to rights. But it was too late: the mast went over the side, along with Midshipman Jarvis, commander of the maintop, and one man he had kept aloft with him to manage the stricken pole. Mr. Jarvis and the seaman were never seen again.

The enemy ship was in worse shape—except she still had her mainmast—and she escaped. Truxton headed for Jamaica, and made it on the canvas of the fore and mizzen masts. Fourteen of his men had been killed and 25 wounded. The French ship, which was later discovered to be the *Vengeance,* had 50 killed and 110 wounded and arrived at Curaçao in a sinking condition. Crewmen said she tried to surrender three times but the *Constellation* kept firing, so she quit trying. That was the problem with fighting at night. A victory was lost in the smoke and haze—and it would have been a signal event, a thirty-eight-gun ship beating a fifty-two.

Even so, Truxton was a hero. He got a gold medal from Congress, and command of the new forty-four-gun frigate *President*.

There was many another fight in this strange war, but most of them were between privateers. In May 1800, Captain Samuel Barron took the frigate *Chesapeake* to sea. She cruised off the West Indies. The captured *Insurgente* frigate was given to Captain Patrick Fletcher, who took her out to cruise between 66° and 68° west longitude and to go as far south as 30°

north latitude. She has never been seen since. Somewhere out there she lies, perhaps in that Bermuda triangle, the cradle of swift storm and graveyard of stout ships, along with the USS *Pickering,* a fourteen-gun sloop under Master Commandant Benjamin Hillar, which sailed in August and never returned, and the *Saratoga,* a sixteen-gun vessel, which also disappeared.

There was one more encounter of French and American warships: the *Boston* versus the French corvette *Berceau,* which was won by the *Boston* because of superior fire power. But then the war slowed down. The French lost their eagerness and much of their seafaring arrogance in American waters. The Americans had captured ninety French ships, and more than 700 naval guns, which were very useful, since in those days naval guns were interchangeable from one navy to another, fired by powder, aimed by eye. At the close of the year 1800 the struggle was really over. The French had been persuaded by many losses to conclude a new "treaty of friendship and alliance," of which there had been neither for some time. The peace came in the early weeks of 1801 and, on March 23 that year, the USS *Herald* was sent down from Philadelphia to round up the various American warships in the Caribbean and send them home.

On March 3, 1801, Congress decided to sell off the American navy and reduce the expenses of defense, since there was nobody on the horizon to defend against, they said. Everything would be sold except the thirteen largest frigates and the schooner *Enterprise.* Most of these were put in mothballs. Of the whole navy only 200 officers were retained, and just enough enlisted men and petty officers to man the handful of ships. The other seamen went back to the merchant trade or drifted into landlubber's occupations. A fine navy was laid to rest.

In 1801 few Americans knew what sort of didoes their government had been up to in its relationship with the pirates of North Africa. The story is the most shocking example of appeasement in all American history.

In the spring of 1795, while those six frigates were being built to show the American flag around the world and put an end to the mistreatment of American ships, a minister named Humphreys was sent to Paris, the center of European political influence, to invoke the assistance of the French government in dealing with Algiers diplomatically, instead of militarily. The theory of the Department of State and those in Congress who approved of this mission was that it was always better to negotiate than to act.

Minister Humphreys arrived in Paris and sent to Algiers, Tunis, and

Tripoli a consul, Joseph Donaldson, who was to divide his time between Algiers, Tunis, and Tripoli.

Once in North Africa, Consul Donaldson decided to go to Algiers and singlehandedly negotiate a treaty with the dey. He did so and in September sent Humphreys the most amazing document yet produced by the State Department: a treaty which promised immediate payment of $650,000 to the dey of Algiers for a guarantee not to attack American shipping. This tribute plus the bribes necessary to quiet the dey's advisers came to nearly $900,000. It was imperative that the money be paid *at once*, said Donaldson, otherwise the dey would send a fleet of xebecs into the Atlantic to find and capture American ships.

Minister Humphreys was shocked, but he sent the treaty, in which Donaldson (without authorization) had guaranteed payment in the name of the United States, on to Philadelphia. Remarkably, Secretary of State Timothy Pickering approved it, and so did a substantial number of members of Congress. The whole came to just about the amount spent on the building of the six frigates.

But that was not all. The first tribute merely established the treaty. To keep it operative after the first year, the United States must pay $21,000 per year. Each time a new consul was appointed, the United States must pay $17,000, and every two years must pay $20,000 to the dey's advisers, plus bribes to lesser officials which came to another $50,000 to $60,000 a year. In this period the average American working man earned $6 a month.

Donaldson then went on to negotiate similar treaties, although cheaper ones, with Tunis and Tripoli.

It took time for the State Department and Congress to swallow the pill, and the dey of Algiers grew impatient. He made many threats, and to quiet him Donaldson and Joel Barlow, the American agent in Paris, promised the dey a fine new frigate. They were apparently under the impression that the United States was going to give up all those frigates built to suppress the pirate trade as Congress had indicated, and that one of them would make a satisfactory tribute to the dey.

So by 1796 the United States had vassal treaties and was paying tribute to Algiers, Morocco, Tunis, and Tripoli.

The undeclared war with France gave the infant American nation all the international trouble it could safely handle in the last years of the eighteenth century. Those six frigates earlier authorized were built for the United States Navy, along with thirty other vessels, and were needed for national defense. But a frigate had been promised the dey, Congress appropriated the money, and one was built at Portsmouth, New Hampshire, the *Crescent.* On January 20, 1798, she set sail.

In America many people held tempers in check as they contemplated the action of Congress that had reduced America to paying tribute to pirates. "Other rights, not less dear to national honour, national character, and national interests, may be sacrificed to a temporising spirit, should not the navy be enlarged, and made the highest aim of national policy," wrote James Fenimore Cooper, the first historian of the U.S. Navy.

But the *Crescent* sailed, and was delivered to Algiers along with twenty-six barrels of silver dollars and a hold full of presents for the rapacious Algerines. She also carried Richard O'Brien, an American who had been one of the original Algiers captives, had remained in North Africa as a prisoner for ten years, and was now going back as consul general to all the Barbary States.

All was well for two years, for the next tribute was not due until 1800. That year Captain William Bainbridge, the hero of the war against the French, was chosen to take the frigate *George Washington* to Algiers to pay the tribute. He sailed into Algiers harbor one September morning and was immediately greeted at dockside by a demand from the dey that he turn his ship around and sail again, bearing gifts from the dey to the sultan of the Ottoman empire, whom the dey had annoyed and who now threatened to depose him. Bainbridge objected. The dey was obdurate. Knowing the temper of the yielding Congress, Consul O'Brien also advised Bainbridge to yield. Otherwise, he said, Bainbridge and his crew would undoubtedly be thrown into prison, and the ship would be confiscated and sent off to Constantinople anyhow. There were at that time some two hundred American merchantmen trading back and forth with North Africa, under the apparent protection of these treaties. Bainbridge's obligation was to them. So Bainbridge also yielded. The dey wanted more. The ship would fly the Algerine flag. No, said Bainbridge: if the American flag were hauled down, the ship would be out of commission, no longer an American naval vessel. The dey responded by sending his minister of marine to the ship to tear down the American flag and plant the Algerine flag at the mainmast head, while Bainbridge watched, under the musket of the dey's guard. Flying that flag, Bainbridge set sail for Constantinople. The moment the ship left port the Algerine banner was hauled down and a new American flag run up.

The *George Washington,* flying the American flag, arrived at Constantinople in November and anchored in the outer harbor. A port officer came aboard, looked at the flag, and asked what it was. The sultan had never heard of the United States of America. Ultimately the confusion was cleared up, Bainbridge saw the sultan, delivered the dey's gifts, and went back to Algiers. This time he anchored in the outer harbor, outside the reach of the dey's shore guns. Despite threats, he would not bring the ship in. The dey demanded that Bainbridge go back to Constantinople, carrying the dey's agent. Bainbridge refused. The dey protested, but to no avail. He could not reach the *George Washington*. Still, he threatened Bainbridge with personal violence, until Bainbridge produced a letter of safe conduct from the sultan at Constantinople, whereupon the dey crumbled. Bainbridge managed to use the sultan's influence to free a large number of European prisoners, carried them off to a neutral port, and then went back to America.

Once again administration and Congress approved of all that Bainbridge had done. Bainbridge was commended and transferred to command of the new frigate *Essex*.

So, for Congress the problem of the Barbary States was again resolved for two years, and when the war ended with France, Congress again made plans to scrap the U.S. Navy. Fortunately, the plans had not been completed when several events indicated that all was not well in the Mediterranean. The bashaw of Tripoli called Consul O'Brien into the presence and informed him that he knew all about the enormous gifts the Americans were giving the dey of Algiers. Why was the bashaw so ignobly rewarded? If this disgraceful situation was not put to rights at once, he threatened, Tripoli would open warfare against American shipping. He would wait six months, said the bashaw. Then he would act.

Consul O'Brien transmitted all this information to the State Department. It was an election year. Jefferson had been elected president and the government was in the process of moving to Washington. Having seen their navy comport itself with considerable success against a great power, Americans had gained a new self-respect. The bashaw's demands did not pay much honor to self-respect, but no one seemed to know quite what to do. The demands languished in the State Department. The six-month deadline passed. The bashaw fumed. The secretary of state wrote a polite letter. The bashaw wrote to President Jefferson:

Our sincere friend: We could wish that these your expressions were followed by deed and not by empty words. You will therefore endeavor to satisfy us by good manner of proceeding. We on our part will correspond with you with equal friendship, as well in words as in deeds. But if only flattering words are meant without performance, every one will act as he finds convenient. Delay on your part cannot but be prejudicial to your interests.

Jefferson did not reply to that letter at all. So the bashaw acted as he found convenient. On May 14, 1801, his men cut down the flagstaff at the American consulate and the bashaw declared war on the United States of America.

At about the same time, and for the same reason, the bey of Tunis wrote Jefferson personally, demanding forty cannon. They must all be twenty-four-pounders he said, and they must be delivered immediately.

And Mr. Jefferson must also send him 10,000 muskets. It was that or war.

The peace lovers could argue that it was cheaper to pay than fight. The North African states were undeveloped nations that obviously needed the money. Should brave American lives be sacrificed just to preserve the pocketbooks of a handful of American shipowners and merchants?

But this time the peace lovers in Congress were going against the national tide. Finally, the Barbary States had pushed the United States too far. Jefferson's answer was to authorize the dispatch of a squadron of American warships to the Mediterranean on permanent duty.

Jefferson had a constitutional problem. He could not declare war. That was the province of Congress. But he could send ships abroad to protect the national interest and the flag. Three weeks after the bashaw cut down the American flag at Tripoli, Commodore Richard Dale was at sea with the frigates *President, Philadelphia,* and *Essex,* and the schooner *Enterprise.* He sailed straight for Tripoli, and disposed his ships so that no vessel could come into or out of that port.

Commodore Dale's orders were very difficult to carry out. He could not take the offensive. If attacked, he could defend himself, but he could not go after the enemy. If he took prisoners in a defensive fight, he must land them ashore as soon as possible. These were the sort of orders that could very easily end a promising naval career.

Considering all this, Dale did very well. He escorted American vessels in the Mediterranean. He sailed to Gibraltar, where he found the Tripolitan admiral, a renegade Englishman named Lisle, with a ship of twenty-six guns and a brig of sixteen guns. Dale left the *Philadelphia,* under Captain James Barron, to keep an eye on these vessels. The Tripolitan vessels were stuck. Dale blockaded Tripoli from time to time. He sailed into Algiers, and the dey suddenly discovered he had no quarrels at all with the Americans. He did not even ask about the semiannual tribute. The schooner *Enterprise* encountered the *Tripoli,* a Tripolitan warship of about its own size, and captured it, after the Tripolitan captain had surrendered three times, only to start firing again as soon as the Americans stopped. The captain, Mahomet Sous, saw finally that the Americans were bent on sinking him and his ship, and got down on the poop to surrender. Fifty of his men had been killed, and the vessel was a wreck, with the mizzenmast shot away. Captain Sterrett assigned Lieutenant David Porter the task of stripping the *Tripoli,* since he was not allowed to capture it. Porter took his men aboard the *Tripoli.* First they threw all the cannon into the sea. Then they ripped off every sail but one, and a single spar, and sent the vessel home to Tripoli as a warning.

When the *Tripoli* arrived in port, Captain Sous was arrested, tied onto a jackass, and paraded through the streets, then beaten with fifty strokes on the soles of his feet with the bastinado. The bashaw did this as a lesson to his people. It was a good lesson: thereafter the Tripolitan navy had a difficult time enlisting anyone.

In December 1801, Dale's squadron went home to America. Then began a debate about the presidential power to order military action.

Jefferson had adopted a strict construction of the Constitution when he forbade Commodore Dale to take offensive action against the Tripolitans, because Congress had not authorized war, even though Tripoli had declared war on the United States. But the principle remained: How far could the president go in authorizing military action? Jefferson said nowhere. Others, particularly the navy and its supporters, held that such construction of the Constitution would tie the hands of the nation's defenders, even when another power was making war. The adherents to strict construction said this was a small price to pay—even if ships and men were lost—for retention of the principle of separation of powers.

But there was also a practical element in the Congress that scoffed at Jefferson's strict constructionism, and did not want to declare war against the Barbary powers, whom they looked upon as a gang of pirates, not worthy of the name *nation*. So Congress passed a law providing for the protection of commerce and seamen. It did not declare war, but it did empower the president to proceed as if a state of war existed. He could issue commissions to privateers, he could equip as many ships as he wished. He could enlist as many men as he thought were needed to man the ships. He could tell the navy to seize, capture, and destroy the goods and vessels of the enemy. Thus Thomas Jefferson was the first recipient of a "War Powers Act" from Congress, for the specific purpose of subduing the Barbary pirates.

For the defense of American shores fifteen gunboats had been authorized even when the navy was being cut back. Nine of them were sent to Africa, and eight made the voyage successfully, although they were so small and built so low that their gunwales were just two feet above still water. It took skilled seamen to get them across the Atlantic even in summer. They found the *Philadelphia,* off Tripoli, maintaining the blockade, and the *Essex* at Gibraltar, keeping Admiral Lisle and his two ships bottled up.

A new American naval squadron was commissioned to go to the Mediterranean. Captain Richard V. Morris, who was an acting commodore because he headed a squadron, was put in command and he had seven frigates. They sailed individually, relieved the *Essex* and the *Philadelphia* to return home, and took station in the Mediterranean, prepared to deal with Tripoli.

Captain Alexander Murray in the *Constellation* was off Tripoli one day when he saw seventeen Tripolitan gunboats that had slipped out to sea in the night and were now trying to make their way back into port. Captain Murray hurried to overhaul them, split the force, bombarded ten of them, and forced nine into shore before the port. They hung about there, under protection of a force of cavalry, and Murray decided against a landing. He kept the Tripolitans bottled up even more tightly from that point on.

For six months the American ships sailed around the Mediterranean, escorting convoys, seeking the enemy, but not finding him. At the end of May the *New York,* the *John Adams,* and the *Enterprise* were standing off Tripoli when a number of feluccas carrying grain were seen, just entering the harbor, and then pulling up under the batteries of the fort. Lieutenant David Porter, the first lieutenant of the *New York,* volunteered to go in with the squadron's small boats and destroy the gunboats on the beach. He went alone at night and reconnoitered the place. The next morning he took in a party of officers and men from the ships. From the shore the Tripolitans opened fire with guns and muskets, but Porter continued inshore. The party landed, burned the feluccas, and then got back into the boats to come out. They spread the boats out, so that the guns from the ships could fire around them and over them at the enemy. But the enemy was too busy putting out the fires started aboard the gunboats. They saved most of them, but not without damage.

The affair was hailed as an example of naval gallantry. Lieutenant Porter had been wounded in the thigh, but he never stopped for a moment. A dozen men were lost but the action was deemed worth it.

In June, Captain Rodgers was left off Tripoli with the *John Adams* and two other vessels. He engaged the bashaw's largest ship, a twenty-two-gun vessel, and was working her over when she blew up. That was a highly satisfactory end of the blockade for the moment, and the Americans sailed for Malta, then Italy.

Congress and the public had expected Commodore Morris to resolve all the problems posed by the Barbary pirates with his little force. He went home and faced a court of inquiry because of public outcry that he had done nothing to the pirates. He could not explain why he had not cleared the seas of brigands, so he was dismissed from the navy. Another precedent was hereby established for the U.S. Navy: Neither zeal nor patriotism were enough; a commander must also have good judgment and good luck, or else woe would certainly come to him. To Americans war was not simply a military exercise but a major political effort.

To rise far a military man not only had to satisfy his superiors in the naval establishment and the executive branch of government, but also to keep Congress happy.

Soon enough, the naval authorities learned that what were needed for a blockade were smaller vessels, preferably fore-and-aft-rigged, with heavy guns for close-in work against shore installations. So in February two brigs and two schooners were built for the Barbary wars.

A new technique and new command were wanted in 1803. Captain Edward Preble was selected as commodore of the new fleet, which consisted of the frigates *Constitution* and *Philadelphia,* and the smaller vessels *Argus, Siren, Nautilus, Vixen,* and *Enterprise.* Captain Bainbridge was in command of the *Philadelphia.*

The *Philadelphia* reached the Mediterranean at the end of July 1803. At Gibraltar Captain Bainbridge learned that two Barbary pirate ships were cruising in the area. A few days later he came upon a strange pair of vessels. One of the ships was a two-masted brig, but sailing only on her foresail, which seemed odd. The other was a warship. On the evening of August 26 off Cape de Gatt, Bainbridge caught up with them, flying the Union Jack flag to make them believe the *Philadelphia* was an English ship. On questioning he learned that the warship was the twenty-two-gun vessel *Meshboha,* which belonged to the emperor of Morocco. The captain was eager to tell the Englishmen of his exploits; he knew the English had little use for the Americans.

Captain Bainbridge asked more questions. Why was the other ship making so little sail? Looking her over, Bainbridge could see that she was very lightly manned. Why? He became suspicious and sent First Lieutenant George Cox with a boat to see what was going on. When the boat reached the brig it was stopped, and the officer, a Moor, refused to let the Americans board. Mr. Cox went back to the *Philadelphia,* and then for a second time his boat rowed for the brig, but this time he was accompanied by heavily armed men. The American flag was run up at the maintop and a gun of the *Philadelphia* was trained out so that the crew of the brig would get the idea.

Lieutenant Cox boarded, and below decks he found the crew of the brig *Celia* of Boston, which had been captured by the *Meshboha.* The crew on deck was a pirate's prize crew. They were now cruising, while the Moroccans waited for more American ships to sail by Cape de Gatt.

So much for tribute. Captain Bainbridge did not hesitate. The new law passed by Congress gave him all the authority he needed. He took the *Meshboha,* but while the men of the *Philadelphia* were transferring the 120-man crew to the hold of the *Philadelphia* as prisoners, the brig escaped in the darkness. Next day the *Philadelphia* caught up with her, steering for Morocco.

Captain Ibrahim Lubarez of the *Meshboha* made all sorts of excuses about his activities until Bainbridge threatened to hang him from a yardarm as a pirate. Then he produced a parchment document signed by the governor of Tangier in Morocco, authorizing him to take any and all American ships. Bainbridge then went back to Gibraltar, left the prizes and captives, and went off to chase other pirates.

When Commodore Preble arrived to take over the Mediterranean command, and learned these facts, he joined up with Commodore Rodgers, who had been left in charge of the Mediterranean by Commodore Morris. Morris was ready to go home, but together they took three frigates and a schooner to make a call on the emperor of Morocco. The three frigates sailed into the Bay of Tangier, guns ready, and anchored so that the emperor and his court would have a clear view of the *Constitution*'s forty-four guns, the *New York*'s thirty-eight guns, and the *John Adams*'s twenty-eight guns.

The two commodores then went to call. They mentioned the incident of the *Meshboha* and that they had discovered the Moroccans had captured another American vessel which was held at Mogadore.

It was all a horrible mistake, said the emperor.

Two horrible mistakes, said Commodore Preble.

Yes, two horrible mistakes, said the emperor.

So he disavowed the governor of Tangier. He disavowed the capture of the other American ship, and punishments followed for the officials. He reaffirmed the old treaty by signing it once more. Commodore Preble went back to Gibraltar and let the *Meshboha* sail home under her own crew, and Commodore Rodgers went home to America. One pirate kingdom had now been settled down.

Commodore Preble at Gibraltar soon learned of new troubles. Captain Bainbridge's *Philadelphia* had sailed off to blockade Tripoli, in company with the *Enterprise*. But the smaller vessel had been sent off to chase a pirate ship, and on October 31 the *Philadelphia* arrived off Tripoli alone. In these unfamiliar waters she was chasing a xebec which was trying to make the harbor; she ran across a bay that the chart showed as perfectly deep, only to run aground on a reef. Captain Bainbridge did all possible to get off the reef. The frigate's guns were thrown overboard to lighten her. She would not budge. Soon the Tripolitans saw her plight and surrounded her with ships. Now she had no guns with which to defend herself. There was no recourse but surrender, and Captain Bainbridge ordered the ship holed for scuttling and surrendered 315 men, including twenty-two officers, to the bashaw of Tripoli.

In a storm on November 2, the ship was floated by the Tripolitans. The scuttling job had been bungled; the holes were stopped up and she was sailed into Tripoli harbor. Later the Tripolitans recovered all the guns and anchors that had been thrown into the shallow water.

Commodore Preble had gone to Cadiz, and when he came back to

Gibraltar he learned of the *Philadelphia* affair. Immediately he declared a full blockade of Tripoli and headed that way with the *Constitution* and the *Enterprise*. En route Lieutenant Stephen Decatur, the skipper of the *Enterprise,* captured a Tripolitan ketch, called the *Mastico*. She had originally been a French gunboat, captured by the English and sold to Tripoli.

Off Tripoli Commodore Preble found storms and a steady northeast wind which endangered his ships at that season, so he went back to Syracuse, Sicily, the port the Mediterranean squadron called home, and waited. During the winter, Captain Bainbridge managed to smuggle several letters out of his prison cell to advise Preble that the bashaw was getting the *Philadelphia* ready for sea. This could be disastrous; the American frigate of thirty-eight guns in the hands of an enemy. So Preble prepared to act.

All Preble's junior officers wanted to attempt to take the *Philadelphia* out of Tripoli. Preble chose Stephen Decatur, and gave him a plan. They were to prepare the *Mastico,* now called the *Intrepid,* to move in alongside the *Philadelphia* and burn her. Use of the *Mastico* gave them a chance for surprise. They could pretend she was a Maltese vessel. She certainly was not American.

Decatur and a volunteer crew went into Tripoli harbor and, under the eyes of the bashaw, burned his new frigate. They backed the *Intrepid* off and, first with oars, then with sails, took her out of the bay, as the *Philadelphia* burned magnificently, her ammunition and cannons exploding and the fire racing up her rigging and lighting up the harbor bright as day. One of her broadsides was discharged into the town of Tripoli. Decatur and his men got off and out to sea to meet the American vessels. They had just concluded one of the most heroic actions in the annals of the U.S. Navy.

All the midshipmen were promoted to lieutenant, the enlisted men were rewarded, and Lieutenant Commandant Decatur was awarded a silver sword by Congress.

In 1804 Congress was fully alive to the dangers in the Mediterranean and finally ready to build up an American navy capable of handling them. But the problem was shipbuilding. Every good shipyard was filled with commissions for merchantmen. American trade had extended all across the world and was prospering. So Congress established six navy yards to build and repair naval vessels. The building then began in a hurry.

In 1804 Commodore Preble began pushing the war against the Barbary pirates in a new way. He saw that the solution was to get at the port of Tripoli itself, and this meant the use of bomb ships and small vessels. On July 25 he assembled a large fleet off Tripoli. He had only one frigate, the *Constitution;* but he also had six brigs and schooners, two bomb ships and six gunboats, and 1,000 men. Inshore the Tripolitans had assembled a naval and military force of 25,000 to defend their city.

On August 3, the Americans attacked. Stephen Decatur led the gunboats in, and they captured three Tripolitan gunboats and sank three more. The bigger ships bombarded the port and the town.

The squadron suffered some damage in this attack and lay offshore for four days repairing it. Then, on August 7, Preble moved in again to bombard Tripoli and her defenses. The bashaw now sent out officers to say he wanted to make a truce and a treaty. But he wanted $400 apiece for the prisoners he had captured, and Preble said no. He prepared for another attack.

Under Stephen Decatur, who had now been promoted to captain in the U.S. Navy for his exploit with the *Philadelphia,* Preble undertook a campaign of bombardment of Tripoli. On August 28, nine gunboats moved in to shore, supported by all the guns of the ships outside. Enemy gunboats came out to meet them, but soon one was sunk, two were beached, and the rest retreated back inside the harbor. The big guns of the warships did much damage to the bashaw's fortress and to the town, as Captain Bainbridge could testify. He was in the prison section, in bed at the moment, when half the wall fell on him, and he was injured by falling bricks and mortar.

The battle continued day after day. The Americans brought up more boats and more ammunition from Malta. In all, within a month the Americans made five assaults on the town.

Then Preble had another idea.

The ketch *Intrepid,* which had been used in the burning of the *Philadelphia,* was converted into a floating bomb. In the magazine stood a hundred barrels of gunpowder, and on deck above were hundreds of bits of chain, shot, and other ironmongery. Preble wanted to send the ketch into the middle of the Tripoli harbor, where it would explode among the bashaw's warships and merchant ships and wreak havoc.

On September 4 Captain Richard Somers, another of the young heroes of the war who had been promoted so quickly, volunteered to take the fireship inside Tripoli harbor. He and Lieutenant Henry Wadsworth and Lieutenant Joseph Israel sailed her in. Behind them were two ship's boats, which were to bring the *Intrepid* sailors out.

The night was gloomy and the Americans outside lost sight of the ketch as she neared the entrance to the harbor. The bashaw's shore guns opened fire. Suddenly the night was brightened by an enormous explosion, and then more shooting and then nothing.

At sea the Americans had premonitions of disaster. The explosion had not been in the right place.

The Americans waited all night, but the ships' boats did not appear. Next day they established what had happened. The *Intrepid* had been sailing in when she grounded near the north battery. She had been a quarter-mile from her destination. A shot from the enemy battery must have fired the "bomb." The ketch had exploded and sunk both the ship's boats behind her. All the heroes were lost. Only a few Tripolitan gunboats nearby were destroyed.

On September 10, Captain James Barron arrived from America to take over from Preble, who sailed, carrying several prize vessels, to Gibraltar. On September 12 Barron's squadron cut off two ships trying to get into Tripoli harbor with grain. The slow process of starving the bashaw out began.

Barron's squadron, as the bashaw could see, was the strongest American force yet sent to Tripoli: five frigates, and five lesser ships. The blockade was maintained during 1804 and 1805.

The American consul at Tunis, William Eaton, now produced another idea. He wanted to organize a land force under the bashaw's brother Hamet, and force the bashaw off the throne. Hamet would attack by land while the Americans attacked by sea.

In March 1805, Eaton and Hamet and the army set out across the Libyan desert accompanied by American marines and cannon. They captured Derne, and Eaton wanted to move on. But the American naval commanders refused to carry out a combined attack on Tripoli, so Eaton had to abandon that plan.

The bashaw was sufficiently frightened by the capture of Derne that he signed a peace treaty. There would be no more tribute, but the Americans paid over $60,000 for release of Bainbridge and his men.

Officially the Barbary pirates were quelled and the war with Tripoli was ended. Actually, the bashaw had no intention of abiding by this new treaty. As soon as the American ships would leave his shores, he intended to prey on shipping once more. Eaton warned of this danger, but the American naval commanders would not listen. Thus, because there was no unified command of land and naval forces, a chance to solve the problem of the Tripoli pirates was lost. The Barbary troubles would erupt again.

CHAPTER 8

Growing Pains

The first decade of the nineteenth century was notable for internal American difficulties with the Indians, caused as always by the same problem: the determination of people in the eastern part of America to move west and find a better life for themselves. Moving west meant coming up against the Indians. In this struggle, William Henry Harrison was to make the military reputation that would catapult him into the presidency. Tippecanoe was not much of a battle, but its significance was not lost on the American people, for the settlement of Indiana meant that the United States' drive westward was not to be slowed.

But internal affairs were only a part of the problem of any nation. The Americans were learning ruefully that they must have a fleet, and an army, and a foreign policy.

Britain was the goad that brought the latter. The British were fighting the French again, and they needed men for their fleet.

*   *   *

One of the complicated territorial exchanges that came out of the Napoleonic Wars involved the acquisition of southern and western territories by the United States. It began with Napoleon's dream of a new French empire in America. Louisiana had been ceded to Spain, but in 1800 in a secret treaty Spain ceded Louisiana back. When this was discovered in Washington, Thomas Jefferson's administration became very much concerned, and opened negotiations to buy these lands.

France, faced by a rebellion of black slaves in Haiti, became disenchanted with the idea of an empire in this area. Ultimately, in 1803, the United States purchased the whole Louisiana territory, 800,000 square miles between the Mississippi and the Rocky Mountains. Questions remained: According to the treaty the northeastern boundary of Louisiana was the Mississippi River "from its source." But no one knew where the source was. The southeastern boundary was also vague, so questions were also left regarding the status of Texas and Florida, but the United States took possession and in 1804 William C. C. Claiborne became governor of Louisiana Territory.

The Americans then set about securing undisputed possession of Florida. This territory had been handed about among France, Spain, and England. Finally, in 1808, Napoleon, riding high in his attempt to conquer all Europe, conquered Spain and Joseph Bonaparte became king of Spain. Virtually every Spanish province in America arose in rebellion, including west Florida which lay along the Mississippi River just across the American border. Most of the people wanted annexation to the United States. The rebels attacked the Spanish fort at Baton Rouge, proclaimed a free and independent state of West Florida, and asked for annexation to the United States as a state. President James Madison replied by announcing the annexation of West Florida as a part of the Louisiana Territory, and ordered Governor Claiborne to see that it was done. The Floridians had already declared themselves a state and elected Fulwar Skipwith as governor. Now they said they would be an independent nation. Skipwith set up in the fort at Baton Rouge, and called his general, Philemon Thomas, to resist Claiborne. The latter raised the American flag at Baton Rouge. The Floridians tore it down and raised their one-star flag instead. General Thomas, in the name of Florida, declared war on the United States. But Claiborne brought up U.S. troops and a flotilla of gunboats from New Orleans, and the Floridians surrendered. Thus the United States for the first time used unbridled aggression to add to its territory. This was truly the beginning of American imperialism.

Baton Rouge was held by the Americans, but in 1810 the situation of Florida was still in dispute.

America was suffering serious growing pains, exacerbated by the question of slavery, which came up every time a piece of the western territory was cut off to make a state. In 1800 Indiana became a territory and a young soldier turned politician named William Henry Harrison became the governor.

The designation of Indiana as a U.S. territory was an indication of the pattern of American growth west. It had come very rapidly, as the list below shows. To qualify for statehood a territory had to have 75,000 inhabitants:

State	Date of admission
13 original states	1787–89
Vermont	1791
Kentucky	1792
Ohio	1803

As the name Indiana indicates, it had been the intent at the time of the great treaty to leave the Indians alone on the western lands. The speed of American immigration and growth was just too much, however, for one generation to keep the promises of the past one. Governor Harrison began buying land from the Indians to sell to the settlers moving into Indiana Territory. By 1805 Harrison had signed three new treaties with the Indians which gave him lands in southern Indiana, Illinois, Wisconsin, and Missouri to sell. That year Congress sliced off the Michigan territory.

More was needed, so in 1809 Harrison called the Indians to a council at Fort Wayne. Three million acres of land on the Wabash and White rivers were purchased this time. Three of the Indian nations of the area agreed. One, led by the Shawnee Tecumseh, who had risen high in the councils of the northwest Indians, declared its opposition.

Tecumseh was the general of this Indian nation. In fact, it was not a nation at all, but a conglomeration of disaffected tribes from many nations who flocked to Tecumseh as a natural leader. His brother Tenskwatawa was the prophet and political leader. For a long time they had been conniving with the British who were interested in lowering their northwestern borders.

Tecumseh declared that the lands sold by the other three Indian nations did not belong to them, but under the treaty belonged to all Indians in common. That was the story he and Tenskwatawa preached in the winter of 1810 at their capital, Tippecanoe.

Governor Harrison learned of the discontent and finally persuaded Tecumseh to visit him at Vincennes. From Harrison's point of view it was not a satisfactory meeting. He suspected that Tecumseh was preparing to go on the warpath, and he wrote to Washington asking for military support. In Washington President James Madison concurred that the Indians must be kept under control, and when Harrison suggested a punitive expedition against Tecumseh, the administration agreed. The 4th U.S. Army Infantry Regiment was sent to Indiana, and Governor Harrison began enlisting militiamen.

Tecumseh, meanwhile, had gone north to Canada seeking support from the British. So when Harrison's 900-man force left Vincennes on September 26, Tecumseh was not in charge of the Indian defenses.

Harrison marched sixty miles, then built a fort. It was named Fort Harrison, of course. From here, in October, the Americans marched along the Wabash River. They stopped again on November 2, 1811, and built another fort. They marched on, and met many Indians. They arranged a meeting with Tenskwatawa at Tippecanoe the next day. That night they camped on ground recommended by the Indians.

At 3:00 in the morning the Indians attacked. The Americans were surprised, but they rallied and drove the Indians into the marshlands below their camp. There the braves examined their wounds. They were not supposed to have any wounds. Tenskwatawa, the medicine man and prophet, had brought out magic beans that would turn the American bullets to drops of water, and his cavalry swords to twigs. But the evidence was incontrovertible. Some Indians had terrible slashes from cavalry swords. Some had wounds caused by bullets. The medicine had not worked. The Indians lost confidence and drifted away from the battle area. Finally the prophet joined them. Next day Governor Harrison led the Americans into Tippecanoe and burned Tecumseh's town. All the Indians of this artificial nation were gone, back to the villages of the Chippewa, Kickapoo, Ottawa, Potawatomi, Sac, Fox, Winnebago, Wyandot, and Shawnee, whence they had come. Tecumseh's lodge and all the others were burned to the ground. Governor Harrison marched back downriver. His force had taken casualties of more than 108 men, but they had cleared the area of the Indians, making the west safe for American settlement.

Tecumseh made a tour to the south with twenty warriors. He went into the country of the Chickasaws and the Choctaws. He visited the Creeks on the Tallapoosa River. He met with the Cherokees. He talked war, and the Indians were ready to listen.

Since the end of the American Revolution, relations between the new American nation and England had been shadowed by one major issue that had political, military, business, and social consequences. It was the impressment of American seamen involuntarily into the British navy.

The British naval system militated in favor of such behavior. A British warship captain was personally responsible for the recruitment and maintenance of his crew. If men were needed to man a warship in an English port, press gangs were sent out into the cities and the countryside to impress men into military service, willy, nilly. The constant warfare in which England was engaged created a constant demand for seamen for twenty years.

This method of recruitment led to many desertions, despite the fierce penalties imposed. Sometimes deserters were "flogged through the fleet," which meant flogged by the officers of every ship in the fleet, which almost always meant the miscreant was dead by the time the last few ships dealt with him: they ended up flogging a corpse. But life aboard a British warship was so awful that many seamen were willing to take any chance to escape. They would jump ship anywhere and then often try to join an American vessel, because the Americans spoke English and because American officers were easier on their men.

The British began to pay particular attention to American ships and to stop them to search for Royal Navy deserters. The practice infuriated American captains, and Congress and a whole succession of administrations tried to put an end to it. In 1792 U.S. Minister Thomas Pinkney tried to negotiate a treaty. It failed. John Jay did negotiate a treaty that dealt with the matter left-handedly, providing for "return" of impressed seamen. That did not resolve the problem of impressment, and it did not stop. In 1796 Britain for the first time impressed five American seamen from the American ship *Lydia*. The result was a Congressional act providing for the issuance of certificates of citizenship to American seamen, passed in March 1796, but the impressment continued and the controversy dragged on.

After 1804 the problem grew worse, largely because the British naval wars dragged on and on. Case followed case, brought up by American diplomats and reported to Congress. Many Americans were demanding direct action: the suppression of commerce with Britain, retaliation by American naval vessels, and even firing on British warships.

Ten, fifteen years passed with the issue paramount in America, where resentments against England left over from the revolution still burned among the revolutionary generation. By 1807, the revolutionary generation had been largely supplanted in the legislatures and in Congress by younger men. The impressment issue carried its own emotional torch, and kept feelings against British arrogance high in the United States. The fact was, too, that there was enough evidence of enlistment of British deserters into American ships, and even into the navy, to keep British national pride and government policy from dealing very generously with the issue.

Thus the stage was set at the end of June 1807 for a major confrontation between America and England.

The thirty-eight-gun frigate USS *Chesapeake* was put in commission early in 1807. She was scheduled to sail soon for the Mediterranean to replace the *Constitution* as flagship of the American fleet watching over the Barbary shores. Captain James Barron, who had commanded the American squadron in the Mediterranean before, was to raise his commodore's pennant in the *Chesapeake* and take over the squadron.

In the spring, the *Chesapeake* was lying in the Washington Navy Yard, taking on stores and her ship's complement. In May, the British minister to Washington informed the Department of State that three deserters from HMS *Melampus* had enlisted in the crew of the *Chesapeake*, and asked that they be given up to British authorities.

The matter came to Commodore Barron. Captain Charles Gordon, the master of the *Chesapeake*, was told to look into it and he reported that, while the men had indeed deserted from the *Melampus,* all three claimed that they were Americans who had been impressed into the crew of the *Melampus* to begin with. One of the men claimed to be a native of Maryland's Eastern Shore. Captain Gordon came from that part of the country; he questioned the man and was satisfied that he was, indeed, an American from the Eastern Shore. The second was a black man, and his credentials were impeccable. The third man's story was a bit shaky, but the American experience with English impressment had been so unfavorable that Gordon and Barron were inclined to give the man the benefit of the doubt. The English minister was informed and no further diplomatic representations were made.

What the Americans did not know was that the British were up in arms about something else. The war between France and Britain had been renewed in 1803. Napoleon had made himself emperor, had captured Italy, Austria, and Holland, and seemed likely to capture the world. Britain had established a blockade of the French coast, and this demanded many vessels and many seamen. The war was also being fought in American waters where both countries had Caribbean colonies. The British lay off American ports, waiting for French vessels.

In March 1807, a number of British sailors had escaped from the British sloop *Halifax,* which was then lying in Hampton Roads. They made their way to Norfolk and joined the crowd enlisting in the *Chesapeake.* One of them was a seaman named Ratford, who enlisted with the Americans under the name Wilson.

The *Halifax* and the *Melampus* incidents were reported to Admiral Berkeley, the British naval commander in Halifax. He issued an order stating that deserters from *seven* British ships had joined the *Chesapeake.*

"These deserters openly paraded the streets of Norfolk in sight of their officers, under the American flag, protected by the magistrate of the town, and the recruiting officer belonging to the above mentioned frigate, which refused to give them up although demanded by His Britannic Majesty's consul as well as the captains of the ships from which the said men deserted."

Any British warship that met the *Chesapeake* outside American waters was to show this order and search the *Chesapeake* for deserters. The British ships were also to allow the Americans to search their ships for American deserters. (This was a nice gesture but an empty one, because practically never did any man desert an American ship for a British one, unless he was accused of some foul crime in America.)

The *Chesapeake* was being hurried to sea, because the relief of the Mediterranean flagship was, as usual, overdue. On June 21, she was loaded and ready to go to sea. She was anything but battleworthy—the crew untried, the guns never yet having been run out, and not all of them secured in place, nor all their supplies of shot and powder at the ready.

That day, the British warship *Leopard*, a fifty-gun frigate, came in and anchored. Next day the *Chesapeake* got ready for sea, and the *Leopard* weighed anchor and preceded her out of the harbor, disappearing behind Cape Henry.

At noon the *Chesapeake* was outside, and the *Leopard* came into view. She was sailing along with the *Chesapeake*, apparently playing one of those games sailors liked to do to check the performance of their vessel against another. At about 3:00 P.M., however, the *Leopard* came around and hailed, telling Commodore Barron that she had dispatches for the American frigate. This was not uncommon, so no particular attention was paid to it, and Barron said he would heave to and receive a boat.

At this time some of the officers of the *Chesapeake* noted that the British vessel had her guns ready for action. But no one reported the fact to Commodore Barron.

The British boat came, and the lieutenant in charge was received by Commodore Barron, and Admiral Berkeley's order was shown to Barron. To it was attached a letter from Captain Humphreys, the commander of the *Leopard*, saying he hoped the matter could be adjusted easily. Barron replied that he knew of no such deserters, that his government specifically ordered him not to enlist English deserters, and that he had not.

The English lieutenant was aboard the *Chesapeake* for about half an hour. Captain Barron finally told him it would be illegal for him to give up one of his men as a deserter. The English lieutenant went back to his ship. Commodore Barron sent for Captain Gordon and told him to clear the gun deck for action. This was already being done, but it was a slow process; the deck was littered with coils of cable and other supplies. Officers' baggage was still standing on deck. The officers preparing the ship for action found that they were short of rammers, wads, matches, and other supplies, all stowed improperly.

The *Leopard*'s boat reached the ship and was taken aboard. A few moments later came a hail from the *Leopard*, which Barron shouted he did not understand. That hail was followed by a shot across the *Chesapeake*'s bow, and then a whole broadside. Barron was wounded, and so was his aide.

The American ship continued to make ready to fight. She still could not fire more than one broadside, after which she would be helpless. The guns were cold, the priming powder not ready, while across the way the British had been preparing for hours. The *Leopard* then began firing steadily on the *Chesapeake* and did so for twelve to eighteen minutes. Finally, to stop the carnage, Barron ordered the American flag to be hauled down.

One American shot had been fired, when a man carried a hot coal all the way from the galley, but that was all. Just then the British fired another broadside, and the flag came down. Three American sailors had been killed and eighteen wounded.

Barron sent a boat to the *Leopard* saying that the ship was now captured and that it was at the disposal of the British captain. Captain Humphreys seemed to be getting an inkling of what he had done, for he refused to accept Barron's sword or responsibility for the *Chesapeake*. Several English officers boarded the American warship. The purser gave up his book and 375 men and boys were mustered (an act of war). Twelve of these were found to be British subjects. The British took off the three men from the *Melampus*. Wilson-Ratford did not appear for the muster. The British searched the ship and found him hiding in the hold. They took the four men and left the ship. (The four "deserters" were then delivered to Halifax, where Ratford-Wilson was hanged, and the three who claimed to be Americans were thrown into jail. One of them died, but ultimately the other two were released.)

Commodore Barron called a meeting of his officers and they agreed that, in view of this act of war by the English, they must return to Hampton Roads. They turned the *Chesapeake* around, and she made her way back to Hampton Roads, with three feet of water in the hold, every pump working, and still half sunk.

At Norfolk the word had come quickly that the *Chesapeake* had been attacked by a British warship and had struck her colors. People did not believe it. But on June 22 many boats went out and they found the *Chesapeake* lying at anchor with no flag flying. At 4:00 in the afternoon one of the *Chesapeake*'s boats reached the wharf with eleven wounded sailors aboard.

Norfolk erupted in despair and fury. Business stopped altogether. Several British officers, ashore on business, fled the town for their own safety and went back to their ships. The British consul locked himself in his house and prepared for a siege.

Some citizens rushed home to cast ball and make cartridges. The rest got together for a town meeting, and resolved to do no business with the British. Any man who served the British would be declared a traitor. The British were to have no supplies. The town meeting asked the major to call out the militia. The men voted to wear black crepe for ten days in mourning.

Watermen went down to the docks and broke up all supplies intended for the British ships. At Hampton a sloop laden with water casks for the *Melampus* was stopped and every cask destroyed.

Captain Stephen Decatur, in command of the Norfolk navy yard, was asked for help and he sent four gunboats, which arrived within twenty-four hours. The British offshore threatened to blockade Norfolk, unless the Americans gave in and serviced their ships. The Americans did not give in.

Captain Douglas, the *Melampus*'s commander, added to the insults and chose a very bad day for it: July 4, 1807. The mayor replied that Americans were not to be "frightened by threats or intimidated by menaces." Captain Douglas then changed his story and claimed to be the aggrieved party. His explanation was received scornfully by the Americans.

Around Chesapeake Bay the Americans were talking war. At Baltimore a meeting of young men called for action. At Wilmingtoon a town meeting said the British had shown hostility to the United States. Philadelphians said the insult could not be accepted. New Yorkers voted the attack "dastardly." Only at Boston was the British action defended, for Boston was the beehive of Federalism, and the Federalists loved the British and hated the French, an attitude that reflected domestic politics. But even in Boston half the people were calling for war.

President Jefferson responded to the overwhelming public outrage by ordering all British warships out of American waters. He could not do less in the temper of the moment. The public went further. If any British ship came into American waters, it would be denied food and water.

The people of the United States were ready for war with Britain. Every national insult of the past was raked up. Jefferson and his cabinet decided to send gunboats to the various ports. They would order the Mediterranean fleet home. They would send a messenger to London with three demands: British disavowal of the "right" to search American ships, return of the sailors taken from the *Chesapeake,* and recall of Admiral Berkeley.

Jefferson was actually talking about invading Canada. But he resisted a call for an immediate session of Congress on the grounds that Washington's climate was too dangerous in the summer (malaria). Congress was called for October 26. James Monroe and William Pinkney were in London, and new instructions were sent to them. All this defused the war bomb, but not the war talk. In the next few weeks seven pamphlets were published by furious patriots, and all seven called for war against Britain.

Nothing more could be done at the moment, said the president. But he was wrong. The public could take out its indignation by demanding the head of the American officer who had surrendered and allowed the British to insult the flag. All along the eastern seaboard, the talk was strong against Commodore Barron, despite the valiant service he had given his country for years. A court of inquiry was held by the navy, and the result was the order of courts-martial for Barron, Captain Gordon, the commander of marines, and the gunner.

Captain Gordon was found guilty of negligence, and sentenced to a reprimand. The marine captain was also reprimanded for not being ready to fight. The gunner, who was really at fault for not having his guns ready, was dismissed from the service. Commodore Barron was found guilty of culpable neglect and suspended from the service for five years without pay.

The British naval captains in American waters comported themselves very badly. They sailed insolently into American ports and demanded what they wanted. In September, the HMS *Jason* and the HMS *Columbine* entered New York harbor. They anchored in the lower bay. The *Jason* hailed a pilot boat and her captain demanded a pilot. He was refused. He sent an armed boat in pursuit of the pilot boat, which got away. The *Columbine*'s captain fired on a gunboat that was sailing in the harbor, stopped it, and ordered an American midshipman to come aboard. Meekly he obeyed. When the collector of customs heard of the rumpus, he sent a cutter to tell the British to get out of the harbor. The cutter was ordered off, and, when he did not go, was stopped and searched by the British.

But the British paid for their insolence. That same day the *Jason*'s barge came up to New York and landed the captain, then pushed off. But six sailors ran ashore, and disappeared into the cheering American crowd. The British officers inaugurated a search but found no one. For the next few days they searched every pilot boat and vessel in the area. A lieutenant stopped a pilot boat near the shore and went aboard to search. His crew manned the oars, took the barge ashore and abandoned it, and disappeared. Next day the whole crew of the *Jason* tried to escape, but the uprising was put down by force.

The excitement in the city and the fleet grew, and finally the *Jason* and the *Columbine* pulled up anchor and headed for Halifax, with fifty men of the *Jason*'s crew in irons.

The news of the *Chesapeake-Leopard* affair reached London late in July. The first report, of course, came from British naval sources, and told the English side of the story, how the Americans were encouraging desertion of British seamen. The *Times* erupted in editorial fury. So did the *Morning Post* and other Tory newspapers. A few weeks of blockade of the American coast, said the papers, ought to teach the rash Americans a thing or two.

On July 25, Special Ambassador Monroe and Minister Pinckney had a note from the British foreign office, with a copy of Admiral Berkeley's orders, and an inquiry as to what had happened outside Hampton Road. His Majesty's government was truly sorry, said the note, and if the British officer in charge should be found to be at fault, prompt reparation would be made. It was six days, however, before Monroe had any information from American sources, and all that time the British press was doing its work. So the three American demands were denied by an indignant British government that had to respond to its own public opinion.

Ambassador Monroe gave up in disgust. With this attitude in Britain nothing at all could be accomplished to bring real peace to the parties. He notified Foreign Minister Canning that he was returning to America without hope for negotiations and turned all his papers over to Minister Pinckney. As Monroe was about to leave the country, Canning realized what such a negative report to Washington would mean, and informed him that a minister would be sent to the United States to adjust the *Chesapeake* affair, that Admiral Berkeley had been recalled and his action disavowed. But public opinion had to be satisfied; Monroe was also told that all English seamen in the service of foreign states were recalled, and that from this point on British ships would stop merchant vessels and warships and demand all British nationals.

So more kindling was to be added to the increasing flames. All discussion of impressment was ended, and the Americans swallowed their pride for the moment. The *Chesapeake* affair lingered on for months. Berkeley was merely transferred to another command.

The English increased the number of warships off the American coast, but one change was notable; they no longer came inshore, but stayed outside American waters, stopping American and other neutral vessels, searching and committing many actions the Americans called outrages. These were duly reported in the American press, and each report raised a cry of outrage.

In the spring of 1811—four years later—the *Chesapeake* affair still smarted, when Commodore Rodgers, commander of the American fleet afloat, learned that a man had been impressed from an American brig off Sandy Hook by an English frigate. Commodore Rodgers's flagship, the *President*, was anchored off Annapolis. He went aboard and ordered the ship to proceed to New York so he could investigate this affair.

On May 16, at noon, the lookouts of the *President* sighted a sail about thirty miles off the land. It soon became apparent from the set of sails that it was a warship.

Commodore Rodgers moved in on her. At 2:00 P.M. the *President* ran up her flags. The strange ship made several signals, but when they were not answered she headed south. The *President* chased and, at dark, about 7:00 P.M., caught up with the other ship, which then raised an ensign, but what ensign no one could tell in the darkness.

The *President* worked around to have the weather gauge, and, at about half past eight, Commodore Rodgers ordered the other ship hailed.

What ship is that?

No answer.

The hail was repeated.

No answer, but the stranger asked the same question.

Commodore Rodgers asked again.

What ship is that?

This time the answer was a shot, which hit the *President*'s mainmast.

The American ship fired one gun in return. The strange ship answered with three guns, and then all of its broadside. The *President* fired a broadside.

But soon it was seen that the ship alongside was very small and not a worthy opponent, so firing was stopped. The other ship started firing again, however. The *President*'s broadside spoke once more, but after that the condition of the smaller vessel was obviously so desperate that Rodgers stopped the action. The ship then identified herself as a British man of war, but the name could not be made out in the rising wind. The *President* remained in the area, waiting for morning. When morning came the *President* found the vessel lying badly damaged off to leeward. Commodore Rodgers sent a boat to offer aid. The ship was the *Little Belt,* a schooner that looked like a frigate because of the spardeck on which no guns were mounted. She carried only eighteen guns as opposed to the *President*'s forty-four, and was no match. She had suffered badly—thirty-one men killed or wounded—but Captain Bingham, her skipper, refused any help from the Americans, and they parted. Bingham's actions were loudly applauded at home and abroad.

The affair was investigated by the Americans, who established the fact that the *Little Belt* fired first. But Captain Bingham denied that; he said the *President* fired a full broadside at him without notice.

So it was another incident, arousing fury in England against the Americans, and doubling the anger of Americans against the British, whom they accused of lying. Each government, of course, believed its own officers. The salient fact is that the British never conducted a court of inquiry into the actions of the captain of the *Little Belt.* That was enough for the Americans—or most Americans. Just then, the remnants of the Federalist party were determined to amplify their differences with the Republican party, and to do so it was handy to take the issue of adherence to Britain as an issue. Particularly in Boston, the Federalists continued to have followers, and they were unstinting in their praise for the English and opposed to Jefferson's policies. All through 1811 the festering sore of "impressment" continued to infuriate most Americans. As for American naval commanders, they were careful not to repeat the error of Commodore Barron—so careful, in fact, that they ran the opposite course.

One day in 1811 Commodore Decatur in the forty-four-gun frigate *United States* came upon two British frigates, the *Eurydice* and the *Atalanta,* off New York. The commanders were hailing one another when suddenly a shot rang out from the *United States*. It was the result of careless handling of a lanyard at a gun. Decatur apologized and explained and all was set to rights for the moment. But the incident showed how American warships traveled with flintlocks cocked and everything in readiness for action at a moment's notice.

The seamen were the same, ever conscious of the vile British practice of impressment, and Britain's cruel treatment of all—even Americans— who had been impressed into the naval service, had escaped, and then were captured again.

Another day in 1811 the frigate *Essex* was in port in England, having delivered some state papers, when someone ashore recognized one of the American seamen as a deserter from a British warship. A British officer came aboard to demand the man's removal. Captain Smith of the *Essex* called the man to his cabin, inquired as to his past, and learned that the man was an American but that he had been impressed into the British navy and escaped from it to join the *Essex*. Captain Smith was in a quandary. The British demanded return of all prisoners. He was in British water and with no hope of fighting. He told the man he would have to go along, but that he would start diplomatic efforts to free him. The sailor was sent to get his belongings. On reaching the gun deck, the sailor saw the carpenter's bench. He went to it, picked up an axe, and cut off his left hand. He picked up the severed hand and marched to the quarterdeck, bleeding, to present himself to the British officer. The officer was so shocked by the action that he left the ship immediately.

There were other incidents, one involving Captain Isaac Hull and the *Constitution*, one involving the *Hornet*, which came to nothing only because of the forbearance of the British officers involved—for many of the Britons knew how angry the Americans were and how they seemed these days to be ready to fire first and ask questions afterward. To anyone knowing the sea and the tempers of the British and American seamen involved, it was apparent that a fight was in the offing, and not long to come.

CHAPTER 9

The War of 1812

The War of 1812 has fascinated many authors, including this one. The company is good: President Theodore Roosevelt was so entranced by the War of 1812 that he wrote a history of the struggle. Largely the interest comes from the war at sea, for this was still the Age of Fighting Sail, and in this particular struggle the Americans showed themselves at their best, particularly in individual ship combat. Except for the Battle of Lake Erie, fought by two tiny squadrons, there was no real "fleet action" during the war for the simple reason that the United States did not have a fleet.

To the world, the War of 1812 is notable for another reason. During that war, the American frigate Essex journeyed to the South Seas in search of a refuge for repairs and Captain David Porter discovered and laid claim to the Marquesas Islands for America. But in 1813, there was very little American interest in the South Pacific and no more in the acquisition of any territory outside the North American continent. So when Porter's men left the islands the American government allowed the claim to die, and it was not renewed. The French came along fifty years later to make a new claim which was never challenged by the United States.

The War of 1812, then, showed the young United States as immature and unrealistic as well as idealistic. Captain Porter was not pleased at the State Department's rejection of his claim, but in that period the American government was almost totally concerned with narrow self-interest.

Another aspect of the War of 1812 that has always interested me is the virtual disloyalty of Boston and New England to the American cause. The war was never popular in New England, which derived most of its profit *from trade that involved England or English colonies. Boston bankers were notorious for trading with the enemy. Indeed, there was secession talk in New England during the War of 1812, and the offshore islands of Nantucket and Martha's Vineyard were split with sympathizers on both sides. The War of 1812 was fought on land and sea, but the land war was tedious and basically inconsequential, not worth describing in detail, since so very little happened. The principal events of the land war were the American burning of the Canadian Parliament buildings at York, and the British retaliation in the burning of the White House and the Capitol in Washington. The American army proved as inept on land as the American navy was skillful on the sea, and the British were properly contemptuous of the Americans, until the Battle of New Orleans, at which they were trounced by Andrew Jackson. But the Battle of New Orleans was fought after the Peace of Ghent had ended the war, so it made no difference (except to history buffs) who won the battle.*

Most fascinating to me is the entirely different frame of reference in which Americans hold the War of 1812, as compared to the British. We have numbered it among our major military struggles. To the British it was as a gnat's sting during the long campaign against Napoleon, and for many years the struggle was not even dignified by British history books with a name.

*　　*　　*

By 1811 the foreign policies followed by President Jefferson and President James Madison were seen by the public and a large segment of Congress as futile. Complaints to the British about impressment of American seamen had not stopped the process. Embargoes against all foreign goods, in complaint against French and British actions, had not succeeded because too many Americans were willing to smuggle. George Washington had warned against "entangling alliances" and here America seemed to be bound up in entangling alliances. Americans had once responded with cheers to the toast "millions for defense, but not one cent for tribute," and now it seemed that the Americans were paying tribute everywhere in one way or another. The public was thoroughly sick of not being able to trade abroad, and not being able to sail the seven seas without threat.

The British in 1811 sent a new minister to Washington to try to settle the differences with America, including the administration's nonimportation policy, which forbade trade and was hurting the English as well as the American economy.

In that summer of 1811, the American press was clamoring for war against England. The *Aurora* and the *Intelligencer*, two of the intensely political papers of the time, scarcely let a day go by without a call to battle. In this atmosphere, in November, the Twelfth Congress assembled and elected Henry Clay as Speaker of the House of Representatives. He was "the mouthpiece of young America," a cognomen bestowed on him after a speech in Congress on the occupation of West Florida (which had been carried out in 1810).

Another legislator had said he feared the American occupation would lead England to make war on America, since England was allied with Spain. Clay replied:

Sir, is the time never to arrive when we may manage our affairs without the fear of insulting his Britannic Majesty? is the rod of British power to be forever suspended over our heads? . . . Whether we assert our rights by sea or attempt their maintenance by land—whithersoever we turn ourselves this phantom incessantly pursues us. Already has it had too much influence on the councils of the nation. It contributed to the repeal of the embargo—that dishonorable repeal which has so much tarnished the character of our Government.

Mr. President, I have said on this floor and now take occasion again to remark, that I most sincerely desire peace and amity with England; that I even prefer an adjustment of all differences with her before one with any other nation. But if she persists in a denial of justice to us, or if she avails herself of the occupation of West Florida to commence war upon us, I trust and hope that all hearts will unite in a bold and vigorous vindication of our rights.

When the men of the House of Representatives chose Clay as Speaker that fall, they knew what they were doing; there was no question about his policy. He was the leader of the group called "War Hawks."

On April 1, 1812, President Madison gave his message to Congress—the administration's order of business for the coming year. Foreign affairs and national defense dominated the paper. He had nothing good to say about France, and nothing good to say about England; both nations had abused American rights. But the wave of indignation in the country was directed against England, and the War Hawks led it. Madison called for strong preparations for national defense, "seeing evidence of hostile inflexibility in trampling on rights which no independent nation can relinquish."

He called for a general embargo for sixty days.

That was all that was needed. In the House, Speaker Clay turned the various paragraphs of Madison's message over to select committees for consideration of legislation. In two weeks they all reported, and every report was warlike. The wrongs of England were recited in the House, and six resolutions were passed:

1.   That the ranks of the regular army be filled up (that meant an increase of the army to 25,000 men).

2. That an additional force of 10,000 men be enlisted to serve for three years.

3. That the services of 50,000 volunteers be accepted.

4. That the president be prepared to call the militia at any time.

5. That all naval vessels fit for sea be put in commission immediately.

6. That merchant ships be armed.

Congressman Peter Buell Porter, the chairman of the Foreign Affairs Committee, announced that Congress had no hope of peaceful settlement of differences with Great Britain.

This was war talk with a vengeance, but it met overwhelming approval in Congress and most of the country was solidly behind it.

In the next few months, however, many people on the eastern seaboard began to falter. They disliked the new embargo because it hurt their pocketbooks. The administration was taxed with all the faults of the three previous administrations and was very unpopular in the central states and New England.

Meanwhile, Britain proved uncompromising in her attitudes toward impressment and trade, and President Madison grew ever more vexed. On June 1 President Madison's secretary delivered to the Speaker of the House and the president pro tem of the Senate two packets of letters. Each contained the expected war message.

Madison began with a recital of events since 1803, charging Britain "with a course of conduct insulting to the independence and neutrality of the United States." Britain had continued her insults to the flag by seizing men sailing under it. Her warships had violated the American coasts, harassed American ships of the coast, and killed and injured Americans. She had blockaded various coasts to the detriment of American commerce. Finally she had passed the infamous orders in council, under which she took the power to blockade anytime and anywhere.

Whether the United States was to remain passive under these provocations or meet force with force, was up to the Congress, said the president.

The debate was short. On June 3, the House of Representatives voted for war. Two weeks of debate followed in the Senate; then it too declared for war. The bill was sent to Madison and he signed it and proclaimed a state of war with Great Britain.

This war, called in American history the War of 1812, was an event of major importance in America. But in England, as noted, it was merely an incident in the middle of the long struggle with France and her vassal states for control of Europe and the seas. It came in the year when Napoleon made the dreadful mistake of invading Russia (to lose more than 90 percent of his army in the subsequent winter retreat), and the year when the Duke of Wellington invaded Spain. English history books scarcely mention the war with America.

The war was fought on land and—more successfully by the Americans—on the sea. On the land the first point of defense had to be Detroit, a remote settlement in gunshot range of British territory, surrounded by unfriendly Indians. The American effort in the west was to defend territory. The British aim, hailed by the Canadians, was to recover territory ceded to America in the revolution and to extend the frontiers of Canada at the expense of the United States.

The American method on land was for General William Hull to invade Canada. First he marched to Detroit, where he arrived on July 5. On July 12 he crossed into Canada. General Henry Dearborn was to go up Lake Champlain for an assault on Montreal. General Stephen Van Rensselaer was to take and control the Niagara area.

But the American army was not much, and had not been since the days of the revolution. In 1808 it consisted of about 6,000 men. By 1812 it consisted of fewer than 7,000. Those were the trained troops. Those in-

THE WAR OF 1812

➡ American routes   ⇨ British routes
–·– Hull's route, 1812   ······ Dearborn's route, 1812–13
▼▼▼ Harrison's route, 1813   –¡– Wilkinson's route, 1813
––– British advance against Washington, 1814

Scale of Miles
0   50   100   150

creases in strength authorized by Congress in the winter and spring of 1812 had come far too late; the troops signed up were little better than raw militia. Most of the generals were politicians, and with one exception (Hull) they had had no military service.

The Americans began by losing the fort on Michilimackinac Island at the Straits of Mackinac, which join Lakes Huron and Michigan. Hull faltered in Canada, retreated to Detroit, and on August 16 surrendered that fortress without a shot being fired. The day before, the garrison at Fort Dearborn (Chicago) had been massacred by Indians, and with the surrender of Detroit the British were in control of the Great Lakes. Hull was disgraced, removed from command, and court-martialed. On March 26, 1813, the court found him guilty of cowardice in the face of the enemy and sentenced him to be shot. President Madison approved the sentence, but remitted the execution in view of Hull's service in the Revolutionary War. His name was stricken from the army rolls.

General Van Rensselaer was charged with the capture of the Niagara River area. He attacked and captured Queenstown Heights against a superior British force (1,000 men to his 600), but was defeated when the New York militia failed to support him on the flimsy excuse that their enlistments did not require them to cross the Canadian border. Van Rensselaer resigned his command and was succeeded by General Alexander Smyth, whose efforts were so puerile that he was quickly dropped from command.

The largest American force was that of General Dearborn at Plattsburg, New York. In November he led the army to the Canadian border, where the New York militia, up to its old tricks, refused to cross. General Dearborn marched back to Plattsburg. The war on land, then, in the year 1812, ended in a series of American fiascoes. The Indians of the northwest, smarting under the westward movement of Americans, joined up by the thousands under Tecumseh to fight with the British.

At sea, the early days of the war were far more encouraging to Americans. The reason was simple enough: while the army had languished under peacetime conditions with an occasional Indian campaign, the navy had been built up to fight the Barbary pirates, and the naval officers and men were experienced warriors. At the outbreak of war the navy consisted of eighteen vessels, ranging from forty-four-gun frigates to twelve-gun brigs. Though there were 176 gunboats, they were useless for a war at sea.

Compared to the British fleet, of course, the American navy seemed laughable. The Royal Navy in 1812 consisted of 230 ships of the line, huge three-deckers with 60 to 120 guns, and six hundred frigates and smaller vessels. To put it another way, the Americans did not have a single ship that the British would have placed in their line of battle to fight against an enemy fleet.

The moment that war was declared, the American navy got into action. The big ships put to sea as a squadron under Commodore John Rodgers. They sighted the British frigate *Belvedira,* but she got away from them. They sailed across the Atlantic, blood in their eyes, but found nary a British ship to fight, and so they sailed home, arriving after a seventy-day cruise.

Hearing of the chase of the *Belvedira,* the British assembled a squadron and sent it across to New York. Outside, the squadron encountered the American brig *Nautilus,* with fourteen guns. Her captain, Lieutenant Commandant Crane, fought; but, seeing that he was being surrounded, he threw his guns overboard and tried to escape. The *Nautilus* was captured by the frigate *Shannon.* She was the first American vessel to "strike her colors" in this war. (Press and public consistently used such heroic terms in connection with the sea battles. Americans were immensely proud of their navy and equally sensitive to any insults to the flag. The flag-burning that became commonplace abroad and at home in the late 1960s, and has persisted, would have been regarded in 1812 as mortal insult. It would have led to duels, arrests, and possibly convictions for treason in terms of individuals, and to breach of diplomatic relations and possibly war with other states.)

On July 12, 1812, the frigate *Constitution* sailed from Annapolis. Five days later the *Constitution* ran into the British squadron off the U.S. coast. Captain Hull wanted to fight *one* of the ships, but the British had no such intention; the whole squadron chased the *Constitution,* and she ran, firing from her stern when she could. The wind raised and dropped, raised and dropped. Sometimes the *Constitution* was towing and kedging, and the British ships were, too, in their effort to capture the American frigate. Finally up came a squall, followed by a fine wind, and the *Constitution* escaped.

A few days later the frigate *Essex* sailed from New York and captured a troop ship from a British convoy. The *Constitution,* out again, harried British shipping off the Bay of Fundy. On August 19 the *Constitution* encountered a British frigate, the *Guerrière,* and got into a fight. They were firing broadside and broadside, and finally they came to close contact, one hull against the other, and fought with muskets until they touched; then marines and sailors of each side tried to board the other ship. But the wind was running, and the ships were carrying heavy canvas, too heavy to allow the men to move freely. Just as the *Constitution* shot ahead of the other vessel, the enemy ship's foremast fell from battle damage and carried the other spars away. The once beautiful frigate lay wallowing, a dismasted wreck. The *Constitution* came around, ready to give her another broadside, but the Union Jack, which had been nailed to the stump of the mizzenmast of the other ship, was torn down; the enemy, no longer able to fight, surrendered. Captain Isaac Hull sent a boat from the *Constitution.*

The captured British frigate was hors de combat, her decks full of dead and wounded men. The prize crew removed the British to the *Constitution,* and the *Guerrière* was blown up and sank. The prisoners were taken to New York.

One American success in individual ship combat followed another. The American sloop *Wasp* defeated the British brig *Frolic;* the forty-four-gun frigate *United States* under Captain Stephen Decatur defeated and captured the thirty-eight-gun British frigate *Macedonian* off Madeira and brought her into Connecticut waters. To celebrate this victory there was an enormous party in New York, where Decatur delivered his famous toast: "Our country. In her intercourse with nations may she always be in the right, but our country, right or wrong."

If there was a slogan for the American navy in the War of 1812 that was it: our country right or wrong.

The *Constitution* spent some time in port after the battle with the *Guerrière* because of damages from that fight, and when she went out again it was under that old hero of two wars, Captain William Bainbridge. This time the *Constitution* went south, and off the coast of Brazil she encountered the British frigate *Java* and again there was a fight. As always it was a fierce one; the British lost 46 men dead and 102 wounded before the *Java* struck her colors. The *Constitution* lost 12 men killed and 22 wounded. This battle, on top of the previous one, brought the *Constitution* a great deal of glory in America. Her men had already christened her "Old Ironsides" because of the way the enemy shot seemed to bounce off her oaken bulwarks. But the fact was that her victories had been against a pair of thirty-eight-gun British frigates, which were much smaller than the American frigates, and this was part of the reason for the American successes. The British claimed that the ships were not matched up and this was true, because the Americans had chosen years earlier, for reasons of economy, to build big frigates rather than ships of the line, and the War of 1812 certainly showed the wisdom of this naval architectural decision. Consistently, the big American frigates could outsail and outfight the British frigates no matter how skillful the British captain and officers might be. As to the ships of the line, those 84- to 124-gun vessels, they were useful for fleet engagements, and the United States had no fleet as such.

Despite the patriotic watchwords, from the outset the War of 1812, except for the heroic ventures of the ships at sea, was not popular on the eastern seaboard of America. The seagoing community—the merchants and traders—wanted the war stopped as soon as possible. As early as August 1812, Secretary of State Monroe was putting out peace feelers to England. But the problem continued to be the British attitude toward impressment; the Americans would make no peace until the British ended that noxious practice, and the British flatly refused to end it. So the peace feelers of 1812 came to nothing.

At the end of 1812, the British announced a new blockade, this time of the Chesapeake and Delaware bays. Later it would be extended to the whole American coast, and it would be extremely effective, because the British were able to employ large numbers of ships for the purpose. The coast was effectively cut off from trade, from Mississippi up through Long Island Sound. Only the ports above New London remained open to neutral trade, and this was because the British were very clever: they knew that New England was generally opposed to the war, and they hoped to put additional pressure on Congress by leaving New England relatively unmolested.

In the fall of 1812, Captain Bainbridge's victory over the British frigate *Java* had come during the American squadron's cruise to the south in pursuit of British merchant shipping. Victories over warships notwithstanding, the squadron's cruise was not very successful. But the cruise of one ship of the squadron was quite something else. This was the thirty-two-gun frigate *Essex*.

She was not ready to sail with Bainbridge on October 26, but moved out of the Delaware River two days later. She sailed south to meet the other ships at a rendezvous point, but did not arrive until after the others had left. Continuing south, she crossed the equator, and shortly afterward captured a British government "packet" (a merchant ship) carrying government documents, supplies, and $55,000 in gold. The gold was taken aboard the *Essex,* a prize crew was put aboard the captive, the *Nocton,* and she was sent toward America. She ran into an element of the new British blockade between Bermuda and Chesapeake Bay, and was captured again. Still, Captain David Porter of the *Essex* had the $55,000 safe aboard his frigate. So it was not a total loss.

The *Essex* missed the American squadron again at the second rendezvous point at the island of Fernando de Noronha. Cruising offshore, Porter captured another English ship and learned that she was one of a convoy of six ships and that she had sprung a leak and been delayed. Porter decided to go after the entire convoy. He did not find it, and he ran short of water, so he put into Saint Catherine's for supplies. While there he realized that the squadron had gone somewhere, he knew not where, and it was no use to keep chasing. So he decided then to carry out the rest of his cruise alone. His mission, he knew, was to disrupt British shipping in the southern seas. How best to do it? He was, in effect, in a great enemy sea, for Britain controlled many of the ports of South and Central America through various business interests. Then, as later, even into the last quarter of the twentieth century, the understanding of the United States government and its people of Latin America was almost totally negative. Virtually no effort had been made to encourage trade with Central and South America; consequently American warships had no provision at all for the equipment and supply of American men of war.

Thus Captain Porter had no more hope for help in these seas than a pirate captain, and would be solely dependent on his own resources.

Remarkably, as seen from the twentieth century, although probably not so much from the viewpoint of his own time, Porter decided that he would go around Cape Horn and attack the English whaling ships that were working in the Pacific, thus striking at a vital resource; for whale oil was the preferred lighting medium of the era. The streets of London might go dark if Captain Porter was successful enough. From what Porter had been able to learn, the British had only a single ship of the line in the South Pacific, and even that was about to leave the area.

On January 26, 1813, the *Essex* left Saint Catherine's, rounded the Horn in a stormy passage, and by March was deep in the Pacific. Porter stopped at Valparaiso, took on supplies and news—mostly bad news about the capture of American whaling vessels by English warships. He rescued two whaling ships from a Peruvian privateer, and then set off to look for British whalers. Soon he had captured six, and then the captures came quickly. Porter's force of men available as prize crews was so small that he could hardly man the captives. He had a fleet of nine ships, one of which, the *Atlantic,* was suitable to become an auxiliary warship, so she was given twenty guns, renamed the *Essex Junior,* and manned with sixty American naval seamen. On July 9, most of the captives were sent off with *Essex Junior* to Valparaiso to prize court. One of the emoluments of a naval career in wartime was the money secured from the capture of prizes, which was shared by every man of the crew of the warship, from captain down to gunner's boy, on a relative basis.

Having sent off this small fortune in prizes, Porter then headed for the Galapagos Islands, captured more British whalers and merchant ships, and made another warship of the whaler *Seringapatam,* which became a twenty-two-gun cruiser. More captures were made, more prizes were sent off to South American ports, and finally, in October 1813, the *Essex* and her entourage landed on the island of Nuahiva, in the Marquesas. Captain David Porter, U.S. Navy, then took possession of the Marquesas Islands in the name of the United States of America, and the United States became a truly intercontinental imperialistic power.

Porter spent six weeks in the Marquesas, a stay similar to the celebrated sojourn of HMS *Bounty* at Tahiti. The girls were beautiful and available, so much so that the chaplain insisted on keeping the ship's boys and midshipmen afloat so they would not be corrupted. In December 1813 Porter was ready to go back to war, his men were not, and a difficulty arose. It had the earmarks of a mutiny, but Porter got wind of it, faced down the leader, and the obdurate captain won out. The *Essex* sailed, leaving Marine Lieutenant John Gamble and twenty-one men to man the fort they had built after they claimed the territory for America. A few weeks later the *Essex* was badly beaten in a fight with two English ships off Valparaiso. Porter and what was left of his crew were captured, and the ship destroyed in the fight.

Back in "paradise," the Polynesian Marquesas, Lieutenant Gamble had his problems. In February four men deserted in one of the whale boats, undoubtedly heading for another island to establish permanent residence with their *wahines*. Eighteen men remained, with the cruiser *Seringapatam* and the captured whaler *Sir Andrew Hammond*. Lieutenant Gamble had been told to wait for the return of the *Essex*. But by April, the lieutenant had the feeling that the *Essex* would never come back, and he decided he must take his ships home. The decision brought a mutiny. Lieutenant Gamble was wounded in the foot and held captive by the mutineers, who intended to stay in their paradise. The mutineers then decided that the *Essex* might come back, and took the *Seringapatam* off to hunt for a new paradise, in the manner of Fletcher Christian and the *Bounty* mutineers, never to be heard of again by the American navy.

Lieutenant Gamble's foot had scarcely healed when the Americans left at Nuahiva were set upon by the Polynesians, many of them angry at the treatment by the foreigners, and the theft of their women. After a pitched battle only eight Americans were left, one badly wounded and one sick. They set sail in the *Sir Andrew Hammond* without a chart, and headed for Hawaii—the Sandwich Islands as they were called then. They arrived at Honolulu and were captured by the British warship *Cherub,* taken aboard, and finally landed at Rio de Janeiro. Lieutenant Gamble got back to New York in August 1815, after the war had ended.

The individual exploits of American naval captains continued, even though they could not lift the British blockade. Given only a relative handful of ships, the U.S. Navy had to devise some policy that would seriously hurt the British, as much as they could without employment of very many vessels. It was out of the question that the Americans could stage with Britain a "fleet battle" of the type that the French and Dutch and Spanish navies had staged. Half a dozen ships of the line could blow the whole American navy out of the water. The 44-gun frigate was a fearsome weapon, when compared to a 38, but not against a 120-gun ship of the line.

In one way, the successes of the American captains were a negative factor. In 1812 Congress did nothing to improve the size or quality of the navy. But in January, buoyed by the performances of the frigates, Congress empowered the president to build four ships of the line, at seventy-four guns each, six new forty-four-gun frigates, six sloops, and vessels to sail the Great Lakes.

There were naval defeats, some of them reflecting very badly on the courage and loyalty of American seamen, even more so on the badly extended naval organization. One such was the battle between the *Chesapeake*—that vessel whose misfortune had been a major cause of the War of 1812—and the British frigate *Shannon*.

Captain James Lawrence had taken command of the *Chesapeake* in May 1813, and set sail to attack British whaling vessels in the Greenland whale fishing area.

The *Chesapeake* was badly manned, not much of a commendation for her previous captain Evans, who had retired because of ill health. In the forecastle burned the coals of disloyalty, fanned by a dispute over prize money from previous captures. In the enlisted crew there were far too many mercenaries who should have been sailing on privateers, if at all, and their ringleader was a Portuguese boatswain who obviously should have been paid off in Boston weeks earlier.

Having just taken over command, Captain Lawrence was not aware of the underlying tensions when he set out from Boston harbor. His first lieutenant, O. A. Page, had been left behind sick. The acting first lieutenant, Augustus Ludlow, had just been commissioned from the midshipmen's ranks and had virtually no experience, and two of the three other officers were midshipmen acting as lieutenants. It was hardly a crew to send to sea in a frigate to fight the nation's wars.

Outside Boston harbor, the *Chesapeake* encountered the British frigate *Shannon*, which was actually waiting for her and seeking single combat. In those days of "fighting sail," a skipper like British Captain Broke could sit down at his sea desk and write to the captain of an American frigate an invitation to combat "at any latitude and longitude that might be agreed upon," and be taken quite seriously. Captain Lawrence had not received such a letter; but now here he was on June 1, 1813, coming out of the bay, and the *Shannon* was bearing down upon him.

Like boxers the captains sparred, each seeking the weather gauge, which meant the wind behind him, or at ninety degrees, to blow him down upon the enemy, and make it easy for him to maneuver and very hard for the opponent. Finally, Captain Lawrence came up on the *Shannon*'s starboard side, planning to move yardarm-to-yardarm, and that way exchange broadsides until one vessel faltered. The *Shannon* began firing from aft to forward, one gun at a time. The *Chesapeake* waited and fired a whole broadside, which was very destructive to British life and limb. But the *Shannon*'s cannon shot away the foresail tie and jib sheet of the *Chesa-*

peake; her foresail blew out, she came up into the wind with a snap, and lay in irons, with her mizzen rigging afoul of the *Shannon*'s forechains. The *Shannon*'s anchor fouled the *Chesapeake* and kept the ships together so that the guns of the *Shannon* were able to rake the decks of the American frigate.

Captain Lawrence was badly wounded. Lieutenant Broom, the marine officer, was killed, and so was Lieutenant Ludlow, Sailing Master White, Midshipman Ballard, the acting fourth lieutenant, three junior midshipmen, and Boatswain Adams.

Captain Lawrence, despite his wound, called for boarders to take the *Shannon,* but the ship's bugler had recently left the *Chesapeake* and the man who had taken his place was so frightened he could not blow a note. Captain Lawrence shouted orders to send men below and bring up the boarders, and then he fell with his second, and mortal wound. He was dying, and he called to one of the midshipmen: "Never strike the flag of my ship." And then he fell unconscious, which was just as well for his last peace of mind.

The crew of the *Chesapeake,* deprived now of any officer above the rank of midshipman—and these were very young midshipmen—went completely to pieces. The spiteful Portuguese boatswain's mate went below, leaving his post, and removed the iron grating above the hatchway as he went. When the British boarded, a few Americans fired back or fought with cutlass and knife, but most streamed down the companionways and hatches to the relative safety of the quarters below. The British came up and fired into the openings, and the colors of the *Chesapeake* were soon hauled down—although, of course, all this was unseen by the dying captain.

The whole battle had lasted only fifteen minutes. Captain Lawrence's sound seamanship had made it appear in the beginning that the Americans would be victorious, for the *Shannon* had twenty-three men killed and fifty-six wounded in those early broadsides. But the tide of war changed, and the poor training of the American seamen, the insufficiency of officers, and what the British captain called the outright cowardice of much of the American crew decided the battle. When it ended the *Chesapeake* had forty-eight men killed and eighty-nine men wounded.

Despite an occasional defeat such as that of the unlucky *Chesapeake,* the remarkable American naval successes at sea continued, and became truly effective in European waters. By the summer of 1814 the Americans had captured 825 British vessels, and the Royal Navy was convoying ships from England to Ireland and into mid-Atlantic, lest they be taken by American privateers or warships. But if the informal American blockade of England was troublesome to London, the British blockade of the American coast was ten times as effective, and literally cut the lifeline of America to Europe.

On land General Harrison's forces were besieged by a British-Indian combination at Fort Meigs at the mouth of the Maumee River. The problem of the Americans in the west was that they could not move as long as the British controlled Lake Erie.

Before 1812 no thought had been given to militarization of the Great Lakes. The only American "warship" there was the *Adams,* a brig owned by the War Department, used for transporting supplies to various military posts. With the British capture of Detroit, the *Adams* fell into their hands and the Americans attacked and destroyed her. The net result was still that the Americans had no warships on the lakes.

Captain Isaac Chauncey was sent to the Great Lakes in November 1812 with a small flotilla, the largest ship being a sixteen-gun brig. He fought a battle with small British vessels, which was indecisive. In December, as the weather was closing in with ice and snow, navigation was abandoned for the winter. The next few months were spent by both sides building ships for fighting as soon as the weather became clement.

American shipwrights were sent up to the lakes from the east, and they started construction of ships from raw timber. There was no time to wait and no transportation to bring the seasoned wood from the eastern ship-yards. Two brigs were built at Erie (then called Presque Isle). In April, a combined sea-land assault was begun against York (now called Toronto), and General Dearborn's troops captured the town, which brought them a large volume of military supplies and several boats and ships.

The fight for York had been more than vigorous. General Zebulon M. Pike (of Pike's Peak) was killed in the fighting. The Americans burned the house of the governor and the Parliament buildings, which the British regarded as an atrocity beyond the call of war.

The war on the Great Lakes continued at a low level during the spring and summer of 1813. A British squadron under Captain Robert Barclay now controlled the lake with six warships. Captain Oliver Hazard Perry was chosen to lead the American effort to take control of Lake Erie. Other American vessels were brought to Presque Isle to join the two brigs, three gunboats, and schooner already there. In May and June the Americans won several victories in the Niagara area and the British withdrew.

In May, the ships that were built at Presque Isle were ready. The problem was to get them across the shallow sandbar from the Niagara River into Lake Erie. The British blockade made this impossible—but Captain Barclay, who needed supplies, took his ships away for just two days and Perry got his ships out. The other vessels had already come into the lake from the river, and in September the Americans had the stronger force on the lake. But the British were ready to contend for that honor, and on September 14, 1813, the two squadrons met in the Battle of Lake Erie. This battle was the first fleet engagement of the Americans against the British, and one of the bloodiest battles of all time. Commodore Perry's flagship, the *Lawrence,* bore on her pennant an idealized version of Captain Lawrence's last plea to the men of the *Chesapeake*—"Don't give up the ship"—and the men of the *Lawrence* did not. They fought until their ship was a smoking hulk, all the guns disabled, the masts down, and the sails strewn across the decks. Perry left the ship and moved to the *Niagara* and fought the battle all over again. This time Perry forced all the British ships to surrender and won a complete victory. "We have met the enemy and they are ours," he wrote in a message to General Harrison, who was waiting for such word to begin to move on land.

So the Americans controlled Lake Erie and could now begin a campaign against Canada. Detroit was taken again, and Harrison sent off a land attack. In the Battle of the Thames, the Indian chief Tecumseh was killed, which dismayed many of the Indian tribes and weakened their faith in the ultimate triumph of the British in this war.

That summer, the officials at Washington became dissatisfied with General Dearborn, as they had with so many of their commanders on the land. He was replaced by General James Wilkinson, who was ordered to attack Montreal along with General Wade Hampton. But the British had 15,000 troops between Wilkinson and the city, so the secretary of war, John Armstrong, who fancied himself as a military man, came up himself to supervise the war in the field. He camped on Lake Champlain with General Wade Hampton, who was to lead the second prong of the attack.

General Wilkinson set out from Sackett's Harbor in mid-October, and managed his campaign so miserably that the British routed his troops. The Americans went into winter camp in November.

Hampton, following the direct orders of Armstrong, moved up to the Canadian border, and then, instead of going north to Montreal, turned west, to wait for General Wilkinson, who did not come. He had abandoned the attack without notice. After a minor battle (Chateaugay) Hampton marched back to Plattsburg. The whole American campaign, involving two forces defeated or stalled by inferior British elements, was a lesson in how not to fight a war, and the presence of Secretary of War Armstrong in the field was not just a nuisance, it was a menace to intelligent command, which contributed to the American delinquency.

That winter of 1813 the war took on many overtones reminiscent of the bitter French and Indian War and the revolution at its worst. The Americans were driven out of Fort George, and they burned two small towns. The British retaliated when they captured Fort Niagara by turning the Indians loose for more of their massacres, and then, when they captured Buffalo and Black Rock, burning the buildings of those two places.

The war was going very badly for the Americans in spite of the heroic fight of Commodore Perry and his success on Lake Erie. The British blockade caused great hardship to Americans, and its success was to be attributed partly to the supplying of British warships by New England and New York merchants. This practice so angered President Madison that he persuaded Congress to a new tough embargo to prevent American citizens trading with the enemy. The result was the complete British blockade of the American coast, and enormous hardship in New England, especially in such outlying points as Martha's Vineyard and Nantucket islands, with those sympathizers for both sides. Those islands—particularly Nantucket—were never quite sure they really wanted to be part of the United States.

The British were not worried about the American armies in the north, based on their experiences. But when the news of Perry's victory at Lake Erie reached London it was annoying far beyond its importance, for the Royal Navy was the apple of England's eye. Parliament, however, could afford to feel expansive at the end of 1813: Napoleon had been defeated at Leipzig and the French ejected from Holland; General Blücher had defeated the French at Wahlstadt and had crossed the Rhine; and Wellington had seized San Sebastian and marched into France. The war against Napoleon, which was the important matter in London, was going very well. The war against the Americans had its ups and downs; the Yankees were like mosquitoes, stinging here and there. If Britain had wished to devote sufficient resources on land and sea in Canada and along the American coast, the mosquitoes could have been eliminated. But was it worth the effort? Lord Castlereagh, the British foreign secretary, with the concurrence of the cabinet, wrote Secretary of State Monroe in Washington, suggesting that the unpleasant war might be brought to an end by direct negotiations. President Madison, who was weary of having the war called "Mr. Madison's War" by the Federalists, and hearing the constant insult that he was "a tool of the French," was quick to appoint a peace commission, which included John Quincy Adams of the famous Adams family and Henry Clay, which meant it went beyond partisanship. Adams and Clay soon set sail for the Flemish town of Ghent, to begin discussions with their British counterparts. The discussions were to begin in August 1814. But, of course, while the politicians were preparing to talk, the war went on. The British moved down into Maine and threatened New England.

Down in Georgia the Creek Indians, brought to fever pitch by Tecumseh in his southern trip several years earlier, had risen up against the American settlers and began burning settlements. They had burned Fort Mims, about thirty-five miles from Mobile, in the summer of 1813, and this led to reprisal from the settlers of Tennessee. Andrew Jackson was the major general of Tennessee militia and he was called on to carry the war against the Indians. His militia began burning Indian settlements (Talladega, for example). The Creeks were infuriated and fought back. They defeated the Tennesseans in three battles, the last at Coffee Creek in January 1814. Jackson stopped and reorganized, and in the spring of 1814 the Tennessee militia invaded the heart of Creek country. The big battle was fought in March at Horseshoe Bend on the Tallapoosa River, and then the Americans continued to ravage the Creek settlements until finally most of the Indians gave up. The Americans took much of the Creek land in southern and western Alabama, and the Creeks moved west.

In the Ohio-Indiana area, the death of Tecumseh put an end to the virility of the Indian war against General William Henry Harrison, and he forced the Indian nations in 1814 to declare war on the British. Their efforts could not make much difference to the conduct of the war in the northwest, but at least the Indians were removed as an irritant.

The defeats on the Canadian front had brought about another reorganization of the American army. This time it began to show some semblance of professionalism. General Wilkinson was fired, and several new generals came into the war, including Brigadier General Winfield Scott and Major General Jacob Brown.

In the summer of 1814, General Brown crossed the Niagara River with about 3,500 men and attacked Fort Erie. The British moved back to a defense line on the Chippewa River, General Brown attacked again, and hurriedly called for General Scott's brigade of 1,300. That force came up and helped Brown defeat the British. It was a real victory, the first that the Americans had won on land against anything like an organized British army force.

But the Americans simply could not pursue the war properly. Army and navy cooperation was almost nonexistent. Commodore Chauncey was given naval forces on Lake Ontario to drive the British off the lake. He failed. Thus General Brown was unable to move up into Northern Canada, although he tried, and by the late summer of 1814, Brown was back at Fort Erie, under siege by a British force under General Drummond. The siege was lifted in an attack by the Americans with heavy British losses, but to little avail: in a few weeks the Americans evacuated the fort as untenable, and their drive on Canada came to an end. As it turned out, the whole campaign was so much military musical chairs.

The Americans on the continent were now definitely on the defensive. On September 11, 1814, General Sir George Prevost began a long-planned campaign southward along Lake Champlain, designed to take Albany and then New York.

Meanwhile events in Europe combined to allow the British government to pay more attention to the American irritation. The allied armies defeated the French in three battles and entered Paris on March 30, 1814. Napoleon abdicated as emperor and was banished to the isle of Elba. A jubilant England prepared for the Congress of Vienna, which was supposed to redesign Europe's geography. Louis XVIII took the French throne, Christian Frederick of Denmark was elected King of Norway, and Europe seemed to be settling down to recover from the revolutionary Napoleonic era.

What to do about the gnats of America? Suddenly there were troops to burn in England, and 4,000 of them were sent off to join the British naval forces blockading the American coast and create a diversion that would draw American effort away from Sir George Prevost's 11,000-man army that was preparing to march down from Canada.

It seemed so much like the Revolutionary War, but it was not. The Americans had no George Washington this time, no Horatio Gates, no Light-Horse Harry Lee. The American military commanders were an uninspired group who bungled effort after effort. Luckily for them, the Americans also had a navy. This time, the key to the American defense lay on Lake Champlain, and the holder of the key was another member of that well-disciplined, tight little American navy. He was Captain Thomas Macdonough, then thirty years old, who had a force of four ships and a dozen gunboats—eighty-odd guns and 850 men. The British naval contingent was about the same, four ships, a dozen gunboats, and 800 men. Sir George Prevost's army came south along the border of Lake Champlain, driving the American military contingent south. But Captain Macdonough placed his fleet on the narrow channel between Crab Island and Cumberland Head, across the bay from Plattsburg, in what became known as the Battle of Lake Champlain. Once again American daring—recklessness, it might be called—won the day, for when the battle was joined, Macdonough ran his flagship *Saratoga* down onto the British flagship *Confiance,* without regard for shot or shell. The swiftness and determination of Macdonough carried the day: the British naval commander, Captain George Downie, surrendered, and the British army had to retreat.

As a battle, it was a minor affair by European standards: American casualties were 110; British casualties were fewer than 130 men. But the capture of all Downie's ships except the gunboats meant the Americans controlled Lake Champlain, and Sir George Prevost could not move any farther south. There was nothing for him to do but retreat back north into Canada, particularly since winter was not far away.

On the East Coast of the United States, Sir Alexander Cochrane was in charge of the sea war against the Americans, and he had carte blanche from London to carry the war as he would.

During the months of June and July 1814, Admiral Cochrane's marines landed time and again at settlements around Chesapeake Bay, burned buildings, and carried off the supplies they could find. Cochrane's purpose was to intimidate the Americans as much as possible, and also to allow the British expeditionary force to live off the land as completely as possible.

When Admiral Cochrane learned that London was sending him those 4,000 seasoned troops no longer needed in Europe, he decided to use them to teach the Americans some lessons they had not learned. The American burning of the government buildings at York (Toronto) still rankled the British, who had a fine sense of the dignity of government. So the Americans had burned York's Parliament; now the British would retaliate by burning the American Parliament—the buildings of Congress and the American government in Washington.

In July Lord Cochrane ordered his forces to land troops, not with the idea of capturing and holding territory in the south, but to lay waste to the American countryside and disrupt American government and communications.

An expeditionary force under Rear Admiral Sir George Cockburn was chosen for the task. The force landed at the mouth of the Patuxent River. As the ships came in, the Americans blew up their gunboats, which were all they had to protect the Chesapeake Bay area, and retreated. The British moved inland to Bladensburg, Maryland.

Secretary of War Armstrong had established nine military districts in the United States. On paper the force looked quite respectable, but actually it was a paper tiger. Now a tenth district was established, to include the District of Columbia, Maryland, and the counties of Virginia adjacent to the capital. The commander was a Baltimore lawyer named William H. Winder, who had seen some service with the incompetent army that had tried to invade Canada; he had been captured in that campaign. Those two factors certainly did not attest to any great competence on Winder's part, but Madison and Armstrong did not seem able either to find anyone else or to cope with the issue of defense. As the British came toward Baltimore and Washington, General Winder prepared to defend the capital. But Winder turned out to be even more incompetent than his detractors had said he was. He did not know how to manage a defense, although he had 7,000 men under his command including 400 tough sailors from the gunboats who had marched inland after the gunboats were blown up.

General Winder was to be assisted in his defense of Washington by Secretary Armstrong, who was prepared to give advice, by Secretary of State James Monroe, who was also prepared to give advice, and by President Madison, who was not quite sure where he should go when the specter of British troops appeared on the Washington doorstep.

General Winder had word that the British were marching on Bladensburg, so he rushed his troops there, leaving Commodore Joshua Barney's 400 sailors to cover the road that led to the District of Columbia. They had half a dozen twenty-four-pound guns, taken from their gunboats. Against them suddenly appeared 4,000 redcoats, veterans of the Napoleonic wars. The American defense lasted half an hour, and then collapsed, with a casualty list of about seventy-five men. The Americans had caused some 250 British casualties, but with 3,700 men left, Admiral Cockburn had no real difficulty in marching into Washington. The British troops bivouacked on the night of August 24, 1814, a quarter of a mile from the impressive United States Capitol building. The American army troops left behind to guard Washington had all fled to Arlington and Alexandria. President Madison and the American cabinet all clustered around Bladensburg, where General Winder had decided to make his stand. When the American order of battle was set up, along came Secretary of State Monroe and Secretary of War Armstrong with free advice which caused the Americans to change their defense plan, until it was a plan no longer. The troops were soon routed back toward Georgetown. Madison, Monroe, and Armstrong fled in different directions. The president of the United States was to go on horseback to Frederick, Maryland, and join the cabinet there, but in the confusion and panic, he did not go to Frederick, but headed toward his family house in Loudoun County, Virginia. He did not get there, either. He stopped at a house a few miles above the lower Potomac Falls. There he spent a restless night, with the jeers of the populace literally ringing in his ears. On August 25, Madison traveled another six miles to an inn, where he was joined by his wife. He was now about twenty miles from the British camp. When he heard that the British were stirring, he fled again to refuge in the Virginia woods. No one the president met had much sympathy for him. Monroe encountered the same sort of treatment.

With a little extra effort the British might have captured the whole American government, but Admiral Cochrane was not really interested in that.

On August 25, 1814, Admiral Cockburn sent detachments out; one to burn down the U.S. Capitol, one to burn down the White House, one to burn the Department of State, another the Treasury, and all the other government buildings. (The only one they missed was the U.S. Patent Office.) They also burned down a number of the houses of the American elite, and the offices of the *National Intelligencer,* one of the more imposing American newspapers.

Rather than see the British get any benefit from American resources, Secretary of the Navy William Jones ordered the sailors at the Washington navy yard to burn it and several naval vessels being built there. They started the fires, and the British came along and stoked them.

The British did not linger long in the burned city. That day a hurricane came blowing up from the south, putting out fires, and making life miserable along the Potomac for a bivouacked army. They moved out on the afternoon of August 25, marched back to the Patuxent River, and rejoined the fleet. A detachment on the Potomac attacked Fort Washington, which was immediately abandoned by the American defenders, and then moved to Alexandria where they captured every ship in the harbor and an immense amount of military stores and foodstuffs, which were loaded into the British frigates. Meanwhile, the Americans across the river in Washington were trying to put their government back together and worrying lest the British navy at Alexandria descend on Arlington and Washington again to see what they could find of value. Many members of Congress were now talking about ending the war by surrendering the country right then to Lord Cochrane.

Now James Monroe took over the defense of Washington. General Winder was still wandering around up country, wasting the talents of his military men.

Slowly the American government reorganized. Armstrong was forced out of the cabinet as a result of the Washington fiasco and Monroe took over the War Department as well as State. The whole government was so shaken that for a month no sensible direction came out of Washington, and the war went on of its own volition, with local military commanders doing as they saw fit. The British continued to roam up and down the Chesapeake Bay, ravaging the shores.

In London, the British government had time, finally, to pay some attention to the long-range questions of the American war. The Duke of Wellington was available for a new enterprise, and Lord Castlereagh suggested that he might be interested in adding to his glories by going to America and resolving the military problem there. But Wellington took a look at the map and the situation reports, and told the war minister that the only way the war in America could be won was to control the Great Lakes and Lake Champlain and that the British had not done so. No land army could do much until the Royal Navy had exercised that control, said the duke, and he respectfully declined the honor.

In September, Admiral Cochrane decided to attack Baltimore. Whether this would be just another burn-and-slash raid or a real attack aimed at occupying the city as well as destroying it would remain to be seen. The troops were landed without difficulty—the American defenses at sea here were nonexistent—and they moved from the landing point on the Patapsco River directly toward the city.

Admiral Cochrane had, however, made one error in his calculations. He had given the people of Baltimore time to prepare defenses, as he had not given the people of Washington. The mayor rallied the defense, and citizens' committees came forth to plan and to toil, moving cannon around the city, building trenches and setting up batteries. By September 1 they had built up a whole system of redoubts and earthworks to protect the troops who would defend them. The batteries were manned by sailors who knew how to shoot, and they were commanded by naval officers. The harbor was protected by Fort McHenry, which was under the command of Lieutenant Colonel Walker Keith Armistead of the U.S. Army Engineers, the first graduate of the West Point military academy (opened July 4, 1802), and a man who knew his military business. He had been responsible earlier for the fortification of Norfolk.

Colonel Armistead had a thousand men under him, artillery men and sailors and regular army troops. Baltimore, in other words, was defended by a force of the size and sort that should have been available to defend the nation's capital, had not the politicians bungled. Altogether, there were about 14,000 fighting men in Baltimore that September.

The defense of the city was commanded by U.S. Senator Samuel Smith, who was then sixty-two. His title was major general of the militia. After the mess Winder had made at Bladensburg and Georgetown, he had headed for Baltimore to take over the defense of the city, but was politely rousted out of town. Winder appealed to the governor of Maryland, who was his cousin, and to President Madison, but nobody paid any attention to him. General Smith remained in command.

The British fleet had stopped at the mouth of the Patapsco and landed the troops of the expeditionary force on the northern point. The naval force, which would bombard the city and its defenses, had only twelve miles to sail in, and the troops had only fourteen miles to march to reach the city. By eight o'clock on the morning of September 12 the troops were moving. Three brigades of troops marched five miles without meeting any Americans, and the fleet moved up the channel toward Fort McHenry and the city of Baltimore.

The Americans were waiting at Fort McHenry. General Smith sent a brigade of Baltimore militiamen down toward the mouth of the Patapsco to slow the British and they met the enemy about seven miles from the north point. Here it was again, raw American recruits trying to fight British regulars trained in the Napoleonic war, with 3,000 Americans facing almost double their number.

By standard military tactics, almost everything the Americans did here was wrong. They divided their force into three lines, without adequate cover of flankers. They sent a force of 400 out to skirmish with the enemy. They retreated when the enemy came up. And yet they managed to shoot down General Robert Ross, the British troop commander, who died not long after. Colonel Brooke took over then, and set his whole force to face and flank the Americans on both sides. In the fighting that followed, the

British routed the Americans, but again the British suffered the most casualties. The fighting was reminiscent of the Revolutionary War, in which the British won most of the victories but lost the campaigns. The delay of this inconclusive fighting kept them back a whole day. That night they bivouacked on the battlefield in the rain. They resumed the march on September 13, but found that the Americans had made roadblocks of trees and rocks in the road. The British were delayed and did not arrive in sight of Baltimore and its new fortifications until evening. Colonel Brooke was taken aback. This was the most competent and formidable defense he had yet seen. The colonel spent the whole day moving around looking at the defenses.

At sea, Admiral Cockburn did the same. He came up that day and found a barrier of sunken vessels outside Fort McHenry and the inner area covered by guns from the fort, by new positions in the revetments, and by gunboats. The admiral began bombarding the whole area with his light vessels, but he was afraid to bring the big ships in lest they be sunk or run aground. So Fort McHenry withstood a bombardment all day and all night. And it was here that Francis Scott Key stood watching "the rocket's red glare, the bombs bursting in air," and was so struck by the beauty of Old Glory flying in the breeze above the fort, that he later composed the American national anthem, "The Star Spangled Banner." Odd that the anthem should come from a little-known and almost totally inconsequential military engagement, but it did; most Americans have no idea of the reason for, or the outcome of, the Battle of Baltimore.

When morning came, the British decided that the defenses of Baltimore were so strong that it would be too expensive and not very useful to breach them, so they turned away and headed back down Chesapeake Bay. On September 19 Admiral Cochrane sailed for Halifax to regroup and prepare for a new expedition. The troop ships that had come from England sailed for Jamaica.

The war was now at a stalemate. The British blockade of the United States was effective and painful. The American harassment of British shipping in European waters and the Caribbean was also painful. Both sides were suffering from exhaustion: the British treasury exhausted by the wars against France and this tiny fillip in America, and the tiny American treasury exhausted by the war against Britain. The disruption of orderly government in Washington caused the big banks in the East to suspend payment of debts in gold and silver. This caused inflation and some panic—a situation that would remain until the British blockade ended. Only in New England, where the bankers were generally in league with the British, did money mean much. In New York the dollar was discounted twenty percent, Baltimore money thirty percent. The U.S. Treasury was bankrupt. This shortage of money also affected the government's ability to recruit and keep troops. The army, supposedly 58,000 men but never having numbered more than 40,000, fell to 34,000. The militia system, on which the Americans depended, was alive with corruption at every level. The troops enlisted served a few days to get on the rolls, then went home and did not appear until the time came to be paid off. It was hard to fight battles with evanescent soldiers.

In England at the end of July Minister of State Lord Bathurst had planned a new expedition for the American expeditionary force. It was to be against the soft underbelly of America, New Orleans. The purpose: to deprive the backwoods Americans of their sources of supply of goods and to capture and hold New Orleans, which could then be traded at the peace table for some other concession, or kept by Britain and added to the empire.

About 10,000 soldiers were committed for the task. After New Orleans was captured, then Lord Cochrane would be free to decide what more, if anything, he wanted to capture.

When General Ross was killed outside Baltimore, Lord Bathurst appointed Major General Sir Edward Pakenham to command the troops for the attack on New Orleans. Pakenham was an extremely capable general and the brother-in-law of the Duke of Wellington, who had been Pakenham's teacher of the arts of war. Obviously in training and disposition Pakenham was in every way superior to U.S. Commander Andrew Jackson; at thirty-eight, he was younger by ten years and his health was better.

The Americans had known nothing about this plan during the summer months. Secretary of War Armstrong had appointed General Andrew Jackson, the hero of the war against the Creek Indians, to head Military District No. 7, which included New Orleans and Mobile, the headquarters of the district. Jackson had arrived there on August 15, without any indication that the British were coming. His real interest was in the seizure of the remainder of Florida from the Spanish, and he had already written to the War Department with that suggestion: "Will you only say to me, Raise a few hundred militia (which can be quickly done) and with such a regular force as can be conveniently collected, make an attack on Pensacola . . ."

Immediately Jackson's attention was drawn to Florida by a small British diversionary force, led by a Colonel Nicholls, which landed at Pensacola, seized the Spanish fort, and began making preparations with the Creek warriors to help them invade Louisiana.

On September 3 the British sloop *Sophie* sailed into Barataria in the Mississippi delta, forty miles south of New Orleans. Barataria Bay was an old-time pirate enclave, under the charge of the three brothers Laffite, Jean, Pierre, and Dominique. For years they had plundered British and Spanish ships and the government of Louisiana and the United States had never been able to bring them under control. The British suggested that if the Laffites would join their enterprise against the United States they would be rewarded richly; if they did not, the British would wipe them out.

That was not the way to talk to the Brothers Laffite. They decided that, many as their past quarrels with the United States had been, Americans were preferable to Limeys, so Jean Laffite sent the letter from the British to Governor Claiborne and offered the services of the pirate fleet and army to the Americans to defend Barataria as U.S. territory.

On September 15, 1814, British Captain W. H. Percy led a fleet of four sloops against Fort Bowyer, an American post built with wild hope on a sandpoint at the entrance to Mobile Bay. There 160 men served with twenty old Spanish guns, most of which were unusable.

Captain Percy landed a force of sixty British marines and about 150 Indians, with one howitzer as artillery. The ships came close in to fire on the fort, but soon two of them, the *Hermes* and the *Sophie,* were damaged by fire from the fort, and the *Sophie* was abandoned. So the Americans won the battle, with three of the fort's guns knocked out and 22 killed or wounded, while the British and Indians suffered more than 100 casualties.

General Jackson was anything but prescient. He regarded the Nicholls force as the wave of the future, and the attack to come as aimed at Mobile, not at New Orleans. The people of New Orleans asked him to pay attention to their defense, but he ignored them and left the problem completely in the hands of Governor Claiborne, while he worked on the defenses of the east, around Mobile.

Then warning came from Washington. There Secretary of State-and-War Monroe had strong indications that Admiral Cochrane's forces would descend on New Orleans after they had regrouped from the Washington expedition. Monroe wrote to Jackson, and sent him men and money, until Jackson had at his disposal 12,500 men. But Jackson was pigheaded and kept talking about attacking Pensacola. Monroe forbade it: "I hasten to communicate to you the directions of the President that you should at present take no measures which would involve this government in a contest with Spain."

Jackson paid no attention. Monroe did everything but order the general to go to New Orleans, and still Jackson remained at Mobile.

Against orders, Jackson marched on Pensacola on November 7, and after a brief struggle raised the American flag there. Colonel Nicholls blew up Fort Barrancas, six miles away, and sailed down the Apalachicola River to await developments.

General Jackson moved back to Mobile, but all his efforts were aimed at pacifying Indians and chasing Colonel Nicholls. He had no time to worry about New Orleans.

Madison and Monroe kept urging Jackson to move, and finally on November 22 he did go to New Orleans, but even then he left the main body of his troops at Mobile. He arrived in New Orleans on December 2. His troops were scattered all over the territory, from Mobile to Florida, chasing Indians, with a few at Baton Rouge. Nothing had been done for the defenses of New Orleans. The people were sullen and seemed indifferent—or that was how it looked to General Jackson. He was not in a hurry. He did not believe half of what he was told. That was why, on December 15, Jackson was out on a leisurely inspection of the area defenses—when the British struck.

Six American gunboats watched Lake Borgne, below New Orleans, through which the enemy ships must pass if intending to attack the city from the lakes. On December 10 they sighted fifty sails, and knew the British were coming. On December 13 the British transferred troops from heavy ships to light ones and moved them into Lake Borgne. The next day the British overtook the American gunboat flotilla and captured all of the boats.

Andrew Jackson was told about the capture the next day, and was summoned back to New Orleans. Now, the general seemed to be convinced that someone was about to attack New Orleans. He called for all his troops everywhere. He declared martial law in New Orleans, and became the dictator of the city.

Jackson was a very lucky man. From east and north came the troops he had been so loath to summon, hurrying to New Orleans. But also up came the British. By December 18 they had moved 7,000 men ashore on the Isle aux Poix in Lake Borgne. Two British officers had hired some Spanish fishermen to take them up by canoe to within six miles of New Orleans to reconnoiter. Three days later an American patrol of nine men visited the fishing village and learned that all the men were gone, all acting as pilots for the enemy.

On December 22 the British were moving; they captured the American patrol, moved up the bayou, and landed three miles from the Mississippi River. Sixteen hundred men of the light brigade formed up in columns and marched up the river; on December 23 they reached a point seven miles from New Orleans, without a gun, a trench, or a soldier, between them and their objective. By allowing the British to march to this point unopposed, General Jackson had just displayed the most appalling degree of incompetence in the matter of intelligence yet shown by an American commander. Had there been anyone above to relieve him, he most certainly would have been fired on the spot. But as it was, there was no one but General Jackson in sight.

News that the British had reached a plantation seven miles from New Orleans reached Jackson on the afternoon of December 23. Jackson then began to organize, and announced that he would attack. He had 5,000 men and two field pieces available. He detailed only about half that force to attack, leaving the other half to defend against a second British assault that he expected from the north.

Jackson also sent the schooner *Carolina,* with six twelve-pound guns on each broadside, downriver to a point where it controlled the British line of advance.

The British, having marched all day, lay down that night at the riverside plantation to sleep. They were awakened shortly after 8:00 P.M. by the booming of artillery. The battle that night was brisk, and the British suffered more casualties than the Americans, but it was not decisive. The Americans withdrew. The British force was intact. Next morning it prepared to move.

Reinforcements were brought up. Major General Pakenham arrived and took command. He had much more highly trained and disciplined troops, most of them veterans of the British peninsular campaign: 6,500 Europeans, plus 1,100 blacks from the Caribbean islands, and 1,200 Royal Navy marines and sailors.

Fortunately for General Jackson, his opponent, General Pakenham, was a British soldier of the European school. He did not move without artillery superiority, and the problem at the moment was that the Americans had the *Carolina* anchored opposite the British camp, and also now the sixteen-gun sloop *Louisiana,* which had been brought down the river to anchor a mile above the *Carolina.* Also Jackson's troops had placed the two six-pound field pieces to command the road. Pakenham sent back for artillery reinforcement, and this gave Jackson three days to work on his defenses. One of his first moves was to bring up more American guns to the bank of the river opposite the British camp.

On December 27 General Pakenham had his artillery, and they proceeded to destroy the *Carolina.* The *Louisiana* sailed back up the river, and the British troops began to march. They moved three miles, and came up against the American troops, who had thrown up breastworks. Instead of attacking, Pakenham retreated. He wanted more artillery. So three more days were spent by both sides moving artillery around. When the maneuvering was complete, the British had twenty-four guns, the Americans fifteen.

On January 1, 1815, the two sides staged an artillery battle, and when it was over the British retreated back to the position they had held before they destroyed the *Carolina.* General Pakenham decided to wait for reinforcements, although he had 5,000 very good troops ready to make the assault on New Orleans.

At New Orleans General Jackson had trouble finding enough weapons for his various militia units. Finally, he had 3,000 men with muskets on

the front line behind fortifications at least five feet high. Jackson expected
a flank attack and held back three regiments of Louisiana militia to meet
it. But he guessed wrong: he expected the flank attack by land, and the
British moved to his right, across the river. And when the attack was ready,
on January 8, General Pakenham had 8,000 men on the front and two
flanks. In the frontal attack, the British were mowed down as they followed
the old European infantry tactics, and General Pakenham was killed. On
the western shore, opposite New Orleans, the British advanced, but the
battle was bloody all the way. The British could have moved on and taken
New Orleans from the west bank, but in the heavy fighting they had lost
three major generals and more than 2,000 men, and the last remaining
major general, Lambert, at the end of the day had no stomach for more
fighting. Nor did Jackson, for when the British retreated he did not pursue.
The British pulled back to previous encampments, remained another two
weeks, and then, on February 8, 1815, made another attempt at the rear
of Fort Bowyer. That was the end of it. It failed and the land war was
over.

Meanwhile, at sea, the Americans and British continued to fight. The
forty-four-gun frigate *President* under Captain Stephen Decatur was captured by the British *Endymion* and three other ships of the blockading
squadron on January 15, and a few days later the U.S.S. *Constitution* fought
the smaller *Cyane* and *Levant,* and captured both.

But on February 13 a messenger arrived in American waters from
Europe, bearing dispatches to the secretary of state which announced that
a peace had been negotiated at Ghent, and that the War of 1812 was over.

On February 15 the treaty was sent to the U.S. Senate and approved
unanimously. The public was delighted, except along the Canadian frontier
where farmers on both sides had made large profits for three years by
supplying the armies of both sides with provisions.

In the American cities, which had been hard hit by the blockade, the
change was instant and enormous. In New York the price of sugar dropped
sixty percent. So did the price of tea. Export crops, like cotton and wheat,
which had been bottled up in America, also rose thirty or forty percent in
market value. So the War of 1812 ended. It had begun with enormous
enthusiasm in America and finished the same way.

Despite appearances of little change, the war had been very expensive
to the American public at large; it had also cost England about £10 million.
One of the major reasons for the war, impressment of American seamen,
was virtually resolved by the surrender of Napoleon and the end of the
war with France. Britain was not impressing seamen, she was paying them
off. The big issues of the peace became territorial claims, the matter of
fisheries, and navigation of the Mississippi River. Since the end of the

Revolutionary War the British had been reevaluating the concessions she had made therein, and hoping to recover some of the enormous block of territory ceded to the Americans. The British expeditions from Canada and the attack on New Orleans were made in the hope of capturing territory to be used in trading for western territorial concessions. But the British efforts had failed, just as the American territorial expeditions had, and so the claims were ultimately adjusted to the reasonable satisfaction of both sides.

Aside from the matter of freedom of the seas, the prime positive result of the war for the Americans was the rise of a new respect for American military prowess on land and sea. When the Americans had gone into the war they were regarded contemptuously by British, French, and other highly militarized nations. But the capture of the British fleet on Lake Erie, the individual exploits of the frigates and other fighting ships, and the stalemates and American victories in the fighting on land had proved an American military prowess hitherto unsuspected.

One loss was in the United States adventure into a new overseas imperialism. For when Captain Porter's men of the *Essex* left the Marquesas, having claimed the territory for America, there was nothing of the American presence left there but the flag and the fort. The flag was soon destroyed by the Polynesians, and the fort pulled down. A few years later the French, in the European rush to claim Pacific island possessions, came into these waters to claim Tahiti and a number of other Polynesian isles. By that time the American claim to Nuahiva was long forgotten.

CHAPTER 10

Nice Little War

The United States came out of the War of 1812 with a certain new cockiness that had not been apparent before that struggle. In the last days of the eighteenth century even President George Washington, certainly no moral coward, had to face the problem posed by the piratical actions of the handful of local despots who ruled the North African shores of the Mediterranean in the name of the Ottoman Empire. They had no respect for the American flag and captured many American vessels; they used the ships, stole the cargoes, and kept the crews in slavery. There were two ways to deal with the Barbary pirates: one could, as did England and France, send punitive expeditions to force the piratical rulers to agree to respect the flag. Or one could pay tribute to the pirates and thus assure freedom of movement. President Washington had agreed with Congress that at the moment it was more expedient to pay the tribute than to fight.

But in 1815 the American attitude had undergone a profound change. The U.S. Navy at sea had proved its worth. The United States had a large number of ships in service. So why not deal with the Barbary pirates in the manner they deserved? Thus began a series of the most exciting naval adventures in the history of the U.S. Navy, the Barbary Wars.

The Barbary Wars held one lasting lesson to America: never pay tribute to despots. Thus the expeditions of Commodore Preble and his boys proved of significance in American history, alas, only to be largely forgotten by the "historyless" generations of the late twentieth century, some of whose representatives do not even know that North and South America are two con-

tinents, much less the historical significance of the breakdown of the Ottoman Empire on the shores of the Mediterranean.

*   *   *

The end of the War of 1812 brought many a toast to "Peace, Commerce, and Prosperity" and the beginning of what a Boston newspaper called the Era of Good Feelings, a slogan that captured the public imagination and is still used by historians.

The cost of the War of 1812 to the American government was remarkably small. Never had more than 30,000 men served in the army during the entire three-year war. Never was a battle fought engaging more than 4,000 American troops. Altogether about 1,600 Americans were killed and about 3,500 wounded, excluding privateers, for whom no figures were kept. But among the privateers the losses could not have been more than a few hundred. The real losses were to merchants and citizens along the eastern seaboard and the Canadian border; no account was ever made of the houses and farms burned and livestock appropriated or driven away by British troops, nor of the burned boats and docks and warehouses along the eastern seaboard. But as for public loss, the White House was rebuilt and so was the partly burned national Capitol.

March 2, 1815, was the day that the Madison administration said would be propitious for the resumption of coastal shipping, after the ratification of the Treaty of Ghent and the process of informing the British had been completed. That day fleets of merchant ships put out from Boston, New York, Philadelphia, and Baltimore; the docks were lined with cheering people as the ships sailed out. The marine insurance companies began writing policies again, the customs houses were opened and swept out, and shipping news returned to the daily newspapers. In the middle of the month the fleets bound outward for Europe and beyond began to sail, and by the end of May the American ports were jammed with vessels from every European nation.

As one contemporary put it, by April 1815 it would have been hard to convince an utter stranger that there had been a war involving America. Business at home boomed and American ships again sailed the seven seas. On November 14 the New York Customs House receipts set a new record: twenty square-rigged ships came up the bay, and that day the value of property entered at the Customs was twice as great as ever before entered in one day.

Still, there were a few military problems remaining, particularly those that concerned nations that had guessed wrong about the course of the War of 1812. Principal among those abroad was the dey of Algiers.

For seventeen years before 1812 the Americans had been paying tribute to the dey in return for his promise, generally kept, to refrain from seizure of American ships in the eastern Atlantic and in the Mediterranean. But when America declared war on Britain in 1812, the British had already been working to undermine this treaty relationship. The dey's advisers came up with a "legal" formula that would allow Algiers to end the treaty unilaterally and then prey on American shipping—which, in effect, would make them an ally of Britain in the war. The mullahs thought long and hard, and found the solution in the calendar. The Christian calendar computes time by the sun, but the Moslem calendar reckons by the moon. Thus the Moslem year was shorter than the Christian year, and over seventeen years six months had been lost, which meant to the dey that he could claim $27,000 more than he had received in the past seventeen years.

So the dey called in Tobias Lear, the American consul at Algiers, and made the demand, sure the Americans would refuse. But Tobias Lear was a consul of the old school, certain that Congress would do anything to avoid a fight. So immediately Tobias Lear paid up the $27,000, to the chagrin of the dey and his English friends.

A new excuse for breach of relations with the United States had to be found. The dey called Tobias Lear once more into the presence. The quality of American goods shipped to Algiers in lieu of money had not been as promised, said the grand vizier.

All right, said Tobias Lear. The American government was ready to make restitution. Let the Algerines state their demands.

As the dey's advisers were shaking their heads over the problem, into Algiers came two English ships loaded with naval stores, anchors, cables, guns, ammunition, and all that the dey would need to put his pirate fleet back into operation, a gift from one emperor to another.

The dey was delighted. Make any excuses you wish to the Americans, he told his advisers, but get Lear out and let the raiding begin at once.

And so it did, but not very satisfactorily considering the volume of American trade in the past. Before long the dey had inveigled from the British five frigates, six sloops, and a schooner, on the promise of using them against the Americans. But the war had brought an embargo on American shipping and trade and the British blockade of the American shores, so there were precious few American vessels in the Mediterranean during the next three years. The British had let New England alone in the beginning, so the brig *Edwin* stood out from Salem bound for Mediterranean climes, and she was captured by one of the dey's new warships. The *Edwin* and cargo were sold to the benefit of the dey, and the crew of ten men were sold into slavery. But that was all. The dey's men were hard put to find Americans, and the only other one who came into their hands was an unlucky American citizen aboard a Spanish vessel. When the vessel was seized he was sold into slavery. The Algerines broadened their activity to include Spaniards, Portuguese, Frenchmen, any ships of any nations but England, whom they respected. By 1815, the Algerine navy and its admiral, Rais Hammida, were hated and feared throughout the Mediterranean and eastern Atlantic.

If, as the Madison administration now declared, Americans had won the freedom of the seas, something was going to have to be done about the Barbary pirates.

Word of the mistreatment of Americans had reached Washington, but in 1813 and 1814 there was little to be done. The American navy was tied up with the war against England. President Madison did not forget, however, nor did Congress. The war ended, and suddenly the United States had what seemed to Americans an enormous navy on hand with no employment. Five days after the proclamation of peace with England, Congress voted to deal with Algiers and the other Barbary States once and for all.

This was a new America speaking.

To Boston, where Commodore William Bainbridge was stationed with a squadron of ships, went the word to sail for the Mediterranean. To New York, where Commodore Stephen Decatur had the flagship *Guerrière* and another squadron, went a similar message. On May 20, 1815, Decatur put to sea with ten ships, mounting 210 guns. The squadron ran across the Atlantic to the Azores, the top of the Barbary pirate hunting ground.

No luck there. Commodore Decatur then sailed to Tangier, Morocco, and visited the American consul. He learned that Rais Hammida had passed the Strait of Gibraltar two days earlier in the forty-six-gun British-built frigate *Mashouda*. Decatur hurried back to his flagship and set sail. At Gibraltar he learned that the Algerine fleet was off Cape Gatta, the old hunting grounds. He also saw two Algerine dispatch boats heading out, one for the admiral's fleet and the other toward Algiers, obviously to warn the dey that the Americans were coming.

Decatur hurried along, and on the morning of June 17 his lookouts sighted the *Mashouda*. The appearance of this American squadron did nothing to excite the crew of the Algerine frigate, which meant that Decatur had beaten the Algerine dispatch boat to the scene, and that Rais Hammida believed the squadron belonged to his English friends.

Commodore Decatur then issued orders to his ship commanders. They were to sail down on the Algerine ship, and when they were challenged were to hoist the British flag first, maintaining the element of surprise for as long as possible.

Along they came, and the Algerines challenged. Up went the Union Jacks on every vessel—save one. The captain of the *Constellation* had run up the American flag instead. The Algerines were immediately alerted. The *Mashouda* began loading on sail, and headed toward Cartagena to escape. But the captain of the *Constellation* retrieved his error by opening fire as soon as he came within range, and the shots from the long guns had some effect.

Commodore Decatur told the captain of the *Guerrière* to hold his fire until they were within broadside range, and the ship sailed on, guns silent, toward the enemy. When the *Guerrière* was yardarm-to-yardarm with the *Mashouda,* Decatur fired a broadside, and then another. The shot and grape did enormous damage to the Algerine ship, and many men were killed, including Admiral Rais Hammida. Still, the Moors tried to escape, expecting that they would all be killed by the Americans. They came straight across the path of the brig *Epervier,* which fired broadside after broadside directly into the Algerine flagship until it was a wreck and struck its colors.

A prize crew was placed aboard the *Mashouda* and she was sent into Cartagena. The American squadron sailed on, looking for the rest of the Algerine fleet.

Two days passed with nothing sighted. On June 19 a single sail was spotted off Cape Palos, and the American squadron headed that way. The ship they were chasing, the *Estido,* moved into water so shallow that the frigates could not continue in but had to leave the battle to the four smaller vessels, *Torch, Spark, Spitfire,* and *Epervier.* As these came up, the Moors ran their brig aground and got into their boats to escape. The Americans captured about half the crew of 180 men, floated the stranded ship, and sent her to Cartagena also.

Decatur now decided it was time to have a talk with the dey of Algiers, so he sailed toward Africa. On June 28 he arrived at Algiers.

The inner harbor was a defensive hive, bristling with a fortress and a mole on which were placed 220 big guns. Another 300 guns were mounted in the high wall that surrounded the city.

The squadron was left outside, ready to sail in and fight if need be. Decatur in the *Guerrière* ran up the Swedish flag on the mainmast and a white flag on the foremast (the former being, again, a common deceit, and the latter an indication of a wish to parley and not fight at the moment). Inside, boats were sent ashore and the Algerine captain of the port and the Swedish consul came out to the *Guerrière.* Decatur identified himself.

"Where is your squadron?" Decatur asked the port captain.

"By this time safe in some neutral port," said the port captain, for word of the coming of the Americans had reached Algiers and he assumed it had also reached Admiral Rais Hammida.

"Not all of them," said Commodore Decatur. "We have captured the *Mashouda* and the *Estido*."*

The Algerines would not believe him, until Decatur produced the first lieutenant of the *Mashouda*, who confirmed the capture of the Algerine flagship and the death of the admiral.

The port captain was stunned, but not for long. In a few moments he was suggesting that Decatur and his officers go ashore and begin negotiations for "peace" at the dey's palace.

But Decatur had learned at Tripoli; he knew his Barbary pirates. If he went to the dey's palace he might very well be clapped into a prison cell, held for ransom, and thus become a subject of barter for the dey.

No, said Decatur, if there was to be peace, it would be arranged right there on the deck of the *Guerrière*. He sent the port captain to the palace to tell the dey the conditions of negotiation and to bring back officials empowered to make terms.

The next day the port captain, who had been second in command of the Algerine navy and was now first, returned to the frigate empowered to negotiate.

Decatur laid down the terms:

1. The Americans would pay no more tribute to Algiers.
2. All American prisoners must be set free immediately, without ransom.
3. The dey must repay in money the value of the goods and property taken from the American prisoners.
4. The dey must pay $10,000 to the owners of the *Edwin* for her seizure.
5. The commerce of America must never again be molested by Algiers.

Coming from a nation that had until now been supine under the Algerine foot, these demands were a great shock. They were too harsh, said the port captain. The war against America was the fault of the late Dey Hadji Ali. The new dey was Omar Pasha. All that had happened was the fault of Hadji Ali.

Too bad, said Commodore Decatur. Those were the terms.

It was too much and too fast, said the dey's representative. His head was spinning. He must have three hours to consider the matter.

*Fletcher Pratt, *Preble's Boys: Commodore Preble and the Birth of American Sea Power*. p. 196.

Not a minute, said Decatur. Not one minute. The envoy could go ashore, and if the dey accepted the terms he was to fly a white flag and return immediately. The port captain was given a prepared copy of the treaty and shown where the dey was to sign, and then he was sent on his way.

An hour passed. No port captain. No white flag. An Algerine ship approached the harbor, and Decatur could see that it was loaded with soldiers. He ordered the *Guerrière* cleared for action. The gunports were opened and the carronades of the frigate rolled out. The men were sent up into the chains and told to prepare to raise anchor. The canvas was unfurled and the yards were manned.

When the Algerines ashore saw the *Guerrière* was getting ready for sea, a small boat set out from the mole, with a white flag flying. In the boat was the port captain, and he had with him the ten prisoners from the *Edwin*. The port captain presented the signed treaty.

That day Lieutenant John Templar Shubrick of the *Epervier* was given the treaty to take to Washington immediately, and custody of the ten freed prisoners, who were to be delivered to their home port. He sailed away. On July 12 the *Epervier* passed Gibraltar, but she was never to reach port. Later, the British West Indian fleet reported encountering an American brig during a hurricane at sea, and the conjecture was that the *Epervier* had foundered during this heavy storm.

Decatur now had some more scores to settle with the Barbary rulers. Tunis had declared herself to be neutral in the late War of 1812, but she had taken the side of the British. The American privateer *Abellino* had sent several prizes into Tunis, but had later learned that the bey of Tunis had turned the ships over to the British cruiser *Lyon*. Now the bey would pay for his two-faced behavior. Decatur dropped anchor in Tunis harbor and demanded, and received within twelve hours, $46,000, the value of those prizes.

Having warned Tunis against any further violations of treaty, Decatur went on to Tripoli. That principality's crimes against the Americans were more serious than those of Tunis; the bashaw had given two prizes taken by the *Abellino* to the British, and had forced the American consul to lower the American flag in Tripoli.

The price, said Decatur, was $30,000 for the prizes and a thirty-one-gun salute to the American flag.

The bashaw threatened. He would declare war on the United States, he said. He had 20,000 soldiers ready to make war.

All right, said Decatur, and he prepared to take the *Guerrière* to sea, and bring in the squadron to bombard Tripoli.

The bashaw remembered the bombardments of 1804 and changed his mind. Decatur grandly reduced the price of the prizes to $25,000 and the salute. The Bashaw complied and released ten Christians he was holding as slaves. None of them were Americans.

The troubles with the Barbary States seemed to be resolved, but Decatur was not convinced that these rulers would live up to their promises. Therefore he went no further than Gibraltar, where he found Commodore Bainbridge's squadron, which had just arrived. The captains agreed to leave about half the ships in the Mediterranean just in case of trouble, and then the two commodores sailed back to the United States.

Decatur obviously knew his Barbary rulers. During the winter, in the belief that the Americans were long gone, the dey of Algiers disavowed the treaty he had made. The residual squadron, under Captain John Shaw, arrived at Algiers, and Captain Shaw delivered to the American consul the treaty signed and sealed by Congress. The dey said the treaty was invalid. His grand vizier returned it to the American consul with such vituperation that the consul hauled down his flag and went aboard the frigate *Java,* which had brought the treaty into Algiers.

Captain Shaw had left his squadron outside, where it was apparently unnoticed by the Algerines. Now he sailed out and brought the squadron back, preparing to bombard the mole, and he arranged the ships' boats, loaded with guns, to attack the land and shore batteries. All was set for the attack, when the commander of a French frigate nearby learned of the American preparations and warned the dey. Immediately the dey changed his mind once again and sent word that he would submit to the terms of the treaty.

Shaw then went on to Tunis where he related the events of this Algerine visit and was assured that Tunis had no intention of violating the treaties with the United States. The same was true of Tripoli, said the bashaw. So Captain Shaw sailed away, but he let it be known that four American ships would remain on the Mediterranean station; that they did, for the next few seasons.

There was no more trouble with the Barbary States for 170 years, until Colonel Muammar Qaddafi began to emulate his predecessor, the bashaw of Tripoli.

CHAPTER 11

The Seminole War

The years after the end of the War of 1812 were generally quiet on the North American continent, except in the southeast corner, where there was considerable confusion as to claims staked by the British, the French, and the Spanish in earlier years. Because of this confusion, the expansion of the Southern states of Georgia and the Carolinas was in doubt. The Americans wanted that land along the Gulf of Mexico and the Florida peninsula. In fact, they were determined to have it. But the Spanish still controlled much of the territory, and they encouraged the Indians to resist American claims and American expansion.

Thus developed the Seminole War, one of the most nagging and exhausting minor military excursions ever to trouble the United States government. Out of this struggle, and in a way because of it, came the Monroe Doctrine, which rejected the generally held European view that the Latin American territories of Spain were fair game for colonization. Thus America, more or less by accident, developed one of the strongest aspects of its international policy, or what was a strong policy until it was allowed to erode in the years after World War II and was finally disavowed as useless by the administration of President Jimmy Carter. This attitude came as a shock to many; the United States is now reaping the harvest and it threatens to become a bitter one.

*   *   *

As the War of 1812 ended, American relations with Spain settled into a peculiarly tangled snarl. Not since 1808 had the United States and Spain maintained diplomatic relations; the breach had come with the conquest of Spain by Napoleon. That conquest and the ascension of the Spanish throne by Joseph Bonaparte had brought rebellion in Spanish America. American shipowners, many of them eager to turn a dollar, no matter how questionably, had cleared vessels at the customs houses at Baltimore and New Orleans as merchant ships, but what merchant ships they were: armed to the teeth. Outside, in international waters, they would hoist the flag of Mexico or of New Granada (Colombia), and then begin plundering the ships of Spain.

But by 1815 Ferdinand VII had brought the legitimate succession back to Spain and diplomatic relations were resumed. The first demand of Spain was that the U.S. government stop its privateers from preying on Spanish commerce. The major problem concerned a pair of freebooters named Jose Alvarez de Toledo and Jose Manuel Herrera, who were recruiting American citizens for filibustering expeditions into Spanish colonies. This matter of American and American-based filibustering—the overthrow of governments in Latin America—was to trouble the United States for many years.

But all in all, the period from 1815 to 1824 was about the quietest in American history in terms of internal and external conflicts. All that energy devoted earlier to conflict was put to building steamboats, canals, lighthouses, and ports, and to extending the frontiers of America west. The Era of Internal Improvements, it was called. If the term seems odd, it meant this was the beginning of the Industrial Revolution that swept across the Western world. In a military sense one of the major developments would be Samuel Colt's invention of the repeating revolver and the assembly line to produce muskets.

The great conflict of the era was a result of the extension of frontiers and the push of the settlers. By the Treaty of Fort Jackson, the Creek Indians had given up several million acres of land that abutted the Spanish holdings in Florida. The idea of the Americans had been most statesmanlike: to put this land buffer between Americans and the Spanish possessions. It might have worked if the recalcitrant members of the Creek nation, who rejected the treaty, had not moved into the Spanish side of the border and joined the Seminole Indians.*

These Creek had been recruited by Colonel Edward Nicholls in his

*Seminole is not a tribal name. It means "runaway" and refers to Indians of various tribes who had sought sanctuary in the Florida swamps, and black escaped slaves who joined them and were accepted as members of the group.

drive to capture Mobile, on the promise that once Britain had won the War of 1812, she would restore to the Indians all the lands taken by the Americans.

When the War of 1812 ended, the legal position of Colonel Nicholls was definitely in doubt. Yet he remained on the Apalachicola River with his little flotilla and his troops. In the name of His Britannic Majesty, Nicholls concluded a treaty with Chief Billy Bowlegs of the Seminole. He rebuilt an old fort on the Apalachicola. He also interceded for the Indians with Colonel Benjamin Hawkins, the Indian agent for the United States in the area, to secure return of Creek lands. He made so much trouble that President Madison took up the Nicholls case with the British, and in the summer of 1815 Nicholls was ordered back to London. He took with him a number of Creek chiefs and left behind more than 750 kegs of powder, 2,500 muskets, and many carbines, pistols, swords, and other military equipment.

So the Seminole and their friends were to have arms. Among their friends were several large colonies of escaped black slaves, about a thousand in all. They lived on the Apalachicola and they were the first to find the abandoned fort with its armaments. They took possession and soon began plundering the frontier of Georgia. They were no longer "friends"; they were foe to the whites, and to the Indians alike.

In 1816 this matter was called to the attention of Secretary of War W. H. Crawford, and he ordered General Jackson to do something about the problem. Jackson then asked the Spanish military commander at Pensacola to suppress the black bandits.

At this time, government and settlers were interested in taking possession of the new lands ceded to the United States by the Creek Indians. They had already forgotten the "buffer zone." General Edmund P. Gaines was supervising the building of a series of blockhouses and forts, and it was his task to protect the surveyors who were running out the section lines and township boundaries of the new lands. In March, Gaines sent Lieutenant Colonel D. L. Clinch and the 4th U.S. Infantry down to the Chattahoochee River. Gaines also asked for permission to build a post on the Apalachicola, near the border with Spanish Florida. The fort, called Fort Scott, was built, not far from the fort held by the blacks. General Jackson also wrote to General Gaines, authorizing him to destroy the black fort and to capture the blacks in the area and restore them as slaves to their "rightful owners."

Supply immediately became a problem. The only sensible way to supply the fort on the Apalachicola, where the Flint and Chattahoochee rivers join, was by sea from New Orleans. Late in June 1816, the schooners *General Pike* and *Semilanto* were loaded, and sent out under Sailing Master Jairus (sic) Loomis and two gunboats.

On July 10 the convoy reached the mouth of the Apalachicola River, where Loomis received a message from Colonel Clinch at Fort Scott: the Indians along the river were dancing the war dance and drinking war medicine. General Gaines was sure the black fort would try to stop the passage of the convoy, so he had ordered Colonel Clinch to march down to the fort. If the fleet was fired on, then Colonel Clinch would burn the fort to the ground. So Clinch now asked Loomis not to enter the river until he reached the fort.

The plan was sensible, but Clinch was delayed. In the meantime a boat crew coming ashore to fill water kegs was attacked by the blacks, and three men were killed and one captured.

Finally, on July 16, Colonel Clinch came floating down the Apalachicola. He met a party of Seminole who were out to take their fort back from the blacks. Near the black fort, the Americans captured a black man wearing a white scalp at his belt. Thus they learned of the attack on Loomis's water boat.

Clinch then surrounded the fort. He sent for the gunboats at the mouth of the river and they came up. The blacks refused to surrender and fired on the Americans. So Captain Loomis's gunboats began shooting. The fort was a tribute to the engineers who built it: the shot from the small guns simply bounced off. Loomis then decided on another tack. He would burn down the wooden fort. Several shot were heated red and fired. One hit the magazine in the fort, and 700 barrels of gunpowder exploded. The whole fort went up in flame and debris. When the smoke cleared the black community inside the fort was gone. Two hundred seventy men, women, and children had disappeared. Most of the sixty-four wounded survivors died shortly afterward.

Among the unhurt survivors was the black leader, Garcon, and a Choctaw Indian chief. In view of the terrible end of the black community in the fort, Colonel Clinch was inclined to be lenient, until he learned that the men of the boat crew had been first covered with tar, and then burned alive by the blacks. So Clinch turned the Choctaw chief and Garcon over to the Seminole, who put them to an equally horrible Seminole death.

One hot cannonball had solved the problem of the black terrorists on the frontier, and the Seminole seemed quite awed. The border was quiet, and it seemed quite likely that all Florida would soon become part of the United States through negotiations with Spain. Tennessee land speculators, awaiting that day, came down by the hundreds to take over land.

All this activity played into the hands of a filibuster named Gregor MacGregor, who had been deeply involved in several of the South American rebellions against Spain. MacGregor appeared in Baltimore in 1817 to raise an army "to wrest the Floridas from Spain." What a patriot! By

June he had enough men to sail with a small fleet of ships for Amelia Island, Florida. He landed there on June 29 with fifty men and after marching ten miles reached the town of Fernandina. There MacGregor demanded the surrender of Don Francisco de Morales, governor of the island.

Who demanded? asked the governor.

"I, Gregor MacGregor, commander in chief of all the forces, both naval and military, destined to effect the independence of the Floridas, duly commissioned by the constituted authorities of the Republics of Mexico, Buenos Ayres, New Granada, and Venezuela."

What Mexico, Buenos Ayres, New Granada, and Venezuela had to do with Florida, no one explained. But Gregor MacGregor needed no logic; he had charisma. "Victory or Death" was his motto. Each of his men wore on his left arm a shield of red cloth with a wreath of oak and laurel leaves embroidered in yellow silk. MacGregor announced a blockade of the entire Florida coast from Amelia Island to the Perdido River.

But MacGregor found that charisma did not supply ammunition and food, and soon Gregor MacGregor disappeared, to be replaced by Louis Aury, another filibuster, who, after he extended his empire to Galveston, decided to take Santo Domingo. This plan fell apart, and in 1818 American troops would replace these freebooters and hold the whole empire in trust for the king of Spain.

Meanwhile, in 1817, on the edge of the old Creek lands, where they bordered the Seminole territory, all was not well. A band of renegade Seminole set up at Fowltown, danced the war dance, and threatened the Fort Scott garrison, now commanded by Major Twiggs. The major descended on Fowltown, demanded its peaceful surrender, was refused, and captured the place. The Indians in the back country danced the war dance and raised 2,700 braves, who vowed to go out and massacre the whites and get their lands back. Thus began the Seminole War.

General Gaines came down to Fowltown. The Indians attacked the American troops as they crossed the Flint River. Americans read in the newspapers of the story of a boat that carried seven women, four children, and forty American troops up the Apalachicola River to Fort Scott. It was attacked by Seminole, who fired from ambush, killed most of the soldiers and their officers with the first volley, boarded the boat, and bashed the brains out of the children. All the women were shot and then scalped, except one who was carried off into captivity. Four men managed to plunge into the river, swim across, and escape to tell the story.

The Indians attacked three boatloads of supplies coming from Mobile. They attacked another military party. When word reached Washington, Secretary of War John C. Calhoun called on Andrew Jackson to take command of the American forces at Fort Scott and pacify the Indians.

Jackson, whose views about the future of Florida were well known, was delighted to serve.

Jackson then moved, sometimes without duly constituted authority, a matter that was to plague him politically later. But he moved. By January 1818 he and a thousand men were marching to Fort Scott. He arrived early in March at Fort Scott and assumed command. Food grew short, so he went into the countryside and foraged. He found the old black fort, and rebuilt it as Fort Gadsden. Ships came from New Orleans with an armed escort; thus reinforced, Andrew Jackson was ready to fight.

General Jackson marched to Saint Marks. General Gaines marched to Fowltown, and burned the place down. Jackson insisted on occupying Saint Marks. Here Jackson found a number of Englishmen who were actively promoting Spanish and Seminole interests against the United States. He also found two Indian leaders who had presided over the torture of Americans in the past, the Seminole prophet Hellis Hajo and chief Hemollemico. They were captured, and, by Jackson's order, hanged.

Jackson then marched on to Suwannee, the capital of Billy Bowlegs, the high chief of the Seminole. His men marched across a hundred miles of swampy wilderness. On April 17 they reached Suwannee and found it deserted. An English trader had warned the Seminole of the coming of the Americans, and they had disappeared into the Florida swamp.

Jackson burned the Indian town, seized several thousand bushels of corn, and declared the Seminole War over. He marched back to Saint Marks, where he court-martialed and hanged two British citizens who had been selling arms to the Indians; then he declared peace. At the end of May General Jackson was at Fort Gadsden when he received astonishing news: Peace had not come to Florida. Five hundred Indians were on the loose, plundering and murdering American citizens, aided by the Spanish governor of Pensacola. So Jackson marched again. This time the Spanish governor threatened that he must quit West Florida or go to war. Jackson marched on. On May 24, 1818, Jackson's military force entered Pensacola without opposition, for the governor had fled to Fort Carlos de Barancas. Jackson brought up two field guns, and in twenty-four hours had the fort in hand. Soon he was on his way home, declaring peace once more.

In Washington, Spanish Minister Don Luis de Onis learned of this activity—which had occurred within the precincts of Spanish Florida. He read about it in the newspapers, specifically the *National Intelligencer*. Don Luis then called on Secretary of State John Quincy Adams and asked for an explanation. None was forthcoming. Don Luis protested the violation of Spanish soil, the capture of Spanish citizens, the destruction of Spanish property, and the capture of Spanish forts.

The reply from the Americans?

Silence.

Silence because President Monroe and the cabinet did not know what to say. Several cabinet members, including Secretary of War Calhoun, said that Jackson had utterly disobeyed the orders from Calhoun, exceeded his instructions, and apparently tried to start a war in the hope that he would then be sent to conquer Mexico.

Some congressmen lamented Jackson's execution of the Seminole prophet and chief. The general had interfered unconstitutionally with the native religion, said these seekers of social justice. The arguments against all that Jackson had done in Florida might almost have been transposed to the twentieth-century debate about American policy in Latin America: the invasion of Grenada, the activity in Nicaragua and El Salvador.

The Monroe administration was torn. Jackson said that he was simply suppressing Indian incursions against Americans. Privately, however, it was known that Jackson believed it was high time the Spaniards were thrown out of Florida and he was simply helping in the expansion of America into territory it must have.

The independent General Jackson—planter, Tennessee politician, and general—was a character very much like General Douglas MacArthur. His strengths and virtues were similar. The early nineteenth century was not blessed with psychiatrists, but had there been one in Washington, he might have seen in Jackson the same combination of paranoia and enormous ego that marked MacArthur's career. Jackson's quarrel with Washington had the same earmarks as MacArthur's quarrel with President Truman: the man on the scene (Jackson) seeing only his point of view, and bucking like a bronco against higher authority.

In the meetings of the Monroe cabinet, John C. Calhoun criticized Jackson. Everyone wanted to disavow Jackson except Secretary of State Adams. Ultimately the Adams view prevailed, and the cabinet united behind it. The Spanish government protested Jackson's activities, and the two nations were close to war, but the furor died down. One reason for the return to calm was Spain's growing weakness. Her government did not really want a war with anyone. A contributing factor was the slowness of transportation. By the time a heated message had been received, the sender had often cooled down. Because all messages went by ship, ambassadors and ministers had to have thick skins and much more power than the envoys of the late twentieth century, when communication anywhere is a matter of seconds, and when the risk of erring by shooting from the hip is so extreme.

The Florida matter became a cause célèbre in the American Congress over the use of troops to march into foreign territory, no matter the provocation to American citizens. The business of Congress was put aside for more than a month that fall of 1818 while every man, it seemed, had his impassioned say, most of the verbiage being anti-Jackson. The debates

were of the sort that raged in America in the 1980s over American involvement in Central America against notably hostile interests. In the end
the Florida issue was laid on the table in the House of Representatives,
and there it died, but not in the hearts of the protagonists in the American
political battles, nor in world affairs. For when word reached Washington
that Jackson had put two British nationals to death, the United States and
Britain were in the midst of negotiations over international fisheries, which
was not a lightweight issue. The British had driven American fishermen
off the Newfoundland banks with the sixty-four-gun ship of the line *Menai.*
Dozens of American fishing boats were captured and sent to Halifax for
trial. That series of events had led to the 1818 negotiations for a fishing
treaty.

The treaty was also to cover the matter of the northern boundary of
the United States. Both America and Canada had sent traders to the
Northwest country. John Jacob Astor had opened a fur trading post at
Astoria on the south shore of the mouth of the Columbia River. The area
had been in dispute for years, furs had been hijacked, ships had been
seized, men had been killed over the question of the boundary and control
of these rich lands.

In spite of the difficulties, both the British treaty, which temporarily
solved the western lands question, and a treaty with Spain giving Florida
to the United States were worked out in 1819, and by 1821, Florida was
safely a part of the United States.

As noted, the next fifteen years were peaceful years for Americans.
The decay of the Spanish empire brought some new problems, for various
European nations were looking to South and Central America and the
Caribbean for new colonies. British Foreign Secretary George Canning
was the leader of the movement to prevent a European rush. The American
administration of President James Monroe supported Canning, but did not
trust the British. The Americans believed that secretly the British were
trying to set up a situation in which they would be welcomed in coming to
Latin America to take over.

Because of all this ferment, in December 1823, President Monroe announced in his annual message to Congress the Monroe Doctrine:

1. The American continents would no longer be considered subjects
   for future colonization by European powers.

2. The political systems of the Americas were essentially different
   from those of Europe (there were no kings).

3. The United States would consider dangerous to its peace and safety
   any attempt on the part of a European power to extend its system
   or control to any point in the Western Hemisphere.

4. The United States would not interfere with existing colonies or relationships between European powers and the new world. She would not interfere in the internal affairs of European nations. She would not take part in European wars *of solely foreign interest.*

And so, in this period of peace, the United States enunciated a hemispheric military and political doctrine that was to serve it well for more than a hundred years, with only one major violation (World War I and the occupations by the United States of Germany and parts of the USSR after World War I), until World War II brought the United States into a European war, and the peace settlements turned the world upside down.

CHAPTER 12

Pirates, Yes; Indians, No

The 1820s were remarkable for several developments in American military attitudes and policies. Alfred Thayer Mahan, the sage of American naval policy (trade follows the flag), had not yet appeared on the scene, but merchants in Boston and naval officers on the Potomac agreed that it was wise and important to send American naval power around the world to establish the American name. Once the Barbary pirates were put down, there were the resources to do just this. There were also problems, including piracy in the Caribbean, and as far west as the Spice Islands of Java and Sumatra. Thus the American navy found a new role, protection of American shipping interests, and this involved such disparate moves as expeditions to Antarctica and missions to suppress piracy in Sumatra.

It was gradually becoming apparent to the government in Washington that the Indian policies it followed were self-defeating, but as the reader will observe, in this period there was no real attempt to make a change. America was pushing westward as fast as the settlers could go. There was no stopping the juggernaut . . .

*   *   *

Except for the Seminole War and minor trouble with other Indians, America enjoyed what was for America a long period of peace—thirty years—between the War of 1812 and the next one.

A large area west of Missouri and Arkansas had been set apart for the Indians, and divided into tracts larger than the territory remaining to each nation in the East. Most of the Indians went west. The Cherokee of Georgia and Alabama and the Creek remained, unwilling to give up their historic homelands.

The large American navy was not immediately cut down, first because of the troubles with the Barbary pirates, and then, following their suppression, because of the rise of piracy in the Caribbean and the Pacific. The end of the War of 1812 in 1815 had caught the navy building big ships. The first seventy-four-gun ship of the line, *Independence,* became Commodore Bainbridge's flagship in the Mediterranean, and the sight of this great ship did much to keep the Barbary States quiescent.

In 1816, when the Barbary pirates were finally being put down, the customs receipts of the federal government had been $36 million. Five years later they had fallen to $13 million in the postwar depression. Since customs receipts were the basic income of the federal government, and deficit spending in peacetime was a long way off, the navy was cut back along with all other services of federal government.

The main tasks of the navy were the suppression of piracy—endemic in the Caribbean and the Pacific—and suppression of the slave trade, which was really the same thing. In 1807 Britain had outlawed the slave trade in the British empire. By 1820, the aid of the American government had been enlisted, and Congress declared the oceangoing slave trade to be piracy, and said that any American citizen found guilty of engaging in the slave trade was to be declared a pirate and hanged. In 1820, President Monroe began sending American naval vessels to the shores of Africa to watch the slave trade and to capture slavers. The problem was that some American naval officers came from slaveholding families, and at the time that they were asked to suppress the slave trade the great debate on slavery in America was beginning and North and South were lining up on opposing sides. Many of these officers simply ignored their duty and nothing happened. There was also the problem of search of vessels on the high seas, to which the United States was extremely sensitive because of past British impressment. So the American attempts to suppress the slave trade were not notably successful, and the trade continued to flourish, with the principal markets in the Caribbean islands and the American South.

There were real pirates, too, of the Blackbeard school, who looted vessels of every nation if they happened to come across them. In 1821 the American navy decided to do something about this raiding, and sent a succession of squadrons into the Caribbean. Commodore Henley went first, then Commodore Biddle, Commodore Porter, and Commodore Warrington. By 1825 the men of the skull and crossbones were flying their flags no more around Cuba and the Caribbean waters.

*   *   *

America and Britain quarreled over the northwestern boundary of the United States, but this was finally settled. There really were no American military excursions; the Indians were quiescent because the Americans were busily engaged in building canals, cities, and there was still plenty of public land left from the purchases made years earlier from the Indians.

By 1819 the picture was changing; the drive west speeded up, and Congress began weaseling on its previous Indian policy. The Cherokee nation was pressed to sell out its lands in Georgia and move west. The Cherokee refused. In 1824 a handful of Creek chiefs were persuaded by fraud and conspiracy to sell the Creek lands in Georgia for $400,000 and a promise of lands "beyond the Mississippi." The agreements led to "the Creek uprising," which was a rebellion of the Indians against their own leaders, and not a fight against the whites. It quieted down in the late 1820s. The prevailing attitude of the whites was that the Indians must be pushed west and controlled; the basis for the future Indian wars of the West was laid in the broken promises of the federal and state governments to the Indians.

Americans of the early nineteenth century were great adventurers. In 1820 the American naval frigate *Congress* made a goodwill voyage to Asia and stopped off at Guangzhou (Canton). After that, scarcely a day went by in New England and the Central States that a ship did not put out for some romantic clime: Polynesia, Java, China. The Americans were quick to learn about the opium trade and were soon deeply involved in it. The slave trade, of course, had its pattern: out from Boston with manufactured goods, sail to the Caribbean to trade manufactures for rum, sail to Africa to trade rum for blacks, sail to America to trade blacks for money, then back to Boston to buy more manufactured goods. And then there was the white ivory trade—to Africa for ivory, to Asia to trade ivory for opium, or pepper, or precious stones.

In 1824, when disputes over fisheries with Britain and other nations were raging, Commodore Isaac Hull was sent down to Callao, the port of Lima, to watch over the South American coasts and implement the Monroe Doctrine. It was the first American move to show that Monroe had meant what he said, and it established the doctrine. Hull's squadron had many duties, among them the suppression of piracy. When the whaler *Globe* out of Nantucket was captured by a mutinous crew who murdered the officers and sailed off, Hull was ordered to find the mutineers. Ultimately the ship he dispatched for the task rescued two young survivors living in the Marshall Islands as captive-adoptees of the islanders.

Then in 1830 and 1831 came a series of incidents which involved Sumatran pirates.

A number of American trading vessels had discovered that excellent pepper was to be found along the northwest coast of Sumatra. They called in there and traded for pepper. The adventure was not always peaceful, and many skippers left the port of Qualla Battoo with casualties. Qualla Battoo was not really a port at all but an indentation in the rocky shore where a ship might lie in clement weather, half a mile offshore, and load and unload the ship's boats with pepper. Occasionally a ship left the place with a handful of wounded sailors aboard and some dead Sumatrans behind. The favorite trick of the Sumatran pirates was to get aboard a small trading ship with a crew of perhaps eight men, in the guise of laborers, take it over, kill the crew, and then sail the ship round to a real port and sell it.

In the winter of 1831 the brig *Friendship* of Salem, Massachusetts, came to Qualla Battoo for pepper. The skipper went ashore, made the arrangements with the chiefs, and the Malays came aboard to load pepper. Seven men had been left aboard the vessel. Three were killed by Malay kris thrusts, and the four others saved themselves by jumping overboard and swimming for the shore.

The captain and the rest of the crew were scheduled to be murdered ashore, but they became suspicious; they came out in their boats, with two canoes full of warriors chasing, and rowed for their lives until they reached the port of Muckie, a few miles away, where three other American vessels were loading spice. The three merchant ships had some cannon aboard; they all came back to Qualla Battoo, and rescued the *Friendship,* but what a wreck they found. The $12,000 in the ship's safe was gone. Virtually all of the ship's equipment had been stolen. The captain and his surviving men limped home with one full load of pepper, which did not make up for the lost cash, men, and equipment of the ship.

When the *Friendship* got back to Massachusetts, its owners made a protest to the State Department and to President Andrew Jackson. This piracy was just the sort of crime that infuriated Jackson, and he ordered the dispatch of the nearest frigate. She was the forty-four-gun *Potomac,* and she was about to take Minister Martin Van Buren to his new post in London. But now the pirates came first, and so Van Buren waited for another ship, while the *Potomac* sailed for Qualla Battoo.

Such matters took time in those days; it was a whole year, February 1832, before the *Potomac* arrived to punish the pirates.

The *Potomac* ran in, flying the Danish flag and pretending to be a merchant ship. When the natives showed enmity, the Americans brought out a small six-pound gun called Betsy Baker by the crew, and proceeded to knock down the Qualla Battoo "fortress," a wooden stockade. Indeed, they attacked and burned a whole series of forts on the Sumatran coast, and ended up their display with a show from the broadsides of the frigate, which awed the Sumatrans into pleading that the bombardment stop. The Americans stopped then, but they told the pirates that if there was any more trouble they would come back and destroy every village in the northwest of Sumatra.

The peace of Qualla Battoo lasted for six years. Then, in 1838, when the ship *Eclipse* was loading pepper at the Sumatran port of Trabang, the local rajah attacked her, killed the captain and some of the crew, and made off with $18,000 in gold. The rajah was so pleased with himself that he went down to Qualla Battoo and Muckie and gave each of those rajahs a piece of the loot, with a promise that they would all go back into the plundering trade.

When the Americans in Washington heard about this breach of the peace, they sent not one, but two, American warships, the forty-four-gun frigate *Columbia* and the smaller ship *John Adams,* to Sumatra. These headed straight for Qualla Battoo. Commodore George Reid discovered that the local rajah had taken some of that loot from the *Eclipse,* and forthwith he destroyed the whole town. He sent a landing party to Muckie, and the men destroyed Muckie. He then suggested that the rajahs might wish to reconsider their actions, the rajahs sued for peace, the Americans granted it loftily, and piracy in the Spice Islands came to an end as far as American traders were concerned.

That was how it had been done for generations. Every country looked out for its own businessmen and none others. Woe to the nation that did not have a navy to protect its traders. It was a lesson the Americans had learned the hard way in the Barbary days, and they did not forget it. Pirates in Cuba and in the other islands of the Caribbean also heard those carronades speak out in broadside, and many a pirate haven was left blasted by the American navy.

Late in the 1830s and 1840s American vessels were sailing everywhere. The navy sent an expedition to the South Seas, where Lieutenant Charles Wilkes found and named Wilkesland of Antarctica. Americans visited Fiji, and when not treated kindly they burned some villages and the islanders subsided. The same happened in the Gilberts. And the same would happen for the next fifteen years as the Americans ranged the Pacific, determined to open every cranny for trade, and for the American traders' search for raw materials and the right to move about without fear of attack by native warriors.

CHAPTER 13

Westward Ho!

In the 1820s, the British and the Indians both recognized the future of the United States far more clearly than did the Americans. British observers could sense the innate power of the young nation on the western shore of the Atlantic Ocean. The Indian chiefs, having observed the fate of their brethren in the past, knew only too well that they faced ultimate extermination. It was a tragedy of history that there was nothing for them to do about it but fight; the even greater tragedy is that their foremost leaders knew that resistance was futile. But in the great American preoccupation with expansion, there was no room for generosity to the Indian.

The pattern of the future was set in the administration of Andrew Jackson. The Americans insisted on moving ever westward, driving the Indians into unfamiliar and unwanted lands, without the slightest interest in the Indian problems of accommodation to strange environment. The Black Hawk War was scarcely finished when the Seminole War began. In terms of the American government's finances and military potential these were major war efforts, taken very seriously by all concerned, from the young Abraham Lincoln in Illinois to General Winfield Scott, the epitome of the military career officer of the first half of the nineteenth century. The idea that a real treaty, irrevocable, might be made with the Indians, giving them forever a part of the lands that had once been all Indian, never crossed the American mind.

*   *   *

The 1820s were marked by a new American confidence in the growing nation, which was manifest by some glaring braggartry in the new media, the magazines. The boasting brought chiding from London, at least one bit of which was uncannily prophetic:

The American propensity to look forward with confidence to the future greatness of their country may be natural and laudable. But when they go further and refer to the wished for period as one in which the glory of England shall be extinguished forever, their hopes become absurdities. Let us suppose the day is come when their proudest predictions are accomplished, when the continent shall be theirs from sea to sea; when it shall be covered by contiguous circles of independent states, each a kingdom in itself, with the great Federal Constitution like a vast circumference binding them together in strength and union and when it shall be the home of countless millions of free and enlightened Americans. Let us suppose the time arrived when American fleets shall cover every sea and ride in every harbor for purposes of commerce, of chastisement, or protection; when the land shall be the seat of freedom, learning, taste, morals, all that is most admirable in the eyes of man, and when England, sinking under the weight of years and the manifold casualties by which the pride of empires is levelled in the dust, shall have fallen from her high estate. . . .

Let the name of England fade from the list of nations, let her long line of statesmen, heroes, scholars, be buried in oblivion, yet so long as an empire of Americans survives, speaking her language, cherishing her institutions, and imitating her example, her name shall be pronounced with veneration through out the world, and her memory be celebrated by a glorious monument.

From the vantage point of more than a century and a half, that London reviewer's observations deserve an A for prophecy. He saw more clearly than the Americans their restless insistence that the continent be spanned and controlled by the United States. He saw the decline of England as a world military power and the rise of the United States—all this a century and a quarter before it occurred.

Other prophets lived within the Indian community, who in the 1820s began to see what King Philip's sachem Passaconaway had predicted back in Massachusetts in the seventeenth century: that the day of the Indian in America was done. In the 1820s and 1830s the scene of the action was Georgia, where the remnants of the Cherokee and Creek nations within the state objected to the state government's claiming power over them and their lands. They were independent nations, said the Indians, living by treaty with the whites. To this, Andrew Jackson's Secretary of War, John H. Eaton, responded with brutal reminders of the past.

During the war for independence your nation was the friend and ally of Great Britain who claimed absolute sovereignty over the thirteen States. By the treaty of 1783 this sovereignty passed to the original States, including North Carolina and Georgia, within whose limits your nation was then living. If you have since been suffered to dwell there, enjoying the use of the soil and the privileges to hunt, it has been because of compacts with your people and affords no ground for a denial of the right of those States to exercise their original sovereignty. . . . Later still in 1802 when Georgia assumed her present limits and ceded all her western territory, the United States bound itself to extinguish your title to all lands within the bounds of Georgia as soon as it could be done peaceably and on reasonable terms. . . . The course you have taken of establishing an independent government within her boundary, against her will, and without her consent, has put an end to forbearance, and forced her as a sovereign, free, and independent State to extend her laws over your country. . . . There is but one remedy: move beyond the Mississippi River. So long as you remain where you are the president can promise you nothing but interruption and disquiet. But once across the Great River there will be no conflicting interests. The United States, uncontrolled by the high authority of State jurisdiction will be able to say to you, in the language of your own people, the soil shall be yours while the trees grow or the streams run. . . .

And President Andrew Jackson himself said this to the Indians: "My children, listen: my white children in Alabama have extended their law over your country. If you remain in it you must be subject to that law. If you remove across the Mississippi, you will be subject to your own laws and the care of your father the president."

The chiefs believed, and once again the Indians moved, adding one more promise to the string made by "the great white father."

The Seminole also agreed to move beyond the Mississippi. The Seminole were not like the Creek and the Choctaw, members of an Indian nation. As noted, *Seminole* means "runaway" in the Creek Indian tongue; the Seminole were a group of Indians of various nations who had banded together in Florida and Georgia for self-protection. Many runaway black slaves lived with them as a part of the community.

Among the Indian nations that had moved to the western territory were the Potawotami who lived at the headwaters of Lake Michigan and the Sac and Fox who lived between the Illinois and Mississippi rivers. It was the habit of the Sac Indians to "go south" for the winter, leaving their old men and women behind in the village at the mouth of the Rock River, and following the game. Imagine their surprise, then, in 1832, when they returned to the mouth of the Rock River. No women. No old folks. No village. The whites had come in, driven out the Indians, and established the town of Rock River. The Indians were camped forlornly on the banks of the Mississippi.

There was nothing to do, said the Sac, but hold a war council. They did, and a chief named Black Hawk took charge. With allies from the Kickapoo and Potawatomi tribes, they assaulted the white village, tore down and burned the houses, uprooted the fences, destroyed the grain, drove away the cattle, and told the settlers to get out or they would be killed.

The whites retaliated. Governor Reynolds of Illinois called on the U.S. Army for help, and ten companies of U.S. soldiers went to Rock Island under General Gaines. At Rock Island most of the Indians agreed to cross the river. Some said they would not. The general then called for help and militiamen came. They all marched to the Indian village, and found it deserted; the Indians had crossed the river and then burned the village. Black Hawk signed a new treaty with the Americans, but over the winter he decided the Indians had been sorely wronged and sought help from the Potawatomi and the Winnebago. There were more army calls, more burning of Indian villages, and more retaliation by the Indians, who invaded a white village near Ottawa and killed some twenty men, women, and children and carried off two young women, then began scourging the countryside.

Thus began the Black Hawk War.

The army came in force. Among the soldiers were Robert Anderson, who in 1861 would be in charge of Fort Sumter, South Carolina; Winfield Scott, who would command Union forces later on; Zachary Taylor, who would fight in the Mexican war and become president; Albert Sidney Johnston, who would be a Confederate general; and Jefferson Davis, who would be president of the Confederate States of America. Into the Illinois militia as a recruit went a young farmer-lawyer named Abraham Lincoln, who soon became a captain. One might say that the Black Hawk War helped shape the characters and attitudes of some very important figures in American history.

After many battles, some won by the whites, some by the Indians, the Black Hawk troops were defeated by the whites at the battle of Bad Axe, on the bank of the Mississippi.

The Black Hawk War had not really ended when another began. In the South the settlers could not wait to get rid of their Indians. In the spring of 1832 the federal government took a party of Seminole chiefs to view the lands they had chosen for the Seminole out to the west in Indian country. Fifteen chiefs agreed to take those lands, and in 1833 a new treaty between the Seminole and the United States was signed. In 1834 the move was to begin. Then came complications. Among the Indians lived a large number of fugitive slaves, some of whom had intermarried, some of whom had been adopted by the tribes. The Americans said the slaves must be captured and returned to their owners, and proposed sending troops into Seminole territory to do so. This insistence blew the new treaty into pieces. Under Chief Osceola the Seminole refused to go. The matter was taken to President Jackson, who said to wait a year before using coercion. So wait it was, until the spring of 1836.

But in November 1835 came word that about 500 Seminole had taken refuge in Fort Brooke, on Tampa Bay, and that many other Seminole had disappeared. The cause was not very complicated: the wife of Osceola was the daughter of an escaped slave. Under the white code of the South, the daughter of a slave was a slave, and when Osceola's wife went to visit Fort King, she was captured by a bounty hunter. Osceola went to General Wiley Thompson, the special Indian agent of the U.S. government, to protest this outrage. He was clapped into irons for his temerity. He feigned penitence, was released from jail, and then declared war on the United States government.

Thus the stupidity of a general of whom virtually no one has ever heard precipitated a war that lasted seven years and cost the U.S. government millions of dollars and thousands of lives.

General Thompson paid the price, however. One day in December 1835, General Thompson went to dinner at the house of a businessman at Fort King, and after a big meal went out to walk it off. Osceola had learned of the affair and lay in wait; he and his men put fourteen bullets into General Thompson, and killed his aide, then killed everyone they could find in the businessman's household and burned the place down, taking scalps. So Osceola had his vengeance. But that was not enough; he now went off to join the Seminole army.

It was only a matter of days before the whites responded. General Clinch of the regular army and General Call of the Florida militia went after the Indians. A battle was fought on the banks of the Withlacoochee River, and the numerically superior whites barely escaped, because the militia faltered. The whites called it a victory, perhaps because they survived.

Bands of Indians and black escaped slaves now took over all Florida east of the Saint Johns River and south of Saint Augustine.

General Winfield Scott was sent down to quell the Seminole. The Indians would hide in the swamps, come out and attack a town or fort or village; the whites would send in troops who would fight the Indians and usually win; but then the Indians would disappear again, back into the Everglades, and it would begin all over again.

General Scott showed so little initiative in this war against the Seminole that he was relieved by General Thomas S. Jesup. More troops were sent south. More guns, more horses, more equipment, more expense. And the war went on.

CHAPTER 14

Beset North and South

Not all military excursions involving Americans were carried out by the United States government. As previously noted, the activities of the filibusters were entirely unofficial. The task of the American military had been to put down the filibusters, just as it had been the navy's responsibility to try to stop the slave trade.

In the 1820s and 1830s the American border with Canada was very vaguely established, and no one was quite sure what fishing rights the Americans had in the productive fisheries off Nova Scotia and Maine. Both matters became sensitive issues, and involved military excursions and diplomatic demarches. In the 1830s the upper Middle West of the United States was seriously disturbed by revolutionary activity in Canada, and many Americans were personally involved. As will be noted, several governors and the federal government stepped in at one time or another to prevent bloodshed. It was even conceivable that the Caroline incident could have led to war between the United States and Canada. Tempers in what was then called the Northwest country were that much on edge. Part of the reason, at least, was the unsettled fate of the far northwest. In the 1820s John Jacob Astor had established a major fur business in the western part of the lands claimed by the United States and Britain, with his major trading post at Astoria, on the south bank of the Columbia River, where the Columbia pours into the Pacific Ocean. This was definitely disputed territory, and the British Hudson's Bay Company, Astor's principal competitor, was agitating in London for action to stop the American expansion. This situation, too, added to the uneasiness along the border.

One of the reasons for the restrained belligerence of United States policy toward Canada in the 1830s was American preoccupation with the nagging Seminole War in the south. Sometimes it seemed that war would never end.

*   *   *

In the fall of 1837 came another threat to American peace and prosperity which nearly involved the United States in a Canadian civil war.

A number of disaffected Canadians decided they wanted their independence from the British Crown and took action. William Lyon Mackenzie was their leader. They included a large number of really disaffected citizens—*les Canadiens français,* who chafed under Anglican rule. They had much sympathy on the American side of the border. At a meeting in Buffalo the loyal Americans who sympathized with them opened the meeting with the singing of the "Marseillaise."

In Buffalo and elsewhere companies of American citizens organized. Rensselaer van Rensselaer of Albany joined up, was elected military commander, and began the fortification of Navy Island, in the Niagara River (the border between the United States and Canada). He also began training the Michigan government's "troops," which included a number of American veterans of the War of 1812. Soon six hundred men were marching on the island.

In Washington, the U.S. government was aroused enough to send troops to the border. The reason: in November revolutionary Canadians had gathered at the Vermont towns of Swanton and Highgate, where U.S. citizens had given them cannon, lead, and powder, and they had "invaded" Canada, been beaten by royal troops, and fallen back into Swanton. Similar tales came from other towns and cities along the U.S.-Canada border. In one suburb of Detroit, hundreds of men were armed and drilling. Each man had signed an agreement to fight in Canada. The village barber was making bullets. A handbill calling for volunteers to fight in Canada was circulated all along the Canadian-American border and literally thousands of Americans were aroused.

Then, on December 28, 1837, a little steamboat, the *Caroline,* was hired by the Canadian rebels to take military stores from the village of Fort Schlesser to Navy Island. She made one trip, on December 29. Colonel McNab, a Canadian officer, was sent down to the area with troops to stop an invasion of Canada by the rebels. When he learned that the *Caroline* had landed cannon at Navy Island the day before, he ordered the destruction of the *Caroline.* He expected her to be found on Canadian territory, or at least the neutral territory of Navy Island, but she was found at Fort Schlesser, very definitely on the American side. The Canadians boarded,

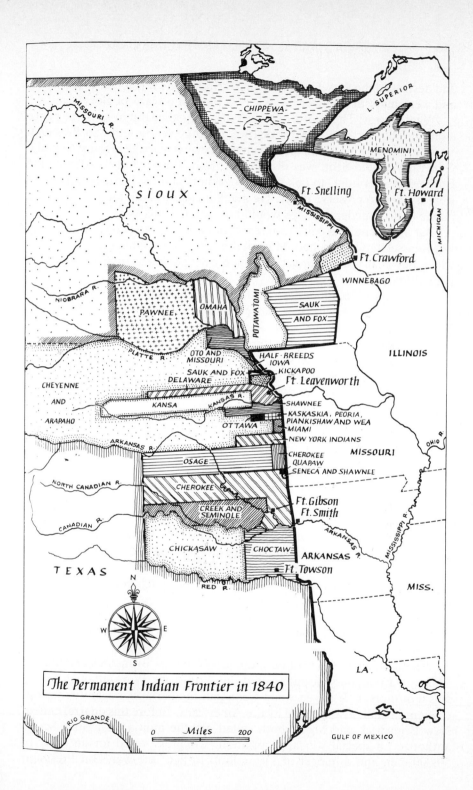

The Permanent Indian Frontier in 1840

and destroyed the vessel in American territory. She was set afire, set adrift, and went majestically over the Niagara Falls in a blaze of glory.

What a furor! The militia of New York was called out to keep the peace along the border. The federal district attorney sent a letter to President Van Buren, warning of wholesale vengeance by Americans against Canada. General Winfield Scott was dispatched from Washington to Albany and Burlington, Vermont, to talk to the governors and see if American troops were needed to preserve order. He made it clear to both the press and the public that the federal troops would be coming if necessary.

But in the end, the American revolutionaries quieted down. Rensselaer van Rensselaer was arrested. Most of the American volunteers surrendered when they heard that their actions could be regarded as treacherous to the United States.

In Detroit revolutionaries raided the Michigan state arsenal, and on January 4, 1838, 400 rifles were seized at the armory in Monroe. The rebels obtained a schooner, the *Ann*, and prepared to sail into Canada. Four hundred men were told to go to the little town of Gibraltar on the Michigan shore, and to wait for the ship. They gathered, but Governor Mason of Michigan came down to investigate and the "patriots" went to a British island in the middle of the river and ran up their flag amid proclamations and bombast. The British troops came after them, but Governor Mason saved the day by picking up the rebels and their arms, and taking them back to Michigan. He landed them at Gibraltar, minus their arms.

The rebellion continued for months. It was serious, so serious that Michigan State and U.S. federal troops were assigned to ride the steamers on Lake Michigan and the Saint Lawrence River to prevent takeover by Canadian rebels.

Ultimately the rebellion collapsed in disorganization. There was never any threat of war between the United States and Canada; the American government backed the Canadian government all the way. But federal troops and state troops were involved, trying to keep American citizens from getting in trouble in the north. It was a near thing, but the government won.

The French Canadians subsided, but did not forget. Their anger and their resistance would come alive again in the following century.

Another Anglo-American dispute involved New Brunswick and Maine. This was a boundary dispute called the Aroostook War, although "war" was a misnomer. It began when Canadian lumberjacks began timber operations in lands also claimed by the Americans. Before this quarrel ended, New Brunswick and Maine both called out the militia, and Nova Scotia authorized a special war appropriation. Congress voted for an army of 50,000 men and a budget of $10 million to fight the war. But President

Van Buren dispatched General Winfield Scott once again to the scene of trouble, and Scott found his shining hour. He arranged a truce. The border matter was settled by the Webster-Ashburton Treaty of 1842, but it would never have been resolved had it not been for Scott. As his Civil War contemporaries used to say, as a general, General Scott was a great statesman.

General Jesup proved more aggressive than General Scott. At the end of 1837 he attacked the Seminole settlement at Withlacoochee and captured some women and children. The Seminole struck back by attacking Fort Mellon. Finally a peace of sorts was arranged; the Seminole agreed to cross the Mississippi and the Americans agreed that they could take their black friends with them. To do this and avoid the issue of the fugitive slaves, the Americans had to declare the blacks to be the slaves of the Seminole, "their negroes, their bona fide property." This was arrant nonsense. The blacks were free men in the Seminole society and always had been. That is why the escaping slaves came to Seminole country. To such strange semantic wrigglings were the authorities reduced in the growing dispute over the blacks in America.

It was all settled. A camp ten miles square was set up at Tampa Bay, the Indians were told to assemble there in April, and ships were brought to carry them all to New Orleans. The ships rode there in the bay in April. The Seminole and the blacks began to assemble.

Then down came slave-owners, seeking their runaway slaves or their descendents. The blacks ran away into the brush. General Jesup seized ninety blacks in the camp and sent them to New Orleans. Then the Seminole deserted the camp and went back into the swamps, and the war was on again.

By a ruse, pretending he wanted a parley, General Jesup captured Osceola and sent him to Fort Moultrie in Charleston harbor, where he was held as a political prisoner. In January 1838, he died.

General Jesup then tricked the Indians again. A delegation of Cherokee chiefs was brought down to Florida to mediate the dispute between America and the Seminole. They met at Fort Mellon. Reassured by the presence of these chiefs that they would be safe, Seminole chiefs came in to talk. The government promised to surrender several hundred Indian wives and children who had been captured and were held at Saint Augustine. All was going well until Jesup learned that Wild Cat, son of Osceola, had just escaped federal custody. He seized the Seminole chiefs who had come in under a flag of truce. Now the Americans had not only exacerbated the Seminole War, they had also infuriated the Cherokee by using them in their ignoble schemes.

A new commander came in, General Zachary Taylor, and he rode down to Florida proudly. Sent off with 1,100 men looking for Indians, he found the Seminole, led by Wild Cat, on Okeechobee swamp. There a great battle was fought. The Americans won again, but had 26 men killed and 112 wounded, and so they retreated whence they had come.

The Seminole War continued. The American generals, with their trickery, were in charge. The president and his cabinet did not seem to know the old adage that war is too important a matter to be left in the hands of generals. The Indians would not forget. The war would cost more thousands of lives and more millions of dollars. Finally, in 1842, the Seminole were exhausted, and peace was finally secured east of the Mississippi. All the Indians, except a few tame tribes of very little size or consequence, had been pushed west. Once and for all, said the pundits, the Indian question had been settled. The border problems with Britain had finally been arranged and stability of the nation seemed assured. It seemed that the time had come for America to settle down and grow up to its geographic limits.

CHAPTER 15

The Mexican War

The most ignoble of American military adventures always seem to be those which have concerned our neighbors to the south. The first of them involved Spain, but the worst was the Mexican War of 1846.

The pressure on America to expand in the Southwest was enormous. First of all the slave states already saw the necessity of maintaining a balance with free states in Congress, and the Southwest was the normal area into which the people of the Southeast might expect to move.

The Mexican War was fought with tactics and weapons largely unchanged from the days of the American Revolution. It was the last American war to be so waged.

Speaking militarily, in the 1830s the American army and navy began to move into the modern era. The old-fashioned musket was being improved rapidly. Samuel Colt developed his rapid-firing six-shot revolver, which would erroneously be called "The Pacifier" and be given credit for the settlement of the Southwest. More important, Colt developed an assembly line for the manufacture of his weapons, and thus added to the industrial revolution. It would not be long before the rifled barrel was introduced to hand weapons, which would mean an enormous improvement in the ability of one man to kill another at a range of 300 yards and more.

Robert Fulton's steamboat was seen as a wave of the future at sea, although it was not until after the Civil War that the real development of a new sort of warship would appear. But the signs were all there, and such men as Matthew Calbraith Perry were leading the pack.

*   *   *

The decade 1830 to 1840 in America was a period of military flaccidity. Virtually nothing happened.

In 1837, the U.S. Navy was in a funk. The steam engine and the steamship were realities, but to look at the U.S. fleet you would never have known it. The American naval vessels of the 1830s differed little from those of the Napoleonic wars. John Paul Jones and Admiral Nelson would have been at home on the decks of the seventy-four-gun *Congress,* all smooth-bore cannon, solid shot, and square rigging.

During the War of 1812 the navy had built a steamship, the 156-foot *Fulton.* It was the first steam-driven warship built for any navy. But with that leap to progress the impetus stopped. The *Fulton* was laid up in the Brooklyn Navy Yard, and was finally destroyed by an unexplained explosion in 1829. Three more steam warships were authorized, but none was built. The seagoing captains who ran the navy were men of the old school. Steam, they snorted, was good for making tea.

Secretary of the Navy Mahlon Dickerson decided in 1834 to build another steam warship, and thus was built the second *Fulton,* which was launched in 1837. But President Van Buren, who took office in that year, cared not a fig for steam warships. "This country requires no navy at all, much less a steam navy," said Van Buren. The captains sniffed again; dirty, filthy steamboats would never replace the clean lines of sail, they predicted.

Right, said Van Buren's secretary of the navy, James K. Paulding. "I will never consent to let our old ships perish and transform our navy into a fleet of sea monsters."

And then along came Matthew Calbraith Perry, brother of the hero of Lake Erie. They put him in command of the *Fulton,* and he became entranced by steam. He went to Europe to study the steam engineering of the British navy and the French navy. He was the captain who broke the hierarchy's solid hatred of steam. In 1839 he supervised design and construction of two new steamships.

The navy, half forgotten since the days of the Barbary pirates, was brought to mind again during several crises with England, one over the arrest of a British citizen for murder, coming out of the abortive Canadian rebellion of 1837, and a second over British interest in Texas, which was populated largely by Americans, and was leaning toward America. A third crisis developed when it seemed that the Canadian-American boundary was not settled after all the difficulties. The British coveted the Columbia River Valley of the west. In the last half of the 1830s, Americans suddenly remembered there was a navy and sometimes a need for it.

In 1835 began a new dispute that was ultimately to push the United States into a new war, this one with Mexico. John Austin and some other Texans had presented a petition to President Santa Anna for admission into the Mexican union. It was ignored and Austin was jailed. Texans rebelled, set up a provisional government, and soon were involved in war with the Mexican government. There were many battles, the most famous of them the battle for the Alamo, at which several well-known Americans died, including Davey Crockett and Jim Bowie.

The fighting continued. Texas became independent. By 1836 she was seeking admission to the United States, and American public opinion generally supported the admission. The rub came with the question of slavery, which had begun to dominate all admissions to the union. Would Texas come in as a slave state or a free state? That meant: Would the Texas representatives and senators vote for or against slavery when the final showdown came? And of course, Texas, populated heavily by Southerners who had slaves, would be a slave state. Thus the issue of admission came to a halt in Congress. When Texas petitioned the U.S. for annexation in the summer of 1837, the petition was refused.

Texas accepted the American rejection and decided to go it alone, developing close relations with France and Britain. This closeness upset the Americans and they began rethinking the Texas question. The more interested the American Congress became, the more coy Texas was. By 1844 the reluctance shown by Texas to talk about annexation spurred the acquisitiveness of the United States and even managed to overcome the slavery issue. In 1845, Texas was annexed to the United States as a state.

Soon there were troubles along the border with Mexico, which was disputed—incursions by Texans and Mexicans. General Zachary Taylor had been ordered from his headquarters in Louisiana to go down to Texas. He went, taking 3,500 men, or about half the American army, with him. He bivouacked on the Nueces River, near Corpus Christi, but suggested that he move down to Point Isabel on the Rio Grande and establish the border there. That suggestion was accepted in Washington, and Taylor marched. By the time he reached Point Isabel, the Mexicans had burned the town and left. So the Americans established themselves there on the north bank of the Rio Grande across from Matamoros, where the Mexican army had 6,000 troops. Both sides began building fortifications.

General Pedro de Ampudia, the commander of the Mexican forces, told Taylor politely that he really ought to move back to the Nueces River country—or else. The "or else" was spelled out: "arms and arms alone must decide the question."

Nonsense, said General Taylor; he knew where the American boundary ought to be. So he stuck fast, and asked Washington to send naval forces to blockade the mouth of the Rio Grande. It was April 1846.

*   *   *

On May 13 Secretary of the Navy George Bancroft ordered Commodore David Conner to take the Home Squadron, as the U.S. fleet was known, and blockade Mexico. The ships were already in the South, and to run to the Gulf of Mexico was no great matter. The blockade began.

It was not easy. Commodore Conner had only two steamers (of a total of seven owned by the American navy) and the rest of his vessels were "fighting sail." The storms in these seas were sudden and fierce; one day the brig *Somers* was blown over, capsized, and sank at Vera Cruz. The crews suffered from scurvy—virtually every man aboard the *Potomac* had it. At Tampico they contracted yellow fever and ultimately the *Mississippi* had to leave her station because 200 men were down with the fever.

The Americans called their fortification across from Matamoros Fort Brown. After asking for naval support, General Taylor marched down to Point Isabel with most of his troops, to receive supplies and protect the supply line. As soon as he left, the Mexicans attacked across the river against Fort Brown. The guns of Matamoros opened up first, on the morning of May 3. Two days later, General Ampudia began his attack. But General Taylor turned back, and the Americans and Mexicans met on May 8 at Palo Alto, five miles from the fort. The American artillery was decisive, and when the struggle ended at dark the Mexicans retreated. The Americans had five killed and forty-three men wounded; the Mexicans took their casualties with them, but General Taylor estimated them at seven times as many.

Next day the battle was resumed at Resaca de la Palma; again the Americans were victorious, and on May 18 they crossed the Rio Grande and captured Matamoros.

General Taylor might have marched to Mexico City just then, had he been given the proper army. The Mexicans were thoroughly disorganized. But so, for that matter, were the Americans. Congress might be ready for war but it had not told the War Department. So Taylor waited for weeks for supply and reinforcement.

President Polk called for 50,000 volunteers for the army. American support for the war was such that he had no trouble finding men; they came in droves. But they had to be trained before they were ready to go into the field, and as the army trained its soldiers, the Mexicans formed a new army and did the same. Now that Taylor had moved across the Rio Grande, there could be no question about his invasion of Mexican territory, and this threat added immeasurably to the strength of the not-so-very-popular Mexican government in raising its new forces.

It was August 1846 before General Taylor was prepared to advance. On September 20 the Americans reached Monterrey. The battle for that city lasted three days, and was marked by many acts of heroism on both sides. The Americans stormed the enemy artillery batteries one by one, and on September 24 they had the city. General Ampudia retired southward.

General Taylor then split his force. General Wool was sent with one body to take Chihuahua. He failed. General Winfield Scott, ever reappearing, appeared again to take charge of the eastern section of the army in an attack on Vera Cruz. Taylor skirmished, then took up a position near Buena Vista where he was attacked by General Santa Anna and his new Mexican army. It was again a tough battle—let no one say the Mexicans did not know how to fight—and at the end Taylor was again victorious, with 700 casualties as compared to Santa Anna's 2,500. But—one reason for the American success in the face of odds (5,000 troops to the Mexican 20,000) was the unpopularity of the Mexican government, which had promised liberal reforms that had not come. So Santa Anna's army, so patriotic, was quickly disillusioned. At this battle 3,000 of his soldiers disappeared into the hills. It was hard to win battles with an army of deserters.

While this war of regulars was going on in central Mexico, Colonel S. W. Kearny was leading an irregular force of volunteers across the desert to attack the Mexicans in New Mexico and California. His 1,800 men were divided that fall: one group moved against Santa Fe while the other headed for California. Chihuahua was captured, and Colonel—now General— Kearny moved on to California. Kearny's force of only a hundred riders was reduced during the march and nearly cut off by a Mexican column.

The navy had been blockading California for months. The navy had ordered the Pacific squadron to "employ its force to best advantage." Commodore Sloat, the commander, had taken Washington at its word. One flotilla moved to capture Monterey (California). Another flotilla captured Yerba Buena (San Francisco). Captain John C. Frémont, an army engineering officer, had been raising the U.S. flag at various points in the interior. Now he joined the naval force at Monterey. In spite of much complaint from the sailors that they were being used as infantry instead of shiphandlers, Commodore Stockton (who succeeded Sloat) formed a naval brigade and marched on Los Angeles, the capital of California. California was then declared to be an American territory, and Captain John C. Frémont was appointed governor.

In September 1846, Mexican Californians pulled themselves together and recaptured Los Angeles, while Commodore Stockton was off with his ships and troops in the north. They besieged the Americans at San Pedro. When Stockton returned, he lifted that siege easily, and then prepared to recapture Los Angeles. General Kearny showed up with the 60 men he had left. They joined up with Stockton's 500-man naval brigade. The com-

bined force marched, fought, and, after battles at San Gabriel and the
Mesa River in January 1847, they won control of California once again.
And so another 600,000 square miles of territory was added to the Amer-
ican claim.

On the east coast of Mexico, the naval blockade continued, tiresome
and expensive. But one by one the positions surrendered: Tampico, Ta-
basco, Alvarado, Tuspan.

But the important place was Vera Cruz. In March 1847, an American
landing force was brought by ship off Vera Cruz. A total of 12,000 men
were transported by the naval squadron, now under command of Commodore Matthew C. Perry.

Surrender, said General Scott to General Morales, the Mexican commander.

Never, said General Morales.

Whereupon on March 9, 1847, American soldiers and sailors began the
disembarkation of the army on Mexican soil, and the building of American
fortifications next to the Mexican fortifications of the city. All sorts of field
guns and mortars were set up in fortified positions, and the navy contributed
a large battery of naval guns, which was planted only 700 yards from the
city wall.

On March 23 the bombardment of Vera Cruz began. It lasted four days,
the navy proudly claiming that its battery did more damage than all the
others put together. Perhaps. Altogether, the artillery was effective: on
March 29, General Morales surrendered the city and the castle San Juan
d'Ulloa, on the reef at the edge of the harbor.

While that battle was going on, in Mexico City another battle was
fought, a revolution, from which General Santa Anna came forth as president of the Republic. More promises of reform. A new army.

General Scott decided to march on Mexico City. He set out, but his
way was blocked by Santa Anna's new army of 12,000 men at the mountain
pass of Cerro Gordo between Vera Cruz and Mexico City. Scott attacked
and was repulsed. Then he put his engineers to building a road around
this mountain, which they did swiftly and skillfully. On April 17, Scott
reached the town of Jalapa (see map), and the next day he attacked Santa
Anna.

Many were the reputations made that day. General Twiggs's division
carried the tower of Cerro Gordo. Particularly notable was the courage of
the men of Colonel Harney. General Pillow's division charged into with-
ering cannon and musket fire, bayonets out front. The Americans were
driven back, rallied, fought harder, and overcame General Vega and his
3,000 men.

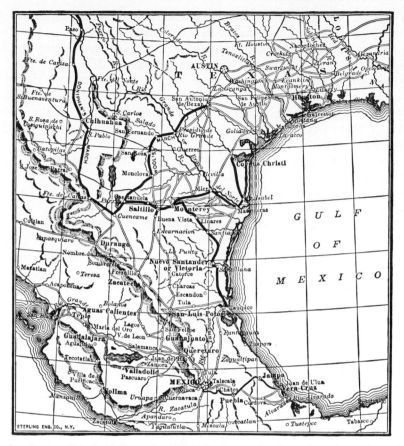

So Cerro Gordo fell to the Americans, and a few days later they captured Vega, and within a month the city of Puebla.

All this fighting had been costly. General Scott set up at Puebla and
remained there during June and July 1847, awaiting reinforcements and
supplies. The troops arrived, still half green, and General Scott's regulars
whipped them into shape there almost on the battlefield. At least it was
better than it had been during the War of 1812, when the American troops
who arrived to do battle did not know one end of a cannon from the other,
and the sight of a bayonet made them dizzy.

Mexico City was going to be a tough nut to crack, as everyone knew.
General Santa Anna had 30,000 troops to defend the national capital.
General Scott marched on August 7, 1847. Three battles were fought in
the next two weeks, at Contreras, Churubusco, and San Antonio. General
Scott's Americans won every battle. But at the end of the fighting, they
made a serious mistake. The politicians back in Washington had appointed
Nicholas P. Trist as special commissioner to arrange for peace with the

Mexicans when the time came. Commissioner Trist thought this was the time. He arranged an armistice with the Mexicans, one Santa Anna was delighted to have. For under the noses of the naive Americans, he used the armistice period to rebuild his shattered military defenses.

And here were the Americans under General Scott, sitting in the midst of enemy territory, holding the roads, but little else, supplied by those roads, with enemy irregulars all around them, and before them the strongholds of Molina del Rey, Casa Mata, and Chapultepec, which must be overcome before they could reach Mexico City.

The idiot armistice came to an end on September 7 and General Scott got ready to move out. General Santa Anna, reinforced and rested, was waiting for him, with his right flank at the fortified Casa Mata and his left flank at Molino del Rey.

The one real help the armistice had given the Americans was a chance to rest and train a little more. They attacked very vigorously, and carried the day again. Santa Anna was defeated and driven back on Chapultepec.

General Scott had on his payroll a Mexican officer who knew all about the Chapultepec defenses. A series of causeways was the key; they guarded the approaches to the capital city. General Scott planned to attack Mexico City from the south. He held a meeting of his principal officers and his engineers. Up stepped one of the engineers, a handsome young man named Robert E. Lee, who recommended a way of approaching the southern front. But Scott's senior officers wanted to attack on the west, so they did.

It was expensive.

Chapultepec was a fort, built against a mountain on one side, and with high stone walls. Inside, everything was reinforced by sandbags put down by Santa Anna's men. At the western wall a deep road ditch protected the wall, and there was a minefield beyond that.

The place looked impregnable, especially to the 7,200 Americans who were now going to assault it.

On September 11 the guns were brought up and on the morning of September 13 began the artillery duel between the Americans on the outside and the Mexicans behind their fortress walls. The American artillerymen said they could batter down the walls themselves. But they could not, and General Scott saw that on the afternoon of the first day. The assault troops and the ladders were readied.

The American infantry were not very hopeful about the result. General Pillow was not happy. General Worth said, "We shall be defeated." Even General Scott admitted, "I have my misgivings."

At daybreak the battle began. For two hours the artillery fired shot and shell at the fort, then, for thirty minutes, grapeshot: those little round balls aimed at soldiers. At 8:00 A.M. the command came to attack, and the 11th and 14th Infantry Regiments attacked, led by an officer who would later be known as Stonewall Jackson. Three other units attacked in slightly different directions, all heading for the fort.

East of the grove, Andrews with his Voltigeurs and Reno with his howitzers turned a little to the right and united with Johnston. This left the Ninth a clear front. Colonel Ransom had promised the day before that he and his men would go into the fort or die. Proudly erect, sword in hand, the beau-ideal of a soldier, he strode in front up the steepest part of the slope, while the Fifteenth marched on his left. The breastwork was captured, and then coming in view of the fort, its buildings almost hidden in smoke, its parapets a sheet of flame, the air filled with the hiss and shriek and roar of missiles—he waved his sword, shouted, "Forward, the ninth," and fell dead with a bullet in his forehead. A terrible cry rose from his men.

"Ransom has fallen. The Colonel is shot." Wild for revenge they all charged on and a part of them reached the fosse.

Was this foolhardiness by the colonel, or sheer bravery? It was augmented; someone had forgotten the boarding ladders, and they were far behind the men. So the soldiers had to stop and seek what cover they could at the foot of the wall, and fire away, waiting. The magnificent impetus of the colonel's sacrifice was all lost, and the battle settled down to slogging, waiting for the equipment.

And so it went all around the fortress, with the 7,000 Americans and the 10,000 defenders. Other Americans attacked the causeways that led into the fortress. At last the ladders came, and the soldiers put them up. The first ladders were thrown down, but the next group came up, and Americans began mounting. At the top they were met by men with muskets firing on them, by men with pistols, swords, and clubs. Many soldiers fell, but some got through, and by 9:30 in the morning the wall was taken and the Americans were firing down on the Mexicans inside the fortress. The fortress soon fell, and the Americans moved onward, toward Mexico City. Santa Anna counterattacked and drove the Americans back. The Americans attacked again and drove the Mexicans back farther.

They reached the causeways that led into the city. By 6:00 at night they were in the outskirts of Mexico City. General Santa Anna retired to Guadalupe Hidalgo and a delegation of citizens came to sue for peace in their city.

At dawn, when the American cannon were about to open fire, a white flag reached the American lines in General J. A. Quitman's sector. Quitman advanced, stopped for half an hour at the citadel, then moved to the Grand Plaza, which fronted on the palace and the cathedral. The United States Marines were there, right out front, with the New York volunteers, General C. F. Smith's brigade, and a battery of artillerymen.

As a triumphal procession the command looked rather strange. Quitman and Smith marched at its head on foot—the former with only one shoe, and behind them came troops decorated with mud, the red stains of battle and rough bandages, carrying arms at quite haphazard angles. Not less astonishing looked the city, for sidewalks, windows, balconies and housetops were crowded with people. Except for the silence, the countless white handkerchiefs and the foreign flags, it might have been thought a holiday. Before the palace which filled the east side of the plaza, the troops formed in line of battle. Officers took their places and when Captain Roberts hoisted a battle-scarred American flag on the staff of the palace at seven o'clock, arms were presented and the officers saluted.

Soon loud cheering was heard. A few squares away the commander in chief escorted by cavalry with drawn swords had reached Worth's command, which had stopped at six o'clock. . . . A clatter of galloping hooves followed, and in another moment amidst the involuntary applause of the Mexicans, General Scott, dressed in full uniform and mounted on a tall heavy bay charger dashed with his staff and Harney's dragoons into the grand plaza—his noble figure with gold epaulets and snowy plumes, resplendent under the brilliant sun, fitly typifying the invisible glory of his unkempt and limping army. Uncovering, he rode slowly along the line of battle to the music of our national airs; the troops presenting arms again, cheered and hurrahed, it seemed as if the earthquake-proof cathedral must be shaking, and the cavalry escort waved high their flashing blades.

In stentorian tones the commander in chief appointed Quitman governor of the city; and then, dismounting in the courtyard, he clanked up the broad stairway of the palace to indite congratulations on the many glorious victories of his army. Presently cross belted American marines were calmly patrolling the halls of Montezuma. . . .

So the war was won, America had seized more territory in its drive south and west, and the United States Marines, present at Tripoli against the pirates, had gotten the rest of the material for their anthem:

> From the halls of Montezuma
> To the shores of Tripoli,
> We will fight our country's battles,
> On the land and on the sea. . . .

The war ended. General Scott, a Whig who was known to have political ambitions that might lead him to the White House, quarreled with Democratic President Polk, and on April 22, 1848, he was relieved of command.

Then, said one cynic, "Major General Butler, who was a Democrat, and who looked well on a horse, bore sway at headquarters."

Sic transit gloria mundi.

CHAPTER 16

Assault on Japan

In the middle years of the nineteenth century the nations of the Western world were on the march, seizing colonies and extending their possessions in Asia. India was so completely dominated by the British in these years that in 1877 Queen Victoria of England was also proclaimed to be "Empress of India." The British were fighting three consecutive wars in these years that ended with the British domination of Burma. In 1855 Britain made a treaty with Siam that brought that small nation within the British sphere of influence.

In the 1850s the French moved into Annam, Tonkin, Laos, Cambodia, and Cochin China, and by 1862 had created a virtual colony, which they would later call Indochina. In the 1850s the British East India Company ruled what became British Malaya, later the Malay States, and now called Malaysia. In the 1850s, the British, Dutch, and Portuguese divided up that area known to us now as Indonesia. In 1842 China ceded Hong Kong to Britain, on a lease that will last until the end of the twentieth century. Britain, France, and Russia were all vying for bits of China.

This drive for control of the wealth of Asia began to infect the Americans in the 1830s and 1840s. By 1850 the United States Navy's leaders were convinced that the United States must expand abroad. The theory of Manifest Destiny, the "natural" drive of the more powerful nations to dominate the less powerful, and, in the name of "civilizing," to milk the new colonies of their wealth, had also spread wide across America.

The U.S. Navy was responding in part to a call from whalers and other ship captains to assure American freedom of navigation of the seven seas.

In Asia and the Pacific some shipwrecked American seamen were held as captives, as a warning to others to stay out of the waters of the captors. The navy was also competing with the navies of other countries to secure coaling stations for the new steam warships that were beginning to emerge around the world.

And so the stage was set for the first great American expedition aimed at creating a climate abroad for the expansion of American business: the opening of Japan.

*   *   *

With the annexation of large chunks of territory that the Mexicans had long claimed, the Americans had definitely joined the colonial powers of Europe in seeking empire. They did not realize it, nor did succeeding generations. If the territory you seize lies next door instead of halfway across the world it is not quite the same, is it? While the United States was digesting California, the British were developing parts of China, which they had seized in the Opium Wars. All very different, right?

Even at the end of World War II, when the people of former colonies called the Americans colonialists, we Americans did not believe it. We had been told for generations that our efforts and our aims throughout the world had been forever benign, directed toward the spread of freedom. This complete nonsense was part of the American school curriculum as long as geography and history were taught in the schools. Small wonder, then, that when others suggested that American motives were dictated by self-interest, the average citizen was ready to believe it was all Communist propaganda.

It was, of course, said to be in the spirit of enlightening the heathen that the United States sent warships to Canton and other ports of China. Enlightenment and trade, they went together nicely. By 1840 American traders were seeking markets all over the world. In 1843 Commodore Lawrence Kearney took two powerful ships to China and "persuaded" the Chinese to sign a trade treaty, as the British had already done. A year later the Chinese erupted in riots against the hated foreigners, and that is when American marines first went to China—"to protect American property." For the next century this slogan would be the colonialists' excuse for a myriad of sins, from murder to extraterritoriality, or the imposition of the law of the conqueror upon the conquered. For the colonies were conquered, no question about that. Sometimes a little king would throw himself under the protection of a colonial umbrella, but only to protect himself from a more ravenous colonial power. The nineteenth and twentieth centuries were still the age of the colonialists, and almost from the beginning the United States was right in there digging, in its own particular way. The only reason the United States did not join the French and British in sawing off parts of Asia and the Pacific in the middle of the nineteenth century was American preoccupation with the North American continent: Florida, Texas, California, and the northwest border, which the Americans wanted to take up to Alaska, then known as "Russian territory." They finally settled with the British on the forty-ninth parallel, the present boundary between Washington and British Columbia, and the middle of the channel between Vancouver Island and the mainland.

But if Americans were too busy to swallow faraway territory and did not possess the means anyhow (in 1845 the United States had six steam warships, Britain had 150) they were not short of greed. It is only fair to say, however, that there were two other reasons for American expansion, at least one of them thoroughly legitimate: the desire to rescue shipwrecked American seamen from Japanese shores, and the growing concern of the United States Navy over the lack of coaling stations abroad in a day of steam, when other nations were grabbing off islands and other territories by the score.

In 1845, without asking the Koreans or the Japanese, Congress decided that these hitherto deprived countries should be granted the boon of American trade. Commodore Biddle took two ships to Japan. The Japanese, who had reluctantly been trading a bit with Europe, although consigning all the traders to a little island in Nagasaki harbor, refused to have anything to do with Commodore Biddle's requests. He had been instructed not to get into a fight, so he did not and came home empty-handed. But in 1846 came word that the whaling ship *Lawrence* had been sunk in a storm off Japan, and that eighteen survivors had been washed up on the beach of Kyushu Island, and were being held in prison by the Japanese. This was all the excuse the U.S. government needed to make a much greater show. Another expedition was dispatched to rescue the sailors and secure a treaty that would protect marooned American seamen and would also open Japan to American trade. The first aim was accomplished, although not without threats of military action, but the second was not.

Congress was becoming annoyed. There was so much about Japan that interested Americans:

The political inquirer, for instance, has wished to study in detail the form of government, the administration of laws, and the domestic institutions, under which a nation systematically prohibiting intercourse with the rest of the world has attained to a state of civilization, refinement and intelligence, the mere glimpses of which so strongly invite further investigation.

The student of physical geography, aware of how much national characteristics are formed or modified by peculiarities of physical structure in every country, would fain know more of the lands and the seas, the mountains and the rivers, the forests and the fields, which fall within the limits of this almost terra incognita.

The naturalist asks, what is its geology, what are its flora and fauna?

The navigator seeks to find out its rocks and shoals, its winds and currents, its coasts and harbors.

The man of commerce asks to be told of its products and its trade, its skill in manufacturing, the commodities it needs, and the returns it can supply.

The ethnologist, curious to pry into the physical appearance of its inhabitants, to dig, if possible from its language the fossil remains of long buried history, and in the affiliation of its people to supply, perchance, a gap in the story of man's early wanderings over the globe.

The scholar asks to be introduced to its literature that he may contemplate in historians, poets, and dramatists, (for Japan has them all) a picture of the national mind.

The Christian desires to know the varied phases of their superstition and idolatry; and longs for the dawn of that day when a purer faith and more enlightened worship shall bring them within the circle of Christendom.

Yes, that was what the Americans wanted, and precisely what the Japanese did not want. They did not want foreign political scientists studying them, nor geographers mapping them, geologists picking amid their sacred rocks, foreigners sailing about learning their secrets of shore defense, traders pushing on them foreign goods, professors bothering their dramatists and poets, and, Buddha forbid, Christian missionaries trying to convert them to a noxious religion from the West.

And what had caused the Americans to want all this?

The immediate impetus was the discovery of gold in California, which turned the attention of the American businessman to the West. Here was America, halfway point between Europe and the Orient.

"It seemed that we might with propriety apply to ourselves the name by which China had loved to designate itself, and deem that we were, in truth 'the Middle Kingdom.' "

So a whole new rationale was born. Trade with the orient suddenly became an obsession. In this modern time, trade would be conducted by steamships, and steamships demanded coal. So the steamer fleet and the navy would have to be supplied with coal. Korea had plenty of coal, thus Korea had to be used. The British were already taking over islands all across the world for no other use than as coaling stations. If the British, why not the United States? And so the idea became fixed in the American imagination. America must expand into the Pacific Ocean.

If General Scott was the tarnished military hero of the Mexican War, Commodore Matthew Perry was his untarnished counterpart in the navy. His brother Oliver, the hero of Lake Erie, had established the family name

and Matthew had doggedly made a place for himself in the naval establishment by his espousal of the steam navy at a time when the senior
captains scoffed. Matthew Perry's enthusiasm was beginning to be shared
by the naval establishment, as England, France, and Russia steamed ahead,
and it was no trick for a man of such probity to secure backing in Congress,
particularly when there was an auxiliary vision of money to be made by
American business.

So an expedition was organized.

This expedition was much more than a military adventure into foreign
seas. There really was curiosity about Japan on every level. Commodore
Perry was given four steamships, the seventy-four-gun sailing ship *Vermont*,
and the sloops of war *Vandalia, Macedonia, Saratoga,* and *Plymouth*, plus
a retinue of supply vessels. President Millard Fillmore took a lively interest
in the expedition (some say it was the only interest he took in anything
while he was in the White House). Daniel Webster supported it. And in
the end, Commodore Perry set off with a carte blanche; he was to go into
the Pacific, establish coaling stations where he wished and could, and spread
American influence around the western Pacific Ocean. He had a letter
from the president of the United States and credentials from the Navy
Department and the State Department; he was general, admiral, and ambassador extraordinary all rolled into one.

As the expedition was fitting out, in came requests from everywhere
to go along. No, said Commodore Perry, seeing the reality better than
anyone else. This was not a scientific expedition, but a political and military
one. There was no room for scientists. "After the accommodation of the
proper officers of the vessels there would be little room left for that of
scientific men, who were accustomed to the comforts and conveniences of
life on shore." Besides, Perry did not want them getting in the way and
causing trouble with the natives.

One man was particularly insistent, the scientist Dr. von Siebold. Perry
immediately turned him down because he was sure in his own mind that
von Siebold was *a Russian spy!*

Commodore Perry had his way. President Fillmore came down to visit
the ships on the eve of sailing. Secretary of the Navy John P. Kennedy
came too, and their wives and children and hangers-on all came, and one
day in mid-November 1852 the expedition sailed from Annapolis down
Chesapeake Bay.

It was a false start. The steamer *Princeton* blew a boiler before they
got to Norfolk and had to be left behind. So the steamer *Powhatan* was
substituted and off they went, heading for the vast Pacific, intending to
touch for refreshment at Madeira, the home of fine wines that naval men
loved so dearly, the Cape of Good Hope, Mauritius, and Singapore. It
was November 24, 1852.

While at sea en route to Madeira, Perry had time to reflect on his mission, and when he arrived he wrote to Secretary Kennedy suggesting that his first step ought to be to occupy the Ryukyu Islands, which belonged to Japan.

These islands come within the jurisdiction of the prince of Satsuma, the most powerful of the princes of the empire and the same who caused the unarmed American ship *Morrison,* on a visit of mercy [to rescue shipwrecked sailors] to be decoyed into one of its ports and fired upon from batteries hastily erected. He exercises his rights more from the influence of the fear of the simple islanders than from any power to coerce their obedience; disarmed, as they long have been, from motives of policy, they have no means, even if they had the inclination, to rebel against the grinding oppression of their rulers. . . .

Now it strikes me that the occupation of the principal ports of those islands for the accommodation of our ships of war, and for the safe resort of merchant vessels of whatever nation, would be a measure not only justified by the strictest rules of moral law, but what is also to be considered, by the laws of stern necessity [read American need for a coaling station]; and the argument may be further strengthened by the certain consequences of amelioration of the condition of the natives, although the vices attendent upon civilization may be entailed upon them . . .

Yes, the white man's burden. See how heavily Commodore Perry carried it as he set forth on his mission of mercy: planning for the good of the natives, and he had not even set eyes on them yet. How right he must have been; had he seized the Ryukyus in 1853 and seized their principal island of Okinawa, there would have been no Battle of Okinawa in 1945.

Having stopped off to pick up coal, water, and the goods of Madeira ("The principal export is wine"), Perry's ships headed south for the Cape of Good Hope and the Indian Ocean.

Colombo, Singapore, Canton, Shanghai—all these romantic places demanded a certain amount of attention. It was the end of May 1853 when the commodore's ships sailed into the harbor at Naha, Okinawa, capital of the Ryukyus, or Lewchews, as Commodore Perry knew them.

No word had come to Perry from Washington authorizing him to seize the Ryukyus, so he did not. He insisted only that he be given a house ashore to entertain his officers, an idea that shocked the Japanese and one they resisted. The British, at gun's point, had forced the Ryukyuans to give them a house, and so Commodore Perry said he would be damned if they would not give the Americans a house as well.

But, said their interlocutor, a minor official who spoke a sort of English: "Gentlemen; Doo Choo man very small; American man not very small. I have read of American in books of Washington—very good man, very good. Doo Choo good friend American. Doo Choo man give America all provision he wants. America can no have house on shore."

But Commodore Perry insisted, and threatened, and got his way, then protested vigorously that all the time the Americans were ashore, the Ryukyuans spied on them.

The expedition visited the Bonins, then returned to Naha. Then it was time to go to Japan. They sailed on July 2, 1853. On July 7, they approached the main Japanese islands. They came into the bay they called Uraga, and they demanded there (in French) to see the highest authorities. The guard boats came out and someone held up a sign in French saying: GO AWAY.

Commodore Perry ignored the message. An official wanted to board.

No, said Commodore Perry, nobody but the highest.

They had the highest, said the Japanese, in Dutch. They had the vice governor.

Not high enough. Why not the governor?

Because he was forbidden to go aboard vessels at sea, for safety reasons.

So the Americans let the vice governor board the *Susquehanna,* the flagship, and confer with the commodore's aide, while the commodore hid in his cabin.

Commodore Perry had already decided on his tack. He was going to be unattainable, available only to the really highest. If necessary, he was ready to land by force. "The question of landing by force was left to be decided by the development of succeeding events, it was of course, the very last measure to be resorted to. . . ."

Perry's refusal to see the provincial governor, and his insistence that if he was unable to see higher authority he would sail right up to Tokyo with his ships and all those wicked looking cannon, caused the Japanese to bring forth the governor. Kayama Yezaimon came aboard the *Susquehanna,* but he did not see Commodore Perry. The commodore stayed in his cabin, and the governor was entertained by two commanders. The commodore, as representative of President Millard Fillmore, the highest official of the United States, would see no one but a representative of the emperor of Japan.

So Japanese and Americans dickered.

The American president's letter could not be received at Uraga, said Governor Kayama. Under the laws of the empire all foreigners were received only at Nagasaki.

No, said the Americans. The commodore would deliver the letter here. If the Japanese would not send someone to receive it, Commodore Perry would assemble a force and march to the capital and deliver the letter.

The governor said he must have new instructions.

He had three days, said Commodore Perry, through his agents, the two commanders. As proof of the importance of the message, the governor was shown two fancy boxes, holding the president's letter and Perry's letter, which must be delivered to high authority.

The governor seemed impressed.

The unlovable Dr. von Siebold had given Perry's expedition some public advice on the eve of departure. The Japanese would try their best to stall, he said. It was too bad they would not use his services, because he knew everything about Japan.

Perry didn't believe that, but he did take heed of the past failures of Americans and others trying to fit the can opener to Japan's hitherto impenetrable interior.

As a man he did not deem himself too elevated to hold communication with any of his brethren in the common heritage of humanity; but in Japan, as the representative of his country, and the accredited guardian of the honor of that flag which floated over him, he felt it was well to teach the Japanese, in the mode most intelligible to them, by stately and dignified reserve, joined to perfect equity in all he asked or did, to respect the country from which he came and to suspend for a time their customary arrogance and incivility towards strangers. The Japanese so well understood him that they learned the lesson at once.

Governor Kayama listened to everything his commander hosts had to say regarding the demands of their leader. The governor sat on the deck of the *Susquehanna* drinking champagne with great aplomb and admiring the military efficiency of the vessel. He called the attention of the Americans to the really impressive aspect of their mission: the great long guns of the ships that threatened the shore. As far as the Japanese were concerned, there was the real message. Japan had no weapons capable of meeting that challenge, and from previous experience they knew it.

In the shogun's palace in Tokyo, the counselors argued. Send the foreigner away, said the traditionalists. But he will then march *here* with his muskets and cannon, said the modernists.

Stop him, said the traditionalists.

We are not sure we can, said the practical.

And the practical won the day. The shogun agreed that a representative would go to the beach at Uraga and meet this strange unseen ambassador from the end of the world.

To Uraga went Toda Idzunokami, first counselor of the empire.

A large and imposing tent was erected on the beach for the formal ceremony.

Perry presented his letter from President Fillmore. It was a remarkably sober and restrained letter, promising that the United States would not interfere with Japanese religious or political affairs, and asking that the Japanese laws regarding trade be suspended for a few years to give trade with America a chance. If the Japanese were not pleased, they could then return to the old ways.

Another aspect: Fillmore asked—did not demand—that the practice of killing or imprisoning shipwrecked mariners be stopped: "Many of our ships pass each year from California to China; and great numbers of our people pursue the whale fishery near the shores of Japan. It sometimes happens in stormy weather that one of our ships is wrecked on your Imperial Majesty's shores. In all such cases we ask and expect that our unfortunate people should be treated with kindness and their property should be protected till we can send a vessel and bring them away. We are very much in earnest in this."

And, Commodore Perry's main interest:

Commodore Perry is also directed by me to represent to your Imperial Majesty that we understand there is an abundance of coal and provisions in the Empire of Japan. [This was not true.] Our steamships in crossing the great ocean burn a great deal of coal, and it is not convenient to bring it all the way from America. We wish that our ships and other vessels be allowed to stop in Japan and supply themselves with coal, provisions, and water. They will pay for them in money or any thing else your Imperial Majesty's subjects may prefer; and we request your Imperial Majesty to appoint a convenient port, in the southern part of the Empire, where our vessels may stop for this purpose. We are very desirous of this.

We ask and expect . . . we are very much in earnest in this: these are polite but insistent phrases. And that is what Perry was, polite but insistent.

So the letter was delivered with great ceremony in the special audience hall erected on the shore at Uraga. The interview lasted twenty minutes. The Japanese said Perry would receive his answer at Nagasaki. Perry said no, the answer would be received at Uraga. Perry informed the Japanese that he would return in the spring for the answer. All bowed, and the Japanese left. The commodore waited for his boat.

To emphasize his determination, Perry then sailed up the bay, toward Tokyo, and the Japanese nearly panicked at the thought of foreign warships in sight of their shogun's capital. Perry's men took soundings until the ships came within sight of Yokohama, port for the capital, and then they turned around. The threat was clearly implied: if the Japanese did not cooperate the Americans were coming anyhow. The implications were not lost on the Japanese.

In March 1854, Perry was back, and this time he anchored in Yokohama Bay.

After fevered debate, in which some samurai offered to attack the Americans and slay them no matter what happened to themselves (they would have been the first kamikazes), the practical voices of Japan won out again. They knew that intercourse with the West was now inevitable; the British were knocking at their door, and a Russian admiral that year presented himself much more properly at Nagasaki and made the same sort of proposals that Perry was making. The Japanese were even then more fearful of the Russians than of the Americans and British, and so when Perry returned, all of President Fillmore's requests were granted.

The seal of Japanese approval came not much later than the formal agreements. One of the marines aboard the *Mississippi* died. He could, of course, have been taken out to sea and buried, but he had not died at sea. Commodore Perry asked for a piece of ground that the Americans could use as a cemetery for the marine and any more Americans who died on Japanese soil.

At first the Japanese were aghast. To let barbarians degrade their sacred soil by living there forever? The idea was appalling to the older generation. Once more the way pointed toward Nagasaki, where a temple had been set aside for the loathsome barbarians. But Commodore Perry would have nought of Nagasaki. He wanted to bury his marine on a small island in Yokohama Bay, called by the Americans Webster Island. But the Japanese objected, and instead let the Americans bury their marine at a spot at the foot of a hill not far from Yokohama. The American chaplain, the Reverend Mr. Jones, read the Episcopal Service of the Dead, and a Buddhist priest did the Americans honor by going through the Buddhist burial ceremony thereafter. The Americans thought it all very strange, and rudely moved away while the priest was still carrying out "the peculiar ceremonies of his religion, beating his gong, telling his rosary of glass and wooden beads, muttering his prayers, and keeping alive the burning incense."

But, said the Japanese in extenuation of the insult: What could you expect of barbarians?

In spite of the American rudeness, the Japanese completed the ceremony. A bamboo fence was put up around the area, and a guardhouse was built and a guard posted to secure the dead marine's peace.

And so the treaty was worked out. The Americans were so naive they had not thought to ask for "extraterritoriality" but shrewd enough that they did ask for "most favored nation" status, which meant that if any other nation got a new concession, the Americans would get it, too. The Japanese entertained the Americans ashore with their strange foods, and the Americans entertained the Japanese afloat with their strange foods.

The Americans delivered many gifts, aimed at impressing the Japanese: fifteen Hall's rifles; three Maynard's muskets; twenty-three cavalry swords; six artillery swords; two carbines, with cartridges; twenty army pistols; one

box of books; one box of dressing cases; one box of perfumery; one barrel
of whiskey; one cask of wine; one box of pistols to distribute to the nobility;
one box of perfumery for nobles; and cherry cordials, baskets of champagne, China ware, bottles of maraschino, one telescope, many boxes of
China tea, two telegraph instruments, three lifeboats, one locomotive,
tender, passenger car and rails, four volumes of Audubon's *Birds of America,* three volumes of Audubon's *Quadrupeds,* several clocks, ten ship's
beakers containing 100 gallons of whiskey, eight baskets of Irish potatoes,
three stoves, boxes containing scales, bushel measures, gallon measures,
and linear measures in yards, a box of U.S. coastal charts, four bundles
of telegraph wires, four boxes of connecting apparatus, boxes of batteries,
a box of machine-made paper, a box of insulators, a box of zinc plates and
other materials for making a telegraph system, seed, and agricultural instruments.

The Japanese responded with a sumo wrestling exhibition, which the
Americans did not like or understand: "This disgusting exhibition did not
terminate until the whole twenty-five had successively in pairs displayed
their immense powers and savage qualities."

There were visits to other Japanese cities, another stay at Naha, with
many Japanese gifts of bells, cloth, swords, and fine metalwork bestowed
upon the Americans. In July the Americans departed. Early in 1855 the
Powhatan returned to Japan, bearing the treaty, signed by the president
and secretary of state, and ratified by the Senate, and the Japanese signed.
The Americans headed home again with their treaty. It was Washington's
birthday, February 22, 1855. Japan was now to be drawn into the modern
industrial world.

The test of the treaty came a month later. The treaty had provided for
the opening immediately of the port of Shimoda for American vessels, and
Hakodate a year later. On February 13, 1855, before the ink was dry, the
firm of Reed and Daugherty, ship's chandlers, sent the American schooner
C. E. Foote from Honolulu, loaded with supplies for the whaling trade,
to establish a base for whaling ships so they could winter at Hakodate
rather than return halfway across the Pacific to Honolulu. Partner Reed
was aboard, with his wife, and a Mr. Doty and his family. It was obvious
that they hoped to establish a trading firm in Japan.

On March 15 the schooner arrived at Shimoda, expecting to find the
American warships *Powhatan* and *Vandalia.* Instead they found the crew
of the Russian naval frigate *Diana,* which had been wrecked off this shore
the year before. The captain of the *C. E. Foote* immediately negotiated a
deal to take the Russians to Siberia, and the passengers then went ashore.
The stunned Japanese assigned them a temple, and it was made Western
enough to suit the Americans as a residence.

The Japanese asked the Americans why they had come to Japan. How long were they planning to stay?

They had come to Japan to live, said Mr. Reed. They were going to confine their activities to supply of American vessels, he added, stopping his selection of a cargo of lacquerware, rice, silks, pottery, and other goods bound for San Francisco to carry out this interview.

The Japanese were more than a little upset. Already, by their interpretation, the Americans were pressing the treaty beyond its limits.

The governor of Shimoda then addressed a letter to Mr. Reed:

. . . You must, on the return of your vessel, leave this place, or should she not return in the declared time, then on the arrival of an American ship you must leave this place, without at that time, expressing any excuse to delay you.

Your present stay among us is found necessary, but it cannot in future be taken as an example.

Never let it be asked again to stay. It is not only so in this place, but also at Hakodate, which you and all Americans are obliged to observe.

But the poor governor of Shimoda did not know his Yankee traders. Once having gotten a foot in the door, Mr. Reed appealed to the next American captain that came along, the appeal was taken back to the U.S. government, and more negotiations began. All a misinterpretation of the treaty, said the Americans, insisting on the right of Americans to reside in Japan. Ultimately they had their way. The Japanese, besieged by foreigners, were perplexed. At Kyoto the emperor's party wanted to throw the foreigners into the sea, but the shogun's party, which had dealt with them, saw the unwisdom of provoking the men with the big cannon. The handwriting was on the wall. They had to join the West or succumb to it as China was doing.

But the Japanese saw very clearly the foreign intentions and their own course. Lord Hatta, one of the imperial advisers, addressed a memorial to the throne, in which he suggested that the Japanese learn from and adopt all the foreign ways, waiting until the foreigners had fallen into a major quarrel among themselves as they were so prone to do, and then to strike, conquer Asia, throw out the foreigners, and assume Japan's rightful place as ruler of the world. Beginning in the 1850s they proceeded to do so.

This was the real result of Commodore Perry's opening of Japan, the opening of a can of worms that would spill over in three-quarters of a century.

If Perry had not done it, a Frenchman, or a Briton or a Russian would have. Perry was just the instrument of the destiny of the West in relation to the East.

CHAPTER 17

The Filibusters

During the 1850s, the concept of Manifest Destiny grew ever more powerful as the Americans saw the Europeans increasing their colonies.

Latin America was a fertile ground for such activity. The Spanish Empire was beginning to collapse. Paraguay proclaimed independence in 1811. So did Uruguay. So did Venezuela. Colombia became independent in 1818. Chile rebelled successfully against Spain in 1818, Peru in 1821. New Spain became independent Mexico that same year. The British were trying to seize control of the Rio de la Plata area, which would ultimately become Argentina. They, the French, and the Dutch were all trying to secure bits of Latin America, and did so in the three mainland colonies of British, French, and Dutch Guiana.

Into this atmosphere came many adventurers who wanted to make millions—and even more, to control the destinies of nations. Thus we have the era of the filibusters.

*   *   *

The filibusters*—adventurers who dreamed wild dreams of empire and sometimes succeeded for a while—would have no place in this study except that they often proved to be nuisances or dangers to the American body politic and had to be dealt with by martial authority. Their ambitions and

---

*From the Spanish *filibustero*, meaning freebooter or pirate.

their activities in the 1840s and 1850s matched those of their government, which was enmeshed in the web of "Manifest Destiny," a theory as old as the American Revolution. Magazine editor John L. O'Sullivan revived it in 1845. The theory held that the United States was destined to spread completely across the North American continent, and this sometimes included Canada and sometimes Mexico. Later the idea was to be extended to American acquisition of colonies abroad.

The American thirst for territorial acquisition seemed only to be whetted by the annexation of Texas and seizure of California. In the summer of 1848, President James K. Polk made a stab at purchasing Cuba from Spain.

Had Polk succeeded, there would have been no Fidel Castro, no seat of rebellion against American suzerainty over the Western Hemisphere, no Cuban troops to be exported to Angola. Cuba would have become another star in the American flag, another slave state.

At about the same time, planters and other businessmen in Cuba, interested in making Cuba American, persuaded Brevet Major General William Jenkins Worth that he could lead an expedition from Mexico to Cuba. They would recruit for him 50,000 troops, said the Havana Club, the principal organization of rich backers. The general would receive $3 million for his trouble.

But the general and his friends were frustrated by President Polk, who did not want a military conquest. He recalled General Worth to the United States and ordered General William O. Butler (General Scott's successor, who sat so nicely in the saddle) to be sure that no American troop ships stopped at Cuba so that American soldiers might jump ship there.

During 1849 the Cuban annexationists operated openly in New York, trying to get an American military man to lead the expedition against Cuba. They approached Jefferson Davis. He refused. An expedition was still planned, with 800 men to invade Cuba from the Mississippi area. Secretary of the Navy William Preston ordered the navy squadron at Pensacola to prevent the sailing of the expedition. Early in September 1849 the navy seized several ships at anchor in New York harbor, loaded to the gunwales with muskets and powder.

Narciso Lopez, a prime leader in the plan for seizing Cuba, actually did land troops there in May 1850, but the expedition failed without official American interference. More expeditions were planned and launched, with private American money readily available, but no official government support. President Zachary Taylor, who did not even believe California could possibly be integrated into the United States, opposed such meddling, and so did President Millard Fillmore. Lopez led another expedition. When it was overwhelmed by Spanish troops, hundreds escaped by small boat back to Key West, but scores of Americans were killed and fifty surviving "of-

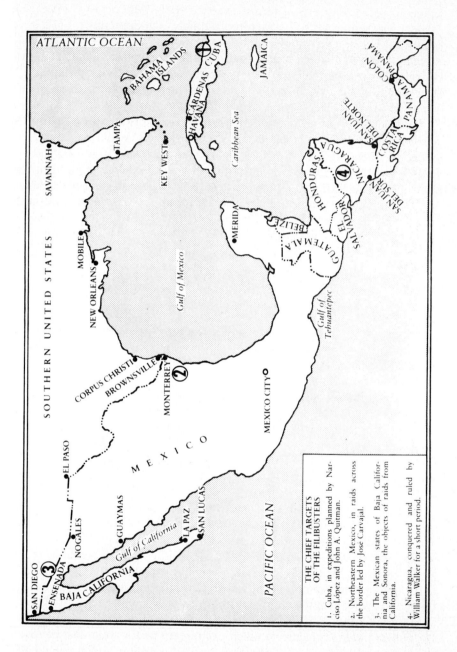

THE CHIEF TARGETS
OF THE FILIBUSTERS

1. Cuba, in expeditions planned by Narciso Lopez and John A. Quitman.

2. Northeastern Mexico, in raids across the border led by Jose Carvajal.

3. The Mexican states of Baja California and Sonora, the objects of raids from California.

4. Nicaragua, conquered and ruled by William Walker for a short period.

ficers" were shot by firing squad. About 200 prisoners were shipped to Spain to serve long prison terms—half of them Americans. Lopez, the leader, was sentenced to be garroted publicly. On September 1, 1850, in front of a Havana crowd of 10,000, revolutionary leader Lopez was duly strangled. He must have bribed the executioner, or had friends at court, for the garrote could kill a man very slowly and painfully or very quickly, depending on the executioner's technique. One quick turn, and Lopez's head fell forward. He was mercifully dead.

The execution of all those American citizens raised storms of protest in the major American cities. Burning Spanish flags became as popular as burning American flags would be later. Signs saying GOD AND LIBERTY—CUBA appeared at parades. Spanish property was in danger and much was destroyed. The Spanish minister protested to the American government.

In the next few years, Cuba was much in the American consciousness:

> The Antilles Flower
> The true key to the Gulf
> Must be plucked from the Crown
> Of the old Spanish Wolf.

So went the impassioned verse.

Cuba was saved from American annexation by the domestic American quarrel over slavery. Since the Cuban economy (sugar) was built on slave labor, the planters were adamant: slavery must remain. After 1850 Congress could do nothing but trade off. A slave state and a free state were admitted simultaneously, thus preserving the ratio in the U.S. Senate. Everybody knew this compromise could not last, if for no other reason than that the population of free states was growing faster than that of slave states. Ultimately the House of Representatives would be controlled by the free states and thus Congress itself would become a danger to the slaveholders. So the Cuba heat subsided.

Leftover soldiers from the Mexican War found it hard to settle down after all the excitement and so the 1850s found them ready recruits for all sorts of military schemes to seize power in Latin America.

José María Jesús Carvajal decided he would set up a Republic of the Sierra Madre in Mexico. He recruited soldiers, including old Texas Rangers and Captain John Salmon Ford, whose big claim to fame was popularizing the Colt revolver on the southern frontier. They failed.

Joseph C. Moorehead, another old soldier, decided to capture Sonora. He failed. Indeed, in spite of much excitement and a good deal of bloodshed, they all failed, these filibusters, until along came a man named William Walker.

Walker was the brilliant scion of a wealthy Nashville family. He studied medicine. He went to France, and Germany, and to Scotland for more medical study. Then he decided he would study law. He moved to New Orleans and passed the bar. He turned to journalism. He moved to San Francisco to work for the San Francisco *Herald*. And then he decided his talents were wasted. He would become a conquistador. He went south to Sonora with 140 men and established the Republic of Sonora. The "republic" was largely illusory, the product of a mind kept active by foraging for food. Then along came Major General John E. Wool, commander of the Pacific Department of the United States Army, who stopped Walker's supplies and reinforcements from coming down from California. And so another dream died. William Walker went back to Marysville, California, to practice law.

Then, in the California rush for gold, various steamship lines began running between New York and the Central American isthmus. A young Californian, Byron Cole, was interested in taking over Nicaragua, and he employed Walker to lead a volunteer force of 300 Americans to do the job.

Walker did it very efficiently and in October 1855, he was dictator of Nicaragua. His grand design called for the unification of the five Central American states into one confederacy.

Because Nicaragua has two rivers and a lake that are suitable for navigation it was the center of American business warfare for control of shipping to and from California. Walker became deeply involved with one shipping faction and made an enemy of Cornelius Vanderbilt, the shipping magnate (later railroad magnate). Vanderbilt financed Walker's enemies lavishly and helped bring about civil war against Walker's government of Nicaragua.

The matter became so serious that President Franklin Pierce declared that a state of civil war existed in Nicaragua and sent an American naval contingent under Captain Charles Henry Davis to protect American interests. Captain Davis was stationed with the ship *Saint Mary's* at San Juan del Sur. A revolutionary group financed by Commodore Vanderbilt was established in Costa Rica and marched into Nicaragua. The struggle went against Walker, and in the spring of 1857, he was on the run. His rag-tag army soon lost most of its weapons. The women and children of the soldiers proved to be a serious liability and Walker was about to abandon them at Rivas, when Captain Davis rescued them under a flag of truce as a humanitarian gesture.

Davis then served as intermediary to persuade Walker to leave Nicaragua so peace might be restored there under a local government. Walker resisted, and Davis put on pressure. He would blockade the area, he said, to prevent Walker from moving troops. Walker said he would take his troops out of Nicaragua in the ship *Granada,* and then return to fight again. But Davis would not let the *Granada* sail; he set up conditions for Walker's surrender.

Walker said that he had no choice but to submit—not to the enemies who were closing in on him—but to the *force majeure* of the United States of America. So he abandoned his troops, and with sixteen of his favorites, he went aboard Davis's flagship, the *Saint Mary's,* and was taken to Panama. His revolutionary force—consisting of about 400 men—was also taken to Panama.

Walker went to New Orleans, where he was greeted as a conquering hero. One citizen wrote a poem that was read at the "victory" celebration, staged for Walker's arrival on May 27, 1857:

> All hail to thee Chief;
> Heaven's blessings may rest
> On the battle-scarred brow of our national guest.
> And soon may our Eagle fly over the sea,
> Plant there a branch of our national tree.

So the passion for more territory burned brightly in the United States, and William Walker was assured of more encouragement and financial assistance in his effort to take over Nicaragua in spite of the *New York Herald*'s prediction that the era of filibustering had ended. The editorial writer of the *Herald* had not taken into account the fever that still raged in America, and the rewards to be won.

Walker had failed in Lower California, but others were not convinced that it was impossible to establish a republic there. Ignacio Pesqueira, who wanted to be governor of the province, staged a revolt against Governor Manuel Gandara. Pesqueira told American friends that he was going to establish a republic. One of those friends was Henry Crabb, who raised a force of thirty men and brought them down to help the "revolution." But by the time they arrived in Sonora, Pesqueira's rebellion had succeeded. Pesqueira, the new governor, announced that Crabb and his followers were "enemy invaders." Pesqueira rushed into action before Crabb could announce their arrangement; he defeated the Crabb force in a battle at the village of Caborca and he executed all but one sixteen-year-old boy. Crabb's head was preserved in alcohol and displayed by the new governor as a symbol of his determination to do right by Mexico.

William Walker ignored all that. He knew that the cause of territorial expansion was very popular in the American South. Using that lever, he managed to get an interview with President James Buchanan. Buchanan was trying to walk a tightrope between North and South; he gave Walker the feeling that he sympathized with Walker's aims, but he said nothing publicly. Walker wrote a public letter blasting Captain Davis and the navy for interfering with his affairs. Walker then went to New York, had his photograph taken by Mathew Brady, the socially significant photographer of the day, and prepared for a new foray into Nicaragua. He was General Walker to everyone, but not a very impressive general to many, with his mild, sharply chiseled features and small slender frame.

Walker spent the summer of 1857 organizing a new expedition. The ministers of El Salvador and Guatemala protested that Walker's shameless promises to reinvade Central America must be stopped. Walker had not for a moment given up his dream of a Central American Federation with himself at the head. Ultimately, he told his Southern backers, this territory would all become part of the United States. Secretary of State Lewis Cass promised to stop any Walker ship from sailing for Central America. Walker was arrested and charged with trying to embark on a military expedition against friendly states. But nothing could be proved. Walker stayed around New York, making court appearances, while his men and equipment sailed south on the steamer *Fashion*. She made Mobile and anchored there. Walker joined ship and sailed for Nicaragua on November 14, 1857.

The U.S. Navy had ordered Commodore Hiram Paulding to take his flagship *Wabash* and several other vessels to Nicaraguan waters to prevent any further military activity by Americans. But their orders did not say what they were to do. Were they to capture the vessels in which Americans were riding? And how was Paulding to know who was a filibuster? For he was warned not to bother legitimate shipping, which meant the thousands of men moving back and forth across the isthmus on their way to and from California, taking ship at New York, getting off on the east coast, crossing the isthmus by coach or steamboat, and then taking ship on the west coast for California. Most of these men were roughly dressed, rough-looking, and carried weapons.

No, the navy had to have real evidence of planned military activity before it could do anything. Thus, when the *Fashion* sailed into Punta Arena, past the U.S. sloop of war *Saratoga,* only fifteen men were on deck and they looked like so many travelers. Next thing Commander Frederick Chatard knew, the ship was belching forth armed men who quickly disappeared.

Walker's men moved fast. They captured three river steamers and a big lake steamer called *La Virgen.* Then Commodore Paulding arrived at San Juan del Norte in the *Wabash.* General Walker had made his camp nearby. Commodore Paulding took 300 armed marines aboard the USS *Fulton,* landed them, and surrounded Walker's camp; the commodore sent Walker a note telling him to surrender, go aboard the U.S. naval vessels quietly, and be shipped back to America where he belonged.

So Walker surrendered again, tears in his eyes, and was shipped to

New York, ostensibly to stand trial for violating U.S. laws. There, there was a furor again. President Buchanan was charged with violating the U.S. Constitution by sending military forces abroad without approval of Congress. Commodore Paulding had exceeded his instructions, shouted elements of the press and public.

President Buchanan, never one to take a firm stand, equivocated. Walker soon saw that he would not be prosecuted for violating American laws (as he had), and he became very noisy. This noise embarrassed President Buchanan, and he then lost all sympathy for William Walker. In the long range this would be disastrous to Walker, but in the short range he could not help but feel victorious.

The fact was that Walker had inserted himself very neatly into the middle of the American political pot, which was boiling furiously, and Buchanan, trying to please everyone, was pleasing no one.

"Grave error," the president called Paulding's arrest of Walker. But Walker's activity: "Such a military expedition is an invitation to reckless and lawless men to enlist under the banner of any adventurer to rob, plunder, and murder the unoffending citizens of neighboring states who have never done them any harm."

So congressmen lined up: the North for the president, but not very vigorously; South against the President, very vigorously. Senator Jefferson Davis brought up a "Constitutional" issue of presidential power. Senator Stephen A. Douglas made remarks accusing Commodore Paulding of filibustering against filibusters. Only Senator James A. Pearce of Maryland supported the president's authority to send a naval expedition beyond the territorial limits of the United States to arrest an American citizen engaged in an illegal activity. In the North, the powerful Senator Seward of New York wanted to forget the whole matter, saying that both sides had done wrong. But Senator James R. Doolittle of Wisconsin demanded that a special medal be struck for Commodore Paulding for "gallant and judicious conduct."

Eventually Congress abandoned the debate from exhaustion. Meanwhile, William Walker basked in the publicity and toured the country, raising money and soldiers for a new expedition. The Buchanan administration's policy toward him hardened, possibly as a result of Buchanan's growing understanding of his own situation: he would never be elected to a second term in office. Three times the government tried to prosecute Walker for violation of the federal neutrality laws. The best they could get was a hung jury. So the government gave up the effort.

Walker's reception in the South and the attitude he saw in Congress persuaded him that he had nothing to fear from anyone in America, so he went about his mission with no attempt to conceal it. He tried to sell bonds, redeemable when he seized power again in Nicaragua. A very risky investment, even among the most voluble supporters of Manifest Destiny. It was not very successful. He encouraged settlers, promising them land. The acting foreign minister of Nicaragua was concerned enough that he issued a statement for the American press noting that only passports signed by him would be accepted for landing anywhere in Nicaragua.

Walker tried to fit out one great ship and send it south, but the revenue authorities frustrated him. Ultimately he sent several vessels with supplies and men. One of his ships, the *Susan,* was wrecked off Guatemala and the survivors were shipped back to Mobile.

In America, Walker began to lose support except from the group calling for "Manifest Destiny *now.*" More and more Americans were turning inward toward their great national problem, the growing distrust between North and South.

In the spring of 1858, Commodore James M. McIntosh had taken over from Commander Paulding as commander of the "home squadron" of the U.S. Navy. He was instructed by Secretary of the Navy Isaac Toucey to use all legal means to prevent a landing of filibusters in Central America. Commodore McIntosh asked for clarifications, offering hypothetical situations, because he knew only too well what had happened to Commodore Paulding—public censure by the president of the United States for doing his duty. McIntosh did not get much satisfaction. The navy could intercept an expedition at sea, said the secretary, but could not land and fight, nor capture a ship within a harbor.

How was a naval officer to know that a vessel was a probable filibuster ship? asked McIntosh. No answer. Should he stop all ships? Of course not.

For reasons of its own, mostly concerning the possibility of territorial acquisition or the right to build a canal across the isthmus, Britain was very concerned about Central America, but was restrained from direct military activity by the Monroe Doctrine. Still, the British had come to distrust American promises of cooperation; many Britons believed that the United States government was secretly behind all this filibuster activity in order to take over Nicaragua and build the Atlantic-Pacific canal by itself.

British policy was simple and direct: the filibusters were to be restrained. Captain W. Cornwallis Aldham, the British commander in Central America, had orders to stop filibusters from landing—no equivocation about how he did it.

William Walker spent January and February 1859 in Mobile and New Orleans, still trying to raise cash and supporters for another expedition. The sinking of the *Susan* had aborted the last one. He went to San Francisco, pretending that he was about to launch a new expedition into Mexico. He returned to New York and gave out publicity about his "new plans."

On June 16, 1860, after leaving many such false trails, Walker landed on an island off Honduras. Some of his suppliers were captured when one of his ships was stopped by customs inspectors and "merchandise" turned out to be guns. But on August 4, 1860, Walker was on the Honduras mainland at Trujillo where he overcame the resistance of the 75 soldiers of the garrison with his force of 110 men.

Walker took over the fort at Trujillo. It was his intention to gain strength in men and get supplies from the United States and launch another attack on Nicaragua. But two weeks later the British warship *Icarus* arrived. Captain Norvell Salmon demanded that Walker lay down his arms and go aboard his ships and leave Nicaragua. He had, in effect, twenty-four hours to make up his mind. That night, Walker evacuated the fort, destroying all supplies he could not carry and leaving his sick behind.

Two days later, in the forest, Walker's band was surprised by a company of Honduran soldiers, but only two men were hurt in the skirmish. Captain Salmon caught up with him three miles from the coast a week later and demanded his surrender, so General Walker surrendered to the British authorities.

Salmon then turned Walker and his principal aide over to the Hondurans. Walker complained that he had been betrayed by the British, and of course he was quite right. General William Walker was court-martialed by the Hondurans, convicted of carrying on warfare against Honduras, sentenced to be shot, and the next morning he was shot by a firing squad.

The news brought no outcry in America. No one in the United States cared very much for William Walker any more, and Manifest Destiny had been submerged in the enormous American concern over the divisive political situation caused by slavery. No one even complained much about the British doing efficiently what the Americans had failed to do because of the outcry about presidential powers. But that does not mean the American body politic learned anything from the experience.

CHAPTER 18

The Ultimate National Tragedy

"From hence, let fierce contending nations know, What dire results from civil discord flow."

—*Joseph Addison*

Since the announced end of the slave trade in the 1820s the American South had been smarting under the restrictions the federal government imposed on its supply of manpower. If the slave trade could be outlawed in America, then so could slavery by some future Congress or Supreme Court decision. With this prospect forever in mind, the people of the Southern states looked upon any change in the status of the union as a possible challenge to their way of life. That is why after 1820 one "compromise" after another was needed to patch up the nation's growing sectional dispute. For nearly forty years the compromisers begged the issue, but finally in 1860 it could be avoided no longer. The political spectrum was changing, the balance of power was moving westward, and the West was not normal slave territory. The sort of agriculture practiced there did not lend itself to the need for concentrated farm labor. And so the issue of slavery and the rights of the Southern states came to a head in the election of 1860. The election of a minority Republican president to the highest office in the land meant the end to the old Democratic party coalition that the South had been able to manipulate for years.

But the dispute had begun a long time before, and for the past twelve years it had been growing in intensity.

The American Civil War was without a doubt the most disastrous and most murderous conflict in the history of this country, bar none, and God and politicians willing, there will never be a military debacle anything like it again. Three-quarters of a million men on both sides died in this struggle, and nearly half a million men were wounded. Thus more than a million men suffered directly from the horror of the war. Nearly 3 million men were under arms in the Union and about 750,000 served the Confederacy. But it would be closer to the mark to say that no American family, North or South, escaped the fury. The American Civil War was a hurricane that swept through every household.

The conflict had been a long time in coming.

*   *   *

The election of Zachary Taylor to the presidency in 1848 brought to a higher pitch the sectional dispute over slavery that had been bedeviling the United States for more than twenty years. Taylor was a man of so little imagination that he could not foresee a United States that spanned the American continent. But perhaps that is harsh judgment, for after Andrew Jackson completed his second term as president in 1837 there would be no two-term president again until Lincoln, and the ultimate reason for the disaffection of the electorate with a whole succession of men was their inability to superintend the resolution of the major national problems, with slavery underlying them all. Thus Martin Van Buren, John Tyler, James Knox Polk, Zachary Taylor, Millard Fillmore, Franklin Pierce, and James Buchanan all came to the presidency with high hope and the high hope of the public, only to fail and be turned out after a single term.

By 1850 North and South were at each other's throats. The people of California had enacted a constitution that forbade slavery—the first ever— and that action was the death knell of any hope for unity. The Compromise of 1850 was regarded by Daniel Webster and Henry Clay as the salvation of the union. Instead it was a Band-Aid applied to a deep wound, which continued to fester underneath. The rapid growth of Kansas and Nebraska territories, the running quarrel over the status of their admission as free or slave states, all increased the growing tension. Duels, fights, quarrels were the order of the day in and out of Congress. John Brown's raid in Kansas renewed the fury. In the South a New England accent became anathema. Where there were no real differences they were created by North and South, until men and women of both regions came to believe that those of the other area were somehow different from themselves.

Finally, in 1860, Abraham Lincoln, a former Whig, now of the new Republican party, was elected president because of a deep split within the majority Democratic party. Many Southerners had vowed that if a Republican was elected, the South would withdraw from the union rather than lose its identity and succumb to Northern pressures to change the Southern way of life. And so it happened.

The first note of physical defiance came at Charleston, South Carolina,

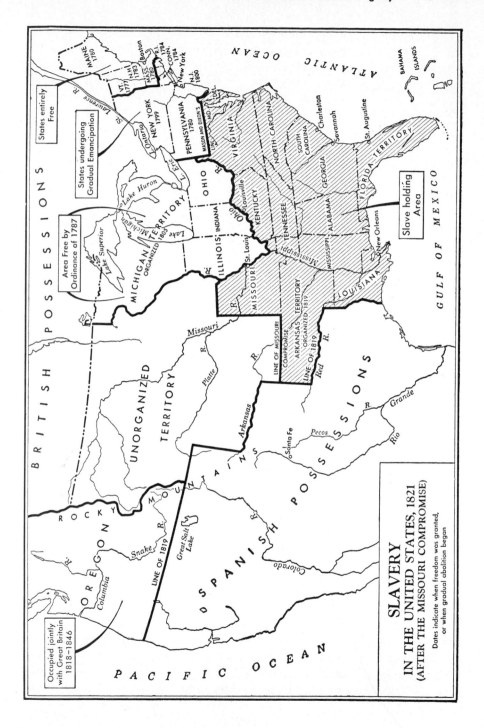

SLAVERY
IN THE UNITED STATES, 1821
(AFTER THE MISSOURI COMPROMISE)

Dates indicate when freedom was granted,
or when gradual abolition began

on November 7, 1860, the day after Lincoln's election. The police arrested a Federal official who was trying to move military supplies from the Charleston Federal arsenal to Fort Moultrie, which was controlled by Federal troops. A few days later the state legislature voted for a convention to consider secession and the two South Carolina U.S. senators resigned their seats. South Carolina was unequivocally the leader of a movement to secede from the union. The legislature voted to raise a force of 10,000 militia. Soon Georgia and other states began voting for state defense forces.

Down in Florida, Navy Lieutenant T. A. Craven wrote the Navy Department that because of threats he was taking new security measures to defend Fort Taylor at Key West and Fort Jefferson at Dry Tortugas Island.

Major Robert Anderson, the commander of Fort Moultrie, asked the War Department for reinforcements and the garrisoning of Fort Sumter in Charleston harbor. He wrote nearly every day. President Buchanan refused to make the reinforcements. The U.S. Army then numbered only about 17,000 men, most of them on duty in the West on watch for Indian troubles.

On December 17, the South Carolina secession convention met at Columbia.

We the People of the State of South Carolina . . . do declare and ordain . . . that the ordinance adopted by its convention on the twenty-third day of May, in the year of our Lord one thousand seven hundred and eighty eight whereby the Constitution of the United States was ratified, and also all Acts . . . are hereby repealed and that the union now subsisting between South Carolina and other states, under the name of United States of America, is hereby dissolved.

The vote for secession was 169 to 0, unanimous. South Carolina was out of the union.

On the day after Christmas 1860, the Federal garrison moved from Fort Moultrie to Fort Sumter in Charleston harbor. The reason: Major Anderson believed that the South Carolinians intended to attack Fort Moultrie, which was not defensible. But Fort Sumter was. Anderson ordered the guns of Fort Moultrie spiked, and he destroyed the place as a military installation. The South Carolinians were furious: an overt act of war, they called it.

Perhaps. But to Major Anderson the occupation of Fort Moultrie by the South Carolinians the next day was the act of war. That day, December 27, the U.S. revenue cutter *William Aitken* surrendered to South Carolina officials. Three days later South Carolina troops seized the Federal arsenal in Charleston. They now occupied all Federal property in the area except Fort Sumter. General Winfield Scott, commander of the United States Army, asked President Buchanan to send 250 troops to reinforce Fort Sumter. A few days later the cabinet agreed and General Scott, to insure secrecy, ordered up a merchant ship, *Star of the West,* for the reinforcements. But Secretary of the Interior Jacob Thompson of Mississippi, the last Southerner left in the cabinet, found out about the sailing, informed the South Carolina authorities, and resigned. At daylight on January 8 the *Star of the West* crossed the bar into Charleston harbor and steamed toward Fort Sumter. Shore guns began firing at her and one ricocheting shell struck the bow. The troop commander aboard the *Star of the West* ordered the captain to take the ship back to New York.

In January, Alabama seceded. So did Georgia, and Louisiana. All along the eastern seaboard Federal revenue vessels surrendered to state authorities, either because their captains were sympathetic to the Southern cause or because the ships had nowhere to go.

In February Texas seceded, as did the Choctaw Indian nation, and on

February 8 the Confederate States of America was formed as a nation at Montgomery, Alabama. Jefferson Davis was elected president.

On March 1, Major Anderson informed Washington that Fort Sumter must be reinforced or abandoned. It was not defensible as it was. At the moment he had good relations with the South Carolina officials, and so supplies were coming into the fort to feed the men. But . . .

On March 4 President Lincoln was inaugurated. The next day he was presented with Anderson's problem. It would take 20,000 men to guarantee the security of Fort Sumter. The president conferred with General Scott. At the end of the week the cabinet considered the problem and the consensus seemed to be that it was too late to do anything about Fort Sumter. How long could it hold out?

General Scott did not know.

The question about Fort Sumter kept coming up. To do or not to do? Lincoln conducted a survey of the cabinet. Everyone but Montgomery Blair, the postmaster general, was opposed to taking any action that would mean war. That meant no reinforcement. Lincoln postponed a decision.

On March 29 the president decided to send an expedition to reinforce the fort, and another for Fort Pickens, Florida. At Charleston the newspapers said this would mean war.

On April 11, a delegation of Southern officials, including one ex–U.S. senator, went to Fort Sumter under a white flag and demanded the surrender in the name of General Pierre Gustave Toutant Beauregard, commander of Charleston for the Army of the Confederate States of America. Major Anderson refused.

At 4:30 on the morning of April 12, the first Confederate guns began firing on Fort Sumter. Fort Sumter fired back, but it was hard: the Federal garrison consisted of eighty-four officers and men with the partial help of forty-three nonmilitary workmen. The men could only manage a few of the guns at one time. On the mainland, firing at them, were four thousand Confederates. On April 13 the fort had to surrender. The war was on.

The relief force arrived at Fort Pickens, Florida, and that fort was saved for the Union.

On April 15 President Lincoln issued a formal proclamation dealing with the insurrection of the Southern states, and began calling for troops and a special session of Congress. He declared a blockade of the South. (It would take some time, but the blockade was one of the most effective actions taken by the Union forces.)

The Federal navy evacuated the Norfolk navy yard when Virginia seceded that month, and Harper's Ferry was taken over by the Confederates. The gun factory located there was torn down and moved to Richmond. Colonel

Robert E. Lee—who had agonized over the problem of his own loyalties, then cast his lot with the Confederacy—was appointed commander of the Virginia military forces.

The U.S. capital at Washington was virtually isolated. The Sixth Massachusetts Regiment, on its way down to the capital, was beset by a mob in Baltimore while changing stations, and four soldiers and nine civilians were killed. The incident raised serious doubts as to Lincoln's ability to bring troops down from the North by rail, since the trains had to pass through Maryland, and Maryland's citizens were not at all sure which side their state was going to support. But the Sixth Massachusetts did arrive in Washington, and so did the Seventh New York Regiment and several other units. As for Maryland, the legislature at Annapolis seemed to be leaning toward the Union, but the agricultural Eastern Shore of Maryland was a hotbed of secessionism. On April 29 Maryland's House of Delegates voted to stick with the Union, 53 to 13. It was the first negative reaction of a Southern state to secession. But antislavery men and Unionists on the Eastern Shore began to close down their houses and move across Chesapeake Bay for protection of their families.

Both sides were furiously raising troops for the war. Arkansas and Tennessee both joined the Confederacy. Riots erupted in the border states, particularly in Missouri. Maryland was pro-Union officially, but so insecure that on May 13 Federal troops occupied Baltimore just to be sure that the railroads continued to be available for maintaining communications between Washington and the Northeast. The South had a big break when England declared herself neutral in this war, which meant she recognized the Confederacy as a legal entity.

On May 24, Federal troops invaded Virginia to capture Alexandria and thus assure the safety of Washington. One man, Private Elmer Ellsworth of the Eleventh New York Regiment, was killed when he tore down the Confederate flag from the Marshall Hotel, shot by the proprietor as he came down the stairs with the flag in hand. Another soldier then killed the proprietor. The newspapers—North and South—had a field day with the death of this young Union soldier: he was a hero or a villain, depending on point of view. Only too soon would the casualty lists become so great that the death of any one soldier would go unannounced save in his home town.

In Western Virginia Major General George B. McClellan was fighting some skirmishes with Confederate troops.

On June 1 Union and Confederate troops skirmished at Arlington Mills and Fairfax Courthouse, Virginia. Captain John Q. Marcy of the Confederate cavalry was killed. His death was greeted in the South as the tragedy of a great soldier. Another hero story, for the fighting had not really begun.

General Beauregard came up from Charleston to take command of the

Confederate forces on the Alexandria line. Seven regiments of Federal troops from Fort Monroe marched out on June 10, and met a Confederate force at Bethel Church. They suffered 76 casualties of a 2,500-man force. Only Major Theodore Winthrop, a "brilliant young author," got much press attention in death. The casualties had risen above the individual level.

The war was more than two months along and nothing much had happened, but there were some actions. The Confederates evacuated Harper's Ferry in the face of moving Federal troops. At Boonville, Missouri, Unionists chased Confederate sympathizer Governor Claiborne Jackson out of the state capital and after a skirmish forced Jackson into the southwest corner of Missouri. Gunboats shelled various positions belonging to the enemy, along the Potomac and Chesapeake Bay and on the Rappahannock. But this was not real war, but skirmish, skirmish, skirmish, the process of feeling out and getting ready.

What was important was the movement of General Irvin McDowell's Federal Army of Virginia against Colonel Joseph E. Johnston's Confederate force that had come out of Harper's Ferry. Johnston was going to Manassas to join up with General Beauregard, who had established a battle line on a stream called Bull Run. An advance force of the Union attacked the Confederates at Blackburn's Ford on July 18 and was rudely repelled with eighty-seven casualties.

On July 21 Confederate and Union forces met in the first real battle, called Bull Run by the Union and Manassas by the Confederacy. This is where Stonewall Jackson got his name. Hundreds of spectators from Washington and the suburbs had come down by horse and buggy and by train to watch the Union army wipe out the Confederates. But the battle went the other way, and by late afternoon, the Union soldiers were streaming back toward Washington. The Confederates, who had fought a hard day, did not follow, but they kept shelling the roads ahead of the Union troops. When the soldiers met the horde of spectators, panic ensued. The casualties: Union, 3,000; Confederate, 2,000. There now was definitely no more room in the papers for long stories about young heroes.

The effect of the first battle of Bull Run/Manassas was extreme. In the Union, gloom descended, matched by elation in the South. General McDowell was fired, although his battle management had been perfectly sound, and General George McClellan, who was doing well over in Western Virginia, was brought east to take over the Federal Army of Virginia, now called the Federal Division of the Potomac. Soon it would be called the Army of the Potomac. Thus began the musical chairs of Union generals that was to last until the coming of Ulysses S. Grant.

The fighting moved west. At Wilson's Creek, Missouri, the Federal troops were whipped and the Springfield area was in Confederate control. In September Confederate troops entered Kentucky, which created a continuous front running from the Atlantic coast to Kansas. A young brigadier general named Ulysses S. Grant won his first victory by capturing Paducah without a fight.

General Robert E. Lee led his troops into Western Virginia. The war staggered along: blockade, skirmish, political overtures from both sides to European nations. The Battle of Ball's Bluff on October 21, involving about 1,700 men on each side, got much publicity because an Oregon politician, Senator Edward D. Baker, a particular friend of Lincoln's, was in command, and he was killed here. The Federals also lost. Baker became the first "martyr" mourned by the Union. Brigadier General Charles P. Stone, who was to support Baker, was accused of everything but treason, clapped into jail without trial, and his career wrecked. The real result was a continued elation among the Confederates over the performance of their troops, and a growing gloom within the Union, which was losing confidence in the Union army and its generals.

The Union was blockading the ports of the South and the blockade was already beginning to hurt. Still, there were many blockade-running captains in the South. That year, 1861, they estimated their chances of getting caught by the Unionists at about one in ten. Those odds were good enough to attract seagoing men to what was an enormously lucrative trade with England, France, and other nations. It was patriotic trade. One blockade runner, later named the CSS *Atlanta,* arrived in Savannah in November with badly needed rifles and ammunition.

The Union was suffering at sea as well. Confederate batteries controlled the Potomac River from the mouth to Alexandria. Out in the west Major General John C. Frémont gave evidence of becoming more political and less general. In Springfield, Missouri, his cavalry routed a small Southern force and the "Frémont press" blew the victory up into major proportions. Frémont did not know it, but President Lincoln had already arranged his removal as commander of the Western Department of the army. When Frémont and his followers learned of this change, they were so furious that they began talking of moving west and setting up their own nation.

General Winfield Scott, the general in chief of the Union forces, was seventy-five years old, corpulent, and wheezing. He boasted the most impressive career of any American soldier, but it was time for him to go, and he agreed to become superintendent of the U.S. Military Academy at West Point, an honorable retirement. And the ambitious thirty-four-year-old Major General George Brinton McClellan replaced Scott as general in chief.

On November 26, 1861, a convention of Virginia Unionists who had seceded from Virginia met at Wheeling to set about establishment of a new Union state of West Virginia. A few days later Missouri was admitted to the Confederacy, although much of the state was controlled by the Union army.

The new general in chief was slow to move the Union armies and Congress did not like it. On December 9, the Senate set up the Joint Committee on the Conduct of the War, which was to oversee and second-guess, with great vigor, the military processes.

Most of the fighting was in the west, and there was not a great deal of that. On January 19, Union and Confederate troops met at Mill Springs on the north bank of the Cumberland River of Kentucky, and General George H. Thomas won the day for the Federals. He broke the Confederate line, which ran from Cumberland Gap to Columbus on the Mississippi.

On the Ohio River, Union Flag Officer Andrew Foote with seven vessels (four of them ironclads) captured Fort Henry, and opened the Ohio to the Union. The gunboats could move into the Tennessee and the Cumberland rivers. Soon the Union forces took Fort Donelson. General Grant was the Union commander. Confederate General Nathan Bedford Forrest and his cavalry escaped, as did Generals Floyd and Pillow (who were later cashiered for their timidity). But General Simon Bolivar Buckner, commander of the main infantry force, had to surrender his troops.

What terms could we have? asked Buckner.

"No terms except unconditional and immediate surrender."

Thus was one old tradition of gentlemanly warfare abandoned and another tradition established. But what could one expect in civil war—the most deadly and emotional of all wars. The Confederates surrendered about 12,000 men. It was by far the most serious defeat they had yet suffered. Their western front was in tatters.

In February Union General Ambrose Burnside made an amphibious landing on Roanoke Island in North Carolina, and began moving inland. His troops captured the island, which gave them a base in the belly of the Confederacy.

In March, at Hampton Roads, the Confederate ironclad *Virginia* (*Merrimac*) destroyed three conventional wooden ships of the Union navy by ramming and gunfire. That night the Union iron ship, the *Monitor,* arrived from New York. Next day the two ironclads fought, to an inconclusive finish. The battle attracted much public attention and brought a visit to the wounded captain of the *Monitor* by President Lincoln. Technologically the battle was important; the term *monitor* came to be generic internationally for the sort of ironclad with a revolving turret. Tactically the arrival of the *Monitor* prevented the *Merrimac* from wiping out all the Federal naval forces in the area.

Slowly, ponderously, General McClellan moved his Army of the Potomac around but did not seem to achieve much. McClellan was very good at staff work, and his several corps commanders held many meetings, but in March the military engagements were out in the west or down south where Burnside was operating in North Carolina.

In April, General McClellan was moving his vast army to the Virginia Peninsula, heading for Richmond. Down in North Carolina, General Burnside was chewing holes in the Confederate midsection. The Union navy controlled Port Royal, South Carolina, and threatened Savannah, a major Confederate port. New Orleans was also threatened by the Union navy's Flag Officer David Glasgow Farragut, who had learned his trade so aptly under Commodore David Porter during the War of 1812. In the Mississippi area, a Federal army was in Tennessee and threatening Mississippi. And another was threatening Chattanooga and Atlanta.

On April 6 came the Battle of Shiloh (or Pittsburg Landing, as it is sometimes called) in Tennessee. Confederate General Albert Sidney Johnston fell upon the unsuspecting army of General Grant. The Union general was at his headquarters in Savannah, Tennessee, when the Confederates charged through the Union line and began firing around Shiloh Church. Grant rushed to the scene, rallied the troops, staved off disaster the first day, and was reinforced that night. General Johnston was wounded seriously and died. The Confederate command fell to General Beauregard, who called for reinforcements.

On the second day the battle began all over again. The Union troops won back ground, the Confederates charged again and took that ground. But by midday it was apparent that Beauregard's reinforcements were not coming, and the Union was getting more and more, so Beauregard had to break off the action and retreat to Corinth. Grant stayed put and reorganized forces that had been badly hurt. About 60,000 Union troops had been involved against about 40,000 Confederates; the Union lost 13,000 and the Confederacy 11,000, and one of their most promising generals.

On April 5, McClellan reached Yorktown. He had with him 100,000 men and he did not believe that was enough to win, although in front of him were only 15,000 Confederates. Instead of attacking, he decided to lay siege. As President Lincoln saw immediately, McClellan's move would give the Confederates time to bring up reinforcements, and that is what they were doing.

Early in May the Army of the Potomac entered Yorktown, Virginia, site of the British surrender that had sealed the unification of the colonies into a nation so long ago. "The success is brilliant," boasted General McClellan, who had not yet fought a battle with this army. The Confederates continued to retreat.

On May 5 the Confederates fought a delaying action east of Williamsburg in a series of fortifications established earlier by General Magruder.

In the evening the Southerners pulled out and retreated again toward Richmond. Stonewall Jackson slashed the Federals at McDowell, Virginia, but returned to Shenandoah. It was still all skirmishing until the Battle of Winchester on May 25 when Stonewall Jackson with 16,000 men defeated General Banks with 8,000 men, and virtually cleared the Shenandoah Valley of Union troops, much to the concern of Lincoln.

General McClellan was still pleading for more troops, more troops. Near the Chickahominy River at Seven Pikes, Union and Confederate forces met again. The battle lasted two days, and the Confederates had the worst of it, with 6,000 casualties to the Union 5,000, but the battle was really a stalemate. McClellan had not been defeated, but he was not advancing on Richmond either.

There was more desultory fighting. Jeb Stuart brought his cavalry completely around the Union army, but that did not stop the threat to Richmond. On June 23 Robert E. Lee, the new overall Confederate commander, decided to take the offensive, and turn McClellan's line away from Richmond. Then began the Seven Days' Battle, fought first in the orchard near King's schoolhouse, then at Mechanicsville, then Gaines' Mill, with the numerically inferior Confederate forces forcing the Union army back, although at heavy cost in casualties. McClellan, the man with the big army, began to retreat to the James River, in what his detractors called "the great skedaddle." The Confederates chased the Union forces across the Chickahominy River, but their drive against the rear guard was disorganized and they lost the chance to split the Army of the Potomac and wreck it. Still, the Union withdrawal was virtually a rout, and McClellan abandoned 2,500 of his wounded and sick at Savage Station. The string of battles ended with that at White Oak Swamp, where McClellan held just north of the James River. But the threat to Richmond was ended. McClellan was blaming everyone but himself for his failure.

For all practical purposes, McClellan was reduced in grade with the appointment of Major General Henry W. Halleck as general in chief of all U.S. land forces. One of Halleck's early orders was to McClellan to move his huge Army of the Potomac north near Fredericksburg and Alexandria where it would be of some use in protecting Washington against a mounting Confederate offensive. McClellan protested.

On August 16 the Army of the Potomac moved. Five days later Lee was moving north, too, and the next day Jeb Stuart's cavalry embarrassed the Union mightily by capturing all of the baggage of General Pope's Union Army of Virginia, including many battle plans. Then on August 26 came the battle known as Second Bull Run, or the beginning of the Second Manassas Campaign. The battle lasted four days, and the Union forces were badly defeated, but Pope's army was not destroyed. The Federal troops had 16,000 casualties, the Southern, 9,000.

The battle cost General Pope his job, and McClellan, for some reason still rather murky, was restored to full command of the troops in the Washington area. General Lee contemplated an attack on Washington, but decided it would be too costly, so he moved across the Potomac into Maryland. On September 6 Stonewall Jackson occupied Frederick, which became the center of Confederate military activity north of the Potomac.

Lee's troops were moving around in the North, when by accident a Union soldier found a "lost" copy of Lee's orders for the whole Maryland campaign. But within hours the Confederates knew the orders had been found by the Union army, and prepared accordingly. McClellan was moving into the mountains west of Frederick. On September 15 the Confederates captured Harper's Ferry and 12,000 prisoners.

Then came the battle called Antietam, or Sharpsburg. McClellan attacked Lee along Antietam Creek. The Union forces outnumbered the Confederate, nearly two to one, but the results did not reflect those differences in strength; both sides lost enormously, 12,000 Union casualties and 14,000 Confederate. On September 18, Lee withdrew. The Maryland campaign was over, but McClellan did not follow. He was afraid of defeat.

General McClellan's failure to follow up his victory at Antietam with a pursuit of General Lee cost him his command. Lincoln was finally completely disgusted with the ambitious young general's tepid performance. General Burnside was ordered to take command of the Army of the Potomac. So McClellan's military career came to an end. He took leave of his army with an emotional, spectacular performance which had his soldiers throwing their hats in the air and cheering him. It was a performance worthy of John Wilkes Booth, the actor, and, in the reading, somewhat reminiscent of the act of General Douglas MacArthur when he made his "Old soldiers never die" speech to Congress after being fired by Harry Truman. McClellan then went away to play politics with the war for the next two years.

Burnside spent the day planning a drive into Virginia against Richmond, and on November 15 the army began to move toward Fredericksburg. General Lee did the same. On December 13, Federal troops, 114,000 of them on the plain southeast of the city, drove toward the hills defended by 73,000 Confederates. The battle lasted all day. The Union suffered 12,000 casualties, the Confederates, 5,000. At the end of the day, the Confederates still held the heights above the city. Both sides were exhausted. On the night of December 14, Burnside withdrew across the Rappahannock.

The action in 1863 began in the West and the South. On January 19, General Burnside began to move back south across the Rappahannock, but the weather, which had been good, turned, and soon the Army of the Potomac was bogged down in mud. They called it the "mud march." By

January 22 the whole supply train was up to its hubcaps in mud and the problem was not how to continue, but how to turn around and get back north to escape both the weather and a lightning slash of the Confederates that would catch them unable to fight. On January 24 the wet army settled into winter quarters across from Fredericksburg.

General Burnside had not wanted the command of the Army of the Potomac in the first place, and after he got it, he did not handle it with much finesse. After two months the command structure was reduced to a bickering committee of dissatisfied generals. Burnside told Lincoln that he insisted that half a dozen of his generals, including Joseph Hooker, be relieved or he would quit. That was not the way to talk to Abe Lincoln, and before the day was out, Burnside was relieved and Hooker was appointed to command the Army of the Potomac.

In March the big action was in the South. Admiral Farragut, who held the Mississippi River with his fleet, was fighting the Confederates who held the banks. He led the squadron up the river past the Confederate batteries of Port Hudson, Louisiana. The ships were hit hard, and the *Mississippi,* which had been to Japan with Commodore Perry, caught fire, exploded, and was destroyed.

The campaign against Vicksburg began.

In April, General Hooker proposed to cross the Rappahannock, make a left turn, and outflank General Lee's army, then drive to cut it off from Richmond. On April 28, Hooker began crossing, upstream in the Wilderness area, and he set up camp around the Chancellor family farmhouse in the community called Chancellorsville. Lee saw the threat and moved out of Fredericksburg to block Hooker's move. Hooker started to advance, met Lee's scouts, and retreated back to Chancellorsville. That night Lee and Stonewall Jackson decided to split the Confederate force and attack. Next morning Jackson moved out in the Wilderness. That night the troops attacked on the flank and the Federals panicked and ran for Chancellorsville. The battle lasted two days, another decisive defeat for the Union, but again the Confederates did not have the strength to follow up the victory. The casualties were enormous; 17,000 Federal and 13,000 Confederate. And Stonewall Jackson was wounded in the battle so sorely that he soon died.

The Confederates advanced into the Wilderness. On June 3, General Lee's army of 75,000 men moved west from Fredericksburg toward Culpeper Court House. The Battle of Winchester was another Confederate victory. The Confederates crossed the Potomac, and Harrisburg, Pennsylvania, went into a panic. The troops reached Frederick, Maryland, again on June 21. Lee was in the North again, and Lincoln did not like it.

On June 27 Hooker lost his job to General George G. Meade. Lee moved into Pennsylvania, a move which had political as well as military overtones. Pennsylvania and Maryland were both chafing under the war, and their loyalty was anything but rock-solid. Lincoln urged Meade to hurry, fight, and win the victory the president needed so badly.

On July 1, Meade obliged. It was the first day of Gettysburg. Inconclusive. The second day: inconclusive. Then came the third day, with Meade and his forces on Cemetery Ridge, where they dug in and placed their cannon. In the afternoon, Lee set off Pickett's charge, the most gallant single action of the war, and one of the most deadly. The Union guns were too many. The result was the bloody retreat from the field of Lee's men. The Federals lost 23,000 men, the Confederates, 20,000.

July 4. Independence Day, 1863. A great day for the Union. Lee was in retreat. Lincoln wanted Meade to pursue, but Meade was in no condition to do so. The threat to the North had ended. Pennsylvania and Maryland were quieting down. Out west in Mississippi, Vicksburg surrendered after a bitter siege, and 29,000 Southern soldiers laid down their arms and marched out of the city. U. S. Grant watched the Stars and Stripes go up. The Western campaign was drawing to a close.

Lee retreated, fighting rearguard actions through Maryland, and on July 13 crossed into northern Virginia, ending the threat to the North.

On August 8, General Lee offered to resign his command, deeply conscious of the failure at Gettysburg. President Davis rejected his offer. The fighting was again in the West, and in Carolina, where it would never be decisive, yet would have great effect on the war. On September 9, the Union troops entered Chattanooga. The battle of Chickamauga was the result, where General George H. Thomas earned his nickname the Rock of Chickamauga. It was another Union defeat, but again not a debacle.

In the East the front was quiet until October 9, when Lee began to move toward Washington. The next day skirmishes occurred along the Rapidan River. Meade fell back as the Confederates moved along his right flank, trying to get behind him.

On October 12, Lee moved, Meade retreated. Lee headed toward Manassas and Washington. The armies faced one another in the area along Bull Run. Meade attacked across the Rappahannock at Rappahannock Station. Maneuvering again.

In the West came the Battle of Lookout Mountain. And then Missionary Ridge. The Federal victories opened the road into Georgia for the Union army and ultimately General William T. Sherman's famous march.

Along the Rapidan, General Meade began to move. But Lee countered and they fenced at Mine Run, Parker's Store, and New Hope Church. Nothing really happened to change the war. The Meade campaign had to be called a failure, although not a disastrous one, or even very costly. On

December 1 Meade gave up trying to break Lee's line and moved back across the Rapidan to go into winter quarters.

The winter of 1863–64 was quiet. Men lost their lives, but in actions that did not affect the course of history. Then, in February, General William Tecumseh Sherman began a march from Vicksburg to destroy Confederate railroads in Mississippi.

In March, both Lee and Meade were waiting. Not Lincoln. Out of the west came a successful general to take command of the Union forces as general in chief, Ulysses S. Grant. On March 8, Grant went to the White House to get his new commission. On March 10 he was down in Virginia conferring with Meade. On March 11 he left for Nashville to confer with Sherman, who would command the Western armies.

At the end of March 1864, General Grant established his "permanent headquarters" at Culpeper Court House, Virginia. *There* was an indication of forcefulness and positive thinking quite new among Lincoln's generals.

Again this spring the action was mostly in the West and South. General Sherman was preparing for his march through Georgia which would begin in May. Lee and the Army of Virginia and Grant and the Army of the Potomac stirred restlessly in their camps, but did nothing. The Confederates waited for the strike that surely would come from Grant, sometime. They were definitely on the defensive; the manpower problem of the South was beginning to make the big difference. The North, with a population of 19 million and immigration at the rate of more than 100,000 people per year, was in a much better position to carry on the war than the Confederacy, with 9 million people and no immigration.

Grant was ready to move on May 4. The night before, he had ordered the army to begin moving across the Rapidan River, march around Lee's right flank, and head for Richmond. The Union army, 122,000 strong, moved. Up to protect the flank came the Army of Northern Virginia.

The Battle of the Wilderness began. It lasted two days, exacted enormous casualties, particularly on the Union side, and ended indecisively.

On May 8 the two forces fought again at Spotsylvania Courthouse. The Union charged and was repulsed on the first day. The second day was perhaps the most murderous day of the whole war, with no real result in terms of territory or strategic advantage. The battle lulled, then fired up again on May 18. There was nothing conclusive, except that the casualties were enormous. In the Wilderness and Spotsylvania engagements the Union had lost 33,000 men of 110,000. The Northern newspapers began referring harshly to the new Union commander as "Grant the butcher."

On May 20, Grant began moving east and south. A few miles south of him, Lee aped the movement, maintaining distance and position. At North Anna, Virginia, an inconclusive engagement was fought on May 23, Lee losing a chance to split the Army of the Potomac. After three days, Grant withdrew across the North Anna River, heading around to Lee's right. Two days later, Lee's army arrived north of the Chickahominy River and Mechanicsville. Grant shifted his line toward Cold Harbor, but Lee shifted to keep Grant from outflanking him and driving toward Richmond. The Army of Virginia built strong fortifications from the Chickahominy on the south to the Totopotomoy on the north. Behind, and not far away, was Richmond.

Grant attacked, and the Confederate artillery decimated his infantry. The battle was not long, but the firing was incredibly fierce. In about an hour the Army of the Potomac lost 7,000 men. The Confederates, with losses of only 1,500, had stemmed the tide, stopped Grant, and saved Richmond for the time being.

On June 2, Grant moved the Army of the Potomac toward the James River, and on June 14 crossed the James. The next day an attack on Petersburg began. The direct assault failed and the Union army began a siege of Petersburg, the vital rail center, also called the "back door to Richmond."

Meanwhile, the two sides fought the battle of Kenesaw Mountain, in Georgia. It was a defeat for the Union but did not stop Sherman's march. At about the same time, General Jubal Early's Confederate cavalry invaded Washington, but the local authorities raised a 20,000-man militia, and Early withdrew. Confederates ranged around the Washington area: they burned Chambersburg, Pennsylvania, and skirmished around the West Virginia border. And in the far South, Admiral Farragut and his fleet invaded Mobile Bay and closed down Mobile as a port for the Confederacy.

All these struggles had their part in the war, but the real action, the struggle that would determine the outcome of the war, was Grant against Lee. The siege of Petersburg went on, and on.

Sherman's inexorable march brought him to Atlanta, and the Confederates evacuated that city on September 1, 1864. In the Shenandoah area, General Early and General Sheridan were fighting battle after battle. Confederate Lieutenant Bennett H. Young and about twenty-five men made a daring raid out of Canada on Saint Albans, Vermont. Confederate agents set a series of fires in New York City (which destroyed Barnum's famous museum, among other sites). These were spectacular and did not help Union morale, but they were stunts that would be of far more interest to Civil War buffs in the twentieth century than to the generals. Still the main contest was Lee versus Grant, and the second most important activity was Sherman's march to the sea. Sherman reached the door to Savannah, and then took the city. Another bastion of the Confederacy was gone.

The struggle in the West ended with the Battle of Nashville, in which

George H. Thomas and the Army of the Cumberland defeated General John Bell Hood's Army of the Tennessee. The Confederates no longer had the military and manpower resources to rebuild that army.

The year 1865 began with talk of peace in the air. On February 3, Lincoln and Secretary of State Seward of the Union met with Confederate Vice President Alexander Stephens in the salon of a steamboat in Hampton Roads. They talked peace. Lincoln said his own disposition was to be liberal, but he could make no promises for Congress. The Southerners said the talk about the authority of the United States being recognized before all else meant unconditional surrender. Lincoln said he had not implied that. But the conference ended without any real results.

The Union forces now began capturing cities. Columbia, South Carolina, was burned. Charleston was taken. Wilmington fell. On March 29, 1865, the Appomattox campaign began when Grant moved 125,000 men of the Army of the Potomac against Petersburg and Richmond. At the battles of White Oak Road, Dinwiddie Court House, and Five Forks, the Union forces came down inexorably, so much stronger than the Confederates, that really nothing could be done. The Confederate government evacuated Richmond on April 2, and Union troops broke the Confederate line at Petersburg. On April 3 the Union forces occupied both cities. On April 4, Lincoln traveled symbolically to Richmond, and he was told there by several former Confederate officials that the war was now over. It was just a question of ending the fighting.

On April 7 General Grant wrote General Lee asking him to surrender to avoid further bloodshed. Lee asked for Grant's terms. Grant replied that his only condition was that the Confederate troops lay down their arms and agree not to fight again until properly exchanged as prisoners. Lee would not accept that, but said he wanted to talk to Grant.

At dawn on Palm Sunday, April 9, 1865, the Confederates attacked near Appomattox Station, hoping to break through the Union line. They failed. Surrounded, Lee admitted that further fighting would lead only to useless bloodshed. He surrendered. The Civil War that had rent the American continent and the souls of 30 million people for four years came to an end.

CHAPTER 19

The End of the Trail

The American Indians were forced steadily westward and by the 1860s, when major settlement of the lands of the Northwest was in progress, they had gone about as far as they could go. The end of the trail was in sight in the 1870s, when American government policy hardened.

In this chapter I go into detail about the Battle of the Little Bighorn because it epitomizes what had happened to the Indians all the way along during the past half century. Little Bighorn was the high-water mark of Indian defiance, and when the Indians won, the Indian chiefs knew that still they had lost. They scattered then, and except for a few more actions, as noted in the text, that was the end of the Indians in America as a social or military force.

*   *   *

The last cogent American government Indian policy before the Civil War was that of John C. Calhoun, President Monroe's secretary of war, who suggested that all the Indians be pushed west of the Mississippi River into that great wide open plains country which no one could foresee ever being used for much of anything else. Let the Eastern Indians go out and learn to hunt buffalo like the Plains Indians, and the Indian problem of America would be solved forever. The fact that many of these Indians were farmers and herdsmen meant nothing to Calhoun.

But at least the Calhoun policy meant freedom for the Indians. The administrations after Monroe's followed this policy until the Civil War.

Then, during the war, some tribes fought with the Confederacy, which did not endear them to the Union later. In the summer of 1862 a gang of four young Sioux Indians murdered two families near the Sioux reservation in Minnesota. They hurried back to their reservation to boast of their prowess. Many of the Indians agreed that the whites had abused them too much, that they must now rise up and drive them from the country. One chief, Little Crow, warned the Indians again, as King Philip's sachem had warned the Massachusetts Indians so long ago: he had been to the white men's cities; he had seen their power. If the Indians fought the whites they would lose, and the loss would mean destruction. Having said that, Little Crow then offered to lead the Indians in battle. Thus, on August 18, 1862, began the Sioux uprising with the murder of all white traders on the Indian reservation.

The Union soldiers at Ford Ridgley were aroused. Captain John Marsh, the commander, believed the uprising was merely local and headed out to stop it with forty-eight men. They were ambushed by a Sioux war party, and only twenty-three men made it back to the fort, which then sent to Fort Snelling for help.

Little Crow attacked Fort Ridgley with 400 warriors. The soldiers inside drove them off with the help of artillery. By August 22, Little Crow had 800 warriors and they attacked again. Again they were driven off. The Indians moved away and attacked New Ulm, which was defended by militia. The defenders held off the Indians, but at a cost of 190 houses burned and only 25 saved, and about a quarter of the defenders killed or wounded. That night the survivors moved to Mankato for safety.

Colonel Henry Sibley of the Minnesota militia came with a force of more than 1,500 men, but he was inept and so timid that very little was accomplished. Ultimately, however, as Little Crow had warned, the power of the whites showed, and the Indians fled into Dakota Territory.

The cost of the Minnesota massacre was inestimable. To the whites, it could be measured thus: twenty-three counties were devastated, a whole strip of the western frontier—50 miles wide and 200 miles long—was depopulated, and 30,000 whites had fled their homes. Some went back east, never to return west.

To the Indians the loss was even greater on a long-range basis. The Minnesota massacre received enormous publicity and was a major factor in the establishment of a new Indian policy by the American government, a policy which basically called for extermination.

When the Civil War ended, General William Tecumseh Sherman was such a hero that he could pick his own peacetime assignment. He had no stomach to become policeman of the South, and he asked for command of the unit that would soon be called the Military Division of the Missouri, which covered the territory from Texas to Canada and from the Mississippi to the Rocky Mountains. Given the attitude of most Americans toward Indians, General Sherman was just the man to command. Asked about good Indians, he made his famous remark: "The only good Indians I ever saw were dead."

The problem of the postwar administration of American Indian territory remained the same as before: white expansion into Indian territory. California brought the miners, and then the settlers across the Southwest and through the Sierra Nevada. Peace brought the expansion—and movement of many discouraged Southerners—across the Oregon Trail, and its tributary, the Bozeman Trail into Montana country. Virtually every mile was contested by the Indians. In 1866 fighting around Fort Philip Kearny caused the evacuation of the fort, and the retaliation of General Sherman: "We must act with vindictive earnestness against the Sioux, even to their extermination, men, women, and children . . ."

Extermination was as much of a watchword as Sherman ever had.

Yet in 1867 vindictiveness was not the national feeling in America. That year Congress ordered settlement of disputes with the Indians without the interference of the War Department. Seven peace commissioners were chosen. Unfortunately, three of these commissioners were generals, and the leader was Sherman.

Even so, the Indians fought so hard that in 1868 a new treaty was signed with the Sioux and Arapaho Indians. All South Dakota west of the Missouri was set aside as an Indian reservation. The Indians could hunt in the North Platte and the Bighorn and Republican river lands as long as the buffalo lasted. The Bozeman Trail and the forts were abandoned: Fort C. F. Smith, Fort Kearny, Fort Reno. Chief Red Cloud of the Oglala Sioux had won one of the few victorious campaigns ever achieved by the Indians over the whites. He had driven them out of the territory they had invaded, and the government in Washington had approved the settlement that gave the Indians the territory for which they had fought. For a short time the Oglala Sioux would have a happy hunting ground. But Red Cloud knew it would not last. He knew his white men. Someone asked him how to become like the whites, and he replied:

"You must begin anew and put away the wisdom of your fathers. You must lay up food and forget the hungry. When your house is built, your store room filled, then look around for a neighbor whom you can take advantage of, and seize all he has."

Eighteen sixty-eight. It was the year that the Kansas Pacific Railroad began selling tickets to the buffalo hunting grounds for "sportsmen." Before this, the sports had simply stuck the muzzles of their guns out of the carriage windows and popped away, letting the bison fall where they might and rot, not even bothering with the skins. The buffalo hunters were legendary men—devils to the Indians—who killed the bison and left the meat, the great wastage that was decimating the plains herds.

By the summer of 1868 along the Kansas Pacific right-of-way the stench was so bad that nonhunting passengers complained. Cheyenne and Arapaho could stand it no longer. About 2,000 Indians went on the warpath in the Solomon and Saline river areas, and the federal troops were once again engaged in warfare.

General Sherman did not waver: "The more we can kill this year the less will have to be killed the next war." General Grant, who was running for president, agreed. It was necessary to protect the migrants crossing the plains, he said, even if it meant the extermination of every Indian tribe.

In command of the 7th Cavalry was Lieutenant Colonel George A. Custer, who preferred the courtesy title general, which he had earned as a temporary general officer in the Civil War. He came up to Fort Hays to participate in the big drive, which was planned for October, against the Indians from Medicine Lodge Creek toward the Wichita Mountains.

The drive was successful. Ultimately every drive against the Indians was successful. Every year they were driven farther west in the compression of Indian territory.

So it went into 1873. That was the year of the Modoc War in California and Oregon. The next year the Comanches rose against the whites. The fighting moved into Kansas, Colorado, New Mexico, and Texas. It was whites against the Osage, Cheyenne, Arapaho, Kiowa, as well as the Comanche. It was called the Red River War of 1874 and 1875. Many men were killed on both sides, by the dozens and scores. The war ended, some Indians were executed, some were jailed, and there was relative peace again until 1878. The main result was that the southern plains hunting grounds were thereafter denied to the Indians.

In the summer of 1875, the Americans began trying to buy the Black Hills from the Indians. When they did not succeed, the Americans turned hostile, and General Phil Sheridan, another hero of the Civil War, set about "rounding up" the Indians, using three converging columns of troops in the Yellowstone, North Platte, and Montana country. The three columns would converge somewhere around the Bighorn and Yellowstone river junction. All the Indians would be vacuumed up and deposited nicely in reservations, never again to disturb the tranquility of the white population. General Sheridan thought there might be as many as 1,500 warriors out there in the Powder River country.

One U.S. column was defeated in the Powder River area and retreated. A spring campaign was planned for 1876, but it was delayed. Finally, on May 17, 1876, a long column set out from Fort Abraham Lincoln near

Bismarck. The center of it was the 7th Cavalry, Colonel Custer commanding. The column reached the Yellowstone River. From here it was to push up the river until it met Colonel John Gibbon's column. Down south, General Crook's column was supposedly driving the Indians northward into the hands of the other two units.

In between the converging U.S. army units were the Indians, some 12,000 of them, with 5,000 warriors, under War Chief Sitting Bull. On June 17, 1876, General George Crook's 1,300 troops set out to do battle with about the same number of Indians under Chief Crazy Horse, one of Sitting Bull's unit commanders. The action occurred on Rosebud Creek, on the eastern side of the Wolf Mountains. The daylong battle was indecisive, although General Crook claimed a victory.

Up north the two other U.S. Army columns established a base at the mouth of the Powder River on the Yellowstone. The camp was supplied by a Missouri River steamboat. Major Marcus Reno, the second in command of the 7th Cavalry, went out to find Indians, and he found plenty of trails, but no Indians on the northern end of Rosebud Creek. He was forty miles too far north, for the day that he reached the creek was June 17, the day of General Crook's big battle down south.

So Reno went back to camp to report no Indians.

General Terry, the overall commander of the army group, decided the Indians had crossed over from the Rosebud to Bighorn River country, west of the Wolf Mountains. He decided to send Colonel Gibbon with one unit up the Bighorn River and the tributary, the Little Bighorn, while Colonel Custer circled around and came along the Little Bighorn from the south. So on June 20 Colonel Gibbon set out from the bivouac on Rosebud Creek and headed up the Yellowstone to the Bighorn, fifty miles away. Colonel Custer was to go up the Rosebud to the point Reno had seen all the Indian signs. If Custer found that the Indian trail turned west and led across the divide toward the Little Bighorn, he was not to, repeat not to, follow it but to continue up the Rosebud Creek. The idea was to surround the Indians. Custer was to travel so that he would enter the valley of the Little Bighorn from the south at the same time that Gibbon entered from the north.

Custer was bragging that his 7th Cavalry could whip all the Indians in the west. General Terry suggested that he take along some Gatling guns and an extra cavalry squadron. Haughtily, Custer refused. It would be demeaning to his troops to carry along Gatling guns. Another cavalry unit would be embarrassing because the 7th Cavalry worked so well together that extra troops would just cause confusion.

On June 22, after a regimental review, Colonel Custer set out. The review was not precisely spit-and-polish. Custer had left his wagon trains behind, and his cavalry was reduced to the old field practice of carrying supplies on packhorses and mules. It had been a long time since some of those soldiers had "skinned" a mule or struggled with a packhorse determined to blow out his belly to avoid a tight cinch. The sloppiness showed through on parade in loose and slipping packs. Custer was embarrassed. General Terry was understanding.

"Now Custer," called Colonel Gibbon of the other column. "Don't be greedy. Wait for us."

"No, I won't," shouted Custer, and he galloped off to join his troops.

Custer was ordered first to survey Tullock's Creek, and then to send a messenger to Colonel Gibbon on the result. Custer ignored the orders, and moved on. He came to the point where the Indian signs showed the trail that many Indians had moved along, and, as General Terry had suggested, it did move over the divide into the valley of the Little Bighorn. But Custer continued to ignore his orders. He would take the trail, he told his officers. The Americans would lie concealed in the rocky high country all day while scouts found the Indians, and then at dawn on June 25, the 7th Cavalry would strike.

So the troops marched far into the night through strange country, until at 2:00 A.M. even Custer decided they had to give up and get some rest.

At dawn on June 25, Custer's Crow Indian scouts climbed to the high point on the divide called the Crow's Nest, where far below and far away they saw an enormous band of ponies, which meant a very large Indian war party. They pointed out the herd to Custer's Lieutenant Varnum, but Varnum's eyes would not see. And below, they saw Custer's campfires, although the Crows had warned Custer not to make campfires.

Custer came up to the Crow's Nest, and the Indians showed him the Sioux camp down below. He could not see the ponies. He could not see the Indian camp. He said there was no camp down there.

Down below, the Indians already knew where Custer was. They had found a box of hardtack dropped from a packhorse during the long night march. The sloppiness noted by General Terry and his staff was now paid for. Custer had lost the element of surprise.

Coming back from the Crow's Nest, Custer decided to move in, and he started the march up to the divide and down the ravine that led to the valley of the Little Bighorn. The men came to a small creek that runs due west into the Little Bighorn. There Custer stopped to organize for battle.

One battalion was given to Captain Frederick Benteen. One was given to Major Reno. Custer kept the other battalion for himself, except one company which was left to guard the pack train.

Captain Benteen and his three companies were ordered off to the southwest, moving off to the left, to reconnoiter that side and then take the first valley and come back to join up. Benteen set out and immediately disappeared from sight in the rough terrain.

Custer and Reno went on to the river with their units, Reno on the left bank of the creek, and Custer on the right. They did not know it, but they were heading for the largest Indian camp ever assembled on the plains.

They passed a single teepee and inside found the body of a dead warrior, probably one of those killed in the fight against General Crook. Then Custer saw something else: a cloud of dust about five miles away and about forty Indians who seemed to be running away. Custer believed that the Indians would run rather than fight when confronting a large unit of U.S. troops. This sight added conviction to his belief. He ordered his Indian scouts to pursue the fleeing men, but they refused. They knew that an enormous encampment was nearby, and they also knew what Indians did to gain time when caught not quite ready for battle; a handful of warriors would mount their horses and begin raising clouds of dust to confuse the enemy while the main band got going.

Custer was never much of a listener, and he had not listened to his scouts this time. He believed he had the Indians on the run, and when the scouts refused to respond, contemptuously he ordered them deprived of their horses and their rifles. Custer then sent an order to Major Reno on the other side of the creek, telling him to make for the dust and charge the Indians. So Reno set off along the creek. Custer had just once again done the unimaginable for a military commander; for the second time this morning he had split his force when apparently confronting a large enemy unit. No wonder he had been at the bottom of his graduating class at West Point!

So Reno went off along the creek, and at about 2:30 that afternoon he crossed the Little Bighorn River and immediately saw that his "fleeing Indians" were coming out to fight.

After Reno crossed the river, he caught glimpses ahead of the teepee camp, which was some two miles away. But he only caught glimpses; the ridges came between. He formed his men into a skirmish line and the battalion galloped toward the village to overwhelm it. But they never got there.

Ahead of Reno's battalion was the cloud of dust, and then figures emerged and Reno could see hundreds of warriors riding toward him. His Indian scouts turned and fled, which left Reno's left flank open. A large party of Sioux rode up to take their place. It was hardly what Major Reno wanted. Where was Custer? He had promised Reno support on the left. But now that the support was needed, Custer was nowhere to be seen.

Reno stopped his men and told them to dismount. The horseholders took the mounts back to the protection of the woods behind the battalion and the troops got ready to fight on foot. Two companies remained, for one company had been sent back to protect the horses. Soon the Sioux were circling the soldiers, whooping, and firing their weapons.

Fortunately the Sioux were more interested in circling and shooting than in hitting anything. A favorite trick was for a warrior to ride in madly, touch a blue-coated soldier or his horse, then turn and ride back into the pack. Such an act was considered a coup, an illustration of bravery in battle. The more coups a brave could count in a battle, the greater his prestige was around the campfire. This day some warriors claimed 80 to 100 coups.

Thus far, the Indians occupied with their own bravery, Reno had not lost a man. He sounded the retreat and the soldiers headed back so that they were all along a bend in the creek. But that position became untenable and Reno then ordered the men to get ready to mount. The order did not reach all the men. The battalion mounted and rode off charging through the Indian line, but leaving seventeen men behind. Soon they would be overwhelmed and slaughtered by the Indians.

The Indians chased Reno's column as it sped along the stream and forced the men into the water from the right; then, as the horses floundered, the Indians on both banks fired down on them. Finally the survivors made the east bank, and found a hill 300 feet high where they organized their defense. Half the battalion was now gone, killed, wounded, or left behind.

Much of Reno's ammunition was gone and the situation looked nearly desperate. Then, suddenly, the Indians seemed to lose interest in Reno's battalion, and rode away to the northeast. The pressure was off. Men could make their way down to the stream for water. The firing became a series of *pop-pops*.

Captain Benteen had been sent on a wild goose chase, and that much was apparent early in the afternoon. Benteen had not seen a single Indian, no matter which valley he searched. He stopped along the creek that was his general guideline (later named Reno Creek) and watered the horses. The regimental pack train found them there, and the pack train moved in for water. Benteen did not wait. He went on. He met Sergeant Daniel Kanipe, of Custer's battalion, who had been sent back to hurry the pack train up to his unit because Custer had finally seen the village and he wanted more ammunition available. Sergeant Kanipe was to rush the pack train up to Custer.

Benteen did not wait, because he heard the sounds of firing; he spurred forward to the Little Bighorn. When he came in sight of the river, he was just in time to see a horde of Sioux warriors riding down the last of the stragglers of Reno's battalion as they ran on foot toward the river. Captain Benteen then encountered one of the Crow scouts, who pointed to the hill where Reno was making his stand. Benteen led his men forward at a trot. They found Reno, pistol in hand, completely confused, and Benteen took over the defense of the hill.

Somewhere to the east, they could all hear the sound of gunfire, a lot of gunfire. But they did not know what gunfire it was, or where. One of Benteen's companies then rode north to a high hill—Weir Point. From the hill they could see a cloud of dust and smoke four miles to the north, and many Indians, some of whom appeared to be shooting into the ground.

Reno was trying to move his wounded up to Weir Point when more of the Indians saw the blue uniforms and turned back. Benteen then saw that the original position was better for defense and moved back to that hill, where Reno was still struggling. There the two battalions set up their line of defense.

The Indians struck just before dark. The fight lasted until after full darkness set in. That night the soldiers dug in, using plates and knives as entrenching tools, for they had only three spades. They were lucky their hill was like a saucer on top, the rim serving as a parapet, hiding the horses and the improvised hospital in the depression below.

That night Indian fires burned down below the army's hill and drums banged as the Indians danced their victory dance. When morning came, the soldiers knew they would be attacked again.

The Indians did not wait for sunrise. Dawn came before 3:00 A.M. and the first rifle began to fire. Soon the crackling was continual. The firing was nearly all from the Indians. Reno and Benteen told their men to hold their fire and only one or two sharpshooters were allowed to use their rifles.

The Indians came close to Benteen's sector. He mounted a cavalry charge, routed them, and came back without a casualty.

Reno also mounted a charge with four companies on the Sioux just as they were gathering to make a charge of their own. The Indians scattered and ran, and the cavalry came back. For a while it was very quiet. When the Indians did return, they were more cautious. The struggle settled into a state of siege, and water became the problem. Soldiers were sent down to the river, while sharpshooters stood on guard over them. The night passed. Morning came, and the soldiers expected another attack. But shortly after noon on June 27, the men could see the teepees in the village down below being dismantled. And that afternoon the whole enormous village of thousands came down and the Indians moved out, toward the Bighorn Mountains. The soldiers did not know it, but the Indians had spotted Colonel Gibbon's column on the way to the meeting place set up by General Terry. They knew Crook was still around. So it was time to go. That night it was absolutely quiet around Reno's hill. The battle was over.

On that night of June 27, Colonel Gibbon and General Terry camped downstream on the Little Bighorn, about ten miles from Reno's camp. Crow scouts had reported on a great battle that had been fought up ahead, with all the soldiers killed. General Terry did not believe that. But where *was* Custer?

At dawn on the morning of June 28 the Gibbon column was moving. Reno's men saw them coming, and two lieutenants rode down to meet them. When they saw General Terry, the two lieutenants rode up, saluted, and both asked at once:

"Where is Custer?"

No one knew.

Lieutenant James Bradley was sent out with scouts to the east side of the Little Bighorn. They had noticed a number of white objects on the ground off in the distance. When they came up they found the objects were naked human bodies, lying scattered among the corpses of many horses, bloating and popping in the sun. Here was Colonel Custer and his battalion, dead to the last man, the only survivor a horse named Comanche.

Lieutenant Bradley counted the bodies—197. He and his men then rode back to Reno's hill to report, and General Terry and Colonel Gibbon went to the site of the battle. Most of the bodies had been stripped. Some had been scalped. Custer had been stripped but not scalped. The scene showed that the battle had been hopeless from the first, that Custer's 200-odd men had been surrounded almost at the beginning, had dismounted and fought on foot, and that literally thousands of the Indians had come at them from all sides with rifles, muskets, and bows and arrows. The battalion never had a chance. The soldiers buried 206 bodies in that field.

Out of Custer's Last Stand came a legend of a heroic cavalry officer in blue, yellow locks ablaze in the sun, cavalry saber in one hand and pistol in the other, going down fighting. The last was true. Custer and his men did die with their boots on. As to the locks, Custer at least had been given the good sense to have them shaved down to a crew cut before leaving Fort Abraham Lincoln that spring. But the Sioux recognized him anyhow. Nor would it have made any difference if they had not. The American Indians were having their last stand, working on their centuries-old grievances against the whites.

Ironically the great victory of the Sioux at the Little Bighorn redounded immediately against them. The temper of America that spring had been generally pro-Indian; there was much lament about the unfair treatment meted out to the unfortunate redskins by the whites. But when the news of the "Custer Massacre" reached America, attitudes changed. The news was accompanied by the most horrible tales of torture, disfigurement, and mutilation. The only actual mutilation discovered was that of the unfortunate men abandoned by Major Reno, who had been turned over to the squaws. The bodies of these men showed they had been tortured and mutilated by experts.

But lack of factual support did not stop the stories. And the army did nothing to remind the public that Custer had been defeated in battle largely due to his own error. General Sheridan ordered a combing of the region for Indians. General Crook set out marching north on Rosebud Creek with more than 2,000 men and Buffalo Bill, who needed the publicity for his wild west show. General Terry and 1,600 men marched from the Yellowstone River to Rosebud Creek. They expected to close like a vise on the Sioux and trap them, but met only one another in a cloud of dust.

The summer became fall, and no Indians were found. Finally the American troops did capture some Indians in the Black Hills region and killed Chief American Horse and destroyed his village. So ended the great campaign to eradicate the Indian. Some statistician figured out that it cost the United States government a million dollars for every Indian the Americans killed.

The Indians had won another major battle and had gotten clean away. But there were too many soldiers. Winter came and the Indians had to move too often. Ultimately Chief Crazy Horse surrendered. Sitting Bull, the supreme war chief of the Sioux, fled into Canada with many lesser chiefs, and remained there for several years.

A new commission set up new rules for the Indians, and, of course, the result was again the seizure of more Indian lands by the whites. The Powder River country was taken, and the Black Hills, and altogether about a third of the previous Sioux reservation.

So 1876 marked the real end of Indian independence in America. There would be more wars and more violence. The Nez Percé were forced across the Snake River into new country, forced to fight, defeated the soldiers, and went into what was called Chief Joseph's Retreat, which ended in the last battle of Bear Paw Mountain. The white soldiers, Colonel Gibbon leading, set to killing Indian women and children, following General Sherman's policy of extermination.

During the next few years that policy underlay the American official treatment of the Indians. Most Indians were sent down to Indian Territory, the malaria-ridden lands of Oklahoma and Arkansas. Ultimately even this land, at one time regarded as too raw and barren for a white man, became attractive to settlers in the drive west.

The Bannocks rose in southeast Idaho. The Cheyenne, banished from their homeland, decided to return in 1878 and moved, fighting the soldiers as they went. The spirit was supreme, but the numbers were weak. There were only 300 of them, and only 70 of these were warriors. They fought four battles against the army, won them all, and moved on. General Sheridan mobilized the entire Division of the Missouri against these 70 warriors. The Indians slipped through the army net, time and again. They headed into the sand hills of northern Nebraska. But in the end, they were captured and mistreated dreadfully. Those who escaped were hunted down by the soldiers. One massacre of Indians followed another. When so charged, General Sheridan complained. "Massacre?" he shouted. "Why do you call it a massacre? A number of insubordinate, cunning, treacherous Indians."

In 1879 the White River Utes rose up against an arbitrary Indian agent named Nathan Meeker. Governor Frederick Pitkin of Colorado again suggested that old strong medicine: "My idea is that unless removed by the government they must be exterminated."

The reason, of course, was that the Indians threatened the white ownership of all that land.

So it went. In 1885 the chief Geronimo led a band of Chiricahua Apaches in flight from the confines of their reservation into the mountains of Arizona and Mexico.

General Crook, who had come to know the Apaches very well, was commander of the Army Department of Arizona then. He fought Geronimo for months, and then persuaded Geronimo to surrender. General Crook believed that almost all the grievances of the Apache were real and their complaints justified, and so said. But General Sheridan was now commander in chief of the army, and he prevailed on President Cleveland to follow the old army policy. Crook's terms of surrender were repudiated and the Apaches were imprisoned. Crook resigned from the army in protest.

Finally in 1890 came the disgraceful Battle of Wounded Knee in which the 7th Cavalry butchered 300 Indian men, women, and children. A line of bodies extended two miles from the Indian camp, all women and children cut down by the American soldiers as they tried to escape the massacre.

The army was true to its motto "The only good Indian is a dead Indian." And in being true in the years after the Civil War the army wrote the most ignoble chapter in the history of the American armed services. The massacre at Wounded Knee was just the finale. The American treatment of the American Indians was as fine a case of genocide as the world has ever seen.

When the first thousand English settlers came to North America in the 1620s, about a million Indians lived there, half a million on the East Coast. Had they been organized they might have made life so difficult for the colonists that they would have gone elsewhere. But they believed the Englishmen's protestations of friendship. In 1675, at the time of King Philip's War, there were more than twice as many Indians as whites in New England, which accounts in part for the fear of the colonists that the Indians might triumph.

Ironic is it not that the man who presided over the beginning of the extermination policy was named for one of the Indians'—and America's—

greatest military heroes, the Chief Tecumseh? General Sherman must have rolled over in his grave on June 2, 1924, when the United States Congress bestowed U.S. citizenship on all American Indians. The handful of Indians lived quietly in poverty on their reservations. The proud Oglala Sioux picked up pocket change by traveling to the Pendleton Roundup, Calgary Stampede, and Cheyenne Frontier Days, to set up a teepee on the fair grounds, dress up in deerskins, beads, and feathers, and dance one or two tired dances that virtually no one in the tribe could remember. Citizenship? Why not? By that time no one cared.

CHAPTER 20

Coal and Colonies

The perfection of the steam-driven warship was the spur for a major American drive toward colonization of the Pacific Ocean. The Americans had their eyes on many bits of territory: Hawaii, Samoa, Japan, Korea, and such mid-Pacific islets as Guam and Midway. Coal was as much the spur here as gold had ever been.

* * *

Manifest Destiny was the high-sounding phrase under which American expansionists worked during the nineteenth century. The followers came in all shapes and sizes, from manufacturers looking for markets to missionaries seeking new flocks. But never in the aft of the craft was the United States Navy, for with the coming of steam and the gradual, reluctant abandonment of fighting sail, the navy looked abroad for bases.

Certainly the U.S. Navy was not alone. Britain was gobbling up stray islands in all oceans. France was moving in the South Pacific. American expeditions to China and Japan had established coaling stations by 1853, when the new navy was still the dream of a handful of commodores.

The navy's foray into colonialism was renewed in 1867 when Midway Island, a deserted atoll about halfway between Hawaii and the western Pacific shores, was occupied as American territory by Captain William Reynolds of the USS *Lackawanna*. The purpose was to establish a coaling base for the navy.

In 1871 Commodore John Rodgers visited Korea with a squadron of five ships. The purpose then, ostensibly, was to secure the safety of ship-wrecked American seamen, some of whom had been murdered and some mistreated by the feisty Koreans. The United States really expected to open Korea for trade, and thus the American minister to China was picked up en route and taken along by the commodore. When they got to Korea the welcome was not overwhelming. A landing party was attacked when it approached a Korean fort and two seamen were killed. Commodore Rodgers demanded an immediate apology and reparations. The Koreans were silent. The commodore then landed a large force of marines and sailors, and attacked several forts and captured them, killing about 400 Koreans. This activity scarcely endeared Rodgers and the Americans to the Koreans. The Rodgers mission could not be called successful since it did not achieve its objectives.

The drive for "coaling stations" and American naval influence contin-ued. For a long time Americans had been interested in Samoa. In 1872 Commander Richard W. Meade negotiated a treaty with the Samoan chiefs which gave the United States Navy a coaling station in the harbor of Pago Pago on the island of Tutuila. The U.S. Senate, going through one of its gyrations against naval expansion, refused to ratify the treaty. The Ger-mans picked up where the Americans had left off and were soon deep in Samoan affairs, which upset the American navy and State Department. Kaiser Wilhelm I was busily building a German empire that he hoped would match the British, although, of course, it never came close. But because of the original rebuff, the Americans had lost ground, and finally in 1878 when they did get their coaling station at Pago Pago it was on a nonexclusive basis, and put the United States up against Germany in the struggle for influence in these islands.

It was ten years after Commodore Rodgers' foray into gunboat diplo-macy in Korea before Commodore R. W. Shufeldt made another trip to that country with much more successful results, achieved by dealing through the Chinese, with whom the Koreans had a vassal relationship.

Americans had been stopping off in the Hawaiian kingdom for a long time, mostly whalers and naval vessels. They were not exactly welcome to the missionaries, but very welcome indeed to the growing business com-munity, especially in Honolulu. Trade in sugar was developing in Hawaii and the problem was marketing. The perfect market for Hawaii was the United States, except that to protect its own growers the U.S. government had imposed a high tariff on imported sugar. The American navy had its eye on the virtually perfect ship haven west of Honolulu called Pearl Har-bor, which was a natural naval base. So a trade was made; the United States would grant to the Hawaiian kingdom special tariff concessions in exchange for the grant of Pearl Harbor as an American coaling station and the promise that none of Hawaii would be turned over to another power. The treaty was enacted in 1875, and thereafter Hawaii moved into a special relationship with the United States. A whole series of American consuls set out to colonize Hawaii for the United States, but many Hawaiians and British businessmen did their best to prevent undue American influence. So the Hawaiian kingdom remained independent.

British and French influence increased, and the Americans became miffed by Hawaii's courtship of the others. The sugar concession to Hawaii had cost heavily in domestic affairs; cane sugar was produced in Louisiana, Texas, and Florida, and Americans had major sugar interests in Cuba and other Caribbean spots. So in 1885 the Senate refused to renew the Hawaii treaty, which brought business in Honolulu virtually to a standstill. Ultimately the problem was worked out, but not before the Americans had a better deal for themselves: they ensured the concession of an exclusive right to establish a fortified U.S. naval base at Pearl Harbor. Thus Hawaii was brought within the American sphere of influence, with American military personnel stationed on Hawaiian shores.

All this was done as the navy was still feeling its way in development. By the end of the Civil War the U.S. Navy was reluctantly accepting iron ships. At the end of the war, the Union navy had 700 ships, 65 of them ironclads. The low-lying monitors with their swivel turrets were much in vogue for harbor defense. Sailing warships were converted to steam, but they still carried their masts and sails. Deliberately, steaming qualities were sacrificed so that sail could be retained. But as every deepwater sailor soon learned, the hermaphrodite ship was neither one thing nor the other, and most unsatisfactory.

Congress, immersed in the problems of Reconstruction, let the U.S. Navy rot. In 1865 the American navy was second only to Britain's. Fifteen years later it was twelfth in the world, behind Chile and China, and there were only forty-eight ships in the whole fleet that could fire a gun. Only thirty of these were fit for service abroad. It was almost as though the navy was back to the days of Commodore Dewey, who had boasted to the Japanese of the enormous naval resources of the United States when actually his ten-ship squadron had represented a third of the whole American fleet.

The major changes in the U.S. Navy began with the establishment of a naval board to recommend new construction. This board asked for thirty-eight steel cruisers and twenty-five gunboats and torpedo boats. These were peacetime years, and Congress was not receptive to defense spending. So the navy got the three unarmored cruisers *Boston, Atlanta,* and *Chicago,* and a smaller warship, the *Dolphin,* called a dispatch boat.

The unarmored cruiser was the ship of the day, the successor to the sailing frigate, a man-of-war suitable for fast action and movement. The

American naval concept (and the German) called for a war of attrition against a possible enemy's shipping, and the best instrument of the day was a fast, relatively heavily armed vessel that could overhaul the enemy's steamers and was still capable of action against naval vessels of its own sort or smaller. Only a navy like Britain's, Russia's, or the one the Japanese were set on building, operated on the concept of fleet battles. The idea was too expensive for most nations, and for the American Congress of the 1870s.

Grover Cleveland's first administration was responsible for the building of the new navy. Secretary of the Navy William C. Whitney secured construction of thirty-three new ships, from the first American "dreadnought," the *Texas,* to the first torpedo boat, *Cushing.*

With this growth the navy looked abroad to see what other navies were doing. They saw Britain, France, and Germany engaged in a struggle for colonies all over the world, with Japan just beginning to join up in the Pacific race. The U.S. Navy, then, became an unashamed advocate of Manifest Destiny. Was it not true that a nation must either grow or decay? Of course. And one grew by expansion. Captain Alfred Thayer Mahan, godfather of the modern American navy, said it all: trade, shipping, colonies, navies, they all went together and let the devil take the hindmost.

By 1880 the United States had bulled its way into a tripartite management of the Samoan islands with Germany and Britain. But again, the U.S. Senate refused to follow the lead of the Hayes administration and would not ratify any of the agreements involved. So they existed, because the U.S. executive branch agreed, but as Britain and Germany knew, the agreements had no force as law.

In the middle 1880s American attention was sharply focused on Samoa, which had not yet fallen victim to the European colonial impulse only because the United States, Germany, and Britain were all maneuvering for the prize. The islands themselves were about to split on the decline of the chief king and the growth of two parties. The Americans moved in on one party and the Germans on the other. The British, with their usual astuteness, saw how the wind was blowing, assessed the difficulties, and persuaded the Germans that they were really on their side; they grandly agreed to withdraw their interests in Samoa in favor of Germany if the Germans would recognize the special British interests in Africa and the Middle East. So the deal was cut.

Meanwhile canny John Bull had cut another deal with the Americans, indicating that Britain would recognize America's special interests in Samoa if the Americans would recognize Britain's special interests in Tonga and the Solomon Islands. So that deal was made as well.

But Count von Bismarck, in the drive to create a quick German empire, was impatient for colonies. When the local Samoan political situation boiled over in 1885, the German-supported faction rebelled in a bid for total power. It failed. U.S. Secretary of State Thomas F. Bayard called for a three-party meeting to settle the matter. Before it began the Germans and British met privately, and the British agreed that if the Germans would give them good opportunity for the Samoan trade, the Germans should have a mandate over Samoa; so the month-long Washington conference was doomed to fail, and it did. Germany then began pressing. The American candidate for king of all Samoa was kidnapped by the Germans and deported in a German warship to sail the high seas while matters were settled. The new Samoan king began to favor the Germans openly, and the German traders reneged on their government's private promises to the British. Not one to be gulled, John Bull began to grumble, and sent a large warship to take permanent station in the harbor of Apia, the principal port on the principal island.

The Germans responded by sending a whole squadron to Samoa. The Americans, piqued by the succession of failures, sent a squadron of their own. In 1888, Apia harbor bristled with foreign warships, whose crews eyed one another balefully and whose commanders tried to keep down incidents of violence ashore.

By the end of the year 1888 the tension was enormous. International communications still rested in fast vessels, so the military commanders on the scene had great latitude for mischief-making. In the islands that year the American and German warships tailed one another around the archipelago, watching, waiting.

So angry did the Americans become that they threatened war with Germany, and by innuendo also with Britain if she did not step out of the way and stop her underhanded support of the Germans. The United States had been at peace for more than twenty years, Indian troubles excepted, and Americans had once again become forgetful of the cost of belligerence, and very mindful of their national ambitions. On January 15, 1889, President Cleveland warned Congress of the machinations in Samoa and asked for Congressional support for his policy: preservation of Samoan independence. What this meant was really overthrow of the German-supported government that claimed power over all the islands.

Congress was still considering the issue in March, and the American force of three ships in Samoa was itching for a fight. So was the German three-ship squadron. The British, who had only one vessel in Apia, but the biggest warship of all, the *Calliope*, were calm, watching and waiting to see what was in the troubled water for them.

On March 15 the Germans were about to steam out of Apia harbor and scour the outer islands to reinforce "their" government. The Americans were prepared to follow them out, and, if the Germans made the slightest misstep, to shoot. But a typhoon blew up that day, so wicked a storm that before it was over it had wrecked all three German ships, with heavy loss of life, and the American warships *Vandalia* and *Trenton*. By the most valiant seamanship the captain of the USS *Nipsic* managed to beach his vessel in the storm, and most of the crew were saved. But as the sky cleared on March 16, there they were, six once-proud warships, not one of them capable of firing a cannon. Only the British *Calliope,* with its more powerful engines and its captain's greater familiarity with these waters, had managed to get out of Apia harbor early, to ride out the storm on the way to New Zealand. The American and German sailors, just hours ago ready to be at one another's throats, found themselves trying to give aid and solace to one another. And so a great natural disaster definitely prevented a major military confrontation which might have well resulted in a war.

While the military men were posturing and threatening in Samoa, the politicians in Washington, Berlin, and London were having second thoughts. The result was a Berlin Conference on Samoa in April, May, and June 1889, which settled the fate of the islands for a time. There was no question of going away and letting the Samoans alone. But the conferees did agree that the "independence and autonomy" of Samoa were to be guaranteed by the three powers under a three-power protectorate. It should be noted that the British, having manipulated the Germans and the Americans for concessions in other parts of the world, ended up with a part of the pie of Samoa, too. And, later, when Germany lost all her colonies, Samoa was split between the United States and New Zealand, a condition in which it remained 100 years later.

CHAPTER 21

Fomenting a Revolution

A military excursion in the nineteenth century could start quite subtly, as did the American effort to annex Hawaii. The idea was first that of the U.S. Navy, which after the Civil War coveted a coaling station and naval base at Pearl Harbor. A succession of Republican administrations looked with approval at this yearning, and made it a diplomatic matter. In effect, the United States traded a preferential policy regarding importation of Hawaiian sugar (which competed with Cuban sugar and Louisiana sugar and later Western beet sugar) for that naval base.

With a foot in the door of the Hawaiian kingdom the United States grew more ambitious, and a number of American consuls and ministers, especially John L. Stevens, who spent many years in the islands, did all they could to encourage American annexation. In this regard they were encouraged by the children of the American missionaries who had come to Hawaii in the early years of the nineteenth century. Many of the children had remained in "the island paradise," had become Hawaiian citizens, and wanted Hawaii to become American.

The combination of circumstances led to the military confrontation in the winter of 1893. Had not Minister Stevens ordered the sailors and marines from the USS Boston *to land in Honolulu harbor on January 14, 1893, the revolution of the sons of the missionaries would never have succeeded. The military gesture was very slight, and yet the consequences were enormous. It was one of the prime examples of a carefully planned military excursion that went much further in its impact than anyone had ever expected.*

*   *   *

Early in the nineteenth century the American missionaries arrived in Hawaii with the intention of dominating the kingdom's moral and intellectual life. But what really happened? It is all summed up in the cynical appraisal of one twentieth-century wag:

"The missionaries came to do good and did well."

The names Thurston, Castle, Cooke, Alexander, Baldwin, Wilcox, Andrews, Bond, and Green are missionary names. They are also names closely associated with the rape of Hawaii by the Americans, and some of them persist in the columns of the Hawaii millionaires today, although all have disappeared from the body politic and the public scene except as names.

Why wouldn't they do well? The Hawaiian kings in their innocence bestowed large tracts of land on these missionaries. A Thurston, for example, was given much of what is today the Kona coast of the big island of Hawaii as a goodwill gesture by the king. In some cases the missionaries, in some cases their children, lived to profit enormously from the growth of the islands under what became a de facto American protectorate before 1890.

In Hawaii the real elements of growth were not the missionaries but the businessmen who came to Hawaii and thrived—Chinese, Russians, French, Englishmen, and Americans, and finally the Japanese, who in the 1950s took over the Democratic party of Hawaii and, safe in that base, began to produce their own millionaires by the usual tactics of force and favor.

But it would never have happened—rather the process would have been cut off in midstream—had the Hawaiians had their way at the end of their monarchical cycle. Innocents that they were in the eighteenth century when British naval Captain James Cook came to call on them, in a hundred years they had learned to distrust the European and the American, and the last gasp of the Hawaiian kingdom was a cry for freedom from the American oppressors. By that the Hawaiians meant the cultural Americans, the English-speaking foreigners with their Yankee ways, even if they were Hawaiian citizens.

Captain Cook came to Hawaii in the second year of the American Revolution. Between his coming and the death of King Kamehameha V in 1872, the island kingdom was a real realm with Hawaiians ruling it. The expiration of the Kamehameha line that year brought a whole new ambience to the islands, and gave the foreigners the chance for which they were waiting.

The fact was, however, that politically many of the foreigners were no longer foreign, but, through the carelessness of the monarchy, Hawaiian citizens. Some Americans, such as John Palmer Parker, a sailing man from Massachusetts, "went native"—that is, they married Hawaiian women, took lands they obtained from the realm, and settled down. Parker and his descendants *became* Hawaiians. But that was not true of the majority of the whites who settled in Hawaii. They married white women and kept their Caucasian ways. In the second and third generations they called themselves *Kamaaiina* (born to the land) but they never really were. They brought America to Hawaii, and gradually imposed American ways on the islands, including a sense of the racial inferiority of the natives that the handful of pure Hawaiians were only beginning to overcome in the 1980s. The missionaries (Hiram Bingham excepted) and their children often opted to spend their lives in what even then they looked upon as a paradise, and had taken Hawaiian citizenship. Still, they were culturally foreign to the Hawaiians, and mostly socially ascendant, their fathers having amassed large fortunes. They had come to dominate the monarchy and the nobility through the church and the educational process. The royal family's degree of adherence to the teachings of the missionaries was really not much more than skin deep, as Queen Liliuokalani showed at the last, when her desire for vengeance against the men who had injured her was so strong that it prompted her into action that cost her the throne. She showed then that she really hated the Americans. It was an attitude shared with many another Hawaiian, then and now, when Hawaii is a state within the union of fifty, courtesy of the Nisei Americans who came to control the Democratic party at its apogee in the islands. When one considers the Hawaii after Kamehameha I, it has to be with a sort of sad sympathy for these noble savages who tried so hard to become civilized, but were overtaken by events. Elizabeth Pauahi Bishop, the last of the Kamehameha line, missionary educated, married to an American banker, left her enormous fortune for one single purpose: to establish a school to make little *haoles* (European-style foreigners) out of little Hawaiians. In the last half of the twentieth century the noble but tenuous experiment seemed just about as tenuous as ever. As of the 1970s the Hawaiians began to regain some pride in their Polynesian blood, tried to revive their old language and their old ways. But it was doubtful if the experiment would succeed. Until about 1980 the Japanese race was ascendant in the islands, with the Caucasian a close second. Sometime in the 1980s the ratio changed and it became apparent even to the most reluctant that Hawaii was moving to become another state dominated by the whites. The handwriting in 1986 was on the wall. Too many Caucasians were making their way to the islands to work and live, and not even the best efforts of Japanese-American Governor George Ariyoshi and his henchmen had been successful in stopping the switch in ratios. Unfortunately for them the U.S. Constitution frustrated their efforts to keep other Americans from moving to Hawaii, even by doing their best

to deny them a livelihood. The processes of natural selection—despite all
the noise from minorities, the majority of Americans were still Caucasians—were working for the Caucasians. Hawaii's real hope was at some
time to become the racial melting pot it had long claimed to be, but in the
1980s there was grave danger that racism was going the other way.

After the death of Kamehameha V the process of selecting a king
became the province of the Hawaiian legislature, which was soon dominated by the Americans. The next king was Lunalilo, who died within a
year. He was followed by Kalakaua, whose missionary education had given
him all the bad habits of the Europeans (drink, women, cards) and none
of the strengths of the Hawaiian aristocracy (bravery, worship of the land,
and love of the people). The American party was first annoyed, and then
furious with the behavior of the Hawaiians. So, they decided to do something about it. Here is the recollection of Lorrin Thurston, one of the
principal American leaders, although a Hawaiian citizen:

On the day after Christmas, 1886, as I stood at the front gate of my residence
on Judd Street, near Nuuanu, Dr. S. G. Tucker, the homeopathic physician,
drew up in his buggy and said:
"Thurston, how long are we going to stand this kind of thing?"
"What kind of thing?" I inquired.
"The running away with the community by Kalakaua, his interference with
elections, and running the legislature for his own benefit, and all that."
"Well," said I, "What can we do about it?"
"I suggest," Dr. Tucker answered, "that we form an organization, including
all nationalities, which shall force him to be decent and reign, not rule, or take
the consequences."
After some discussion I said I would consider the idea.
In the afternoon, I went to the residence of William A. Kinney at the corner
of Judd and Liliha Streets, told him of Dr. Tucker's suggestion and asked him
what he thought. We discussed it at some length, Kinney taking to the proposal
enthusiastically. He was more belligerent than Dr. Tucker or I and suggested
if Kalakaua did not come to time, that conditions justified a revolution and
deposition.
He continued. "I have a book in my library describing the French Revolution which I will show you."
He got the book and pointed out the declaration made by the revolutionaries
and some of their orders. Among others, one called upon citizens in sympathy
with the revolution to declare themselves, and requested that all arms be turned
in to support the revolution. Those orders so impressed me that I took copies. . . .
After interviewing Mr. Kinney, I discussed Dr. Tucker's suggestion with
others. . . . I found them all in favor of the plan. . . . I was to submit a draft
of a constitution. A meeting was held. . . . After thorough discussion we agreed
to form an organization on the lines above suggested, to be known as the

Hawaiian league. I submitted a draft of a constitution which was unanimously accepted.

From this point the rebels—note the Anglo Saxon names—proceeded to stage the first Hawaiian revolution. Colonel C. W. Ashford, leader of the Honolulu Rifles, apparently one of the chowder and marching societies common throughout America in those days, but really a much more sinister organization, suggested that they shoot King Kalakaua and hang his "renegade" American adviser, Walter Murray Gibson. That was too much for the "missionary boys," the children of the missionaries, who still thought occasionally about doing good while they were doing so well, at least as long as it did not inconvenience them. But Colonel Ashford was talked down.

On July 1, 1887, the rebels learned that the government had just brought in a large shipment of arms, which would give it weapons superiority over the rebels. The shipment was still aboard a ship just in from Australia. Colonel Ashford assembled his Honolulu Rifles, with their weapons. They "arrested" Prime Minister Walter M. Gibson and his son-in-law Fred Hayselden, and confined them in a warehouse on the wharf.

Rebel Thurston then came into the picture.

When I arrived at my law office, about eight o'clock in the morning, I learned of the events. My partner, William O. Smith, was leaving the office with a rifle in his hand. "W. O.," said I, "what in thunder are you doing with a rifle?"

He answered: "This is one of those times which show what a man is made of. Where is your rifle? Get it and come down here as quick as you can." He told me of the arrival of the arms on a steamer and what was occurring. I returned on horseback to my home, got my rifle and ammunition belt, and again went to my office. Telephoning to the executive committee of the League, I called a meeting to be held at once in the law library of the Honolulu Bar Association, upstairs in the Campbell Block at Fort and Merchant streets.

Then I went to the water front to learn what was occurring. At the open front door of the warehouse, Mr. Gibson sat on a nail keg, with Hayselden standing beside him. A member of the Rifles stood guard at the entrance. Everything appeared to be quiet; I went to the law library to meet the League executive committee at 9 A.M. On the way there I was informed that Colonel Ashford intended immediately to hang Mr. Gibson from the yardarm of a sailing vessel then lying opposite the warehouse in which Mr. Gibson was confined. I informed the executive committee; it immediately summoned Colonel Ashford and interrogated him. He replied that he intended to strike terror into the community, so that all might understand that no one could do, with impunity, the acts of which Gibson had been guilty. Immediately and unanimously the executive committee repudiated the colonel's plan, and directed that Gibson be transferred to Oahu jail. There he was given an option, to remain and stand trial for "high crimes and misdemeanors," whatever that might have meant, or to depart for San Francisco. Mr. Gibson chose the latter, and he died in San Francisco within a short time.

So here were the revolutionaries, taking the law into their own hands. They framed their constitution and forced Kalakaua to sign it. And the king was made to form a new government. Who was in it? Mr. Green premier; Mr. Brown, minister of foreign affairs; Mr. Ashford, attorney general; Mr. Thurston, minister of the interior.

This was a government of Hawaii?

But yes. The *new* Hawaii.

It was a very nice government. All the stationery was expensive and most of it imported from San Francisco, just as in the most flamboyant days of the monarchy. All the seals were gold and red wax. The imposing arms of the kingdom (drawn from the British, like the Hawaiian flag) were very impressive.

And so those Hawaiians with the names of Ashford, Thurston, Green, and Brown ran the country as they pleased.

The revolutionaries fell out among themselves. Colonel Ashford found it more advantageous to play the king's game than the League's, and he did. But then, Kalakaua died on a trip to California (where he was taken by an American navy cruiser, the *Charleston*). Princess Liliuokalani, his sister, succeeded him. The American party expected Liliuokalani to be a more or less placid instrument of their will. But they were to be rudely disabused of this notion almost immediately. What they did not know about Liliuokalani was that her missionary education had turned her irrevocably against the missionary party. Although she had married an American, her dream was to restore Hawaii to the Hawaiians. One of the queen's first actions was to demand the resignation of the league cabinet. Soon she had a cabinet with some real Hawaiians in it. By 1892 it was apparent that Liliuokalani intended to rule, not reign, and that she had very little use for the children of the missionaries, whom she had watched raping the country. To be sure, her Hawaiians had some bad habits, a fine love of fornication like the Polynesians of the story books, opium trading, and a great taste for liquor. But it was their country.

Or was it? Not according to the Annexation Club, formed by Thurston and his friends in 1892, preparing for Hawaii to be taken over by the United States.

As Queen Liliuokalani kicked up her heels, Thurston and the others agreed that annexation was the only answer. Thurston went to Washington to seek American support for annexation of Hawaii. He saw James G.

Blaine, secretary of state, B. F. Tracy, secretary of the navy, Congressional leaders; President Benjamin Harrison sent word through Blaine that the United States would look kindly on annexation of Hawaii.

So Thurston went home happy. Soon he had a letter from Washington saying that the United States would pay Queen Liliuokalani $250,000 if she would sell them Hawaii.

What cheapskates! The queen already had an income of about $100,000 a year. Why would she sell her kingdom for a mere $250,000? She would not, of course. But what Mr. Thurston did not seem to realize was that the queen would not sell it at all. What she wanted was to get the missionary influence out of Hawaii altogether. That was the end to which she was moving in her own way, as Thurston and his friends schemed for American annexation.

Thurston suggested that they work on buying off native leaders, who would sell out, he thought, for from $500 to $5,000 each.

It all came to a head in January 1893. The queen knew what the American party was up to, and she was doing her best to get power into her own hands, and then to put a very quick end to the rebellion of the pro-American group. On January 14, 1893, one of Thurston's old schoolmates, John F. Colburn, came to him to report that the queen had drawn up a new constitution that made her absolute monarch, and was prepared to promulgate it within hours.

What to do? The revolutionaries' problem was that the royal government had just about as many rifles as they had, and they might conceivably lose in a confrontation.

One of the revolutionaries remembered that the U.S. cruiser *Boston* was in harbor, as she often was these days. She had every right to be, as the Americans had leased the naval base at Pearl Harbor. But of course, if one looked deeply there was another reason for her presence: something to do with the navy's feelings about annexation of Hawaii to the United States. And of course, as had been indicated, the navy was not alone.

The revolutionaries went to see the American minister to Hawaii, John L. Stevens, a well-known advocate of annexation, who had been working for American control of Hawaii for many years.

Now was the time to act, said Thurston and his friends. Let Minister Stevens land American troops and take over Hawaii right now.

Minister Stevens replied:

I do not know what your plans are, gentlemen [an untruth if there ever was one, since for years he had made it his business to know] and I cannot afford to take chances and find out what the plans of the government may be. The conditions are so serious, and the possibilities of trouble so great, that it is my duty to protect the lives and property of American citizens with every available means within my power; and I am going to land American troops immediately for that purpose. I have already given orders to that effect and it will not be long before the troops are ashore. That is all I have to say.

It was enough. Thurston and his friends felt that the success of their rebellion had been ensured by the United States of America.

They went down to the landing at the foot of Nuuanu Street. It was 5:00 P.M. They saw the troops landing from the *Boston,* carrying rifles, with ammunition belts about their waists, with Gatling guns and small field pieces. The troops in a column marched from the wharf along Queen Street to Fort Street, up Fort Street to King Street, and then out toward Waikiki.

It was all satisfactory to Thurston and the other revolutionaries, who followed the troops for a while, then tired of the fun.

At the corner of Fort and Hotel streets, Thurston met W. H. Rickard, manager of the Honokaa Sugar plantation and a supporter of the queen.

"Damn you, Thurston, you did this," shouted Rickard, shaking his fist in Thurston's face.

Thurston put on his choirboy visage, learned so well in Grandpapa Thurston's Kona church.

"Did what?"

"Had those troops landed."

"You credit me with considerable influence to be able to direct the United States troops. I had no more to do with their coming than you did, and I have no more idea of what they are going to do than you have."

What a lie! Thurston was the man who consorted with the U.S. secretary of state and the U.S. secretary of the navy, and who received private messages from the president of the United States. But Thurston maintained his innocent façade all his life and included it in his *Memoirs of the Hawaiian Revolution,* a book which reveals to the careful reader just how the American party in Hawaii went about its planning to seize the Hawaiian kingdom.

Thurston then began planning how to manage the revolutionary government. He dug up those notes taken from Mr. Kinney's book on the French Revolution, and used them to prepare the new government's proclamation deposing the queen.

There was nothing to fear from the queen's army. It was not nearly so strong as the American landing force, and the fact that the Americans had landed troops at this hour was proof to the queen that the United States was behind the rebellion. Force majeure had won again without more than a single shot being fired in protection of the kingdom.

It was, said Thurston, in tones that did not disturb the butter sitting so stiff in his mouth, "the result of fate, foreordained from the beginning of things." Or, as more cynical observers noted, foreordained from the moment King Kamehameha I was persuaded against his best judgment to let that first shipload of American missionaries land at Kona instead of sending them away. Foreordained and helped along by the American-Hawaiian revolutionaries, and ensured by American troops.

The next day all was ready. The committee went to the government building, which it had seized, and Henry E. Cooper read the proclamation deposing the queen and establishing a provisional government to exist until the terms of annexation had been arranged with the United States.

But the revolutionaries and Mr. Stevens had failed to reckon with the turn of events in the United States. After November 1892, they should have been talking to Grover Cleveland, not President Harrison. Cleveland had been defeated for the U.S. presidency in 1888 by Benjamin Harrison. He had, in turn, defeated Mr. Harrison in 1892. And while the revolutionaries and Mr. Stevens were playing out their triumph, President Cleveland was preparing to rearrange matters in the White House. He was not a man of Manifest Destiny—anything but. Nor did he look kindly on a revolution staged under American management during a Republican administration.

Minister Stevens and his American-Hawaiian friends knew that Cleveland was not enamored of the seizure of Hawaii or the American role in it. But they hoped to present the new administration with a fait accompli, always difficult to undo. They wanted to rush annexation through the Congress before March 4, the date that Cleveland came into office. They did not have much time, and they knew it. Immediately they chartered a steamer and on January 19, 1893, they left Honolulu for San Francisco. They arrived in San Francisco on January 27. There Claus Spreckels, the sugar king, gave them his blessing and his private railroad car to speed them on their way. The car was hitched onto a train of the transcontinental railroad and took them to Washington. While they were en route, back in Honolulu, Minister Stevens quite illegally hoisted the American flag over the Hawaii Government Building, and proclaimed a temporary protectorate.

The revolutionary committee arrived in Washington on February 3. The next day they presented the American secretary of state with a proposal for annexation. So eager was the Harrison administration to do the job that a treaty was prepared by the State Department in record time; it was signed on February 14 by the Hawaiians and Secretary of State Foster. Foster then rushed the treaty to the U.S. Senate for ratification.

Then the plans of Mr. Stevens and Mr. Thurston and friends suddenly came up against a problem. In the 52nd U.S. Congress, elected in 1890, the Republicans had a comfortable majority in the Senate, but in the 53rd Congress, elected in the fall of 1892, they did not.

The lame ducks of the 52nd Congress might have bulled the Hawaii treaty through before the Congress ended in March, but the Republican senators who would continue in the 53rd Congress knew that if they did so even over determined opposition, they would have a difficult time in the next two years. So very wisely the Republican senators opted to lay the Hawaii treaty on the table for the next Congress.

Grover Cleveland took office on March 4, 1893. Five days later he withdrew the Hawaii Annexation Treaty from consideration, and appointed a special commissioner to investigate the overthrow of the Hawaiian monarchy. He was former Congressman James H. Blount, a man of great probity and influence in Washington.

Blount came to Hawaii with a mind set, if anything, toward return of the kingdom to Queen Liliuokalani, so overt and disgusting to Cleveland had been the behavior of the Americans in Hawaii and so apparent their conspiracy with the American-descended Hawaiians who formed the rebellion. But the queen made a fatal error. Blount was ready to recommend the return of the kingdom. He had only one demand: that the queen pardon the rebels and leave them alone if they chose to continue to live in Hawaii. Liliuokalani refused indignantly. She intended to hang Thurston and several other ringleaders, and seize all their property. Other revolutionary leaders would also be punished to lesser degrees.

As Blount knew very well, the American party of Hawaii had strong ties to America, family and other, and such punishment would create political difficulties for the administration. This was explained to the queen, but she was obdurate, and thus Blount recommended that the United States steer clear of the whole matter. The revolution would not be undone by America, but neither would Hawaii be annexed.

So the uneasy Hawaiian-American revolutionaries had to go their own way for the next few years. Then, on November 3, 1896, Republican William McKinley was elected president, and Manifest Destiny was once again the foreign policy of the United States. The United States leapt back into the swirl of colonial acquisition. Even before McKinley's inauguration in March 1897, he let it be known that Hawaiian annexation would be welcomed. On June 16, Secretary of State John Sherman signed the Hawaii treaty, as did Thurston and friends. The Hawaiian legislature ratified within days, but the Japanese appeared on the horizon, fearful lest the acquisition by racist America interfere with the rights of Japanese citizens who had been brought by the thousands to work in the Hawaii sugar fields. It took months to resolve this problem, because the Japanese were dead right, American racism was a major factor in U.S. foreign policy. Particularly Americans of the west opposed any act that would bring more Orientals under the American flag.

In spite of Manifest Destiny, Hawaii might not have been annexed at all except for two new issues raised. One, the Japanese had been interested in Hawaii for years. During Kalakaua's reign, overtures were made to marry a Japanese prince to Hawaii Princess Kaiulani, third in line for the throne, which might have meant an ultimate annexation of Hawaii to Japan. Washington had come to fear that, if the United States did not take the islands, the Japanese soon would, because the Oriental population there was by this time the greatest of all. Second, in the spring of 1898 the United States went to war with Spain and the U.S. Navy needed a major Pacific base from which to launch the attack on the Philippines. Thus, Congress accepted the new offer to take over Hawaii, and on Friday, August 12, 1898, at 11:30 A.M., the flag of the republic was hauled down from the staff at the Executive Building in downtown Honolulu and the flag of the United States was run up. Hawaii had gone from coaling station to colony in twenty-three years, with scarcely a drop of blood shed. America was showing the way in the simple acquisition of colonies, and the U.S. Navy was leading the way.

CHAPTER 22

The Spanish-American War

In the last years of the nineteenth century the American jingoists and advocates of Manifest Destiny looked around them to see the nations of Europe devouring territory at a furious rate. Africa was partitioned by France, Britain, and Germany. Asia was being swallowed by Britain, Russia, France, and Japan. American business looked longingly at Latin America, but the government was pursuing the Monroe Doctrine, and preferred to see economic domination of Latin America rather than political suzerainty.

The great exception lay in the remnants of the Spanish empire, and particularly Cuba.

Cuba had been penetrated very heavily by American business and American plantation owners, who grew sugar and cattle there. They would have liked nothing better than to see Cuba as a new state in the union. The big objection was that the Cubans represented an alien society, Spanish for the most part, and an alien language. These were important issues in the 1890s.

There was another element in America, the political evangelical bloc, which wanted to further the cause of Cuban independence. What was most interesting about the result was the alliance that it created: President William McKinley's Republicans wanted Cuba as a colony and they played successfully on the heartstrings of Americans who wanted Cuba free. The combination led to a general public support for American intervention in the Cuban independence movement, which was well along by 1895. Many congressmen and many ordinary Americans really believed the McKinley administration's motivation was sublime. Thus there was virtually no opposition to the administration's movement to intervene.

*   *   *

What is most remarkable about the Spanish-American War is not that it was fomented by a pair of greedy newspaper publishers—which is only marginally true—nor that America won the war, which it was apparent that it would from the earliest moment, but that, if territory had to be seized, the territory seized by the United States as a colony was the wrong territory, and that if the right one had been seized, a lot of trouble would have been avoided by the United States in the following century.

The newspaper publishers were William Randolph Hearst, owner of the *New York American,* and Joseph Pulitzer, owner of the *New York World,* who in the 1890s were locked in deadly struggle for the allegiance of the citizens of New York City, which, even if much smaller in those days, was still the largest media market in America.

The wrong territory was the Philippine Islands. The right territory would have been Cuba. In fact, millions of people believed it was going to be Cuba right up until the end.

After the U.S. Civil War, Cuba continued to interest American adventurers. In 1868 a rebellion broke out in Cuba, and this one was serious enough that the American government persuaded U.S. commercial interests to recognize the rebel government. But Secretary of State Hamilton Fish persuaded President U.S. Grant not to recognize. The struggle went on and many Americans were involved as soldiers, more as gunrunners, or in other ways. The most serious incident, over which the United States might have gone to war, was the seizure of the gunrunning ship *Virginius* in the fall of 1873. The *Virginius* was manned partly by Americans, and was flying the U.S. flag when she was captured by a Spanish government gunboat off Jamaica. The authorities were thoroughly aroused over their troubles, and nervous; after they took the ship into Santiago de Cuba, they summarily executed fifty-three men aboard, including thirty Americans. The war cry went out across America. Secretary of State Fish termed the executions "brutal butchery" and many congressmen wanted to declare war against Spain for seizing an American ship and murdering Americans.

But it soon came out that the *Virginius* was not what she seemed. She was owned by the Cuban revolutionary junta, and her American papers were forgeries. The Americans aboard the vessel knew precisely what they were doing, involving themselves in a foreign revolution. The Spanish, sensing the tenor of American opinion, calmed down and returned the ship and the surviving 102 members of the crew to the Americans. Secretary of State Fish was a moderating influence, and some even said that he prevented war with Spain by moderating the official demands of the United States for reparations. In the end the Spanish government paid an indemnity of $80,000 to the families of the executed American gunrunners, and war was averted.

The U.S. Navy was disappointed. This would have been a good time to have tested the American monitors against the new Spanish naval vessels, built by the British, with armored hulls. What was really wanted by the navy was a "nice little war" to advance the causes of nautical science and ship construction.

That war fever was never far beneath the surface. It went right along with Manifest Destiny. The guns of the Civil War had scarcely stopped booming when Manifest Destiny reared its head again.

Secretary of State Seward had negotiated a treaty with Denmark to take over the Danish Virgin Islands, but President Johnson was so hated that nothing he did could be accepted by the Senate, and the measure died. America had to wait until 1917 to secure the islands. When Grant came to the presidency in 1869, he had wanted to take over the island of Santo Domingo and a treaty was drawn, but the Senate killed that one, too.

Many Americans, as well as the naval establishment, were concerned about the whole Latin American area in these post–Civil War years, far more seriously than Americans were in the 1980s when the Monroe Doctrine was unceremoniously buried and no cogent policy emerged to take its place. The navy knew what it wanted: a canal across the Central American isthmus to link the American oceans, and naval bases where coal could be stockpiled and arms laid down.

After French engineer Ferdinand de Lesseps made such a success of the Suez Canal, at the end of the nineteenth century the French company's eyes turned to Central America. Arrangements were made with the government of Panama, and de Lesseps brought his steam shovels to the isthmus to create another canal. In Washington the admirals shuddered. James G. Blaine, secretary of state in the cabinet of President Garfield, tried to persuade the British to relinquish the influence in the area granted them by the Clayton-Bulwer treaty (by which neither the United States nor Britain would try to expand without consulting the other). But the British, who had just taken over Suez and Egypt, had ideas of their own about the ultimate control of the isthmus, and they refused. So the Americans fell back belligerently on the Monroe Doctrine. Central America was a sphere of American interest.

Garfield was shot, died, and was succeeded by Chester Arthur as president. Blaine was succeeded by F. T. Frelinghuysen as secretary of state. But Manifest Destiny lived on, and in 1884 Frelinghuysen negotiated a treaty with Nicaragua for a canal, in violation of the Clayton-Bulwer treaty with Britain. Fortunately for amicable British-American relations the Nicaragua treaty finally died in the Senate. Fortunately, also, for world peace, the de Lesseps company had financial troubles, and yellow fever for the moment proved to be a blessing, preventing anyone from looking at the Central American isthmus too seriously.

The captains thought they had their little war in 1882 when Chile and Peru began fighting over territory. The U.S. Navy wanted to intervene, but wiser heads prevailed and reminded the hotheads that Chile had four big ironclad warships, British-built, which were better than anything the United States could put to sea. To be defeated by Chile was something that even the most ambitious navy career man could not have explained, so the war fever died down again.

But the ambitious were forever there. In 1891 Chile erupted again in revolution, and the rebels sent a ship, the *Itata,* to San Diego to pick up arms. Part of the U.S. Navy's job was to prevent just this sort of meddling in Latin American affairs, so the USS *Charleston* was sent to pursue and catch the *Itata.* She did. Unfortunately for the United States, this time the rebels won the war, and they did not forgive. So relations between the United States and Chile were deplorable. In this atmosphere the United States sent a cruiser to Valparaiso "to assure the safety of American lives and property."

Despite the tension, on October 16, 1891, the commander of the USS *Baltimore* let a shore party of sailors go to the town. In a tavern an argument began. It became a fight. Two sailors were killed and seventeen injured. Commander W. S. Schley, who had let the sailors go ashore knowing there might be trouble, got belligerent. The Chileans got belligerent. Within several months affairs deteriorated rapidly, and President Benjamin Harrison issued a special message to Congress calling for war.

The admirals said no. The Chilean navy was still more powerful than that of the United States, and it would be months before the United States could make any kind of a naval showing. Temporization was the only solution.

So the diplomats temporized. So did Commander Robley D. Evans, sent down to Valparaiso in the USS *Yorktown* to replace the belligerent Commander Schley. The Chileans paraded their gunboats and torpedo boats and handsome armored warships in front of Evans, just tempting him to some hostile act. In the end, more reparations were paid to American families, and peace was declared.

Something warlike skidded across the skyline in 1895, during a phase of the long dispute between Venezuela and Great Britain, which managed a colony (British Guiana) on the Venezuelan border. The new phase of the dispute was an attempt by the British to punish the Americans for having had the temerity to try to junk the Clayton-Bulwer treaty. But the

Americans were still feeling belligerent after Chile. When the British re-fused American mediation, President Cleveland announced that the United States *would* arbitrate the dispute, since it came within the Western Hemi-sphere and thus under the Monroe Doctrine, and that if the British did not like it, that was unfortunate.

This was hardly the sort of "nice little war" the navy was looking for, since the Royal Navy did indeed at that time rule the waves of the world, and the sun never set on all those British navy coaling stations. The admirals were inclined to ask Congress how quickly they could build twenty-seven battleships, for that was what was needed to face up to Britain. She had thirty, the United States had three.

Fortunately, without really wanting to help the Americans, Kaiser Wil-helm announced Germany's support of a rebellion of the Boers in South Africa. The anger of Britain was diverted from Washington to Berlin, and soon Britain was so deeply immersed in the Boer War that few in England could become excited about the placement of the British Guiana boundary line. The American arbitration was accepted.

During the next three years after 1895 the navy was busy trying to stop filibustering expeditions to Cuba. The admirals counted seventy-one ex-peditions launched from American shores. Thirty-three of these were bro-ken up by the Americans, five by the Spanish, and the rest died aborning. The reason for all the activity was a new rebellion in Cuba, one that was lasting unusually long. This one was creating havoc. Americans had an enormous amount of money invested in Cuba, in sugar, shipping, ranching, and real estate. U.S.-Cuban trade had amounted to more than $100 million. (The entire federal income ran about $375 million in those days.) After three years of revolution, that trade with Cuba was virtually ruined. The Americans with interests in Cuba, quite naturally, believed that the United States ought to step in and "restore order" no matter how that had to be done. President Cleveland, who had a soft spot in his heart for bankers, agreed with them and so warned Spain just as he was getting ready to go out of politics.

The admirals agreed with Cleveland. The troubles between Chile and Britain had helped the navy's building program. Captain Mahan's theory that trade follows the flag and the navy must be paramount had become American naval doctrine. The presence of an American cruiser or other warship in any troubled waters of the Western Hemisphere was to be expected.

The armored cruiser *Maine* had been built, and the battleships *Indiana*, *Massachusetts*, *Oregon*, and *Iowa* (10,000 tons, with 12- or 13-inch guns), and the fast armored cruisers *New York* and *Brooklyn*. On the naval front, affairs were looking up; looking over the Spanish navy, the admirals had to agree that it was just about the right time for a "nice little war." Spain had only four 7,000-ton armored cruisers. The rest of her navy, except for a dozen torpedo boats, was virtually useless.

Generally speaking, Americans favored the Cuban revolution against Spain, although neither President Cleveland nor President McKinley did. Congress, however, resolved in 1896 to accept the "belligerent" status of the Cuban revolutionaries, which meant official recognition of the uprising; yet Cleveland refused to grant the rebels belligerent rights.

In 1896, when McKinley was elected president, many Americans thought he would stand for Cuban independence and offer the rebels some help. But Senator Henry Cabot Lodge, one of the most powerful figures in Congress, advised McKinley to declare war on Spain immediately and seize Cuba as loot. Whitelaw Reid, editor of the *New York Tribune*, said the same in more honeyed words. No one in authority in the Republican camp suggested that McKinley even think about independence for Cuba. Indeed, the pressure was all toward the United States intervening to stop the rebellion in the interests of American shipowners and other businessmen. So McKinley began to exert pressure on Spain, but in behalf of American business, not in behalf of the Cuban people. By the fall of 1897 the American policy was settled: peace must be restored in Cuba. If the Spanish would not do it on their own, then the Americans would step in and put an end to the rebellion. If that seems an extremely high-handed policy on the part of the United States, it was indeed.

In October 1897, the Americans forced a change in the administration of Cuba and a promise from the Spanish that they would offer the Cubans autonomy within the Spanish structure. Many Republicans thought that a good idea, since autonomy would be a training ground for the Cubans, after which they would want annexation to the United States.

But the Spanish reforms, according to consular reports reaching Washington, were not effective. Was more going to have to be done? On December 15, 1897, the *Maine* was moved to Key West. Her captain and the American consul in Havana established a code: the message "Two Dollars" meant the consul wanted the *Maine* to come to Havana immediately. In Washington Secretary of the Navy John D. Long, Assistant Secretary Theodore Roosevelt, and several admirals met and decided that the cruiser *Marblehead* should also be sent to Havana when needed.

On January 1, 1898, the Spanish gave the Cubans the promised autonomy. But the Cuban revolution had gone beyond the point where this move was acceptable. Theodore Roosevelt and other activists had already decided that war with Spain was inevitable, because the Spanish had not solved the problem. The Navy Department issued unusual orders to forcibly retain in service all men whose enlistments were about to expire.

In Havana the autonomist government was under attack from the revolutionaries on one side and Spaniards who favored strict controls on the other. Riots disturbed the tranquility of Havana. The American consul suggested that it would be a good idea to send an American warship to Havana at the end of January. The relations between the United States and Spain were so tense that it had better be done under a ruse. The captain might indicate that his coal supply was exhausted.

In Congress, the move to recognize the Cuban rebels came up again, and again it was knocked down by a Republican administration. But this time it was apparent that the American people were restless, and congressmen were being pressured to favor the Cuban rebels.

As with the Indians, as it would be many times in the future, the American people were generally on the side of the oppressed, and favored the peoples' rights to self-determination everywhere. As with the Indians, and as it would be many times in the future, the American government lagged behind or was at odds with the people. In 1898 the people favored Cuban independence. The Congress favored Cuban independence. Two administrations had stood fast in favor of the vested interests of business and capital against independence. Unfortunately, events could move more quickly than the people, and the opinion-makers in Washington could pervert facts and influence attitudes.

One analyst suggested that unless McKinley did something spectacular, the resolution favoring the Cuban rebels might pass within a few weeks. So McKinley decided to send the *Maine,* that powerful (24-gun), modern "pocket battleship" so dear to the hearts of America's navy buffs, to Havana harbor. It was decided that the visit would be one of friendship, a gesture of support for Spain for having granted the benevolence of autonomy to the Cubans.

The Spanish were not fooled. Nor were the Cuban rebels. Perhaps many Americans were, but certainly Theodore Roosevelt was not. He saw the end approaching rapidly. The Spanish attempt at establishing an autonomous Cuban government would most certainly fail, and the Americans were then committed to stepping in to bring peace to Cuba. Afterward, many Americans seemed to think that Teddy Roosevelt brought on the Spanish-American War—along with those two newspaper publishers. But the fact was that it was a considered Republican policy, and Roosevelt was merely an instrument—willing as he might be—and a second-level instrument at that.

What had to be done, from the official American point of view, was to prevent chaos in Cuba, or, to state it another way, to prevent the revolutionaries from taking over.

So on January 25, the *Maine* arrived in Havana harbor. Documents came out at about that time, indicating that the Spanish "reforms" were simply a façade. Publication of these in America stirred a storm composed equally of Manifest Destiny adherents who wanted excitement and colonies, and people who wanted to see the Cubans free. At this point it seemed that just about everyone in America had a stake in Cuba. It was a brotherhood similar to that formed in June 1941, when the Germans attacked the Soviet Union. Suddenly, not very comfortably, people who had been shouting at each other from opposite sides of the political fence found themselves on the same wagon.

Autonomy really was acceptable only to the Cuban businessmen, the Spanish businessmen, the American businessmen, and the U.S. government. Everybody else wanted something else. One of the Cuban leaders tried to explain it to McKinley, who had asked why the Cubans, so long associated with Spain, now wanted to get away from her. For the same reason that the Americans decided to get away from England, said the Cuban. The irritations had just become too great to live with.

On the evening of February 15, 1898, the American consul in Havana sat at his desk in the consulate overlooking the Havana harbor. He was writing a letter back to Washington. He had just finished one sentence when he heard an enormous racket out in the harbor. He rushed to the window and looked out, to see the mighty *Maine* sinking off the mole, flames shooting high in the sky as she sank. The consul rushed out and headed for the harbor, along with thousands of people who had been out in the streets that evening. He met the captain of the *Maine* and a handful of officers. They had been saved. But 264 sailors and two officers had gone down with the ship, probably most of them killed instantly by the explosion that blew beneath the crew quarters. What had caused the explosion?

The consul, the captain, the Spanish authorities, the State Department—all agreed that the explosion had been internal, and was probably caused by overheating of coal dust in the bunkers to the point of spontaneous combustion. Such accidents were woefully common in those days of coal-fired steam boilers. (The battleship *Indiana* had already suffered *seven* such accidents.) In the case of the *Maine,* the compartment next to the coal storage had been, unfortunately, an ammunition locker which had then blown up.

Several high-ranking naval officers rejected the theory. It was impossible, they said; safety precautions in modern ships prevented such accidents. (Not so for the *Indiana,* the *Oregon, Boston, Philadelphia, Cincinnati, New York,* and *Atlanta;* all recently had suffered such impossible accidents.)

The Spanish made an investigation of the explosion on the *Maine* and concluded that it had been caused by something internal. They asked the Americans to cooperate, letting them see the bottom of the ship and interview the crew. The American government refused. The U.S. Navy secretly conducted its own investigation.

The jingoes in the administration and Congress called for war. Captain

Sigsbee of the *Maine* was convinced that the explosion was internal, and he asked that the public suspend opinion. Secretary of the Navy Long announced that in his opinion an internal explosion had caused the sinking. So did McKinley. But the Manifest Destiny men in the administration and the business world saw their chance to inflame America, and they did it adeptly. The situation was made to order for William Randolph Hearst of the *New York American,* who was engaged in a desperate circulation battle with Joseph Pulitzer of the *New York World.* In the first week after the explosion, Hearst devoted eight pages per day to the *Maine.* Circulation of the *World* jumped from 400,000 copies a day to more than a million. Hearstlings (as they later came to be called) faked interviews with Spanish authorities and Cubans, and published "eyewitness" accounts of the bombing of the *Maine.* Editor Pulitzer picked up the sensational material and did the same. And so did newspapers all across America. WE SAW THE TORPEDO . . . was the headline in a story in the *Kansas City Star.* Americans who lamented the lack of objectivity of the American media in the 1980s could learn something from a trip to local libraries to look up the newspaper treatment of the sinking of the *Maine.* It is also an excellent object lesson in the short-term manipulation of public opinion.

So the nation was aroused, believing, as it then tended to do (unlike in the 1980s), what it saw in the media.

> Remember the *Maine*
> To Hell with Spain

That was the new slogan of 1898.

The navy's admirals were pleased. The American consul assured the State Department that the explosion was caused by a torpedo or a bomb used by the Spanish authorities. He recommended immediate occupation of Cuba by the United States, and then annexation. "American capital and enterprising spirit would soon Americanize the island."

American diplomats in those days had great influence on the State Department and the president. Like Minister Stevens of Hawaii, the consul was a strong Manifest Destiny supporter, and he was in the right place to make his influence felt.

So was Teddy Roosevelt. On February 25, taking advantage of Secretary Long's absence from the office, Assistant Secretary of the Navy Roosevelt alerted the fleet to prepare for war. His message was particularly effective with Commodore George Dewey off in Hong Kong with a squadron. When Long came back he was dismayed by the actions of his admittedly "jingo" assistant, and vowed that Roosevelt would never be allowed to have his hand on the tiller again.

McKinley was playing politics with the problem. Personally he was as great an advocate of Manifest Destiny as America had. But he knew the temper of the American people, so he went slowly. But he could talk, and he did. One of his suggestions made to a number of powerful Republican senators was that America purchase Cuba from Spain. No, said they. It was too expensive, and besides, Cuba was about to fall off the Spanish tree, to be picked up by the United States at will.

The public still pictured McKinley as a man of peace, and the newspapers railed at him as favoring peace at any price. But McKinley was preparing for war. The preparations included a new military budget of $50 million. In Congress the debate centered on recognition of the Cuban rebels, but the forces for recognition lost. So the danger that the forces favoring recognition of the Cuban rebels could somehow push through such a measure, which would be certain to be greeted by public favor, was gone.

The navy solved the problem. On March 28 the result of the secret investigation of the sinking of the *Maine* was released. *Maine* had been sunk, said the navy, by a submarine mine which caused the explosion of two magazines. Such was the power of the jingo element in the navy and elsewhere that the report was accepted. It was too late for the forces of peace. As several senators pointed out, relations with Spain had so deteriorated in those last weeks that if the *Maine* had never sunk the war would have come anyhow.

McKinley tried to buy Cuba. The Spanish refused and war was then indeed inevitable. But some time was needed to build up American weaponry, so the U.S. government stalled. No one asked the Cubans if they wanted American intervention. No one in the administration cared. The war for Cuba was not being fought for Cubans, but for American interests in Cuba. McKinley made all this clear in a message which indicated the United States would alone decide what was to happen to Cuba. But if the motives of Americans were mixed, by April 25 their intent was solidified. On that day Congress declared war on Spain.

The navy was mightily pleased. It would be a naval war for the most part. On land in Cuba, despite the indication in America that Teddy Roosevelt's Rough Riders won the war alone, most of the fighting was done by the Cubans. All they really wanted from America was military supplies. But the Americans insisted on landing a force, and fighting the war. The American military men had no regard for the brown-skinned Cubans. *Niggers* was the word used by soldiers and newspaper correspondents. On land the Spanish fought hard. The famed "Battle of San Juan Hill" was actually a disaster for the Rough Riders and the Americans. But ultimately, without giving the Cubans credit for their efforts, the Americans won the war and controlled the Cuban countryside.

At sea, the war was more romantic. Admiral Pascual Cervera sailed

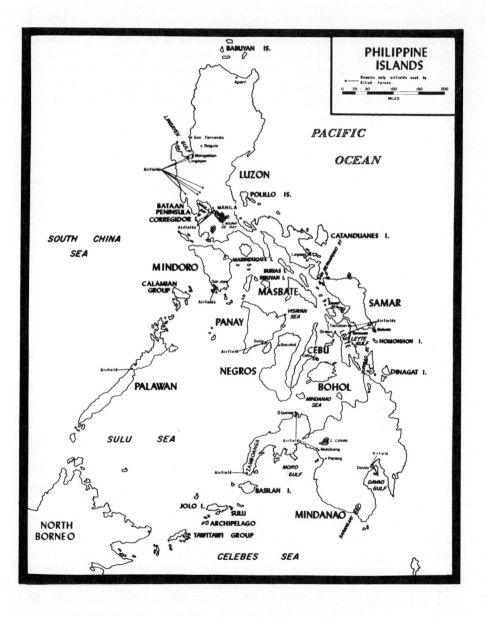

BABUYAN IS.

Aparri

PHILIPPINE
ISLANDS

Denotes only airfields used by
Allied Forces

0   25   50   100   150   200

MILES

San Fernando
Baguio
Mangaldan
Lingayen

LINGAYEN GULF

Airfields

PACIFIC

OCEAN

LUZON

POLILLO IS.

BATAAN
PENINSULA
CORREGIDOR I.

MANILA

LAGUNA
DE BAY

Airfields

CATANDUANES I.

SOUTH   CHINA

SEA

MINDORO

MARINDUQUE I.

Legaspi

BURIAS
TICAO

CALAMIAN
GROUP

San Jose

MASBATE

Airfields

SIBUYAN I.

SAMAR

PANAY

VISAYAN
SEA

Leyte

Tacloban

Airfields

Guiuan

Airfield

Doilo

Bacolod

CEBU

Ormoc

LEYTE
GULF

HOMONHON I.

Cebu

DINAGAT I.

NEGROS

BOHOL

PALAWAN

MINDANAO
SEA

Dipolog

Airfield

SULU   SEA

Airfield

ZAMBOANGA

L. Lanao

Malabang

Parang

Airfield

Davao

DAVAO
GULF

MORO
GULF

BASILAN I.

NORTH
BORNEO

JOLO I.

SULU

ARCHIPELAGO

TAWITAWI GROUP

MINDANAO

CELEBES   SEA

across the Atlantic with four cruisers and three destroyers, the only ships he had that could be effective against the American fleet. One cruiser broke down en route and was left behind at Martinique.

Slowly the U.S. fleet assembled. The battleship *Oregon* had been at Seattle on March 7 when the navy began ordering ships about, and she had been called to sail 14,000 miles around Cape Horn. She did, and joined the North Atlantic Squadron at Key West. It took her sixty-six days, which reminded the navy how badly the United States needed a canal across the Central American isthmus. In the Caribbean, the Americans waited for the coming of Cervera, and meanwhile blockaded Cuba.

The first naval action occurred in the Pacific. Commodore Dewey was ready, having been alerted by Teddy Roosevelt to keep his coal bunkers full. And he had. By the time war broke out his squadron included seven ships. He had bought two British ships to be used as colliers, and leased Mirs Bay, twenty miles from Hong Kong, where he could operate without concern over British neutrality regulations. He was ready, and on April 27 he sailed for the Philippines.

The squadron arrived on April 30 and searched Subic Bay but did not find the Spanish fleet. Admiral Montojo had just moved his ships up to Manila Bay. On May 1, Dewey attacked.

What did he attack?

Seven ships, the 3,500-ton *Reina Cristina;* the old wooden *Castilla,* which had no engines, and was moored; five small gunboats; and a number of small vessels. The Spanish had thirty-one guns to the American fifty-three. It was no contest—or, as an English historian put it, it was "a military execution" rather than a battle.

Dewey moved into Manila Bay for the exercise. Even the watchword of the day was reminiscent of a war game. It was not "Don't give up the ship," which has a desperate ring, nor "We have met the enemy and he is ours," which has the exultant sound of battle hard fought, but "You may fire when you are ready, Gridley."

In the action that followed, the overwhelmed Spanish suffered hundreds of casualties from the "big" eight-inch guns of the Americans. The American ships were hit only fifteen times by Spanish shells and only one did any real damage; a shell exploded inside the *Baltimore* in a box of 3-pound gun ammunition, wounding two officers and eight men. That was the American casualty list.

By noon the battle was all over. The Americans were embarrassed because they had no troops to occupy Manila, and there in Manila Bay assembled the vultures: British, Germans, and Japanese, hoping to find some profit for themselves. The Germans were most obvious, having brought up a fleet of five ships that was stronger than Dewey's fleet. Admiral von Diederichs would have been happy for a little war of his own. He acted as if he were occupying the Philippines, landing troops for "exercise" and disregarding American orders about ship movements in Manila Bay. Finally Dewey was pushed too far. He warned von Diederichs that the Americans were in charge.

"And I tell you if Germany wants war, all right, we are ready . . ."

Von Diederichs would have been glad to oblige. But the British and the Japanese were not with him. If they could not have the Philippines, and it seemed just then that they could not, then they would prefer to have the Americans there rather than the Germans, who were so rapidly and aptly building empire. So von Diederichs faced not only the Americans, but the British and Japanese as well, not knowing what they would do if he started shooting; he got no support from home, and ultimately he moved his ships elsewhere.

The Spanish-American War had scarcely begun, and America, its eyes on Cuba, was suddenly faced with the need to occupy the Philippine Islands and take over administration of an utterly foreign Asian colony.

In the Caribbean the sea war was more exciting. Commodore William T. Sampson sailed out and bombarded Puerto Rico, then sailed back to Havana, waiting for Admiral Cervera to show up. Cervera came to the Dutch port of Curaçao, coaled, and then sailed into Santiago de Cuba, which was not blockaded by the Americans. Commodore Winfield S. Schley was in command of the "flying squadron," and Commodore Sampson had ordered him to move against Santiago de Cuba because he thought Cervera was there. But Schley moved like a snail. He was worried about coaling; he had a collier along, but the time never seemed right to take coal aboard. Several of his scout ships had sniffed around outside Santiago de Cuba and not seen anything on May 26, so instead of blockading Santiago de Cuba as ordered, Schley put on full steam for Key West. The next morning Schley had a "rocket" from the Navy Department indicating that the Spanish were at Santiago de Cuba—*where* was he?

Schley regretfully informed the Navy Department that he could not obey orders. He was short of coal. And besides he had not seen anything of the enemy.

But Schley obviously began to think over the reaction that might be expected, and suddenly he discovered that the weather was not so bad after all and he could coal from his collier. He did so, and went to Santiago de Cuba. There, he found, were the Spanish. What to do?

For two days he did nothing but cruise back and forth outside the entrance to the port, giving an excellent display of what a later court of inquiry called "vacillation, dilatoriness, and lack of enterprise."

Having Schley on hand, the Americans were lucky to have the Spanish to fight. For as Captain Mahan said in his study of the war, "We cannot expect ever again to have an enemy as inept as Spain showed herself to be.''

Commodore Sampson was as put out with Schley as was the Navy Department. He brought his squadron up on June 1 and started a real blockade of Cervera. Inside, Cervera was glum and uneasy. The port facilities were inadequate; he had gotten little coal and not much else here.

At 9:30 on the morning of July 3, Admiral Cervera brought his squadron out of Santiago Bay. The battle that followed was notable for some bad American ship handling (the *Brooklyn* nearly ran into the *Texas*) and the superior American firepower that destroyed the whole Spanish squadron in about four hours.

Superior American firepower? The term is relative. The Americans fired 1,300 shots and hit forty-two times for an average of 3.2 percent. They were lucky that their hits were in such spots as the *Vizcaya*'s magazine and the *Teresa*'s steam lines. The fact was that the American shooting was very poor, and was matched only by the worse performance of the Spanish.

There were a few more naval actions in the Spanish-American War. But it was not much of a war. In the whole conflict the U.S. Navy lost 18 men killed, 67 wounded, and 6 men invalided out sick. The army suffered 4,000 casualties, but more than half of these were from fever, and of the battle casualties 1,500 were wounded, nearly all of them at the avoidable Battle of San Juan Hill.

So the ''nice little war'' against Spain ended, leaving the Americans in control of Cuba, which they would now have to run for several years, a colony in Puerto Rico, a little colony suitable as a coaling station in Guam, and a dreadful political mess in the Philippines.

CHAPTER 23

"My Legation Is in Danger . . ."

The end of the Spanish-American War posed the United States with the enormous problem of administering the colonies captured from Spain, right?

Wrong.

The people of Cuba wanted independence, and had been fighting for it for years. They were perfectly capable of assuming control of their country in 1899. Instead they had to wait for three more years while an American military government tidied up affairs, leaving a multimillion-dollar American business imprint on the island in the process.

The people of the Philippines wanted independence and were ready for it. Aguinaldo, the Filipino leader, thought that Admiral George Dewey had guaranteed it to him. But the Filipinos were wrong. The United States was ruled by politicians who believed that the white man had a responsibility to "train" the brown man for independence. It did not make any difference that the brown man resisted. In January 1899 Aguinaldo protested the American "betrayal" and called on Filipinos to fight for their liberty. The Americans promised them freedom, but not just at the moment. So the revolt began. In February 1900, William Howard Taft was sent to the Philippines to set up a civil government. Still the rebellion went on.

The American insistence on granting the Filipinos independence under America's own conditions was quite in keeping with the times. These were the days of the "white man's burden" in Asia, and nothing showed that quite so clearly as the multinational intervention in the affairs of the Manchu Empire of China in the year 1900.

*   *   *

Nineteen hundred. China was the scene. China, the land of incense and opium, mystery and misery, the largest empire in the world, yes, even including the British Empire; but an empire crumbling with age and senility, weakened by a hundred years of corruption. The Mings had fallen to the Manchus (Ch'ing), and, after a very short era, the Manchus were falling because they had lost the art of government and because the harpies of the West were gnawing at their vitals.

Espionage was so endemic within the empire that the launching of an internal rebellion was most difficult. That is why, when a group of anti-foreign young rebels wanted to take action, they banded together as a brotherhood of Boxers, or practitioners of the martial arts. They had many meetings and engaged in strange activities. They believed in the cult they had invented, believed that the practice of their art made them superior to all foreigners in all things.

The Boxers began by attacking foreign institutions and peoples, particularly the missionaries, and, more important, the Chinese who had become Christians or westernized. There followed a whole series of murders against "primary devils" (the missionaries) and "secondary devils" (the converts).

Secretly, many officials at the court in Peking applauded the Boxers, although the guns of the foreigners prevented them from saying so openly. The foreigners, particularly the British, were never loath to use gunboat diplomacy to enforce their views. The Chinese had suffered the embarrassment of losing the Opium Wars and had been forced to give up territory to Britain, including that island that would become a glittering jewel in the British crown, Hong Kong. The Chinese were shy of provoking the Western powers that were gnawing away at China, but nonetheless resentful of all foreigners.

Murders of missionaries were followed by attacks on other foreigners, and by the spring of 1900 the legation quarter of Peking was under siege by the Boxers. That quarter was cut off from the rest of the city by a high wall, erected originally to keep the foreigners in. Now it became their fortress, and in spite of international tensions among nations outside this wall, inside the Germans, French, British, and Americans worked together in the common defense.

In May the U.S. legation at Peking sent an urgent call home for military help, and the navy dispatched the cruiser *Newark* to Taku Bar at the mouth of the Pei-Ho on the coast near Tientsin. The ship arrived at the end of May and sent a force of more than fifty U.S. Marines and sailors by train to Peking for the defense of the legation. Similarly, other governments with interests in China were doing the same. The number of the American force shows how little the Americans at home understood the problem that was developing in China. Thousands of Boxers were in motion in Peking and all around north China. Milling around Taku Bar were vessels of Britain, Russia, Germany, the United States, France, Italy, the Austro-Hungarian empire, and Japan, all either sending troops up to Peking or making plans to do so.

From Peking came news of Boxer attacks on the legation quarter and fighting on the wall. The Chinese government was supposedly intervening to protect the foreigners, but actually its intervention was halfhearted and useless. Suddenly on June 9 came word that the Boxers had cut the rail and telegraph lines from Peking and Tientsin and the legation quarter was surrounded.

Then, no more news.

The foreigners outside Tientsin pondered and ultimately conferred. It was obvious that the Chinese Imperial Army would be of little use. Some elements of the army openly sympathized with the Boxers; the rest would not act.

Captain McCalla of the *Newark* declared, "I don't care what the rest of you may do, but my legation is in danger and I am going immediately to start for its relief."

Other military men were there for the same reason as Captain McCalla. But—they were off the shore of an independent nation, China. What right did they have to send in troops? There were no international lawyers present and the need seemed imperative.

The ships shelled the Taku forts, which were occupied by the Chinese Army, and the forts replied until they were knocked out. Victory number one, over the wrong people, to enable the troops to go ashore. A relief expedition was formed that day, with Vice Admiral Seymour of the British Royal Navy in charge, because he was senior officer present and because the British presence was largest. But the force was a real international brigade, with troops from all the nations mentioned earlier, 2,078 officers and men.

They commandeered a train and set out by rail. The first day the expedition covered forty-eight miles of the eighty miles to Peking. But that night the Boxers tore up the rail line ahead. The Boxers attacked, not just on that night but at every opportunity for the next week. The attacks would have been pitiful had they not been so seriously launched by so many. Up came the Boxers, some with rifles or pistols, but many with lances or knives, or cudgels. They charged, truly believing that their "magic" would protect them against the foreigners' bullets, and they fell, dead and dying. But more came. They swarmed all around the expeditionary force, tearing up the rail lines in front of the train and behind it. Details were sent to protect ammunition dumps, and the details were attacked. In ten days perhaps a thousand Boxers were killed, but they inflicted many casualties on the international relief force, too, and prevented it from reaching Peking. The legation quarter of Peking was under constant attack, and many were the tales of heroism on the wall.

Ultimately the relief expedition itself had to be relieved. On June 25 new forces from Tientsin began to arrive at the expedition headquarters, now outside Tientsin. The Americans had five men killed and twenty-six wounded.

On June 16 orders had been sent to General Arthur MacArthur (Douglas MacArthur's father) at Manila to rush a regiment to Taku for reinforcement of the international brigade. The general complied. The 9th Infantry Regiment was sent through a typhoon to Taku Bar. It arrived July 8. Troops from other nations arrived that week also, and on July 13 an allied army attacked Tientsin, fighting both Boxers and the Chinese Army, which refused to give control of its territory to foreigners. The battle lasted fifteen hours. Then Tientsin was in Western hands, and could become the headquarters for a new effort to relieve Peking.

Major General Adna R. Chaffee was the general in command of the American army forces that came to China, 900 marines and 1,400 soldiers, as part of the 8,000-man international army that now set out to relieve Peking.

There were fights at P'ei Ts'ang and Yang Tsun. The heat of the China plain was terribly oppressive but the campaign went on. Finally, on August 13, the relief army reached a point only twelve miles from Peking. The troops stopped for a rest, and agreed to reconnoiter that day and fight the next. But the Russians, who had been lagging behind all the way, now came up and launched an attack on the Tung Pien Men gate to steal the thunder of the rest of the force; and so every man had to stop resting, pick up his rifle, and charge. The Russians got there first, but the fighting was heavy and they barely made it through the entrance before the other troops came up to help.

General Chaffee's Americans arrived on the morning of August 14 at 11:00 A.M. Two companies of the 14th Infantry scaled the great stone wall and planted the regimental flag. They drove the Boxers off the wall as far as the Sha Huo (East Gate) into the Chinese city. The main force came up, the troops rushed into the legation quarter, and the Boxers melted away.

But the job was only half done. Peking was to be occupied by this foreign army.

General Chaffee rode on his horse to the American legation, where he was greeted by the minister: "The patriotic purpose with which you hurried more than half around the world, the heroic courage displayed, and the tremendous sacrifices made in your victorious march from Tientsin to Peking deserves a more fervent expression of our sincere appreciation than can ever be given. . . ."

It was reported that someone was firing at travelers and troops around the outside of the Forbidden City, the imperial palace of China. This would not do. On August 15, the international army set out to crush the resistance. The American artillery moved up outside the palace wall and began banging away.

It was no easy job against the Chinese Army defenders who objected to the foreigners attacking their empress's house. Captain Reilly, the commander of the battery, was standing next to General Chaffee, watching the effect of the fire, when a bullet struck and killed him. A few minutes later the artillery fire blasted a hole in the gate, and the infantry began to move through. It was now August 28.

What happened in Peking in the next two weeks was so objectionable that most modern Western histories do not mention it. Suffice it to say that Peking was raped by the allied armies that had come to save the legations. Physical evidences are still available in museums and curio shops around the world. But what happened to the people of Peking remains locked in the Chinese memory.

General Chaffee was shocked:

The city of Peking has been sacked, looted from corner to corner in the most disgraceful manner imaginable. I had no idea that civilized armies would resort to such proceedings. It is a race for spoil. I have kept my own command relatively clean, thank God, but with all my efforts it is not spotless. It requires but one example of the sort I have witnessed to convince one that every nation's hand is against the Chinese people.

What could be done?

Not much.

For example, the Germans had not arrived in time for the fighting into Peking, but they arrived in time to loot. General Chaffee complained to Count von Waldersee that the German forces had walked off with ancient Chinese astronomical instruments from the royal Chinese observatory. The Germans loaded them up and took them to Berlin for display.

Small wonder that the Boxers were anti-foreign. The entry into the Forbidden City (so called because it was specifically forbidden to foreigners) was, as General Chaffee put it, "an exercise in curiosity" which, to the general's eternal credit, he had opposed, to be overruled by the generals of the other nations (i.e., Britain). And, after all, had not General Chaffee been the one to batter down the wall into the Forbidden City? All Chinese resented this intrusion by the foreign devils.

In fact American conduct was the most exemplary of that of all the nations involved in putting down the Boxer rising. The reason was simple enough: only the United States among all these nations had no territorial ambitions in China. Lest Americans puff up too much at this, as they have over the years, let it be said that the reason could be found in Cuba, Central America, the Philippines, and Hawaii, where the United States had already bitten off more than it could chew satisfactorily. Just at this time there was no room for extension of Manifest Destiny. The effect was salutary.

The various nations involved demanded reparations for the damages. The fact is that they probably should have paid the Chinese reparations for the damages they did in China, but once again force majeure ruled, and the Chinese swallowed their imperial pride and paid, and paid, and paid. The foreigners' arrogance grew, their chunks of Chinese territory became greater, their control of the rivers and cities increased, and so did the Chinese hatred.

From China's point of view the Boxer Rebellion had its positive side. It certainly prevented the outright partition of China by the European powers into a number of colonies. For the Chinese had fought well—both the army, defending its territorial integrity against the Europeans, and the miserably armed Boxers. They had fought well enough to give the Europeans pause. What if Europeans did partition China? Then they might expect a whole series of anti-foreign uprisings (for they understood well enough what the rebellion was all about).

The Europeans (and Americans) contented themselves with stationing troops in Peking, a direct violation of Chinese sovereignty, and garrisoning any point they wished between Peking and Shanhaiguan on the sea. The French and British insisted on taking further "leased territories"; the Americans did not. But the Americans did participate in the demands for extensions of the concessions in such cities as Shanghai, and in the making of new treaty ports.

The Americans also made much of their refusal to accept reparations, and their decision to turn the reparations over to scholarships for the education of Chinese students in America, and it is indeed one of the most lasting memorials to one speck of American official generosity. American policy in China in the early 1900s and until World War II called for an open China, with equal opportunity for trade for all nations and no further seizure of territory by the foreigners. That, too, was generous and of enormous benefit to such organizations as Standard Oil Company and other industrial giants, which moved into the China trade. But American marines remained in Peking, and in Shanghai, and in Canton, and the Americans had extraterritorial rights in China.

CHAPTER 24

Philippine Morass

The Boxer Rebellion had been a punctuation mark in the history of American-Asian relationships. Some Americans saw the American policy in the Philippines for what it was: outright aggression. Those Americans, however, did not include the Republican administrations of William Mc-Kinley and, after his assassination, of Theodore Roosevelt. Manifest Destiny was their motto.

But the trouble with Manifest Destiny, as the United States was learning in the Philippines, was that it was expensive, far beyond the benefits to American business. The U.S. Navy was the only real beneficiary of the U.S. policy, with its very strong presence in the Philippines giving it an important voice in Asia. But for America by and large, the first sixteen years of the twentieth century were a nightmare in the Philippines.

* * *

On May 1, 1898, Commodore Dewey won his easy victory at Manila Bay and controlled the Philippines.

So now what?

Back in Washington, President McKinley said he was hard put to figure out where the Philippine Islands were located. Perhaps. But such was not true of the United States Navy. What a good base Cavite made!

Commodore Dewey had no intention of leaving the Philippines to the tender mercies of the British and the Germans, whose warships now clustered around Manila Bay like turkey buzzards, waiting to see if the Americans would be so stupid as to leave and let them fight over the body.

In fact, a decision to send an army expeditionary force had been reached in Washington before Dewey won his little battle.

The Manifest Destiny people were pleased. "Unless I am utterly and profoundly mistaken," said Senator Henry Cabot Lodge, "the Administration is now fully committed to the large policy that we both desire."

Of course, said McKinley, the United States was now going to establish sovereignty over the Philippines, not because America wanted any colonies, but, because, as long as the United States had to take responsibility for its little brown brothers in these islands, law and order must prevail. McKinley assured everyone that America wanted only to protect the Filipinos. The best way to do that was to take over public property and start collecting taxes.

The State Department added its endorsement: "The United States . . . will expect from the inhabitants . . . that obedience which will be lawfully due from them."

While all this was happening, Aguinaldo, the leader of the Filipino revolution against Spain, was in Hong Kong, where he had been seeking foreign support. Commodore Dewey had agreed to take him back to the Philippines, and on May 16, Aguinaldo and his staff boarded the USS *McCulloch* for the journey.

At Manila Bay, Aguinaldo was met by Dewey, now Rear Admiral George Dewey. Dewey and Aguinaldo agreed to cooperate against the Spanish. Later the two gave totally irreconcilable accounts of their talks, but that was understandable. Probably neither was listening to the other.

The word that Aguinaldo was back rushed like fire through the Philippines, and Aguinaldo's supporters began seizing Spanish vessels and Spanish armaments wherever they could. On May 24 Aguinaldo proclaimed a temporary war government, with himself as head of it. This pained Dewey, for he was waiting for the arrival of American troops to batter down the walls of Manila, and capture it from the Spanish defenders.

On June 18, Aguinaldo compounded matters by issuing a Philippine Declaration of Independence. His followers began seizing territory and soon held most of Luzon. Dewey's dispatches home indicated his sympathy for Philippine independence. But who was Dewey? Just a military man who was charged with carrying out military duties entrusted to him by his political superiors.

And how did they feel about the Philippines?

They wanted them.

"We find that we want the Philippines," wrote the *Chicago Times-Herald*. "We also want Puerto Rico. We want Hawaii now. We may want the Carolines, the Ladrones, the Pelews [Peleliu], and the Mariana groups. If we do we will take them."

Admiral Dewey and Generalissimo Aguinaldo were waiting for the American expeditionary force, which had to be organized from scratch. The first contingent of American troops sailed from San Francisco on May 25. They stopped by to capture Guam, which took thirteen shells from the USS *Charleston* and a boatload of U.S. Marines to raise the flag. Now the United States had another colony. Manila changed hands in August. The Spanish, worn down by all the waiting, fired a few token shots and surrendered the city.

But the trouble had not yet begun.

On September 26 proceedings began in Paris to bring an end to the Spanish-American War. The treaty signed there gave the United States possession of the Philippines, and the Americans gave the Spanish twenty million dollars.

President McKinley, who had not been at all sure a few weeks earlier about what to do with the Philippines, now knew:

"There was nothing left for us to do but to take them all, and to educate the Filipinos and uplift and civilize and Christianize them, and by God's grace to do the very best we could by them, as our fellow men for whom Christ also died . . ."

Not everyone agreed. Some foot-draggers on the road to colonialism pointed out that the Filipinos were already mostly Christian, courtesy of the Spanish, that they had a workable civilization of their own, and that they were aware of the need for education. First of all, however, they wanted their independence.

Andrew Carnegie, the multimillionaire, wrote a magazine article opposing the annexation of the Philippines: "The Philippines will be to the United States precisely what India is to England, a nation of incipient rebels."

But no one was listening. "Andrew Carnegie really seems to be off his head," said Secretary of State John May.

The United States Senate decided. It accepted the Treaty of Paris. The Philippines now belonged to America.

But the Filipinos had yet to be heard from.

On February 4, 1899, U.S. troops along the San Juan River were attacked by Filipino troops. The Filipino insurrection had begun.

No one in Washington expected this uprising to be very important. The *New York Times* predicted that Aguinaldo would not have much staying power: after one or two skirmishes, the insurgent army would break up.

"These babes of the jungle . . . are veritable children. They show the weaknesses and the vices of the resourceless and unmoral human infant.

Aguinaldo is a vain popinjay, a wicked liar, and a perfectly incapable leader. His men are dupes, a foolish, incredulous mob.''

That was a "responsible" American newspaper talking, saying what was being said all across the country by the hopers of hope, the followers of Manifest Destiny.

February became March, and the "popinjay" was still strutting his plumage and crying his cry of "Freedom." The fighting did not slacken. The "babes of the jungle" did not disappear in confusion.

April came, the fighting grew worse. The Americans captured the towns, and the Filipinos held the villages around them. The Americans got sick. In May, of 4,800 troops in the San Fernando area, 2,160 were down with dysentery, malaria, or just plain "fever." In one skirmish an American regiment lost 3 men killed, 10 men wounded, and 84 men with heat prostration. The Nebraska volunteers crossed the swampy Rio de Pampanga, and 108 new cases of malaria showed up.

The monsoon came, rain by the bucketful, and slashing winds of hurricane force.

On June 10, between Manila Bay and Laguna de Bay, 4,000 American troops were caught between two units of Filipinos, 3,000 in all. In the fighting the whole American division fell apart. Reinforcements were rushed to the scene, but 1,000 men had already staggered off into the jungle, discarding their equipment, most of them never to return. By June, American battle casualties were 2,000.

Racism played a nasty role. Some black American soldiers found their sympathies were with the Filipinos, particularly since they were segregated by their own countrymen. One American deserter, a black named David Fagan, joined the Filipinos, asked custody of a number of white American prisoners, and shot them all dead. Later the Americans put a price of $600 on Fagan's head, and it was delivered in a wicker basket to officers of the 38th Infantry. The Fagan story and others not nearly so dramatic did much to set back the cause of blacks in the American military service.

The Americans called the Filipinos "niggers." Soon they announced that they were not taking prisoners. Why? Because American bodies, found in the villages, often showed signs of the most intensive torture before death.

It worked both ways. The Americans used the "water treatment" to elicit information from reluctant prisoners. Four or five gallons of water forced down the throat of a victim changes his appearance remarkably, and was intended to change his mind. Squeezing the water out by kneeling on his stomach changed the picture again. Usually the prisoner died, but not quickly.

The Filipinos put out white flags and lured the Americans into death traps. The Americans stopped paying any attention to white flags.

Everyone suffered enormously, but the Filipinos would not give up and the Americans would not let the Filipinos have their country.

And how did the American soldier behave?

In December 1899, the American 33rd Infantry was pursuing Aguinaldo through the mountains. The commander of Aguinaldo's rear guard was General Gregorio del Pilar, Aguinaldo's best friend and one of his most faithful soldiers. On December 2, Pilar fought a delaying action at Tirad Pass to give Aguinaldo time to reach safety in the mountains. In the fight, General Pilar was shot off his horse by an American sharpshooter and died. Richard Henry Little, a correspondent for the Chicago *Tribune*, was there:

We went up the mountainside. After H Company had driven the insurgents out of their second position and killed Pilar, the other companies had rushed straight up the trail.

Just past this a few hundred yards we saw a solitary figure lying on the road. The body was almost stripped of clothing, and there were no marks of rank on the bloodsoaked coat.

A soldier came running down the trail.

"That's old Pilar," he said. "We got the old rascal. I guess he's sorry he ever went up against the Thirty-Third.

"There ain't no doubt its being Pilar," rattled on the young soldier. "We got his diary, and letters and all his papers, and Sullivan of our company's got his pants, and Snider's got his shoes but he can't wear them because they're too small, and a Sergeant in G Company got one of his silver spurs, and a lieutenant got the other, and somebody swiped his cuff buttons before I got there or I would have swiped them, and all I got was a stud button and his collar with blood on it. . . ."

The man who had the general's shoes strode proudly past. A private sitting on a rock was examining a golden locket containing a curl of woman's hair. "Got the locket off his neck. . . ."

The year 1899 passed and became 1900. Soldiers wrote home. Some bragged, as did Sergeant Howard McFarlane to the Fairfield (Maine) *Journal:* "On Thursday March 29, eighteen of my company killed seventy-five nigger bolomen and ten of the nigger gunners. When we find one that is not dead, we have bayonets."

But not all the soldiers liked what they were doing, and some brought charges against others for murder and mistreatment of prisoners. The mistreatment was brutal; five times as many Filipinos were killed as were wounded, a complete reversal of the usual. When asked about this, General Arthur MacArthur said with a straight face: "Our soldiers know how to shoot." Someone might have rejoined, "Yes, how to shoot fish in a barrel."

*   *   *

That spring, reaction set in at home. Congress began to investigate the unseemly conduct of the American army in the Philippines. All was not well, and President McKinley soon recognized it. So he dispatched to the Philippines Judge William Howard Taft, a huge, benign Republican of stature as enormous as his girth.

"I don't want the islands," Taft said to McKinley.

"Neither do I," said the president (having exhibited a change of heart). "But we've got them."

And so Judge Taft sailed for Manila, to take control of the Philippines away from the army and set it up in civil hands—his hands.

The year 1900 was again a presidential election year, and the American army in the Philippines must have been Republican. For the army was ruthless in its censorship of newspaper dispatches and letters home telling about conditions. Anything written that indicated any lapses of protocol (torture, murder, etc.) by the American troops never made it home. But as always, censorship failed. They could not keep the newspaper correspondents in the Philippines forever. When the correspondents got home, like Moscow correspondents of another generation, they let loose with their blasts. The Anti-Imperialist League in America was glad to hear them, and a reaction against imperialism set in.

By the winter of 1900–1901 Taft had begun organizing his Philippine commission, and he was appointing some Filipinos to it; the Americans were going to let the Filipinos have a say in their government. On the Fourth of July, 1901, military government would be terminated except in those areas where the rebellion had not been quelled.

It sounded good. But it sounded much better than it was; most of the Philippines was still in rebellion.

As long as Aguinaldo fought, so would many millions of Filipinos be with him in spirit. The Americans would continue to be "an occupying power" no matter what they called themselves.

Then General Frederick Funston's troops captured one of Aguinaldo's couriers, Cecilio Segismundo. He was questioned (tortured, said the Filipinos) and under questioning he revealed Aguinaldo's hiding place: Palanan in Isabela Province in northeast Luzon. General Funston was one of those short, wiry, Napoleonic figures that may in times of crisis go far, no matter the impression they make on their comrades. He was then thirty-six years old and full of ambition. He decided that he, Funston, would capture Aguinaldo.

Leading a handful of renegade Filipinos, Funston and ninety men sailed around Luzon in the gunboat *Vicksburg* and were landed at Casiguras Bay on February 4, 1901. The *Vicksburg* left them there, promising to return in five weeks. Meanwhile the troop was to move up country, kidnap Aguinaldo, and return to Casiguras Bay.

Pretending to be American prisoners of a guerrilla band, General Funston and his men found their way to Aguinaldo's camp and captured him. They took him back to the coast and were met by the *Vicksburg* and taken back to Manila. General Funston delivered the rebel leader to General MacArthur.

The capture of Aguinaldo impressed the whole world. General Funston was appointed a brigadier general in the regular army and awarded the Medal of Honor. But not everyone was complimentary. The British said that Funston's method, employing trickery, disguises, forgeries, mercenary soldiers, and bribes, was "not cricket." One London paper spoke of the Americans fighting "to deprive the Filipinos of their liberty" and called the capture of Aguinaldo "a piece of sharp practice thoroughly in keeping with the rest of the war." Hypocrisy, they said, was the hallmark of the Americans.

General MacArthur kept after Aguinaldo to tell his friends to lay down their arms.

For three weeks Aguinaldo refused. The Americans brought his family. They treated him well. They argued with him. But, as a friend put it, Aguinaldo objected to the idea of having "lots of American school teachers at once to set to work to teach the Filipino English, and at the same time to keep plenty of American soldiers around to knock him on the head should he get a notion that he is ready for self-government before the Americans think he is."

But ultimately Aguinaldo accepted American sovereignty over the Philippine Islands in order to stop the bloodshed.

On July 4, 1901, William Howard Taft became the first civilian governor of the Philippines. General Arthur MacArthur sailed for America, replaced by General Chaffee, who had commanded the Americans in China. But all this talk of civil rule was still illusory. Fifty-five of the seventy-seven Philippine provinces were still under army rule. Fighting was still going on. The army was up to its old tricks of harshness and Taft did not like them. He argued so constantly with General Chaffee that finally President Theodore Roosevelt* felt impelled to write Chaffee and call to his attention the fact that the president of the United States knew what was going on and did not like it.

Taft said the secret of American success in the Philippines lay in education. No one heard much about rebellion in northern Luzon, any more—perhaps because the army had wiped out a sixth of the Luzon population in its relentless campaign against the insurgents.

In the fall of 1901 came several dreadful uprisings, the most notable being in the village of Balangiga on the southern tip of Samar Island, where

---

*President McKinley had been assassinated.

knife-wielding bolomen massacred most of Company C of the U.S. 9th Infantry. These massacres brought a reign of terror by the U.S. Army. As General Jacob Smith put it in his orders: "I want no prisoners. I wish you to kill and burn; the more you burn and kill the better it will please me."

If his troops could turn all Samar into a wilderness he would be delighted; all persons who had not surrendered and who were capable of carrying arms were to be shot on sight.

Who was capable of bearing arms?

Anyone over ten years of age, said General Smith.

In six months Samar was as quiet as a cemetery. In fact, it *was* a cemetery.

The same attitude was taken by the army throughout the Philippines. If an American soldier was killed, a native prisoner was selected by lot and he was executed immediately. Does it sound like the Nazis at Lidice? Occupying forces have a dreadful similarity.

These harsh policies were enforced in Batangas Province, in Cavite, and Tabayas. In six months 54,000 civilians were killed by the army in Batangas alone.

Slowly the warring ended. The Moro tribesmen of the southern islands were the last to give in. For several months they staged their terrible raids with bolos, fully expecting to be cut down by the troops but vowing under the protection of Muhammad in the name of Allah to take as many American soldiers with them as they could. Sometimes a Moro could take a dozen men with his bolo before he fell. The Americans took to using weapons with heavy-caliber slugs capable of knocking a man down even if hit in the shoulder or the side. The .45-caliber Colt automatic pistol was designed for this purpose.

Terror did its ugly work. In April 1902 the last of the big guerilla bands surrendered. On July 4, 1902, President Roosevelt declared the Filipino insurrection at an end. Amnesty was granted to all who would take the oath of allegiance to the United States. Everywhere but in the Moro islands the civilian government came into power. President Roosevelt praised the army: the Democrats in Congress called the soldiers murderers.

The cost of the war was never fully assessed. Four thousand American soldiers had died and were buried in the Philippines. More than 20,000 Filipino fighters and about 200,000 Filipino civilians had been killed or died of disease brought on by the war. The water buffalo population, on which the farmers depended, had been reduced by ninety percent. The cost of the war to the United States was estimated at $170 million. And when the dreadful struggle came to an end, nobody in America was watching. They were much more interested in the Panama Canal.

No one paid much attention to what happened in the Philippines from this point on. Many of the facts were unknown. An infantry captain, John

J. Pershing, was nearly killed by insurgents in the spring of 1903. But officially the Philippines were "pacified," so such incidents were ignored at home. In 1906 there were so many Moro murders that the army made an expedition on the island of Jolo. No prisoners were taken. Dead on the field were 600—men, women, and children.

The same story was repeated in 1916 on Mindanao. That year Congress passed the Jones Act, sometimes called the Organic Act of the Philippine Islands, reaffirming the intention of the United States to withdraw from the islands and give the people real independence "as soon as a stable government should be established." The law set up suffrage for males, established a bill of rights and an elected senate, and put executive power in the hands of the American-appointed governor general of the islands.

In 1933 Congress decided that by 1941 the Filipinos would be ready for independence, and that year was set for granting complete freedom. It was a great day to one particular man in the islands, although he had to have some reservations about it. Aguinaldo was still alive and thinking his own thoughts about the way the Americans conferred freedom on brown-skinned people.

CHAPTER 25

Cuba Libre and Other Troubles

The one positive element to emerge from the American decision to maintain control of the Philippines in 1899 was that it created an awareness of the negative side of colonialism. This new awareness—spurred by the enormous difficulties of the Americans in trying to "pacify" the Filipinos—played a major role in the struggle in Congress over the fate of Cuba. The Filipinos gave the Cubans their independence, one might say. Seeing the trouble that was involved in administering an unwilling colony, Americans backed away from actual administrative control of Cuba. Nevertheless, under Theodore Roosevelt, the economic *penetration of Latin America, with many outright military interventions, reached a new high.*

*　　*　　*

In May 1902, Governor Leonard Wood turned the affairs of Cuba over to President Tomas Estrade Palma and the Cuban congress, and the American government of the island came to an end. Yielding to American public opinion, the Republican administration had promised not to annex Cuba, but that did not mean the Americans did not feel a proprietary interest in this "Pearl of the Antilles." This interest was most often described in terms of "a special relationship." A shorthand description of that relationship is embodied in the career of Frank Steinhart, General Wood's administrative assistant during the American occupation of Cuba, who became successively U.S. Consul to Havana and then president of the Havana Electric Railway Company.

But the cynical appraisal of American greed in relation to Latin America, typified by the stereotype of United Fruit Company as the great banana exploiter, is misleading. Exploitation was never the basic American interest in the Americas.

America was very proud to announce that after the Spanish-American War it had not annexed Cuba and had no colonial office to manage Puerto Rico and the Philippines, which it had annexed. The reason is simple enough: the American public and government never considered the colonies to be colonies in the European sense. All those relationships were "temporary." The basic concept was always that the territories would "some day" become independent or full partners in the American nation. How well that concept worked is another matter. In the case of the Philippines, integration did not work at all, and ultimately Americans realized it, as they had done so early in Cuba, and granted the Philippines release. In the case of Puerto Rico it did not work very well either.

What Americans wanted in 1900 (and still wanted in the 1980s) was to be sure that the political climate of the American sphere of influence was complementary to the American system. Far more than economic penetration, this has been the keystone of American policy wherever Americans have trod.

As one of the leading students of Latin American affairs has noted, the American effort in Latin America has always been to produce and maintain an orderly society populated by the law-abiding. "These were the values not of Wall Street, but of Main Street."

In a sense, then, the American attitude has been far more arrogant than that of Britain, France, and other imperial powers; our nation has believed in playing God to others with what we consider to be the most benevolent of motives. (As of 1987 as a nation we still had not learned that the evangelist is seldom a successful politician.)

The key to the American attitude toward Cuba since 1900 is to be found in what is called the Platt Amendment. (The name comes from that peculiarly American device of attaching an amendment onto an appropriations bill to secure passage of a controversial measure. In this case the Platt Amendment was part of the Army Appropriation Bill of 1901.)

The Platt Amendment stated: (1) that Cuba would never enter into any treaty with any foreign power impairing Cuban independence; (2) that the Cuban government would not run up a deficit; (3) that the United States was authorized to intervene in Cuban affairs to "preserve Cuban independence" and law and order; and (4) that Cuba would lease military bases to the United States.

Until 1934 these provisions were part of the Cuban constitution. They are still the basis of the attitude of some Americans about Cuba, particularly part one. The special relationship between Cuba and the USSR is more than irritating to Americans. Part four, which covers the American maintenance of a naval base at Guantanamo, is more than irritating to the Cubans.

No sooner had the Americans moved out of Cuba than they found themselves involved in another matter in which national honor and the strictures of the Monroe Doctrine had to be maintained. In 1902 the Venezuelan dictator Cipriano Castro defaulted on his international debts. He owed money to German banks, and the German government was furious, threatened action (combined with the British who were then playing politics with the Germans), and announced a blockade of the Venezuelan coast. Here was a clear challenge to the Monroe Doctrine, and President Theodore Roosevelt and Admiral George Dewey, chairman of the navy general board, so saw it. Dewey took command of a special Caribbean Fleet and sailed for the south.

Indeed, Teddy Roosevelt's administrations were marked by enough military excursions to satisfy half a dozen ordinary presidents. Long before he uttered the immortal words "Speak softly and carry a big stick, you will go far," Roosevelt was going far.

Before his assassination, President McKinley had persuaded the British to give up their claim to the isthmian canal, all put in order in the Hay-Pauncefote treaty in 1900. Once Roosevelt took over, he moved rapidly through shark-infested political waters. The big decision was where to put the canal. The Nicaraguan route, favored by Commodore Vanderbilt so long before, was also favored in 1901 because the successors to the bankrupt de Lesseps canal company wanted too much for their holdings in the Panama sector. But when the Americans indicated that they would go to Nicaragua to build their canal, the Panama price suddenly dropped to about thirty-five percent of the original. The Americans bought the holdings and rights, but then had to get the Republic of Colombia to lease its Panama territory "forever." Colombia balked; it wanted a lot of hard cash. Teddy Roosevelt blustered that he felt like invading Colombia, but he did not. Instead he smiled benevolently on a rebellion of "Panamanians," backed by American and other capitalists interested in the canal; he sent American warships to the area to help out, and generally guaranteed the rebellion. The cruiser *Nashville* was sent down to Colón, Panama, and a string of orders from the Navy Department came after it. Marines were landed, and they took over the railroad office at Colón.

On November 3, 1903, the Colombians landed a force of soldiers who were planning to take a train across to Panama City to fight the rebels. The marine officer demanded a ticket from every Colombian soldier. The commander of the Colombian troops did not have the money to pay for tickets for his men. The Americans provided the commander with personal transport to Panama City, promising that his troops would come along in a special train. But somehow the cars could not be found to make up the special train. When the commander got to Panama City he was arrested by the rebels.

Back at Colón the lieutenant in charge of the Colombian troops was furious. He demanded the immediate release of his commander, and, knowing where the responsibility lay, threatened to kill all the Americans in Colón. Since there were only about fifty marines ashore, as compared to several hundred Colombian troops, the situation was difficult until November 5, when the USS *Dixie* arrived at Colón, carrying a whole battalion of marines led by Major John Lejeune. The Colombian commander was bribed ($8,000 bought a Colombian troop commander in those days), and a British steamer took all the troops aboard and returned them to Colombian land far from the isthmus. The crisis was ended.

In later years Lejeune became a part of marine legend. The real legendary figure should have been that unknown marine who invented the ploy of charging for individual tickets for the Colombian soldiers and thus holding up the whole troop transport.

It was a surprise to no one that the Panamanian revolution succeeded— and this in days long before the Central Intelligence Agency began its spotty record of covert operations to destabilize Latin American governments.

On November 6, 1903, the United States recognized the government of Panama, and two weeks later Panama gave the United States control of the Panama Canal Zone, ten miles wide across the isthmus, "in perpetuity," plus the rights of fortification, for $10 million and an annual payment of $250,000. Everybody was happy except the Colombians and various resentful European powers.

More trouble for Roosevelt came on the island of Hispaniola, which had been a thorn in the American side since the days of the pirate Henry Morgan. At one point the black government of Toussaint l'Ouverture had dominated the whole island. But for sixty years half the island had been governed under the Dominican Republic, as crooked and cruel a succession of administrations as ever existed anywhere. From this island emerged many of the tales of Latin America that delighted and horrified American readers, such as this story of Ulises Heureaux, one of the early dictators:

One evening the dictator invited an old opponent to dinner. Eager to bury the hatchet, the old enemy came gladly, for el presidente Señor Heureaux was a powerful and dangerous man, whose friendship gave, and took away, fortunes.

They shook hands, the dictator smiled. They talked. Dinner was served. The wine was vintage French. The food was excellent, the conversation was pleasant. The service was unexceptionable. At the end of the meal, a servant came with a box of the finest Havana cigars. The guest was replete, and he indicated that he might pass until the next time.

"Next time?" said the dictator. "Have a cigar. Enjoy it. It will be your last. When you finish it you will be shot."

In the Dominican Republic the white man's burden was often heavy, as Roosevelt found in 1903. The Dominican government was always in financial trouble and in the nineteenth century had adopted a system of satisfying its creditors by turning over to some foreign power the right to collect the customs duties and parcel them out to the government and the creditors. The Americans, of course, had the job. But just now the Dominican government was having difficulties with rebels and the army wanted more money.

Roosevelt was not averse to the idea. Indeed, it played into an idea of his own. For several years the United States Navy had been agitating for bases in Hispaniola, at Manzanillo and Samana Bay. So a team of navy intelligence men, disguised as journalists, went down to Hispaniola. They returned full of enthusiasm for Hispaniola naval bases. But just then a revolution broke out, and then another, and the island was beset during 1903 and 1904. Since there were a number of American business establishments there, the U.S. Navy sent a succession of warships to "protect the property," and in various ways they interfered with the rebels and the government. In January 1904, for example, Commander A. C. Dillingham of the USS *Detroit* landed at Puerto Plata and told both sides that fighting was forbidden in towns that contained large numbers of foreigners. When an American sailor was killed by the rebels, the U.S. Navy sent a whole squadron down to Hispaniola to bombard them.

In 1904, the Americans were virtually the force maintaining law and order on the north coast of the island. Some in Washington urged annexation, but President Roosevelt wanted a simpler solution. All he really wanted was to install American collectors of revenue so that the taxes would be paid and the creditors would get the money. He managed it, although in 1905 he did so by maintaining seven warships in Dominican waters. Ultimately one of the many Dominican generals, General Ramón Caceres, triumphed, and established a relatively stable government.

By that time the Americans were back in trouble in Cuba. The peace established in the Cuban republic in 1902 had brought back American investment, which soon hit the $100-million mark and climbed ever upward. The navy was greedy for bases, but ultimately had to content itself with the one at Guantanamo Bay. So the United States had a continued stake in Cuba. All went well until the time of the administration of Tomas Estrade Palma ran out. In the campaign that followed, the opposition saw that it was going to lose and so rebelled. Another Cuban revolution.

So in the summer of 1906, American warships were again sent to Cuba, their captains enjoined to discover what was happening. Commander J. C. Colwell of the USS *Denver* sailed into Havana harbor, donned civilian clothes, called on President Estrade, and learned that the president was nervous about his ability to hold the capital if any more trouble came. Colwell began landing American marines and sailors on September 13.

The day before, Secretary of State Robert Bacon had sent a telegram to the American mission at Havana, warning that no troops were to be landed. Yet there they were, with two machine guns and an artillery piece. The next week, Bacon and a special envoy from Roosevelt arrived in Havana to mediate the dispute between government and rebels. The envoy was William Howard Taft. He investigated. He recommended patience and the landing of more troops. Roosevelt was so sick of the mess in the Philippines and so reluctant to plunge into an equally sticky morass in Cuba that he delayed. Meanwhile Estrade forces and the rebels were eager to be on with the fighting. Estrade resigned. Cuba had no government. Taft was there, so he took over the rule, and another 2,000 marines were landed. Cuba was occupied by the Americans for the second time in five years.

This second occupation lasted three years. In 1909, again, the Americans left, sure that they had established a stable government and that the political process would be observed. But in 1912 the Americans were back in Cuba in military occupation for a third time, putting down a rebellion by Cuban blacks who apparently intended to take over and massacre the whole foreign population. Once again American intervention was made in behalf of American lives and property. After a few months government control was assured and the Americans left, offering no promises that they would never again return.

Indeed, to the military it seemed almost inevitable that they would be back again to deal with some other evidence of political incapability.

CHAPTER 26

Bullets and Bananas

The seeds of anti-Americanism in Latin America, which has grown so powerful in the 1980s, were scattered widely in the first quarter of the twentieth century. The Dominicans of the 1980s are the grandchildren of the Dominicans of 1910. The Haitians and the Nicaraguans are the same. Most Americans do not realize how many times we have invaded these little countries of Latin America. To Americans the interventions of the past were justified by the need for law and order to permit the orderly processes of American business. In the 1920s and the 1930s that was quite enough justification for the United States.

*   *   *

The island of Hispaniola, which houses the republics of Haiti and the Dominican Republic, is not very far from Guantanamo Bay, the American naval base in Cuba. So it was not hard for the American navy, with its strong interest in Latin American affairs, to keep an eye on the succession of events in Hispaniola. And what a tangled web of events occurred in the early years of the twentieth century!

The U.S. Navy would have liked to have a base in Haiti, but the Haitians would not permit it; they opposed all foreign bases. Being black, they did not trust whites, a compliment that was returned by the U.S. Navy. So the proposed base at Môle Saint Nicolas was never to be.

With the Americans collecting the customs of the Dominican Republic in 1907 and after, that government did fairly well. President Heureaux had been assassinated in 1899. After that came all those civil wars that had brought the American intervention. In 1906 President Carlos Morales was evicted from office by President Ramón Caceres, one of the assassins of Heureaux who was then assassinated in 1911. If the Dominican Republic was stable, its stability was more or less measurable in five-year spurts, followed by a "lead bullet election."

On the Central American mainland the concatenation of revolutions in the first and second decades of the twentieth century was so confusing that even Richard Harding Davis, the American journalist who specialized in pocket revolutions, was hard put to separate them. Guatemalans plotted against Hondurans and Salvadorans. War sometimes came for strange reasons: in 1906 El Salvador invaded Guatemala because the Salvadoran secretary of war hated the Guatemalan president, got drunk one night, and sent off the troops. That struggle was mediated aboard the USS *Marblehead*.

American warships were constantly roaming about Central American waters in these years, stopping fights, shelling rebels who were shelling towns where American citizens had interests, rescuing women and children from revolutionary forays, and generally "policing the area," as they called it. Whether or not they had a right to do it is a matter that was debated endlessly in the cafés of Central America and sometimes in Congress. But generally speaking, the American government took the position that the Monroe Doctrine had two responsibilities: first to be sure that no Europeans came in to take over colonies, and second, to be sure that the Latin American nations governed themselves in a manner that made for stability of enterprises and general peacefulness. The American success at the latter was not particularly notable.

In 1907 Guatemala invaded Honduras. American vessels patrolled the Honduran coast and maintained a certain amount of order by preventing all sides from fighting in towns where foreigners lived. Finally a certain tranquility was established when five Central American states held a peace conference in 1907.

But many American residents of Nicaragua hated José Santos Zelaya, the president of Nicaragua, because of his manipulation of concessions in a manner they disliked, and so they supported rebellion. The American consul, Thomas Moffatt, was deep in the conspiracy. In some ways the situation was reminiscent of the old days of the filibuster William Walker. Two Americans who were laying dynamite charges for the rebels, aimed at sinking Zelaya's navy in the rivers, were arrested and summarily executed. The revolution continued and in 1909 was going strong until the chief rebel announced early in 1910 that he could not hold the town of Bluefields, a center of American influence, and that Zelaya was likely to

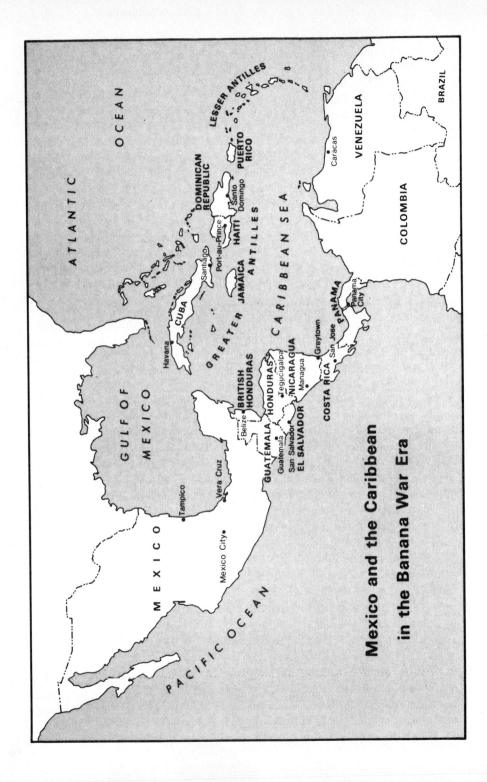

Mexico and the Caribbean
in the Banana War Era

come in and execute everybody, including the American residents. So Moffatt cabled for the marines. Major Smedley Butler was sent from the Canal Zone with 250 marines to police Bluefields.

The American marines were again running affairs in a Latin American country. Major Butler was a real purist. When he was told to run something, he ran everything, even garbage and trash control (he issued orders that all garbage in Bluefields was to be buried at least two feet deep).

On the political level the interference was just as complete. President William Howard Taft and his secretary of state, Philander C. Knox, interfered openly in Nicaragua against President Zelaya and in favor of his various enemies. Zelaya's major opponent was Juan Estrada. Taft and Knox declared that Estrada had the broad support of the Nicaraguan people (about as likely a claim as the claim that the Contras of the 1980s had the broad support of the Nicaraguan people). But in 1909 the Taft administration did not have a Vietnam behind it or a sensitive Congress, and so Americans backed their political decisions with military force. A large naval squadron commanded by Admiral W. W. Kimball was ranging off Central America—nine ships loaded with marines. The Americans helped in many ways to overthrow Zelaya, whose major crime was his antipathy to foreign interference in Nicaraguan affairs. Finally American interference created an impasse in the revolutionary situation, and President Porfirio Diaz of Mexico arranged for Zelaya to step down in favor of Dr. Jose Madriz, who was considered to be more to America's liking.

The American squadron arrived at Corinto, Nicaragua's west-coast port, in early December, and Admiral Kimball stood by while President Zelaya was whisked out of Nicaragua by a Mexican warship sent by Diaz.

Zelaya out of the picture, all should be well.

The yanquis, however, did not like Madriz. He was just another Zelayista, said Secretary Knox, preferring to believe the reports in the newspapers, based on tales from businessmen in Nicaragua, rather than those of Admiral Kimball, on the scene. The admiral, seeing what was happening, wrote that Estrada wanted to be another Zelaya. No, said Knox. Perhaps Knox was right; Dr. Madriz fought the rebels until the Americans made it impossible to win, by protecting the rebel ports and shipping. So Dr. Madriz also fled the country, and then Señor Estrada declared himself president.

The Americans then continued to interfere in the Nicaraguan revolution. General Estrada, appealing to the Americans, said he was committed to new elections and financial stability. Ah, yes, said Secretary Knox, this was just what was wanted. Maybe a customs receivership in the hands of the Americans, as with the Dominican Republic. Much better to use money than to send troops, the Taft administration told Congress. Thus came into being the concept of using dollars instead of bullets to maintain stability in Latin America—"dollar diplomacy."

Secretary Knox sent an emissary to Managua to help prepare Nicaraguans for those new elections, and also to be sure that no Zelayista remained in any position of importance. He was Thomas Dawson. He would soon be the chief of the Latin American Division of the Department of State, a post created to watch over affairs south of the border. Dawson supervised an agreement among the various rebel leaders that would give America the customs concession and also guarantee payments to foreigners for all losses suffered in the civil war.

But no sooner had Knox's man left Managua than the agreement fell apart. President Estrada really did want to be another Zelayistic dictator after all, it seemed. He quarreled with his other generals, and on May 8, after he lost his bid for absolute control, he fled the country.

The new president was Adolfo Diaz. He nicely put all the American demands into a treaty package and sent it to Washington, but it arrived too late for the Senate to consider before going into recess for the season. In the interim, American investment bankers raised the money for Nicaragua's survival, and the customs collections passed into the hands of private Americans.

But competition for power within the Diaz administration continued. General Luís Mena rebelled against Diaz. One of the really dangerous aspects of this new rebellion was that Mena's troops threatened the railroad, which was operated by Americans. As if illustrating the reality of the threat, the rebels captured two lake steamers on Lake Managua and Lake Nicaragua—steamers owned by the rail company.

This was unacceptable behavior.

Up to Managua from the USS *Annapolis* came 100 bluejackets, to protect American lives and property once again. In the second week of August General Mena attacked Managua and bombarded the capital with field guns. Americans sought refuge in the Hotel Lupon, which was shelled by Mena's troops as a focal point—more serious threats to American lives. Out went a message for more help. Major Butler came with a battalion of marines.

In Washington, the American authorities were comparing the Managua situation to that of Peking in 1898, and there was talk about sending a whole army infantry regiment to Nicaragua. But the navy objected. Admiral W. H. H. Southerland, who was in charge in the south, had six ships full of marines and fighting sailors, and they had the resources in Panama. So sailors landed from ships, and marines landed, and from Panama came a whole regiment: the 1st Provisional Marine Regiment was put together and brought to Nicaragua under Colonel Joseph H. Pendleton. By September the United States had a thousand marines in Nicaragua, and everybody guessed that the railroad was going to be safe.

But the rebels and the government forces were fighting along the railroad, and many incidents threatened the peace of the banana shippers. American marines got involved. Major Butler was in the thick of it, running up and down the railroad on a train, fighting engagements, keeping the line open. For months the fighting went on. The most serious battle was the Battle of Coyotepe, fought in October 1912, involving nearly 1,000 marines. They won, of course. The marines marched around Nicaragua then to impress the people, distributed Red Cross packages, and prepared to go home. The 1,100 marines in Nicaragua had suffered 37 casualties. In November new elections were held. President Diaz, who was favored still by the Americans, won the election easily, since all his potential opponents had the good sense to agree not to run, and peace came to Nicaragua once again. The Americans went away, official lock, stock, barrel, marines, fleet, and admiral, leaving the businessmen and a legation guard of 100 marines, and advice that Nicaragua needed civilian rule.

The United States, said Colonel Pendleton on the eve of his departure, "does not intend longer to tolerate Central American revolutions."

CHAPTER 27

"The Pall of Negro Despotism"

Americans really did not know very much about Latin America, even in the first decade of the twentieth century. Nor did American politicians and diplomats seem to believe that it was important to learn. They were not even sure of the languages that were spoken in the south, except to be annoyed that the people did not have the courtesy to speak English. They were bliss-fully unaware of the cultural histories of these countries. They knew virtually nothing of the heritage of despotism and fierce independence left by Toussaint L'Ouverture, the former slave who rose to become dictator of the black nation of Haiti on Hispaniola Island.

During the administration of Grover Cleveland the United States had tried to clean up its foreign service and civil service corps. The civil service had remained cleansed, but in recent years the foreign service had become tainted again, particularly at the top levels where party hacks were the rule, not the exception. Both parties were guilty. From 1896 until 1912 the Re-publicans were in office, and not particularly well-informed. Nor were they sympathetic to the problems of the region as the quotation from Henry L. Stimson in this chapter shows. In 1912 the Democrats captured the White House, and then the usual "housecleaning" of the "scoundrels" (read other party) began. But as will be seen, the Democrats for all their political piety proved no more of a bargain to Latin Americans than had the Republicans.

*   *   *

"Hispaniola lies under the pall of Negro Despotism," wrote United States Secretary of War Henry L. Stimson of the Republic of Haiti and the Dominican Republic when he visited the island of Hispaniola in 1911. In the Dominican Republic things seemed to go from bad to worse. Late in 1912 the Dominican legislature had chosen a cleric, Archbishop Adolfo A. Nouel, as president, and he proved to be a very bad apple from the American point of view. Soon the word came to Washington that the archbishop was exhausting the national treasury in suppression of a rebellion. The Americans came to investigate, aided by a team of 750 marines, found that the charges were true, and forced the archbishop out of office by threatening to deny the government all the customs receipts.

But the Americans were too late. The republic had virtually dissolved into factionalism and for the next few years the country was shaken by one rebellion after another, so thoroughly that Thomas Morris, an American and a customs agent, observed that there was no law at all in the republic except that of the customs service.

When Woodrow Wilson became president of the United States in 1913, he began a Latin American policy more stringent than that of any of his predecessors. Secretary of State William Jennings Bryan began "cleansing" the U.S. foreign service, a process that involved appointment of a whole regiment of Democratic party hacks who were either incompetent or corrupt or both. The average service of an American minister in Latin America under the Republicans had been fifteen years, and the ministers all spoke Spanish. Wilson fired them and Bryan hired men with almost no experience and no Spanish. The worst was the new minister to the Dominican Republic, James Sullivan, a former fight promoter whose sole qualification was that he was a "deserving Democrat."

The Wilson administration brought a basic change in the approach to Latin American policy. Dollar diplomacy administered by the bankers gave way to dollar diplomacy administered by the government. It was easier to control Latin American governments that way. Interference in Dominican affairs became the rule. The same was true for Haitian affairs.

A State Department official had described Haiti as a public nuisance. When Secretary of State Bryan came to office in 1913 he did not quite understand that—but then he did not understand anything about Haiti until briefed by an American official of the Haitian Banque Nationale. That was a revelation to Bryan.

"Dear me," said the secretary of state. "Think of it! Niggers speaking French!"

For years, the American navy had patrolled around Haiti. However, financial control was not in American hands—the Banque Nationale had headquarters in Paris—but three Americans were members of the board of directors and they kept track of its affairs.

Politically one Haitian regime drove out another, hiring the professional *cacos* (bandits), who made their livings at other times by robbing the farmers. A president would leave office usually by being shot, blown up, or poisoned.

In the fall of 1914, when Secretary Bryan became seriously disturbed at reports that the money of the Banque Nationale was being used to finance a revolution, the Americans sent 800 marines to Haiti and told the various warring groups to accept the government of Joseph Theodore.

In 1915 the United States got a new secretary of state, Robert Lansing, and a new Haiti policy, which was bent on reform, just like the policy being pressed upon the Dominican Republic next door. In a phrase, it was a clean-government policy, prompted by that great American fervor for the management of other people's business.

Early in 1915, to help the policy along, the navy sent Rear Admiral William Banks Caperton and a cruiser squadron down to Haiti to assess the political and military situation there. Caperton anchored off Cap-Haïtien in the north, and there he met General Vilbrun, also known as Guillaume Sam, the current revolutionary front runner. "A very gorgeous black gentleman arrayed like a head bellhop at the Waldorf." Guillaume Sam promised not to carry out any massacres and to agree to an American customs receivership. But by the time the admiral had moved the fleet around to Port-au-Prince, the black bellhop had conquered his enemies and entered Port-au-Prince in triumph.

The Americans were not sure what they thought about Guillaume Sam. The navy was ready to launch a full-scale invasion of the whole island, to hold Santo Domingo and Port-au-Prince. But despite Guillaume Sam's comic-opera appearance, the admiral was concerned about law and order and he called home for reinforcements.

Admiral Caperton went to Vera Cruz, but he was on his way back in a few weeks, having learned of disturbances in Haiti brought about by Europeans. Indeed, affairs had deteriorated even more than he had feared: Dr. Rosalvo Bobo, a graduate of the Sorbonne, had raised an army of *cacos* and was threatening Guillaume Sam, whom he charged with selling out to the Americans. Guillaume Sam responded by bringing a reign of terror to Port-au-Prince, where many of Bobo's friends lived. Bobo in turn responded with an attempted coup in which Sam was wounded. Sam retaliated with the execution of 160 of Bobo's adherents who were being held in prison.

Such executions! The warden of the prison was an expert. Some were strangled. Some were hacked to death. Some had their eyes gouged out.

When the people of Port-au-Prince learned of these grisly events, they rioted. They rushed the prison, but the warden had taken refuge in the Dominican legation. They invaded the legation, seized the warden, slaughtered him, and then burned his body.

The mob soon learned that Admiral Caperton was on his way back to Haiti with the marines, and so some young revolutionaries attacked the French consulate, where Guillaume Sam had taken refuge. The American chargé d'affaires was coming up the street as the rebels came out with their president, and watched as they hacked him to death. One man went running past the American chargé carrying a bloody hand in his teeth; behind him were men with the feet and the other hand and the head. The body was dragged along by the crowd, screaming and shrieking revolutionary slogans.

When Admiral Caperton arrived, he was greeted by representatives of the foreign community who were frankly terrified. Haiti had its reputation: when Toussaint L'Ouverture had run the French out of the country he had then massacred all the whites who had not left with the troops. It was not hard to convince the admiral that a dreadful threat to law and order existed, so he landed the marines. It was July 28, 1915, the day that Guillaume Sam had been killed. The revolutionaries had vowed to fight to the death, but when Caperton's aide explained that the United States was prepared to throw the whole U.S. Navy into Haiti, they saw the problem of resisting force majeure and quietly disappeared—except for twenty-five stalwarts, who barricaded themselves in a post in mid-city, draped the gate with the Haitian flag, and vowed to fight to the last. Nobody bothered them, and after a week a young marine picked the lock to the gate, took down the flag, and opened the gate. The soldiers gave up.

Admiral Caperton set up his occupation, assuring Port-au-Prince that he did not intend to stay long. But he told Washington he needed more troops and more ships and more supplies for this difficult task. Actually, Caperton governed through the Haitian revolutionary committee, which did just about everything he asked them to do, except that the committee announced it supported Bobo for the presidency and asked Caperton to call for elections so that Bobo's popularity would become official. The admiral, not having any orders to cover this situation, temporized.

The press, always suspicious of Americans, and freer and more responsible than anyone believed, looked with grave suspicion on the occupation. Their worst fears were realized on August 4 when the 2nd Marine Regiment showed up to take on occupation duties. From that moment, so far as Haiti was concerned, affairs went from bad to worse.

The admiral had been looking over the potential candidates for the presidency and he had decided that Bobo was not the man. Being a naval gentleman of the old school, he felt the responsibility to tell Bobo so before he could come into Port-au-Prince and cause trouble. The Haitian leader boarded the flagship *Washington* in top hat and frock coat, carrying an oversized attaché case with the legend *Dr. Rosalvo Bobo, Chief of Executive Power,* stenciled on it, and followed by four of his chosen officials. He was taken to the cabin of the admiral's aide and given the bad word: he could not be president because the American government in Washington forbade it.

This was true. President Wilson was not behaving like a man about to save the world for democracy. He had insisted that any Haitian president must accept American control over Haitian customs, and any other controls the Americans found necessary. Appropriately, when the Haitian legislature was called upon to select the new chief executive not long after this, they chose Philippe Sudre Dartiguenave, the American candidate. In Haiti it was all done with proper solemnity. But in Washington, the wags began calling Secretary of the Navy Daniels "Josephus the First, King of Haiti."

More marines came to Haiti. They decided to get rid of the *cacos,* which was easier said than done, but they did push them out of the cities and towns, and harried them until the *cacos* put up a fight. On October 24, 1915, about 400 *cacos* ambushed an American force near Fort Rivière. It was just what Smedley Butler, now a marine general, and marine Colonel L. W. T. Waller were waiting for. They launched an offensive, the *cacos* took refuge in the old Fort Rivière, and the marines killed them and blew up the fort.

Rebellions continued, but to a lesser degree. By the end of the year Haiti was "pacified." Admiral Caperton could turn his attention at this point to the Dominican Republic, which was also not behaving the way President Wilson wanted. General Desiderio Arias, the minister of war, was anti-American. This shocking situation could not be permitted, particularly after Arias rebelled against American-backed President Jimenez and seized control of Santo Domingo. In came the United States marines and sailors, 600 of them, from Admiral Caperton's ships. On May 13 they occupied the shore—but not the hearts of the people. The Dominican legislature had been wavering; now it became openly anti-American. The Americans took Santo Domingo and set up a military government. More troops came in, because the rebels had fled to the interior and the admiral expected to launch an offensive against them. Politicking began, the Dominicans hoping to get their country back from the Americans. More marines were landed. They seized Puerto Plata. The admiral announced his intention of occupying Santiago, Moca, and La Vega. As the Americans seized territory the admiral explained: he was not seizing territory, he was just suppressing revolutionaries who were against reform.

So the nonwar went on, and the Dominicans died. One small marine unit was attacked by a large rebel unit that had never seen a machine gun.

Thirty-nine rebels were cut down before the mob went yelling off in re-treat. It was a no-contest war all the way. A few marines died. The first was Captain H. J. J. Hirshinger, shot in the temple while landing on the beach at Puerto Plata. One had to regard the event as a lucky shot for some rebel and a very unlucky one for the captain. But the Dominicans continued to fight, and they fought on through Christmas in the hills and in the valleys.

By July 1916 the Americans had pacified most of the countryside, but they had not won the hearts of the people. The Dominican assembly was even more anti-American than before. By fall it became apparent that the Americans might be able to occupy the country, but they would be unable to get a Dominican government to do their bidding.

On October 31, 1916, officials of the State Department and the navy met to discuss the problem. They had lost the battle for the Dominican heart. Now they could either get out or declare military government. So the decision was made in Washington to overthrow the Dominican gov-ernment and declare an out-and-out American military government. That great lover of freedom President Wilson so declared on November 22, 1916.

In 1918 the Haitians voted to legalize the American occupation of their country. Most of them thought they were voting for a new president, and one thought he was voting for a new pope. The marines fought the *cacos* from time to time, the most serious uprising being that of Charlemagne Peralte in 1918. A young marine officer named Lewis Puller fought in that campaign and learned a great deal about tropical warfare and guerrillas.

The occupation of Haiti and the Dominican Republic transcended American politics. It survived World War I, it survived the election of 1920, in which Republican candidate Warren G. Harding castigated the Democrats for their "bayonet rule" of Hispaniola. But in 1921 the Amer-ican press demanded an investigation of charges of atrocities and harsh treatment of the people of the island by the marines. A Senate committee investigated, produced two volumes of detailed testimony including some damning statements, but then recommended continued occupation in both countries which grew even harsher. The results were to be seen all through Central America.

In Managua, the newspaper *La Tribuna* published a little poem in 1921.

> With folded arms, with mouth gagged,
> Without a press to denounce their laws of
>   terror,
> What atrocious infamies, what vile torments, in
> Four long years of wicked intervention.

The poem referred to events in Haiti and the Dominican Republic, but the marine guards at the legation in Managua were so furious that they attacked the offices of *La Tribuna* and ransacked the place.

In 1922 the occupation became so much of a problem in America that the navy was forced to pull out. In 1924 the last American marines left the Dominican Republic. But the occupation of Haiti continued until 1934, when it was ended by President Franklin D. Roosevelt.

Nineteen fifteen to 1935. It was a long, long time, and it was not forgotten in the Caribbean.

CHAPTER 28

Mexican Hat Dance

One of the most interesting aspects of the succession of American inter-ventions in Latin America after 1912 is the responsibility born by President Woodrow Wilson for a policy whose excesses have left embers that burn today. The American invasion of Veracruz in April 1914 is a plain case of unwarranted interference in the affairs of another nation. President Wilson was an advocate of peace and reason for European nations; it is remarkable that he could justify an opposite policy of naked force in the Americas.

*　　*　　*

One could write a book about the history of the American interference with the nations "south of the border," and Lester D. Langley has: It is called *The Banana Wars: An Inner History of American Empire, 1900–1934,* and it is a detailed chronicle of military and political events, about 80,000 words long. It takes at least that much space to do justice to the subject. The operations of the navy and the Marine Corps in southern waters comprise a large portion of the book, and from these tales one can gather that the latinos know Americans a great deal better than most Americans believe. From these chronicles what seems remarkable is not that the United States faced as much hostility as it did during the 1980s, but that the hostility was as limited as it was, particularly given the activity of Woodrow Wilson, the greatest meddler of all in Latin American affairs.

Mexico was a case in point. President Porfirio Diaz was faced by Fran-cisco Madero in 1911. From a base in Texas, Madero challenged the Mexican elections, which had been won by Diaz, and declared that he, Francisco Madero, was the rightful president of the Republic of Mexico. Madero soon had the support of several revolutionary leaders—or bandits, depending on point of view: Pascual Orozco, Pancho Villa, and Emiliano Zapata. By the beginning of 1911 the revolution was serious enough to worry President William Howard Taft, and he sent the navy down the Mexican Gulf Coast, and mobilized 20,000 troops on the Mexican border. It was the same old American-life-and-property theme. President Madero's troops beat President Diaz's troops, and Madero took over the palace in Mexico City. But he was ruling only through a cabal of generals, whose loyalties ebbed and flowed.

Madero was also hampered by the activity of U.S. Ambassador Henry Lane Wilson, who did not believe in democracy for Mexicans. They were not ready for it, he said. When Madero did not respond properly, the ambassador made the U.S. embassy into a fortress, and then conspired with Victoriano Huerta, another presidential aspirant. Huerta seized power, Madero was shot, and the drama continued. Ambassador Wilson was urging recognition of Huerta's government.

The Republican administration in Washington was fretting over the course to be pursued, when the American elections intervened, and Taft no longer had to worry. It was Woodrow Wilson's problem.

The new American president was a very moral man. He did not like Huerta's morals (murderer, he called him), so he refused to recognize the Huerta government. President Wilson decided to make good, freedom-loving people out of the Mexicans.

So at Guantanamo, the Cuban naval base, along the coast of Cuba, and in Texas, American forces prepared for action. They were ordered, under the plan, to occupy most of northern Mexico, but they never did.

A new general now entered, Venustiano Carranza, who challenged Huerta. He marched on Tampico, and U.S. Admiral Frank Friday Fletcher, who was itching for some action, warned Carranza that he intended to safeguard American and foreign lives and property. But nothing came of that immediately. In the meantime, Huerta was losing power to Pancho Villa and Carranza and other generals, all fighting for power. As everyone knew, because of President Wilson's policies, the Americans were supplying guns and military hardware to the rebels.

It was spring in Tampico, April 1914. In command of the U.S. Navy 5th Division at Tampico was Rear Admiral Henry T. Mayo. He really wanted a fight. On April 9 a party of American sailors from the USS *Dolphin* was arrested for trespassing on Mexican federal territory without permission, and marched through the city. When governor Morelos Zaragoza heard of the incident, he apologized to Admiral Mayo and let the men go. But Admiral Mayo's dander was up. He demanded a written apology, the hoisting of the American flag to show deep respect, and a twenty-one-gun salute to the flag. The admiral informed Washington. By the time the story got to President Wilson it was surrounded by endorsements of higher officials, all indicating American righteous indignation.

In Mexico City the upset continued. Huerta's government took the position that Tampico was a federal city besieged by rebels, and that it was understandable that the military men there would be nervous, particularly since the Americans were supplying the enemy.

It was, as President Wilson believed, really a minor incident. But it was almost immediately out of hand. On the weekend of April 18–19, while President Wilson was in West Virginia, the general board of the U.S. Navy met to consider policy. A ship called the *Ypiranga* was about to land in Veracruz bringing arms for President Huerta's forces. It would be an excellent time to seize the docks at Veracruz, thus teaching the Mexicans a lesson (what lesson was not explained). And so President Wilson went before Congress with a joint message, and the House and the Senate both approved. By the time they did so, American troops were already ashore in Veracruz.

And so, on April 20, the Americans landed at Veracruz to seize the customs house and wait for the arms shipment which they would also seize. The first shot was fired by a Mexican policeman. Then fighting began between Mexican troops and sailors and the Americans. Admiral Fletcher decided to land more troops, because at the end of the first day the Mexicans still held the Plaza Constitución and the naval academy. At the end of the second day the American casualties numbered two dead and twenty men wounded. That news, when it reached Washington, was a shock to President Wilson. He had not really wanted any *violence*. As one marine fresh from the Far East said, he had been making landings of that sort since the turn of the century, and the Filipinos and the Chinese had not shot at him.

But now what had been planned in Washington as a show to impress President Huerta and make him either accede to American wishes or step down, had become something far more serious. In the fighting, the Americans had killed the son of the Mexican naval commodore, José Azueta, who was directing the defense of the naval academy, and made a martyr of him. The Mexicans would not forget José Azueta or the other Mexican dead in the fighting.

How many were there? Nobody knows. Veracruz is a very hot place, and meat decomposes rapidly there. As soon as the fighting ended, and sometimes before, American burial parties went through the streets of the city picking up corpses and carrying them off to the central squares, where they were buried. The count was not very careful. And then there were other ways—a unit of sailors from the USS *New Hampshire* piled a heap of bodies on top of a pyre of railroad ties, and set the creosote on the ties on fire. The bonfire was spectacular, the creosote hid most of the smell, and the laws of sanitation were enforced. How many Mexicans were killed? Nobody knows, but the official tally was 126. The real number was probably three times that.

The Americans, with their superior firepower, suffered too, 17 men killed and 63 men wounded. It was not a war, or even a battle, but it was another one of those too-common American military forays of the early twentieth century, another prime aspect of gunboat diplomacy that showed the very definite imperialistic thinking of the United States government. President Wilson said several times that the United States had no territorial ambitions in Latin America. American imperialism here was all bright-eyed, with the school-teacher determination of Woodrow Wilson to make better people of the latinos, and the determination of the admirals, marine generals, and army generals to do it by the numbers.

And so in 1913 the United States was involved in a military situation with Mexico, which, to President Wilson's dismay, created almost universal condemnation in Latin America. "My ideal is an orderly and righteous government in Mexico," said President Wilson. And on April 26, the Americans declared martial law. Orderly yes; righteous, no.

For the task of imposing martial law on Veracruz, President Wilson chose General Frederick Funston, the captor of Aguinaldo. Funston was eager for action, so much so that Navy Secretary Daniels suggested to Wilson that if Funston was appointed, he might get the country into a major war in Mexico. President Wilson, never a great listener, did not listen. On May 2 the Funston military government took over.

And so "clean government" came to Veracruz, emphasizing reform and honesty. The number of prostitutes had swelled to such an army that they overran the bordello district and spilled beyond it. The army moved the girls into houses in the suburbs and set up a system of medical examinations. Funston created a new district for prostitution, over the objections of the suburbs, where the climate and conditions were more salubrious. Citizens of downtown Veracruz threw their garbage out the window and urinated in the gutters. Urination in the gutters was forbidden, and Funston announced a campaign against dirt. Garbage disposal was strictly regulated, and the citizens of Veracruz were told to use garbage cans. The hardware shops soon ran out of garbage cans, so the Americans supplied them, at two dollars each.

That summer, the Huerta government fell and General Carranza took over in Mexico. With his candidate in, President Wilson felt a real pressure to withdraw the American troops, and so on November 23, 7,000 American soldiers marched down to the docks and boarded American transport ships. The next day the ships sailed.

The Mexicans were delighted that the American presence was gone. Away went the garbage cans, and into the streets went the garbage. The whores moved back to their old district, and Veracruz tried to forget that the Americans had ever been there. It took a long time. Americans forgot about the occupation in a matter of months; by the time the smoke from World War I had settled, scarcely an American who had not been there could remember Veracruz at all. But the Mexicans still remember. To an American of the 1980s, the name Frederick Funston means little. But every Mexican schoolboy knows the name of José Azueta, and how he died that day in 1913.

CHAPTER 29

From the Mexican Border to Mobilization

It was true that after war broke out in Europe in August 1914, the United States had some special difficult problems in the Mexican region. Germany and Britain both maintained warships in these waters up until the fighting began. Afterward, the Germans tried to use Mexico as a base for their cruiser war against British commerce in the Atlantic and Pacific oceans. This situation created a threat to American neutrality, and had to be watched by the U.S. Navy.

It was also true that Pancho Villa, the revolutionary bandit general (he was all of these), created many problems by crossing the American border with Mexico and raiding American ranches and robbing American banks. Yet President Wilson's dispatch of an American expeditionary force into Mexico created a whole new set of political problems, and was partly responsible for the entry of the United States into the European War in April 1917, after having remained aloof for two and a half years. The Zimmermann telegram, described in this chapter, would never have been sent, had not the Americans so angered the Mexicans that the climate was right for this German demarche. It was another indication that any sort of military excursion has enormous lasting political consequences. A look at Latin America in the 1980s does not offer much indication that Americans as a nation have learned that lesson, with one exception: Grenada, which will be described later.

*   *   *

When war broke out in Europe in 1914, President Wilson warned Americans to be neutral "in thought as well as deed." But it was hard. The Germans were not very good at the sort of propaganda that would enlist sympathy to their cause, and their ruthless drive through Belgium turned many Americans to the Allied side. Most German sympathizers in America were of German descent, and the number did not increase as the war rolled on. The adventures of some of the German cruisers, fighting lonely battles and fighting them bravely, did bring the admiration of the world. The *Emden* caused an enormous amount of trouble for the British before being sunk in the Indian Ocean, the *Königsberg* fought bravely off Africa and then in the Rufiji River where she was embattled. The *Karlsruhe* set out for South America, sank several ships, and then mysteriously disappeared (victim of an internal explosion). The German East Asia Cruiser Squadron started home, fought a winning battle at Coronel off South America, and then was destroyed in battle off the Falkland Islands in what was to be the major naval action of the war.

With the start of the war in Europe, some Americans had begun campaigning for a strong national defense system for the United States: men like Theodore Roosevelt, Henry Cabot Lodge, and Henry L. Stimson. General Leonard Wood now called for universal military training. Out of this ferment came the Plattsburg idea for a private citizens' training camp. Actually, before the Plattsburg camp was established in the summer of 1915, others had already begun training men at Gettysburg and Monterey. But Plattsburg captured the imagination of the Eastern establishment.

Secretary of War Lindley M. Garrison was ceaseless in his campaign for defense. He pointed out that in 1915 the American army had twenty-one airplanes, 634 modern field guns, two days' supply of artillery ammunition, and 1,000 machine guns, most of them Gatling guns of the sort used in the Boxer Rebellion. The United States Army might fight a war with Nicaragua, but not with a modern military power, said Garrison. What was needed was a modern military force, a volunteer army under federal control.

Not so, said the states. Did they not have the National Guard?

Not so, said Henry Ford, the motor car manufacturer, who was a leader of the pacifist movement. Ford chartered a ship, the *Oskar II,* and sent it to Europe as a "peace ship" to negotiate an end to the war. It was a genteel idea but neither the Triple Alliance (Germans) nor the Triple Entente (British) were interested.

Nor were many Americans, by the time Henry Ford's ship got to Europe, for in May 1915 support for Germany was all but wiped out when a

German U-boat sank the steamer *Lusitania* without warning, causing the loss of American lives. The Germans blustered. They made error after error in dealing with American public opinion. The error of carrying out the unrestricted submarine warfare campaign, and German truculence in so doing, lost the kaiser's government support in America and made war supporters of many pacifists.

Three days after Ford dispatched his "peace ship," President Wilson asked Congress for a comprehensive national defense plan.

The plan called for expansion of the regular army to 175,000 men and a National Guard of state militia of 450,000 men. On this point Secretary of War Garrison resigned; he wanted a federal force, not a mixed force. Wilson could see the point, but he was a politician, and he did not want to lose state support by invading states' rights. Nineteen sixteen was a presidential election year.

An army was created, and, inexorably, it had to be used somehow. Sixty-five regiments of infantry, twenty-five of cavalry, twenty-one of field artillery, ninety-three companies of coast artillery, eight air squadrons, seven regiments of engineers.

How to try it out?

How better than on the Mexicans?

President Carranza, Wilson's creation, was having trouble with some of the rebel generals. Now they became "bandits." Actually they had always been bandits, but in Mexico a bandit could be a real revolutionary at the same time, his ambition to establish a regime of his own, rather like the Horatio Alger hero's ambition to run his own company.

Pancho Villa was the particular thorn in the side of President Carranza in 1916. Villa controlled much of northern Mexico, particularly the lands along the United States border, and he supported his army by banditry on both sides of the border. He killed a whole troop of American engineers who had been invited by the Mexican government to reopen abandoned mines at Santa Ysabel. He also raided ranches and towns in Texas and New Mexico in that spring of 1916, and one raid in which the Villa bandits killed seventeen people at Columbus, New Mexico, particularly aroused the ire of Americans. So President Wilson called out 150,000 militia and stationed them along the Mexican border. He told Carranza he intended to send a military expedition into northern Mexico, and the Mexican president reluctantly said it was all right. Wilson then dispatched General John J. Pershing with 15,000 soldiers on a punitive expedition into Chihuahua and other areas of desert Mexico. That was not appreciated by the soldiers, who suffered great hardships in the intense heat of day, the cold of night, and the shortage of water. It was not appreciated by the Mexicans either, for Veracruz was remembered bitterly. Carranza grew restless, and took the position that the visitors had overstayed their welcome and were out of line in trespassing across the border. The legalities were lost in the realities, finally; Pancho Villa proved most elusive, and Black Jack Pershing never did catch him. Relations with Mexico grew ever worse because of the American presence inside the Mexican border.

Then came a bombshell.

The Germans had given up unrestricted submarine warfare after the enormous international outcry in 1915. First over the *Lusitania,* and then the *Arabic,* another British steamer sunk without warning with more American lives lost. Count von Bernstorff, the German ambassador in Washington, promised an end to surprise sinkings of ocean liners. The Germans were trying hard to keep the United States out of the war.

But the German general staff was not sympathetic. War was war and every means should be used to prosecute it. The argument continued all the rest of 1915 in Berlin, and finally the warriors had their way. In January 1917, the German foreign office sent out a message announcing the new war policy. This was the famous Zimmermann Telegram, sent from the German foreign office to the German ambassador in Washington laying out German hopes for the immediate future.

We intend to begin on the first of February unrestricted submarine warfare. We shall endeavor in spite of this to keep the United States of America neutral. In the event of this not succeeding, we make Mexico a proposal of alliance on the following basis: make war together, make peace together, generous financial support and an understanding on our part that Mexico is to reconquer the lost territory in Texas, New Mexico, and Arizona. The settlement in detail is left to you. You will inform the president [Carranza] of the above most secretly as soon as the outbreak of war with the United States of America is certain and add the suggestion that he should, of his own initiative, invite Japan to immediate adherence and at the same time mediate between Japan and ourselves. Please call the president's attention to the fact that the ruthless employment of our submarines now offers the prospect of compelling England in a few months to make peace.

What the German foreign office did not know was that British naval intelligence had broken the German codes. The airwaves buzzed; about the time Count von Bernstorff received the message in Washington, Lord Balfour, the British foreign secretary, was reading it to Walter Hines Page, the American ambassador to London, and a little later President Wilson had it.

What to do? American relations with Mexico were not such that President Wilson could dismiss the threat. The idea of getting back Texas, New Mexico, and Arizona was very attractive to the Mexican mind. And, although there is no record that Wilson mentioned it, he must have understood the resentments against his highhandedness at Veracruz. Suddenly

Mexico seemed much more important than in the past, an entity deserving some serious attention.

Then, on January 31, 1917, the Germans announced a total blockade of the British Isles. It was time to shore up all defenses. In February 1917, President Wilson told Black Jack Pershing to give up his counterproductive wild goose chase and withdraw the expeditionary force from northern Mexico. He even recognized the Carranza government after Carranza was elected president under a new constitution. The threat across the Atlantic had done marvels for Mexican-American relations.

As far as Germany was concerned, Wilson had announced that he would await an overt act of war before reacting. Wilson now suspected that war was inevitable. War. That would mean alertness in defense against sabotage. It would mean an upgrading of the supplies sent to Europe, more ships, more guns, more planes. It would mean loans to England, France, and Italy so they could buy more munitions in the United States. All during the European war, Britain and France had been sending purchasing commissions to America. The British and French knew how little support for foreign excursions, outside the Western Hemisphere, was to be found in the United States. Their message had been carefully put: Help us by delivering the weapons, and we shall win our war. That concept had been deeply embedded in the American consciousness. Wilson had been slow to recognize the needs that would have to be met by America, but now he acted.

In March a German submarine sank the U.S. steamer *Algonquin* without warning. Two weeks later other German submarines sank three American steamers in one day. On April 2, President Wilson appeared before a joint session of Congress in the House of Representatives. Everyone knew what was coming.

I advise that the Congress declare the recent course of the Imperial German government to be in fact nothing less than war against the government and people of the United States; that it formally accept the status of belligerent which has thus been thrust upon it. . . . We shall fight for the things which we have always carried nearest our hearts—for democracy, for the right of those who submit to authority to have a voice in their own governments, for the rights and liberties of small nations, for a universal dominion of right by such a concert of free peoples as shall bring peace and safety to all nations and make the world itself at last free.

There was the Wilson doctrine, in its most direct and simple form. The same motives that had led him to interfere mercilessly in the affairs of other American states to establish moral governments now led him to put the fate of the United States of America on the line. He stood for right and justice, and there was no doubt about that in his own mind. As to what he had been doing and was doing in Latin America, that simply was not considered by the American establishment to be in the same category as the German threat.

In London the British government declared "American Day," April 20. "It was not for nothing that the flags of Great Britain and America hung side by side under the chancel arch of St. Paul's Cathedral on Friday morning."

And from Paris came Gallic applause from the Chamber of Deputies: "The cry of children and of women from the depths of the abyss into which they have been hurled by an abominable crime, has echoed to the ends of the earth. The ashes of Washington and Lincoln have stirred; their mighty souls inspire America."

So America had taken the plunge, joining the Allies in the war. Now what to do to bring the war to an end in a hurry? A few score ships to be built? A few hundred million dollars to be loaned out on favorable terms? Perhaps an American naval contingent, a unit or two of marines? Surely that should tip the tide for the Allies in a matter of weeks.

So went the talk in Washington.

The talk lasted fourteen days. Then on April 16, 1917, Lord Balfour and a band of British military and political leaders arrived in Washington. Four days later in came Marshal Joffre and the French. In painfully clear terms they laid out the picture for the Americans: The Germans had been very nearly right when they had predicted that a few weeks of unrestricted submarine warfare would force Britain and France to their knees. The great Allied drive on the western front, so heavily ballyhooed in Europe and America as the drive to push the Germans back, had failed. Russia, rent by revolution, was dropping out of the war. There was no hope for immediate victory. There was no hope of victory at all unless the badly shaken morale of Britain and France were restored. It was up to the United States now to restore that morale, and that was going to take a lot more than a few million dollars and a few ships.

The bad news brought a few hard swallows in Washington, and then a plan. The United States would provide money, food, antisubmarine warfare, and troops. First would go a small contingent to show the American intent. Then, as soon as it could be made ready, a large American expeditionary force would prepare to take part in the major Allied campaign of 1918.

America had been making slow, steady preparations for defense, but now much more was needed in a hurry. A winter of desperation faced the Allies at home and in the field if food and supplies did not arrive in time. And so America mobilized for war.

CHAPTER 30

The War in Europe

How one estimates the role played by the United States in World War I depends on which side of the Atlantic one inhabits. The Americans emerged from the war with the belief that they had won it for the French and the British. The truth to that claim is that the Americans had come in when the French, British, and Germans were all exhausted by nearly three years of grueling combat in which the total casualties were 37.5 million men. Look at these figures to get the picture:

	Dead	Wounded	Total (includes missing)
Russia	1,700,000	4,950,000	9,150,000
France	1,357,000	4,266,000	6,160,000
British Empire	908,000	2,090,000	3,190,000
U.S.	126,000	234,000	350,000

Russia and France really lost almost an entire generation of men, as did Germany and the Austro-Hungarian empire. The vast majority of British Empire casualties were from the British Isles. Small wonder that the British and the French scoff at American claims about World War I.

The casualty figures, however, do not tell the entire story. The Americans after April 1917 supplied vast resources of food and war supplies. American industry built thousands of tanks, thousands of aircraft, hundreds of thou-

sands of vehicles, and machine guns, mortars, field pieces, aircraft, and millions of small weapons. American productivity, and particularly the food, played an enormously important role in winning the war. But America emerged unscathed, so to speak, with no cities bombed, no fields laid waste, while France was decimated. For years after the war in every growing season the newspapers carried reports of French farmers being blown up by plowing into "dud" artillery shells or bombs or mortar rounds.

The American attitude toward the war, too, was quite different from that of the other Allies. There was a sort of light-hearted braggadocio about the Americans, and a soppy sentimentality, illustrated here by the war songs and the slight anecdote about Verdun Belle as told by Sergeant Alexander Woollcott. He was a correspondent for Stars and Stripes *and wrote many such tales, which were devoured by the American soldiers in France. After the war, Woollcott dined out on this story for years; his friend* New Yorker *editor Harold Ross claimed that Woollcott was the only writer he knew who made a career of plagiarizing himself. Woollcott used the Verdun Belle story in magazine articles, books, and on the radio. Again this is important in showing the American attitude, because Woollcott became the critic, the American tastemaker in the 1930s and 1940s.*

For America World War I was something of a lark; certainly not for the 350,000 casualties, but for the four million other Americans who served. They came home full of tall stories about French girls, and a yen to see Europe again—some of them. One of the important results of the war was a realization by millions of Americans that there was a Europe across the sea. Soon enough the Americans sank back into their old insularity, but never quite as much as before.

But the casualty figures do tell the big difference—and why, when the United States refused to back its brave words of peace with deeds, the League of Nations, formed out of the Versailles Treaty of 1919, would be doomed to failure. That is a big difference, and it accounts for a different view of the war on the two sides of the Atlantic. It also would account later for an entirely different approach to risk-taking in World War II.

*   *   *

Nineteen seventeen. Black Jack Pershing was chosen to tell it to the people.

"We must not only feed our soldiers at the front but the millions of women and children behind our lines," he said for a war poster, just before he sailed for England.

The British had been completely frank about the desperate situation. In April 1917, U-boat sinkings had hit their peak, with 875,000 tons sunk. Allied shipyards were building only at the rate of 3 million tons a year, and the U-boats were sinking at the rate of 10 million tons. Unless American food arrived in quantity in the winter of 1917–18, there would be starvation in England and in France.

"They will win," said British Admiral Jellicoe, "unless we can stop these losses and stop them soon."

What a time the Allies had chosen to run out of food! The average American export of grain was 89 million bushels. Europe had to have 225 million bushels that winter, said the experts, and America was faced with a short crop. The planting had to be increased.

Under Herbert Hoover, the president's chairman of food supply and prices, it was done, one of the least heralded and most important initial acts of the American war.

Meanwhile, Black Jack Pershing and a staff of 200 officers and men went off to win the war. On June 26 the U.S. 1st Division arrived in Paris and joined Black Jack at the tomb of Lafayette, the French officer who symbolized Louis XVI's assistance to the American Revolution.

"Lafayette we are here," said Black Jack, and, according to the press, the statement electrified the French nation.

The U.S. Navy rushed destroyers overseas to help the English fight the U-boats. By July, there were thirty-four American destroyers in British waters. They were quite valuable to the British in the matter of escorting convoys, for there were never too many escorts available. But as U-boat killers, they did not have much of a record. In November 1917, the U.S. destroyers *Fanning* and *Nicholson* did depth-charge the *U-58* just outside Queenstown and damaged her so badly that her captain scuttled her. But American assistance at sea was more valuable in mine-laying.

In the air, the Americans were also active. The Yale University Naval Aviation Unit was the first American force to reach France, arriving at Saint-Nazaire in June 1917. By the time of the armistice, naval air had big plans. Its center of activity was at Pauillac, France, and there accommodations for 20,000 men were finished just before the armistice. Actually in France, naval air accomplished very little.

The navy also contributed battleships and transports to the Allied cause. Some transports, such as the *President Lincoln,* were torpedoed in convoy. The *President Lincoln* was hit by four torpedoes from the *U-90* in May 1918 and sank. Discipline was so good aboard this vessel that of a total 715 people on board all but 26 were rescued.

The fact was, however, that American involvement in the sea war was minimal. Britain had the most powerful surface navy in the world and really did not need much help at sea. The army's contribution was far more important. On June 5, 1917, 9.5 million young Americans registered for the draft. Already thousands of volunteers were in training. For the United States had promised to participate in the Allied offensive of 1918 and there was scarcely time to get the new soldiers outfitted and dried behind the ears before they would be pressed into action.

Everywhere America was preparing for the struggle. Camps, each large enough to house a division, sprang up all across the country. The public often gave the money to buy the land for the camps, as in Pierce County, Washington, where the people donated 90,000 acres. Citizens of Linda Vista, California, put up a camp near San Diego, also with donated land.

This American army that was developed was an odd mixture of regular army, National Guard, and national army. In the summer of 1917 the regular army and National Guard numbered 650,000, but Secretary of War Baker announced that the United States Army the next year would number over 2 million men. That meant the draft had to move fast. In the U.S. Senate Office Building on July 20 the secretary of war reached into a big glass bowl and drew out one of 10,500 capsules of black celluloid, each containing a number. The number in the capsule was 258. In America there were 4,557 draft registration districts, and number 258 belonged to one man in each district. For sixteen hours the drawing in the Senate Office Building continued, and at the end, 1,374,000 young men had just joined the army. It was the cleanest, fairest way known to organize a people's army.

By September 5, the camps were built, the officer and noncommissioned officer cadres from the regular army had been filled out with "ninety-day wonders" and sergeants rapidly promoted, and it was time for the first thirty percent of the first quota of draftees to start to train. On September 3, President Wilson sent a message to the new men:

"The eyes of all the world will be upon you, because you are in some special sense the soldiers of freedom. . . ."

And that was the feeling among the doughboys, as they came to be called. They were heading for foreign soil to perform a great mission: not to conquer territory, but to preserve freedom. Theirs was the same sense of moral imperative that had led to all the many U.S. incursions into the Americas, once again the Wilsonian imperative. The men took it seriously, as one officer wrote: "Our men know this war; they followed it in the press since its outbreak. They are going into it dogged and grim; theirs is a solid courage—which is the most sublime."

But the war was not all grim determination. At home, wives, parents, and little brothers could read Lieutenant Edward Streeter's letters from "Bill" to "Dere Mable":

"We're still up at the artillery range shootin. I don't know what at. Our guns is pointed right at some woods. We've been shootin at those woods now for a week and haven't hit them yet. . . ."

So the Americans prepared to go into war, a new sort of war to them.

The Germans had developed the gas attack, spraying clouds of gas—mustard was the worst—which immobilized troops, tore out their lungs, and left them wrecked for life if they managed to survive. The Germans had also perfected the flamethrower, which could roast a man to a turn in ten seconds. The British invented the tank, which pulverized machine gun positions and trenches. Both sides struggled to gain superiority with the airplane. Both sides developed new methods of wireless and telephone communication. Wires and trenches—all this was material to be mastered. Trenches were built in New Jersey and all over America, trenches where Americans played at assaulting one another. The grenade, a weapon from the eighteenth century, was refined and became a major means of organized murder. The French had the best grenades and were best at using them.

The bayonet, that old French weapon so prized by the British infantry of the 1800s, was again prized in the attack across "no-man's-land" to the enemy's trench. The machine gun, the modern fast-firing, water-cooled machine gun, was another new weapon of enormous destructive power that had to be mastered.

As the American troops in training were deemed ready for combat, they were shipped to France. There they waited to see what would be done with them. At Allied headquarters, where General Pétain had taken over after the failure of General Nivelle to complete his 1917 offensive, the Allied leaders tried to decide what was to be done with the Americans. The Europeans still talked in terms of the war of position. But Pershing demurred; the war could not be won thus, he said. The Americans, fresh and vigorous, would break the will of the enemy. And that is the word Pershing sent home to Washington: perfect the men in the use of the rifle and the bayonet. They would be leading the charge. And, as Pershing said, "Plans should contemplate sending over at least one million men by next May."

Where would the Americans fight?

The British held the north end of the Allied line. They were used to it and their bases on the Channel were close by. There was no room for the Americans in the north. The French absolutely had to fight in front of Paris for reasons of national pride. There was no room for the Americans in the center.

So to the Americans was allotted the southern front in Lorraine, from Verdun to the Swiss border: Château-Thierry, Saint-Mihiel, Nancy, Neufchatel, Épinal, Belfort . . . names that would be remembered by thousands of Americans. If they could capture Metz, they could secure the Briey iron mines and foul up the German munitions industry. The France where Americans would be fighting was a France unknown to most Americans: its ports were Saint-Nazaire, Nantes, La Rochelle, and Bordeaux.

On September 3, 1917, General Pershing established his headquarters at Chaumont, a castle town on a road that ran more or less back to Paris and forward to Neufchatel. As one visiting journalist recalled: "GHQ a shock. Expected to see General Pershing like Napoleon at Friedland on white charger, spy glass under arm, surrounded by gold-laced officers in swords and high boots. Found instead group huge stone barracks, around court, with million typewriters clicking at once. Reminded me of Sears Roebuck. More field clerks and stenogs than soldiers."

The 1st Division went to Gondrecourt for training. The 26th Division, made up of New England National Guard units, came in September and was sent to Neufchatel. Marine and regular army troops arrived in September and were organized into the 2nd Division. In October came troops from everywhere in America, and they became the 42nd—the Rainbow Division. Valcoulers was their destination. In December came the National Guard of the northwestern American states, and it went to Saint-Aignan and lost its name. It became the 1st Depot Division. Its function was to train recruits and make "replacements" out of them. Some people had another name for them: cannon fodder.

The German offensive was still weeks away, so the Americans had a chance to fraternize with the French. Generally speaking, fraternization turned out to be fighting with the French soldiers and chasing French girls.

But all too soon the fun and games ended, and the stark matter of war appeared. The first Americans to enter the front line, October 20, 1917, were the regulars of the 1st Division. The French were not at all sure of the Americans, so they alternated French and American units all along the line just in case the Americans should panic and run. French generals still held the command. It was a very quiet sector, and very little happened.

On January 15, 1918, the 1st Division took over part of the Toul sector of the front, flanking Saint-Mihiel on the south.

German General von Hindenburg's plan for the 1918 spring offensive was to break through the Allied line from the Ardennes, at the point where the French and British lines met. The offensive began on March 21. No American troops were involved and on March 31 the German drive stopped. It had hit a British wall.

But the Allied high command was nervous. They wanted fresh troops to throw in where necessary. The Americans were the freshest troops, and the British and French proposed to use them piecemeal under British and French commands. Now came the first disagreement of the war. Black Jack Pershing knew what America would think of the European proposal. He dragged his feet. In America his position was totally supported. The Allies got some American troops to throw into the line as corks, but not many.

The Germans, who had very little respect for this new citizen army from America, decided on a raid to show that the Americans were inferior

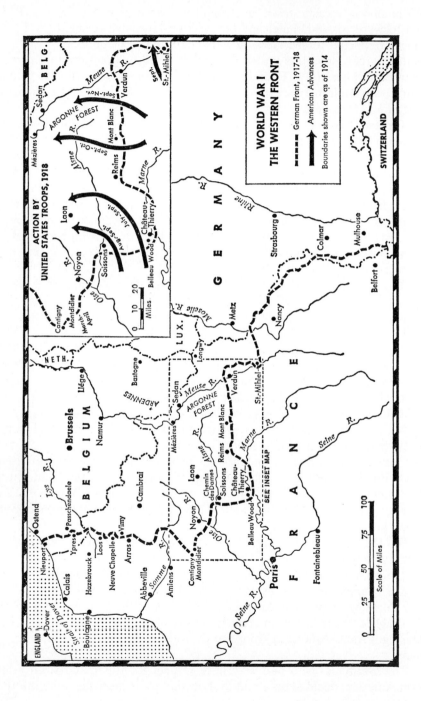

fighters. On April 20, 1918, the Americans relieved tired French troops at Seicheprey. That night the Germans put down a box barrage, plastering three sides of the village, and then sent the infantry in front. They captured the whole American front position, 179 men and twenty-four machine guns. The Germans remained in Seicheprey for twelve hours, the press and propaganda corps making hay every hour. Finally they were driven off by the French. Within hours German aircraft were dropping photos of the raid on British and French troops in the line. Here was a propaganda coup: those Americans were useless. They could not fight! Here was the proof; pictures to the front, radio broadcasts to the world.

When Black Jack Pershing had the news, he fumed. He went to Paris and insisted on a quick chance for retaliation in the interest of American morale at home as well as in France. So the U.S. 1st Division was brought north from Toul. It would, said Pershing, attack and hold the tip of the German salient that had pierced the French line from Amiens to Paris.

Preparation took some time, but by May 27 the Americans were in position. The Germans knew something was up; that day they threw 15,000 shells of mustard gas into the area. They conducted raids all along the line, but they caught only one prisoner and he knew nothing of what was going to happen.

At 5:45 on the morning of May 28 the American artillery opened up on the German lines. An hour later it began firing a rolling barrage; the shelling advanced 100 meters every two minutes. Then the infantry, tanks, and flamethrowers began moving forward. All were American save ten French tanks and a platoon of French flamethrowers.

The U.S. 28th Infantry led the charge. In eighty-eight minutes they captured Cantigny. Next morning the Germans counterattacked, but the Americans held.

Said General R. L. Bullard: "The moral effects to flow from this proof of the reliability of the American soldier in battle far outweigh the direct military importance of the action itself."

The general, obviously, was not much of a propaganda phrase-maker, but the point was well taken at British and French headquarters. Still, the German derision of the Americans did not end.

The Germans launched another major thrust—forty-two divisions and 4,000 pieces of artillery were involved. The British and the French held. But no matter how the Americans felt about fighting under foreign generals, they were needed to plug some holes in the line now, and the 2nd and 3rd divisions were sent to hold the line of the Marne.

May 31, 1918. Château-Thierry, the crossing point for the Marne. The French had destroyed the bridge, but the Germans were determined to swim, ford, do anything to get across. They were stopped by the machine guns of the 7th Machine Gun Battalion of the U.S. 3rd Division, firing from a group of houses on the bank. The Germans turned and crossed the Marne at Jaulonne, several miles to the east. French and American troops made a forced march, turned the Germans, and made them cross back over the Marne again. The drive was stopped. But there was more fighting for the Americans on the Marne. Le Champs de Mars—the Field of Mars: the British and the French had fought for it for four years, and given it the name. It had been blasted, bombed, shelled, tunneled, dredged. Every living thing had been killed by guns, shells, bombs, daggers, knives, bludgeons, gas, liquid fire, and hand grenades. It was one great hilly field of blasted petrified earth. And the Americans fought there, and died there, too.

June 1. North of the Marne. An emergency on the Paris road between the French 7th and 38th corps. The Germans threatened the line from La Nouvette farm through the Bois des Clermebauts. The American 2nd Division was rushed in to replace the exhausted French 21st Corps.

June 4. German infantry sighted plodding along the road toward the Americans. The word flashed back to division. Artillery fire called. And what artillery fire! The German columns were plastered, turned, and beaten back. The American artillery had proved itself. The German drive was stopped.

June 5. The Germans held the Bois de Belleau—Belleau Wood as it would always be known in America. Behind them were three villages. The wood was thoroughly fortified, with interlocking fields of fire from machine gun nests, and vertical support as well, which meant that if the Americans overran one machine gun nest they would come under fire from one immediately behind.

June 6. The Americans attacked. This time it was the marines of the 4th Brigade. Hand-to-hand encounters. Grenades and bayonets.

Three weeks—a few days out of the line, then back into the line. June 26. The village of Bouresches and Belleau Wood were American. Bouresches looked like a Hollywood set for a war movie, a blasted French village, a great tree standing leafless and virtually branchless in the town square. What sort of tree? Who knew? How would you identify a shell-blasted relic of a tree trunk?

July 1. Vaux la Roche fell to the Americans. "A great victory," announced Premier Clemenceau to the French people.

July 13. The Germans were preparing for a new offensive in the Champagne area. The names: Rheims, Épernay, Châlons, Verdun. This battle would be called the Second Battle of the Marne, and intelligence was the key. The Germans had worked hard to conceal their movements from the Allies; surprise was everything in these titanic struggles between the European behemoths. On the night of July 14 French General Gouraud ordered suicide patrol raids to capture prisoners. Brave men died, but other brave men brought back the prisoners. Their information: The Germans had amassed an enormous army. Artillery barrage to begin at midnight. The infantry to march at 4:30.

Warned, Gouraud acted. French artillery began at 10:45 and caught the Germans massing behind the lines. The casualties were atrocious. But at midnight the Germans opened their greatest barrage of the war. The whole area was illuminated for fifteen miles; the flashing of the guns could be seen in Paris. Four American divisions joined the French to hold the line that day east of Rheims.

West of Rheims. Château-Thierry again. July 14. Bastille Day. Dawn. Fog and smoke. To begin with the French commander drenched the Germans with gas. The Germans replied with shells from 500 batteries. Three German divisions charged the U.S. 3rd Division. The objective: cross the Marne. The Germans surged forward. The American machine guns on the west bank spoke up from their nests.

And the Germans came, they crossed the river under gunfire, and then rushed the guns, overran them and reached the rail line. The American machine gunners had lost half their men. Now the Germans wanted to reach the Paris road. But here the 3rd Division stopped them.

"No German soldiers crossed the road," said General Dickman proudly, "except as prisoners of war. And by noon of the following day there were no Germans in the foreground of the Third Division sector except the dead."

Somewhere in Washington there is a picture of the railroad embankment at Mezy, a drawing by Captain J. Andrew Smith of the U.S. Signal Corps, showing a rail line, telegraph poles, low hills in the background, and a long line of white crosses to the left of the tracks. Graves. Graves of American soldiers buried where they died to stop the Germans from reaching the Paris road.

One regiment, the 38th U.S. Infantry, stood fast here virtually surrounded, firing in three directions, throwing two German divisions into confusion, turning encirclement into victory, and capturing 600 prisoners of war. "One of the most brilliant pages in our military annals," wrote General Pershing.

And who was in charge? Colonel Ulysses Simpson Grant McAlexander—an American name for an American commander. Colonel McAlexander's men had been trained and trained and trained in the use of the rifle and the bayonet. They knew what they were doing and they did it. Captain Wooldridge's Company G alone took 400 prisoners.

Still, the war went on. Frenchmen, Englishmen, Germans, and Americans died. So did Chinese porters and mules and horses—and dogs and cats and women and children. Women and children, along with the dogs and cats, did not even know why. At least the Chinese porters and the mules and horses were in the military service.

The Soissons offensive. The German railhead at Soissons was the key to von Hindenburg's penetration. The Americans set out to take it. The 2nd Division advanced for two days, captured 3,000 prisoners, advanced eight miles, and suffered 3,788 casualties. It was relieved from the line, replaced by the 1st Division. The 1st advanced for three days, then was stopped by powerful German counterattack and consolidated to hold for two more days. Three thousand eight hundred German POWS, but 7,000 American casualties. Seventy-three percent of the infantry field officers were among them.

At home mothers knitted and prayed, daughters worked in the canteens, fathers and brothers worked in the factories, and everyone bought War Bonds. Americans, except for a handful of German-descended diehards, were firmly behind the war. Morning and night they picked up the newspapers to read of exploits of Eddie Rickenbacker, the racing driver turned aviator, and his Hat in the Ring Squadron. Soon enough he was an ace, with five planes destroyed. His achievements brought wonder into the eyes of small boys.

And yet, the Germans' Baron von Richthofen, France's Georges Guynemer, and Britain's Albert Ball all had many, many more victories in the air. The Americans were still neophytes in war, although this truth could not be stomached back at home. General von Ludendorff, the German chief of staff, never did gain much respect for the American military presence, although he did for the American soldier.

Speaking of the Second Battle of the Marne, which had ended in stalemate, Ludendorff said:

The German losses through the battle had been so heavy that we were compelled to break up about ten divisions and use their infantry as reserves for others. . . . The Armies of the Entente had also suffered; the battle cost the enemy as much as it had cost us.

The American units engaged in this battle had suffered most severely without achieving any successes. . . . Notwithstanding the gallantry of the individual American soldiers, the inferior quality of the American troops is proved by the fact that two brave German divisions were able to withstand the main attack made by very superior American forces for several weeks, and these two divisions, the 4th Ersatz and the 201st, I had up to then considered no better than the average.

But the key to truth was: ". . . the attempt to make the nations of the Entente inclined to peace before the arrival of the Americans' reinforcement by means of German victories had failed. The energy of the army had not sufficed to deal the enemy a decisive blow before the Americans were on the spot in considerable force. It was quite clear to me that our general situation had thus become very serious. . . ."

But the war went on.

In July the French decided to take the offensive, and strike the Amiens salient, thus freeing the Paris-Amiens rail line. They would hit the Germans in the north, and hit the Saint-Mihiel salient, to free the Paris-Avricourt rail line.

On August 8, 1918, the British 4th Army struck in the north with 400 tanks and seven divisions. In that one day they took 13,000 prisoners. "The blackest day of the war," said General Ludendorff and asked to be relieved.

The Americans and the French attacked at Lys, at Amiens. General Pershing now insisted that the Americans must fight as a unit. The U.S. 1st Army was organized in August. On September 2 it was ready for action. It was to fight for the Saint-Mihiel salient, a German finger that poked into the French line southeast of Verdun.

On September 12 the Americans attacked.

September 12. One A.M. The artillery bombardment began. The sky burst into a sheet of flame when every gun of the American army fired in unison the opening shot of this, the first American offensive. . . . Then, at 5 A.M. . . . before daylight on the foggy raining morning, the rolling barrage began. Up came the infantrymen. The major looked at his watch, then at the barrage, then at his watch again and gave the signal to advance. In the darkness the lines moved forward until the men reached the German barbed wire. Under cover of intense American artillery barrage, the infantry cut their way through the belts of barbed wire. Never before in the whole four years had infantry dared to assault until the artillery had, by heavy concentration, cut the enemy wire. . . . The wire was soon cut, and the infantry moved forward in wave after wave, toward the German front line.

The Americans suffered 7,000 casualties at Saint-Mihiel, but they captured 16,000 prisoners.

September 25. The first phase of French Marshal Foch's offensive ended. The Germans had been forced back beyond land they had held in France for four long years. And great as was the German generals' contempt for the American military organization, the Americans were arriving in France at the rate of 10,000 a day. On September 12, another 13 million Americans registered under the Selective Service Act. By the spring of 1919 4 million more Americans would be in France. The German armies had been worn down by battle after battle. There simply were no more reserves at home.

But in France the Americans and the French did not agree. Like the Germans, Marshal Foch was not impressed with the American military leadership. He wanted to cut the 1st Army down to size and use most American troops under French command alongside experienced French divisions. Pershing refused. What was Foch to do? Here were the new troops he needed desperately after four years of heavy Allied losses; he knew quite well that their army command was incompetent, but. . . .

So with Gallic smoothness Foch accepted the inevitable and gave the Americans their choice of two areas for the coming offensive, Champagne or Meuse-Argonne. Pershing chose the Meuse-Argonne.

The American army assembled north and west of Verdun and faced Sedan. Here the Germans had been in "trenches," which after four years were really complicated strongholds.

The offensive began. At Apremont, at Dead Man's Hill, the Americans were fighting on ground where the French had alone already lost more men than the Americans would lose in the entire war. On September 26 the Americans captured Montfauçon. They moved toward Varennes.

Now came the offensive that produced the "Lost Battalion," and made one of the most poignant tales of the American war. The scene: the Argonne Forest. Major Charles Whittlesay, commanding a mixed battalion of infantry and machine guns, was ordered to take and hold a ravine on the front. After heavy losses the battalion took its objective. But the units that were to come up on either side failed. The Germans infiltrated, surrounded the battalion, and strung new wire behind them, cutting them off from their lines. Whittlesay had been told to hold. So he held. The Germans attacked. The battalion held. The Germans attacked again. The battalion held. On October 4, Whittlesay sent back to regiment his last carrier pigeon with this message: "Men are suffering from exposure and hunger and wounded are in very bad condition. Cannot support be sent at once?" It seemed a reasonable request, given the circumstances.

The Americans, suffering from their usual organizational problems, had not been able to bring any help for a hundred hours. They had tried to air-drop supplies, a new technique for aircraft. The bundles had gone into "no-man's-land." Nine men had gone out from the battalion to bring them in; five were killed and four were captured.

One man, Private Growell R. Hollingshead, was blindfolded and sent back to Major Whittlesay with a message from the Germans, asking the major to surrender: "The suffering of your wounded can be heard over here in the German lines and we are appealing to your human sentiments." (Pretty good English. Indeed. The German commander, Lieutenant Heinrich Prinz, used to live in Seattle.)

Major Whittlesay did not reply. Ultimately the brass of the 79th Division pulled themselves together and men fought their way to the battalion, then brought them out. Whittlesay had attacked with 550 men; 194 walked out.

*   *   *

Then there was Sergeant York.

He wasn't really Sergeant York at all, but Corporal Alvin York, a Tennessee hillbilly who, with his little Hitler mustache, looked more like a German soldier than an American. Maybe that had something to do with what happened next:

The 328th Infantry of the 82nd Division was attacking toward the Decauville railroad when it found itself under a hill, being assaulted by German machine-gun fire. The guns on the left flank were particularly ominous, and a sergeant ordered a patrol of fifteen men to quiet those guns. Corporal York and the others squirmed around behind the Germans. The patrol then surprised a German command post and took three officers and several enlisted men prisoner. The inhabitants of a machine-gun nest not far off shouted at the Germans, who dropped, and the machine gunners then shot up the Americans. Six of the patrol were killed and three wounded, including the sergeant in charge.

Corporal York was then senior officer present. He ordered six men to guard the prisoners, and he attacked the machine gun. He moved slowly, shooting Germans with his 1903 Springfield rifle. He shot twelve. Then a lieutenant and seven men charged.

York fired one shot from his Springfield 1903, but the rifle did not work fast enough for him. He had a Colt .45-caliber automatic pistol, which held seven shots, and he lifted it and fired at the oncoming men. The Colt .45 was designed to stop berserk kris-swinging Malays as they ran amok during the Philippine insurrection. Its slug was intended to knock a man down, and these slugs did, to the surprise of the German major in charge of all the machine-gun positions on the hill. He shouted to all his men to surrender, and they did. York moved back to his own men with the major. He put the major on one side of himself and a lieutenant on the other. The rest of his patrol brought up the rear, behind the German prisoners. Then Corporal York found himself disoriented.

Which way to go to the Allied lines?

The major pointed.

York took the opposite direction. He kept running into machine-gun nests, and each time he would prod the major with his .45. The major would yell at the men to surrender, and the Germans would surrender, drop their arms, and join the crowd.

They came to the American line. York saw a lieutenant.

"Corporal York reports with prisoners, sir."

"How many prisoners?"

"I don't know."

The lieutenant counted 132. Corporal York became Sergeant York and Sergeant York was awarded the Medal of Honor.

*   *   *

On October 11 the Americans of the 18th Infantry were in the Ardennes. Casualties were heavy. One battalion began the day 1,000 strong and ended it with 285 men on their feet.

The German positions fell one by one. The marines took Blanc Mont, the key to Rheims.

On November 1 the French 4th Army and American 1st Army were poised to cross the Aisne and advance against Sedan. By November 6 they had reached the heights above Sedan. They were ready to attack. Then, November 11: armistice. The Germans had given up. The war was over.

The world, said President Wilson, was now safe for democracy. The American boys had done the job, and the task ahead was to make sure that no Americans ever had to fight again. The idea was to establish a League of Nations, a podium for peace.

CHAPTER 31

Forgotten Occupation

One aspect of World War I that is virtually unknown to three generations of Americans is the part the United States played in the Allied occupation of portions of Russia in 1918 and 1919. It came about because the British enticed Woodrow Wilson into the joint venture, on the premise that it was essential to protect lines of communication and prevent the Germans from taking over arms and supplies shipped to the Russians before the October Revolution of 1917, the rise of the Bolsheviks to power, and the establishment of the Union of Soviet Socialist Republics.

The British fears were reasonable enough. The Germans intended to do just what the British general staff suspected: to make a deal with the Russians to take over those military supplies and turn them back against the Allies. A German military mission was in Moscow when the occupation of the port of Archangel began.

The second aspect of the American occupation of Russia was the move into Siberia. The purpose of this occupation was to clear the railroad so that prisoners of war from Slovakia and Moravia, who called themselves Czechoslovaks, could move in units across the Trans-Siberian railroad. The Americans would then undertake to ship these soldiers back to the western front where they would change sides and fight for the Allies, as they had earlier fought (mostly unwillingly) for the Austro-Hungarian empire against the Allies. It was all part of the very complicated European political scene and was not at the time understood by very many Americans.

The net result, as will be seen in these pages, was to create in the historiography of the Soviet Russians the distinct impression that the United

States had proved to be an enemy of the Soviet revolution. Soviet-American relations never did recover from that blow, even when the United States and the USSR became allies by chance in the war against Hitler a generation later. The scars remain even yet. The irony is that the American occupation of north-central Russia and Siberia accomplished virtually nothing. In the long run this occupation was one of our most destructive military excursions.

*   *   *

The fall of 1918 found the harbor at Vladivostok alive with shipping. On the docks and in the warehouses were piled a billion dollars' worth of war material shipped largely from the United States and Japan for the Russian war effort against Germany. But there was no Russian war effort any more; the Russians had rebelled against their czarist leadership, the Bolsheviks had captured the Russian revolution, and the Allies with Pacific interests were milling around, trying to decide what must be done. The USS *Brooklyn,* flagship of the American Asiatic Fleet, was in Vladivostok harbor, flying the Stars and Stripes so all could see. The Chinese *Hai Jung* was there, and the British cruiser *Suffolk.* It was significant that the Japanese had three warships in the harbor, the *Asahi, Iwami,* and *Asakage.* The preponderance of Japanese naval power was an indication of the great national interest of Japan in what was happening in Siberia.

The collapse of Russia in 1917 had brought all sorts of complications. British naval forces were stationed at Archangel and Murmansk, to protect supplies shipped to Russia from falling into German hands. In Pacific Russia, Bolsheviks tried to take power. At first the Chinese stopped them, driving the Bolsheviks out of Harbin in northern Manchuria on what was really a spur of the Trans-Siberian Railroad. The Chinese also sent thousands of troops to guard the rail lines of Manchuria. This activity upset the Japanese, and particularly the Japanese army, which would have liked nothing better than to rip off a large part of western Siberia and add it to the growing Japanese empire. So the "Plan to Send Troops to the Russian Far East to Protect Foreign Residents" was offered by the Imperial Japanese Army. The real purpose of the plan was not to protect foreign residents, but to establish a base for future Japanese army operations in Pacific Russia.

Early in December 1917, the British were trying to organize some sort of joint Allied occupation of Siberia. The Americans were approached but refused to participate. On January 1, 1918, the British sent the cruiser HMS *Suffolk.* Not to be outdone, the Japanese immediately sent the warships *Iwami* and *Asahi.* The Japanese arrived first. On learning that the

Japanese were there, the Americans changed their minds and sent the USS *Brooklyn,* flagship of the Asiatic Fleet.

The British and the Japanese laid plans to land marines to patrol Vladivostok. Almost immediately they learned of the breakdown of law and order: a gang of forty armed men wearing Russian militia uniforms entered the luxurious Versailles Hotel and stole a million rubles in valuables and money from the safes and patrons of that establishment. One American lost his passport and all his pocket money.

Further, the Bolsheviks had seized Khabarovsk and Irkutsk. Major General Masatake Nakajima was sent by the Japanese army to land in Manchuria and Siberia, and survey the situation, preparing for Japanese troop movements. He landed at Vladivostok on January 22, 1918. Soon the Japanese plans for Pacific Russia included two landing forces, one to take control of Vladivostok, Nikol'sk, Ussuriysk, and Khabarovsk, and the Amur River basin, and a second force to advance to Chita and control the trans-Baikal territory.

By March, the American consul in Harbin was reporting to Washington on Japan's plans for seizure of suzerainty over the area. The Americans were extremely distrustful of the Japanese, and had been for a long time. Part of this distrust was American racism; the Oriental had become anathema to the American working class in the 1860s when Leland Stanford and associates used Chinese labor to build the Pacific railroad with enormous success, and the Chinese had remained in California and the West until most of them were driven out by the Chinese Exclusion Acts a few years later. The Japanese had inherited the Chinese mantle of most dangerous Orientals when they began settling in California, and outproducing the local farmers. Thus had come the "Gentleman's Agreement" of 1907 which was one of the most ungentlemanly matters of all diplomatic history. The Japanese had accepted a refusal of the Americans to tolerate Japanese labor in the United States rather than have specific exclusionary laws passed against Japanese, but in Japan people were extremely resentful against the United States. At that time, the United States became designated by Japan's navy and government as that country's primary enemy in the Pacific, a designation the U.S. was to share with the Soviet Union because of the Japanese army's ambitions in Asia. It was a designation that would never be lost until World War II was fought. In 1907 Theodore Roosevelt had sent "the Great White Fleet" to Japan to awe the Japanese. It did not do so, mainly because the fleet was largely a paper tiger built of outmoded vessels. Since that time the Japanese and Americans had maintained a cautious peacefulness, like a pair of tomcats walking carefully along the contiguous borders of their territory, careful to stay on their own side but not by much. World War I had brought an uneasy alliance; the Japanese had joined in 1914 and the Americans in 1917. Relations were again threatened when the Americans saw how the Japanese were using the war to add to their empire (they took the Shantung Province of China, and the Mariana, Marshall, and Bismarck islands).

The Americans were interested in Pacific Russia for two reasons: the possibility they then saw of economic penetration and profits, and the maintenance of the railroads so that the war in Europe could be brought to a successful conclusion. A few visionaries saw in Asiatic Russia a different country from European Russia, but there were not many of them.

On March 24, 1918, the Bolsheviks seized the Vladivostok telegraph office and the anti-Communist employees went on strike in protest. The Allied officials were furious and threatened intervention. The Bolsheviks then restored the service. A few days later Red Guards began arriving from the east, and then came a commission of German officers. Since the Soviets had signed a peace treaty with the Germans at Brest-Litovsk, the two countries were not at war, and the Germans were trying to get hold of all those military supplies in Pacific Russia for use on the western front against the Allies. The British wanted to stage a united Allied landing. The Americans refused to participate. As Secretary of the Navy Josephus Daniels stated in a message that reflected the Wilson policy: "During disturbed conditions in Russia this government most anxious that nothing be done that could in any way affect the confidence of the Russian people in our sincere desire to help them establish and maintain government of their own choosing."

The Russians forced the issue. On April 4, several armed men in uniform entered a Japanese shop in Vladivostok and demanded money. Refused, they shot and killed three Japanese. The Japanese admiral then landed marines "to protect the life and property of Japanese citizens." The British followed with a landing of their own. The Americans did not land any marines, but the Soviets, in their paranoia, assumed that the British and Japanese would never have landed men unless they had conspired with the Americans to do so. The Soviets were immediately suspicious. From Moscow, Lenin warned the local Vladivostok authorities to expect Japanese advances and Allied assistance to the Japanese. The Americans refused to participate, but in Soviet eyes they were part of the Allied cause, and therefore they were suspect.

Now came another complicating element.

During the war, Czechs and Slovaks living in Russia had been organized in a special Russian army unit called the Druzhina, which fought with the rest of the Russian army, mostly under Russian officers. A large number of Czech and Slovak soldiers in the Austro-Hungarian armies had deserted to the Russians. Others had been taken prisoner. With the overthrow of the czar's government, the provisional government had permitted expansion of the Druzhina until it grew to two full divisions. When the Bolsheviks seized power, the Czechoslovak army was authorized to move across Russia to Siberia, and then leave Russia via Vladivostok. The Allied plan was then to ship the Czechoslovak army around the world to fight on the western front.

So the movement (by railway) of the Czechoslovak army across Siberia began. By the beginning of May 1918, the Czech army was spread out from Pena, just west of the Volga, to Vladivostok. The first trains were just arriving at Vladivostok. The Soviets then had a change of heart, and Leon Trotsky ordered that the Czechoslovaks be taken off the trains and organized into labor battalions or drafted into the Red Army.

The uneasy truce between the Czechoslovak army and the Soviets then came to an end, and the Czechoslovaks decided they would shoot their way through to Vladivostok rather than remain prisoners in Russia.

Meanwhile, in the spring of 1918 relations between the Soviets and the Allies grew progressively more strained. The Soviets labored under twin problems: their treaty with the Germans, and their natural suspicion that the world was against their revolution. As time went on, the Allies began to regard that revolution as an international threat and became equally suspicious of the Bolsheviks, a matter not helped by the Bolshevik assertion that they would bring the same sort of bloody revolution to all the capitalist countries of the world. Thus by the spring of 1918 the American sympathy for the Russian revolution was on the wane, and President Wilson was persuaded to send the USS *Olympia* to join the French and British warships in the far northern Russian port of Archangel, to prevent the Soviets from shipping war supplies stored there to the Germans for use on the western front. Arthur Bullard, an official of the U.S. Committee on Public Information (the American war propaganda agency), was in Russia, and he took a train trip from Moscow to Archangel. Along the route he saw much of the war matériel.

I have never seen anything more desolate, more depressing—more maddening. Acres on acres of barbed wire, stands of small arms, cases of ammunition, and pyramids of shells of all calibers, great parks of artillery, motor trucks, field kitchens, ambulances,—thousands of them; railroad iron, wheels, axles, rails, coils of precious copper telegraph wire; most important of all, the regularly piled, interminable rows of metal pig—the alloys so essential for artillery production—and the sinister looking sheds where the TNT was stored. It was all worth its weight in gold to Berlin. It was all so terribly needed by our friends before Amiens, on the Chemin des Dames. So much of it would be valuable to our own men when the time would come.

In Moscow the Allies tried to negotiate with the Soviets over the disposition of these military supplies. The Soviets made many excuses, but continued to move supplies, and the Allies were convinced that some of those supplies were going to the Germans, even though Lenin declared that they would not. By spring most of the supplies had been moved, and the Allies did not know where. The ships at Archangel, loaded with still more military supplies ordered and sent before the Russian capitulation, were not allowed to unload. With their food and supplies, they represented one of the few weapons the Allies had with which to negotiate with the Soviets, who wanted the supply. So the lives and safety of a number of Allied citizens were secured by trading supplies to the Soviets. Ultimately some of the ships returned to the West still bearing their loads.

The British were the first to intervene in Murmansk, sending a force of 600 "military advisers" who would train the Czechoslovaks in the area. The British saw the Soviets slipping into the hands of the Germans, and they were determined to keep a foothold in Russia, in case they had to make a serious landing there to fight the German enemy. By the beginning of June, the British were putting serious pressure on the Americans to join in the occupation of Russian territory at Murmansk and Archangel. On June 1, President Wilson agreed with this idea in principle, if Marshal Foch would also agree.

On June 3, the matter of northern Russia was considered by the Supreme War Council meeting at Versailles. Marshal Foch and the others agreed that to keep the Russian ports out of German hands, something had to be done. England, France, Italy, and the United States ought to be prepared to supply four to six battalions of troops, under British command, to train the Czechs and supply them.

On June 11, 1918, 150 American marines were put ashore to help patrol the railroad. So, Americans had landed in Russia, with what were obviously the best intentions in the world as far as the Allies were concerned. President Wilson had steadfastly refused to become involved in the politics of the Russian revolution, even though the Bolsheviks were almost impossible to deal with. Still, on June 11, American troops landed. This fact was something the Soviet government would never let the Russian people forget.

The British wanted the Americans to send three battalions of infantry, two batteries of field artillery, and three companies of engineers.

The tension in the north grew, not just between the Allies and the Soviets, but within the Soviet forces. Finally, Comrade Yhuryev, the local commander, was outlawed by Moscow and declared to be a tool of the Western European capitalists. Moscow-backed soldiers blew up the rail line and cut the telephone and telegraph wires from Murmansk to Moscow. The Allies made an agreement with the Murmansk government which justified the intervention. And so the Americans sent 4,500 troops of the 339th Infantry Regiment, the 337th Field Hospital Company and the 3109th

Engineers Battalion to Russia. They went ashore at Archangel on September 4, 1918, under British command.

The Americans were concerned with the situation of the Czechoslovak Legion in Russia, particularly at the end of May 1918. The name of this military organization symbolized the dreams of several groups of nationalists in the eastern area of the old Austro-Hungarian Empire. When war had come in 1914, the people of Prague and the other cities in this region had been conscripted along with Austrians and Hungarians to fight for the Hapsburg empire. Many thousands of them had been taken prisoner by the Russians. But also, in 1914, the Czar's government had established a small brigade of Czechoslovak volunteers in the Russian army. It was called the Czechoslovakian Druzhina. It represented the 100,000 Czechs who lived in Russian territory. By 1916 the revolutionaries Thomas G. Masaryk and Edouard Benes were plotting to achieve the independence of that area which would be known as Czechoslovakia. By 1917 they had persuaded the leaders of France and Britain of the value of a buffer state in the New Europe to be formed after Germany and Austria-Hungary were defeated. The rebellion in Russia in 1917 brought matters to a head. In December that year at Paris, the Western Allies agreed to the establishment of Czechoslovakia under the peace treaty of the future. The Czechoslovak Legion began forming up in the prison camps and outside them, as the Russians let the prisoners go.

But at the end of May 1918, Leon Trotsky ordered the Czechoslovak troops disarmed and converted into Soviet slave laborers or soldiers. Soon fighting broke out all along the railroad, and along the rail lines that fed into the Trans-Siberian. Some 15,000 Czechoslovak troops had already reached Siberia and they were not directly concerned at first. But the world was watching the Czechoslovak Legion progress, and most American sympathy was on the side of the new army representing the new nation (Czechoslovakia) that was being born out of the European war. For the first time in history one might say an army was giving birth to a nation.

By July 6 the Czechoslovak units in the west had managed to fight their way to Ufa where they made contact with the rest of the Czechoslovak body. Then they moved toward Lake Baikal. It was the end of August before they reached Chita.

All this while the war situation in Europe, and particularly in Russia, was enormously confused. The White Russians were fighting with the Finns in the west against the Bolsheviks. The Czechoslovaks were convinced that the Germans were trying to capture Siberia, and half convinced that the Soviets were in league with the Germans. If that were true, and the Germans were to win, then the dream of a free Czechoslovakia would die.

The Soviets, of course, were deeply involved in their revolution, and suspicious of everybody. Seldom has there been military confrontation anywhere as confusing as that inside Russia in 1918.

American views of what was happening in Russia were also confused. One factor was a belief that Americans should show the new government a friendly American interest. To do this was hard, when dealing with someone like Lenin. When asked how he felt about Americans sending food to Russians, Lenin's sharp question was: Which Russians? And his next statement was equally indicative: "Food is a weapon." Given that attitude, almost any assistance the Americans were inclined to offer was bound to be misunderstood. Americans on the scene, along the Trans-Siberian Railroad and elsewhere, saw clearly that any action the Americans took, whether by sending food or by mediation, would be regarded as intervention.

In the spring of 1918, among those Americans who knew Russia and who had begun to have grave misgivings about the direction of the Bolshevik revolution, there was a growing feeling that Siberia should be detached and assisted in gaining its independence from the Soviet revolution. The Czechoslovak Legion provided an army with which to work.

By the Fourth of July, 1918, the Czechoslovak Legion had captured control of Vladivostok from the Soviets. Thomas G. Masaryk, the Czechoslovak leader, had met with President Wilson and secured support for the establishment of his new nation in Eastern Europe, and thus the American attitude toward what was happening in Siberia was profoundly affected by the situation of the Czechoslovak Legion. It was, as President Wilson said, an American responsibility to aid the Czechoslovaks. He proposed to send an American force of 7,000 men to Siberia, to guard the lines of communication of the Czechoslovak Legion, and to land more forces in Vladivostok if necessary to hold that city.

"The public announcement by this and the Japanese governments is that the purpose of landing troops is to aid Czechoslovak prisoners against Germany and Austria, that there is no purpose to interfere with internal affairs in Russia, and that they guarantee not to impair the political or territorial sovereignty of Russia. . . ."

And so on August 3 orders went to the commanding American generals in the Philippines to send the 27th Army Infantry Regiment, the 31st Army Infantry Regiment, a field hospital, ambulance units, and a communications battalion to Siberia. The Americans began landing on August 16.

Washington had played into the hands of the Japanese army, which was delighted with the turn of events. Instead of sending 7,000 troops as proposed, the Japanese sent 72,000 to Siberia and another 12,000 to the Chinese Eastern Railway Zone of Manchuria. This move was a major action in the Japanese plan for control of all East Asia, but the Americans did not know that. When Wilson learned how many troops the Japanese were sending he was appalled. But by then it was too late; the principle of major intervention had been established.

In Murmansk and Archangel, the breach with the Soviet authorities led to efforts by the British to undermine the Soviets in the area, and to espionage and activities that aroused enormous fury in Moscow.

In August the Allies participated in several actions against Soviet forces to assure control of the Murmansk area, and American marines from the cruiser *Olympia* were involved in the fighting. One marine lieutenant and a handful of men seized a train at Bakaritsa and chased Soviet troops along the railway line for seventy-five miles before the Russians stopped and burned a bridge.

The main American force of 5,500 men was stationed largely at Murmansk. One battalion went up the Duna River to help the British capture Kotlas. Another battalion went to Archangel. Another battalion joined the British on their drive to capture Vologda.

The Americans, babes in the woods that they were, did not realize that they were being used for purposes President Wilson had never considered. The purpose of France, in particular, was to support a friendly government, really a puppet, in northern Russia. So Americans fought and died without knowing why, and at home in America most people did not even know what was going on. The imbecility of the whole situation finally caused the Allies to abandon Archangel at the end of September 1919, and Murmansk two weeks later.

The Allied intervention destroyed whatever chance there was for reasonable relations with the Bolsheviks. Americans, British, and other nationals were captured and held in Moscow and elsewhere. World War I ended in November 1918, but the military mess in Russia continued.

In what had been eastern Russia, attempts to prevent Bolshevik takeover lasted much longer. The United States found itself involved in the "White counterrevolution," willy-nilly, simply by being in military occupation. The American participation was relatively small, but it was still an invasion of the territorial sovereignty of the Russians, and, although American history teaches virtually nothing about this invasion, as with the Archangel and Murmansk invasions, the USSR has not forgotten. Ultimately, beginning in 1920, the Americans and the other nations got out of Russia. The Japanese were the last to leave and managed to hold troops in Siberia until 1926. The Japanese army never did relinquish its plans to add Siberia to the Manchurian holdings of the Japanese empire.

The American intervention in Russia at the end of World War I turned out to be one of the least useful, least self-serving, and most damaging forays of American arms abroad. President Wilson's instincts were against intervention at all, and he was really persuaded to intervene in northern Russia only because he had been convinced that such U.S. intervention would help shorten the war in France; in Siberia he was persuaded by his recognition of the validity of the Czechoslovak dream of nationhood. As it occurred, the intervention was a fiasco, and one that in the 1980s still added to the complications of Soviet-American relations.

CHAPTER 32

The Banana Wars

Most of America's military excursions between the two world wars involved Latin Ameria. It must be surprising to the 1980s generation to realize just how much military activity was involved. If we study what happened in the Latin countries in the 1920s and 1930s it is much easier to understand the resentments of the Latin people in the 1980s. Since the 1920s American political evangelism in the Latin countries has far outweighed crass financial concerns in the matter of our interventions. Of course one might say that our political concern (worry about communism) is a direct result of our capitalistic notions about the way in which the Latin countries ought to be run. But it is important to realize that the hatreds and anxieties of Central Americans about American intentions toward their countries go back a very long way.

*   *   *

In the 1920s the banana companies struggled for power and profit in Central America. The action was in Honduras in 1923 and 1924 when the U.S. Navy's Special Service Squadron patrolled the isthmian waters and America tried to keep the peace among various conflicting factions. The cry supporting various minor invasions of Latin American sovereignty by American troops was almost always the same: "the protection of American lives and property." And, of course, there was a certain justification to this theme: in the Honduran revolution, in one battle between factions in La

Ceiba, the American consulate was hit with so many shells that the consular staff fled to the protection of one of the big banana plantations.

During the 1920s the "banana republics" were stirred by rebellions so often that the American military and naval presence in Central America was constant. Honduras, Nicaragua, El Salvador, seemed to be always in a state of uprising, threat, or preparation for war against one another. The Americans dealt with these people as though they were constantly bickering cousins who could not survive unless the United States set down the ground rules. This policy was rooted in American history, and apparently fated to continue throughout the twentieth century. In 1923 this attitude was established in a Central American Conference run by Sumner Welles. Out of the conference came multiple treaties governing the actions of the Central American states, stemming from a combination of the policies of Theodore Roosevelt and Woodrow Wilson, brought up to date: if a political aspirant took power by force, he would not be recognized by the United States or the other nations of the conference, and would get no loans from American banks.

By manipulating the banana companies and other American interests in the area, and the American government itself, various conspirators in Central America would make a laughingstock of the treaties that came out of this conference. But as long as the area remained quiet—and by this time, economics *was* playing a major role, even above the traditional American do-goodism in Central America—then Washington was not too dismayed. What really bothered a succession of American administrations was the sort of Central American leader who looked upon the United States not as the great Uncle Sam, but as a powerful nation pursuing its own interests, often in conflict with those of his little country. It was unthinkable in Washington that American interests and those of the Central American republics could differ. The sort of leader who believed that was happening, and that his country ought to have the right to pursue different interests, was the sort of leader the Americans could neither abide nor understand.

Nicaragua was a case in point. In 1912 Adolfo Diaz had become president of Nicaragua. The United States had marines protecting the legation, which was not so unusual. But the United States still supervised collection of Nicaraguan customs taxes and the United States also got a new canal treaty concession, in case the Americans wanted to build a second canal across the isthmus, for $3 million and a guarantee of Nicaraguan independence. American bankers gave the Nicaraguans what they wanted and guaranteed the monetary system.

In the early 1920s the U.S. Marines committed what was probably the worst break of discipline in the history of the corps. Several policemen and others were killed in fighting that erupted when the marines decided they could do as they pleased in Managua. The scandal was so great that one Nicaraguan legislator dared demand the removal of the marine guard from the U.S. legation. He did not get that, but he did get the removal of the entire personnel contingent of the guard, and the transfer in of a whole new unit.

Diaz, Emiliano Chamorro, and Diego Chamorro (uncle of Emiliano) were all eminently satisfactory presidents as far as the Americans were concerned, but in 1923 Diego Chamorro died, and the vice president, Bartolome Martinez, decided he wanted to be president. Unfortunately for Nicaragua, Emiliano Chamorro decided he wanted to be president again. The code for the election of 1924, drawn up by the Americans, was violated vigorously by the Martinez faction, which elected Carlos Solorzano. But the Americans had given a pledge that they would remove themselves from Nicaragua, and after the election they did. The marines went home. The Nicaraguans bought their national bank back from the Americans, and everything looked positive.

But in a series of comic-opera kidnappings and political incidents, Nicaragua's independence became displaced. For two years Emiliano Chamorro conspired against President Solorzano, and finally the president resigned and fled the country, along with vice president, Dr. Juan B. Sacasa. Emiliano Chamorro took control of the country again. But Vice President Sacasa had not resigned, and this omission became the excuse for the anti-Chamorro faction to rebel. In America up to this point the attitude was generally "a pox on both your houses," since by no test could the political didoes of Nicaragua be reconciled to the American political theory. The American minister to Nicaragua, Charles C. Eberhardt, knew all the politicians. Indeed, most of them were related, by blood or marriage, for Nicaragua's elite was a tight little community. Eberhardt was able to play both sides.

In the need for capital to finance their rebellion, the rebels turned to Bluefields, that center of the American colony, and raided the national bank, taking $160,000. This action brought the cruiser *Cleveland* to Bluefields, and the marines landed again "to protect American lives and property."

But Minister Eberhardt suddenly went home, leaving as chargé d'affaires Lawrence Dennis, a State Department man who decided he was an éminence grise. His dispatches to Washington resulted in a buildup of the American naval presence at Bluefields and Corinto and the landing of more marines. So while no marines were officially involved in internal Nicaraguan problems in 1926, physically they were very much in evidence.

And now, into American foreign policy came a new element that was to last, and last, and last, as a trigger and an excuse for intervention in Latin American affairs: *communism*.

American participation in the 1918 "intervention" in the Russian revolution destroyed irrevocably the relations of the United States with the new government of Russia, and created a feeling of revulsion in the United States. This distaste, accompanied by an inchoate fear that communism just might be, as Lenin said, "inevitable," was enormously magnified by the birth of the Communist International and the attempted export of the Communist revolution to China. There the Communists were very visible to Americans, since Chiang Kai-shek, a puzzling figure, had made an alliance with them. Also communism in other countries, including the United States, had attracted the adherence of many of the old bomb-throwing radicals. In America a small but extremely vocal group of anti-Communist intellectuals virtually paralyzed the American political vision for half a century. Fifty years? Perhaps an underestimate; even in the 1980s, to shout the word *Communist* in the State Department was not only to raise a red flag but to start the shivering processes from which assistance to any sort of "anti-Communist" movement flowed.

In 1926 the feeling was certainly understandable, and became more so as the convolutions of Soviet government policy were faithfully aped by the foreign sycophants, and as various spy rings were disclosed. But never has a political movement engendered quite as much fear for quite as long as the Communist movement has. And in Latin America anticommunism became a political way of life that threatened to become permanent in the wake of *norteamericano* paranoia.

In 1926, the United States was again having its troubles with Mexico. The government of President Plutarco Calles had turned left in the face of the American Big Brother. Among other changes, he was proposing the nationalization of oil and other industries in which American capital had made significant contributions and now had important holdings. President Calles was often accused in Washington of "Bolshevik tendencies." One of the Bolshevik tendencies was an inclination to help other Latin American states beset by American meddling. Nicaragua's Dr. Sacasa went to Mexico City, and there secured Mexican arms and Mexican "volunteers" for his attempt to unseat President Chamorro. Soon Mexican arms and Mexican nationals were being captured in Nicaragua by President Chamorro's forces, who immediately called foul and "Bolshevism," and succeeded in arousing the American press and government to a terrible new hemispheric threat. Probably the Comintern had a hand in it all, but the Comintern's resources were extremely limited and not very effective in changing governments. Yet to understand the American attitude of 1926 one would have to look to Russia, where Stalin had just ousted Leon Trotsky in the struggle for sole leadership of the Communist movement, and to China, where Soviet General Vasily Konstantinovich Blücher, using the nom de guerre Galens, was advising Nationalist Generalissimo Chiang Kai-shek how to win his northern campaign. In the American eye, Bolshevism seemed to be grasping the imagination of the subject peoples of the world in a manner previously reserved for the American Revolution.

And so in the fall of 1926, a frightened Washington arranged for another conference to settle the internal affairs of Nicaragua.

The conference was held at Corinto—symbolically, on the deck of the USS *Denver* with Chargé d'affaires Dennis presiding. Out of this came a complicated maneuver, which sent President Chamorro to Europe as a general minister, and made Adolfo Diaz president. President Diaz was an artful fellow, and he knew how to manipulate the Americans with announced worries over Bolshevism, and over Mexican meddling in Nicaraguan affairs, which was the next worst thing in the Washington view.

Just before Christmas 1926, President Diaz expressed new fears, and Admiral Julian Latimer, head of the American squadron, sent more marines ashore. They came to protect American life and property, and the government. The Americans did not now content themselves with protecting Americans; they surrounded the presidential palace in Managua. This put them in the position of interfering in the Sacasa rebellion, for Dr. Sacasa's army was still very much organized and awaiting events.

In January 1927 President Coolidge issued a special message to Congress. Conventional historical wisdom has it that Coolidge did little in the White House. But the fact is that President Coolidge established a new official, anti-Bolshevist policy for Latin America. And so, as Senator William E. Borah announced with disgust, Coolidge fabricated this new "mahogany and oil" policy, which was patently contrived to maintain American meddling in Central America. The policy was for the interests of American business, said Senator Borah, who never really appreciated the paranoia of so many of his compatriots. So the Americans had again been entrapped to do the bidding of a Nicaraguan political leader.

Thus American marines held several centers in Nicaragua: Bluefields, Prinzapolca, Puerto Cabezas, León, and Managua. These were all called "neutral zones"; they were neutral because the Americans protected them. The result of this American protection was to push Sacasa's revolutionary army into the interior.

Americans, driven by the profit motive or anti-Communist ideals, provided an aviation corps for Diaz, and some fought on the ground. But the Diaz forces did not do very well against the rebels even so. In several battles the rebels routed the government forces. Minister Eberhardt, who had returned, wrote gloomily to Washington that unless the Americans intervened completely Diaz was likely to be beaten.

Henry L. Stimson was sent down to Nicaragua to solve all the problems, and he spoke of free elections and the spirit of fair play, words not well

known or well understood in Managua. But Stimson did bring a halt to
the military processes, by a meeting with General Moncada, the rebel army
commander. Out of the meeting came the Tipitapa Accord, by which the
policing of Nicaragua was turned over to the marines, and General Moncada agreed to keep his troops from action until after he saw how free the
new elections would be.

The marine policing was violent. There were firefights with rebel groups.
A number of Nicaraguans were killed, and the marines suffered some
casualties. But true to the spirit of the accord, most of Dr. Sacasa's troops
surrendered their weapons to the Americans. Diaz's did not, and Sacasa
saw the handwriting on the wall, and fled the country.

The most flamboyant military figure to emerge in this confusion was
Augusto C. Sandino, a "bandit" who was to operate for five years in
Nicaragua. His activities brought more marines and the first of the "jungle
wars." At one point Sandino surrounded a mixed force of American marines and Diaz guardsmen at Quilali, providing the marines with an opportunity to show off their new air force. One lieutenant saved the day
for the marines by flying in medical supplies and flying out eighteen wounded
men.

The war went on in 1928. The marines got good experience on the
ground and in the air in jungle fighting. Remember the names Chesty
Puller, Merritt Edson, Julian Smith, Matthew Ridgway, Edward A. Craig.
They will reappear in greater glory in the annals of the American military.
The careers of these men were forged partly in the jungles of Nicaragua.

To some of the American press it seemed that the United States government was involved in a "fury for annihilation" of one guerilla leader
in one small Central American country. Sandino had his own view: "We
are not protesting against the size of the invasion, but against invasion.
The United States had meddled in Nicaragua for many years. We cannot
merely depend on her promise that some day she will get out."

In the spring of 1928 the Americans were anything but out. Nearly
4,000 marines were ashore in Nicaragua, fighting the rebels, and American
cruisers patrolled the Nicaraguan shores.

Elections were held in Nicaragua in 1928, and critics agreed that they
were quite fair. The Americans supervised. They prevented repeat voting
by making everyone, including President Diaz, dip his fingers in Mercu-
rochrome after voting.

The Liberals won. That is, the anti-Diaz government party won, which
meant General Moncada. But, of course, in the interim, General Moncada,
who had been an ally of General Sandino, had made his bargain with the
Americans.

At the Sixth Pan-American Congress in Havana in 1928 the United
States was charged with aggressions in Latin America. Former Secretary

of State Charles Evans Hughes defended American interventions in Latin America as "interposition of a temporary character," to protect American lives and property, and incidentally other lives. By 1929 the United States had 5,000 marines in Nicaragua. Then the Hoover administration came to office, and Henry L. Stimson became secretary of state. Sandino despaired of winning his struggle and slipped out of Nicaragua, giving the government no further reason for the bandit chase. Urged by Stimson, the United States began withdrawing the marines and moving toward a more civil— as opposed to military—policy toward Latin America. The change was hastened by the crash of the American stock market in the fall of 1929 and the onset of the Great Depression. Now Congress was not interested in spending any money abroad. In 1931 Secretary Stimson told the marines that they would have to be out of Nicaragua by June, except for a small contingent left to train the Nicaraguan national guard.

Sandino had come back to Nicaragua to fight again. "Sandinistas," his rebels were now called, no longer just "bandidos." In March 1931, an earthquake destroyed most of Managua. General Sandino said it was a sign that God was on his side. And he attacked. Here came the marines again, to drive the Sandinistas back into the interior. But that was just a temporary action; the ravages of depression at home were more important, and on April 18, 1931, Secretary of State Stimson announced that the United States could no longer provide general protection of Americans in Nicaragua. This statement was really revolutionary. It announced the abandonment of an extraterritoriality that had never been officially claimed, a dumping of the American residents of Nicaragua (and of all Latin America) into the hands and legal arms of local government. After the spring of 1931, Nicaragua and the rest of the Caribbean could be said to be truly independent of American military meddling for the first time since the Spanish-American War. The American policy of military interference had been abandoned in favor of political and economic maneuvering. But how long this would last was another matter.

CHAPTER 33

Trouble on the Yangtze

America's interest in China goes back to the 1820s, when many Boston sailing ship captains were engaged in the opium trade as well as the slave trade, and sometimes in both callings at once. China meant wealth and mystery to Americans then and it still does in the 1980s.

With trade, and the opening of Canton to American vessels, came consular relations. With the consular relations came American marines to guard the American installations and protect American lives and property. We simply followed the French and British in their scheme of maintaining gunboats on the major waterways, to make sure that the many Chinese pirates did not hijack American shipping, and to ensure that the Chinese government lived up to the concessions wrung from Peking, usually at gunpoint.

The American position regarding China was always somewhat different from that of the Europeans, which ought to be a matter for self-congratulation. We never did sink to the level of the Europeans in sawing off pieces of Chinese territory. Our most flagrant adventure was during the Boxer Rebellion, but there was some justification then in the murderous treatment of American missionaries in China.

As time went on, however, we did yield to the general call for extraterritorial concessions, and began to regard China as an international marketplace, with ourselves as most favored buyers and sellers. We began to lose sight, in the 1920s, of the reality of Chinese nationalism. All this was a forerunner to a state of mind that developed in America in the next generation, the 1940s, and it accounts for some very peculiar American reasoning, and a complete misreading of the situation in China in the 1940s, that caused us to lose touch with the de facto government for a quarter of a century. It all began just after the Boxer Rebellion.

*   *   *

Although the United States did not have any colonies in China, from the middle of the nineteenth century the Americans had maintained a powerful presence there. It was not to be compared to the British presence, with Hong Kong and Weihaiwei and the great tobacco and other trade concessions, but it was still considerable, and based on the American premise of freedom of trade for American businessmen throughout the world.

The early activity was limited to the coastal waters of China, but in 1869 the Shanghai Chamber of Commerce (a body of Westerners) suggested that the Yangtze River be opened for trading up as far as Chungking, in Szechuan Province, 1,400 miles upstream.

Trade follows the flag, said Captain Mahan, and he was right in this case. The Americans did not have a naval vessel in China waters powerful enough to navigate the dangerous Yangtze gorges, where the currents and whirlpools vie to see whose devils are the worst. So British warships went upriver, and so did British traders, and the Americans were left behind— but not for long. By 1871 there were 145 Americans in Hankow, on the Yangtze, and more drifted westward year by year. Following Mahan's doctrine, the U.S. Navy produced stronger vessels for the Yangtze. Soon the American navy too was "protecting" the riverbanks. In 1874 Commander E. O. Matthews took the gunboat *Ashuelot* 1,000 miles up the river to Ichang. By 1880 American vessels had navigated virtually every oceanic waterway in East Asia; the flag was well known, and trade was increasing.

As noted, American marines first landed in Canton; then marines came to Peking, Tientsin, and Shanghai, for protection of consulates, legations, and American life and property.

In 1901 the United States gunboat *Vicksburg* was sent up to Newchwang (Yingkow) on Liaotung Bay, 150 miles north of Port Arthur. This was Russian territory at the time; the Russians had built their big naval base at Port Arthur. The American (and British) presence at Newchwang was just to remind the Russians that they did not own China.

In 1902 Rear Admiral Robley D. Evans brought the United States Asiatic Squadron to Amoy for maneuvers. All the Europeans—British, French, and Germans—did something of this nature too. The squadrons would assemble and carry out their war games ashore and their maneuvers at sea, their competitions at shooting and marching and rowing boats. Sometimes the squadrons would compete against one another. Generally speaking, in this period, the Americans and Europeans were one big family, exchanging visits and gossip and even port facilities and equipment. Even their quarrels were more or less family quarrels, over protocol and naval niceties. The British were particularly helpful to the Americans by letting them use docks and repair facilities at Hong Kong. The American squadron soon became the U.S. Asiatic Fleet, but after 1902 its influence in Chinese waters was limited because the Americans were tied up with the nasty mess involving the Philippine insurrection. As many ships as could be released were sent up to North China to summer. Chefoo was the port. It got everyone out of mosquitoland.

Even wives and children came from Manila and Cavite to live in hotels for the summer months, although wives were forbidden by naval regulations. They came independently, and the Navy Department could not do anything about it. But life was not all tennis and racing and swimming clubs. In August 1903 American merchants and missionaries in the Poyang area were threatened by "bandits," which meant a warlord on the loose, and Admiral Evans sent the gunboat *Villalobos* (captured from the Spanish in the late war) up there to show the flag. The gunboat did the job.

The Chinese government protested. The American minister tended to agree with the Chinese government that Admiral Evans had violated Chinese sovereignty. But this was 1903 and what was Chinese sovereignty? The admirals had already decided that it was not much, and the Evans policy became American policy when Secretary of State Hay sided with the admiral against the minister.

Thereafter the American gunboat became a common sight on the rivers and in the bays whenever there was trouble. The year 1903 marked the beginning of the Yangtze River patrol, under the control of the *Monadnock,* the U.S. station ship in Shanghai. She was a floating fort built to fight the Civil War, and she had ten-inch guns. Other more maneuverable ships on the river were the gunboats *Elcano, Pompey,* and *Villalobos.* But 1903 was also the year that America in the form of the Naval War College made the major decision that destroyed the fighting effectiveness of the U.S. Asiatic Fleet until 1942. To save money, all the battleships were withdrawn and moved to the Atlantic side of the United States as part of the main U.S. fleet. From that time on, the name Asiatic Fleet was really a misnomer for a naval organization of which the largest ship was an armored cruiser.

The Americans maintained a careful but properly belligerent neutrality in China waters during the Russo-Japanese War (the American naval officers were very pro-Russian, or very anti-Japanese, however one viewed it).

By 1908, life was so quiet along the Yangtze that the Yangtze River patrol was all but abandoned, and then a dispute between warlords in the Hankow area sent American businessmen and missionaries ducking for cover, and they found the protection of the British. This created some reverberations in Washington, and without fanfare the gunboats came back to the river within six months. Two years later the cruiser *New Orleans* was assigned to the China station and spent part of her year on the Yangtze.

With the establishment of the Chinese Republic in 1910 by revolutionaries and the struggle with the feudal warlords, the international community (British, French, Germans, Americans, and Japanese) decided they had to increase naval forces in Chinese waters to keep such rivers as the Yangtze open to trade. So all of them dispatched more ships and more gunboats to China, where they flew the flag, "protected citizens and property," and maintained a fair semblance of order along the waterways. From time to time the gunboats would launch shore excursions to punish a warlord or save a community of missionaries or businessmen.

In the early 1920s the civil war—the Republic's campaign against the warlords—threatened to disrupt trade with the interior. The foreign powers, including the United States, were not loath to send warships to the trading cities to demonstrate their power and warn the various Chinese factions against disturbing foreigners. After the death of President Sun Yat-sen in 1925, the commandant of the Whampoa Military Academy, Chiang Kai-shek, decided that he was the man to reform the Chinese Republic. He secured Soviet help and made an alliance with the Chinese Communists. But in March 1926, he broke off relations with the Soviets and began the unification of China. That year, Chiang also planned a great northern expedition, to bring the warlords into line and unify China. In two months, under Chiang's direction, his revolutionary armies swept through south and central China and entered Wuchang. But Hankow and Hanyang were in the hands of the Communist element of Chiang's forces, and so was the arsenal. The Communists' loyalty to Chiang was questionable at best. A great deal of fighting was conducted along the Yangtze River, so the gunboats of the foreign powers were often at work, showing the flag and preventing the Chinese armies from destroying the property of Western traders.

By 1928 Chiang began to push the Communists out of the government. He then had three years to further consolidate his country, before the Japanese bit off their first piece of China, the five northern provinces of Manchuria. At that time, had the Americans but put up a show of force, threatened to take military action, the Japanese would have backed away. But the Americans did not know, and frankly they did not care, for in 1931 the United States was buried deep in the economic depression, and foreign affairs were very low on the list of priorities of the Hoover administration and then of the early Franklin Roosevelt administration.

In 1931 the Chinese in Shanghai and several other Yangtze River cities began a boycott of Japanese goods. This hurt the Japanese quite severely, for their textile industry had made great strides in China sales in the past two years, so in 1931 and 1932 the Japanese were eyeing China proper. The first incident created by the Japanese in Shanghai occurred on January 18, 1932. In front of a Chinese factory in the district of Chapei several ultra-Nationalist Japanese Shinto priests began throwing stones and assaulting Chinese workmen. In the scuffle, two of the priests were seriously hurt. Two days later fifty Japanese came back to the factory and set it afire. The Municipal police came, and the Japanese fought them. Three Japanese and three Chinese policemen were wounded and one of each died. On January 20 the Japanese consul in Shanghai demanded a formal apology from the mayor of Shanghai, reparations, outlawing of anti-Japanese activity, and dissolution of all anti-Japanese organizations.

The Japanese sent marines into Chapei on January 28, 1932, and they clashed with Chinese soldiers. Japanese bombers came over and bombed the Chinese positions. Thousands of Chinese civilians were killed and a quarter of a million refugees streamed out of Chapei that day and the next.

One of the factors that made the Japanese go as slowly as they did after the seizure of Manchuria was the presence of the Western powers and their military contingents in China or nearby. The British maintained their fleet at Singapore, with elements in Hong Kong and at Weihaiwei on the north coast of the Shantung Peninsula. The major American presence was in the Philippines, but half a dozen American gunboats were stationed in Chinese waters, as far up the Yangtze as Chungking.

To the Americans in central China the increased Japanese military activity after the Manchurian takeover was easy to understand. Soon Japanese cruisers, battleships, and carriers began calling at Shanghai, and remaining for long periods of time. A number of other incidents between Chinese and Japanese were arranged by the Japanese, and each one cost the Chinese dearly in prestige and money. Despite boycotts along the Yangtze the Japanese had continued to develop the China market, until they sold more goods than anyone but the Americans. The Shanghai boycott was the most effective and it was renewed each time the Japanese created some problem. Then negotiations would begin, and finally the boycott would be lifted, only to be renewed again a few weeks or months later.

Then, in 1937 the Japanese Kwantung Army of Manchuria struck again in an "incident" at Marco Polo Bridge in north China and the Sino-Japanese* war began. By August Peking had fallen to the Japanese. That month the Japanese army and a major fleet unit attacked Shanghai. The Chinese fought valiantly, but they were outclassed by the Japanese military equipment, including many land-based aircraft and bombers from the Jap-

---

*For the "now" generation, Sino-Japanese means Chinese-Japanese.

anese aircraft carriers, an air element developed largely by Admiral Isoroku Yamamoto.

The American and British naval units in China had a very difficult task, to protect their citizens, and their property, which even the Japanese respected at the moment, and to try to prevent incidents arising from clashes caused by the growing Japanese arrogance, an arrogance born of a new sense of power over Asia. Japanese ship commanders, once the most polite, were likely to edge in on foreign vessels, threatening collision unless the foreigners gave way. Japanese shore parties were likely to be looking for trouble. And since the Allies did not want trouble in China, the Western navy men were ordered to take it easy, go slow, and put up with many insults.

But on December 12, 1937, came an action that not even the most forbearing of peace seekers could accept. On that day the Japanese attacked British and American gunboats on the Yangtze River.

The Japanese army and navy were attacking toward Nanking, the Chinese government capital, 150 miles west of Shanghai on the Yangtze. As the Japanese approached, many Americans and Britons prepared to flee the besieged city, and several gunboats moved along the river to Nanking. The British HMS *Cricket* and HMS *Scarab* came to protect Britons. U.S. Ambassador Nelson Johnson moved out of the American embassy to the safety of the *Luzon,* and that gunboat took him to Hankow, 600 miles farther inland. He went to join the Chinese government, which had also moved upriver. The gunboat *Panay* was ordered to Nanking to stand by and help all Americans who needed it. The American embassy's second secretary, George Atcheson, was given the task of calling on all Americans left in Nanking, and urging them to take sanctuary on board the *Panay*. The Japanese ambassador also urged the Americans to take shelter on the gunboat—a very good indication of what was going on in Japan just then, where the foreign office and the military ministries were almost out of touch with each other.

On Saturday, December 11, the safe exits from Nanking had been reduced to one, the Hsiakuan gate, and the Chinese commander of Nanking told Secretary Atcheson he did not know how much longer he could keep that open in the face of Japanese attack. So Secretary Atcheson went around to the few remaining Americans and told them the time had come. If they wanted to get out of Nanking before the Japanese came in, they had best go board the *Panay* without further ado.

Down on the bund, the long, broad avenue of docks, the Americans found a *Panay* launch waiting. They boarded the *Panay* and Captain James Joseph Hughes, a lieutenant commander in the U.S. Navy, notified the captains of three Standard Oil tankers in the river that he was going upriver, and would escort them if they wished to come along. Of course they wanted to come along. They had passengers of their own, Standard Oil employees and Americans affiliated with the company. The little flotilla almost immediately raised anchor and steamed up the river twelve miles to get away from the Japanese shells that were falling around the city and too often in the river.

The night was quiet, but when dawn came, the Japanese started shelling the river again. A number of Chinese junks were anchored in this area and these were the apparent targets, but some of the Japanese shells were coming a lot closer to the American vessels than they ought to. So Captain Hughes decided to move farther upriver, to get away from the Japanese army forces closing in on Nanking from the west.

As the four ships steamed upriver, they were stopped by a Japanese signalman, who pointed to a field gun trained on the river. The ships stopped, a Japanese lieutenant came aboard the *Panay,* and insisted on being allowed to inspect the ships. In no uncertain terms, Captain Hughes told the lieutenant that this was United States property and he had best get off the deck of *Panay* forthwith. The Japanese lieutenant looked around at the armed American sailors, smiled, bowed, and went away.

Captain Hughes and his four ships sailed upriver. At 11:00 A.M. they reached a point twenty-seven miles above Nanking, the Hohsien cutoff, a good anchorage. There was no sound of gunfire, no indication of any trouble on the shore up here. So the captain ordered the *Panay* anchored, and the three Standard Oil tankers anchored too.

Second Secretary Atcheson used the ship's radio to inform the embassy at Hankow and the U.S. consulate at Shanghai that the *Panay* was in this spot, so that the Japanese could be informed and take care not to attack by mistake. There was not likely to be a mistake, as everyone knew. When the siege of Nanking began, the crew of the American gunboat had painted two huge American flags on the awnings that covered the upper deck. Any airplane pilot could not help but see them from far off. Besides, the *Panay* was flying an enormous ensign from her mizzenmast. There was no possibility of error.

The morning was quiet. It was Sunday so a big noon meal was served, and afterward everyone relaxed. Because of the dictum issued by the secretary of the navy during World War I, and never rescinded, no liquor could be served aboard the *Panay.* Some of the civilians wanted a drink, so boats were lowered and took the civilians over to the tankers which were not bound by naval restrictions. The boats plied back and forth, carrying visitors from one vessel to another. After the fighting died down, the *Panay* would go back downriver to Nanking to check on the safety of the handful of recalcitrant Americans who had refused to leave the city. But this Sunday everybody was going to take it easy.

Then, at 1:35 that afternoon, the bridge watch of the *Panay* reported to the captain that strange aircraft were coming toward the ship from the southwest. Captain Hughes went to the bridge. He saw aircraft strung out in a long line, coming in on the *Panay*. And then three planes began to drop into bombing formation. From the cabins and the wardroom, officers, men, and civilians came to the rail to see what was happening.

Captain Hughes was just about to pay the price for ordering that Japanese army lieutenant off the deck of his ship the day before. The lieutenant, having lost face before his men, had gone back to shore, and reported to his superiors that the ships were loaded with Chinese soldiers, escaping from the trap of Nanking and heading upriver. They must be stopped. The way to stop them was by bombing the ships. The bombing force belonged to the Imperial Japanese Navy's 13th Naval Air Group. So the army headquarters near Nanking got in touch with the navy headquarters, and passed the word. By that time the number of ships involved was reported to be seven. Soon it became ten. So six Japanese dive bombers and six level bombers were sent out to bomb those ships and stop the Chinese army. As they approached the Hohsien cutoff, they saw the four vessels anchored, and a number of small boats moving around between them: obvious indication that the boats were loading Chinese soldiers, said the Japanese air commander. They attacked.

Admiral Yamamoto could be proud of his boys that day. The first bomb hit the *Panay* and the second struck just off to port, causing heavy damage to the ship. The people at the rail were knocked off their feet and half-drowned in the water that spouted across the deck from the near miss. The captain and one junior officer were wounded. The radio mast was down. The three-inch gun in the bow was smashed. Down below the black gang began trying to raise steam. The Americans manned the machine guns and began firing. The bombers kept coming in to bomb. Soon more men were wounded; the fuel lines of the engine room were ruptured, and it became impossible to get up steam.

In twenty minutes the *Panay* began to sink. The only way to move would be to slip anchor and put her into the current of the Yangtze, but if this were done she might well capsize, because, like all the gunboats, she was of shallow draft and extremely topheavy. So the captain decided to abandon ship. The tanker captains started to ground their vessels and get the passengers off before the Japanese turned the ships into flaming pyres.

The men of the *Panay* put their boats over the side, and began moving the personnel and passengers to the shore. During the process the Japanese planes returned and strafed the boats, wounding more men.

Late that afternoon word reached Shanghai that the *Panay* had been sunk, the three Standard Oil tankers had been attacked and run aground, and two British gunboats on the river had been attacked. The Japanese navy and the Japanese government were quick to apologize, and to make amends, and that quickness seemed to quiet the American and British anger. The Japanese admiral in charge of the China force was recalled in disgrace. The Japanese navy apologized abjectly to Ambassador Grew. But when President Roosevelt demanded reparations and complete apology, the affair reached a new level, that of top government. The Japanese stalled, which should have been a warning to the Americans. Finally, they said it had been an accident (which it most certainly was not), but they did pay indemnity of more than $2 million for the loss of the ships and the deaths of two Americans and injuries to seventy-four others.

The Americans and the British knew that the *Panay* bombing was no accident. The whole attitude of the Japanese in China at this point was arrogant and belligerent, representing the Japanese military leaders who by this time controlled the government. From now on the relations of the Americans and the Japanese along the Yangtze would grow worse, as the Japanese won what seemed to be continuing victories in China. Americans on the China station saw the situation clearly and knew very well that the time would come when America and Japan would go to war.

The United States Navy had lost the initiative, the superior striking power. The change had occurred midway in the 1930s. After the Japanese had wrenched Manchuria away from China, the League of Nations condemned Japan and made her an international outlaw. In a flurry she resigned from the League, and thereafter her army-dominated government did not even pay lip service to such international agreements as those controlling naval armament. Secretly, the Japanese began to build dozens of warships, and by 1937 she had the most powerful fleet in the Pacific, far stronger than the American Asiatic Fleet and Pacific Fleet combined. No longer could American saber-rattling prevent the Japanese from doing what they wanted to do.

The thoughtful people in Japan, the naval strategists in particular, knew that Japan's course was virtually suicidal, and in spite of Japan's growing strength, the strategists did not want conflict with the United States, knowing that in the long run they must lose. Thus, although the American Pacific strength did not justify it, when Admiral Henry Yarnell, the commander of the American Asiatic Fleet, spoke, the Japanese listened. After the *Panay* incident, the new Japanese naval commander in China suggested that if foreign warships in Chinese waters would clear their movements with the Japanese, the danger of incidents would be less. Admiral Yarnell minced no words. He told the Japanese admiral to "go to hell."

The State Department shivered. Yarnell's attitude was well known: the only way to deal with the Japanese was from strength, to show them a face of steel at all times and be ready to fight at the drop of a hat. The slightest indication of weakness would be greeted by the Japanese with contempt and with incursions into the rights of the weak.

Yet even with their growing power, the Japanese did not relish a fight with the British, the Americans, the Dutch, and the Chinese all at once. Indeed, by 1937 it had already become apparent to the Japanese army's best strategists that Japan was mired down in China, and that the sensible thing to do was get out quickly. So a strong policy by the Allies in the later 1930s still would have worked wonders. But a strong Allied policy would have had to be accompanied by an arms building program and by the staffing of Asian military establishments with trained men under strong leaders with excellent weapons. None of this was done. Admiral Yarnell would have been happy to serve longer facing the Japanese, but he was relieved. He had caused too many shudders to the diplomats. The junior admiral in charge of the Yangtze River patrol was William A. Glassford, a temporizer who took the view that since the Japanese were in charge, they had to have their way. Yarnell's successor in command of the Asiatic Fleet was Admiral Thomas Hart, who agreed with Yarnell. But by that time—1939—World War II was beginning in Europe, and Washington found it convenient to listen to Glassford and not to Hart. It was a tragic error, but that viewpoint on the Far East was one supported by U.S. Secretary of State Cordell Hull.

There was going to be a war, as every foreigner in Asia knew by 1941. But the Japanese were going to decide where and when. All that remained now was for them to pick the time and place.

CHAPTER 34

America's World War II Begins

American participation in World War II came as a surprise to many Americans. As far as Asia was concerned the American failure to stop the Japanese from seizing Manchuria in 1931 was the key. Japanese leaders later admitted that if the United States had taken a strong stance then, Japan would have backed away. But we equivocated, and thus made it inevitable that the Japanese would move to swallow China in 1937. Again we equivocated, and only in 1940, after the European war had begun, did we begin to take a strong position against Japanese expansion. American cutoff of Japan's oil resources was the immediate reason for the attack on Pearl Harbor that brought declarations of war against America by Germany and Italy, Japan's allies.

And yet, as this chapter shows, the American navy was already at war with the Axis in 1941.

When the war became a reality on both sides of America, the decision as to which enemy must be first addressed with the might of America had to be made. The popular choice was Japan, but Winston Churchill persuaded President Franklin D. Roosevelt to turn the principal effort against Germany. Thus the decision was made to abandon the Philippines and the Dutch East Indies, and to set up the Pacific line of defense at Australia. For that reason no attempt was made to halt the Japanese juggernaut until the summer of 1942.

*   *   *

For Americans the war began on September 3, 1939, the day that Lieutenant Fritz Lemp's *U-30* sank the British liner *Athenia* off the Irish coast
and killed American citizens. In the United States that week no one knew
that this European struggle would be known as World War II, or that
ultimately there would be a war in the Pacific. No one even knew that a
German submarine had sunk the *Athenia;* the Germans denied it and sent
up a very effective smokescreen to conceal Lemp's egregious error, and
for a year convinced at least some Americans that the British had sunk
their own ship in a plot to destroy Hitler's reputation in America. The fact
that this wild propaganda campaign was partly successful is an indication
of the confusion of millions of Americans, and their unwillingness to see
what was happening in Europe, where Hitler was already engaged in his
campaign to exterminate a whole race—the Jews—and to establish a dictatorship over Europe. The climate of 1939 was not the same as that of
1914, when Germany had sympathy in America from millions of new immigrants from the old country. Those immigrants had been totally integrated into American society in the following generation. The American
reluctance to believe the truth of what was happening in Europe in 1939
was occasioned by the American people's revulsion against the last war,
that struggle characterized by President Wilson as a fight to "preserve the
world for democracy." Ultimately the fruits of that victory were lost; the
Americans refused to participate in the League of Nations,* and withdrew
to isolation behind their two oceans, thoroughly disgusted with European
politics.

Americans had watched as the Russians slaughtered their own people
by the millions to establish "the perfect state." They had watched as Benito
Mussolini established his Fascist movement in the name of "state socialism"—which indicated it was for the benefit of the people, and then turned
it into a dictatorship and vehicle for conquest of part of Africa while Britain,
France, and the League of Nations looked on, paralyzed. They had watched
as Spain was rent by civil war, in which major unofficial protagonists were
the USSR on one side and Germany and Italy on the other, and they had
seen the Fascist side win victory.

The shadow of the Soviet Union loomed large. The essential disloyalty
of the American Communist movement to the United States was proved
a hundred times in the years between the wars, as the American Com-

---

*Some scholars still hold that the failure of the League of Nations as the inter-
national peacekeeper it was supposed to be was the fault of the United States for
not joining. But the abysmal record of the United Nations, to which the United
States did adhere through thick and thin, ought to lay that ghost.

munists aped the Soviet line. But the radical movement in America, immeasurably strengthened by the dreadful economic strictures of the Great Depression, allowed itself to be swayed by the Communists, in some cases (notably among labor unions) to be captured by them.

Across the Pacific the Japanese drive for empire became noticeable to Americans with the virtual annexation of Manchuria—but there were some Americans who fooled themselves into believing that "Manchukuo" was, as the Japanese insisted, an "independent state." This was a convenient attitude, making it possible to ignore all the realities of Asia. Orientals were not popular in America anyhow, so when China was attacked again in 1937 Americans followed their government in a general wringing of hands.

The brave, vigorous, and often pathetic defense of the Chinese came as a surprise to the world, and gradually began to attract American sympathy. The most famous war picture of the time was that of a Chinese baby sitting, crying, in the bomb-wrecked Shanghai railroad station, destruction and death all around him. At a glance it told the story of China and the horror of war.

Of course, there were Americans who started to fight very early in this war, just as there had been idealistic Americans who went to Spain to fight for the Republic in the International Brigade. The Eagle Squadron of the Royal Air Force was made up of Americans who wanted to shoot down Hitler. The Flying Tigers under Claire Chennault went to China, some of them as mercenaries, some of them because they believed in fighting aggression.

But generally speaking, in the late 1930s as the separate wars in Europe and Asia raged on both sides of them, Americans wanted above all to stay out of the conflicts. A number of peace organizations began and prospered, most important of them the America First organization, whose membership held views which ranged from those of Senator Burton K. Wheeler, with his "pox on everyone's house" attitude, to those of Charles A. Lindbergh, who had outright praise for the Germans. In between were millions of Americans whose major concern was that the nation be kept out of foreign wars.

That concept, of course, was very old. George Washington warned his fellow Americans against foreign entanglements, and that warning had long dominated American foreign policy outside the Western Hemisphere, which a succession of U.S. administrations had regarded as the particular American bailiwick. As noted, this concern had two edges: on the one hand it had certainly prevented European powers from taking over various Latin American states after the fall of the Spanish empire. On the other hand, it had been the reason prompting United States intervention in the affairs of various Latin states, sometimes for hardly hidden commercial motives, but more often because of the American political evangelical motif.

After Nazi Germany and democratic Europe went to war, a new element crept into American thinking, most certainly into that of the White House. What if Hitler conquered Europe? What would that mean to the United States?

Hitler did conquer continental Europe in the spring of 1940. He set about then to conquer Britain, the last bastion to hold out. He failed in the air Battle of Britain and abandoned the invasion of England, which had been all set to go that fall. Hitler's attention then was turned to destroying England by starving her out—through the U-boat campaign against shipping. And by the spring of 1941, that campaign was so successful that it looked as though Hitler had a good chance of destroying Britain.

That is when President Roosevelt really became concerned. Britain's desperation was apparent when she asked for fifty obsolete American destroyers, to protect convoys from submarine attack. America's response was apparent when she gave the destroyers in exchange for lease on British territory as bases (Bermuda), and when the Lend-Lease program of long-term financial aid to Britain was begun. Obviously this was support of the British, but it was not a military adventure.

The military excursions, however, began soon.

Occasionally, after 1939, an American ship had been stopped or shelled or even sunk by a U-boat. But generally speaking, Hitler was so anxious to keep the United States from entering the war on Britain's side that he bent over backward not to antagonize the Americans. By the spring of 1941, however, the United States had already been drawn into military excursions, which took the form of United States naval patrols in neutral waters to prevent submarine attacks. Then, in April 1941, the USS *Niblack* was on destroyer patrol off Iceland when she received an SOS from the Dutch freighter *Saleier.* She rushed to the scene, saw the U-boat which had just torpedoed the *Saleier,* and she attacked it and dropped depth charges. The U-boat got away and the *Niblack* rescued the survivors of the *Saleier.* The rescue was fine charitable work. The depth charges were an act of war.

The U.S. public was not informed of this act or of the naval policy, straight from the White House, that had dictated it.

The next move came on June 9, 1941, when the Germans acted. A U-boat sank the U.S. freighter *Robin Moor* although she was clearly flying the U.S. flag. She was in mid-Atlantic, and the Germans had declared the whole Atlantic a war zone.

In July, American warships ventured ever farther into that war zone, patrolling and even convoying British merchantmen. One day the battleship *Texas* was patrolling near Greenland when she was discovered by the *U-*

203. The captain would very much have liked to sink her. He got her in his sights, and wondered if he dared. The issue—what would Admiral Dönitz say—was resolved when the *Texas* turned away and the chance was lost.

The captain of the *Texas* knew what was happening. He turned on purpose and dispatched two destroyers to sink the submarine. They did not get close, but the principle was established: Sight submarine, sink same.

On September 4, 1941, the USS *Greer* engaged a submarine near Iceland. The *Greer* was warned by a British flying boat, which added the dimension of British-American cooperation to the incident. The *Greer* dropped depth charges and the U-boat fired a torpedo. Both missed.

September 14. The USS *Truxton* encountered a U-boat. The destroyer attacked. The U-boat dived and got away.

October 16, the USS *Kearny* and four other American destroyers came down from Iceland to help a British convoy under attack by a German U-boat wolf pack. The *Kearny* was hit by a torpedo and eleven American sailors were killed and twenty-four wounded. Here was an absolute encounter, an act of war. The American people heard little of it. But the United States Navy was at war with Germany, and the Germans knew it and had responded.

On October 31 the destroyer *Reuben James* was even farther afield, escorting British ships off Ireland. She was torpedoed by a U-boat. This sinking was a tragedy. The *Reuben James* sank with all but forty-five members of her crew. Once again, most of the facts were suppressed by the U.S. Navy. President Roosevelt was actually at war, but he knew the nation was not yet ready for a declaration.

Still, here was a definite military excursion, a whole series of them—evidence of a policy of assisting the British in their war against the U-boats. How much longer could this policy be kept from the American people?

The answer came on December 7, 1941.

CHAPTER 35

Hitler First

Until December 7, 1941, Americans had been of two minds about the events in Europe and those in the Pacific. Japan had sacrificed whatever sympathy she had in America by a long succession of annoying actions. She had begun with such minor irritations as confiscating the cameras of tourists and arresting them for "espionage" when they were doing no more than taking tourist pictures. She had then moved to control the foreign correspondents by charging them with espionage offenses anytime they tried to get at some aspect of Japanese life that the army held sacrosanct. American sympathy was very much with the Chinese and it grew as Madame Chiang Kai-shek's propaganda campaign swung into high gear. But this was not tantamount to American belligerence.

Most Americans did not want to go to war with Japan.

The same was true in Europe. President Franklin Roosevelt saw the ultimate danger to America of a world controlled by Hitler and his allies, Japan and Italy. Most Americans did not. The America First Committee and like organizations were eminently respectable. Many college students joined anti-war organizations. One did not have to like or respect Hitler to feel that the United States should remain free from European problems. The Neutrality Patrol of 1940 was an attempt by the United States to stay unentangled. But it did not succeed very well, particularly when President Roosevelt began leaning very strongly toward Britain. The trading of fifty overage destroyers for American bases in the Atlantic was one aspect. Another was lend-lease, a sort of emergency loan for the British in their hour of need. Some Americans joined the Canadian army. Some joined the Royal Air

Force. Some went to Africa with Red Cross and Friends ambulance services to show their adherence to a free way of life as opposed to totalitarianism. On December 5, 1941, the nation was really quite badly split in a way that it would not be again until the Vietnam War, three decades later.

*   *   *

When war came to the United States on December 7, 1941, the initial American reaction was to fight the Japanese. They were the ones who had attacked American territory (Pearl Harbor), sunk American ships, and snuffed out American lives in what Americans regarded as the most treacherous strike in history. They did not realize that the sneak attack was an accepted Japanese practice; the samurai had been using it on one another for a thousand years before they unleashed it against the Russians at Port Arthur in 1904. "Win first, fight later" was an old Japanese proverb. What the Japanese did not understand was that their sneak attack had instantly unified a very badly disunited America and created a powerful war spirit.

Americans were puzzled, then, when almost immediately the major U.S. war effort was turned toward Europe. Nor could the people then be told the reason: the fear that Germany was winning the war. As for the Pacific, the Japanese had made their enormous gains in a few weeks. The worst might happen, and all the European colonies in the Pacific might be lost. But the recovery of them would have to wait. The immediate problem—Prime Minister Churchill brought a high-level delegation to America to make the point—was the U-boat menace. Soon enough the Americans learned of this menace. The Germans dispatched a handful of submarines against the East Coast of the United States in January 1942, and followed them with more as they became available; it was a spotty process because Hitler was demanding major U-boat effort in the Mediterranean. That handful of submarines arrived off the American coast and found no convoys, no air defenses, no naval defenses. The fact was that although the United States Navy had been given every access to the British antisubmarine warfare operations for two years, the American naval leaders were contemptuous of the convoy system; they had virtually no antisubmarine patrol aircraft and no antisubmarine patrol vessels. For the U-boat commanders it was like fishing in a stocked lake, no game wardens, no limit. After a few weeks of wallowing in plenty of victims, they concentrated on tankers, and in three months sank so many that oil was actually running up the beaches around Cape Hatteras and threatening to soil the bathers along the Florida coast. The big oil companies lost so many tankers that they were predicting a freezing winter for New England, and the British feared their North Africa war against the Germans would come to a sudden halt for lack of fuel.

That is why the U.S. Navy's major emphasis was on the Atlantic in those early months. That is why the Americans fighting in the Philippines could not be reinforced or saved, why the gallant U.S. Asiatic Fleet was nitpicked to destruction in the Philippines and the Dutch East Indies, and why only a handful of strikes were made by American carriers against Japanese-held islands. Then, in April 1942, the spectacular but militarily, tactically, and strategically debatable B-25 bomber raid against Japan was staged by Lieutenant Colonel Jimmy Doolittle from one of Admiral Halsey's carriers. That raid did indeed help the morale of an American people who were badly confused by their government's apparent inability to fight the war. That was the reason the raid was authorized by President Roosevelt, who was ever alive to the fluctuations and importance of public opinion. In that sense the Doolittle raid was an enormous success. But at what cost! Generalissimo Chiang Kai-shek had been against the grandstand gesture from the start. It would prompt the Japanese to fury against the Chinese people, he said, because Doolittle's fliers were to land in China after bombing Japan, and the Japanese would surely retaliate. And that is precisely what happened; not one of the aircraft survived, but many Doolittle fliers parachuted or crash-landed in China. The Japanese then detached an entire army corps to comb the areas of the landings, destroy the airfields, and take vengeance against the handful of Doolittle raiders they caught and the Chinese people who had helped them. Chiang's government estimated that the Doolittle raid cost 250,000 Chinese lives. There was the balance: 250,000 Chinese lives against American morale.

The reason for the fury was General Hideki Tojo's ego; the Japanese prime minister had promised the people of Japan that they would never be bombed, and they had been. No matter how he shouted that the raid had been a fluke, they had been bombed. The Japanese people had been shown a vision of the future, and it was not a happy one. Thus came the immediate and vicious retribution. Militarily, the raid was all a tempest in a teapot, not affecting the war outcome a whit. The Doolittle raid did not, in fact, even prompt the Japanese to perfect their air defenses.

In the spring of 1942 the Japanese war machine drove ahead like an unstoppable juggernaut, reaching the South Pacific, halting only when the inertia expired at New Guinea. With a few more troops they could have invaded Australia and New Zealand and all the islands around. When the men of the Japanese Imperial General Headquarters saw the way the Japanese army cut through the Allies in the Philippines and Malaya and the Dutch East Indies like a knife through cheese, their egos became overblown, and they decided to forge on. For May an invasion of Port Moresby was planned, plus establishment of air bases in the Solomon Islands that would control Australian airspace and prevent the Americans from launching a counterattack, as they had indicated they would do by bringing General Douglas MacArthur out of the besieged Philippines to command all American forces in the South Pacific.

That spring, the major American effort was devoted to building ships—merchant ships, carriers, and submarines for the Pacific, destroyers and the new destroyer escorts for the Atlantic—and aircraft, thousands of aircraft for both wars. The most serious problem was manpower: how to train an American army of millions to be prepared to strike a major blow against Hitler, and soon? Considering the fact that American military maneuvers of just a year earlier had been conducted by artillerymen with tree trunks as field pieces, machine-gunners with branches as machine guns, infantrymen with sacks of Bull Durham tobacco as grenades, and fliers dropping flour-sack "bombs," the task of arming and training that army was staggering. Lord Ismay, the British chief of staff, came to see the Americans train and snorted that they would never stand up to a German army. But to make them stand up was the task, and that is where the effort was directed. At first the Americans and British talked about a 1942 drive for a second front across the English Channel. Then they sobered and began talking about 1943. But something had to be done in 1942, to encourage a beleaguered Soviet Union to hold out on the eastern front, and to put a crimp in Hitler's North Africa victories. So the Americans and the British agreed on a fall North African offensive in which the Americans would land in French North Africa and join up with the British fighting German Field Marshal Rommel. American troops were trained at home to a certain degree of proficiency, ready to go to the British isles for more training. In Britain they would free the better-trained British troops for battle. Also, as planes became available and fliers trained, they were shipped to Britain to assist in the major air war against the Germans. The contributions at sea by the U.S. Navy and in the air by the U.S. Army Air Forces were the first effective acts of the Americans in the war against Hitler.

In the Pacific, the Japanese pursued their timetable. They launched the invasion of Port Moresby and the southern Solomons in May, but were met by two American carrier task forces. In this Coral Sea Battle the Americans lost one carrier (the *Lexington),* which they could ill afford to lose, the Japanese lost one light carrier and had two big carriers damaged, and the fight was really a toss-up. The truly important factors were that the Port Moresby invasion was scrapped, a Japanese seaplane base at Tulagi (in the Solomon Islands) was wrecked, and the carriers *Shokaku* and *Zuikaku* were not going to be available to Admiral Yamamoto. Yamamoto, now commander of the Japanese Combined Fleet, planned a new strike to take Midway Island as a forward Pacific base for an attack on Hawaii, to establish Aleutian Island bases for a future attack on the U.S. mainland, and to destroy the U.S. Pacific Fleet carriers, which had been missed by the timidity of Admiral Nagumo, commanding the Japanese attack force. It was a very ambitious plan. And it failed utterly. The Americans scored a triumph of intelligence (breaking the Japanese naval codes) and daring which extended from the level of a whole squadron of pilots who sacrificed themselves, attacking the Japanese carriers in obsolete torpedo bombers, to the American high command which put its three Pacific carriers at risk. When the Midway Island battle was over, the Japanese fleet limped back to Japan without four precious carriers, without a base on Midway, and with a base in the Aleutians so small and extended that it could not be satisfactorily resupplied. As quickly as possible, the whole enterprise was abandoned.

July 1942. The Americans prepared feverishly for the coming invasion of North Africa. In Washington there was little time for worry about the Pacific. But then, Admiral Ernest J. King, the chief of the American navy, noticed one day that the Japanese were building an air base on Guadalcanal Island. Immediately he saw what it meant: the Japanese attempt to take control of the Australian airspace. It had to be stopped.

The other members of the joint chiefs of staff were inclined to scoff. Not now, they said, we are too busy. But King persisted. The building of that air base had to be stopped at any cost. And he demanded an immediate invasion of Guadalcanal Island.

The others, and this included General MacArthur and Admiral Robert Ghormley, the chief of naval operations in the South Pacific for Admiral Chester Nimitz in Hawaii, said that it was impossible. King said: Do it.

And so Guadalcanal was invaded by the U.S. Marines, who had a very bad time of it as the Japanese counterattacked. Major Lewis Edson, trained so well in Nicaragua, was one of the brave defenders here. But there were thousands of others, on the ground and in the air and on the sea. The Japanese had air superiority and fleet superiority. They sank dozens of American warships, but they lost almost as many themselves in the end; and while the Americans were furiously building ships in the United States at some 300 shipyards, there were only half a dozen yards in Japan that could turn out a naval vessel, and these were already desperately short of materials.

But, more important than anything else, the Americans held Guadalcanal through bravery and sacrifice until the material forces could come creeping along. The Japanese miscalculated from the beginning, sending first a battalion to oppose the Americans, then, when it was swallowed up, sending only slightly larger forces, until finally they had two divisions on the island. But by then it was hopeless. The Americans had won air superiority, the naval situation was a toss-up, and at the end of 1942 the Japanese evacuated Guadalcanal. They did it very skillfully—but they evacuated, and that meant Admiral King had his way. For the next two years the Americans pushed the Japanese back in the South Pacific with scarcely a hiatus, stranding hundreds of thousands of Japanese troops on little islands and big ones by the process of island hopping, one of the best strategic inventions that the Joint Chiefs ever devised. There would be many points at which the experts suggested that the war had changed. Was it at Guadalcanal? Was it the capture of Saipan in 1944, breaking the inner ring of empire and causing the fall of the Tojo government? Japanese and American historians have placed the change point here and there. But for the Japanese people, who had developed a sort of sixth sense to augment the sparse flow of truthful information from their government about the progress of the war, the fall of Guadalcanal was the point at which they knew the war had changed. No longer were the Japanese troops master of all they surveyed. The Pacific war had become for Japan a desperate enterprise.

CHAPTER 36

The Invasion of Europe

The reason for the slow movement of America to fight back against the Axis powers was lack of American preparation in the early months of the European war. In the early months of 1942 the Americans were playing "catch-up." No one knew this better than General George C. Marshall, commander of the U.S. Army.

It had to be that way. The fact was that the American military machine was infantile in the spring of 1942. The navy had no shore defenses against German U-boats. In the North Carolina maneuvers of 1941 soldiers were using sticks for machine guns and large saplings for 37-mm antitank guns. In fact, the real 37-mm antitank guns were already outmoded, although the United States was building them as rapidly as possible. Soon enough, in North Africa, the Americans would begin to learn how much they had to learn about war. As noted here, in the Battle of Kasserine Pass the Americans took a dreadful beating because of inexperience and inferior weapons. The American tanks were never in this war equivalent to those of the Germans or the Russians. The American bazooka (rocket launcher) was only about half the size of the German.

Where the Americans excelled was in aircraft and artillery. The B-17 and the B-29 were the best long-range bombers. The B-24 was a superb antisubmarine craft. The American carrier planes of wartime manufacture were the best in the world. And although the Germans had the finest single piece of artillery, the 88-mm gun, the American 105- and 144-mm howitzers and guns were the most formidable artillery, and the Americans knew how to use them.

*   *   *

November 1942. In the Pacific, the battle for Guadalcanal was coming to an end, even though the United States had been able to supply General MacArthur and Admiral Nimitz with only a minuscule part of the men and supplies they needed. In New Guinea, MacArthur fought with the Australians at his point; Aussies and New Zealanders came to the Solomons, and with U.S. Army and marine troops held the Japanese and pushed them back. A mixed air force and navy of Australians, New Zealanders, and Americans fought on the seas.

The Americans, typified by "Big Red One," the U.S. Army 1st Division, were going to fight the enemy in North Africa: in Algeria, Morocco, Tunisia. The French had resisted German advances here, and then the resistance had ended. But where French resistance ended, German attack began. The Americans learned how not to fight an armored battle at Kasserine Pass. The Americans were simply too green to understand why.

But the Germans knew. In November Colonel General Jürgen von Arnim's army had been attacking the American forces in Tunisia with great success. The U.S. 168th Infantry Regiment lost about 600 prisoners to the Germans in these battles. From questioning American troops, General von Arnim learned that they were not very well trained and their morale was good but not strong. Further, and this was most important to the Germans, the Americans were badly led by their officers. The American armored troops chattered over their radios so much that the Germans had no difficulty in figuring out what they were up to. The American artillery and tanks seemed to be very timid and more than once fired on their own men. The British and French officers referred to the Americans as "our Italians," and the Germans knew what they meant: the Germans had been fighting with badly led and badly armed Italians for two long years.

With this information in hand, Field Marshal Alfred Kesselring, the commander of all German forces in Italy and North Africa, decided to attack the Americans and wipe them out. The place chosen was Kasserine Pass, a narrow defile that encased the road from Sbeitla to Feriana. The Americans were on the northwest side, protecting the flank of General Keith Anderson's British army. Two German forces would do the job; Field Marshal Erwin Rommel's Afrika Korps would attack the Americans to the south at Gafsa and General von Arnim would attack at Sbeitla. Once they had gone through the narrow mountain passes to the east, the two German armored divisions making the attack would sweep north toward the port of Bône. This move would remove a growing threat to the Afrika Korps flank, and cut off General Sir Keith Anderson's First British Army in the north.

On February 12, General Dwight D. Eisenhower, commander of American forces in North Africa, went up front to see the American positions in this area of Tunisia. He found Major General Lloyd Fredendall's command post in a remote canyon eighty miles behind the front. Fredendall was commander of II Corps, the major American offensive command. Eisenhower did not like what he saw: Fredendall was way too far back from the front. Eisenhower also learned of an argument between an American intelligence officer and the British intelligence officer, who had access to secret messages decoded from the German dispatches. The British officer tried to convince the American that a German attack was coming and it would be in the north, not through Gafsa, as the American insisted. The Briton was unable to shake the American's confidence.

Later that day Eisenhower was even more appalled. General Fredendall's men had done nothing to set up minefields or other defenses in the passes. They had not dug any defensive positions, although they had been there two days. They would do that the next day, they said. Eisenhower continued to look around. The Germans, he noted, would have built defenses within two hours of taking a position. He saw that the Americans were spread out all over the area, because General Fredendall had not left his command post, but had disposed his troops from maps laid out on the floor of the operations office. The dispositions made no sense in terms of the terrain. Eighty miles is a long way.

That night the front was quiet. Up on the left of the American positions were the heights at Lessouda. Off to the right were the mountains called the Djebel Ksaira. Up there were the men of General Orlando Ward's 1st Armored Division, the best American troops available. They were crouched down in their foxholes, trying to get some sleep in the chill night.

The next morning was Saturday, February 14, Saint Valentine's day.

At 4:00 on the morning of Saint Valentine's day, the observers at the forward observation post of the 1st Battalion of the 1st Armored Division climbed up to the top of Djebel Lessouda and trained their binoculars across the Faid Pass. But the wind was blowing, and sand hung in the air, obscuring the view, so they could see virtually nothing. A few minutes later the observers heard something: the rumble of artillery fire. It was coming from the road between Faid and Lessouda.

The Germans were attacking. Two battle groups of the German 10th Panzer Division were advancing on the U.S. 1st Armored Division's Combat Command A. That meant sixty-ton Tiger tanks, and they were already moving through Faid Pass. The American infantrymen in their foxholes watched them come and the American artillerymen with them watched too. But what could they do against these monsters with their 88-mm guns? The Americans began falling back.

"The Tigers are coming," somebody shouted, and the rout began.

The American area commander, Lieutenant Colonel John Waters, ordered fifteen of his tanks to move forward. And what were these tanks? They were the American Honey tanks, too tall for their breadth, and mounting only one 37-mm gun. How could they stand up against the German tanks with 88-mm and 75-mm guns?

They could not. That was the answer. One by one the American tanks were knocked out. They fired, but their 37-mm shells bounced off the German Mark IV and Tiger tanks. Not one American tank did any damage to a German tank.

Then the Germans added a new dimension. They brought in the Luftwaffe. Dozens of Messerschmitt fighter planes appeared, machine guns snarling and cannon cracking, as they shot up the American rear lines. Only four American planes appeared, and they were soon routed.

Colonel Waters looked down and saw Germans in front and on the flank. He began moving up the hill with his command post, in a jeep and a halftrack. Higher up, he looked down again. Germans were all around; he counted sixty tanks below.

It was five hours after the beginning of the German attack before General McQuillan, commander of Combat Command A, ordered the 2nd Battalion of the 1st Armored Regiment to attack. Almost immediately Colonel Hightower discovered that he was outnumbered and outclassed. He radioed back to McQuillan that he could slow the Germans but he could not hold them.

The American Sherman tanks moved into action, firing their 75-mm guns. But the Germans knew the Sherman tank's weakness. One shot glancing off the rear sprocket of the tank would turn it into a fiery furnace. The tank's armor was very thin and it burned gasoline, not diesel fuel. The Americans knew too; they called the Sherman "the Ronson," which was the name of a general issue cigarette lighter.

One after another the Sherman tanks were hit and blew up or blazed up into infernos. The five-man crews scrambled out and ran, followed by machine-gun fire from the Germans.

Hightower of the armored battalion fought on, but not all his men did. A reconnaissance company of 100 men surrendered en masse. The artillerymen ran back across the desert not even bothering to destroy the firing pins of their guns. That was the ultimate sin of an artilleryman. The artillerymen rushed into the position of the 168th Infantry.

"The Germans are coming," they shouted, and ran straight through. Officers tried to stop them with drawn pistols, but the men paid no attention. They were panic-stricken and they ran.

Lieutenant Colonel Drake, commander of the 168th, picked up the field phone and told General McQuillan that his men had panicked. McQuillan did not believe it.

Up on the heights, Colonel Waters decided it was time to try to break out. He had seen Colonel Hightower's unit destroyed. He wrote a note to McQuillan. He was going to move as soon as darkness fell, he said. One of his men volunteered to take the message, but half an hour later he appeared, blood streaming down his side. He had been shot by one of the trigger-happy American soldiers.

Down below, on the road, the Germans were sending out patrols to look for American survivors. The Arabs were helping them—having seen the two armies and chosen what they thought to be the winning side.

Down there, Colonel Hightower's tank, already hit three times, was hit again, and the crew abandoned it just before it blew up. They hitched a ride back to the command post. Hightower had just seven tanks left out of an original fifty-one. His battalion had been wiped out.

Up on the hill, Colonel Waters heard footsteps. He turned around to face two Arabs and seven men with the peaked caps of the Wehrmacht on their heads. They were pointing machine pistols at him. It was all over for Colonel Waters.

Down below, the 168th Infantry was surrounded. Major Robert Moore's 2nd Battalion was the last to retreat, and as they went through the night they passed through German infantry and artillery positions. Six hundred men set out to make it through the lines. Eighteen of them made it.

Colonel Drake had set out with 1,000 men to try to make it back to the American lines. They passed through the German lines. They did not make it. Drake refused three times to surrender, but finally a command car pulled up alongside and an officer said to get in. There was nothing else to do. When he got to the headquarters, he was saluted by a German general. "I want to compliment you on your command for the splendid fight. It was a hopeless thing from the start. . . ."

Indeed it had been. Back at McQuillan's Combat Command A headquarters they counted up the losses. Colonel Drake's 168th Infantry had lost 2,728 men and 139 officers. McQuillan had lost 52 officers and 1,526 men. And down in Kasserine Pass lay forty-four tanks, fifty-nine halftracks, twenty-six artillery pieces, and twenty trucks all abandoned by their American crews, most of them burning.

The battle was just beginning. Before it was over General Fredendall had lost 6,000 men and his command. It was true: the Americans had been very badly commanded. And up to command II Corps came Lieutenant General George S. Patton, Jr. So, the learning process had begun, and the sorting out of the fighters from the barracks soldiers.

The next spring, U.S. General Omar Bradley was leading the Americans of II Corps to join the British 8th Army in Tunisia and capture the cities of Tunis (British) and Bizerte (Americans).

From the outset, friction between the British and the Americans was a serious problem. Could anyone expect it to be otherwise? The Americans insisted on having overall command of the new invasion, and Prime Minister Winston Churchill was prescient enough to know that it had to be this way, although nearly every military man in Britain cavilled at the thought. So General Dwight D. Eisenhower was made commander. The British regarded him as a paper shuffler, an administrator who knew nothing about fighting troops. The British took the position that they had been fighting the war for three years, and knew how to beat the Germans. The Americans took the view that the British were far too timid, and not properly respectful of their American allies.

This last was certainly true, the British commanders did not think much of the Americans. Perhaps the best judges were the Germans, who did not think much of the Americans at the beginning either.

After Kasserine Pass the Germans tried to launch a propaganda campaign based on the idea that the American soldier fought only for money. *That* was a mistake that was corrected before the African campaign ended. Still, the German ideal of a fighting man on the American side was Patton, the flamboyant armored commander, who began the war in North Africa but was shifted to planning for the next phase of fighting, the invasion of Sicily. Patton did possess a lot of qualities the Germans respected. He was hard as nails (on the surface, at least; but he used to say his prayers every night). He was fearless and even brash. He struck hard and fast. And he also had a very well developed feeling for the use of troops.

July 1943. The Sicilian invasion. Patton led the Americans, angry all the way because he figured the British were upstaging him and using the American force to protect their flank, while they got all the glory. To be fair to British General Bernard Montgomery, it was not quite that: the British knew and trusted themselves; they did not know and did not much trust the Americans. So Patton hurried along and captured Gela and raced the British to the end of Sicily. The competition hurried the war along and Sicily was secured with the fall of Messina in mid-August.

Patton, the new American caesar, blotted his copybook in Sicily and very nearly got himself cashiered from the battlefront for mistreating wounded American servicemen. As a general who fought the war, flitting about, mostly behind the lines, he simply did not understand what it meant to be under shell fire for long periods of time, and the words *combat fatigue* and *shell shock* to Patton meant cowardice and malingering. He was dead wrong, and his abuse of two soldiers caught up with him. Eisenhower put a stopper on his career right there. Patton could be used in the future and would be, but never as more than the commander of a field army; he would have no advance in the world of command that was shaping up in this war.

*　　　*　　　*

Sicily won, the Americans and British turned their attention to Italy in the hope that they could land at Salerno, near Naples, and roll the Germans back to the Alps. But Hitler had other ideas; he was going to contest the attack on the underbelly of Europe every foot of the way. So what looked like an easy route to Rome bogged down. Through some very bad planning the Americans failed to take Cassino, ended up by uselessly destroying the old monastery there, which will never be forgotten nor forgiven, and made a terrible mess of crossing the Rapido River, an enterprise that cost General Mark Clark, the overall American commander, the respect of the 36th Division (Texas National Guard), which suffered enormous casualties; ultimately it also cost him his chance to rise to become army chief of staff.

The Allies landed again, at Anzio and very nearly got knocked out there, but recovered and fought on. The Italian campaign was notable for disputes between American and British commanders, for a mouselike advance, and for one frustration after another. Paratroopers, who found they were thrown into the lines to fight as ordinary infantry (a skill for which they had not been trained), believed it was because somebody up there did not like them, but the fact was that the Allies got themselves into so much trouble in the Italian campaign that several times they found themselves in desperate situations where anybody who could move had to be thrown in to stop the ferocious German counterattacks. It was lucky for the Americans that they had with them the 100th Infantry Battalion, and later the 442nd Regimental Combat Team—the Japanese-American Nisei, volunteers to a man, who had come from Hawaii and the West to fight their country's battles, even if a lot of people in their country did not believe the "Japs" were real Americans. The Nisei fought like bulls, and any Nisei soldier who did not have three or four Purple Hearts was plain lucky.

The Western Allies had argued with the Russians that Africa, Sicily, and Italy were all the "second front," which Stalin had urged since the German invasion of Russia in June 1941. But Stalin was not satisfied, and he never would be satisfied until the Allies took a shot at Fortress Europe across the English Channel. That had been the British-American plan from the beginning, once called Operation Roundup.

The realities of the difficulties of a cross-Channel invasion had caused a postponement of the plan from 1942 to 1943 and then to the spring of 1944. By this time the Americans had plenty of soldiers, and some of them were very well trained. The 1st Division had been in battle in North Africa and Sicily. So had the 9th, and the 2nd Armored Division, the 82nd Airborne Division, and a number of other units. Some, like the 1st Armored Division, were bogged down in Italy. ("Bogged down" became a sort of general watchword in Italy, and was celebrated by *Yank* magazine's cartoonist Bill Mauldin's drawings of a pair of bewhiskered, bedraggled, and bemused GIs marching along in the mud or the dust.)

In England were some of the other American divisions that had fought in Africa and Sicily. They would be used along with the untried 4th Division, the 101st Airborne Division, and the 29th Division to assault the Normandy beachhead in May 1944.

By the early months of 1944, the war at sea had really been won by the Allies. The U-boats, once the hunters, were now as much the hunted. Lucky indeed was the U-boat captain who could come back to the French ports flying two or three pennants to indicate sunken ships. The loss ratio of submarines to ships sunk was going up, up, up; Dönitz was building more submarines than ever before, but more were being sunk. Most of the old tried-and-true U-boat captains had either been promoted out of danger, or were dead or captives of the Allies. New inventions kept coming on both sides: radar and sonar, long-range antisubmarine air patrol, the escort carrier, the Lear Light, the Hedgehog, and the radio direction finder for the Allies; the schnorkel, radar, and the homing torpedo for the Germans. But the threat of the U-boat diminished steadily, the sinkings were now counted in thousands of tons per month, not hundreds of thousands.

The buildup for the cross-Channel invasion continued in England until it is a wonder the British isles did not sink under the weight of men and matériel. Indeed, the invasion came at just the right time: there were so many Americans in Britain that life was growing most uncomfortable for the home folks.

June 1944. The invasion of Fortress Europe could not be managed in May, as had been hoped, because of a shortage of shipping. But it was brought off, after a false start, on June 6, and the luck of the Allies held; over 1,000 ships crossed the Channel and got a tentative lodging on the shore between spring storms. As the ships crossed the Channel, the men learned of the Allied capture of Rome. Everyone cheered, although exactly what it meant was not certain, for the Germans had not quit but were planning more defenses in northern Italy.

In Normandy, the Utah Beach landing was, as the British called such things, "a piece of cake." The Omaha Beach landing was a potential disaster, caused by poor intelligence and errors in landing, errors in air bombardment, and all sorts of other errors. But the errors, in a sense, canceled one another out; the American airborne troops were scattered all over the area and thus confused the Germans.

The British landing around Caen, the capital of Normandy, drew the preponderance of German armor, because the Germans knew and respected Montgomery, and they did not know nor much respect the Amer-

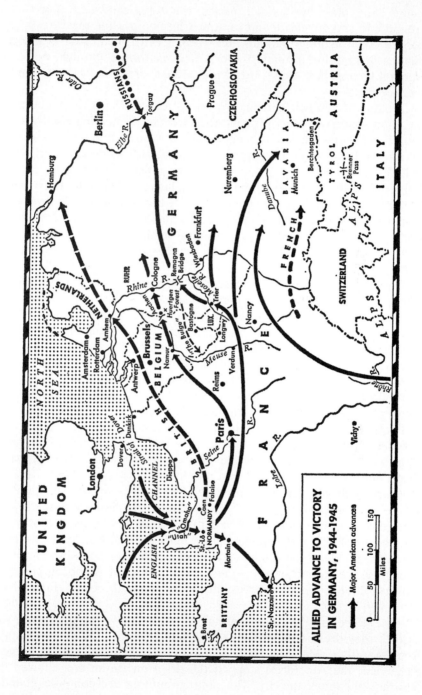

ALLIED ADVANCE TO VICTORY
IN GERMANY, 1944-1945

➤ Major American advances

0   50   100   150
Miles

icans. Thus, after the initial troubles, the Americans were able to run around end and penetrate and capture Cherbourg while the British were bogged down fighting German tanks near Caen. Then, after nearly two months fighting in Normandy, the Americans broke through, delivered General George S. Patton's 3rd Army to the shore, and Patton began the race for Paris.

In August, another landing, not really necessary as it turned out, was staged in southern France. It gave the Germans something else to worry about, and these Americans headed east, toward southern Germany.

But the big action was up north, where the Allies liberated Paris, after waiting for the French to come and do the official liberating for reasons of French pride. They then liberated Belgium and Holland. There was a certain difficulty in these lowlands, when the big airdrop of Allied airborne armies got into trouble trying to outflank the Germans. The plan did not work, and the war settled down to autumn weather and hard fighting. The U.S. 1st Army entered Germany in September at Eupen, and the armored troops came across near Trier.

They moved ahead. The war seemed very nearly over, but the Allies forgot the adage of the old Japanese general who warned, "When you have won a major victory it is time to tighten your helmet straps." Instead of tightening up their helmet straps, the Americans in the French-Belgian border area more or less adjourned the war for Christmas, 1944. They forgot to consult with the Germans. And that was the moment at which Hitler struck with all the power left in his western reserves. General Karl von Rundstedt hit the thin American lines in the Belgium and Luxembourg areas, places where so many men had died in the 1914–18 war. More men died now in the snows. A whole raw American division, the 106th, was completely disorganized and torn to pieces. It actually had no business being where it was in the front lines. But generals did like their Christmas cheer, and many of them were in London when the Nazis hit.

Fortunately for American prestige, and for the war effort, the 82nd Airborne Division was on hand, and once again the paratroopers were pressed into service as ordinary infantry. Death and heroism, that is the story of the Battle of the Bulge: death, heroism, and murderous counter-attack by the Germans, using every device, including American uniforms, to confuse the American troops, and the slaughter of American prisoners of war at Malmédy. All this was part of the death throes of Hitler's Nazi Germany.

As 1945 began, the Americans had recovered and, with the French and British, they drove for Germany, in conjunction with the Soviets coming from the other side. For political reasons which turned out to be very misguided, the Americans stopped the drive on Berlin and allowed the Russians to capture the city. This politico-military decision precipitated a geographic division of Germany and Berlin that would become a permanent fixture of Germany, at least as far as the twentieth century was concerned. In May the Germans surrendered and the war ended.

Immediately a very uneasy peace was brought about in four sectors of Germany and four sectors of Berlin by Allies who really did not trust one another—the Western Allies versus the Soviets most of all. Hitler's overlay on the map of Europe was now torn away, but the map would never be the same as it had been in 1939. And Americans, having hoped that they were going to win a war and get out of it, found themselves firmly bogged down in European military and political affairs. Forty years later they still would be there.

CHAPTER 37

Pacific Victory

One of the myths of World War II is the myth of atrocities. By our lights, only the enemy committed atrocities, and we can point to U-boat outrages, the Bataan Death March, the rape of Nanking, the capture of Hong Kong, the fall of Singapore, and a dozen other stories. The building of the Bangkok-Rangoon railroad cost thousands of Allied lives, due sometimes to inattention and sometimes to Japanese cruelty. The Japanese did commit atrocities, there is no doubt about it. The reason for their atrocities is that they were determined to destroy the myth of European (and American) racial superiority over the Asian peoples. To show an American or Australian prisoner of war sweeping a street like a common coolie was very beneficial to the Japanese view of the Caucasian peoples as weak and decadent.

But we had our own atrocities as well. Some submarine commanders went far beyond the call of their orders, to machine-gun the survivors of sunk vessels as they struggled in the water. "Mush" Morton of the Wahoo *was a case in point. Some marines picked up Japanese skulls and bones from the South Pacific battlefields and sent them home as souvenirs to the enraged disgust of the Japanese people. But the bombing of Japan, had we somehow lost the war, would have been the most significant war crime with which Americans could have been charged.*

In March 1945, General Curtis LeMay, commander of the 21st Bomber Command, set out to destroy Japan's ability to fight by firebombing her cities. On the night of March 10 the Americans sent more than 300 B-29s loaded with firebombs over Tokyo, and created firestorms that destroyed twenty square miles of the city, killed so many Japanese that the numbers

400

*can only be estimated (estimates run between 85,000 and 200,000), and
destroyed the homes of a million Japanese people. This raid was followed
immediately by four more on Nagoya, Osaka, and Kobe. The firebombing
of Japan had begun. In the end dozens of Japanese cities were burned, and
perhaps 10 million Japanese people were left homeless. The casualty figures
rose well above 250,000. Then came the two atomic bombs, which killed
another 160,000 people.*

*The one possible justification was that this was war, and in war anything
is fair.*

So when one speaks of atrocities . . .

*   *   *

June 1944. At home in the United States the news was completely dominated by the war. Of course the war had filled the newspapers and the
airwaves since December 7, 1941. But now in 1944 the Allied drive for
victory everywhere seemed overwhelming.

In China, the Japanese were completely bogged down in a war with an
army that kept eluding them, and had been for seven years. The Japanese
held the cities, the major ports, and the rail lines. But between the cities
were the towns and the villages, and the rivers and the roads. And the
Japanese did not hold these. In the northeast the Chinese Communists
fought unceasingly against the Japanese. In southern and central China,
various resistance groups moved about, some Communist, some Nationalist, some adhering to warlords. The Japanese dared not move except in
military column lest they be ambushed by Chinese fighters. In the west
and southwest, Chiang Kai-shek's Nationalist government held power,
sometimes a little tenuously, as in Yunnan Province, still controlled by a
warlord, who showed his independence during the war by remaining on
standard time while all the rest of Free China went on daylight saving time.
But Yunnan at least paid lip service to Chiang Kai-shek.

Try as they might, the Japanese had never been able to bring Chiang
to his knees, nor to make an agreement with him. American aid to China
during World War II had been slight enough—for many months almost
all of it coming in by air across the Himalayas—but it had been sufficient,
particularly the financial aid, to permit Chiang to survive. Millions of Japanese troops, thousands of Japanese tanks, trucks, aircraft, and field guns
were kept pinned down on the China mainland, although the major fighting
was elsewhere.

The Americans had taken the initiative in the war in the Pacific. American submarines were driving the Japanese from the seas; the Imperial
Japanese Navy was so short of oil that the main elements of the fleet could
not return to Japan for organization between fleet operations, but had to

stick close to the fuel supply of the Dutch East Indies. This made for a highly disorganized Japanese fleet. But by the middle of June 1944 it no longer mattered.

In 1942 Japan's Admiral Yamamoto had hoped for a major fleet battle with the Americans, which he expected to win because of Japan's more powerful carrier force and battleship force. Yamamoto was dead, victim of an "assassination"—an ambush—ordered by President Roosevelt, based on information secured through the breach of the Japanese naval command code; but Yamamoto's doctrine lived on, for there was no other in Japan who had his imagination. Had Yamamoto lived, his policy would undoubtedly have changed, for the relationships of the Japanese and American fleets were now completely different.

In this summer of 1944 the Americans had fifteen carriers available in their Pacific striking force. The Japanese had nine. Nor was that all the difference: nearly all the American carriers had been built since the war began; none of the Japanese carriers had been built since the war began. As serious a problem was the disparity in naval air crews. The American air crews were all highly trained, under the intensive program begun by Washington before America entered the war. Some of the Japanese crews were not well trained, for only a few months before, Admiral Takejiro Ohnishi, then perhaps the brightest living air admiral, had pressed on the Japanese naval general staff a new pilot training program, replacing the old prewar system which required four years training before a pilot was considered proficient. There were some excellent fliers still, but the number had been gravely diminished by the sacrifices of pilots and planes in the battles of the Coral Sea, Midway, and the attrition campaigns of Guadalcanal and the Solomons and New Guinea. Furthermore, the Japanese began the war with the best naval fighter plane in the world, the Mitsubishi Zero, and two of the best bombers, the Mitsubishi bomber (Betty) and the Nakajima 96 dive-bomber. Now the Americans had surpassed them with the Grumman F series of fighters, a new dive-bomber, and the TBF Avenger torpedo and level bomber.

In the Battle of the Philippine Sea, the Japanese and Americans held a major confrontation between carrier forces. Admiral Ozawa, the Japanese fleet commander, might not have been much of a strategist, but he was a cunning tactician who wanted to make the best use of his resources. The Japanese had a master plan to make up for their numerical inferiority in carriers. They would use the Marianas airfields as "fixed carriers," flying planes from the carriers to attack the U.S. fleet, then landing on the islands, refueling and rearming, and flying back to attack the U.S. fleet again before returning to the carriers. The only trouble was that the American planes shot down the Japanese attackers and most of them never reached the islands. Or if they did, they were shot down as they took off again from

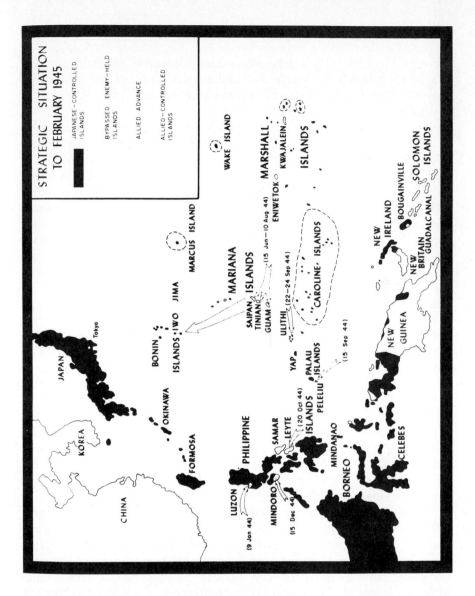

STRATEGIC SITUATION TO FEBRUARY 1945

JAPANESE—CONTROLLED ISLANDS

BYPASSED ENEMY—HELD ISLANDS

ALLIED ADVANCE

ALLIED—CONTROLLED ISLANDS

the islands. The result was a disaster for the Japanese fleet at the Philippine Sea, the sinking of two major carriers, damage to three, the retreat of the fleet, and the loss of nearly all the remainder of Japan's skilled naval pilots. A sign of the times was the fate of Admiral Nagumo, the failed commander of the carrier fleet whose timidity in not pressing his attacks for a second day had cost the Japanese major victories in his strikes at Pearl Harbor, Trincomalee, Midway, and in all the carrier battles of the Solomons. Admiral Nagumo finally had been reduced to command of the fleet air arm in the Marianas, and ultimately he died in the fighting on Saipan. The Imperial General Staff managed to send a submarine to rescue some of the downed pilots in the Marianas, but there was no submarine for Admiral Nagumo. The Imperial General Staff had a good sense of its priorities by this time.

The Japanese were defeated at the Marianas, and they knew it. At that point they knew there was no chance at all of winning the war, even through some miracle that would give them all of China and free those millions of troops. General Tojo, who had promised victory all these years, was forced to resign as head of the government. Had there been some reasonable alternative, perhaps so slight as keeping Korea and Taiwan, a surrender government might have been appointed. But the Japanese faced a stark reality: the U.S., British, Soviet, and Chinese allies had stated flatly since 1942 that only unconditional surrender would be accepted. And, to the Japanese, unconditional surrender conjured visions of Japan becoming a slave society, a colony of the West. To the vast majority of Japanese, death was preferable to such a course, a truth they showed the Western nations at Saipan where thousands of women and children committed suicide rather than be captured by the "barbarians." The gulf of cultural misunderstanding was so wide that there was no one in authority in the American military who understood the Japanese attitude. And so the war went on, to assume an even more deadly guise; the general turn of the Japanese toward suicidal action.

No one, not yet even the emperor, dared make overtures for peace in such a framework. The Japanese reaction to defeat, now that it was coming more and more often, was resignation and a new fury at the same time. Out of the defeat in the Marianas arose the specter of the kamikazes, the suicide pilots who would cause enormous difficulty to the Allied navies in the next fourteen months.

October 1944. In Europe, Paris was in Allied hands and the drive for Berlin had begun. The success of the Allied invasion of Fortress Europe had taken an enormous strain off the American navy and the production lines. Now, for the first time, the Pacific could receive a major share of the productivity of the American military machine. Ships, guns, planes were no longer in short supply. The battles for the Solomons, for the Gilberts, for the Marshall Islands, had all been conducted on an Allied shoestring. But no more.

In the South Pacific, General MacArthur moved up to the northern side of New Guinea and prepared for the next step. In a masterful polemical coup at Pearl Harbor meetings between MacArthur, Admiral Chester W. Nimitz (commander of the U.S. Pacific Fleet), and President Roosevelt, MacArthur had secured the president's agreement that the next step in the

Pacific would be the invasion of the Philippines—to redeem the American promise to return, liberate the islands, and give the Filipinos the freedom they were supposed to have had in 1942. It was a grand idea, showy and positive, the sort of thing that President Roosevelt did best. It also was designed to give hope and create good will for the Allies among all the people held in bondage by the Japanese. The chief objection to this plan came from the United States Navy, for the move to the Philippines with MacArthur in overall command meant that the control of the Pacific war passed from the hands of Admirals Ernest J. King (chief of the U.S. Navy) and Nimitz to Generals George C. Marshall (chief of the U.S. Army) and MacArthur. But what could not be changed must be borne, and the navy prepared for its new role.

In the third week of October an enormous armada steamed toward Leyte Gulf bearing the invasion forces. The Japanese planned to counter with "the last great battle"; this time they would utilize army and navy forces together. But since the army and navy forces had never worked together in all their existence, the hope for success had to be dim. Further, the Japanese fleet was strung out, part in Japan, part in the Celebes, part near Singapore. The American selection of Leyte for the invasion was a brilliant idea, it was far over to the eastern side of the Philippine archipelago, reachable from Japan and Singapore only through the narrow Sulu Sea and several narrow straits. The American battle fleet was larger than ever, so large that the task of protecting the invasion ships could largely be left to three groups of escort carriers. Two elements of the Japanese fleet were blasted as they came in from the south. The main element, coming around through San Bernardino Strait, came within sight of the landing forces it was supposed to destroy, but instead it was battered and turned back by a combination of destroyers, destroyer escorts, and the planes of the escort carriers. Not seeing the battle for the victory it was because of the loss of two carriers and several destroyers and escorts, the conservative admirals "blamed" Admiral William F. Halsey for leaving the scene with the U.S. Third Fleet to go off northeast and destroy the remainder of the Japanese fleet. The argument went on for years, and historians still played with it in the 1980s. In my opinion Halsey was precisely correct in this action.

The invasion of the Philippines was marked by the advent of the kamikazes, army and navy suicide planes that dived on Allied ships. The kamikazes were spectacular, deadly, and futile. The Allied advance went on, although the casualties of ships were much greater. No panacea was ever found to combat the kamikazes. They became, like the cockroach, a misery that had to be borne.

Soon Americans landed on the major Philippine island of Luzon, and the final battle for the Philippines began. It would last until after the end of the war, with Japanese soldiers hiding out in the mountains of Luzon, some of them for twenty years.

The next stage of the Pacific war was further indication to the Japanese people that, since victory was denied them, death or slavery was the only course.

Since 1942 the Americans had been working hard to develop a long-range bomber that could strike Japan from the west China bases. In 1943 it was perfected: the Boeing B-29 bomber. The planes were shipped to India and China, and raids began. But the winds and weather were such that the results were disappointing. Raids were conducted against Manchurian targets and some installations in southeastern Japan, on Kyushu. The major Japanese targets, the industrial centers of Honshu Island, were beyond the range of the bombers.

But when Saipan was captured, that island and neighboring Tinian and Guam became bases for the B-29s. The bombings from the Marianas began in November 1944. The run to Honshu was very easy. The bombers could attack from 30,000 feet, and the Japanese, who had not developed high-altitude fighters or high-altitude antiaircraft guns, could not touch them. The Japanese responded by stripping aircraft down to the necessities, and by using suicide tactics, and they began to shoot down B-29s. There were still plenty of difficulties for the Americans, too. One was the long flight over water, which brought casualties to planes with engine trouble or battle damage. Too many went down in the sea. The establishment of "lifeguard" submarine service did not solve the problem. So in February 1945 Iwo Jima was invaded, to provide a base from which long-range American fighter planes could accompany the B-29s on their raids.

Still the American air force faced the problem of what to deliver where, now that the system was perfected. Some strategists wanted concentration on industry; Admiral Nimitz wanted concentration on airfields and airplane factories. But General Curtis LeMay, a rising star in the air force system, offered a new plan for "strategic bombing." This plan called for the United States to conduct murderous bombing raids on the civilian population and bring Japan to its knees. Over strong opposition, LeMay had his way because the B-29s did not seem to be producing enough damage to warrant their expense. On March 9, 1945, LeMay had his first experiment. Some 300 B-29s loaded with small incendiary bombs attacked Tokyo and set fire to the paper and wood houses. A firestorm developed, far more deadly than the controversial one created by the Allies at Dresden, and in that one night perhaps 200,000 Japanese lost their lives in Tokyo. Most of the dead were women and children.

General LeMay was elated. The Tokyo raid was followed by a series of raids on the civilian populations of Nagoya, Osaka, and Kobe, and similar results were obtained. Altogether perhaps half a million people were killed, 10 million made homeless.

The result of these raids, and other firebombings that continued right up to the end of the war, was to persuade the Japanese people that, indeed, the Americans intended to destroy the Japanese race or enslave them, and this attitude made it easy for the cabal of generals running the government to persuade the people to a policy of death but no surrender.

The Allies moved forward in April to Okinawa, where the kamikaze attacks grew worse. But to brighten the picture, in May the Germans surrendered, which meant that most of the enormous American and British military strength in Europe could now be transferred to the Pacific. Finally, on the first day of summer, organized resistance on Okinawa ended; but the kamikazes from Kyushu still kept coming.

The Americans planned twin invasions of Kyushu and Honshu, worriedly expecting casualties of perhaps a million men in just getting ashore and established. In light of the Japanese homeland preparations and attitude, the figure does not seem in any way exaggerated.

But there was one key element in Japan that could rise above all: the emperor. Emperor Hirohito, Son of Heaven, had received a very liberal, spartan education. In his youth he had made a trip to Europe and had been entranced by the manner in which the Windsor family reigned over England. This relationship of royalty to subjects was the sort of imperial relationship that Hirohito wanted. He had been frustrated through the years by the rise of the Japanese militarists, but he did not share the fears of his subjects. He was sure that the Japanese would not all be murdered, nor enslaved, and that ultimately somehow they would be freed. Hirohito had taken one of his rare visits outside the palace grounds after the March firebombing, and he saw what the Allies could do in devastating the population. Then came a rapid succession of events: the atomic bombs on Hiroshima and Nagasaki, and the entry of the Soviet Union into the war. The Soviets were racing through Manchuria. It was not inconceivable that they would mount an amphibious attack on Hokkaido. So Hirohito decided that the war must end, and he was supported by the growing antiwar faction within the government. In mid-August 1945, in the face of an army rebellion from the militarists who wanted to fight to the end, the emperor surrendered Japan.

So the war was over. But American military involvement in the world was not. Unfortunately the Congress and the public did not understand that, and once the shooting stopped, the shouting began: "Bring the boys home." In Italy the GIs had a little song that told it all:

Please Mr. Truman, let the boys come home.
We have conquered Naples, we have conquered Rome.
We have beat the Master Race
And we have———in Hitler's face.
Let the boys come home,
Let the boys at home see Rome.

The attitude was the same everywhere that Americans were to be found, in Australia, the South Pacific islands, and a hundred tropical isles that housed airfields and communications installations; in the Philippines, Okinawa, Iwo Jima, Japan, Korea, China. From Italy, from England, from France, North Africa, and from Germany came the same pleas. And they were repeated within the fleet—the greatest naval establishment in the world. The war was over, said the American people and their congressmen. Now let us hurry back to the business of peace and the peace of business.

All the furor and all the response were an indication of how much the Americans had yet to learn about what had happened to them in the past five years. For the sort of peace they wanted was not to be found again, at least not in their lifetimes.

CHAPTER 38

Aftermath of War

In August 1945 the Americans had the mightiest military machine in the world. A year later it was virtually disassembled, ships were in "mothballs," laid up in estuaries and in long lines in backwaters, thick grease coating their moving parts, with no one anticipating that they would ever be used again.

By 1945 the Americans had become adept at the arts of war, but they showed dismal mismanagement in the arts of peace. At first they misread Soviet intentions, and expected the Soviets to share the Western Allied view of peace. Soon enough they learned that to the Soviets the end of World War II was but a phase of the international revolution by which all the world was supposed to turn red.

In the fall of 1945 and winter of 1946 some bitter lessons were learned. And they continued. Joint Allied control of occupied territories, Germany and Japan, fell completely apart. The Americans assumed sole control of Japan, paying only lip service to the Allied Control Commission. The same was true, almost, in Berlin and Vienna, except that all European Allied powers were represented. But the Russians had control of access to Berlin, and this led to more complications.

In the Far East, the Americans completely misread the signals sent by the people. In China, the Nationalists of Chiang Kai-shek were trying to manage a failed revolution with a growingly corrupt government. They had lost the confidence of the people. The Communists, who had the people's confidence far more than the Nationalists, were written off by the Americans as subservient to Moscow, a judgment that proved to be erroneous, but one that determined American China policy for twenty-five years.

In Indochina, the Americans failed to recognize the social revolution of the people for what it was and sided with the French, a disastrous decision that was to have dreadful consequences for America. We were not directly concerned with events in Indonesia, but again we tended to be on the wrong side, with the Dutch against the Indonesians. What we failed to recognize was the enormous success the Japanese Greater East Asia Co-Prosperity Sphere plan had enjoyed, simply because it held that Asia was for the Asiatics.

All over the world the common people were determined to be freed of the colonial yoke, and too often the United States found itself on the side of the oppressors. Such military strength as we retained up until 1950, and it was not much, was turned too often to this end.

*   *   *

When what is now known as World War I ended in 1918, the Western Allies were more or less united in their aims, and so the occupation of Germany was brief and dedicated to disarmament of the Germans and establishment of a democratic government.

At the beginning of 1945, with military successes everywhere, the realization that some provisions had to be made for the victory that was coming led the Allies to meet in what was then called the Crimea Conference but has since come to be known as Yalta. On February 7 President Roosevelt, Prime Minister Churchill, and Marshal Stalin met at Yalta and established the conditions of peace. It was a meeting at which Stalin won an enormous diplomatic victory over the Western Allies, one that continued to plague them and had not been really resolved by the late 1980s.

The Soviet diplomatic victory was based on a basic difference in assumptions by the Western Allies and the Soviet Union. The United States and Britain worked on the principle that the war was ending, and this conference was to agree on the manner of cleaning up the debris. The Soviet Union worked on the principle that the war was no more than a phase of the Soviet drive for a world dominated by communism. The next phase would be the bringing of Communist governments to the beaten countries and the countries subjected by the Axis powers.

And so, trading on the good will and myopia of the West, Stalin managed to secure concessions that shaped the future of the entire world. Germany was to be occupied by the four powers—the United States, the Soviet Union, Britain, and France—until a democratic German government could be established and a nonaggressive economic system secured.

The same would be true for Austria, which was to be separated from Germany. The Eastern European countries were also to be treated in a more-or-less similar manner. Had the Westerners been more aware of Soviet plans, they would have seen a vision of the future in Poland. During World War II, the Polish had flocked to England to fight for the Allies. The Germans and Russians had partitioned Poland in 1940, a move the Polish government-in-exile in London had refused to accept. As the war wound down and Poland was occupied by Soviet troops on their drive to Berlin, the Soviets began deporting Polish political leaders and transferring whole elements of the population from Poland to the Soviet Union. These people were regarded as politically unfriendly to "socialism." Even as the Crimea Conference was in session, the Polish government-in-exile was pleading, without success, with the Western Allies to take cognizance of what was occurring in Poland.

So complete was the disaster of the Crimea Conference, as seen by few people, that when the anti-Communist paranoia seized America in 1947, fingers of suspicion were turned on civil servants of the State Department, and charges made that they were actively working for the Communists all the time. A senior civil servant and one of the architects of the conference was Alger Hiss, later convicted in a complicated case that involved membership in the Communist party in the 1930s and active employment as a Soviet agent while a civil servant (quite a lowly one) in the Department of State. To accept the theory that Hiss was a Soviet agent in the mid-1940s, one would have to believe that the U.S. government, from the presidency to the messengers, was equally divided between fools and knaves, a difficult proposition to accept.

Yalta was followed in the summer of 1945 by another conference at Potsdam. President Roosevelt had died by that time, and Prime Minister Churchill had been defeated in a British election, so Prime Minister Clement Attlee came to represent a new British government, socialist by its own definition, and President Harry S. Truman came to represent the United States. The result was another attempted coup by Stalin, but one that did not fare so well. The Russians, who had remained aloof from the Pacific war when their assistance would have helped a great deal, suddenly opted in August 1945 to come in, patently in order to share in the loot and control of the future in the Pacific and Asia. Their entry certainly contributed to the emperor's decision to take Japan out of the war. The Soviets were amply repaid for that by the equipment they stripped from Manchurian factories, and the slave labor they forcibly enlisted from the Japanese army. Some soldiers never came home. Some were held captive for ten years and more.

The Soviets had also hoped to have a finger in the occupation of Japan, but here they failed on the practical level. The Soviets were hoping for a four-party occupation by the United States, Britain, China, and the USSR. General Douglas MacArthur, who was in Tokyo, refused absolutely and was backed by the Truman administration. The British and the Chinese were shut out as well, and all the other powers had to be satisfied with token representation on the Allied Control Commission, which represented China, Britain, the USSR, the United States, and Australia, with MacArthur and the Americans in charge. The occupation of Japan became a model for the resurrection of a conquered country to make it into the victor's most serious economic rival. But politically, the results were all the Western world could hope for, with a democratic government established where even the Communists were tolerated if not accepted. Once again, the essence of American political evangelism triumphed.

Elsewhere, the Western world wanted a peaceful and bright future in a United Nations world, expostulated during the war and apparently established at San Francisco in the formation of the United Nations organization.*

Now, all Americans wanted was to bring the boys home from World War II. Instead, the United States found itself thoroughly entrapped in policing actions all across the globe. In Germany, after the second meeting of the Allied commission that represented the four powers, it became apparent that no agreement on the future of Germany or even of Berlin could be expected, unless the West was prepared to give up and let the Russians have the boodle. That meant American troops would be bound up for years in the occupation of Germany. The same would be true in Austria, but because Austria was of little importance in the world political scene, and valuable as a buffer state between the Eastern and Western political blocs for trade and espionage, it was ultimately detoxified, neutralized, and made into a little Switzerland. The American soldiers left in the 1950s.

In Asia and the Pacific the Americans found it impossible to disengage. They were responsible for the occupation of Japan. They also occupied half of Korea, with the Russians in the other half. This agreement, part of the Yalta coup of the Soviets, achieved for them an end sought by the

---

*Alger Hiss was also one of the principal architects of the UN, and whenever anything went wrong for the United States at the UN during the early postwar years, the right wing pointed to Hiss and again claimed treason. The fact is that if Alger Hiss invented the dual system of a general assembly (one nation, one vote) and a big-power security council (unanimous agreement essential), he should have had a medal. In the past fifteen years only the U.S. veto, used against political enemies and questionable allies, has saved the international organization, for whatever that is worth.

czars in the nineteenth century, control of a warm-water port in the Pacific. Wonsan, the principal port, was just barely warm water. But appearances are deceptive; the real reason for Soviet insistence on the division of occupation at the thirty-eighth parallel was to prevent the formation of a government hostile to the Soviet Union. The joint occupation began with a big friendly bang; border parties by Americans and Russians and lots of toasts in whiskey and vodka, a few social forays by military parties into the depths of the other's territory; and then a sudden freeze. The amicability all came apart at once in November 1945, when it became apparent to the world that Soviet and Western interests were in collision, that the Soviet evangelism was apparently equal to the American. Impasse. It began in the troubles over Berlin, and spread across the world.

It was impasse everywhere, in Germany, in Austria, in Korea, even down in the Adriatic corner of Italy and Yugoslavia, where in 1945 a Communist, Marshal Tito, took control of the new Soviet-style government of Yugoslavia. In 1945 and 1946 American troops stationed in the Trieste area of Italy were clashing with Yugoslav troops occupying the new areas of Yugoslavia seized as a part of the war loot.

The Americans had other postwar military complications. They inherited much of the broad Pacific, including some of the Old German colonies over which Japan had held a League of Nations mandate in the 1920s and 1930s. Some of Japan's own colonies, including the major island of Okinawa, and a number of small islands demanded American attention, economic aid, and military presence.

The Philippines also had to be tidied up, politically washed, and prepared for independence, a task accomplished by the Fourth of July, 1946. The United States, of course, maintained major naval facilities in the islands.

At war's end, the United States found that the China that had aroused enormous American public support was largely an illusion, created by the publicists of the Nationalist government of Chiang Kai-shek. The fact was that Chiang's revolution of the 1920s had grown old by the 1940s, and in the war years corruption had sapped its vitality at the core. A later look at the fortunes of the Soong, Kung, and other prominent Chinese Nationalist families would tell the story of how billions of dollars of the tax money of the American people were siphoned off into the pockets of a handful. On the lower levels it was a story common enough elsewhere—generals keeping the payrolls of their troops to themselves, falsifying the troop figures, and pocketing the money for supplies, guns, and ammunition as well, bankers using inside information to inflate and deflate the money markets and profit enormously on the results, civil officials stealing from the public funds.

The American involvement with Nationalist China was cemented by the formation of the United Nations. The United States either had to support Chiang or make a major shift in its Far Eastern policies, which at that time seemed unimportant and unnecessary. A number of well-grounded, loyal, and observant State Department officials warned Washington that the Nationalist government was a house of cards. The military, unfortunately, in the person of General Albert C. Wedemeyer, who was in command in China, did not concur. There was also a faction of Americans dreamily looking at China's "third force," the Democratic League, forgetting that third forces never have armies and that armies decide the political issues in civil disputes.

The American hope in the summer of 1945 was that the Chinese Nationalists and Communists could be forced into a working coalition by American mediation. General George C. Marshall, freshly released from the duty of running the land war everywhere, went to China to mediate. In Peking, which was more or less neutral ground, in the center of the Chinese Communist north country, but also surrounded by Nationalist troops, the United States set up an "executive headquarters" with the Chinese Communists and the Chinese Nationalists, to work out the details for a unified China.

Meanwhile the United States Navy continued to be deeply involved in China, policing ports such as Shanghai and Tsingtao, moving Chinese Communist troops to one location and another as agreed by the executive headquarters, and moving Nationalist troops on the same terms. Marines kept the roads open in disputed territory, as between Tientsin and Peking. There was trouble, and there were American casualties, as at the village of Anping on the Tientsin-Peking road, where an American marine patrol was ambushed for no reason that ever became understandable; perhaps it was just the belligerence of the Communists.

That ambush came in August 1946, at just about the point when General Marshall was ready to quit. In 1947 he finally saw that the mediation was impossible. Neither side would budge on the issues; Chiang did not trust the Communists, Mao Ze Deng did not trust Chiang. Both had good reason for their suspicions. So by the summer of 1947 the attempt to form a government of unity was all over.

The United States then made another egregious error of policy, led by the military men and not the diplomats. Had General Joseph Stilwell been alive it would hardly have happened; he knew the failings of Chiang Kai-shek and the Nationalist armies so well that finally he had been removed from command in China shortly before war's end. His replacement, General Wedemeyer, really believed he could shore up the Nationalists, and this is where the American politicians should have stepped in with a realistic assessment. That they did not was the failure of the Truman administration, which was already becoming distracted by fears of Communism. The majority of Americans on the scene in China recognized the weakness of the Nationalist forces, their corruption and the growing futility of supporting them, but this attitude did not get back to the American administration, or to the American people, by and large because of the success of the China Lobby, a pro-Chiang group in the United States supported with millions by the Nationalists, and given credence by such homespun figures as the Time empire's Henry Luce, son of missionaries in China, who was still living in the dream-world China of his boyhood.

The American people, in other words, were duped by experts, and the Truman administration was duped as well. In the general American revulsion against Communism, Truman was persuaded to support the failing Nationalist government because its opponents were Communists. And so the United States failed to make the admittedly difficult transition of ideas in 1947 and supported the Nationalists in the civil war with aircraft, guns, rifles, ammunition, supplies and plenty of publicity in the United States. But with all this aid—much of it immediately sold to the enemy or on the market to line the pockets of Nationalist officials and generals—the Nationalists could not win the civil war. Through the reluctant courtesy of the Russians, the Chinese Communists had gained almost immediate control of Manchuria at the end of the war, and most of the equipment of the Japanese Kwantung Army. They captured some of the equipment of the Japanese China Army as well. That was about all the help they got from the Russians; it was certainly no help to have the Soviets strip every major factory in Manchuria and thus deprive the Chinese of a chance to gain industrial resources.

One could say that the Chinese Communist forces won the civil war. It would be more to the point to say that Nationalist forces lost it, with generals changing sides, or selling their armies to the Communists. By 1949, when Chiang's armies lost the Battle of Tientsin, it was all over. Chiang raided the Chinese treasury and the museums and fled with the loot to Taiwan, followed by parts of his political and military organization. It was all temporary, he said. The China Lobby in America responded, and the result was the maintenance of an American naval presence in China waters, and a guarantee that Taiwan would be protected from Chinese Communist invasion (although there was no such guarantee that Communist China would be protected from Nationalist invasion) which dominated American Asia policy for the next twenty-nine years. The military cost to the United States of maintaining the 6th Fleet ready for action against Red China could be measured in the hundreds of millions of dollars.

So the aftermath of World War II was not at all what the American people had expected. The military reacted on one level; grateful for the maintenance of a relatively strong military organization, the professional soldiers did their best to police the world with diminishing resources. To the professional military men the shock was not immediately too great; the resignation of the citizen soldiers up to the ranks of generals and admirals gave the promotion boards the slack they needed to keep from demoting high-ranking officers, as had been done at the end of the Civil War, Spanish-American War, and World War I. But Congress, beginning in the fall of 1945, diminished these physical resources with a vigorous will. Ships by the hundreds were put in mothballs. Billions of dollars' worth of military equipment was destroyed, abandoned, or sold off at pennies on the dollar.

The process was slowed somewhat in the spring of 1947 when, to the surprise of the world at large, Great Britain announced that she could no longer police the Mediterranean area, which had been her lot at the end of World War II. Anyone watching Britain would have known that she was in desperate times. Her old colonies, beginning with India, were demanding independence. What could a socialist government do but grant it? And so under the Labor government the British Empire was decimated. Would the situation have been different under a Conservative government? Winston Churchill thought so and said so.

The Americans were told then that unless they took over policing of the Mediterranean there would be no cop on the beat, this at a time when the Communists of Greece had sanctuary in Bulgaria and Yugoslavia and threatened to overthrow the government. Turkey was also threatened, but more by exterior problems. So President Truman in 1947 enunciated the Truman Doctrine, which, in effect, promised economic and military aid to countries opposing Communist takeover. Militarily the direct result was the establishment of American military presences (called "military advisory missions") in these countries. This practice would spread until it became virtually worldwide, and it would continue into the 1980s in Central America. It created further employment for the military and assured a continuing strong military flavor in American foreign relations.

The Truman Doctrine was followed in 1948 by the Marshall Plan. Theoretically the Marshall Plan was purely economic, providing credits to European governments to rebuild their economies after the debacle of war. It was even offered to the Soviet bloc, which had, as Winston Churchill observed in 1947 in a famous speech in America, pulled down an Iron Curtain between the Soviet satellite countries of Europe and the West. There is no doubt that the Marshall Plan frightened the Soviets. It was too good, too honest, and too much above anything they could do to counteract it. They retreated behind their curtain, forcing their satellites to do the same (Yugoslavia broke away). And the military confrontation grew more serious than ever.

Nineteen forty-eight. Three years after the war and the world was still armed to the teeth. This was certainly not what the Americans had intended when they recovered from the initial shock of Pearl Harbor and plunged so hopefully into the war to end aggression.

CHAPTER 39

The Berlin Blockade and What It Wrought

The misreading of Soviet intentions by the Americans began in the war years, and the result was the Yalta agreement, which set up the partition of several countries between Western and Eastern blocs. The Americans had come out of the war hoping for "one world" with the United Nations as a general policeman and judge and welfare agency all rolled into one. But the world would not conform to this American view. The result, as described in this chapter, was a long series of confrontations, given the name "The Cold War." Some of the confrontations were military, and some were not. But by 1947 it had become apparent that the United States must maintain a strong military presence in the world—apparent, that is, to just about everyone but Congress, which was back to saving money again.

The Berlin Blockade was followed by the establishment of the North Atlantic Treaty Organization (NATO), and that begot the Warsaw Pact and the establishment of a Soviet bloc. The Americans were pact-crazy for a time, and SEATO (Southeast Asia Treaty Organization) was the next attempt. It never did very well to bring the Southeast Asian nations together. One reason was the write-off of Indochina, which was involved in a civil war, with the Americans on what ultimately proved to be the wrong side.

The American system of alliances never did hold together very well. The French pulled out of NATO. The Greeks became disenchanted when NATO would not side with them against the Turks, but the Turks, right on the Soviet border, were deemed more important than the Greeks. And so it went. In the middle 1980s the salient factor in European international politics was the steady growth of neutralism, epitomized by the general French complaint when the Iceland summit meetings of October 1986 failed to produce nuclear arms agreement. The French blamed the Americans. It had become fashionable in Europe to do that, not a very good augury for the future of European-American defense plans.

*   *   *

When the war in Europe ended, the Americans approached the peace in the fashion so familiar; their aim in Europe was once again to promote political, social, and ideological change that would lead to the sort of stability in the world that the Americans always wanted. It was political evangelism again, accompanied, of course, by a healthy respect for the free enterprise system.

As the occupation of Germany proceeded, the Americans discovered that their aims and those of their old allies were not the same. The French wanted to dismember Germany. Their attitude toward the Germans was pretty well summed up in the experience of one German prisoner of war, captured in North Africa. He was shipped to a prison camp in America, where before long he had a large amount of freedom and worked on a farm, for which he was paid. About a year or so after the war ended he was shipped homeward, with all the money he had earned. But he was stopped in France, reimprisoned, and all his American earnings were taken from him—a sort of reparations. He was then held as a prisoner of war for five more years by the French before being repatriated. There had been no pay from the French.

The French attitude toward Germany was not the American. Nor was the Soviet attitude. The Soviets wanted a reunited Germany, but to them that meant a Communist state. The first months of occupation showed that to be impossible, and the Russians grew restless. Berlin, the old capital of Germany, was located near the eastern end of the Soviet occupation zone, and it was an irritant to the Soviets that the Westerners came and went through their zone, flaunting goods not available in Soviet areas. The arrangement was all very unsatisfactory and became more so as the Allies disagreed more and more openly on matters of policy toward the reconstruction of Germany.

After Secretary of State George C. Marshall had taken a commencement speech at Harvard as an opportunity to enunciate his new plan for the redevelopment of Europe, based on American assistance but European control, the plan delighted Western Europeans but immediately frightened the Soviets because of the implications. If the Soviet-bloc nations accepted Marshall Plan assistance, they would inevitably be drawn into the Western orbit and Soviet control would be lessened at the very least. So the Soviets refused to consider the Marshall Plan and forced their satellite nations into a similar position. They embarked on a plan of their own; the big difference was that the United States had the material resources to supply the needs of European industry, and the Soviets did not.

By 1948 the Americans were also growing restless with the continued partition of Germany and all the difficulties that it brought, and with the British were pressing for the reestablishment of a German state. The Soviets were opposed. As the argument grew, so did the difference between what was happening in western Germany and what was happening in the east.

By the spring of 1948 the Soviets were so upset about what was going on in the west, and so worried lest the cancer of economic independence be transferred east, that they decided something had to be done. In April the Western powers reversed the policy of dismantling German industry. The Soviets were alarmed. Their solution was to begin making it difficult for the Westerners to come into Berlin. A selective blockade was established. Roadblocks stopped cars and convoys and sometimes turned them back. Trains were stopped and rerouted. The supply of the British, American, and French sectors of Berlin became more and more difficult. And then finally, on June 24, 1948, the Soviets imposed a total blockade on transport into Berlin.

Or so they believed. The Potsdam Agreement, which broke up Germany and Berlin into occupying zones and sectors, had not stipulated that the Western allies would have transport access to Berlin, since no one in the West had considered the denial of such access to be a realistic possibility at the time. Now the Soviets said no more cars, no more trains. The idea was to starve the Westerners out of Berlin, and take control of the city as the capital of a new East Germany.

But General Lucius Clay, the American commander in Germany, did not intend to be so defeated. He suggested that the United States Air Force could operate a shuttle supply service, bringing food and other supplies into Berlin in sufficient quantity to feed the 2 million people of West Berlin and support the Western forces there. On an emergency basis he began the supply. The plan was endorsed by President Truman, and the Berlin airlift began.

The planes were harried by the Soviets, and there were some accidents. It was not a war. The planes of the airlift were not armed, and the confrontations were relatively rare—except that the whole enterprise was a confrontation. At some point the Soviets might have considered shooting down some aircraft; had they followed that policy most certainly a "hot war" would have followed immediately. But they did not. The impasse continued.

The Western powers had their little revenge. The Soviets said they would no longer participate in the joint government meetings of Berlin, and the Westerners said all right, and they went on to govern their sectors without Soviet participation. That was scarcely a victory for the USSR. It did create the two Berlins, the eastern capital of the Democratic Republic, and the western commercial center. It also convinced the Soviets that the impasse was not going to be resolved by establishment of a Communist state of Germany. The blockade lasted for 321 days and virtually every day the sky was darkened by the caravans of transport planes landing at Berlin airport. The Americans indicated that they were willing to accept the resupply of Berlin as a way of life.

Finally on May 5, 1949, the Soviets admitted that they were defeated. They offered to lift the blockade in exchange for East-West meetings to determine the future of Germany and Berlin, and Austria. So, after 277,000 flights into Berlin, the airlift ended, a triumph for one American military excursion with scarcely a shot fired. East and West met again, but out of these meetings came only a peace treaty for Austria, which was neutralized.

Two Germanies were created that year by Western and Eastern powers, the beginnings of the Federal Republic, at Bonn, and the German Democratic Republic, in East Berlin. The creation of these states was recognition by the big powers that the world was divided into two spheres of influence and that compromise was a long way off.

The schism between the Germanys was complete. Later there would be more difficulties, particularly in the days of Nikita Khrushchev, an expert saber-rattler, who as much as threatened war if the Westerners did not get out of Berlin. They stood firm, and finally the Soviets built the Berlin wall to keep Easterners inside East Germany and Westerners out. The wall was a symbol of Soviet acceptance of their failure in Germany; they were reducing the East Germans to the level of the Soviet people, prisoners inside their own country, except that, in the case of the Germans, some of them at least had known another way. The awkward situation was dictated by the Soviets as a new way of life. From that point on there would be a number of incidents involving the shooting of Western military men in East Berlin—even as late as 1985, when an American major on perfectly legitimate intelligence business was shot by a Soviet sentry and allowed to bleed to death. These unpleasantnesses were always protested, but it was apparent also that the situation was acceptable to the United States as a modus vivendi in Berlin.

The real problem for the Americans was that the situation that had evolved tended to tie them into Berlin and West Germany; it was a situation that was restrictive, to say the least.

If there had ever been any serious possibility that the Americans and the Soviets could agree upon a government for Germany, it had ended with the Berlin blockade. As a tactic, the blockade failed. As a strategy, it failed as well, for this proof of the Soviet willingness to use naked force was an important factor in the establishment of the North Atlantic Treaty Organization, a mutual defense pact for the protection of Western Europe against Soviet designs.

The NATO idea came from the American government, but not from the American people. When it was introduced, many Americans of differing political views opposed the idea, but President Truman enunciated the persisting American idealism and rejection of the old prewar isolationism: "No one nation can find protection in a selfish search for a safe haven from the storm."

And so NATO was formed, and the United States committed itself to the defense of Europe. An attack on any one NATO nation would be considered to be an attack on all.

The original members were the United States, Great Britain, Canada, Belgium, the Netherlands, France, Luxembourg, Italy, Denmark, Norway, Iceland, and Portugal. Later Greece and Turkey joined. Germany was brought in, and Spain in 1984. The United States agreed to station American military forces permanently in Europe, as a deterrent to the Soviet bloc. The Soviet response was the Warsaw Pact, in which the Soviet-bloc countries established a military alliance of their own, and thereafter held frequent maneuvers to rattle the sword a little. So too did NATO hold its maneuvers. Europeans were reminded that there really was no peace.

But whether or not an international organization like NATO could prove really successful was another matter. In 1966 the French withdrew. The cause: a combination of French arrogance, pique, weltschmerz, and disbelief in the effectiveness of the organization. The NATO professionals had to leave their comfortable ambience just outside Paris and move to Brussels. Then in 1974 the Greeks quit NATO because they were quarreling with the Turks over Cyprus and the NATO powers would not take their side.

These two desertions disproved the entire principle on which NATO was founded: that the common defense was more important than any quarrels. So NATO failed; although its body continued to function like a zombie, the soul had gone out of it. Thirty years after the end of World War II the salient fact of Western European life was its neutralism. Britain had lost virtually all her colonies, and her spirit of enterprise. France had retreated into a never-never land of her own. Germany had begun reaching for world economic power, had faltered, and was facing a growing popular feeling for neutrality and a longing for reunification of the old country.

The quibbling and public outcry of the 1980s against the stationing in Western Europe of American missiles to face the missiles of the East indicated the unreality of NATO's defensive posture. The organization might be supported by the governments involved, but not by the publics. And NATO was now the subject of almost total cynicism by all concerned.

The Americans continued to station their troops in Germany, where they were more-or-less welcome except by the Bader-Meinhof gang and its sister organizations. But what troops! When maneuvers were held, the troops were issued live ammunition, and when the maneuvers ended, the ammunition was collected, cartridge by cartridge. The authorities were not willing to leave in the hands of these troops the wherewithal of death, so fearful were they of incidents. And why should they not be? The troops were too often drug-ridden and badly disciplined, out of condition, fat, and woefully trained. They were as poor an argument for the volunteer army as existed anywhere west of the Korean demilitarized zone. To try to beef up some spirit, the American military authorities took to airlifting National Guard units to Germany for training programs, the idea being to emphasize the American commitment to Europe. But in Europe, as in American military circles, it was known that the American troops in Germany were not a military force, but a hostage force, kept there to force American participation in anything untoward that happened in Europe. That had not been quite the intent of the NATO founding fathers.

The disarray of European defense postures was clearly indicated in the Gulf of Sidra incident in 1986 when the United States decided to raid Libya in retaliation for Libyan terrorist activity, and France refused to allow American planes to fly through French airspace. Of all the NATO members, only Britain gave support to the American action, and the British government's support was not widely shared by the British people—an indication for the future.

So it was apparent in 1987 that NATO had run its course as an effective mechanism of mutual defense. What would replace it, if anything, remained to be seen, but if it was not replaced, and a time came when it was to act, it seemed probable that the entire mechanism would collapse and disappear in its own smoke like the wonderful one-hoss shay.

CHAPTER 40

Aggression in Korea

If any proof were needed for the contention that war is the result of failed foreign policy, the Korean War is certainly more than adequate. It would never have happened if the United States had not invited North Korean aggression.

Having done so, the U.S. government then changed its mind when the aggression came. General MacArthur, the occupation commander in Japan, was given the responsibility of saving Korea from the Communists. Morally, he was certainly behind that policy, for MacArthur was convinced that the war against international Communism was going to have to be fought in Asia. His preference would have been to take on the Chinese Communists in a no-holds-barred war. But he was not given his preference. MacArthur in the war in Korea in the summer and early autumn of 1950 proved himself a brilliant tactician.

*　　*　　*

Winter 1949. For four long years the Americans and the Soviets had occupied Korea, the Americans in that area below the 38th parallel to the southern tip at Pusan; the Soviets northward from that 38th parallel to the Yalu River that borders on Manchuria.

Their announced purpose, agreed upon at the Yalta conference, was to restore to Korea independent government. Their real purposes were slightly different: the Soviets wanted a government that was pro-Soviet. They had never deviated from that goal. To be pro-Soviet in the Soviet sense the government had to be Communist. That had been shown in Hungary and Czechoslovakia, where postwar governments that were not Communist had been converted by Soviet backed "revolution." The Soviets, one might say, had a clear policy from the beginning.

The Americans did not. The Americans had gone into Korea in 1945, hopeful, not quite sure what to expect from their Soviet allies in Asia or in Europe. They soon found out. The Soviet blueprint for a Communist world had not changed. The purposes had changed; no longer were the Soviets so naive as to believe they could persuade the world to accept the form of government that had failed to bring the Russian people a decent living. So the old Communist International, officially disbanded, would not be rejuvenated. *Autres temps, autres moeurs.* Communist governments would be imposed by force where they could be without endangering the Soviet state. After all, the Americans had the atomic bomb, and although some helpfully disloyal Americans and Britons had handed Moscow important parts of the atomic technology, the nuclear power was still American. Until that problem could be solved, the Soviets had to go slow, taking advantage of their opportunities and the errors of the Americans.

In Korea, the incoming Soviets were greeted by the people as liberators, which they were. Since a "people's government" had already been established there, the Soviets did not have to face that problem. Everyone knew it was the Russian-American obligation to restore self-government to the Koreans. The Soviet opportunity came in the spring of 1946, when the Soviet-American talks on Korea failed. The Soviets established a "government" in the north. They called it a People's Republic, and Kim Il Sung, a Korean patriot who had fought the Japanese with the Chinese Communist armies in north China, was chosen by the Soviets as the president. It was understood that Kim's government would give way to the final government established for all Korea.

The Americans geed and hawed. When they had landed in South Korea at the time of the Japanese surrender, they had been greeted by a People's Republic, led by a group of idealistic leftists, mostly socialist in outlook. True to his orders, Major General John R. Hodge brushed them aside. His orders were to establish a military government, and then negotiate with the Russians for a real Korean government.

By 1948 no progress at all had been made in establishing a popularly elected government for all Korea. The Americans wanted a government that was friendly to the United States. By 1949 one might as well add the word *anti-Communist,* so far had world affairs deteriorated.

The South Koreans were very restless, and so the United States permitted the establishment of a civilian government of South Korea, called the Republic of Korea, in the hope that ultimately the North Koreans would join up. No one with a lick of sense expected that to come peacefully.

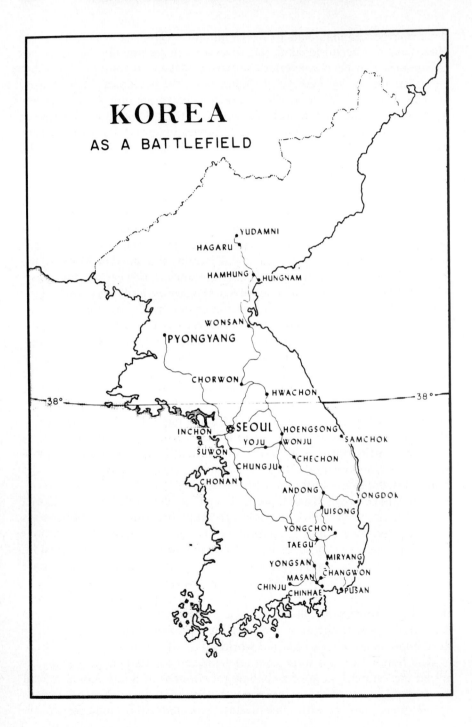

KOREA

AS A BATTLEFIELD

Dr. Syngman Rhee, a very old Korean patriot, who had conspired for years against the Japanese and had lived in Hawaii and Washington, was the man chosen by the Americans to become president.

Almost simultaneously, the Soviets canonized the Kim Il Sung government by calling it the Democratic People's Republic. Each government now claimed to represent the Korean people. The problem remaining for each side was to get rid of the other government and the dividing line at the 38th parallel.

Thereafter, Korean problems for America did not diminish, they multiplied.

The Soviets, wise to the ways of the world, immediately began building up a North Korean army. By 1949 it was second in power in Asia only to the Soviet army itself. The central element was the armored corps, with its Soviet T-34 tanks armed with 85-mm guns.

The Americans, restless under so much world responsibility, were loath to arm the South Koreans. They did not entirely trust Dr. Rhee's judgment. He spoke often of unification of Korea, and there was more than a suspicion that if he had the might he would use it to attack the north. Consequently all the South Koreans got from the Americans was a police-force type army, with 37-mm antitank guns, whose shells were bound to bounce off the T-34 tanks. The comparison was generally the same in the whole pantheon of armament.

Sometimes historians and journalists refer to the "Pax Americana" of post–World War II. *Pax* in that sense, as the Pax Romana, the Pax Britannica, refers to a period of time in which one great power so dominated the world that no one challenged it. The Pax Americana never really existed at all. The moment the European war ended, the Americans found themselves abutting Soviet power, and trying to contain its expansion.

In 1949, hemmed in by a cost-conscious Congress and growing military commitments around the world, the Joint Chiefs of Staff discussed the perimeters of the American sphere of influence—that area which the United States would defend against attack. The most knotty situation was that of Korea. From the first days of the American military occupation, General Hodge had observed wryly that, if attacked from the north (a contingency a general must always consider), he could defend "for about fifteen minutes." South Korea, the rice bowl of the country, is largely one great plain, with clusters of mountains, mostly in the east. There is no terrain between the 38th parallel and Seoul to slow down an army on the move.

With only ten army divisions and only two marine divisions, all under strength, the Americans would have been hard put to defend anywhere. Their major consideration was Europe; China had been written off, and the new American policy called for ignoring Red China and expecting it somehow to go away. Korea: that was the problem. Many in the Pentagon wanted to write it off as indefensible.

And that is why, very early in 1950, when speaking to the National Press Club of Washington, Secretary of State Dean Acheson noted that the American defense perimeter included Japan. He did not mention Korea. He could not have chosen an audience better suited to send a signal, and the signal was to the Soviet Union and the North Korean Democratic People's Republic. The message, in essence, was: "If you attack South Korea, the United States will not defend."

If the Tass correspondents were not at the luncheon, all they had to do was read the *New York Times* the following morning. The word sped to Pyongyang, the capital of the North Korean government. The green light was on for the absorption of South Korea by North Korea.

Early in June the North Koreans announced elections to be held throughout Korea to choose a parliament. It would meet on August 15 in Seoul and take over the government of a united Korea. This "National Front" call was flatly rejected by President Rhee. Two days later the North Korean defense minister and the military men met, and the invasion of South Korea was on. It began on June 25 when the North Korean tanks rolled across the 38th parallel and began speeding south. Three days later the North Koreans occupied Seoul.

The South Korean army virtually disintegrated before the North Korean forces. The South Koreans did not have the weapons to resist properly, and they became quickly dispirited, except for one division, the ROK (Republic of Korea) 1st Division, which never did lose its spirit.

Nor were the South Koreans alone. In Japan, when the blow struck up north, General MacArthur looked around. He did not have a single division of troops ready for combat. The American forces in Japan had been established as occupation forces. The old combat readiness of the World War II years was far behind them. Most of the troops lived a pleasant life, many with their mama-sans (Japanese mistresses). The life of the occupying soldiers was not a demanding one, and they had grown fat and lazy. MacArthur shipped the U.S. Army 24th Division to Korea to try to stop the North Korean tide. The Americans began to fight—and fall back. Their arms were no match for the North Korean arms either. They, too, had 37-mm antitank guns, although they had proved ineffective in World War II against German tanks. They had the old World War II bazooka, which had proved ineffective as well. A new bazooka had been designed, but was not in production because the Pentagon had to save money.

Nor could the out-of-shape troops stand up against the lean North Koreans. So for two weeks the war went very badly. It is surprising, however, how quickly the fat comes off in combat, and the 24th Division began to shape up. On the field there were individual acts of great heroism, such as that of Colonel Jay B. Lovless of the 34th Regiment. He had just come to Japan to find that the regiment given him was out of training and commanded by inept officers. He took them into combat. He was able to bring into the regiment one or two men whom he knew and trusted, but the 34th was unable to stop the tide of North Koreans, and Colonel Lovless, a fine officer, was the first victim of the inexorable system that demanded the relief of any unsuccessful commander in the field.

But the relief of the colonel did not make the 34th any better a fighting outfit. Colonel Robert R. Martin, another good officer, was given the command, and the task of stopping the North Korean drive at Chonan, before it could reach Taejon in central South Korea, the next key point. Colonel Martin could not stop the North Koreans, although in the end he tried to do so singlehandedly. He took a bazooka into a hut and lay in wait for North Korean tanks. One came up and pointed its 85-mm gun at him. He fired the bazooka. The rocket bounced off the armor of the tank, but the 85-mm shell cut Colonel Martin in two.

On came the North Koreans, and General MacArthur rushed all the American troops he could find to stop them. In Washington, the army realized it had been caught with its defenses down, and scurried around, stripping the U.S. continental forces below the safety level always maintained. That had to be done if the threat in Korea was to be countered.

And the fact that the threat must be countered was established. President Truman and the military men met and the president said Korea had to be defended. The matter was taken up with the United Nations, which was taken seriously in those days. Surprisingly, the Soviet representative on the Security Council was absent at the time, protesting another matter. Why should he not be absent? The Americans had already said they would not defend Korea. And now the Americans had reneged on this position, and before the Soviets could move, the Americans rushed a motion through the Security Council, condemning the North Korean invasion as aggression, and authorizing the use of United Nations troops to stop it. That meant the United States had the formal backing of the whole United Nations, which put pressure on American allies and on uncommitted nations such as India to help in the general effort. It did not, however, solve the military problem of American unpreparedness for action. So the North Koreans drove on south. They had a timetable. They wanted to clean up all South Korea, force the Americans out, and force the South Korean army to surrender, so that those Korean elections could be held and the parliament convened on August 15, the fifth anniversary of the Japanese surrender.

By July 10 the North Koreans were right on schedule, perhaps a little ahead. That day General Lawton Collins of the U.S. Army and General Hoyt Vandenburg of the U.S. Air Force arrived in Tokyo to assess the situation. Was there really any hope of holding the North Koreans?

General MacArthur said yes, if Washington would give him the reinforcements he needed. And it was absolutely essential that the position be held; otherwise the American strategic situation throughout the world would turn immediately to the defensive.

The Joint Chiefs of Staff and the president had already realized this. Collins and Vandenburg went home and began to make the fur fly. On July 13, General Walton Walker came to Korea to take over command, and he installed his headquarters at Taegu in the southeast sector of South Korea. It was just a few miles below the line the Americans had chosen for defense, the line that was to be known as the Pusan Perimeter, running in a rough semi-circle from Chinju on the south to Pohang-dong on the east coast.

More troops began to arrive: the 25th Division, the 1st Cavalry, and various smaller units, including the 1st Provisional Marine Brigade, made up by stripping various marine units in the United States. Edward A. Craig, one of those tough, Nicaragua-trained officers of the corps, was now a brigadier general.

In these early days, the Americans had difficulty in even mounting a naval force, so drastically had defense expenditure been cut in the past four years. Fortunately the Pacific fleet's most powerful elements, including one aircraft carrier, the *Valley Forge,* were engaged in amphibious training just as the North Koreans struck, and so a small naval force could be sent. But one aircraft carrier! In World War II fifteen or twenty could have been focused anywhere in the Pacific. Pax Americana indeed! Fortunately for the Americans, the North Koreans were not strong on air power, and in short order United Nations air superiority was established and maintained by American, British, and Australian planes.

But the difficulty of holding on to the Pusan Perimeter remained. The North Koreans threw everything they had at the perimeter, determined to keep to their political schedule. On July 29, General Walker announced to his subordinate commanders that they must hold along the Pusan Perimeter. "There will be no more retreating, withdrawal, or readjustment of the lines or any other term you choose," he said.

And they held. The U.S. troops from Japan were growing tougher. New troops and new weapons were coming in to help. As of August 3, hope began to rise. A major North Korean assault was stopped on the Pusan Perimeter. Marines arrived from the West Coast of the United States and were rushed into the line in the Chinju-Masan area. They stopped the North Koreans and began to drive them back. The 5th Marine Regimental Combat Team stopped the North Koreans at the Naktong Bulge.

New spirit was engendered in the UN forces. No longer did the battle look desperate, doomed to end in failure. The marine M-26 tanks were proving equal to the North Korean T-34s. New guns, 75-mm and 105-mm, and the new bigger bazooka were also helping change the equilibrium.

By mid-August, the North Koreans were showing the strain. The halcyon dream of uniting Korea under the Red banner by the fifth anniversary of the Japanese surrender had gone by the boards. Several high-ranking officers had been removed from command because of the failure of the troops to keep to schedule. Pusan, said the word from Pyongyang, had to be captured by September 1.

Back in Japan, General MacArthur was planning a surprise for the North Koreans. The United Nations would launch a counterstroke, an amphibious landing, and the army of General Walton in the south would rush north to join up with the landing forces, and seal off the North Korean troops in South Korea. Already the North Koreans were having difficulty with supply because of United Nations air power. This landing would finish them.

The North Korean high command now lashed its forces in the field, demanding victory, and the field commanders began a new offensive at the end of August. They struck on three sides of the Pusan Perimeter and seemed near breaking through, particularly on the east, where much of the fighting was in the hands of the South Koreans. Reinforced by American units, helped by air power and by a sealift, the South Koreans rallied, and the line was held. As of September 15, 1950, the Pusan Perimeter was quiet. The major Naktong offensive of the North Koreans had failed.

Now it was MacArthur's turn to take the offensive.

September 15, 1950. U.S. marine and navy planes blasted military installations in the harbor of Inchon, the port city west of Seoul, the capital of South Korea now held by the North Koreans as it had been since June 28. Then came the marines, first the men of the 3rd battalion of the 5th Marines. They landed on the little island of Wolmi Do. The amphibious invasion of the northern offensive was on. In spite of a good deal of calamity-howling in the planning stages, and dire predictions all the way along, General MacArthur had achieved total surprise of the North Koreans, and in the south, when the enemy armies heard of the move, they began immediate withdrawal.

By the night of September 15, the American marines were established in and around Inchon. There were virtually no North Korean troops in the area to oppose them—that is how great the surprise had been. One of the key figures in the fighting was Colonel Lewis M. Puller, another of the Nicaragua marines. Whatever else the American interventions in Latin America had done, they had certainly contributed to the training of some highly skilled fighting men.

General MacArthur did not like General Walker, and in this new landing he showed his dislike by putting his own man, Major General Edward M. Almond, in charge of X Corps, as the northern invasion's land forces were known. General Almond had been MacArthur's chief of staff in Japan, and MacArthur knew he could trust Almond to carry out his wishes.

Down in the south General Walker's army was supposed to break through the North Korean lines and hurry to link up with the Inchon landing, thus cutting off the North Korean line of retreat. This was easier said than done. The North Koreans still had a major force in the south and, in planning his own invasion, General MacArthur had shorted Walker in terms of replacements and resupply. Walker's force was split into two corps, I Corps and IX Corps. Altogether he had 157,000 men, compared to about 100,000 North Koreans.

The breakout, then, should have been easy. But of the total UN forces, 73,000 troops were South Koreans, and the Americans had very little confidence in them. It took the U.S. 8th Army several days to get going, and by that time, the North Koreans were beginning to move fast, using every road north so that they would not be cut off from their own lines. By September 23 there was no more Pusan Perimeter. The 8th Army was in a position to move north and join the new landing.

From Inchon the marines moved toward Seoul. They captured Kimpo airfield two days after the landings, and then Yongdungpo. As they moved closer to Seoul, the North Korean opposition began to stiffen.

Back in Tokyo, General MacArthur informed General Almond that he wanted Seoul captured by September 25. Here was another case of a general playing politician. September 25 would be three months to the day since the North Koreans had moved across the 38th parallel, and how nice it would look in the newspapers to see that they had got their comeuppance. In 1948 General MacArthur had felt some political stirrings toward the Republican presidential nomination. Nothing had come of them, but the raising of MacArthur's name had made of him a political figure, and neither he nor anyone else in politics forgot it. Thus, even if the general had not been grandstanding (which he was very much inclined to do) he would have been accused of it. In the case of the capture of Seoul, MacArthur, through General Almond, became extremely difficult. Almond did not believe the marine regimental commanders were moving fast enough, so he issued direct orders, over the head of General Oliver Smith, the 1st Marine Division commander. Smith was furious. Almond backed down when confronted, but the interference continued. On September 25 the marines did enter Seoul, but they did not control it. Almond insisted that they attack. He heard a report that the North Koreans were streaming north from Uijongbu, headed for Pyongyang. He immediately jumped to the conclusion that the defenders had fled Seoul and ordered an immediate attack. The fact was that some of the units from the south had come along and passed through the city, but the force designated to defend Seoul was in place and fighting as hard as ever. Almond announced that the attack was on. Back in Tokyo, MacArthur's public relations men seized on this information and announced that as of 2:00 P.M. September 25, Seoul was in UN hands. This announcement was not true, but it made fine headlines in America.

It did something else. It blasted any trust the marines had in General Almond, and it drove a wedge between the news reporters and the military. True enough, in previous wars there had been friction between news correspondents and the military. But generally speaking, the correspondents respected the rules, abided by censorship, and refrained from engaging in feuds. MacArthur and Almond, however, made such efforts to utilize the press for MacArthur's personal ego gratification and as a fulcrum to secure his way with the Joint Chiefs of Staff and the Truman administration, that the press began to balk. What had always been an uneasy alliance between press and public relations officers became even more uneasy. Some of the communiqués issued by the MacArthur headquarters were found to be false, and after that the military-press relationship was never the same. When, on September 27, the North Koreans were still fighting in Seoul, and Almond had already "captured" the city two days earlier (according to MacArthur's announcement), many members of the press were disgusted.

On September 27 General Walker's forces from the south finally forced their way up to join the troops that had landed at Inchon. On September 29 MacArthur came over from Tokyo for the ceremony of handing back Seoul to President Syngman Rhee. In the fashion of a Roman conqueror, MacArthur ordered the marines to build a special bridge so he could travel in style from Kimpo airfield to Seoul. Then they had to stand at attention while he gave his speech, in which he gave credit for the capture of Seoul to none other, thus taking it for himself. The fact was that MacArthur deserved much of that credit; his had been the plan for the lightning attack, and the choice of Inchon for the landing, both opposed by many. It was MacArthur's hour of triumph and he savored every moment of it. Standing in the National Assembly Chamber of the battered National Capitol Building in Seoul, amid the rubble of the fighting, MacArthur spoke loftily of hope and inspiration, and "the grace of a merciful Providence" that had allowed the forces "fighting under the symbol of that greatest hope and inspiration of mankind, the United Nations," and he used the words "despotism and Communist rule" together, and "primacy of individual liberty and personal dignity." But throughout it sounded somehow as though General MacArthur had granted all these gifts personally. When he had finished he called on all to say the Lord's Prayer and they did, even the Confucians and Buddhists among them. And then the general outdid himself, turning to President Rhee: "My officers and I will now resume our military duties and leave you and your government to the discharge of civil responsibility."

It was all a grandstand play, and among the observers could be heard murmurs that were not entirely commendatory. But the general had his day and he had earned it. The press and public in America granted him the laurels he had heaped upon himself, for he had turned defeat into victory. There was no doubt about that. Having reminded the world of that, in this simple ceremony, the general then went back to Tokyo to prepare for even greater glory.

CHAPTER 41

Failure in Intelligence

General MacArthur's brilliance as a tactician was overshadowed in the fall of 1950 by his failings as a strategist. Never has the old adage "war is far too serious a matter to be entrusted to the generals"* been better proved than in the Korean War, when General MacArthur was allowed by President Truman to direct the strategy of the war far beyond the original aims of the United States and the other United Nations members.

The original aim had been to stop North Korean aggression. MacArthur's aim was to destroy North Korea, and he would have liked to add Red China to that. It was, as will be seen, a policy of disaster, and it could never have happened if the United States government had not made the error in 1946 of backing the wrong side in the China civil war, and compounded the error in 1949 by refusing to accept the reality that the forces of Mao Tse-tung had won. If there was ever a case that proved the inseparability of political and military decisions, it was certainly Korea all the way through, but the most disastrous aspect was the American political miscalculation that made the war against the Chinese a reality.

---

*Sometimes attributed to Georges Clemenceau, French prime minister in World War I, and sometimes attributed to Lloyd George, British prime minister in World War I.

*   *   *

The major role of intelligence in military operations is nowhere better illustrated in history than in the third phase of the Korean War. The American failure to properly assess the character and aims of the armies opposing the United Nations forces resulted in an error of judgment that changed the whole character of the war, very nearly lost it in a few weeks, and ultimately prolonged it for years.

The original war aim of the Truman administration, supported overwhelmingly in the United Nations, was to repel the aggression of North Korea and drive the North Korean military forces back behind the 38th parallel. This was accomplished by October 1950, just a little over three months after the war began.

Shortly after the war began, even as the South Korean government was fleeing from one temporary refuge to another, President Syngman Rhee announced that once the North Koreans were driven back, they must be defeated totally and made incompetent to try again. He went further: he said the 38th parallel no longer existed as a political issue. The North Korean aggression had relieved the South Koreans and the Americans of the obligations of Yalta. It was his intention to unify the country under the Republic of Korea banner.

In Washington, several State Department advisers held the same view. One was John Foster Dulles, then a Truman associate. Another was John M. Allison, a civil servant whose career went back to the days in Shanghai when as a consul he had been slapped by a Japanese officer. In 1950, Allison was director of the State Department's Office of Northeast Affairs. The position of the hawks was that to allow the North Koreans to go unpunished for their aggression would be to invite aggression elsewhere.

In a world of law that position would have been unassailable. Unfortunately, despite the existence of the United Nations and its backing of the American defense of South Korea, the world was not a world of law. Everyone knew that the Korean situation was the result of a fluke, and did not in any way represent the real divisions of nations. The reality was an American bloc and a Soviet bloc. What Dulles and Allison were suggesting was the extension of the police action to change the political balance in Asia. History shows that political balances are changed only by successful wars. That is the course they wanted to follow.

It might possibly have been workable, had the Americans not painted themselves into a corner with their China policy. If, once the Chinese Communists had won their civil war against the Chinese Nationalists, the United States had acknowledged that fact and given diplomatic recognition to the de facto government of China, then this government, the Peking government, would have inherited the China seat in the United Nations

Security Council and some sort of relationship would have been established with China that would permit discussions. It would scarcely have been a perfect situation, but it would have been better than what developed.

In 1950, however, in America the myth of the Chinese Nationalists as the Chinese government still persisted, and the Nationalists had the China UN seat, at the insistence of the United States government. The Chinese Communists did not exist, since they were not recognized by the United States. Therefore the United States had absolutely no contact with Peking.

The Department of State's highest advisory group, the policy planning staff, warned that under the circumstances that existed in Asia, a movement north of the 38th parallel would court the risk of starting World War III. George Kennan, expert on the Soviet Union and director of the policy planning staff, was very much opposed to the move as a dangerous adventure. Secretary of State Acheson called the issue of the 38th parallel "explosive." The CIA, using all the resources it had, suggested that the crossing of the parallel might bring the Chinese Communists into the war.

One of the problems of the State Department in this period was that there was really no one left in the department who could (or would) speak authoritatively about China. In the paranoid years 1947–1950, all the China experts had been forced out of the department, tainted with a red or at least a pink brush, or they had submerged for survival.

John Allison called his contemporaries who opposed a U.S. move north of the 38th parallel "appeasers," a term picked up by many Republicans in Congress. Part of the reason for this attitude was the deep frustration of most Americans, who had hoped that the end of World War II would produce a peaceful and benign world. Another part was the political ambition of the Republicans, who, after eighteen years in the political wilderness, were willing to try any tactic to embarrass the Democrats and win victory for the Republicans in the Congressional elections that year. Allison and the other hawks were willing to start World War III. They said it was inevitable, and the Americans should start it while they could win, before the Soviets got the atomic bomb perfected. Actually, many of them did not believe the Soviet Union would fight, and they disregarded the China they did not know.

General MacArthur's attitude was well known. Late in July he had made an unauthorized trip to Taiwan to visit Generalissimo Chiang Kai-shek. His purpose was to explore the possibility of using Chinese Nationalist troops in Korea, a thought that sent shivers up the spines of the diplomats because of all the complications it might bring. MacArthur's view was that, having started the cleanup of Asia, the Americans ought to finish the job, and that meant going right on into Communist China. But even MacArthur did not dare say that openly.

As for the 38th parallel, MacArthur intended to cross it and occupy all

of Korea right up to the Yalu River. Whether or not he crossed the Yalu
was a more important question in the minds of the MacArthur claque. He
believed that Chiang Kai-shek should be "unleashed" from Taiwan to
conquer Red China. *Unleashed* was scarcely the word: the Communists
had already beaten Chiang once, the power he had in 1950 was nothing
like that he had held in 1948, and the only way he could come back would
be through American might.

President Truman by 1950 was desperately trying to avoid the issue of
Chiang Kai-shek. President Truman seriously considered replacing
MacArthur that summer with General Omar Bradley, a really nonpolitical
general. But Truman did not because of the political implications; he knew
that such a move would turn many votes to the Republicans, particularly
those influenced by the veterans' organizations. So in the end Truman
gritted his teeth, bore with MacArthur, and thus began an enormous mistake. For from this point on, General MacArthur was determined to force
American policy to his own wishes; to carry the war against the Korean
Communists and if possible to move against the Chinese Communists too.

MacArthur laid it all out for Washington, America, and the world in
August 1950, when he was trying to persuade the Joint Chiefs of Staff to
allow him to strike at Inchon. General Lawton Collins, the army chief of
staff, had come to Tokyo to hear the MacArthur plan. The general then
treated him to a view of the MacArthur world strategy: "It is plainly
apparent that here in Asia is where the Communist conspirators have
elected to make their play for global conquest. . . . We have joined the
issue on the battlefield. . . . If we lose this war to Communism in Asia,
the fate of Europe will be gravely jeopardized. . . . I can almost hear the
ticking of the second hand of destiny. We must act now or we will die."

As always, MacArthur was long on rhetoric. He linked irrevocably the
Soviet and Chinese Communists. Some day, he was known to have said,
the Americans would have to fight the Communists *à l'outrance*. Why not
now?

MacArthur did not worry about the Chinese. He had no respect for
the Chinese Communist military system. Also he had no understanding of
it.

As always, MacArthur was very persuasive. General Collins went back
to Washington to present the MacArthur view. And the debate began:
What to do when the 38th parallel was reached?

Such a debate in August, with the UN still in South Korea, was easy
to conduct in the abstract. But by October, the moment was arriving. A
decision had to be made.

The military men were swayed by the philosophy of their training: one
fought a war to win. Victory could not be accomplished until the enemy's

will or ability to fight was destroyed. Those were the views of General Collins and Admiral Forrest Sherman, the navy chief of staff.

But soon they were also the views of Dean Acheson, Dean Rusk, John K. Emmerson, a State Department man who *did* know China, President Dwight D. Eisenhower of Columbia University, the national commander of the American Legion, and other Americans. In other words one could never say that the political leadership of the United States was opposed to the extension of the Korean War and was dragged in by the military. It was a discussion that involved civilians as well as the military.

President Truman was cautious, as well he might be, for he was the man who would have to bear the responsibility for the decision. But he was definitely impressed by the attitudes of his advisers, and when George Marshall, general, super ambassador, one time secretary of state, and now secretary of defense, added his argument to those in favor of crossing the 38th parallel, Truman was convinced. The wheels began to move to authorize General MacArthur to destroy the North Korean army. He was to be warned only not to involve the Chinese or the Russians by violating their territory.

The die was cast.

And as it was done came the word that it was the wrong thing to do if the United States did not want war with Red China. For on the day that the directive was sent to General MacArthur, September 27, 1950, the Americans had their first warning: if the Americans crossed the 38th parallel, the Chinese would join the war on the side of North Korea.

The warning was indirect. It had to be. There was no agency through which the Chinese government could address the American government. So it was done through the Indians, who were neutral, although involved in the UN effort symbolically with an ambulance unit in Korea. Chou En-lai, the Chinese prime minister, informed the Indian ambassador, with the definite implication that he should inform the U.S. through Delhi, that the Chinese would not stand by idly if the United States crossed the 38th parallel. That very day the Indian foreign minister told the American ambassador. Washington had the message. There was also one from the British ambassador, who was concerned enough (particularly since Britain was also involved militarily in Korea with two brigades of troops plus naval and air forces). Washington also received supporting messages from the American ambassador to the Soviet Union, warning of possible Chinese entry into the war.

But the hawks refused to believe.

Two days later, September 29, Prime Minister Chou made the warning publicly, to be sure the American media had it.

Bluffing, said the hawks.

So October 1950 began with the United Nations forces driving hard above the 38th parallel. On the west, General Walker was told to start for Pyongyang, the North Korean capital, to capture it and drive to the Yalu River. On the east General Almond's X Corps was to land, and drive up to the Manchurian border.

Politically the MacArthur directive was a challenge to the Chinese. Militarily it was potentially suicidal, because the general had split his forces. Down the middle of Korea, he had left a fifty-mile gap between General Walker's army and General Almond's. Anyone who looked at the map could see it, but was likely to be told that it was all mountain country and impassable; there were no roads. No one was to worry about it.

During September, as the Chinese were issuing their warnings to Washington and New York, more than half a million Chinese were moving to the borders of Korea. O. Edmund Clubb, an "old China hand" and head of the China desk in the State Department, reported that the 4th Field Army had just moved from North China to Manchuria. There was no reason for that—there were already half a million troops in Manchuria—unless the Chinese government had decided to intervene in Korea.

And so the UN forces moved quickly. President Truman was still enough concerned (and concerned about the coming Congressional elections) that he met MacArthur at Wake Island for a conference on the war, and was assured by MacArthur that it was most unlikely that the Chinese Communists would enter the war, and that if they did not to worry, he, MacArthur, would handle it.

How swiftly the UN forces moved. By October 20 Pyongyang was in UN hands and the soldiers were making jokes about the North Korean ways of government. On the east, on October 26 the U.S. Marines landed at Wonsan, the North Korean port, and prepared to move north to the Manchurian border. There was not a sign of a Chinese anywhere. The North Korean government seemed to be totally shattered; deprived of its capital, the political leaders fled into Manchuria.

And then, the commander of the ROK 1st Division, who ought to know a Chinese when he saw one, reported his first Chinese prisoners of war.

At first General Walker did not believe this report. He sent his intelligence men, who questioned the new prisoners. They were Chinese, all right. They did not even speak Korean.

MacArthur did not believe. Walker sent the evidence. Just a handful of misfits, said MacArthur's intelligence officer. There was absolutely no evidence of the presence of any sizable Chinese unit in Korea.

This view represented the MacArthur command's readings of the interrogations of the Chinese prisoners. Unfortunately there was no one on the MacArthur staff who had had any experience with the Chinese Communists in World War II. It had been their technique, when captured by the Japanese and faced with torture, to give information. But the information they gave was not helpful to the enemy. In Korea prisoners reported on their battalion and "unit." Such reports seemed thoroughly sensible to the Japanese (and now to MacArthur's staff), because a private soldier, and particularly a "wog," was not supposed to know much; if he knew only his battalion and his regiment, that was about right. Actually the Chinese common soldier knew far more about the operations and organization of his army than did the American. It was part of the military-political philosophy to keep the troops informed. So when the prisoner said he was from the 1st Battalion of the 10th Unit, it would mean 1st Division of the 10th Army.

On October 24, Mao Tse-tung had presided over a meeting of the government ruling committee at which it was decided that, since the Americans had ignored their warning, intervention was the only answer. Twenty Chinese armies were dispatched to Korea. On the night of October 26 a Chinese unit launched the first attack on Onjong. The next day a small unit of the United Nations 8th Army reached the Yalu. It was the ROK 7th Regiment's reconnaissance platoon, and it was the only part of the 8th Army ever to reach the river.

"There are no indications of open intervention on the part of Chinese Communist forces in Korea," said the communiqué from MacArthur's headquarters.

That day hundreds of thousands of Chinese troops were moving in Korea. They moved by night for the most part, or in snowstorms, from one forested area to another. If they had vehicles, and these were few, the tracks were carefully wiped out by a rear guard. The Chinese lay concealed from UN aircraft all during the daylight hours.

As October drew to a close, the acrid smell of smoke drifted down upon the UN troops from the north. From the air, observers could see great smoke clouds in the Onjong and Unsan areas. They were forest fires. At first MacArthur's people could not figure them out. They were the age-old method of making a smokescreen. Concealed by those screens, by the end of October hundreds of thousands of Chinese had crossed the border, some in the 8th Army's area in the west, and some in the X Corps area of the east, and some right down the middle where, as General MacArthur's staff would say, there was no possible danger.

The Chinese struck in small units, here and there. General MacArthur's intelligence men were completely confounded. They did not know what to think, and that confusion was indicated by MacArthur's statements. On November 1 MacArthur still questioned the commitment of the Chinese government to send troops to Korea.

On November 1 the Chinese attacked the ROK II Corps in the west, and virtually destroyed it. The 8th Army's right flank was opened up for Chinese soldiers coming down the middle of Korea.

On November 2 General MacArthur said the Chinese now constituted a serious threat to the UN forces.

On November 2 the 8th Army was in retreat south of Unsan, pursued and partially cut off by Chinese forces.

On November 4 General MacArthur said the Chinese were in Korea in such numbers as to threaten his whole command and demanded reinforcement from Washington.

On November 4, in response to the orders from Peking, the Chinese were moving a million men into Korea. They had captured Unsan and were mopping up the surrounded UN forces in the area. There was little but patrol activity on the east side of Korea, where the marines had landed.

On November 5 General MacArthur told the Joint Chiefs of Staff that he did not believe the Chinese would really enter the war.

On November 6 the Chinese gave up all concealment, and sent troops across all six of the Yalu River bridges. UN pilots flying in the Yalu area saw them coming, a steady stream, as far as the eye could reach. But the front was strangely quiet. The Chinese remained in place or moved back everywhere. Prisoners were released and told to tell the Americans that the Chinese did not wish to fight. One last message was being sent by Peking to Washington. Unfortunately, it was shortstopped in Tokyo. Probably it would not have made any difference. So completely had the Americans constructed the tower of their misunderstanding of the Chinese Communists, that nothing Peking might have said would have been likely to convince them. The Americans seemed bent on expanding the war. No one in Washington spoke of the possible costs or the possible outcome.

CHAPTER 42

The Long War

It ought to have been apparent at the moment that the Chinese attacked the United Nations forces in Korea that this war would be a disaster. Ironically, it was recognized, and the United States would very much have liked to review the bidding. But by this time, November 1950, the Chinese had "psyched themselves" into as jingoistic an attitude as General MacArthur ever had, and they demanded nothing less than a complete victory over "American imperialism" that would include the abandonment by the Americans of the Chinese Nationalist government on Taiwan.

The Chinese made the serious error of misreading the old American adage "Never get involved in a war on the continent of Asia." The front side of the coin said that in such a war the Americans would be bogged down. The obverse side, however, said that the Americans would be forced into a long, long war, and that they had the staying power to continue it.

So at the end of 1950, Americans and Chinese were killing each other for all the wrong reasons and neither side was able to get out of the morass that political error had forced upon them.

*　　*　　*

On November 6, 1950, General MacArthur issued one of his strangest communiqués. He announced that he had already won the war in Korea, with the capture of Pyongyang.

Then why did he not stop then and there? Instead he ordered the "end of the war offensive" to continue, and the air force to bomb the Yalu

443

bridges over which the Chinese troops were streaming. That order was countermanded in Washington and the bombing did not happen.

General MacArthur then began a political campaign against his opponents in Washington that was as powerful as the military campaign he was waging in Korea. He was now a man possessed by the paranoia that had threatened him all his life. At Inchon, he had made the greatest coup of his career, and turned defeat into victory. Now the combination of the Chinese in Korea and the foot-draggers in Washington was about to deprive him of his victory. This would not do. He set out to conquer Washington first of all.

And he did conquer Washington, because in principle the military men were on his side: a war should be won; and the politicians simply did not know what to do. They were the victims of the position into which they had fallen at the end of the Chinese civil war. It was the old American attitude that only "sanitary" governments were fit to be recognized by the United States. And, in the past few years, *sanitary* had taken on a new meaning: anti-Communist. Almost any government could get recognition and even foreign aid from the Americans if it was anti-Communist. America dealt with unsavory governments in Spain, Portugal, South Africa, Iran, and half of South America without a whicker; they were all sanitized, they were all anti-Communist. Only recently, since 1947, had there been any question that there might be more than one sort of Communist in the world. The Yugoslavs had broken with Moscow. But Washington was still not sure this was not some sort of a trick, and the American dealings with Tito's Yugoslavia were at arm's length.

There was no way at this time that President Truman could undertake a reassessment of the American position toward Red China. In the elections that week of November 1950, public reaction against eighteen years of Democratic rule had set in; the Republicans had won control of Congress, and there was little possibility that the general belief that the Chinese Communists were devils could be controverted. President Truman was reaping the harvest of his truckling under to the overblown anti-Communist fervor of the late 1940s.

So the war continued, but now the Chinese Communists took the offensive. They poured hundreds of thousands of men into Korea, to fight the well-armed UN forces. The Chinese did not have good arms; their soldiers were badly equipped. But their morale was very high, and they marched into the American artillery bravely, and were cut down. They were decimated by bombing and naval gunfire, and they kept coming. Their casualties were enormous, but they kept coming. That sacrifice of manpower was the Chinese military philosophy, the only one they could possibly hope to succeed with, given their military situation. And it very nearly did succeed. Once again the United Nations forces were forced back, back, back. In New York, at the end of November the Americans and British supported a UN resolution to condemn the Chinese Communists for aggression in Korea. But the Soviet representative to the Security Council had come back from his self-imposed exile, and he vetoed it.

The war was completely changed; even the enthusiasm of the United Nations General Assembly members now wavered and in some cases disappeared altogether. The Americans and their allies, the Anglo-Saxons for the most part, were stuck.

In the winter of 1950–51, for a competent general, MacArthur was making the most shocking mistakes. The split in the UN forces had been disastrous. Only through sheer guts did the marines fight their way out of the trap in the northeast, and evacuate Wonsan. Not all the army troops up there made it.

The Chinese kept driving south.

In the UN the Americans encouraged a move in the General Assembly to set up a mechanism to bring the war to an end. But the Chinese, scenting victory, now became as arrogant as the Americans had been. No, said the Chinese, the war would go on, unless the Americans withdrew entirely from Korea, and from Taiwan.

One could say that the Americans had erred first by announcing that they would not defend Korea; the North Koreans had erred by attacking South Korea; the Americans had erred again by trying to push the war too far; and now the Chinese erred by not knowing when to quit.

The Chinese would, said Peking, now drive the Americans into the sea, and reestablish the Korean peninsula's unity under a People's Republic of Korea. In January they started a new offensive and recaptured Seoul on January 4, 1951. The capture was greeted by a new round of Communist rhetoric to match General MacArthur's of the past. The Chinese arrogance created in America a new stubbornness for the execution of this war. MacArthur got everything the United States could give him. By March, under a new field commander, General Matthew B. Ridgway (another veteran of the Latin American wars), the UN forces recaptured Seoul. This time there was little bombastic rhetoric. This time, the UN forces having reached the 38th parallel again in a ragged line, there was no enthusiasm in Washington for a "clean sweep." The costs of the past had been assessed, and they were too high. The real effort of the political leaders was now devoted to attempts to find a political solution to the war and the future of Korea.

The Chinese were very good at suffering, and they had not yet suffered enough to reduce their arrogance. They still believed in Peking that the armies could drive the Americans into the sea. So they tried again in April 1951 in a new spring offensive. It failed. In the middle of the offensive, General MacArthur was suddenly relieved of command by President Truman. The reason was MacArthur's complete intransigence. He had never given up his belief that the war must be fought to a successful conclusion, and now he admitted that he meant the defeat and destruction of the Peking government, and even attack on the USSR if necessary. This attitude was so thoroughly at odds with the attitude shaping up in America, where the difficulties of recent months had produced an acceptance of the limitations of economic and military technological power, that when MacArthur took it upon himself to threaten China with air and naval attack, adding further complications to the diplomatic negotiations, Truman decided he had had enough. He consulted the Joint Chiefs of Staff, who had also been forced by grim reality to change their views, and they agreed that it was time for MacArthur to go. And so on April 10, 1951, MacArthur was fired. His supporters raised an enormous hue and cry, and he was accorded a caesar's return, even addressing a joint session of Congress at which he made the best theatrical performance of his long life, and retired, as generals do, to a huge salary and all the perquisites of a thankful armaments industry. Oddly enough, after the bath of tears, he was almost immediately forgotten by the public.

The Chinese Communists may have been buoyed by the confusion in which they saw the UN command as General Ridgway took over as field commander. They launched an offensive that spring, supported by 1,000 aircraft secured from the Soviet Union, from which they expected great results. The 1,000 aircraft were decimated by the UN forces. A second offensive also failed. The Chinese were learning, the hard way, the limitations of manpower alone.

The war dragged on. The relief of MacArthur had established in Washington with all parties the new policy of seeking a political rather than a military settlement. But the Chinese still had much to learn and they were not quick in learning it. So the months went by and thousands more lives were lost, ten times as many on the Chinese side as on the UN side. And the war settled down to a static war, something like the European war of 1914–18 in France, where the troops fought and died, and where they created poetic names for their battlefields: Heartbreak Ridge, Bloody Ridge, the Punchbowl, Bunker Hill . . .

Finally, the Chinese realized that they could not win the war, and that the Americans, whom they had underestimated, were not going to give up. Then meaningful negotiations began at Panmunjom. The Chinese–North Korean side was as difficult and circuitous as it could be, but the Americans were patient, and ultimately, the Korean War ended right back where it had started, at the 38th parallel.

To the Americans the Korean War should have been the ultimate lesson in the course of study involving foreign wars. It had taught the politicians and the military the dangers of caesarism. It seemed unlikely that any general in America would ever be allowed the political latitude that MacArthur had managed to wrench from the politicians before he abused it and brought about his own downfall.

The war had certainly shown the Americans the need for vigilance; the state of readiness of the American military forces in June 1950 was a disgrace for any country that called itself a "power." This failure was almost entirely that of the politicians. Congress had whittled away at American defense appropriations steadily since 1945, aided by weak resistance from the Truman administration.

It was true that the war had hastened the military rehabilitation of Japan, which manufactured more and more war materials for the Americans as the Korean War continued. The war had also convinced the Pentagon of the need for development of Japan as "our best friend in Asia," and had put an end to any forlorn hopes of the China Lobby that the United States would pull Chiang Kai-shek's burned chestnuts out of the fire and reinstall him in Nanking.

But the major lesson to be learned from the Korean War was not learned at all. In World War I the Americans had found themselves in France, as guests of the French, and no matter how great the strains, they were allies among allies. In World War II in Europe they had again fought with equal allies for basically the same ends. But in the Korean War, from the beginning, the Americans were carrying an ally whose aims were not precisely their own. As they drove north they found themselves in unfriendly country. After the crossing of the 38th parallel and the entry of the Chinese, the political climate in the United Nations became lukewarm, and then almost unfriendly. The Americans were fighting too far from home, against an enemy whose home was just next door. And above all, they found themselves for the first time fighting a limited war, in which they could not use all the weapons at their disposal because of political considerations. They could not bomb inside Manchuria, lest they bring the Soviet Union into the war. They could not use the atomic bomb, because the people of the United States would not stand for it. So the military should have learned of the limitations of power, in a complicated world. Instead, they continued to behave as if they were operating under a Pax Americana which in fact, as the Korean War showed, had never existed at all.

CHAPTER 43

Vietnam Beginnings

One might expect that the Americans, having seen the effects of political error in China and in the Korean War, would have somehow managed to disengage themselves from the French who were fighting in Indochina against Ho Chi Minh's indigenous revolution. But in fairness to the Americans it must be said that American involvement in Indochina was largely on account of American involvement with France in Europe. As it turned out it was more than foolish, because in the end the French deserted the Western camp to go it alone in Europe; but by that time America was already stuck with the mess the French had created in Indochina.

The entire imbroglio could have been avoided if the United States had paid more attention to its professional diplomats who served in Asia in the World War II years, and less attention to the generals and admirals. Vietnam and virtually every other disaster we suffered in Asia was directly attributable to the failure of foreign policy, and it all goes back to that same root: the blind American anticommunism of the 1940s, which allied generals and politicians against the diplomats.

*   *   *

Hanoi, September 1945. You had to be there to understand what was happening, because very little accurate information about the first postwar weeks in Indochina has ever come out at all. I happened to be there, as correspondent for the United Press Associations, arriving just too late to see the Japanese surrender. What I wrote then, I later discovered, was

448

almost all consigned to the wastebasket in Chungking. At war's end United Press correspondents had fanned out all over the Japanese-occupied sectors of the Asian mainland, leaving only a Chinese assistant in the press hostel in Chungking. His assigned UPI task was to assemble all the news dispatches sent to Chungking by the handful of UPI correspondents (mostly by U.S. Army radio) and transmit them in Morse code on the United Press radio frequency to New York. His actual task was to censor the dispatches to conform to Chiang Kai-shek's policy lines, a task assigned by Chiang's propagandists, for he was a Chinese Nationalist agent. So he doctored the reports, and UPI New York got a combination of Chinese Nationalist propaganda to disseminate to the world. Specifically what was missing from my articles was reportage on the ravages of the Chinese Nationalist troops on the North Vietnam countryside, the self-enrichment program of the Nationalist officers,* and, much more important, the results of my almost daily interviews with Ho Chi Minh for about three weeks, in which the Vietnamese leader laid out his political views, his hopes for the future, and his pleas to the United States for assistance.

Hanoi was filled with posters and slogans, most of them lionizing the Viet Minh, Ho's political faction. Ho and the Viet Minh were perceived by the people of Hanoi to be pro-American, and the initial Vietnamese perception of the Americans, widely spread by Ho, was that they were pro-Ho.

When I had left Kunming by plane for Hanoi I was given an American-flag armband and told to wear it on the right arm of my khaki shirt. Not knowing quite why it was very important, I did so, and on my second night in Hanoi I found out why. I was riding in a ricksha along the Boulevard Gambetta, one of the broad avenues in the French residential district, when I heard sandaled feet padding swiftly up behind the ricksha. My ricksha man shouted something. With a prickle in my neck I stuck my right arm out so that the American flag showed brightly in the moonlight. The running footsteps suddenly stopped and we proceeded with only the sound of the ricksha man's clopping feet and the swishing of the ricksha along the road. It was dangerous, Ho told me the next day, for anyone to be out at night in Hanoi in these uncertain days. But not for an American.

On August 16, the Viet Minh army marched into Hanoi with orders from Ho to avoid fighting with the Japanese if possible. It was very possible; the Japanese, having been told to surrender, were not going to fight anyone if they could avoid it. They had already been confined to their barracks by the Japanese high command, except for those soldiers who were essential

---

*One of them presented me with a fine camera which had been taken from a Chinese merchant. I had to accept. He already had three of his own. I took it. It was later stolen from my room in Shanghai by another Chinese.

to run such services as the airfield where they would be welcoming Allied troops and Allied officials.

The Viet Minh troops then took over the city. The French police and military had been disarmed by the Japanese in March on the eve of an aborted French attempt to take over Indochina, in the misunderstanding that a powerful American task force off the Indochina coast was en route to support them.

So began the new era in the old French colony. Its name was already changed by the local people to Vietnam, although the French of de Gaulle, who had also just arrived, did not seem to notice the change. All they knew was that General Lu Han, Chiang Kai-shek's commander of the forces that would occupy (by the Yalta agreement) Indochina north of the 16th parallel, had arrived and taken over the governor's palace on the outskirts of town, and Ho Chi Minh, the Vietnamese nationalist leader, had arrived and taken over the Gouvernement Général, the administrative buildings in the center of the city, leaving the French out in left field, which they resented mightily.

Ho had come out of the jungles and grasslands of northern Tonkin, where he had been fighting guerilla war against the Japanese and conspiring against the French.

During most of the Pacific War, Ho Chi Minh, who in the 1930s had been imprisoned in Hong Kong, moved around in northern Tonkin and in Yunnan Province of China, fighting the Japanese, planning the independence of Vietnam, and seeking assistance from the Americans, who were the strongest Western Allied presence in China. Kunming, the capital of Yunnan Province, was the headquarters of General Claire Chennault's American 14th Air Force, and, after the Americans had built the Burma-Ledo road in 1944, the U.S. supply headquarters for all China. The Office of Strategic Services and the Office of War Information both had centers here, and Ho visited both. At one point he tried to secure a visa to visit America and was sponsored by an OWI official. But the move failed because of the intransigence of an American consul in Kunming, who did not think the French would like it if Ho got to Washington. Thus do decisions by low officials in far-off places high policy make!

The OSS offered Ho more than the OWI, for the former was not only a propaganda agency, but an action unit of the sort that the CIA would later be, and it had funds, and could secure and dispense arms. The OSS gave Ho arms, he gave them intelligence about the Japanese, and his people rescued downed American fliers. By the spring of 1945, Ho controlled six provinces of northern Indochina with his guerillas.

Late in August 1945, Ho had arrived in Hanoi, where he wrote a declaration of independence on his portable typewriter, using a copy of the American declaration borrowed from Major A. L. A. Patti, an American OSS officer whose job was to rescue Allied war prisoners. The declaration was also deeply influenced by the Atlantic Charter of 1941 in which President Roosevelt and Prime Minister Churchill had promised the restoration of sovereign rights and self-government to those people who had been forcibly deprived of it. To Ho, that included the people of Indochina, which he now declared to be the nation of Vietnam. There were some difficulties in all this, particularly the fact that the people of Cochin China in the south, where Saigon lies, were of quite different racial stock than those of Tonkin. But that was the sort of difficulty that Ho, as a politician, was prepared to pass off.

On September 2 Ho spoke to a rally of half a million people before the Gouvernement Général building, and announced Vietnam's independence. As far as he was concerned, from that point on there was no going back. He might—and later would—be prepared to make concessions on the timing of the independence. But he and that half-million agreed on one thing: Vietnam had the right to be independent, and it would be. Like all powerful ideas it was very simple. But, as far as the United States was concerned, too many promises had been made to too many people—including one by President Roosevelt to General Charles de Gaulle, that France would get her colonies back. Later it appeared that the promise to de Gaulle did not actually represent Roosevelt's thinking, but by that time Roosevelt was dead and anyone had the right to interpret what he had meant. Unfortunately, President Truman was more short-term pragmatist than long-term idealist, and his mind was turned more to Europe than to Asia. That is why events in Asia in the next few years were disjointed, and American policy contradictory.

In the weeks that followed Ho's return to Hanoi, he buttonholed every American who would listen, hoping to get his views through somehow to Washington. He used even such leaky and imperfect vehicles as this callow young UPI correspondent who in no way deserved the respectful attention granted him by Ho. But Ho Chi Minh failed. My dispatches were gutted, so I was of no use in telling his story, much as I tried. I was thoroughly sympathetic to the Vietnamese desire for independence, indicated to me by dozens of people, young and old. I was thoroughly out of sorts with the French officials I met, who seemed as arrogant and presumptuous as the French can be, an opinion I shared with such disparate characters as the correspondent of the Associated Press (Australian) and the Press Trust of India (Bengali). What disappointed me most was to see the manner in which the United States government handled the emergence of Indochina from five years of Japanese rule. First came a military mission, headed by Brigadier General Philip Edward Gallagher, whose previous command had been the U.S. Military Academy at West Point, a man who as far as I could see had no experience or aptitude for the delicate sort of political-military liaison he was to accomplish. He seemed to me to be in league with the French. Second was the dispatch from Shanghai of a vice consul whose major interest in Hanoi seemed to be to secure the best possible personal accommodations and live like an ambassador. With this pair, Ho Chi Minh's pleas to reach the ear of President Truman did not have a chance.

From the beginning, the Americans played into the hands of the French and thus soon convinced Asians that the United States was bent on the perpetuation of colonial power wherever it had existed before. Even that highly publicized and quite honest grant of freedom to the Philippines in 1946 was not enough to convince the American movers and shakers that this policy of granting independence, framed a long time before, was a good policy and should be followed in Asia.

That failure of American political philosophy was not confined to Vietnam. Events in China, Indonesia, and all over the Far East and Pacific could have been altered by a different American approach. It would have required, however, a much greater imagination than that of Harry Truman, and a willingness to break with the traditions of the recent past, or rather to return to the original traditions of America.

The official Americans in Hanoi in the summer and fall of 1945 were only observers. The policing of Indochina was in the hands of the Chinese in the north, who quickly made a deal with Ho and kept out of sight. In the south the police power was in the hands of the British army, which made the mistake of watching the Vietnamese, but not the French. The French in Saigon were rearmed, staged a coup, and controlled Saigon. Under the British aegis, the French gained a touchy control of southern Indochina, and then the British left Saigon.

The Americans should have had nothing to do with this situation and the war that followed. But the anti-Communist crusade that developed in the United States decreed otherwise. Having missed the chance to be Vietnam's saviors in those early days by supporting Vietnamese nationalism against French colonialism, the Americans should have become no more than neutral observers, but they turned out to be observers who would take the French side.

Most Americans believe their country was not at all involved in Indochina in those early days, and so did I for a long time. But American air force officers were flying the Civil Air Transport Company (CAT) planes that supplied the French garrison, particularly when the French began to lose control, and ended up at Dienbienphu, their Asian Waterloo. The Americans were flying in order to familiarize themselves with the area in case the U.S. military forces had to go in.

Had to? Why would Americans have to devote themselves to trying to preserve for the French a colony that did not want to be a colony? By the time of Dienbienphu it was 1953. The Communist scare was still endemic in America. Ho Chi Minh was a Communist; the Viet Minh were Communist: they obviously had to be allied with Red China and Moscow; and therefore they were the enemies of the people of the United States. That perverted view had come to dominate American foreign and military policy. General Dwight D. Eisenhower was now president. The secretary of state was John Foster Dulles, one of the greatest anti-Communist hawks and most misguided diplomats of American history. Dulles may have been called "the lone eagle" because he almost never took advice from his subordinates, no matter their expertise and his lack of it. The rueful joke was that as long as America had John Foster Dulles it did not need ambassadors—and Dulles would not permit them anyhow. The title *ambassador* hid the errand-boy nature of the job, as Dulles conceived it. After Dulles had left, the State Department was a long time in picking up the pieces. He was undoubtedly the most disastrous secretary of state of modern history.

Until the end of 1953, American assistance to the French in Vietnam was indirect; the United States gave the French military and economic materials, shipped them to Vietnam, and used them to fight the Viet Minh. This action was not really a military excursion. But the United States was paying for a third of the French war effort in Indochina. Americans were directly supplying arms, and had sent to the French 200 U.S. Air Force technicians.

Senator Richard B. Russell of Georgia said sending 200 technicians was the prelude to disaster. Soon the French would have 2,000 technicians; the number would reach 20,000 all too soon, said Senator Russell, and then go to 200,000.

The Truman Doctrine theory of supplying military missions all over the world was a part of the general policy that put American fingers into just about every war on the globe.

In 1953, General—now President—Eisenhower was persuaded by his advisers that China, Vietnam, Korea, and Malaya were pieces of the same machine, a great international Communist plot to take over the world for the Soviet Union. Three decades later it is interesting to see what happened: the Communist rebellion in Malaya was quelled by the Malayans themselves, with British assistance that was effective only when the Malayans took over. The Korean War ended in 1953, leaving the festering sore of the demilitarized zone of the 38th parallel, with two Koreas yapping at each other like junkyard dogs on opposite sides of the divide. China, having been the American enemy (a concept largely in the American mind until the Americans *made* China the enemy in the fall of 1950), eventually became the American friend, and Vietnam, after enormous bloodshed and dreadful expense of every sort to the United States, did in fact become independent, and turned to Soviet Russia, but almost immediately found itself immersed in a border war with China.

So much for world Communist solidarity. But in 1953, that was how it looked to the Eisenhower administration, and that is why the Domino Theory was invented, and why the American military went in to replace the French military after the French had lost in Vietnam.

In the spring of 1954, when Dulles and the other hawks were putting the pressure on Eisenhower to take over from the French, army chief of staff Matthew Ridgway had sent a team of army experts to Vietnam to survey the requirements for a military victory—which was what the administration was talking about. The experts estimated that between half a million and a million men would be needed. To secure that force the draft would have to call 100,000 men per month. And even worse than in Korea, the Americans could not expect much, if any, support from the people of Vietnam. In other words, the U.S. Army had learned something from the costly experiment in overseas military excursion in Korea. But, as events would only too soon prove, the politicians had not.

CHAPTER 44

Bay of Pigs

In the late 1940s and 1950s everyone who followed Latin American politics knew that General Fulgencio Batista's government was corrupt and repressive. I spent some time in Cuba in those days and realized that whatever passed for freedom there was almost totally illusory. Thus it was not hard to sympathize with Fidel Castro and other young rebels who wanted to get rid of Batista.

The American government, of course, took a different stance. Batista was anti-Communist, and that was about all that was necessary in those days (and still is, unfortunately) to assure American approval.

The ease with which Fidel Castro and his handful of revolutionaries took over Cuba should have been indicative to Americans of something more than lassitude on the part of the Cuban people. But the U.S. government was not prepared to deal with anyone who declared himself sympathetic to Marxism.

A truly intelligent policy followed in the late 1950s would have put Fidel Castro into the American pocket and avoided much anguish and the expenditure of millions of dollars in the rest of Latin America to try to counteract "Castroism." We should have bought all his sugar and made him thoroughly dependent on us. Instead in a very short time we threw Castro into the lap of the Soviets. The American relationship with Cuba was one of the few post–World War II examples of a bipartisan foreign policy, but in this case it was a totally wrongheaded one. Both parties declared a pox on Castro's house, and agreed to destroy American relations with Castro. The Eisenhower administration went out of office in 1960 and the Democratic Kennedy administration came in. In the period of hiatus the Republicans completed planning a revolution for Cuba and the Democrats agreed to take it over. It was probably a very bad idea from the start, but, the Republicans having planned it and put the wheels in motion and the Democrats having agreed to the plan, they should have gone ahead and finished the revolution and Castro. Instead, as will be seen, the Democrats bungled the job because of the ineptness of the new Democratic president, John F. Kennedy. It was another case of a military excursion planned by the politicians, and in which the politicians interfered at the operating level to wreck the whole plan and create untold difficulties for the future.

*   *   *

In the winter of 1957, Fidel Castro and a couple of hundred followers were holed up in the mountains of the Sierra Maestra in Cuba and plotting the downfall of President Fulgencio Batista.

The Columbia Broadcasting System had sent a free-lance correspondent in to live with Castro in the mountains and he had come back with some footage that showed Castro in his beard and cigar and something about the life in the guerilla camp. The CBS television news department decided that a show could be made of the film. And so, under the supervision of Leslie Midgley, one of the earliest of CBS News producers, a show was prepared.

Tony Motolla and his guitar provided the music, which was probably the best feature of the show. Castro and his interlocutor did a good deal of talking about the essential friendship of the rebels for the United States, and everybody at CBS seemed to believe it. Certainly no one had the idea that Fidel was going to become a Soviet client when he came to power. In those days he gave the impression that he favored the U.S. side. The *New York Times*'s Herbert L. Matthews, who went down to Cuba to see for himself, came back with such a conviction that he destroyed a flourishing career by taking Castro's side in the international political debate after Fidel had opted for the Marxist way and began expropriating American investments.

The United States did not decide immediately upon a military excursion of the sort that would have settled the problem as late as the 1930s. That sort of gunboat diplomacy was frowned upon in a postwar world which was supposed to be dependent (but never did become dependent) on the principles of the United Nations. Government under international law, that was the idea. And the Americans then believed enough to allow their hemispheric thinking to deteriorate. Castro proved to be not as painted by CBS News or the *New York Times*. Later Fidel claimed that it was all a Fidelian plot; that he had intended to become a Soviet adherent all the time and had deceived the Americans. Perhaps that is so, but at least the Department of State should have known.

U-2. Washington was embarrassed in the spring of 1960. For the first time an American president was caught outright in a flat lie about important affairs. The Soviet Union had reported that an American spy plane had been shot down over the USSR. President Eisenhower had been asked the direct question: Was this true? He had denied that the United States did any airplane spying over Russia. Of course the Russians knew this was not true, and had known for months. But the world did not know, and Americans, in particular, believed their president. Then Nikita Khrushchev unveiled the wreckage of the U-2 spy plane that had indeed been shot down, and produced in the flesh pilot Gary Powers, who in a split second had opted to parachute over the USSR and surrender rather than take the cyanide pill he was supposed to swallow as a CIA contract spy.

So the United States had been seriously embarrassed. Nothing was helped by the publicity of the Powers trial and the sentencing, covered by the world press.

It was the most serious gaffe of the postwar world, creating a crisis in confidence in the statements of the leaders of the United States, or, one might say, destroying a confidence that had been built up over the years.

Indeed, for all the expertise and experience of the men of the Eisenhower administration, there were a large number of gaffes and policies that were not useful.

As for Cuba, in 1960 Washington's interest was just beginning, for then it became apparent that the Monroe Doctrine was seriously threatened by the new sort of foreign meddling that the Soviet Union had discovered in the Korean War: their ability to find client nations to further their foreign policies.

The Soviets had fallen on hard times since the succession of diplomatic demarches executed by Premier Joseph Stalin during World War II. The agreements for Allied management of the peace had given the Soviet sphere of influence Eastern Europe and North Korea. But they had been firmly excluded from Japan and pushed out of Iran, and the flourishing rebellion they were supporting in Greece had collapsed under pressures of the Truman Doctrine and the Marshall Plan. Germany had split and the Soviets did not even get all of Berlin. China, which the United States had tried to push into Soviet arms, had resisted and gone its own way. Yugoslavia had flown the coop, and little Albania had cut off with a more scathing denunciation of Soviet shortcomings than of the wickednesses of the capitalists. Communist parties in Italy, France, and Belgium had failed to ignite the people, and the Communist leaders in these countries were becoming old, tired, and uncertain.

Suddenly, the United States offered Cuba to the USSR on a platter. Who would be foolish enough not to accept, particularly when the USSR was being ringed uncomfortably by American bases.

And so the rapport between Moscow and Havana began.

Also in 1960 began a plot by the Central Intelligence Agency to do away with Castro. Assassination was considered and then rejected. It was decided to stage a coup, using Cuban refugees trained, supported, transported, and given air cover by American military personnel, and thus to destroy the government of Fidel Castro "from within" and create a government more to the American liking. This was to be accomplished through a small amphibious invasion of Cuba at the Bay of Pigs. The hope was that once the invaders got ashore they would be joined by thousands of Cubans who would welcome them as liberators.

In the spring of 1960 Fidel Castro visited New York to address the United Nations. While American newspaper publishers, networks, and magazines were lionizing Fidel, Vice President Richard M. Nixon spent almost three hours with him.

Free elections? Nixon asked.

The people don't want free elections. They make bad government, Fidel said.

Fair trials of the political accused? asked Nixon.

The people don't want fair trials. They want them shot.

Nixon emerged from the confrontation convinced that here, indeed, was a dangerous man, not because of what he stood for, but because of his cynical betrayal of all the hopes of his people. From that point on, Nixon became one of the stoutest supporters of the Bay of Pigs excursion.

The planning continued during the fall of 1960. Most of the people involved, like Douglas Dillon, the undersecretary of the Department of State, were certain that the plan would involve a standby combat unit of the U.S. naval air force, to see that the landing was successful once it began. The planning and the training of the Cubans continued. So did the assembling of ships and boats, and the procurement and allocation of weapons for the Cubans.

The administration of the United States changed hands; John F. Kennedy replaced Dwight D. Eisenhower, and a whole new set of inner-suite executives became involved in the Cuba plan. Now a large number of people knew about the Bay of Pigs enterprise (probably way too many). But still it went on.

Kennedy could easily have stopped the whole adventure the moment he took office. He did not.

Of course, the Kennedy administration was not the Eisenhower administration. Kennedy and the people around him were new in the matter of dealing with the Soviets, full of bright ideas like the Peace Corps, and not at all cynical about the Soviet Union. For many reasons, many people in the Kennedy administration did not like the Bay of Pigs plan, particularly the American-air-cover aspect to it. Did they really have to have the air cover? Kennedy asked.

There were objectors. Senator William Fulbright of Arkansas objected. Paul Nitze of the Pentagon did not like the plan. But on April 4, President Kennedy's advisers, in a meeting at the White House, voted to go ahead.

James Reston, the chief of the *New York Times* Washington bureau, knew about the invasion, and he was opposed to it. For years he had watched successive American administrations working "to put some kind of ethical base under the new world order." It seemed to him that the Bay of Pigs invasion would be a cynical betrayal of all that idealism, a violation of American principles. In his column in the *Times* on April 14 he asked the question: If Cuban refugees did invade Cuba, what would the United States do to help them? This was an inside question, really, addressed to the president of the United States. The real question within the question was the degree to which the U.S. naval air force would participate.

Perhaps the Reston column raised new doubts in President Kennedy's mind (the major American media had an enormous amount of influence in the Kennedy administration). At this time he and the State Department were very concerned about a crisis in Laos, which seemed all-important. They also worried lest Nikita Khrushchev take some action to drive the Westerners out of Berlin as he had been threatening to do. Khrushchev was the extra man at the conference table. What would Khrushchev do, the participants kept asking themselves, as they worried about proceeding in Cuba?

That day Kennedy called the CIA man who was managing the whole operation, Richard Bissell, and told him he wanted American air support to be minimal.

And so the Bay of Pigs attack was on, but already it was hamstrung.

Fidel Castro, of course, knew that it was coming. Too many people in too many countries knew too much about the operation to keep it any sort of secret. But what Castro did not know was when, where, and how many.

The plan was certainly sound, and it could have worked. Admiral Arleigh Burke, who had studied the situation, told President Kennedy just that when asked. In those last days, a nervous Kennedy was asking that sort of question—will it work—of everybody he met who was in the confidential circle.

And so the invasion was launched. But even as it began President Kennedy consulted with liberals in his administration, such as Adlai Stevenson, who were totally opposed to the action and who reiterated all of Senator Fulbright's and columnist Reston's complaints that this was a departure from the American dream. Kennedy now had such serious doubts that he called off the American air strikes. The reasoning seemed to be that thus the administration could deny responsibility. But the fact was that the responsibility remained, while the chance of success vanished. The whole invasion had been built around the assistance from the air, and when this assistance did not come, the plan fell apart. The Bay of Pigs affair was a total fiasco and it collapsed in a hail of Castro's laughter. He could not have been laughing so hard as Nikita Khrushchev.

The result of the fiasco was an investigation. Kennedy asked General Maxwell D. Taylor, retired U.S. Army chief of staff, to make it, and he did.

But in the end, the president of the United States had to assume the responsibility. He had accepted the plan (which he could certainly have rejected after he came to office), and, having accepted it, he had allowed it to develop. Then at the last minute he sabotaged it by tearing out one of the essential parts at such a late date (the day of the invasion) that no alternatives could possibly be worked out, nor could the whole affair be scrapped.

Here then was a military excursion that brought as much obloquy on President John Kennedy as the U-2 incident had brought to President Eisenhower. Many, however, were inclined to forgive him when he appeared in his boyish way and said the invasion had all been a horrible mistake. It was, but not the way he meant it. It was another gaffe that brought disrespect for the American presidency at large, for Kennedy's courage and judgment in particular, and for the Washington political community in general.

What were Americans to believe? That our foreign policy was based on the broad principle of liberty and justice for all, as our political leaders had been saying for 200 years on the Fourth of July? That our policy was based on self-interest, the best results for the Americans? That our policy was based on the new *realpolitik*, as all those bright young advisers around Kennedy who were so confident that they knew how to make history were advocating? Or that our policy was based on confusion, a failure to understand the world around us, a continued naiveté, accompanied by the old political evangelism, with an icing of anti-Communist hysteria?

Who knew?

And that was the trouble, which led to Fidel Castro becoming a Soviet client, the establishment of Soviet submarine and air bases in Cuba, and the extension of Soviet military influence into the Western Hemisphere.

In terms of success and failure, the military demarche known as the Bay of Pigs turned out extremely badly, because it convinced Nikita Khrushchev that in dealing with John F. Kennedy he was dealing with a weakling and a fool. Khrushchev and Kennedy met in Vienna a few months later, and Khrushchev set out to terrorize Kennedy with threats about Berlin, missiles, and atomic war. What saved Kennedy was his political sense of survival. He knew that if he backed down to Khrushchev he was finished.

The Soviets then brought missiles into Cuba. It took Kennedy a flat-out confrontation and threat of war to convince the Soviet leader to remove them. In the 1980s the threat still remains.

In his study of the Bay of Pigs fiasco, Peter Wyden notes that shortly after the Bay of Pigs invasion failed, President Kennedy asked his special counsel, Theodore C. Sorensen, "How could I have been so stupid as to let them go ahead?"

A day or two after the failure of the Bay of Pigs, Kennedy invited his political enemy, Richard Nixon, to the Oval Office to discuss the matter. "What would you do now in Cuba?" Kennedy asked.

"I would find proper legal cover and I would go in," said Nixon.

Kennedy then began talking about the difficulties. Nixon left with the Cuba question still up in the air, and he had the definite feeling that nothing was going to happen. He also had the feeling that in the crisis, Kennedy had lost his nerve, a conclusion that is hard to escape. In the months ahead the foundation was quietly cut out from beneath the Monroe Doctrine and it was soon to crumble and fall apart. Cuba, an American problem and sometime irritation for 200 years, was made into a cancer that at some point would have to be dealt with one way or another.

CHAPTER 45

Wrong Time, Wrong Place, Wrong War

The perennial struggle between media and government that is an integral part of the American scene reached its apogee during the Vietnam War. It would be wrong, however, to believe that relations between media and the military somehow suddenly turned sour in the 1960s and 1970s. The distrust between military and media men goes back a long, long way. During the Civil War several Union generals had quarrels with the newspapermen that resulted in their preferring charges, one of treason, against reporters. Many reporters were thrown out of Union army camps. A newspaper in Chicago that was critical of the Union policies was burned down. So it is apparent that the troubles between press and military were nothing new.

During the Spanish-American War, most of the reporters sent out to Cuba and the Philippines comported themselves properly, and very jingo-istically, in their relations with the military. It was a sign of the times. Manifest Destiny controlled.

During World War I the media were mostly very tame. Roy Howard of United Press Associations disgraced himself by breaking the release date on the armistice of 1918, but the war was over then anyhow.

In World War II the war correspondents operated under censorship and generally comported themselves well, with some notable exceptions. The Chicago Tribune *started off 1941 by disclosing the American secret naval plan for war against Japan, Plan Orange. Some people, who did not like the owner of the* Chicago Tribune *anyhow, said he should be tried for treason. When the Americans broke the Japanese naval codes in 1942, a* Tribune *correspondent also disclosed that fact. Fortunately the Japanese did not believe it, for the codes became a vital factor in U.S. submarine operations. And, at the end of the war in Europe, an Associated Press correspondent violated the code of ethics and released the news of the German surrender ahead of time.*

Even so, the relations between media and military remained decent enough until the Korean War. Then General MacArthur's bald attempts to use the media to further his own ambitions backfired and the journalists began to grow suspicious.

All this was but prelude to the Vietnam War, when the relations between media and military became downright inimical. One reason for it was the emergence of television on the battlefront. Television told it like it was— well, at least like the television cameraman and the television commentator said it was. And the military often disagreed. Further, the military tried to feed the media the military line, and when some media men disagreed they found themselves given the cold shoulder by the generals.

There was nothing new in that. There was nothing new in the enmity the media showed toward the military. No one gave the media any franchise to go along on military operations, and no one gave the military any license to control what was said. Censorship had to concern itself only with military operations as such.

*   *   *

The basic problem in Vietnam was that neither President Harry Truman nor anyone else in authority in America in the late 1940s and 1950s understood the nature of communism. Had they known what the world knows now (barring perhaps the Americans, still)—that no matter how hard they tried the Soviet Communists could not control any countries except those in which they could keep troops—then anticommunism would not have become the cornerstone of American foreign policy, and we would never have become mired in the Vietnam War. It was the politicians and not the military that put America into the quicksand.

But to lump all Communists together was obviously the thing to do in that period. China fell. The North Koreans attacked South Korea. All this seemed to redound to the benefit of the Soviets, and that is how it was seen in the United States. So the decision was made that no matter where communism reared its head, it would be countered. And so came the simplistic American view that Ho Chi Minh was a puppet on strings pulled by Moscow. Secretary of State Dean Acheson, for one, did not believe this, but he let himself be persuaded.

General Eisenhower, the great simplifier, simply put the troubles in Korea, China, Indochina, and Malaya all in the same dish. It was a Red dish. The Soviet Union, said John Foster Dulles, his secretary of state, was determined to have the Southeast Asia peninsula, the rice bowl of Asia. If the Soviets got it, what they were going to do with it no one said.

By 1953 the Eisenhower administration had highly overemphasized the strategic importance of Indochina ("The loss would be critical for the security of the United States").

Vice President Richard Nixon was one of the most open advocates of American interference. If the French were defeated, he said, they would have to be replaced by American soldiers; Vietnam was that important in the struggle with the Soviet Union.

The military, not yet caught up in the emotional issues, was much more hardheaded. In May 1954, the Joint Chiefs of Staff said: "From the point of view of the United States, Indochina is devoid of decisive military objectives and the allocation of more than token U.S. armed forces to that area would be a serious diversion of limited U.S. capabilities."

Was it true that Indochina really was not of any strategic importance, as the Joint Chiefs of Staff of 1954 said? Or is it of the utmost strategic importance, as the Joint Chiefs of Staff of 1987 say?

In February 1954 the Eisenhower administration was beginning to go astray in Vietnam.

The situation recalls that of 1949, when the United States military forces were removed from South Korea and the military drew the American regional defense line around Japan, but not Korea. The politicians in 1950 overrode the military decision, just as the politicians in the middle 1950s would override the military decision in terms of Vietnam.

But what if the military men of 1949 had been right? That Korea was not worth the candle? Could the United States live without a South Korea that manufactures automobiles, computers, and now threatens the economies of Japan and Taiwan? The Japanese in the 1980s might be pleased to let the new Kim Il Sung (son of the old Kim Il Sung) have South Korea if he would promise to stay home.

Could it also be true that there was no possible advantage for the United States to get involved in Vietnam except to provide an easy testing ground for an American power that seemed in the 1950s to have disintegrated?

The first 200 U.S. Air Force men were sent to Vietnam with forty B-26 fighter-bombers given the French. The American Military Advisory Group, that force that Senator Russell said would rise to 200,000 men, was formed.

In the summer of 1954, after the partition of Vietnam into two Vietnams, the decision was made by the Eisenhower administration to intervene on the side of the French-created South Vietnamese government. The reason was a unique concept called the Domino Theory, which controlled American policy in Southeast Asia for twenty years.

The Domino Theory, espoused by John Foster Dulles, held that if Vietnam fell to Communist rule, some electric force would cause Thailand, Malaya, the Philippines, and just about every state between China and California to also go Communist. One could test the theory by setting up a whole ring of dominoes each close enough to the next so that the toppling of the first caused all the others to fall. It was a nice exercise in design, but a poor example of political consequence. As events proved, it is not contiguity of territory that makes Communist conspiracies triumph or fail, but conditions of life inside the countries involved. If conditions are desperate enough and the people have no hopes to live for, then communism is not at all frightening to them. The obverse is that when people gain even a small economic foothold in the status quo, they have no further use for Communist propaganda. The examples were there in 1954: India, Malaya, Singapore, the Philippines. It is a lesson the policy-makers of the United States were very slow to learn, although in 1946 they had granted freedom to the Philippines as promised by another generation, and could see the positive results.

In 1946, the Hukbalahap (Communist) guerillas had been powerful throughout the Philippines. The Hukbalahaps were subdued by the creation of the Philippines Republic. When, in the 1970s, Ferdinand Marcos turned to dictatorship to try to maintain personal power indefinitely, the Huks came back. The Marcos murder of Benigno Aquino in 1984 strengthened the forces of communism immeasurably. Only the American support of really free elections and the denunciation of Marcos's rigging of the elections of 1986, followed by U.S. support of the government of Corazon Aquino, turned the tide away from the chaos in which the Communists would thrive. Somehow Washington had learned something from all the failures all across the years—in spite of a dreadful few hours during the crisis when it seemed that President Ronald Reagan was going to run true to American presidential custom and support the dictator. But wise heads prevailed, and Marcos fled to the security of Hawaii.

In Vietnam, the Eisenhower administration's answer to political challenge was the creation of a treaty organization. NATO was in force. In 1954 John Foster Dulles virtually singlehandedly gave birth to SEATO, the Southeast Asia Treaty Organization, designed to confound the Communists and prevent the dominoes from toppling. SEATO never amounted to much, because it was founded on sand. The threat it was designed to withstand was that of aggression of one nation against another. No one but perhaps the American government ever believed that the war between the Vietnams was one nation against another. From the beginning, South Vietnam was a foreign creation. I happened to be in Saigon on the day that it was created, and it was apparent then among the cynical French that they knew that *they* had created South Vietnam. Only a naive Washington could have been fooled.

And not even Washington was really fooled or truly fooled itself. Ngo Dinh Diem worked his way to the top of South Vietnam. But in 1955, the Americans wanted to drop him, and John Foster Dulles told the U.S. Embassy in Saigon to find a new man. *This was an independent government?* Diem fought a decisive battle against dissident elements in Saigon, and won the hearts of John Foster Dulles and Dwight D. Eisenhower. The order for Diem's demise was revoked.

In May 1955, the French withdrew from Indochina, emotionally and financially exhausted. Did it mean nothing at all to the Americans that the French, supported fully by American money and American armament, had finally given up all hope of influencing events in Vietnam and had pulled out everything including the Bank of Indochina? It did not. Americans have never been long on history.

The Americans in 1954 were in no emotional condition to think of Vietnam in terms of history. Having erred grievously after winning a victory in Korea, they had nearly turned it into a defeat, and for thirty years would continue to regard their conditional victory as a defeat because they did not get everything they wanted. In Indochina, the Americans needed a victory.

Ho Chi Minh wanted to talk unification of Vietnam, but by this time it was probably too late for unification; the American refusal to help Ho and then the American support of the French had forced Ho into the hands of the big Communist moneylenders, China and the USSR. They were not great supporters, but they were better than nothing, which was the alternative. Supported by the United States, Diem refused to negotiate. He knew very well that in the end Ho Chi Minh and the Viet Minh would win out over his very personal and not very popular government. The United States continued to give Diem support; eight of each ten dollars was spent by Diem for various forms of internal security, to protect him from the people of South Vietnam.

That is how matters still stood in 1960. Gradually the American expense and the American military involvement had escalated.

The election of John F. Kennedy brought a new approach. The Kennedy "whiz kids" knew everything, it seemed, including how to manage Southeast Asia and prevent the dominoes from falling. They did not even stop to examine the domino premise, but forged onward.

In 1961 John F. Kennedy told associates that the United States was in its most dangerous period in history. It was true. Kennedy had made it so, by his blundering in the Bay of Pigs matter, which had cost him the respect of every knowledgeable political leader anywhere, including his enemies the Muscovites. The Kennedy weakness had very nearly prompted the Soviets to try military action to knock out the Americans. One crisis had come after another: new Soviet ultimatums about Berlin had brought an enormous crisis that ended in the building of the Berlin wall. Khrushchev had sent Soviet missiles to Cuba, and the Americans had had to threaten war to get them out. At that time all America was rocked by serious concern over the possibility of war.

Public confidence in the Kennedy administration's ability and courage was eroding. To recapture a measure of that confidence Kennedy had to call up the U.S. reserve troops (which had not been done since the Korean crisis of June 1950), triple draft calls, order ships and aircraft out of moth-balls, and generally show that America was prepared to go to war if nec-essary. He came within a shadow of declaring a state of national emergency.

As Khrushchev later indicated, the Soviets viewed the success of Castro in Cuba as an indication of the decline and approaching collapse of the capitalist world. ("We will bury you," Khrushchev told the Americans.) Khrushchev also made another prediction when the Americans got involved in Vietnam: the United States would be bogged down there for twenty years. He was very nearly correct.

In 1961, to John F. Kennedy, beset by the consequences of his dreadful errors, Vietnam ceased to be a small country in Southeast Asia beset by civil war, and became a proving ground for the United States under a Kennedy administration. "We have a problem in trying to make our power credible," he said to James Reston of the *New York Times,* "and Vietnam looks like the place."

Kennedy sent Vice President Lyndon Johnson to Southeast Asia, and after a whirlwind tour Johnson returned to recommend all the aid that Diem's government wanted. Diem, the vice president had seen immedi-ately, was a "good ol' boy."

Diem just then wanted to add 250,000 soldiers to his army at the U.S. expense. He also wanted American troops to fight in Vietnam. Diem knew: once in, never out.

The Pentagon, stung by the revelations of American weakness and world contempt, now turned hawk. So did the State Department. So did the Kennedy advisers. Harvard seer William Bundy suggested that if the United States backed Diem and they struck together, they had a seventy percent chance of knocking out the Viet Minh altogether. Other Kennedy insiders were even more optimistic; so was the National Security Council. Paul Kattenburg, of the State Department, suggested in the National Se-curity Council that the best thing the United States could do was disengage from Vietnam before the Americans were completely beaten. Kattenburg labored under one serious burden: he alone, among the National Security Council, knew what he was talking about. He had spent several years in Vietnam and knew that the war was already lost in the hearts of the

Vietnamese people. He tried to explain the difference between an indigenous revolutionary group (Viet Minh) and a foreign-inspired government claque (South Vietnam). But Kattenburg was put down for his views, shifted about and finally hounded out of government altogether. The "whiz kids" of the 1960s did not like to be disputed.

Kennedy sent a fact-finding mission to Vietnam, the Taylor-Rostow group, which included General Maxwell Taylor ("If they trained Generals at Harvard, Max Taylor would have been a Harvard man") and advisor Walt Rostow (who *was* a Harvard man). They approved of more help for Diem. The Vietnamese people were clamoring for American troops, said the advisers.

So now the Kennedy administration was committed to the buildup of American ground troops in Vietnam. But, if the Americans were going to spend so much, they wanted a hand in running the Vietnamese government.

Diem knew what the Americans wanted: sanitization of the South Vietnam government—less torture, fewer murders of opponents and critics, less thievery of millions by generals, a broadening of the government to include people other than Diem's family, friends, and sycophants. Especially disliked was Diem's brother, Ngo Dinh Nhu, a flamboyant high-liver with a stunning wife who looked a little like Jackie Kennedy, but whom the press soon christened the Dragon Lady.

Naturally President Diem did not want to turn his government over *completely* to the foreigners. He objected. He brooded.

In August, John F. Kennedy, president of the United States, decided that Ngo Dinh Diem, the president of that great "democracy," the Republic of South Vietnam, must go. Diem had no intention of giving up power; but John Fitzgerald Kennedy had spoken from the Oval Office. It would be as he wished.

Henry Cabot Lodge, the U.S. ambassador to Vietnam, discovered that a plot existed to overthrow Diem. Which plot? For months Diem's security forces had done little but squelch plotters. Now there was another, manned by high military officials. What should the United States do about it?

Support it, of course, was the word from Washington. Had not President Kennedy said that Diem was an embarrassment and must go? And so word went to the generals in Saigon that the plot was approved by Washington, and on November 1, 1963, the plotters rose up. Diem heard the bad news from the plotters. He holed up with his brother and called Ambassador Lodge to ascertain the American position. Lodge's equivocation told him all he needed to know. He made a deal with the plotters for sanctuary, and surrendered along with his brother. The two of them were massacred in the back of an armored personnel carrier on their way to the "safety and exile" promised by the cabal of generals.

Twenty days later President Kennedy was murdered in Dallas, and a new administration began. But Lyndon Johnson was already entrapped in the errors of his predecessors: the ignorance of Harry Truman about the facts of Asian life; the genial disinterestedness of Dwight D. Eisenhower, who did not believe in meeting any problem unless stunned by it; the determination of Eisenhower's éminence grise, John Foster Dulles, who vehemently hated Communists and found their evil hand in every wrong-doing; and the weakness of John F. Kennedy, who never learned how much power he controlled—how a gesture from the Oval Office could bring an assassination in Saigon—and who cynically set out to sacrifice the people of Vietnam to prove that the Americans could win a war.

"I am not going to lose Vietnam," said President Lyndon Johnson. "I am not going to be the President who saw Southeast Asia go the way China went."

This was reminiscent of a quotation from Prime Minister Winston Churchill. "I have not become the King's First Minister in order to preside over the liquidation of the British Empire," said he. And yet he did.

The year was 1963. The new president was now going to forge on to astound all the world with his victory in Vietnam.

CHAPTER 46

How to Win Every Battle
and Lose a War

The American dilemma in Vietnam was compounded by the media approach to the war. On the battlefield the reporters gathered, ever more loquacious, ever more concerned with putting across their own points of view. The problem with American journalism did not start on the battlefield; the "star system" of journalism was a development of television soon transferred to all media, in which the journalist became more important than his story. That is why the vital war of Vietnam was fought in the American living room, with Walter Cronkite* against the generals and the president of the United States ultimately. No one won that war. The losers were the American people.

*   *   *

President John F. Kennedy had turned on the time bomb in committing American forces to the Vietnam War. When President Lyndon Johnson came to office, he had the option of stopping the time bomb or continuing. Without a qualm, he opted for the latter.

In January 1964 Major General William C. Westmoreland took command of American forces in Vietnam. His meteoric military career had

---

*I use Walter Cronkite symbolically. John Chancellor was as much a part of it, and dozens of correspondents for CBS, ABC and NBC. The fact is that not everyone in America watched Walter Cronkite even in his finest years. Thus he cannot be blamed for all the ills of television journalism.

been aided by John F. Kennedy as part of the Kennedy program to replace experience with youth wherever possible. Westmoreland came armed with the knowledge that President Johnson wanted action, and so action began. The Americans, unknown to Congress and the American people, became active participants in the war against North Vietnam.

Now the U.S. Navy crept into the fray. Admiral Ulysses Grant Sharp, Jr., commander in chief of naval forces in the Pacific, was a believer in action. To support an American air strike in the Gulf of Tonkin, the destroyers *Maddox* and *C. Turner Joy* were sent into the gulf, which was patrolled by North Korean warships. An action ensued, the Americans claimed they had been attacked by North Korean warships (although this was not certain), and reprisals were ordered. What President Johnson needed was authorization to make a real war out of the skirmishes. He got that authorization from Congress in August 1964. The bill was called the Tonkin Resolution, which created the right of the president of the United States to take the country into war without a declaration from Congress.

Consonant with the Constitution of the United States and the Charter of the United Nations, and in accordance with its obligations under the Southeast Asia Collective Defense Treaty, the United States is, therefore, prepared, as the President determines, to take all necessary steps, including the use of armed force, to assist any member or protocol state of the Southeast Asia Collective Defense Treaty requesting assistance in defense of its freedom.

So President Johnson could go into the Philippines to fight Communist guerillas, he could go into Thailand to destroy the growers of poppies, he could go into Pakistan to fight the enemies of the government. All he needed was a request from the government involved to plunge the United States into anyone's civil war.

And that is what President Johnson did in Vietnam. Or perhaps one should say he accelerated the plunge begun by John F. Kennedy.

In April 1965 the U.S. commitment was raised to two divisions: 20,000 troops; they were authorized to undertake offensive operations within fifty miles of their bases. By the end of April the troop count was up to 82,000 Americans and 7,250 from Australia and South Korea. By June, President Johnson had granted General Westmoreland authority to commit American troops to battle as he saw fit.

The American purpose was to persuade the North Vietnamese that they could not win the war. How many men would that take? Secretary of Defense McNamara asked.

"It was virtually impossible to provide the secretary with a meaningful figure," said Westmoreland.

So America was committed to fight a war for no real purpose except to persuade a revolutionary government that it could not complete its revolution. A backward look at America's own revolution and the attitude the Americans had toward the British might have convinced someone in Washington that something was wrong.

But the stark fact is that no one in power in Washington understood the Vietnamese, or even cared to. The war was being fought primarily for the prestige of the United States, to show the world that America was not, as it was being called, "a paper tiger."

Thus logic had no place in the assessment of this war.

Nineteen sixty-five. Very soon the Americans discovered that many Vietnamese did not want them in the war. Too soon those Vietnamese began joining the Vietcong, the supporters of the North Vietnamese army living in the south.

Meanwhile, the Americans yearned to make a real people's government, an honest government, an effective government, of the government of South Vietnam. Somehow this generation of Americans had failed to study the history books well enough to discover that it was not possible to impose a people's government on a people. The South Vietnamese were drafting 3,000 men a month, but 7,000 men a month were deserting to join the Vietcong forces.

Bombing was the answer, said the military experts. Bomb Ho Chi Minh into submission. The man in command of the air force bombings of North Korea was General Curtis LeMay, who was responsible for the decision to try to destroy the whole Japanese civil population when, as noted, in March 1945, as bombing commander of the 20th Air Force, he killed about a half-million Japanese with a series of firebomb raids on civilian targets in Tokyo, Nagoya, Kobe, and Osaka. Saturation bombing of every conceivable target in North Vietnam was General LeMay's solution to the war. "We should bomb them into the stone age."

The politicians—the McNamaras, the Bundys, and other thinkers— had a different sort of plan for the air war: selective bombing. The bomber pilot has his target, a gun factory in the midst of a housing district. He plunges down, drops his bombs with precision, and buzzes off. The gun factory goes up with surgical precision, not even hurting the children playing in the street outside.

Fact, however, was that if the bombs hit the gun factory, the resulting destruction would devastate the whole district. More likely, most of the bombs would hit the housing district.

The men around President Johnson, who were making the decisions, were not overly familiar with the realities of war, though many had served in the armed forces. They did ask questions. Secretary McNamara went to Saigon and asked General Harkins, the head military adviser, how long it would take to "pacify" the country. Harkins said if he were given command of the Vietnamese he could do it immediately. McNamara asked General Westmoreland; he said it would be a long, hard war with no end in sight—a "bottomless pit." McNamara did not like that. (Westmoreland did not quote one of his favorite military authorities, the Chinese philosopher General Sun Tzu, who had said: "There has never been a protracted war from which a country has benefited.") When pressed, Westmoreland said that eventually he could win if he were given enough wherewithal.

But if money could have won the Vietnam War it would have been over in a year, for the money kept coming.

But from the north were coming regular North Vietnamese troops to reinforce the Vietcong, and the Vietcong was growing: it controlled eighty percent of South Vietnam.

Nineteen sixty-six. A Japanese observer who had been through the China War would have recognized the American dilemma in Vietnam. It was like the Japanese dilemma in China by 1940. They had control of the cities and were hated by the people, and unable to move on the ground without either risking life and limb or going in enormous convoy.

To any objective observer, the situation had to be called impossible.

So why did it continue?

Because the political leaders of the United States did not understand their own recent history. They and the military leaders still lived with the phantom of the "lost war" of Korea, and were visibly desperate for a military victory.

The escalation of the American war against North Vietnam went on. Secretary of Defense McNamara might say "Don't take a chance on killing innocent people in order to kill a few Viet Cong." That was an eminently comfortable Washington rationale, but the war did not go that way.

Nineteen sixty-seven. Washington basked in the comfortable feeling that it was fighting a sanitary war. But in Vietnam, the bombing continued. (The air war was ultimately stepped up by President Nixon, in the operation called Linebacker II, to the point where it was really giving the North Vietnamese pause. The bombing would possibly have won the war, but at the height of its effectiveness, Nixon stopped it.) The land war progressed and progressed and progressed. More North Vietnamese were killed. The United States now had 465,000 troops in Vietnam, 265,000 more than Senator Russell had prophesied. Ten thousand of them had died in the fighting.

Nineteen sixty-eight. The Americans continued to win battles. The Tet offensive of the North Vietnamese was crushed. The Vietcong suffered blows from which they never recovered.

The people of the United States suddenly realized that this was going to be a long, long war. They did not like it. President Johnson discovered the bitter truth: one day Walter Cronkite on the CBS Evening News commented that the war could not be won. "If I've lost Walter," said President Johnson, "I've lost the support of Mr. Average Citizen."

And he was right.

Nineteen sixty-nine. The new president, Richard Nixon, took over the Vietnam mess. Once again there was the opportunity for immediate disengagement, and it was lost. Nixon proceeded to make almost all the same mistakes that Johnson had made before him. He, too, believed the war could be won even though there was no plan for winning it or any objective. He, too, believed that with training the South Vietnamese army could be made effective, not realizing that the South Vietnamese army did not really believe in its cause. He underestimated the American public discontent with the war. He lied to Congress and the people about the bombings. He extended the war to Cambodia, and began the destruction of that country.

Nineteen sixty-nine, My Lai. The little village where Lieutenant William Calley did his duty and helped kill a whole village full of women and children. The American press publicized the story. A villain was needed, and Lieutenant Calley was it. But there were hundreds of Lieutenant Calleys.

Nineteen seventy. The American people knew that something was very wrong. Desertions from the U.S. service grew greater. In 1967 President Johnson had committed 465,000 military men to Vietnam. That year there were 27,000 desertions. By 1970, when the personnel level had been dropped by the Nixon administration to 334,000, there were 64,000 desertions. That is to say nothing of the young men who evaded the draft, who fled to Canada; to say nothing of the protesters.

As the war continued, with no victory in sight, nor any plan for victory, and no sense to be made of the war at all, the objections became more strident. As with the Germans in the last days of World War I, and the Russians at the time of the revolution, American soldiers began to kill their own officers rather than fight. Literally hundreds of overeager officers were "fragged"—shot or blown up by fragmentation grenades thrown by their own troops. In 1970 alone, one army study put the number at 209 fraggings. It was probably an understatement.

Another alarming aspect of the war was the breakout of racial violence between whites and blacks. There was nothing new about racial violence in the service. It had occurred in the Spanish-American War. It had occurred in World War I, and in World War II.

But the Korean War inadvertently gave an enormous boost to military racial relations. Black soldiers at that time were still organized into all-black units; the 24th Army Infantry Regiment was an example. But in the desperate days of the Pusan Perimeter, blacks had been ordered to previously white units out of sheer necessity. The brass found that the black-white mixture worked, and army integration truly began.

In Vietnam, racial integration was set back years. The reason: black irritation at being forced to carry more than their share of the load. Too many white youngsters managed to escape the draft; as the war wore on the black faces increased, and so did tensions.

In one year the 1st Marine Division reported on more than eighty racial incidents, including the explosion of a hand grenade in an enlisted men's club, with sixty-three casualties.

Toward the end of the Vietnam War America was badly split—father against son, brother against brother—on such questions as the legitimacy of fleeing the country to avoid the draft. By 1968, Lyndon Johnson had been crushed by what he had done to the country, and knew that he could never again be elected, so he opted not to run. Heartbroken by this war, President Johnson lived only five more years and died at sixty-five, on January 22, 1973, the day before Secretary of State Henry Kissinger and North Vietnamese Foreign Minister Le Duc Tho agreed to end American involvement in the Vietnam War.

What a war it was! Helicopters! The Americans kept unveiling new techniques, new weapons, and new ideas. Most succeeded, but in the end all failed, not because there was anything intrinsically wrong with them, but because no weapons can defeat a nation fighting on its own soil against a foreign invader, when the people of the embattled nation are willing to take unlimited casualties to preserve the land from the foreigners. And that was the situation in Vietnam. The Americans lost 57,000 young men fighting for no cause at all. The North Vietnamese lost 500,000. Six hundred thousand Vietnamese civilians were killed, and by 1969 a million and a half had been made homeless. The figures kept rising every year, until war's end.

Much of the responsibility for this holocaust had to be attributed to the egos of a succession of American presidents, John F. Kennedy in particular, for setting in motion the time bomb. President Lyndon Johnson was the particular stubborn victim. He would not give up. President Richard Nixon, by 1972, had realized that the war was lost, and he enunciated the Nixon Doctrine: supplies but no more American men to die (except in the air).

Late in 1972 Nixon's secretary of state, Henry Kissinger, had begun negotiations for the retreat of the Americans. In January 1973 the United States bought its way out of the war, promising the North Vietnamese $3.25 billion in reparations as part of the agreement that North and South Vietnam would stop fighting, and that all foreign troops would be withdrawn from Vietnam.

On March 23, 1973, the last American troops were ordered home from

Vietnam. They had fought the nation's longest war, one of its bloodiest and most expensive, and certainly its most unpopular. The American soldier went home unwelcomed; he felt used and abused. The nation was ashamed. Once again it had "lost" a war—America, the "paper tiger."

Militarily all this talk was nonsense, some of it perpetuated by unfriendly news media. The American soldiers had acquitted themselves well until they lost faith. Even then there had been no Dienbienphu for them; they had not lost a battle. Their political leaders had just lost a war.

The inevitable end came in the spring of 1975. There were no more Americans to shore up a deteriorating South Vietnam. North Vietnamese troops moved south; the crumbling South Vietnamese government could no longer hold the allegiance of troops or citizens. In March, the North Vietnamese army cut the country in two, took Danang and Hue, and captured millions of dollars' worth of equipment that the Americans had given the South Vietnamese army. In April the fighting was within 100 miles of Saigon. The U.S. influence was back down to former levels: 50 military advisers and 7,500 civil employees of the U.S. government, still sorting out affairs. On April 30, 1975, American Ambassador Graham Martin was whisked away from the U.S. embassy by helicopter, just as the North Vietnamese came in to take over Saigon. It was all over at last.

Vietnam had been a very expensive way of propping up egos. The Americans spent $25 billion to aid South Vietnam. They also spent $165 billion on war expenditures of their own. It was a most costly war in terms of money—but, of course, it propped up the American and Japanese economies into a sort of perpetual boom until the day the shooting stopped.

Socially speaking, the impact of the Vietnam War on America was enormous. The war came at a time when American society was in the midst of great change. Television had come to rule the American home. The change was so profound that it affected the whole of American life, from breakfast to bedtime. Children got up with Captain Kangaroo and their parents went to bed with the late show. Morning newspapers, long on the decline, suddenly picked up because few read evening newspapers any more. They watched TV. One by one the evening newspapers died. In 1950 the *Denver Post* (afternoon) circulation was twice that of the *Rocky Mountain News* (morning). In 1986 the positions were nearly reversed. Television news, once called the "ghetto" of TV, became prime entertainment, certainly sparked by the ability of this new medium to cover the war pictorially. Books began to go out of style. Television became the great entertainer, the great babysitter, the central factor in nearly every American home.

The new medium and the war clashed from the beginning, because the pictures did not back up the generals' observations. Also, the star system of television so affected the journalism business that reporters for all media began to take themselves more seriously; they were not just messengers, but commentators whose opinions seemed important. The "anchor men" who came into everybody's house every day, were better known to Americans than U.S. senators.

Since the television reporters were mixing opinion with fact, so, too, did the print and radio reporters. Thus what had been called journalism became "newsbiz." And with the decline of the American newspapers also went the decline of the fighting editor. Newspaper publishers, in more and more "one paper towns," did not see any reason to "rock the boat." Which boat? Any boat. Newspapers settled down to printing classified ads, the local supermarket advertising, which were the lifelines of their business, and letting the news alone. The forthright editorial page became an item from the past; and why not? No one had time to read editorials anyhow. The Honeymooners would be on at 8.

In the war field, the irritations between military and media people that had sprouted during the Korean War became endemic. By 1970 military people and media people looked upon each other with grave suspicion. The body counts in Vietnam, for example—one of the principal manners in which the Americans assessed "victories"—were swiftly appraised by the media as false. But the media, ever more competitive—particularly the networks—often revealed information to the point of endangering military operations, and here the military drew a line. Out of it came a return to a suspicion between military and media that took them back to the relationships of the Civil War.

Suspicion, disbelief, loss of confidence of Americans in their government and in the media, and a new American isolationism; those were the heritage of Vietnam.

CHAPTER 47

Reign of Terror

Terror is an effective weapon for a time. The terror wrought by the firebombing of Japan in the spring of 1945 was definitely an element in bringing about the Japanese surrender in August. It convinced the one man who could make the decision that the war was lost and that to continue it would mean the end of Japan as a nation: Emperor Hirohito.

But terror is very difficult for the military to combat, because it is basically a political problem. Solve the political differences of the parties, and terror immediately vanishes. Menachem Begin was once a terrorist. So was Anwar Sadat. They survived to become respected statesmen in Israel and Egypt, thus, I think, proving the point.

In the last quarter of the twentieth century, terror dogs the world. In Northern Ireland terror had become a way of life, and the British military was not notably successful in containing it. So it was with the Americans in many places. Iran, Beirut Airport, Libya, all represented problems in the management of terror. Military excursions in two of the areas were utter failures. In the Libyan bombing attack of 1986 it was a different story, and a more positive one. The United States political leaders determined a limited policy and commissioned the military to carry it out. It was clean and surgical and it cleared the atmosphere and warned the terrorists for the future.

*   *   *

There is nothing new about terror as a political and military weapon. The Mongols practiced terror in the eleventh and twelfth centuries, knowing that the very name of the horde struck fear into the hearts of its enemies and made those enemies much easier to conquer. The Catholic Inquisition was an adventure in terror: horrible examples of torture and killing frightened the people into submission.

Nihilist and anarchist bomb-throwers of the late nineteenth century used terror as a means of gaining attention. One of the Americans who started the revolution in Hawaii suggested a "reign of terror" to bring the Hawaiians into line. In the twentieth century terror has again come into its own: terror in Northern Ireland and England, terror in Tehran, terror in Beirut, the Bader-Meinhof terror in Germany, Arab terror in France, and above all Palestinian terror, on the ground, on the sea, and in the airlanes of the world.

America became seriously involved in the terror only in 1979 when Iran's Ayatollah Khomeini's terrorists seized the United States embassy in Tehran, killed eight marines, and held fifty-three Americans as hostages.

When the seizure happened, no one in Washington seemed to know what to do, and the impotence of President Jimmy Carter's administration was frightening and maddening to Americans. Fifty years earlier an American administration would have sent a fleet, if necessary, to extricate the Americans and put down the terrorists. But these were new times, Americans were still suffering the shocks of two major wars that had not gone as planned, and they did not know how to react to this new (to them) phenomenon.

At first the U.S. government did nothing but wring its collective hands publicly in its self-inflicted impotence. Inaction was the worst possible move. The ayatollah took immediate advantage of it.

President Jimmy Carter publicly renounced the use of force to rescue the hostages. Again, Carter made a mistake. Even if he meant not to use force, he should never have said so. Also, his announcement was a lie. He was already planning to use force. And the lie, intended to persuade the Iranians that America would do nothing to rescue the hostages, had a deleterious effect. In effect, Jimmy Carter told the ayatollah that, no matter what he did, he was safe enough. The American media, exercising its valued First Amendment rights and no restraint whatsoever, played into the hands of the Iranian terrorists time and again. In the beginning the newsmen showed the terrorists poking and defiling the bodies of the dead Americans. Later they faithfully recorded the burning of dozens of American flags, and other insults to the United States.

The Pentagon was about as little prepared in 1979 to deal with terrorism against Americans as it had been in 1942 to deal with the U-boat menace off the American shore. But now it was better late than never: a few days after the seizure of the embassy, the Joint Chiefs of Staff were ordered to

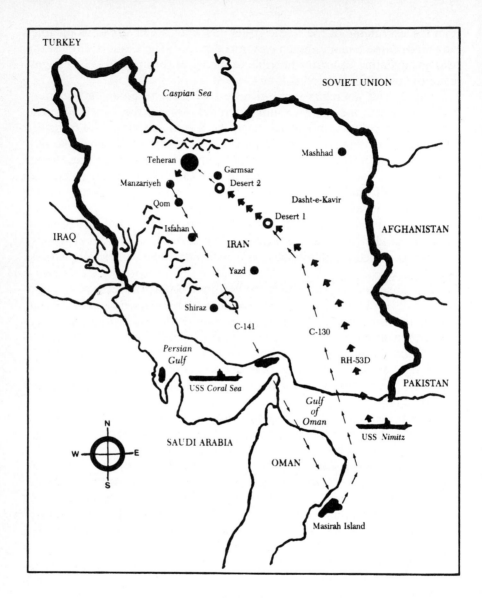

set up an organization and make plans for dealing with terrorism, including the hostage situation.

Thus began another American military excursion, the Iran rescue mission, which was to be accomplished by air. Six C-130 aircraft were to take a rescue team into Iran. Eight helicopters were then to move by stages into Iran, finally descend on Tehran, and rescue the hostages.

But two hours out from the carrier USS *Nimitz,* Helicopter Number 6 was abandoned in the desert because of supposed mechanical difficulties. Actually there was no mechanical difficulty, but a warning light had flashed and the crews of these helicopters were unfamiliar with the machines.

Four hours out, Helicopter Number 5 got a warning light, and abandoned the mission. And when Helicopter Number 2 reached the landing site, it had real mechanical difficulty and had to abort the mission.

At the landing site for the C-130s, the first plane hit an Iranian truck on the highway on its landing attempt, went around again and finally landed. But the truck incident compromised the mission's security.

When the helicopters and planes got on the ground finally, Colonel Charles Beckwith, the commander, discovered that he had only five helicopters instead of the six minimum called for in the plan, so he aborted the whole mission. Then in taking off one helicopter struck a C-130 tanker just behind the cockpit, the tanker blew up, the five-man crew was killed, and the ammunition aboard the C-130 began exploding. Some of the rockets struck other helicopters. Leaving all the classified material on the helicopters and leaving them for the Iranians to examine (and turn over to the Russians if they pleased), the Americans boarded the remaining C-130s and fled the scene.

And so the Iran air rescue mission was a failure, with eight Americans dead, a number of others wounded or burned, and what was left of American military prestige going up in smoke with the C-130. The ayatollah told the world that America was not a paper tiger, but a paper pussycat.

Americans were stunned but not very surprised. By this time the American military was perceived at home as self-serving and incompetent. Discussions of pay and pensions in connection with the federal budgeting process over the past few years had revealed that many military men these days were in the service only for the money, the lifelong medical and dental care, the liberal pension program, and the willingness of the government to let highly trained and very expensive military people retire at the end of twenty years and begin new careers. The average citizen perceived the American military system as a legalized racket, and seeing generals and admirals slide from command jobs into the seats of captains of industry did nothing to dispel the public impression. The public cynicism was capped by revelations of former high officers of Pentagon officials peddling influence and military wares to the Pentagon.

Richard A. Gabriel, a former army intelligence officer turned professor, wrote a book on the whole general subject, called *Military Incompetence.* His main point was that the restructuring of the Pentagon, largely by Secretary of Defense McNamara, had been a fatal error. The military

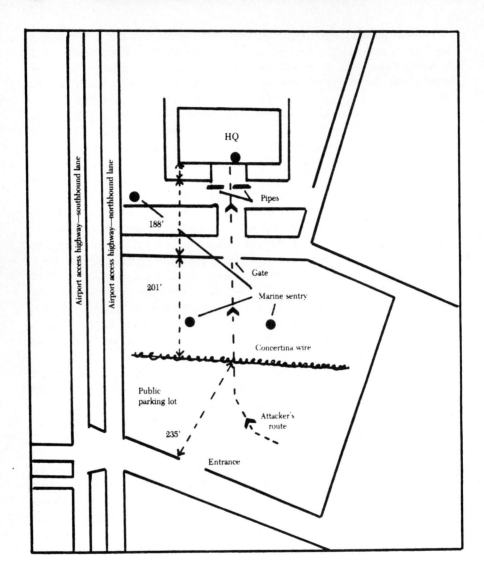

organization had been rebuilt to resemble American business. Thus all the dedication and almost religious sense of duty of the past was wiped out. Perks became the name of the game for the new volunteer army.

Ultimately, the failure of the Iran rescue mission did much to cost Jimmy Carter the presidency. It was a convenient symbol of the indecisiveness and incompetence the public perceived in the White House. In the election of 1980, Carter was perceived (and portrayed by Ronald Reagan) as a wimp. It was a low blow of fate, for unlike the Vietnam War, where most of the errors were made by politicians and White House advisers playing general, in the Iran rescue mission *all* the errors were made by the military. It was a totally incompetent military operation.

Nineteen eighty-two. The Americans still had not learned about terrorism. In an attempt to put an end to the 1982 Israeli invasion of Lebanon, the Americans had agreed to send a protective force to Beirut. On August 25, 1982, 800 marines of the 32nd Marine Amphibious Unit landed and took up positions between the Israelis and the Palestine Liberation Organization's troops, while the PLO withdrew. On September 10 the marines were withdrawn and taken back aboard their ships. Then violence broke out in Beirut. The Christians, with no military force to stop them, began attacking Shiite Muslims. Christian President-elect Bashir Gemayel was killed by a bomb. The violence in Beirut spread. Swiftly a multinational police force was assembled: British, French, Italian, and American. Twelve hundred marines went ashore again.

What was their mission?

To present an American "military presence." Was that a policy? It was the only one the United States had.

Colonel James Mead, commander of the marine unit, was ordered to garrison the Beirut airport. He planned to put his troops on the high ground to the east of the airport, with just a few marines at the airport itself. That installation was indefensible, located on a small plain with mountains on two sides and the sea on the third side. Mead called it a death trap.

But the White House intervened, and ordered the marines to occupy the airport. Colonel Mead moved his men into the death trap.

On November 3, the 32nd MAU was replaced by the 24th MAU.

All was quiet, until the Pentagon thinkers intervened. They decided that the way to bring peace to Lebanon was to establish a powerful Lebanese National Army. This showed their ignorance of the Lebanese political alignments. For centuries the Christians and the Shia and Sunni Muslims of Lebanon had warred on one another. In recent years the emotions had begun to run higher than ever, and broke out frequently in assassinations, murders, and firefights between militia organizations. If there was ever to be a Lebanese National Army, there would have to first be a Lebanese united nation, and that could only originate in Lebanon. It could not be imposed from the Pentagon. But the Americans said there was a Lebanese Army. It was a Christian Army.

Having established the premise, the Pentagon began implementing it. Arms and American Special Forces advisers were brought in to train the Lebanese army. All Lebanese perceived this as American support for the Christian Phalangists. The Christians bragged about the support. The Shiites and the Sunnis believed them. For in fact it was U.S. support. The Americans were again playing God. This time they announced that peace talks between the Lebanese government and Israel would begin, the object being to guarantee Israel's northern border.

In Lebanon this announcement was regarded as further proof that American policy in Lebanon was an extension of Israeli policy.

The trouble now came from the Israelis. They were very aggressive and attempted to push the American marines. On February 2 a unit of Israeli tanks started to penetrate the American defense position. Captain Charles Johnson jumped on the command tank, drew his pistol, and pointed it at the tank commander. At the same time several marine helicopter gunships took off, and orbited and kept their weapons pointed at the tank column. The Israelis withdrew, but that was the sort of treatment the marines had to be prepared to give.

The marines then were popular in Beirut. But Washington changed all that. The Americans in Washington continued to support the Christian government and strengthen it with arms.

Whatever happened to the original American policy of simply maintaining a presence? It had evaporated. The new policy, never really enunciated, was to support the Christian government. Anyone who knew anything about Lebanon knew that that support meant trouble.

The Lebanese National Army began arresting Muslims. A thousand disappeared. The two Muslim communities then resorted to violence, and general fighting broke out. The marines were now perceived as supporters of the Christian government.

On April 18 the American embassy was bombed and fifty-seven people were killed, seventeen of them Americans. Fighting broke out in the mountains.

The Americans began making joint patrols with the Lebanese army, more proof to the Muslims that the marines were in league with the Christians. And indeed they were.

In the mountains the Druse artillery began shelling the airport. On July 22, three marines were wounded and the airport was closed. After that it was often closed. On August 28, the marines began firing on the Druse artillery positions in the mountains. Now there was no question of whose side they were on.

The Druse force captured one of the mountains overlooking the airport, and the shelling of the airport increased. On September 7 the navy got into the fight, first with airborne reconnaissance for the marine gunners, then on September 8 with naval gunfire against the Druse artillery.

On September 12 the White House interfered again, and commenced naval and marine gunfire support of the Christian army. The new marine commander, Timothy J. Geraghty, had the option to call the fire. He refused, saying it would be a disaster to the marines, ending in their massacre at the indefensible airport.

By mid-September the Americans were shipping the Lebanese army large quantities of arms, and were firing artillery in support of their soldiers. When the American ambassador's residence was shelled, the firing became general. Then the battleship *New Jersey* came to the coast, and it began firing on the artillery positions in the mountains. The Americans were deep in the Lebanese civil war.

On the morning of October 23, 300 marines were asleep in the airport headquarters building when a suicide driver drove a flatbed truck loaded with 12,000 pounds of explosives wrapped around butane gas canisters into the compound. He crashed through the barbed wire, went past the sentries (whose guns were not loaded by order), and crashed through barriers into the lobby of the building, where he detonated his explosives. The explosion was so powerful that it lifted the building off its foundations and drove the floor eight feet into the earth. The sleeping marines were massacred.

The military, who had not liked the policies forced on them from the White House, now began leaking reports of their past objections. The public was aroused, but the White House refused to back down. It had to show support for the Christian government, was the argument advanced by National Security Adviser Robert McFarlane. Defense Secretary Weinberger and the marine high command wanted the marines out of Lebanon. Secretary of State Shultz wanted them to stay to support his policy of supporting the Christian government. President Reagan agreed with Shultz. The marines stayed and continued to get hurt.

The navy decided to give the Druse something to think about and sent an air attack against their artillery positions. The Druse antiaircraft gunners went into action. Twenty-eight planes attacked; two were shot down and one was damaged, without causing any appreciable damage. It was apparent that this carrier's airmen had something to learn. The attack was not repeated.

Finally the embarrassment of President Reagan's Lebanon policy became too great, and he had to abandon it, although he did so with a fierce show of truculence for the world. On February 26, 1984, the marines were withdrawn from Lebanon. On March 30 President Reagan announced that the Americans were also withdrawing from the multinational police force. They had been there for 531 days and had suffered nearly 400 casualties—and they had not affected the outcome of events in Lebanon a whit. Once again a military excursion had gone astray. The problem was political: the military men had been given an impossible assignment by the White House in furtherance of a murky policy that changed to become a wrongheaded policy. Once again the U.S. military presence was in the wrong place at the wrong time for the wrong reason.

*   *   *

After the event, Americans were inclined (led by the White House) to equate the Iran-embassy hostage affair with the Beirut bombing; and when a TWA passenger liner was forced down at Beirut, an American sailor killed, and more than seventy hostages held for days, this, too, was added to the "terrorist" file. Then came the hijacking of the cruise ship *Achille Lauro,* the massacre at the Rome airport, and the bombing of a German nightclub frequented by American servicemen, and these events too were added to the file. But the fact is that the Beirut bombing had to be separated from the rest. It was a military action carried out by a military (or at least a paramilitary) force engaged in civil war, against an American military establishment. The other terrorist events were something quite different.

In facing those acts of deliberate terrorism against civilians, the Americans showed that at last they had learned something about fighting terrorism. In the Barbary Wars back in the eighteenth and nineteenth centuries, a weak young United States first opted to pay tribute to terrorists, and did so until it learned the price. Through the efforts of Commodore Preble and Stephen Decatur and William Bainbridge and a dozen other brave naval captains, the North African terrorists were finally overcome, but only when the United States quit paying tribute and mollifying the terrorists and adopted a policy of blasting them.

In 1986 President Reagan authorized a "surgical" mission against Libya, whose government had adopted a policy of encouragement of terrorist organizations aimed at embarrassing the Western powers. The action might have been taken from a page of the history of the American war against the bashaw of Tripoli and the dey of Algiers.

In the spring of 1986, from the carriers and from shore bases in Britain, the Americans launched a strike against Bengazi and Tripoli. The Reagan move was part of a greater policy which placed American warships in the Mediterranean, skirting the edges of Libya on war games, in the hope of provoking Libyan President Muammar Qaddafi to foolish action. Qaddafi responded once, and he lost some aircraft for his pains. Thereafter he turned to posturing and striking through terrorism against civilians.

Then came the American air strike. The American attack was extremely successful and informative. The French, who had previously refused to take united action against the terrorists (although they suffered as much as any nation from terror raids in France), refused to let American planes fly over French airspace, showing how little value France had as an ally. The Germans wrung their hands, and so did most of the other NATO countries. The British government stood by Reagan, but the Labour party criticized (an indication of what to expect from a Labour government). The strike itself very nearly killed Qaddafi, but just missed, and it had an excellent purifying effect, particularly after President Reagan warned that the United States was prepared to strike again against any country that encouraged terrorism. In Tripoli and Damascus there was silence.

Finally, America had indicated a new awareness of the uses to which power could be put by a major government: extreme power quickly applied and quickly withdrawn to accomplish a limited objective was a solution that did not create new problems.

What remained to be seen was whether or not the Reagan administration's hard-learned lesson could be transmitted to a future administration; for the American nation has already shown that it has lost its sense of history, and no administration of recent years has been able to profit from the lessons of the past. There was a time when politics stopped at the water's edge; those were the days of bipartisan foreign policy. Basically bipartisan policy has worked only in times of crisis, notably wars. It worked during the revolution, but it did not work in the War of 1812, when the Federalists did all they could to sabotage the war effort. It worked in the Civil War and in World War I (except for the Socialists who were flung in jail for opposing the war). It worked in World War II, but failed in the peacetime years over China and communism.

If there was ever a time when bipartisan foreign policy was needed it was the 1980s, with an America recovering from the bruises of recent years, and still not quite sure where it wanted to go or how to get there. But the horizon looked very, very blank.

CHAPTER 48

The Usual (Unusual) Crisis in Latin America

In this book I have been quite critical about the military and political failures in connection with America's military excursions, and particularly those of recent years, wherein the Americans so often seemed inept, ill-informed, and lackadaisical in performance. Certainly the American policy toward Fidel Castro remains ridiculous, based on old slights and scratches, and not in tune with the world politics of today. By reaching an accommodation with Castro, the United States could pull a plug that would drain Soviet influence right out of all Latin America. The only problem remains the American political evangelism that forces one military excursion after another in Latin America.

There is one American excursion which I applaud in its entirety: the Grenada invasion. It came at a time when American morale was sagging badly, so it served the purpose of buttressing the civilian self-respect as well as the military self-respect. It was handled intelligently, with proof being given to the world that the airport under construction on Grenada was destined to carry Soviet bombers.

President Reagan and his advisers did not go in alone. They fabricated a special alliance of Grenadian neighbors to join in the operation, thus rendering it an international service rather than a Big Brother putdown. And when the Americans went in, they went quickly, accomplished their task of overthrowing the "bad guys" and installing the "good guys," and then got out.

There is still another respect of the Grenada invasion that I applaud: the flat refusal of the military in this instance to have anything to do with the media. The grounds were that the Grenada invasion was a secret operation and the media could not be trusted. The journalists were allowed to come in only after the fact. Thus there was no chance that they could, inadvertently or deliberately, forecast the American maneuver. I find that quite acceptable, given the media behavior in Vietnam, and I gather that the American people at large feel the same.

The media set up a hue and cry at the time, but finding very little public support, backed off. I am hopeful that the media learned something at Grenada that will be useful to all of us: that is, a bit of humility, an understanding that the military has an obligation to succeed in its undertakings and has no obligation to the media to provide special access. It would be best if an accommodation could be again reached, wherein the media agree to abide by the rules of the game, and the military agree to provide as much access as possible. But that is all for the future. It really does not hurt the media to have to scratch for their stories, or to lose the silver platter on which they have been dished their information by the military since the beginning of the Vietnam War.

The media really ought to welcome the change. They might have devoted some of their zeal at Grenada to reporting on the number of medals the generals, colonels, light colonels, and majors gave one another—enough weight in metal probably to pave the main road of the island. But that, of course, is in the military tradition. Bankers get money, soldiers get medals.

*   *   *

The history of American interventions in Latin America over two centuries would fill a five-foot shelf, and has already taken up a good amount of space in this book. The interventions before World War II have been described in earlier pages. But after World War II American attitudes underwent some changes. The result has been a stumbling in Latin American policy that has destroyed the old tenets of the Monroe Doctrine and replaced them with nothing more than reactions of the moment. The marines used to think they knew what was wanted in Latin America; they had been there so long some of them felt like natives. But no more. The Vietnam syndrome controls policy; no American military intervention could be carried out without an enormous public backlash.

The problems in Latin America have not changed significantly in a hundred years. The problems are violence, greed, and poverty. All have been sustained by the wealthy ruling class, very similar in nearly every state, which keeps the poor in a state of poverty. The result, of course, is that radicalism flourishes like mosquitoes on a pond.

From time to time the American government and American institutions have attempted to deal with this central problem of poverty, but to little avail. The only way to solve the problem of poverty is to restructure the society that spawns it, and, try as they might, the Americans have never been able to restructure Latin American society with any long-range success. Revolutions, social or political, proceed from within; they cannot be successfully imposed. If there is one lesson still apparently unlearned from Vietnam, that is it.

In 1956 dictator Somoza was assassinated in Nicaragua. His heirs carried on the dictatorship.

One night in May 1961, dictator Rafael Trujillo of the Dominican Republic came to the end of a lonely road. He was assassinated. The Dominican Republic then went into a period of almost constant change. Juan Bosch elbowed his way to the top. At first the Americans thought Bosch was fine. Elections held in the republic were declared by all concerned to be the freest in its history. But then Juan Bosch proved to be too thoroughly imbued with Dominican nationalism. He said he wanted friendship with the United States, but he refused to take actions that the American ambassador wanted him to take, and he often honored guests from other Latin countries who were not regarded by the Americans as friends. Juan José Arevalo was a case in point: he was the former president of Guatemala and an ardent anti-American. In the Organization of American States, a sort of United Nations of the hemisphere, the vote of the Dominican Republic in favor of American propositions could no longer be assured.

One example: the Kennedy and Johnson administrations wanted to conduct a "holy war" against Castro; Bosch's Dominican government refused to participate.

Consequently, when dissatisfactions arose in the Dominican Republic, the American embassy did nothing to stop them or to assist the Bosch administration. Some say various American embassy officials gave as much aid and comfort to the dissenters as possible. Bosch was too close to the Communists for American comfort. In any event, Juan Bosch was overthrown and deported in September 1963 by a triumvirate, which lasted only from September 1963 to April 1965. Then the civil war began. Juan Bosch wanted his job back. There were Communists in the underbrush, and they scared the Americans thoroughly.

Very shortly the United States was involved in the Dominican revolution. The involvement began with the matter of moral support for Colonel Pedro Bartolome Benoit, Colonel Enrique A. Casado Saladin, and Navy Captain Olgo M. Santana Carrasco. Their junta was recognized by the U.S. government on April 28, 1965, and the first thing President Benoit did was call for the American marines to come in and preserve order.

And so back came the marines to the Caribbean, five hundred of them,

landed from the U.S. naval task force that was off the coast of the Dominican Republic that day evacuating American civilians from the civil
war zone. As a "humanitarian gesture" the marines landed, to protect
United States lives and property, of course, but to protect everyone else
as well.

President Johnson: "I have ordered the Secretary of Defense to put
the necessary American troops ashore in order to give protection to hundreds
of Americans who are still in the Dominican Republic and to escort them
safely back to this country. This same assistance will be available to the
nationals of other countries, some of whom have already asked for help."

This action was not an intervention, it was indicated—just plain hu-
manitarianism.

The marines landed, and were placed around the American embassy
and the Hotel Embajador. They waited for Colonel Benoit to organize his
revolution.

But . . . Colonel Benoit did nothing. The Americans would have to do
it for him. Juan Bosch's army took advantage of the lull in fighting and
attacked the Fortaleza Ozama, captured the post and its 4,000 stand of
arms, and planned to move against national police headquarters. Soon,
his forces said, the Bosch government would be reestablished.

The marines of the task force had landed, and the 82nd Airborne
Division sent men. (This was the army's most effective strike force.) A
buildup of 20,000 American troops was begun.

"Communist leaders, many of them trained in Cuba, seeking a chance
to increase disorder, to gain a foothold, joined the revolution. They took
increasing control. . . ."

So to save their friends, the Americans were forced to act. On April
30 the American paratroopers moved out of San Isidro and headed for the
capital. The marines occupied San Isidro and set up a corridor bisecting
the island.

The Dominican rebels, calling themselves the Constitutionalists, continued to fight. But the new American special ambassador, John Bartlow
Martin, arranged for a new Government of National Reconstruction. The
generals of the military junta were deported to Puerto Rico.

In Washington, the headquarters of the Organization of American States,
the Latin countries were not pleased with this new evidence of American
interference in hemispheric affairs. As in the United Nations, the members
of the Organization of American States talked and talked, but nothing
happened, because the United States could always muster the proper votes
to avoid being condemned for interference.

An inter-American force was authorized. Honduras became the first
contributor of troops (250). Brazil contributed, as did Paraguay, Nicaragua,

Costa Rica, and El Salvador. The headlines were more powerful than the force; El Salvador's contribution was 3 soldiers. Of the contributors, five of the nations were dictatorships.

Fine company for the Americans! That is what one would say if one shared the general American revulsion against dictatorships. But here again the U.S. government was playing its usual hand: the dictatorships are bad, admittedly, but the Communist alternative is worse. And the Communist alternative was always the only alternative mentioned.

In Washington some senators and representatives began to question the validity of the "Communist threat." To quiet the rumblings, the Johnson administration sent envoys from Washington to negotiate a settlement among the parties. The American troops prevented any military solution; in other words, had the troops not been there, the revolution might have succeeded.

The negotiations, presided over by American representatives from Washington, seemed endless. But in September 1965 a provisional government was installed. The chief of it was Hector Garcia Godoy, a member of the elite. Fighting continued on and off for the rest of the year. In June 1966 elections were held. Juan Bosch was a candidate, but his life was constantly threatened and he left his house in Santo Domingo only three times during the campaign. The American-backed candidate won. He was Juan Balaguer, and he collected fifty-seven percent of the vote to Bosch's thirty-nine percent. No one ever claimed that the elections were fraudulent, and it was true that they were free enough. As historian Piero Gleijeses noted in his study of the Dominican revolt, it was notable that thirty-nine percent of the people had the courage to vote for Juan Bosch, considering the American posture. The whole affair had been nicely arranged in Washington.

This time, however, there was a notable reaction to the intervention, in the place where it mattered: in Washington. For five years the American people had been responding to alarums and excursions of the Kennedy and Johnson administrations against communism, and particularly Castro communism. Having broken relations with Fidel Castro in Cuba, having isolated him by trade and travel bans, having forced Castro into the arms of the Soviet Union, the U.S. government never stopped complaining.

The history of El Salvador is again a history of poverty. In a nutshell: in 1961 seven-tenths of one percent of the people held forty percent of the land. Forty-one percent of the people had no land at all. Eighty percent of the people lived in poverty. They still do.

In October 1979 El Salvador had a coup d'état. President Humberto Romero was deposed by the organization called Young Military. After that, junta followed junta until 1980, when the United States intervened politically in the usual evangelical fashion to try to stabilize the country. "Law and order" was the watchword. But instead of law the Americans got the assassination of one of the major Christian Democratic leaders, Mario Zamora. The junta fell apart again. And José Napoleon Duarte came to power.

The Americans at this stage were expending much time and money trying to build El Salvador's agricultural economy. But their efforts were constantly undermined by internal security forces and death squads. Instead of improving, the economy declined.

In 1982 the United States set out to legitimize the Duarte regime, a policy advocated by the Carter administration and followed by the Reagan administration. Voter turnout was said to be seventy-five percent (the U.S. turnout is often just over fifty percent), but Duarte got only thirty-five percent of the vote, which was a problem. The United States began its usual fulminations against the revolutionary movement in El Salvador. But this was 1982—the American people had some inklings from Vietnam, although one could hardly say they understood what had happened there. But what could be understood is that Americans were overwhelmingly opposed to interference in the affairs of any nation that would bring about the involvement of American troops again. The rebels were called Communists and stooges of Moscow and stooges of Castro. Probably they were Communists, or, if not, they soon would become Communists, since that seemed even in 1986 to be the only way out for Latin American rebels. A whole succession of American administrations from McKinley on had steadfastly refused to acknowledge the existence of home-grown revolution.

In 1979 the Sandinistas (the revolutionaries who had adopted the name of a rebel leader of the 1920s) overcame the government forces and took control of Nicaragua, in spite of American attempts to prevent the take-over. President Jimmy Carter had done everything but send troops; that he could not do, for the temper of the American people, after Vietnam, forbade it. But at the last minute the Carter administration welcomed the change in Nicaragua. Then they turned against it when the Communists took control.

The Reagan administration was no different. Using old clichés and observations to quell revolutionary movement in El Salvador and a revolutionary government in Nicaragua seemed unavoidable. But in the 1980s the Pentagon, and Congress, to say nothing of the American people, forced the White House to go slowly. The Duarte government in El Salvador was backed up, but not like in the old days of El Salvador. There would be no marines. The contras in Nicaragua were backed up. Were they the answer to the failed revolution? After several tries, in 1986 President Reagan

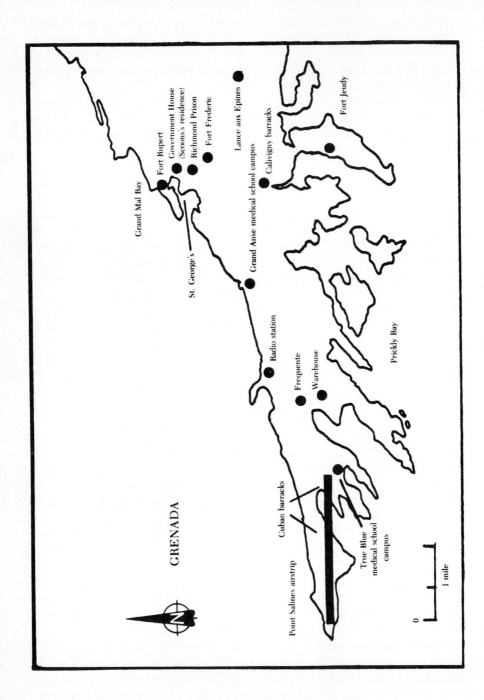

managed to get them $100 million, which would be spent on arms for the most part. It would go down the drain, and Reagan or his successor would be back to Congress for more, unless by some modern miracle American policy in Latin America could be brought to change the realities of the twentieth century.

In 1983 the Pentagon showed that it had learned something in Vietnam and something in Latin America. The concern was over a 12,000-foot airstrip being built on the little island of Grenada. The situation was complicated by the fact that the island republic had been taken over by a group that American intelligence termed Communist, and indebted to both Castro and the Soviet Union. This seemed a legitimate concern, since Cuba is an acknowledged client state of the USSR, and Soviet planes and submarines have the use of Cuban bases, which could at some future date be very harmful to the United States.

The Pentagon launched a surgical operation against Grenada. It sent in marines, rangers, and part of the 82nd Airborne Division to take the airport and the island. A complicating factor was the existence on the island of a medical school which was educating a large number of American students. Quite rightly in the 1980s, the White House also had concern over the possibility of a hostage situation. So the surgical operation was the answer, and it went very well, in spite of complaints of "overkill."

The Grenada invasion solved two problems for the Americans. It removed the danger of the 12,000-foot runway as a base—but only so long as a government friendly to the United States could be kept in Grenada. If that were to change, then the problem would arise again.

Second, the Americans had finally achieved the splendid little victory that American presidents had been wanting since John F. Kennedy, to prove anew the ability of the American military to win.

CHAPTER 49

Space Ships and GI Shoes

Amid so much criticism of American military policy in recent years and so little regard for American military performance, perhaps it seems odd that I should advocate the removal of the American space effort from the hands of the National Aeronautics and Space Administration into the hands of the air force. But the reason for my advocacy comes out of a number of years of observing NASA's arrogance and incompetence, and the determined policy of concealment of its errors. True, the military has its own level of incompetence and confusion, but the military is responsible through a chain of command to the president of the United States, and, generally speaking, the military men (at least before McNamara's "industrialization" program) have shown a degree of selflessness and dedication to service unmatched in the other sectors of government. NASA has always seemed to me to be a tight little kingdom in which the baton is passed from one ruler to another, and the general public and even Congress get as short shrift as the bureaucrats can manage.

From the outset of the American space effort, NASA has operated as an entity unto itself. It set up rules under which the original astronauts sold their "stories" to Life *and the* New York Times *for personal profit. The bureaucrats allowed the original astronauts to capitalize on their star status to own and operate a motel in Cocoa Beach, Florida, which they did with gusto, misusing the public weal for private profit, until the scandal got too bad and they were forced to sell out.*

Time and again the standards of the space programs have virtually collapsed, under pressures from the agency chiefs to "make it look good," the

Challenger disaster being only the most recent. Anyone asking questions around NASA headquarters is quietly rebuffed or loaded down with a mountain of statistical material that has no relationship to the questions asked. I encountered that wall of resistance time and again when writing a book called The Space Dealers *some fifteen years ago. My opinion is that NASA should be disbanded, that a truly vitalized Aeronautics Administration be established to manage aeronautical affairs, and that space be left to the military men, who in this sense could be likened to a transportation agency, carrying the scientists, and ultimately perhaps the businessmen, to the places they want to go.*

*   *   *

The American military tradition has come a long way since the days of the Massachusetts colonists and King Philip's War. The fact is, however, that in the 1980s the American military is still a questionable force. The first problem, as always, is that American foreign policy has become more and more "pragmatic," which is a euphemism for responsive, rather than generative. Soviet policy, on the other hand—and that is what the United States is up against—is remarkably solid and evocative of the policies of the past. The czars dreamed of fleets in far oceans; the Soviets have attained them. The czars dreamed of surrounding Russia with controllable governments: except for China, the Soviets have attained that dream. The czars dreamed of empire; the imperialist Soviets are creating it.

For nearly forty years the American policy has been response: response in Korea, response in Vietnam, response in Europe, response in the Western Hemisphere. Only in the Pacific, where the war and the peace brought the United States into close alliance with Japan, and where Richard Nixon dared to bring the United States into friendship with China, has the policy shown any vigor of its own.

Until very recently, the batterings of Korea and Vietnam caused the American military to live in a state of severe paranoia. Its doubts were not helped a bit by the McNamara restructuring of the Pentagon in the image of General Motors.

In Grenada as well as in the Gulf of Sidra, the American military has proved itself. But politically, in Latin America, U.S. policy is approaching a dead end. More and more Americans have begun doubting the efficacy as well as the morality of the policies followed since the 1800s. But what to do? That is the new question.

The fact is that American policy in Latin America and elsewhere is still confined to opposing "communism" wherever it raises its head, and no difference even yet can be seen between native radicalism and Soviet adherence in the American responses.

China is the lesson, if one does not like Yugoslavia. China is Communist, yet the Chinese have disavowed Marxism now because they say it does not work. So what is there to be afraid of with China? Nothing for Americans, and there never was anything to be afraid of unless the United States threatened China, which it did in 1950, thus provoking the Chinese entry into a war America had already won against the North Koreans.

That aspect of the Korean War remains almost totally undiscussed in America in the 1980s. It is not the sort of subject that political and military leaders savor.

In the 1980s, Americans continue to talk about defense, but to make the most appalling errors in the application of defense policy. One can laugh about $600 toilets for airplanes, and $500 bolts for spare parts. But there is something wrong with the system that allows the excesses to continue. The pattern continues even in space, which may indeed become the frontier of national defense, despite the scoffings of some elements of the political and scientific communities. Those same elements opposed atomic development.

Space is a far more serious matter than most Americans realize, although they are beginning to see that something is drastically wrong with the American space program. The Challenger disaster proved this beyond doubt.

The American space program, like most American external policies, began as a response. The challenge was Sputnik in 1957. The shock caused the Eisenhower administration to begin a crash program of science and space development. But it was put into the wrong hands when the administration created the National Aeronautics and Space Administration, and the failure was proved with the Challenger disaster. It left the United States with no adequate manner of launching space vehicles. In the summer of 1986 Janes, the publisher of *Janes Fighting Ships* and paramount world observer of the military capabilities of nations, observed that the United States had fallen so far behind the Soviets in the space race that it would take until the late 1990s to catch up.

Americans had no suspicion that this was so. But as the various investigations of the Challenger disaster continued, it became ever more apparent that NASA was reduced to a bureaucratic shambles.

The solution is not to try to prop up a failed agency, but to remove the entire space program from the hands of NASA, to destroy NASA and put the space program into the hands of the military where it has always belonged and where the Soviets have quite properly relegated it. The other uses of space—civil communications, satellites, and the like—can quite properly be handled by an arm of the military, just as community relations are. For with all the difficulties of military management and procurement, and all the errors of abandoned projects, the elements of the military space program have been far more cleverly managed over the years than the NASA programs. And when it comes right down to it, where does NASA get its astronauts? From the military. And that is the way it will always be. Space should be taken out of bureaucratic politics, and the sooner the better.

As for defense in the last part of the twentieth century, the legitimate American concern is the safety of the United States, and in the 1980s that means safety from Soviet encirclement. There is a way to ensure it, and that is to treat first of all with the root problem: the Soviet Union itself. Tentative advances have been made from time to time in this regard, but always they have ended in some irritation caused by the basic distrust of the two parties. Make no bones about it, Nikita Khrushchev was not posturing when he said to Americans "We will bury you." He was just talking out of turn. The Soviet Union intends to destroy the American government and its capitalist system. The Soviets are dedicated to it and always have been. No change has ever been indicated. It is the task of the United States to prevent it from happening if America is to survive.

But preventing the victory of Soviet imperialism does not mean seeing a Communist under every national bed.

What the United States ought to be doing with the Russians is trading off. The United States might trade Soviet abandonment of Castro and removal of Soviet bases in Cuba and Soviet influence in Nicaragua for American noninterference in Afghanistan. Let the Soviets enjoy their counterpart to Vietnam. They may be there another ten years before they finally decide to cut their losses. They have already shown that they have failed to learn from the American Vietnam experience. Eventually they will have to get out, for the same principle applies: a people can be subjugated by another only so long as the subjugating power has the will to maintain troops in the land of the victims. As General Westmoreland's favorite military philosopher, Sun Tzu, put it, there is no profit for a big country in a long war.

To reach an accommodation with the Soviets, it might be useful for the United States to remove the missiles from Western Europe. It might even mean an end to NATO, which for the United States would be a blessing, since more and more people in the NATO nations have shown that they are far more interested in neutrality than in mutual defense. In case of trouble, NATO is more likely to collapse than to produce European warriors.

In the Pacific, the most important area of the world for the American future, the United States for once finds itself in a positive position. Japan is a firm ally, the only fear being that she will be pushed too far and back into her old militarist-imperialist pattern by excessive American demands on her. China is a natural ally of the United States against the Soviet

Union; one might say it the other way about—the United States is a natural ally of China against Russia—because the long Sino-Soviet border and the continuing disputes over its exact location is a problem that will never go away.

The American defense position in the Pacific, then, is sound and workable, and should be extended.

For once, an American administration with only the slightest bit of hesitancy did the right thing in a serious political matter abroad. When Ferdinand Marcos rigged the Philippine elections of 1986, the Reagan administration came out on the side of the angels; Marcos, whose dictatorship had grown ever more oppressive, tried to give the impression that Corazon Aquino's party was a Communist stooge or would soon be taken over, but for once the old Red flag trick did not work on the Americans. Marcos and his wife were forced out, and it was all done without an increase in the American military presence, a remarkable display of good luck and forbearance.

At some point the Americans are going to have to come to grips with the incompetence of the nonprofessional volunteer army. The training manuals have been rewritten time and again to take account of the lowering ability of the American soldier to read and write. In a word, there are too many virtually illiterate persons in the service; military service represents to young people perhaps the best job they can get. But as Vietnam showed, the overenlistment of minorities creates a whole set of new problems for the military. The real solution has to come out of the past, and it has to be a military of obligatory service, with no special deals for anyone.

The American military always has been a mirror of the American nation, and it still is, reflecting the racial and social problems of the country. What it has lost in recent years is the pride of the profession. And that lack of pride shows most particularly among the officer corps. In America no one likes to keep track of the statistics of dropout from the military services after the young officers serve the mandatory five years to pay the government back for their education. At the end of the five-year period, the current dropout rate is enormous; with the navy it has been as high as forty percent. In Japan, for example, there is virtually no dropout for Defense Academy graduates—less than one percent. The Japanese choose the military as their profession just as Americans used to, and then they stick with it for the rest of their working careers. That is a very big part of what is needed by the American military to regain its own sense of pride. The politicians have always been the burden the military must bear, and always will be under the American system of political control of the military. But before the 1960s, the military maintained its sense of dignity and duty. That has suffered seriously since.

The military has learned much about when not to get involved in other people's business, and in recent years the political institutions have also been impressed by a series of American failures. Given a positive political policy, to replace the old Monroe Doctrine, the failed United Nations, and the moribund defense treaty system, and given a renewed sense of dedication and purpose by the military, the United States might be able to look forward to a decade or so in which America is not involved in any wars at all.

Bibliography

Unpublished Manuscripts

Hoyt, Edwin P. "Richard Harding Davis."
———. "The Parkers: A Family History of Hawaii."
———. "Leland Stanford."
———. "The Death of the U-Boats."
———. "The GI War."
———. "The Nisei Warriors."

Published Works

Adams, Henry. *The War of 1812*. Washington: Infantry Journal, 1944.
Alden, Carroll Storrs, and Allan Westcott. *The United States Navy*. Philadelphia: J. B. Lippincott Co., 1943.
Alden, John R. *A History of the American Revolution*. London: MacDonald and Co., 1969.
Ambler, Charles H. *George Washington and the West*. New York: Russell and Russell, 1936.
Andrist, Ralph K. *The Long Death: The Last Days of the Plains Indians*. New York: Macmillan Co., 1964.
Bailyn, Bernard. *The Ideological Origins of the American Revolution*. Cambridge, Mass.: Harvard University Press, 1967.
Bancroft, George. *History of the Colonization of the United States*. Boston: Charles C. Little and James Brown, 1846.
———. *The American Revolution*. 10 vols. Boston: Little, Brown & Co., 1875.

————. *History of the United States of America.* 6 vols. Boston: Little, Brown & Co., 1879.

Barr, Pat. *The Coming of the Barbarians.* New York: E. P. Dutton, 1967.

Bassett, J. S. *A Short History of the United States.* New York: Macmillan Co., 1939.

Beach, Stewart. *Samuel Adams.* New York: Dodd Mead and Co., 1965.

Beirne, Francis F. *The War of 1812.* Hamden, Conn.: Archon Books, 1965.

Bill, Alfred Hoyt. *Rehearsal for Conflict.* New York: Alfred A. Knopf, 1947.

Bird, Harrison. *War for the West, 1790–1813.* New York: Oxford University Press, 1971.

Boettcher, Thomas D. *Vietnam: The Valor and the Sorrow.* Boston: Little, Brown & Co., 1985.

Boyd, Thomas. *Mad Anthony Wayne.* New York, n.p., 1929.

Brown, Charles H. *Agents of Manifest Destiny: The Life and Times of the Filibusters.* Chapel Hill, N.C.: University of North Carolina Press, 1980.

Browne, Dee. *Bury My Heart at Wounded Knee.* New York: Holt, Rinehart, and Winston, 1984.

Burgess, John W. *The Middle Period.* New York: Charles Scribner's Sons, 1897.

Buttinger, James. *Vietnam: A Dragon Embattled.* New York: Praeger, 1967.

Catton, Bruce. *This Hallowed Ground.* Garden City, N.Y.: Doubleday, 1956.

Churchill, Winston S. *The Second World War.* Boston: Houghton Mifflin, 1949.

Clay, Lucius D. *The Papers of Lucius D. Clay.* Edited by Jean Edward Smith, Bloomington, Ind.: Indiana University Press, 1974.

————. *Decision in Germany.* Garden City, N.Y.: Doubleday, 1950.

Connell, Evan S. *Son of the Morning Star.* San Francisco: North Point Press, 1984.

Cohen, Warren I. *America's Response to China.* New York: John Wiley and Sons, 1971.

Coleman, R. V. *The First Frontier.* New York: Charles Scribner's Sons, 1948.

Cooper, James Fenimore. *Naval History of the United States.* 2 vols. Philadelphia: Lea and Blanchard, 1840.

Corrison, D. J. *The United States Navy.* New York: Praeger, 1968.

Cumming, William P., and Hugh F. Rankin. *The Fate of a Nation.* London: Phaidon Press Ltd., 1975.

Dangerfield, George. *The Awakening of American Nationalism.* New York: Harper and Row, 1965.

DeConde, Alexander. *Entangling Alliances: Politics and Diplomacy under George Washington.* Durham, N.C.: Duke University Press, 1958.

Dewey, Admiral George. *Autobiography.* New York: Charles Scribner's Sons, 1903.

Fishel, W. P., ed. *Viet Nam: Anatomy of a Conflict.* Itasca, Ill.: Peacock Publishing Co., 1968.

Fiske, John. *New France and New England.* Boston: Houghton Mifflin Co., 1902.

Foner, Philip S. *The Spanish-Cuban-American War and the Birth of American Imperialism, 1895–1902.* 2 vols. New York: Monthly Review Press, 1972.

Gabriel, Ralph Henry, ed. *The Pageant of America.* New Haven, Conn.: Yale University Press, 1928.

Gabriel, Richard A. *Military Incompetence.* New York: Farrar, Strauss and Giroux, Hill and Wang, 1985.

Gimbel, John. *The American Occupation of Germany.* Stanford, Calif.: Stanford University Press, 1968.

Gleijeses, Piero. *The Dominican Crisis: The 1965 Constitutionalist Revolt and American Intervention.* Baltimore: Johns Hopkins University Press, 1978.

Hamilton, Milton W. *Sir William Johnson, Colonial American, 1715–1763.* Port Washington, N.Y.: Kennikat Press, 1976.

Harris, William. *A Rhode Islander Reports on King Philip's War: the Second William Harris letter, of August 1676.* Edited by Douglas Edward Leach. Providence: Rhode Island Historical Society, 1963.

Hawks, Francis. *Narrative of the Expedition of an American Squadron in the China Seas and Japan, Performed in the Years 1852, 1853, and 1854 under the Command of Commodore M. C. Perry U.S. Navy.* Washington, D.C.: Beverly Tucker, Senate Printer, 1856.

Higginbotham, Don. *The War of American Independence.* New York: Macmillan Co., 1971.

Hitti, Philip K. *Lebanon in History.* New York: St. Martin's Press, 1957.

Holmes, W. J. *Double-Edged Secrets.* Annapolis, Md.: U.S. Naval Institute, 1979.

Hoyt, Edwin P. *The American Attitude.* New York: Abelard Schuman, 1970.

———. *The Bloody Road to Panmonjum.* Briarcliff Manor, N.Y.: Stein and Day.

———. *Blue Skies and Blood.* New York: Paul Eriksson, 1975.

———. *Closing the Circle.* New York: Van Nostrand Reinhold Co., 1981.

———. *On to the Yalu.* Briarcliff Manor, N.Y.: Stein and Day.

———. *The Glory of the Solomons.* New York: Stein and Day, 1983.

———. *Guadalcanal.* New York: Stein and Day, 1982.

———. *Japan's War.* New York: McGraw-Hill Book Co., 1986.

———. *The Lonely Ships.* New York: David McKay Co., 1975.

———. *The Militarists.* New York: Donald A. Fine, 1985.

———. *Pusan Perimeter,* Briarcliff Manor: Stein and Day.

Hsu Long-Hsuen and Chang Ming-Kai. *History of the Sino-Japanese War of 1937–45.* Taipei: Chung Wu Publishing Co., 1971.

Hubbard, William. *The Present State of New England, Being a Narrative of the Troubles with the Indians, 1677.* Introduction by Cecelia Tichi. Bainbridge, N.Y.: York Mail-Print, Inc., 1972.

Jackson, Don, ed. *Black Hawk.* Urbana, Ill.: University of Illinois Press, 1964.

James, Marquis. *The Life of Andrew Jackson.* Indianapolis: Bobbs-Merrill Co., 1938.

Jennings, Francis. *The Ambiguous Iroquois Empire.* New York: W. W. Norton & Co., 1984.

Johannsen, Robert W. *To the Halls of Montezuma.* New York: Oxford University Press, 1985.

Jones, Virgil Carrington. *The Civil War at Sea.* 3 vols. New York: Holt, Rinehart, and Winston, 1960.

Karnow, Stanley. *Vietnam: A History.* New York: Viking, 1983.

Kennan, George F. *Soviet-American Relations, 1917–1920.* 2 vols. Princeton, N.J.: Princeton University Press, 1956.

Khrushchev, Nikita S. *The Soviet Stand on Germany*. New York: Crosscurrents Press, 1961.

Lamb, Roger. *An Original and Authentic Journal of Occurrences During the Late American War*. New York: New York Times, Arno Press, 1968.

Langley, Lester D. *The Banana Wars*. Lexington, Ky.: University Press of Kentucky, 1983.

Linderman, Gerald F. *The Mirror of War*. Ann Arbor, Mich.: University of Michigan Press, 1974.

Liu, F. F. *A Military History of Modern China, 1924–1949*. Princeton, N.J.: Princeton University Press, 1956.

Long, E. B. *The Civil War Day by Day*. Garden City, N.Y.: Doubleday, 1971.

Long, J. C. *Lord Jeffrey Amherst*. New York: Macmillan Co., 1933.

Ludendorff, Erich. *Memoirs*. Berlin: Hoff Verlag, 1919.

Mahan, A. T. *Sea Power in Its Relations to the War of 1812*. 2 vols. Boston: Little, Brown & Co., 1905.

Martin, Christopher. *Damn the Torpedoes: A Biography of David Glasgow Farragut*. New York: Abelard Schuman, 1972.

———. *The Boxer Rebellion*. New York: Abelard Schuman, 1970.

McDonald, Forrest. *E Pluribus Unum: The Formation of the American Republic, 1776–1790*. Boston: Houghton Mifflin Co., 1965.

McMaster, John Bach. *A History of the People of the United States*. 8 vols. New York: D. Appleton and Co., 1919.

Miller, John C. *Sam Adams*. Stanford, Calif.: Stanford University Press, 1936.

Miller, Stuart Creighton. *Benevolent Assimilation*. New Haven, Conn.: Yale University Press, 1982.

Miller, W. *The Martial Spirit*. Boston: Houghton Mifflin Co., 1931.

Montgomery, Tommie Sue. *Revolution in El Salvador*. Boulder, Colo.: Westview Press, 1982.

Morley, James William. *The Japanese Thrust into Siberia, 1918*. New York: Columbia University Press, 1957.

Morris, Richard B. *The Era of the American Revolution*. New York: Harper & Row, 1939.

———. *Encyclopedia of American History*. New York: Harper & Bros., 1953.

Parkman, Francis. *France and England in North America*. 2 vols. Boston: Little, Brown & Co., 1898.

Richardson, James L. *Germany and the Atlantic Alliance*. Cambridge, Mass.: Harvard University Press, 1966.

Roberts, W. Adolphe. *The Caribbean*. Indianapolis: Bobbs-Merrill Co., 1940.

Smith, Justin H. *The War with Mexico*. 2 vols. Gloucester, Mass.: Peter Smith, 1963.

Spears, J. R. *Anthony Wayne*. New York: n.p., 1903.

Sprout, Harold and Margaret. *The Rise of American Naval Power*. Princeton, N.J.: Princeton University Press, 1946.

Stewart, George. *The White Armies of Russia*. New York: Macmillan Co., 1933.

Thurston, Lorrin A. *Memoirs of the Hawaiian Revolution*. Honolulu: Advertiser Co., 1936.

Turner, Frederick Jackson. *The Frontier in American History*. New York: Holt, Rinehart, and Winston, 1947.

Walker, Thomas W. *Nicaragua, the Land of Sandino*. Boulder, Colo.: Westview Press, 1986.

Warren-Adams Letters, Being Chiefly a Correspondence among John Adams, Samuel Adams, and James Warren. Boston: Massachusetts Historical Society, 1925.

Wellman, Paul I. *The House Divides*. Garden City, N.Y.: Doubleday, 1966.

Winsor, Justin. *Narrative and Critical History of America*. Boston: Houghton Mifflin Co., 1888.

Wolf, Leon. *Little Brown Brother*. New York: Kraus Reprint Co., 1970.

Wood, William and Ralph Henry Gabriel. *In Defense of Liberty*. New Haven, Conn.: Yale University Press, 1928.

Wright, Robin. *Sacred Rage: The Crusade of Modern Islam*. New York: Simon and Schuster, 1985.

Wrong, George M. *The Conquest of New France*. New Haven, Conn.: Yale University Press, 1920.

Wyden, Peter. *Bay of Pigs*. New York: Simon and Schuster, 1979.

Zimmerman, James Fulton. *Impressment of American Seamen*. New York: Columbia University Press, 1925.

Acknowledgments

The author is much indebted to Olga G. Hoyt for research assistance and editing of the raw manuscript, and to Leslie Meredith, editor, and Lisa Frost, assistant editor, for suggestions and much patience in the process of putting together this book.

A great deal of the research for the book was done at the Miller Library of Washington College in Chestertown, Maryland, a small liberal arts college with a marvelous collection of American history materials. Librarian E. C. Butts and his staff were invariably helpful to an outsider to whom they had no possible obligation.

Other materials for the book came from the U.S. Naval History Division in Washington, the Office of the Army Historian, and several other libraries, including the Library of Congress. Some of the material is from the author's notes made over a period of forty years. The author has also quoted and cited unashamedly from his own previous works, nearly all of them based on original research in the American, British, and Japanese archives. If this seems to present the reader with a distillation, that is what this whole book really is: a distillation of what the author has learned over a half-century about the military aspects of American history.

That history has sometimes shown America at its finest, generous beyond belief, and has sometimes shown less pleasant aspects of the national character, such as a cruel selfishness. Sometimes the leaders have been far-seeing, and sometimes they have been myopic beyond belief. But what emerges from the whole is the picture of America as it really developed, not so innocent as my generation was led to believe when we were in school, but by world standards quite generous and truly believing in the American dream that men should have the right to choose their own form of self-government. That belief has led us to some errors of our own; noting that the Communist revolutions deny the majority the right to rule, we have taken stands against communism that sometimes have been against our own self-interest. Certainly our policy from 1946 to 1970 regarding China was a primary example. We cut off our nose to spite our face and the result was the war between the United States and Red China fought in Korea. It could have been avoided so easily if we had only maintained lines of communication between Beijing and Washington. But that is a matter for perusal in the text of this book.

Chapter Notes

1

In this chapter I relied for various materials on Harris's *A Rhode Islander Reports on King Philip's War: The Second William Harris Letter of August 1676,* and on Hubbard's *The Present State of New England, Being a Narrative of the Troubles with the Indians, 1677.*

2

A great number of varied sources contributed to my account of events in this chapter. Fiske's *New France and New England* was useful, as were Wrong's *The Conquest of New France,* Parkman's *France and England in North America,* and Ambler's *George Washington and the West.* I found many insights in Bancroft's works about the history of the United States for use here and elsewhere in the book. The *New York Mercury* of May 1754 reported Delaney's speech to the New York assembly, April 23, 1754. Morris's *The Era of the American Revolution* was helpful, and of course, the song quoted is the Amherst College song.

3

Smith's volumes on the war with Mexico were useful for this chapter, as was Higginbotham's discussion of the War of American Independence. Morris and Bancroft were consulted again, here, and Beach's *Samuel Adams* was helpful for specific material.

4

The Fate of a Nation by Cumming and Rankin was of interest for this chapter, and the continuing story of American history contained in Bancroft, especially the volume on the revolution, was helpful. Morris's books were again consulted.

5

In addition to referring to Bancroft and Higginbotham, Cooper's two-volume *Naval History of the United States* was pertinent, as was Alden and Westcott's *The United States Navy,* Lamb's *An Original and Authentic Journal of Occurrences During the Late American War,* and my own *The Damnedest Yankees.*

6

Books by both Boyd and Spears on Anthony Wayne were useful for this chapter. *Narrative and Critical History of America* by Winsor provided material, as did Bird's *War for the West, 1790–1813.* Volume 1 of Cooper's work also was utilized.

7

Most of the material in this chapter is from James Fenimore Cooper's history of the United States Navy, written just after the War of 1812, and really going no further than that. It is particularly valuable for detail about the early years of the U.S. Navy. Other sources consulted were Cooper, Winsor, my own *U-Boats Offshore,* Christopher Martin's *Damn the Torpedoes,* Zimmerman's *Impressment of American Seamen,* and the 1969 *World Almanac.* The second and third volumes of McMaster's eight-volume *A History of the People of the United States* offered significant insights.

8

Morris, McMaster, Winsor, Zimmerman, and Cooper all played important parts in the writing of this chapter. Also useful was Bill's *Rehearsal for Conflict.*

9

Again I consulted McMaster, Winsor, and Cooper. Adams's *The War of 1812* was also a useful source, as was Beirne's book on the same topic. The August 15, 1812, *New York Post* was quoted.

10

Here I relied heavily on McMaster and Cooper.

11

McMaster, Morris, and Winsor all were helpful in the continuing story of America's wars and military excursions. James's *The Life of Andrew Jackson* also was helpful for this period.

12

I got much material for this chapter from my own *Pacific Destiny*. As always, Bancroft was useful, as was Corrison's *The United States Navy*.

13

Jackson's *Black Hawk* provided interesting information for this chapter, as did Bassett's *A Short History of the United States*. Volume 4 of McMaster was useful here.

14

Volume 6 of McMaster had much significant material. Morris was also used to tell this story.

15

The classic volumes of McMaster were again consulted; of importance were volumes 5 and 6. Again Corrison and Bill related telling events. Burgess's *The Middle Period* was also helpful in this chapter.

16

The basic story line for this chapter comes from Francis Hawks, who was commissioned by the U.S. Congress to write the official history of the Perry expedition to Japan. I also used material from my own *Pacific Destiny* and an unpublished manuscript about Leland Stanford. The communication of Commodore Perry to the secretary of the navy was dated November 1852. Millard Fillmore to the emperor of Japan is also from 1852. Material about Congressional action is from records of the U.S. Congress, 1855. The Lord Hatta memorial is from imperial Japanese records, 1853.

17

Brown's *Agents of Manifest Destiny: The Life and Times of the Filibusters* was exceptionally useful here. Morris and McMaster's works were also helpful, as were my own *Commodore Vanderbilt* and *The Vanderbilts and Their Fortunes.* Newspapers cited were the *New Orleans Picayune,* May 28, 1857, and the *New York Herald,* September 10, 1849, and June 1, 1857.

18

Long's *Civil War Day by Day,* Jones's three volumes on *The Civil War at Sea,* Morris's work, and many other general books on the Civil War were most useful for this chapter.

19

Connell's *Son of the Morning Star* gave a good account for this period, as did other volumes too numerous to mention. McMaster and Brown were again good sources.

20

Several of my own books were helpful here, namely *Pacific Destiny, The Typhoon That Stopped a War,* and an unpublished manuscript, "The Parkers." Mahan's two-volume *Sea Power in Its Relations to the War of 1812* was extremely significant for material contained in this chapter, for Mahan's observations, in magazine articles as well as in this major work, were the foundation of American naval policy of the late nineteenth century. Quoted also is material from the report of the secretary of the navy, 1865.

21

Thurston's *Memoirs of the Hawaiian Revolution* contained many facts and quotations about events during the revolution. My unpublished manuscript on the Parkers also was most useful here, as was my *Jumbos and Jackasses.*

22

Brown and Morris were source materials for this chapter, as was George Dewey's autobiography. I made much use of my own works mentioned in notes for previous chapters, with the addition of my *The American Attitude,* and an unpublished manuscript on Richard Harding Davis. The Report of the Secretary of the Navy, 1899, was used, as were the files of the *New York Times* for February 1898.

23

Gabriel's *The Pageant of America* was helpful, as were Martin's books on the Boxer Rebellion, and my own *Pacific Destiny.*

24

Miller's *Benevolent Assimilation,* Dewey's autobiography, Gabriel's work, all were important in forming this chapter. The *New York Times* material was from the February 5, 1899, issue, and the files of the *Chicago Tribune* for November 1899 were used.

25

The Banana Wars by Langley gave much insight for this chapter, as did Gleijeses's work on the Dominican crisis. Morris was again helpful.

26

For this chapter again Langley and Gleijeses were basic.

27

Langley and Morris were of paramount use here.

28

Again much material for this period was gained from the works by Langley, Gleijeses, and Morris. The *New York Times* of April 19–23 and April 27, 1913, were consulted.

29

Gabriel's *Pageant of America* was useful here, as were several of my works cited in the chapters above. The *New York Times* for September 1914, and April 3, 1917, were useful.

30

The American Legion History of the Great War, volume 2, contained useful material. Again Gabriel's work, cited above, was helpful, as was Ludendorff's *Memoirs.* The *New York Times,* the chronicler of events, was again consulted, specifically the issues of June 6, 1917, July 1, 1917, September 4, 1917, and July 16, 1918.

31

George Kennan's work on Soviet-American relations was important here, as was Stewart's volume on the White Army of Russia. My own *Japan's War, The Lonely Ships,* and *The American Attitude* provided other material for the chapter.

32

Langley, Morris, and Gleijeses all helped buttress the author's observations for this chapter.

33

My own works helped a great deal for this chapter, namely *The Lonely Ships, Pacific Destiny,* and *Japan's War.* Several volumes about Yamamoto were also useful here.

34

This chapter contains many observations of the author, including the material about Kunming, China, which was the headquarters of the U.S. 14th Air Force, General Claire Chennault's command. Here some of the people connected with the Old Flying Tigers remained during the war, and they had many a tale to tell. Material about the submarines comes from my *U-Boat Wars.* Various writings of Winston Churchill, especially his six-volume history of World War II, also gave insight into the activities of this period.

35

Holmes's *Double-Edged Secrets* was extremely useful, as were several of the Churchill volumes, and Japanese documents contained in a series of books giving the Japanese viewpoint of the Guadalcanal battles. A great number of my own books concerning the Pacific war were essential in writing this chapter, especially those on the U-boats, on the Guadalcanal campaign, and on Nimitz, and *Japan's War*.

36

The bulk of this chapter was written based upon my own published books about the Pacific war, and research material for two unpublished manuscripts, one on the GI war, and the other on the Nisei warriors.

37

Of importance here was the oral history by Curtis LeMay, which is available at the Air University at the Maxwell Air Force Base in Alabama. This chapter contains much of the author's observations when in China during World War II, and research and material on the many books I have written about the Pacific war, in addition to an interview with Senator Ed C. Johnson of Colorado in 1947. Senator Johnson was one of the most prominent members of Congress to call for immediate return of "our boys" at the end of World War II.

38

Again this chapter contains material based on the author's own observations not only in China—especially Peking and Chungking—but also from experience in Korea, Japan, Austria, Germany in 1945 and 1946, and in Trieste and Venezia-Giulia in 1947. Churchill's volumes on World War II were also useful here, and the *New York Times* told much about the events of 1949.

39

Here again, material is based on interviews and observations by the author. In addition the author received many letters from retired professional soldiers who were much disaffected with the "new army." One sent a photo from the European edition of *Stars and Stripes,* showing a "typical squad" of infantrymen in West Germany, obviously overweight and out of condition.

40

Some of the material in this chapter is based on observations of the author as a UPI correspondent in Korea, 1945 and 1946. The State Department's John Davies statement to the author was made in the fall of 1947. Army records, 8th Army, for August 1950 were used, as was much material gathered for my three books on the Korean War.

41

My books on the Korean War were useful here. Also the Syngman Rhee interview with the author in 1946, and the author's observations through the years. Most of the old China hands of the Department of State were forced to retire or resign during the McCarthy era. A few, like Edmund Clubb and John Emmerson, survived. But the State Department attitude became definitely hawkish and opposed to any contact with Red China. The author, who disagreed with this policy, found that it was not only a matter of official government attitude, but a national attitude that permeated every aspect of American society. He was an editorial writer on the *Denver Post,* and later editor of the editorial page, in the late 1940s and early 1950s, having served as the newspaper's correspondent in Asia and Europe for several years. He soon learned that although the *Post* was generally liberal in its outlook, virtually no one from the publisher down could accept the author's contention that Red China had won the revolution, Chiang's Nationalists had lost it, and that the American attitude and actions had been really irrelevant to the outcome. The author then subsided on the China issue, not to emerge again until Richard Nixon confirmed his view in the 1970s and took steps to undo the enormous damage the United States had done to itself over a quarter of a century. Some others, like William Powell and Israel Epstein, pursued the view that U.S. policy was wrong, and found themselves either in serious difficulty or living in Red China. Powell was actually tried for disloyalty during the Korean War, but exonerated. Still, his was another of the careers smashed by the great ideological conflict.

42

The official history of Marine Corps operations in Korea was most useful here, as were the various books by the author on the Korean War.

43

This chapter contains much material based on the author's observations as a correspondent in Indochina in the fall of 1945, and in Malaya and Singapore during the period 1945–47.

44

Wyden's *Bay of Pigs* contained much significant information, as did H. L. Matthews's articles on Cuba and American policy in the *New York Times* during 1957.

45

Buttinger's *Vietnam: A Dragon Embattled,* and Karnow's *Vietnam: A History* were important to this chapter. The Joint Chiefs of Staff papers for May 1954, found in Washington, D.C., were also utilized.

46

Viet Nam: Anatomy of a Conflict by Fishel had good material, as, of course, did Le May's oral history, and Karnow's *Vietnam: A History*. Official U.S. Marine Corps records were used, as were reports of the trial of Lieutenant William Calley in the *New York Times* and the *Washington Post* in 1971. The *New York Times* was also consulted for the period of fall 1972, and May 1, 1975. An autobiography of Westmoreland was also consulted.

47

Richard A. Gabriel's *Military Incompetence* played a significant role in forming this chapter, as did the material in the author's manuscript on the Parkers, and studies for a biography of Stephen Decatur. As usual, many points made are based on the author's observations.

48

Gleijeses, Langley, and Walker were all helpful here, as was the *New York Times* for 1956, and the period January to July 1986. As always, the author's observations appear throughout.

49

Since the late nineteenth century the Russians have moved steadily to broaden their foreign bases, and in recent years with a good deal of success. My views about NASA are disputed by some space experts, notably Ms. Marcia Smith of the Library of Congress. She is not convinced by this author's arguments, nor he by hers. This exchange of viewpoints was conducted by interviews.

My *The Militarists* was utilized in this chapter. The statistics about the military posture of Japan come from the Japan Defense Agency, 1984. Since that time there has been some backlash in the Japanese defense organization, and some hitherto eager sailors in particular have suddenly discovered that they do not like sea duty for long periods of time. Some have resigned from the service for that reason. Generally speaking, however, the Japanese defense force has the most impressive record of career adherence in the world of America's allies.

Index

Abdul Hamid I, 94
Abenakis, 18
Acadia, 18–20, 23–24, 28–30, 34
Acheson, Dean, x, 428, 437, 439, 463
Adams, Boatswain, 147
Adams, John, 48, 49, 50, 52–53, 59, 64, 80, 85
Adams, John Quincy, 150, 177, 178
Adams, Samuel, 42–43, 46, 48, 50, 52, 54, 56, 59, 62, 63, 71, 74, 84
Addison, Joseph, on civil discord, 229
Aguinaldo, Emilio, 291, 298–300, 301, 302–303, 305, 328
Alamo, the, 199
Albany Congress, 27
Aldham, Captain W. Cornwallis, 227
Aleutian Islands, 386, 387
Algiers (see Barbary pirates)
Allen, Ethan, 63, 70
Allied Control Commission, 409, 412
Allison, John M., 436–437
Almond, General Edward M., 431–433, 440
Alvarez de Toledo, José, 173
America First Organization, 380, 383
American Horse, Chief, 257

American military incompetence, 480–483, 496, 500
American military and professional pride, 500–501
American Revolution, xii, xv, 39–67, 68, 126, 220, 267, 338, 365, 472, 487
    causes and early stages, 1–2, 38–39
    Lexington and Concord, 64–67, 68, 70, 73, 74, 76
    resistance to military control, 55, 57–64
    taxation and trade controversy, 38, 40–54, 56–57
    (See also Revolutionary War)
Amherst, Lord Jeffrey, 33, 34, 36, 41, 62
Ampudis, General Pedro de, 199, 200, 201
Anderson, General Keith, 390
Anderson, Major Robert, 189, 232–233, 234
André, Major John, 86
Anne, Queen, 18, 21
Antietam, 241
Anti-Imperialist League, 302

Anvile, Asmiral le Duc, d', 24
Anzio, 395
Apaches, 258
Appomattox, 246
Aquino, Benigno, 465
Aquino, Corazon, 465, 500
Arapaho, 249, 250
Archangel, occupation of, 351, 355–357, 359
Arevalo, Juan José, 490
Argonne Forest, 348–349
Arias, Desiderio, 322
Aristotle, 106
Ariyoshi, George, 268
Armistead, Colonel Walker Keith, 156
Armstrong, Captain John, 97
Armstrong, John, 149, 153, 154, 155, 158
Army Appropriations Bill of 1901, 307–308
Arnim, General Jürgen von, 390
Arnold, Benedict, 70, 82, 86, 87–88
Aroostook War, 194–195
Arthur, Chester A., 279
Ashford, Colonel C. W., 270, 271
Associated Press, 463
Astor, John Jacob, 179, 191
Atcheson, George, 373, 374
Atlantic Charter, 451
Atomic weapons, 401, 407, 419, 422, 425, 437, 447
Attlee, Clement, 411
Attucks, Crispus, 50
Aury, Louis, 176
Austin, John, 199
Azueta, José, 327, 329

Bacon, Robert, 311
Bader-Meinhof gang, 423, 479
Bainbridge, Captain William, 105–107, 112–113, 117, 118, 119, 120, 121, 142, 143, 167, 171, 182, 486
Baker, Edward D., 237
Baker, Secretary of War, 339
Balaguer, Juan, 492
Balfour, Arthur James, 333, 335
Balfour, Colonel, 86
Ball, Albert, 346
Ballard, Midshipman, 147
Ball's Bluff, 237

Banana Wars, The (Langley), 325
Bancroft, George (historian), 65
Bancroft, Secretary of the Navy George, 200
Banks, General, 240
Barbary pirates; Barbary Wars, xiv, 93, 94, 95, 101–102, 103, 110–121, 126, 140, 164–171, 181, 182, 198, 206, 486
Barclay, Minister, 102
Barclay, Captain Robert, 148
Barlow, Joel, 111
Barney, Commodore Joshua, 154
Barnum's museum, 245
Barras, Count, 88
Barreault, Captain, 106, 108
Barrett, Amos, 66
Barrett, Colonel, 65, 66
Barron, Commodore James, 114, 120–121, 126–127, 128–129, 130–131, 133
Barron, Captain Samuel, 109
Barry, Captain John, 104
Bathurst, Lord, 158
Batista, Fulgencio, 455, 456
Battle of the Bulge, 398
Bay of Pigs, 458–461, 466
Bayard, Thomas F., 264
Beach, Stewart, 43
Bear Paw Mountain, battle of, 257
Beauregard, General Pierre Gustave Toutant, 234, 235–236, 239
Beckwith, Colonel Charles, 481
Begin, Menachem, 478
Beirut, 478, 479, 483–485, 486
Belcher, Corporal, 6
Belle Isle, Duc de, 33
Belleau Wood, 344
Benes, Edouard, 357
Benoit, Colonel Pedro Bartolome, 490, 491
Benteen, Captain Frederick, 252, 254–255
Berkeley, Admiral, 127, 128, 130, 131, 132
Berlin, 398–399, 404, 409, 412, 457, 459, 461, 467
  blockade and airlift, 418, 420–422
Bermuda triangle, 109–110
Bernard, Governor, 46, 48, 49
Bernstorff, Johann-Heinrich von, 333
Bethune, Nathaniel, 43

Biddle, Commodore, 182, 209
Biddle, Captain Nicholas, 78
Billy Bowlegs, Chief, 174, 177
Bingham, Captain, 133
Bingham, Hiram, 268
Bipartisan foreign policy, 487
Bishop, Elizabeth Pauahi, 268
Bismarck, Otto von, 263
Bissell, Richard, 459
Black Hawk War, 186, 188–189
Blacks in American military service,
    300, 474–475
Blaine, James G., 271–272, 279
Blair, Montgomery, 234
Blanchard, Luther, 66
Blainville, Celeron de, 25
Bloody Swamp, battle of, 22
Blount, James H., 275
Blücher, General Gebhard Leberecht
    von, 150
Bluecher, General Vasily Konstanti-
    novich, 364–365
Bobo, Rosalvo, 320, 321–322
Bonaparte, Joseph, 123, 173
Boone, Daniel, 49
Booth, John Wilkes, 241
Borah, William E., 365
Bosch, Juan, 490–491, 492
Boston Cadets, 58
Boston Massacre, 50, 57
Boston Port Bill, 56
Boston Tea Party, 51–54, 56
Bowie, Jim, 199
Boxer Rebellion, xiii, 292–296, 297,
    303, 331, 368, 369
Braddock, General Edward, 28–29, 30
Bradley, Lieutenant James, 256
Bradley, General Omar, 393, 438
Bradstreet, William, 15
Brady, Matthew, 225
Breed's Hill, battle of, 71–74, 75, 76,
    79
Broke, Captain, 146
Brooke, Colonel, 156–157
Broom, Lieutenant, 147
Broughton, Captain, 77
Brown, Colonel, 87
Brown, General Jacob, 151
Brown, John, 230
Brown, John (merchant), 52, 65
Brown, Jonas, 66
Bryan, William Jennings, 319, 320

Buchanan, James, 224–225, 226, 227,
    230, 232, 233
Buckner, General Simon Bolivar, 238
Buffalo Bill, 257
Buffalo (bison) hunters, 249–250
Bull Run (see Manassas)
Bullard, Arthur, 355
Bullard, General R. L., 343
Bundy, William, 467, 472
Bunker Hill, 71, 73
    (See also Breed's Hill)
Burgoyne, General John, 62, 71, 81–
    83, 84
Burke, Admiral Arleigh, 459
Burke, Edmund, 61
Burnside, General Ambrose, 238, 239,
    241–242
Butcher, Captain Lloyd, 107
Butler, General William O., 206, 220
Butler, Richard, 98
Butler, General Smedley, 314–315,
    316, 322
Buttrick, Major John, 66

Caceres, Ramon, 310, 313
Calhoun, John C., 176, 178
    Indian policy, 247
California, 209, 220, 223
    goldrush, 210, 223, 249
    and Mexican War, 201–202, 208,
        220
    and slavery, 230
Call, General, 190
Calles, Plutarco, 364
Calley, Lieutenant William, 474
Cambodia, 474
Canada, 38, 39, 41, 57, 97, 124, 130,
    191–195, 198, 220
    border skirmishes, 14–22, 23–24,
        28–32
    boundary disputes, 179, 183, 191,
        194–195, 198, 209
    fishing treaty, 179, 191
    French settlement, 11, 23
        French vs. English, 192–194
    siege of Quebec, 33–36
    War of 1812, 139–140, 148, 149–
        152, 153, 162, 163
Canning, George, 132, 179
Canonchet, Chief, 9

Cantigny, 343
Caperton, Admiral William Banks, 320, 321–322
Caribbean Sea, 309–310, 312–313, 315, 318, 319–324, 330, 367, 488, 490–492
   piracy in, 181, 182, 185
   (*See also* Cuba)
Carnegie, Andrew, 299
Caroline incident (1837), xiii, 191, 192, 194
Carranza, General Venustiano, 326, 328, 332–333, 334
Carter, J. E.: Carter administration, xiv, 172, 479, 482–483, 493
Cartier, Jacques, 12
Carvajal, José Maria Jesús, 222
Casado Saladin, Colonel Enrique A., 490
Cass, Lewis, 225
Cassino, 395
Castlereagh, Robert Stewart, Viscount, 150, 155
Castro, Cipriano, 308
Castro, Fidel, 220, 455–460, 488, 490, 492, 493, 494, 499
CBS News, 456, 470n, 474
Central America, 179, 279–280, 288, 296, 313–317, 323, 361–367, 416, 490, 492–493
   and filibustering, 222–228
   Panama Canal, 304, 308–309
Central American Conference, 362
Central Intelligence Agency (CIA), 309, 437, 450, 457, 458
   (*See also* Bay of Pigs)
Cervera, Admiral Pascual, 286, 288, 289, 290
Chaffee, General Adna R., 294–295, 303
Challenger disaster, 497, 498
Chamorro, Diego, 363
Chamorro, Emiliano, 363, 364, 365
Champlain, Samuel de, 11, 12–13
Chancellor, John, 470n
Chancellorsville, 242
Chatard, Commander Frederick, 225
Château-Thierry, 340, 343–344, 345
Chauncey, Commodore Isaac, 148, 151
Chennault, General Claire, 380, 450, 514(34)

Cherokee, 182, 183, 187, 195
Chesapeake–Leopard incident, 126–132
Chesapeake/Shannon battle, 146–147
Chiang Kai-shek, x, 364, 365, 371, 385, 401, 409, 413–414, 415, 437, 438, 447, 449, 450, 516(41)
Chiang, Madame, 383
Chicago *Times-Herald,* 298–299
Chicago *Tribune,* 301, 462–463
Chickahominy, 240
Chickamauga, 243
Chile, 280, 281
China, 183, 207, 208, 210, 218, 261, 291, 296, 327, 368–369, 436, 452, 453
   Boxer Rebellion, xiii, 292–296, 297, 303, 331, 368, 369
   Communist, 364–365, 371, 401, 409–410, 413–415, 424, 425, 427–428, 435, 436–437, 441, 444, 457, 463, 487, 497, 498, 499–500, 508, 516(41)
      Korean War, 424, 435–446, 447, 498, 508
   and Japanese, 371–377, 378, 380, 385, 401, 404, 473
   and Nationalist government, 414–415, 437–438
   Peking, sack of, 295–296
   and World War II, 380, 385, 401, 404, 413, 450
   Yangtze, opening of, 369–377
China Lobby, 415, 447
Chou En-lai, 439
Christian, Fletcher, 145
Christian Frederick of Denmark, 152
Church, Captain Benjamin, 10
Churchill, Winston S., xiv, 378, 384, 394, 410, 411, 416, 451, 469
CIA (*see* Central Intelligence Agency)
Civil War, x, 195, 229–246, 247–248, 250, 258, 266, 278, 279, 370, 416, 487
   and border states, 235, 236–237
   first skirmishes, 235–237
   Georgia, 243, 244, 245
   national disaster, 229–230
   naval action, 236, 237, 239, 242, 245
      blockade of South, 234, 237, 245
      Monitor and *Merrimac,* xv, 197, 238, 262

Civil War *(cont.)*:
  and the press, 462, 477
  Richmond threatened and taken,
    240, 244–246
  secession, 230, 232–234, 235
  Shenandoah Valley, 239–240, 245
  and Southern manpower problem,
    244, 246
  Union generals, 236–237, 240, 241,
    242, 243
  Washington invaded, 245
  western front, 238, 242–243, 244,
    245–246
  (See also entries for specific battles,
    actions and campaigns)
Claiborne, William C. C., 123, 159
Clark, General Mark, 395
Clarke, Richard, 52
Clay, Henry, 137, 150, 230
Clay, General Lucius, 420
Clayton-Bulwer treaty, 279, 280–281
Clemenceau, Georges, 344, 435n
Cleveland, Grover; Cleveland admin-
  istration, 258, 263, 264, 274–275,
  281, 282, 318
Clinch, Colonel D. L., 174–175, 190
Clinton, General Henry, 62, 71, 72,
  73, 79, 82
Clubb, O. Edmund, 440, 516(41)
Coaling stations, 208, 210, 211, 212,
  215, 260–261, 266, 276, 290
Cochrane, Admiral Sir Alexander,
  152–153, 154, 155, 157, 158, 159
Cockburn, Admiral Sir George, 153,
  154, 157
Colburn, John F., 272
Cold Harbor, 245
Cold War, the, 418–423
Cole, Byron, 223
Collins, General Lawton, 429–430,
  438–439
Colonialism *(see* Imperialism)
Colt, Samuel; Colt revolver, 173, 197,
  222
  .45-caliber automatic, 304, 349
Colwell, Commander J. C., 311
Communism in America, 379–380,
  411
Communism, combating, 363–367,
  410–411, 415, 416–417, 424, 452–
  454, 455–461, 463, 487, 490, 491,
  492, 493–494, 497–501, 507–508

Communism, combating *(cont.)*:
  (See also Cold War; Korean War;
    Vietnam war)
Compromise of 1850, 230
Confederacy, the, 189, 234, 235, 238,
  248
  (See also Civil War)
Congress of Vienna, 152
Conner, Commodore David, 200
Constitution (frigate—"Old Iron-
  sides"), 141–142
Continental Congresses, 27, 44, 57,
  60, 61, 70, 78
Cook, Captain James, 267
Coolidge, Calvin, 365
Cooper, Henry E., 274
Cooper, James Fenimore, 112, 510(7)
Coral Sea, 386, 402
Corn, Ira B., 38
Cornstalk, Chief, 96
Cornwallis, General Lord Charles, 81,
  83, 86, 87–88, 89–91
Cox, Lieutenant George, 117
Coyotepe, battle of, 317
Crabb, Henry, 224
Craig, General Edward A., 366, 430
Crane, Lieutenant Commandant,
  141
Craven, Lieutenant T. A., 232
Crawford, W. H., 174
Crazy Horse, 251, 257
Creeks, 150–151, 158, 173–174, 176,
  182, 183, 187, 188
Crockett, Davey, 199
Cronkite, Walter, 470, 474
Crook, General George, 251, 253,
  255, 257, 258
Cuba, 185, 220–222, 262, 277, 278,
  281, 291, 310–311, 312, 326
  Castroite, 455–461, 466–467, 488,
    490, 491, 492, 493, 494, 499
  independence, x, 277, 278–284, 291,
    296, 306–308, 310–311, 455–
    456
  (See also Spanish-American War)
Cuban missile crisis, 461, 467
Cudworth, Captain, 7
Cunningham, Colonel William, 86–87
Custer, (General) George Armstrong,
  250–253, 254, 255–256
Czechoslovakia, establishment of,
  357–358, 360

Dale, Commodore Richard, 114, 115
Dana, Richard, 43
Daniels, Josephus, 322, 328, 354
Dartiguenave, Philippe Sudre, 322
Dartmouth, Lord, 62
Dartmouth (ship), 53–54
Davis, Captain Charles Henry, 223–
   224, 225
Davis, Captain Isaac, 66
Davis, Jefferson, 189, 220, 226, 234,
   243
Davis, Richard Harding, 313
Dawes, William, 64
Dawson, Thomas, 315–316
Dearborn, General Henry, 139, 140,
   148, 149
Decatur, Commodore Stephen, 104,
   118–120, 129, 133, 142, 163, 167–
   171, 486
Declaration of Independence, xii, 38,
   79, 84
Deerfield massacre, 18
de Gaulle, Charles, 450, 451
Delancey, Lt. Governor, 28
DeLancey, Oliver, 31
Dennis, Lawrence, 363, 365
Denver *Post,* 516(41)
"Dere Mable," 339
Deux Ponts, Count, 90
Dewey, Admiral George, 262, 285,
   288–289, 291, 297–299, 308
Diaz, Adolfo, 316, 317, 362, 363, 365–
   366
Diaz, Porfirio, 315, 325–326
Dickerson, Mahlon, 198
Dickman, General, 345
Diederichs, Admiral, 288–289
Diem, Ngo Dinh, 466, 467, 468
Dienbienphu, 452, 453, 476
Dillingham, Commander A. C., 310
Dillon, Douglas, 458
Dinwiddie, Robert, 25–26, 27, 75
Dollar diplomacy, 315, 319
Dominican Republic, 309–310, 312–
   313, 315, 319, 320, 322–324, 490–
   492
Domino theory, 464–465, 466
Donaldson, Joseph, 110–111
Dönitz, Admiral Karl, 382, 396
Doolittle, James R., 226
Doolittle, Colonel Jimmy, 385
Douglas, Captain, 130

Douglas, Stephen A., 226
Downie, Captain George, 152
Drake, Colonel, 393
Druce, Trooper John, 7
Drummond, General, 151
Duarte, José Napoleon, 493
Dudington, Lieutenant, 51
Dulles, John Foster, 436, 453, 454,
   463–464, 465, 466, 469
Dunmore, Lord, 74, 78, 79
Duquesne, Governor, 25
Dutch in America, 2, 3, 14

Early, General Jubal, 245
East India Company, 51–52, 53, 56,
   207
Eaton, John H., 187–188
Eaton, William, 121
Eberhardt, Charles C., 363, 365
Edgar (flagship), 21–22
Edson, Major Lewis, 387
Edson, Merritt, 366
82nd Airborne Division, 395, 398, 491,
   494
Eisenhower, Dwight D., 439
   general, 390–391, 394
   president, ix, 453, 454, 455, 457,
      458, 460, 463–464, 465, 466,
      469, 498
Ellsworth, Private Elmer, 235
El Salvador, 178, 492–493
Emerson, William, 64
Emmerson, John K., 439, 516(41)
England, maritime trouble with, 105
   (*See also* Impressment of seamen;
      War of 1812)
Epstein, Israel, 516(41)
Era of Good Feelings, 165
Era of Internal Improvements, 173
Essex (frigate), 143–145, 163
Estrada, Juan, 315, 316
Estrade Palma, Tomas, 306, 310–311
Evans, Admiral Robley D., 280, 369,
   370

Fagan, David, 300
Fairfax, Lord, 25
Fairfield (Maine) *Journal,* 301

Farragut, Admiral David Glasgow, 239, 242, 245
Federalism, 130, 133, 150
Ferdinand VII of Spain, 173
Filibusters, xiii, 173, 175–176, 191, 219–228, 281, 313
  and the British, 227–228
Fillmore, Millard, 211, 213–215, 216, 217, 220, 230
Fish, Hamilton, 278
Fletcher, Admiral Frank Friday, 326, 327
Fletcher, Captain Patrick, 109
Florida, 22, 23, 39, 123, 137, 209
  and the Civil War, 233, 234
  Pensacola, 158, 159, 177
  Seminoles, 172–178, 179, 181, 186, 188, 189–190, 195–196
Floyd, General, 238
Foch, Marshal Ferdinand, 347–348, 356
Foote, Flag Officer Andrew, 238
Ford, Henry, his peace ship, 331–332
Ford, Captain John Salmon, 222
Forrest, General Nathan Bedford, 238
Fort McHenry, 156–157
Fort Moultrie, 232, 236
Fort Sumter, 189, 232–233, 234
France and the American Revolution, 69, 84–86, 88–91, 93, 103
Franklin, Benjamin, 26, 27, 33, 39, 56, 61, 63, 80, 84, 86, 91
Fredendall, General Lloyd, 391, 393
Fredericksburg, 241
Freeman's Farm, battle of, 82
Frelinghuysen, F. T., 279
Frémont, John C., 201, 237
French in America, 2, 3, 4, 11–37, 39, 41, 42, 58, 123
  Canada, 11, 14–22, 23–24, 28–30, 31–37, 39, 41, 192–194
  colonialism, 12–16
  Louisiana, 33, 36, 39, 123
  Mississippi Valley, 23, 25, 33
  Ohio Valley, 25–28, 30–32, 39, 75
French and Indian wars, xi–xii, xv, 1–2, 12
French Revolution, the, 93–94, 103, 269, 273
Frontenac, Comte de, 13–14, 15–16, 17
Fulbright, William, 459
Fulton, Robert, 197

Fulton (steamship), 198
Funston, General Frederick, 302–303, 328, 329

Gabriel, Richard A., 481–482
Gage, General Thomas, 41, 44, 45, 46, 47, 57–59, 60–62, 63, 69, 70, 71, 74, 76
Gaines, General Edmund P., 174–175, 176, 177, 189
Galens, 365
Gallagher, General Philip Edward, 451–452
Gamble, Lieutenant John, 145
Gandara, Manuel, 224
Garcia Godoy, Hector, 492
Garcon, 175
Garfield, James A., 279
Garrison, Lindley M., 331, 332
Gates, General Horatio, 75, 82, 86, 152
Gemayel, Bashir, 483
George III, xii, 2, 38, 41, 44, 55, 56–57, 60, 61, 62, 63, 68, 70, 84, 91–92
Geraghty, Timothy J., 484–485
Germany, partition of, 420–422, 457
Geronimo, 258
Gettysburg, 243
Ghormley, Admiral Robert, 387
Gibbon, Colonel John, 250, 251, 252, 255, 256, 257
Gibson, Walter Murray, 270–271
Gilbert, Sir Humphrey, xii
Girty, Simon, 98
Glassford, Admiral William A., 377
Gleijeses, Piero, 492
Gordon, Captain Charles, 126–127, 128, 130
Gouraud, General, 344–345
Grant, Ulysses Simpson:
  general, 236, 237, 238, 239, 243, 244–246
  president, 250, 278, 279
Grasse, Admiral Comte de, 88–89, 91
Graves, Admiral Thomas, 88
Gray, Sam, 49, 50
Green Mountain Boys, the, 63, 70
Greene, General Nathanael, 70, 83, 86, 87

Grenada, xiv, 178, 330, 488–489, 494, 497
    and news media, 488–489
Grenville, Lord, 38, 39, 41, 42, 43, 44, 45, 46
Grew, Ambassador, 376
Gridley firing when ready, 288
Guadalcanal, 387–388, 390, 402
Guam, 290, 299, 406
Guantanamo Bay, 308, 310, 312, 326
Guillaume Sam, 320, 321
Gulf of Sidra, xiv, 423, 478, 486–487, 497
Gunboat diplomacy, xiii, 212, 261, 263–265, 292, 308–310, 327–328, 368–376, 456
    Commodore Perry, 210–218
Guynemer, Georges, 346

Hadji Ali, 169
Hadley, Samuel, 65
Haiti, 312, 318, 319–324
Hall, Lyman, 70
Halleck, General Henry W., 240
Halsey, Admiral William F., 385, 405
Hamet, 121
Hamilton, Alexander, 90
Hamilton, Colonel Henry, 85
Hammond, William, 6
Hampton, General Wade, 149
Hancock, John, 47, 48, 52–53, 54, 58, 59, 60, 63, 64, 71, 74, 84
Harding, Warren G., 323
Harkins, General, 472–473
Harmar, General, 96–97
Harney, Colonel, 202, 206
Harrington, Caleb, 65
Harrington, Jonathan, 65
Harris, Toleration, 5
Harrison, Benjamin, 272, 274, 280
Harrison, William Henry, 122, 123–125, 148, 149, 151
Hart, Admiral Thomas, 377
Hatta, Lord, 218
Havana Club, 220
Havana Electric Railway Company, 306
Hawaii, 261–262, 298
    annexation of, 266–267, 296, 479

Hawaii (cont.):
    missionaries in, 266, 267, 268, 269, 270, 271, 272, 274
Hawkins, Colonel Benjamin, 174
Hay-Pauncefote treaty, 308
Hay, John, 370
Hayes, Colonel, 87
Hayes, Rutherford B.; Hayes administration, 263
Hayselden, Fred, 270
Hearst, William Randolph, 278, 285
Hellis Hajo, 177, 178
Hemollemico, 177, 178
Henchman, Captain Daniel, 6, 8
Henley, Commodore, 182
Henry VIII, 12
Henry, Patrick, 44, 49
Herrera, José Manuel, 173
Heureaux, Ulises, 309–310, 312–313
Hightower, Colonel, 392–393
Hillar, Master Commandant Benjamin, 110
Hindenburg, Marshal Paul von, 341, 346
Hirohito, 404, 407, 411, 478
Hirshinger, Captain H. J. J., 323
Hispaniola, 309–310, 312–313, 315, 318, 319–324, 490–492
Hiss, Alger, 411, 412n
History, teaching and sense of, xiv, 466, 473, 487
Hitler, Adolf, ix, 33–34, 352, 379, 380, 381, 383, 384, 386, 395, 398, 399
Ho Chi Minh, 449–452, 453, 463, 466, 472
Hodge, General John R., 425, 427
Hollingshead, Private Growell R., 348
Holmes, Oliver Wendell, 90
Honduras, 361–362
Hood, General John Bell, 246
Hooker, General Joseph ("Fighting Joe"), 242, 243
Hoover, Herbert, 338, 367, 371
Hopkins, Commodore Esek, 78
Hopkins, Captain John B., 78
Horseshoe Bend, 151
Hosmer, Abner, 66
Howard, Roy, 462
Howe, Admiral Lord Richard, 68, 79, 80

Howe, Captain Tyringham, 78
Howe, General Lord William, 62, 70–73, 76, 78–79, 80, 83, 85
Hoyt, Edwin P., 448–449, 450–451, 452, 455, 465
Hudson's Bay Company, 191
Huerta, Victoriano, 326, 327, 328
Hughes, Charles Evans, 367
Hughes, Captain James Joseph, 373–375
Hull, Cordell, 377
Hull, Commodore Isaac, 134, 141–142, 183
Hull, General William, 139–140
Humphreys, Captain, 128, 129
Humphreys, Minister, 110–111
Hundred Years War, the, xii, 12
Hunt, John, 80
Hurons, xii, 11, 13, 18, 23
Hutchinson, Thomas, 45, 49, 50, 52, 53, 54, 56, 63

Iceland summit meetings, 419
Ideas, power of, xv
Imperialism, American, 123, 135, 144, 163, 208–209, 220–222, 224, 260–265, 296, 302, 306–308, 328
    (See also Hawaii; Latin America; Philippine Islands)
Impressment of seamen, 125–134, 136, 142–143, 162
    (See also War of 1812)
Indiana, 100, 122, 123–125
Indians, American, ix, 1–10, 39, 41, 58, 66, 93, 95–100, 122, 123–125, 140, 186, 264, 283
    and American Revolution, xii–xiii, 82, 85, 87, 188
    Black Hawk War, 186, 188–189
    and broken promises, 183, 186, 188, 195–196
    citizenship for, 258–259
    and Civil War, 248
    and extermination policy, xi, xiii, 9, 96, 248–250, 257–258
    and the French, xi, 11–12, 29–30, 32, 36
        (See also French in America)
    Indian Territory, 181–182, 183, 188, 247, 249, 250, 257

Indians, American (cont.):
    King Philip's War, xi–xii, 3–10, 14, 97, 187, 248, 258, 497
    Little Bighorn, 247–257
    Ohio Valley, 25–28, 30–32, 39, 75, 96–100
    Pequots, xi, 2, 10
    Seminoles, 172–178, 179, 181, 186, 188, 189–190, 195–196
    in Virginia, 2
    and the War of 1812, 140, 149–151
    and the West, 232, 247, 250, 257–259
    Wounded Knee massacre, ix, 258
    (See also entries for specific tribes and leaders)
Indochina, 410, 418, 464
    and the French, 448–454, 464
    (See also Vietnam)
Industrial Revolution, the, 173, 197
Intelligence, military, role of, 436
Intervention, 178–179
Intolerable Acts, 57, 60
Iran hostage affair, xiv, 478, 479–483, 486
Iron Curtain, 416
Iroquois, 11, 13–14, 15, 17, 18, 44
    (See also Mohawks)
Ismay, Lord, 386
Israel, Lieutenant Joseph, 120
Italy, invasion of, 395, 396
Iwo Jima, 406, 408

Jackson, Andrew, 136, 151, 158–159
    New Orleans, 158–162
    president, 184, 186, 187, 188, 190, 230
    Seminole War, 174, 176–177, 178–179
Jackson, Claiborne, 236
Jackson, Thomas Jonathan ("Stonewall"), 205, 236, 240, 241, 242
Janes (Janes Fighting Ships), 498
Japan, Japanese, ix–x, 353–354, 457
    American curiosity about, 209–210, 211
    and American racism, 353
    and American trade, 209–210, 215
    treaty, 216–218

Japan, Japanese *(cont.)*:
  in China, 371–377, 378, 380, 385,
    401, 404, 473
  imperialism, 218, 410
  naval power, 263, 353, 373, 376,
    386–387, 401–404
  aviation, 375
  Nisei, 268, 395
  and the Pacific, 353–354, 378
  and Perry's gunboats, 210–218, 242,
    262
  postwar development, 447, 499–500,
    518
  Russo-Japanese War, 370, 384
  and the Ryukyus, 212–213
  and shipwrecked American seamen,
    209, 212, 215
  in Siberia, 352–354, 358–359
  and the "white man's burden,"
    212
  in World War I, 353–354
  in World War II, ix–x, xv–xvi, 353,
    377, 378, 382, 384–387, 400–
    408, 411, 429, 431, 449–450,
    472, 478, 497
Jarvis, Midshipman, 109
Jay, John, 126
Jefferson, Thomas, 49, 74, 103, 113–
    114, 115, 130, 133, 136
Jellicoe, Admiral John, 338
Jenkins, Thomas; his ear, 22
Jesup, General Thomas S., 190, 195
Jimenez, President, 322
Joffre, Marshal Joseph, 335
Johnson, Andrew, 279
Johnson, Captain Charles, 484
Johnson, Ed C., 515(37)
Johnson, Lyndon B.; Johnson admin-
    istration, 104, 467, 469, 470–472,
    473–474, 475, 490, 491, 492
Johnson, Nelson, 373
Johnson, Samuel, 63
Johnston, General Albert Sidney, 189,
    239
Johnston, Colonel Joseph E., 236
Jones Act, 305
Jones, John Paul, 78, 84, 85, 101, 102,
    198
Jones, the Reverend Mr., 216
Jones, William, 154
Joseph, Chief, 257

Kaiulani, Princess, 276
Kalakaua, King, 269, 270, 271, 276
Kamehameha I, 268, 274
Kamehameha V, 267, 269
Kanipe, Sergeant Daniel, 254
Kansas, 230
Kansas City *Star,* 285
Kasserine Pass, 389, 390–394
Kattenburg, Paul, 467–468
Kayama Yezaimon, 213–214
Kearney, Commodore Lawrence, 208
Kearny, Colonel S. W., 201–202
Kenesaw Mountain, 245
Kennan, George, 437
Kennedy, Jacqueline, 468
Kennedy, John F.; Kennedy adminis-
    tration, 455–456, 458–461, 466–
    468, 469, 470, 471, 475, 490, 492, 494
Kennedy, John P., 211–212
Kesselring, Field Marshal Alfred, 390
Key, Francis Scott, 157
Khomeini, Ayatollah, 479, 481
Khrushchev, Nikita, 421, 457, 459,
    460–461, 467, 499
Kilroy, Private, 49, 50
Kim Il Sung, 425, 427, 464
Kimball, Admiral W. W., 315
King, Admiral Ernest J., 105, 387,
    388, 405
King Philip; King Philip's War, xi–xii,
    3–10, 14, 97, 187, 248, 258, 497
King William's War, 11
Kinney, William A., 269, 273
Kissinger, Henry, 475
Knox, Colonel Henry, 78
Knox, Philander C., 315, 316
Knyphausen, General William von, 83
Korea, 312–413, 423, 464
  and American seamen, 261
  coal in, 210
  partition of, 424–428, 445, 446–447,
    453, 457
Korean War, x–xi, xvi, 424–447, 448,
    453, 454, 457, 463, 466, 467, 473,
    497, 498, 508, 516(41)
  air, 430, 431, 441, 446
  and China, 424, 435–446, 447, 498
  Inchon landing, 431–432, 433, 444
  lesson of, 447
  and military racial relations, 474
  naval action, 430, 431–432

Korean War *(cont.)*:
  and the press, 433, 463, 477
  Pusan Perimeter, 430–432, 474
  ROK 1st Division, 428, 440
  and Russian diplomacy, 424–428
  24th Division, 428–429
  United Nations participation, x, 429,
    430, 431, 432, 433, 435, 436,
    438, 439, 440, 441–442, 443,
    444–445, 446
  U.S. Marines, 427, 430, 431, 432,
    433, 440, 442, 445

Lafayette, Marquis de, 87–88, 103,
  338
Lafitte brothers, 158–159
La Jonquiere, Admiral, 24
Lake Champlain, battle of, 152
Lake Erie, battle of, 149, 150
Lambert, General, 162
Lameth, Charles de, 90
Langley, Lester D., 325
Lansing, Robert, 320
LaSalle, René Robert de, 11
Lathrop, Captain Thomas, 8
Latimer, Admiral Julian, 365
Latin America, 306–307, 309, 312,
  318, 319, 325, 330, 335, 361, 367,
  380–381, 431, 488, 489–490, 494,
  497
  (*See also* Caribbean Sea; Central
    America; Mexico; South Amer-
    ica)
Laurie, Captain, 65
Lawrence, Captain James, 146–147,
  149
League of Nations, 337, 350, 376, 379,
  413
Lear, Tobias, 166
Lebanon, 478, 479, 483–485, 486
Lee, General Charles, 75
Lee, General Henry (Lighthorse
  Harry), 86, 152
Lee, Richard Henry, 49
Lee, General Robert Edward, 204,
  235, 237, 240–241, 242–246
Lejeune, Major John, 309
LeMay, General Curtis, 400, 406–407,
  472, 515(37)

LeMoyne, Charles, 17
Lemp, Lieutenant Fritz, 379
Lenin, V. I., 354, 356, 358, 364
Lesseps, Ferdinand de, 279, 280, 308
Levis, General, 36
Leyte Gulf, 405
Liberty Tree, 44–45, 49, 52
Libya, xiv, 171, 423, 478, 486–487,
  497
Lidice, 304
Life magazine, 496
Liliuokalani, Queen, 268, 271, 272,
  273–274, 275
Lincoln, Abraham, x, 186, 189, 230,
  232, 234, 235, 237, 238, 239, 240,
  241, 242–243, 244, 246, 335
Lindbergh, Charles A., 380
Linebacker II, 473
Lisle, Admiral, 114, 115
Little Bighorn, 247–257
Little Crow, Chief, 248
Little, Richard Henry, 301
Little Turtle, Chief, 97–99
Livingston, Robert R., 91
Lloyd George, David, 435n
Lodge, Henry Cabot, 282, 298, 331,
  468
Long, John D., 282, 285
Longfellow, Henry Wadsworth:
  Evangeline, 29
Lookout Mountain, 243
Loomis, Sailing Master Jairus, 174–
  175
Lopez, Narciso, 220, 222
Lost Battalion, the, 348
Loudon, Earl of, 30, 31, 32
Louis XIV, 13, 14, 17, 20–21
Louis XVI, 90, 93, 103, 338
Louis XVIII, 152
Louisiana, 33, 36, 39, 123, 136, 158–
  162, 163
Lovless, Colonel Jay B., 429
Lu Han, General, 450
Lubarez, Captain Ibrahim, 117
Luce, Henry, 415
Ludendorff, General Erich von, 346–
  347
Ludlow, Lieutenant Augustus, 146,
  147
Lunalilo, King, 269
Lusitania sinking, xiii, 332, 333

McAlexander, Colonel U. S. G., 345
MacArthur, General Arthur, 294, 301, 303
MacArthur, General Douglas, x, 178, 241, 294, 386, 387, 388, 390, 404, 405, 412, 424, 428–435, 437–447, 463
McCalla, Captain, 293
McClellan, General George Brinton, 235, 236, 237, 238–239, 240, 241
Macdonough, Captain Thomas, 152
McDowell, General Irvin, 236
McFarlane, Sergeant Howard, 301
McFarlane, Robert, 485
MacGregor, Gregor, 175–176
McIntosh, Commodore James M., 227
Mackenzie, William Lyon, 192
McKinley, William; McKinley administration, x, 275, 277, 282, 283, 284, 285–286, 297, 298, 299, 302, 303n, 308, 493
McNab, Colonel, 192
McNamara, Robert, 471, 472–473, 481, 496, 497
McQuillan, General, 392–393
Madero, Francisco, 325–326
Madison, Colonel, 58
Madison, James; Madison administration, 123, 124, 136, 137–138, 140, 150, 153, 154, 156, 160, 165, 167, 174
(*See also* War of 1812)
Madriz, José, 315
Magruder, General, 239
Mahan, Alfred Thayer, 181, 263, 281, 289–290, 369
Maine (ship), 281–286
Malcolm, John, 56
Manassas (Bull Run), 243
  1st, 236
  2nd, 240–241
Manifest Destiny, 186–187, 207–208, 219, 220, 227, 228, 260, 263, 274, 275–276, 277, 279, 283–286, 296, 297, 298, 300
Manly, Captain John, 77
Mao Tse-tung, 414, 435, 441
Marcos, Ferdinand, 465, 500
Marcy, Captain John Q., 235
Marianas, 299, 402–404, 406
Maritime expansion, 181–185

Maritime troubles, early, 103–110, 122, 125–134
(*See also* Barbary pirates; War of 1812)
Marlborough, John Churchill, Duke of, 19
Marne, second battle of, 344–347
Marquesas, 135, 144–145, 163
Marquette, Pierre, 11
Marsh, Captain John, 248
Marshall, General George C., 389, 405, 414, 419, 439
Marshall Plan, 416–417, 419–420, 457
Martin, Graham, 476
Martin, John Bartlow, 491
Martin, Colonel Robert R., 429
Martinez, Bartolome, 363
Masaryk, Thomas G., 357, 358
Mason, Governor (Michigan), 194
Massasoit, Chief, 3
Mather, Cotton, 15
Matthews, Commander E. O., 369
Matthews, Herbert L., 456
Mauldin, Bill, 395
May, John, 299
Mayo, Admiral Henry T., 326
Mead, Colonel James, 483
Meade, General George G., 243–244
Meade, Commander Richard W., 261
Meeker, Nathan, 258
Memoirs of the Hawaiian Revolution (Thurston), 273
Mena, Luís, 316
Meuse-Argonne, 348–349
Mexican War, x, 197, 199–206, 208, 210, 222
Mexico, 219, 220, 222, 223, 224, 325–330, 331–334, 364–365
  Veracruz, xiii, 325, 327–329, 332, 333
Miamis, 96–99
Midgley, Leslie, 456
Midway, 260, 386–387, 402, 403
Military Incompetence (Gabriel), 481–482
Militia forces, limitations of, 9, 15, 46, 80, 97, 158, 190
Mill Springs, 238
Minnesota massacre, 248
Minute Men, 60, 64–66, 76
Missionary Ridge, 243
Modoc War, 250

Moffatt, Thomas, 313, 314
Mohawks, 12–13, 19
Moncada, General, 366
Monitor and *Merrimac,* xv, 197, 238, 262
Monroe Doctrine, xiv, 172, 179–180,
     183, 227, 277, 279, 281, 308, 313,
     380–381, 461, 489, 501
Monroe, James; Monroe administra-
     tion, 130, 131–132, 142, 150, 153,
     154, 155, 159, 160, 178, 179, 182,
     183, 247
Montagu, Admiral, 53
Montcalm, Marquis de, 30–36
Montgomery, General Bernard, 394,
     396
Montgomery, Hugh, 50
Montojo, Admiral, 288
Moore, Captain, 76–77
Moore, Major Robert, 393
Moorehead, Joseph C., 222
Morales, Carlos, 313
Morales, Don Francisco de, 176
Morales, General, 202
Morelos Zaragoza, Governor, 326
Morgan, General Daniel, 82
Morgan, Henry, 309
Moros, 304, 305
Morris, Commodore Richard V., 115,
     116, 117
Morris, Thomas, 319
Morton, "Mush," 400
Moseley, Captain Samuel, 6–7, 8
Motolla, Tony, 456
Munroe, Robert, 65
Murmansk (*see* Archangel)
Murray, Captain Alexander, 115–116
Mussolini, Benito, 379
Muzzey, Isaac, 65
My Lai, 474

Nagumo, Admiral, 387, 403–404
Nakajima Masatake, General, 353
Napoleon, Napoleonic wars, 103, 122,
     123, 127, 136, 138, 150, 152, 154,
     156, 162, 173, 198, 341
Narragansetts, 8–10
Nashville, battle of, 245–246
National Aeronautics and Space
     Administration (NASA), 496–
     497, 498–499, 517(49)

National Intelligencer, 136, 154, 177
National Security Council, 467–468
NATO (*see* North Atlantic Treaty Or-
     ganization)
Naval precedent and tradition, 105–
     107, 116, 288
Naval War College, 370
Nazis, 304, 379, 381, 398
     (*See also* Hitler, Adolf; World War II)
Nebraska, 230
Nelson, Admiral Horatio, 198
New Guinea, 385, 386, 390, 402, 404
New Orleans, battle of, 136, 158–162,
     163
New York *American,* 278, 285
New York *Herald,* 224
New York Times, The, 299–300, 428,
     456, 459, 467, 496
New York *Tribune,* 282
New York *World,* 278, 285
Newcastle, Duke of, 28
Nhu, Ngo Dinh, and wife, 468
Nicaragua, 178, 279–280, 308, 312,
     313–317, 323–324, 331, 362–367,
     387, 430, 445, 490, 493–494, 499
     Sandinistas and Contras, 315, 366–
          367, 493–494
     and Walker's filibustering, 223–228
Nicholls, Colonel Edward, 158, 159,
     173–174
Nicholson, Colonel Francis, 20
Nimitz, Admiral Chester W., 387, 390,
     404, 405, 406
Nitze, Paul, 459
Nivelle, General, 340
Nixon, Richard M., 458, 461, 464,
     473, 474, 475, 497, 516(41)
Normandy landing, 395–399
North Atlantic Treaty Organization
     (NATO), 418, 422–423, 465, 486,
     499
North, Lord Frederick, 47–48, 51, 59,
     68, 84
North and South, 227, 229, 230
     (*See also* Civil War)
Northwest country, territory, 179, 183,
     191, 209, 247, 257–258
     (*See also* Little Bighorn)
Nouel, Archbishop Adolfo A., 319
Nuahiva, 144, 145, 163
Nuclear weapons, 401, 407, 419, 422,
     425, 437, 447

Oaks, Lieutenant, 7
O'Brien, Captain Jeremiah, 77
O'Brien, Richard, 112, 113
Occupation, military:
  Dominican Republic, 322–324, 490–
    492
  Europe, 412, 413, 416–417
  Germany, 409, 410–411, 412, 413,
    419
  Grenada, xiv, 178, 330, 488–489,
    494, 497
  Haiti, 319–322
  Japan, 409, 411–412, 428, 432, 464
  Korea, 412–413, 424
  Lebanon, 478, 479, 483–485, 486
  Philippines, 297–305, 307, 349, 370,
    413
  Russia, 180, 351–360, 364
Office of Strategic Services (OSS),
  450–451
Oglethorpe, James Edward, 22
O'Hara, General, 91
Ohio Company, 25–26
Ohio Valley, 25–28, 30–32, 39, 75,
  96–100
Ohnishi, Admiral Takejiro, 402
Okinawa, 212, 407, 408, 413
Oldham, John, xi
Oliver, Andrew, 45
Omar Pasha, 169
Onecas, 8
Onis, Don Luis de, 177
Opium trade, 183, 368
Opium Wars, 208, 292
Organic Act of the Philippine Islands,
  305
Organization of American States, 490,
  491
Orozco, Pascual, 326
Osceola, 190, 195
OSS (see Office of Strategic Services)
O'Sullivan, John L., 220
Otis, James, 48–49
Ottoman Empire, 94, 95, 114, 164–165
  (See also Barbary pirates)
Ozawa, Admiral, 402

Pacific Ocean, expansion in, 185, 210,
  211, 215, 260–265, 353
  (See also Hawaii; Japan)

Paddon, Captain, 21
Page, Captain, 8
Page, Lieutenant O. A., 146
Page, Walter Hines, 333
Pakenham, General Sir Edward, 158,
  161–162
Panama Canal, 304, 308–309
  Canal Zone, 309
Panay incident, 373–376
Parker, John, 64
Parker, John Palmer, 268
Parker, Jonas, 65
Parkman, Francis, 29–30
Passaconaway, Sachem, 4, 97, 187
Patti, Major A. L. A., 450–451
Patton, General George S., Jr., 393,
  394, 398
Paulding, Commodore Hiram, 225–
  226, 227
Paulding, James K., 198
Pawtuxet raid, 5, 9
"Pax Americana," 427, 430, 447
Peace of Paris, 36, 41
Pearce, James A., 226
Pearl Harbor, ix–x, 261–262, 266, 272,
  378, 382, 384, 403, 417
Pendleton, Colonel Joseph H., 316,
  317
Pequots, extinction of, xi, 2
Peralte, Charlemagne, 323
Percy, Captain W. H., 159
Percy, General Lord, 59, 63, 66, 70
Perry, Commodore Matthew Cal-
  braith, 197, 198, 202, 210–216,
  218, 242
Perry, Commodore Oliver Hazard,
  148–149, 150, 210
Pershing, General John J. (Black
  Jack), 304, 332–333, 334, 337,
  338, 340–341, 343, 345, 347,
  348
Pesqueira, Ignacio, 224
Pétain, Marshal Henri Philippe,
  340
Petersburg, 245, 246
Philip (see King)
Philippine Islands, x, 276, 278, 296,
  306, 307, 311, 327, 372, 500
  and American racism, 300
  and Communists, 465, 471, 500
  independence, 291, 297–305, 307,
    349, 370, 413, 452, 465

Philippine Islands *(cont.)*:
  and Spanish-American War, 288–289, 290, 297–299, 462
  and World War II, 378, 385–386, 405–406, 408
    Philippine Sea, battle of, 402–404
Phillips, Captain, 105, 106–107
Phips, Admiral Sir William, 14, 15, 16–17, 19
Pickering, Timothy, 111
Pickett's charge, 243
Pierce, Franklin, 223, 230
Pierce, Captain Michael, 9
Pigott, General Robert, 72, 73
Pike, General Zebulon M., 148
Pilar, General Gregorio del, 301
Pillow, General, 202, 204, 238
Pinckney, Thomas, 126
Pinckney, William, 130, 131–132
Piracy, suppression of, 182, 183–185
  (*See also* Barbary pirates)
Pitcairn, Major John, 64–66, 72, 73
Pitkin, Frederick, 258
Pitt, William, 32–33, 34, 36
Pittsburg Landing, 239
Platt Amendment, 307–308
Poland, 411
Polk, James Knox, 200, 206, 220, 230
Pomeroy, Seth, 62
Pontiac, 41
Pope, General John, 240–241
Porter, Asahel, 65
Porter, David, 108, 114, 116, 135, 143–145, 163, 182, 239
Porter, Peter Buell, 138
Potsdam Agreement, 411, 420
Powell, William, 516(41)
Power, precision use of, 486–487
Powers, Gary, 457
Preble, Commodore Edward, xiv, 101, 116, 117–120, 164, 486
Prentice, Captain, 7, 8
Prescott, Samuel, 64
Prescott, Colonel William, 71, 73
Preston, Captain, 50
Preston, William, 220
Prevost, General Sir George, 151, 152
Prinz, Lieutenant Heinrich, 348
Privateers, American, 104, 109–110, 115, 165
Pueblo incident, 107
Puerto Rico, 289, 290, 298, 307

Pulaski, Count Casimir, 86
Pulitzer, Joseph, 278, 285
Puller, Colonel Lewis ("Chesty"), 323, 366, 431
Putnam, General Israel, 70, 71, 80

Qaddafi, Muammar, xiv, 171, 486
Quartering Acts, 47, 57
Quebec, siege of, 33–36
Quinnapin, Chief, 10
Quitman, General J. A., 205–206

Racial violence, U. S. Army, 300, 474–475
Rais Hammida, Admiral, 167–168, 169
Randon, John, 74
Ransom, Colonel, 205
Ratford (Wilson), seaman, 127, 129
Reagan, Ronald; Reagan administration, xiv, 465, 482, 485, 486, 488, 493–494, 500
Red Cloud, Chief, 249
Red River War, 250
Reed and Daugherty, 217–218
Reid, Commodore George, 185
Reid, Whitelaw, 282
Reilly, Captain, 295
Reno, Major Marcus, 251, 252–256
Reston, James, 459, 467
Revere, Paul, 60, 64
Revolutionary War, xii, xv, 1–2, 38–39, 64–92, 140, 152, 157, 163, 197
  American army established, 69–70, 75–76
  American intelligence service, 83
  English viciousness, 68, 69, 73, 85, 87
  and France, 69, 84–86, 88–91, 103
  Hessians, 79, 80–81, 82
  and Indians, 82, 85, 87
  Lexington and Concord, 64–67, 68, 70, 73, 74, 76
  naval action, 76–78, 84–85
  New Jersey, 80–81, 85
  New York, 79–80, 81–83, 88
  Philadelphia, 83–84
  in the South, 86–91, 93

Revolutionary War *(cont.)*:
  and Spain, 85
  (*See also* entries for specific battles
    and campaigns)
Reynolds, Governor (Illinois), 189
Reynolds, Captain William, 260
Rhee, Syngman, 427, 428, 433, 434,
  436, 516(41)
Richardson, Colonel, 21
Richthofen, Baron, 346
Rickard, W. H., 273
Rickenbacker, Captain Eddie, 346
Ridgway, General Matthew, 366, 445,
  446, 454
Roberts, Captain, 206
Robinson, John (customs commis-
  sioner), 48–49
Robinson, John, 66
Rochambeau, Count, 88
Rockingham, Earl of, 45, 62
Rodgers, Commodore John, 108, 116,
  117–118, 132–133, 141, 260–261
Rogers' Rangers, 31
Romero, Humberto, 492
Rommel, Field Marshal Erwin, 386,
  390
Roosevelt, Franklin D., ix, 324, 371,
  376, 378, 381, 382, 383, 385, 402,
  404–405, 410, 411, 451
Roosevelt, Theodore, 135, 282, 283,
  285, 288, 331
  president, 297, 303, 304, 306, 308,
    309, 310, 311, 353, 362
    Rough Rider (San Juan Hill), 286,
      290
Ross, Harold, 337
Ross, General Robert, 156, 158
Rostow, Walt, 468
Rotch, Quaker, 53–54
Rouville, Hertel de, 18
Royal Auvergne Regiment, 90
Rundstedt, General Karl von, 398
Rusk, Dean, 439
Russell, Richard B., 453, 464
Russia:
  diplomacy after World War II, 409,
    410–412, 413, 415, 416, 419–
    420, 424 425, 488, 497, 499–
    500
    Cuba, 457–461, 488, 494
    Germany; Berlin, 418–422
    Korea, 424–428, 457

Russia *(cont.)*:
  occupation of during revolution,
    180, 351–360, 364
    and Czechoslovaks, 354–355, 356,
      357–358
  World War II, 387, 395, 398–399,
    407, 411
Russo-Japanese War, 370, 384
Ryukyu Islands, 212–213, 407, 408, 413

Sacasa, Juan B., 363, 364, 365, 366
Sadat, Anwar, 478
St. Clair, Arthur, 96, 97–98
St. Laurent, Captain, 106
Saint-Mihiel, 340, 341, 347
Saint-Pierre, Legardeur, 27
Saipan, 388, 404, 406
Salmon, Captain Norvell, 228
Saltonstall, Captain Dudley, 78
Samoa, 261, 263–265
Sampson, Commodore William T.,
  289, 290
Sandino, Augusto C.; Sandinistas,
  315, 366–367, 493–494
Sanford, Captain Peleg, 10
San Juan Hill, 286, 290
Santa Anna, Antonio Lopez de, 199,
  201, 202–203, 205
Santana Carrasco, Captain Olgo M.,
  490
Santos Zelaya, José, 313–316
Saratoga, 82–83
Satsuma, 212
Sausaman, John, 5
Savage, Ensign, 7
Savage, Captain Ephraim, 16
Savage, Major Thomas, 7–8
Schley, Commander Winfield S., 280,
  289–290
Schuyler, Peter, 17
Schuyler, General Philip, 81, 82
Scott, General Charles, 99
Scott, General Winfield, 151, 186, 189,
  190, 194, 195, 201, 202, 203–204,
  206, 210, 220, 233, 234, 237
Seamen, American, protection of, 183,
  208, 209, 212, 215
  (*See also* Impressment)
SEATO (*see* Southeast Asia Treaty
  Organization)

Secession (*see* Civil War)
Segismundo, Cecilio, 302
Seicheprey, 343
Seminoles; Seminole War, 172–178, 179, 181, 186, 188, 189–190, 195–196
Sepoy Rebellion, 31
Seven Days' Battle, 240
Seven Pikes, 240
Seven Years War, 29
Seward, William Henry, 226, 246, 279
Seymour, Admiral, 293
Sharp, Admiral Ulysses Grant, Jr., 471
Sharpsburg, 241
Shaw, Captain John, 171
Shawnee, 96, 99, 124–125
Sheridan, General Philip Henry, 245, 250, 256–257, 257–258
Sherman, Admiral Forrest, 439
Sherman, John, 275
Sherman tanks, 392
Sherman, General William Tecumseh, xiii, 243, 244, 245, 248–249, 250, 257, 258
Shiloh, 239
Shirley, William, 23–24, 30
Short, Captain, 14
Shubrick, Lieutenant John Templar, 170
Shufeldt, Commodore R. W., 261
Shultz, George, 485
Siberia, occupation of, 351, 352, 354, 357–359, 360
Sibley, Colonel Henry, 248
Sicily, invasion of, 394–395, 396
Siebold, Dr., 211, 214
Sigsbee, Captain, 284–285
Sioux, 248, 249, 251–257, 259
Sireuil, Captain, 90
Sitting Bull, 251, 257
Sixth Pan-American Congress, 366–367
Skipwith, Fulwar, 123
Slavery, slaves, 123, 229, 230
    and Seminoles, 173n, 174–175, 176, 182, 188, 189–190, 195–196
    slave trade, 182, 183, 191, 229, 368
    spread of, 197, 199, 220, 222, 228, 229, 230
Sloat, Commodore, 201
Smith, Captain, 134

Smith, Colonel, 63, 64, 70
Smith, Captain J. Andrew, 345
Smith, General C. F., 205–206
Smith, General Jacob, 304
Smith, Julian, 366
Smith, Marcia, 517(49)
Smith, General Oliver, 432
Smith, General Samuel, 156
Smith, William O., 270
Smyth, General Alexander, 140
Soissons, 346
Solomon Islands, 385–386, 390, 402, 403
Solorzano, Carlos, 363
Somers, Captain Richard, 120
Somoza, Dictator, 490
Sons of Liberty, 44–45, 52
Sorensen, Theodore C., 461
Sous, Captain Mahomet, 114
South (*see* North and South; Slavery)
South America, 183, 219
    rebellion against Spain, 173, 175–176, 219
South Pacific, 135, 144–145, 163, 260–265
Southeast Asia Collective Defense Treaty, 471
Southeast Asia Treaty Organization (SEATO), 418, 465–466
Southwest, expansion in, 197, 249
    Indian fighting, 250, 258
    (*See also* Mexican War)
Space Dealers, The (Hoyt), 497
Space effort, 496–501
Spanish in America, 2, 23, 39, 69, 172, 173
    and Revolutionary War, 85
    and southern American colonies, 22
    (*See also* Cuba; Florida; Latin America)
Spanish-American War, x, 277–290, 291, 297–299, 307, 367, 370, 416, 474
    and the press, 462
Spanish Civil War, 379, 380
Spotsylvania Courthouse, 244
Spreckels, Claus, 274
Stalin, Joseph, 364, 395, 410, 457
Stamp Act, 44–46, 56
Standard Oil Company, 296, 373–374, 375
Stanford, Leland, 353

"Star-Spangled Banner, The," 157
Stark, General John, 70, 71, 73, 82
Stars and Stripes, 337, 515(39)
Steamboats, steamships, 197, 198, 200, 208, 209, 210, 211, 260, 262
 coaling stations, 208, 210, 211, 212, 215, 260–261, 266, 276, 290
 and internal explosions, 284
Steinhart, Frank, 306
Stephens, Alexander, 246
Sterrett, Captain, 114
Stevens, John L., 266, 272–273, 274, 285
Stevenson, Adlai, 459
Stilwell, General Joseph, 414
Stimson, Henry L., 318, 319, 331, 365–366, 367
Stockton, Commodore, 201–202
Stoddart, Benjamin, 104
Stone, General Charles P., 237
Streeter, Edward, 339
Stuart, General James Ewell Brown (Jeb), 240
Submarine warfare (*see* World War I; World War II)
Sugar Act, 41–43, 44
Sullivan, James, 319
Sullivan, General John, 83
Sumatran pirates, 183–185
Sun Tzu, General, 473, 499
Sun Yat-sen, 371

Taft, William Howard, 291, 302, 303, 311, 315, 326
Taiwan, 415, 437–438, 443, 445, 464
Talcott, Major, 10
Taylor, General Maxwell D., 460, 468
Taylor-Rostow group, 468
Taylor, Zachary, 189, 195–196, 199, 200–201, 220, 230
Tea tax, 48, 51–54
Tecumseh, 99, 124–125, 140, 149, 150, 151, 258
Television journalism, ills of, 463, 470, 476
Tenskwatawa, 124, 125
Terrorism, 423, 478–487
 (*See also* Barbary Wars)

Terry, General, 251–252, 255–256, 257
Texas, 123, 198–199, 209, 220
 in the Civil War, 233
 (*See also* Mexican War)
Texas Rangers, 222
Theodore, Joseph, 320
Tho, Le Duc, 475
Thomas, General George H., 238, 243, 246
Thomas, General Philemon, 123
Thompson, Jacob, 233
Thompson, General Wiley, 190
Thurston, Lorrin, 269–274, 275
Ticonderoga, 31–33, 70, 76, 78, 81
Tiger tanks, 391–392
Tipitapa Accord, 366
Tippecanoe, battle of, 122, 124–125
Tito, Marshal, 413, 444
Toda Idzunokami, 214–215
Tojo, General Hideki, 385, 388, 404
Tonkin Gulf, 104, 471
Tonkin Resolution, 471
Toucey, Isaac, 227
Toussaint l'Ouverture, 309, 318, 321
Townshend Acts, 46–48, 51
Townshend, Charles, 45
Tracy, B. F., 272
Treaty of Fort Jackson, 173
Treaty of Ghent, 136, 150, 163, 165
Treaty of Paris, 95–96, 99, 299
Treaty of Versailles, 337
Trent, William, 26, 27
Tribuna, La (Managua), 323–324
Tripoli, 118–121, 169, 170–171, 206, 486, 487
Trist, Nicholas P., 203–204
Trotsky, Leon, 355, 357, 364
Trujillo, Rafael, 490
Truman, Harry S.; Truman administration, x–xi, 178, 241, 408, 436, 438, 439, 440, 444, 445–446, 447, 451, 452, 463, 469
 Truman Doctrine, 416, 453, 457
Truxton, Commodore Thomas, 107–108, 109
Tucker, S. G., 269
Tunis, 170, 171
Tunisia, 390–394, 395, 396
Twiggs, Major, 176, 202
Tyler, John, 230

U-Boats (*see* Submarine warfare)
Uncas, Chief, 8, 9
United Fruit Company, 307
United Nations, 379n, 412, 414, 418,
    436–437, 439, 443, 445, 447, 456,
    458, 471, 490, 491, 501
    (*See also* Korean War)
United Press, 448–449, 451, 462
U.S. Army, foundation of, 95
U.S. Asiatic Fleet, 370, 376, 385
U.S. Committee on Public Informa-
    tion, 355
U.S. Marines, 325, 327, 489
    China, 208, 292, 294, 296, 327, 368,
        369, 414
    Corps established, 104
    Cuba, 311
    Dominican Republic, 319, 322–323,
        490–491
    Grenada, 494
    Guadalcanal, 387–388
    Guam, 299
    Haiti, 320, 321–322, 323–324
    Korea, 427, 430, 431, 432–433, 440,
        442, 445
    Lebanon, 483–485
    Mexico, 205, 206
    Nicaragua, 314–315, 316–317, 323–
        324, 362, 363, 365, 366, 367,
        430, 431
    Panama, 308–309
    Tripoli, 206
    Vietnam, 475
    World War I, 341, 344, 350, 356,
        359
U.S. Navy around the world, 181,
    183–185, 207–208, 209, 260–265,
    266, 280, 297, 310, 313, 319, 320–
    321, 325, 361, 414, 415, 486, 491
    Great White Fleet, 353
    (*See also* Gunboat diplomacy; Ha-
        waii; Spanish-American War)
U.S. Navy, founding of, 100–105
U-2 spy mission, 457, 460

Van Buren, Martin, 184, 194–195,
    198, 230
Vandenburg, General Hoyt, 429–430
Vanderbilt, Cornelius, 223, 308

Van Rensselaer, General Stephen,
    139, 140
Van Rensselaer, Rensselaer, 192, 194
Varnum, Lieutenant, 252
Vaudreuil, Marquis de, 34, 35, 36
Vega, General, 202
Veracruz Expedition (1914), xiii, 325,
    327–329, 332, 333
Verdun, 340, 344, 347, 348–349
Verdun Belle, 337
Vetch, Samuel, 19, 20
Vicksburg, 242, 243
Victoria Regina, 207
Vietcong, 472, 473
Viet Minh, 449–450, 453, 466, 467,
    468
Vietnam:
    and Chinese Nationalists, 449
    and French, 450–454, 465–466
Vietnam war, ix, xvi, 104, 315, 384,
    453–454, 462, 463–477, 482–483,
    493, 494, 497, 499
    air, 464, 472–473, 474, 475
    and American deserters, 474
    and Cambodia, 474
    lessons of, 490, 499, 500
    My Lai, 474
    naval action, 471
    and news media, 462, 463, 470, 474,
        476–477, 489
    and racial violence, 474–475
    social impact in America, 476–477
    Tet offensive, 473
    weapons, 475
Vilbrun, General (*see* Guillaume Sam)
Villa, Pancho, 326, 330, 332–333
Virginius incident, 278
Vladivostok, 352, 353, 354–355, 358
Volunteer army and incompetence,
    480–483, 496, 500

Wadsworth, Lieutenant Henry, 120
Waldersee, Count, 295
Walker, Admiral Sir Hovendon, 21–22
Walker, General Walton, 430–432,
    433, 440
Walker, William, xiii, 222–228, 313
Waller, Colonel W. T., 322
Wampanoags (*see* King Philip's War)

War of 1812, 135–163, 164, 165, 166,
    170, 172, 173, 174, 181, 182, 192,
    203, 239, 487
  Baltimore and Washington, 153–157
  and Canada, 139–140, 148, 149–152,
    153, 162, 163
  Congressional feeling, 137–138
  economic factors, 157–158, 162, 165
  and merchants and traders, 142–143
  naval strength and battles, xv, 135,
    140–148, 152–155, 162, 163
    Great Lakes, 148–149, 150, 151,
      155, 163, 198, 210
    steamship, 198
  and New England, 135–136, 138,
    143, 150, 157
  New Orleans, 136, 158–162, 163
War of Jenkins' Ear, 22
War of the League of Augsburg, 11
Ward, General Artemus, 62, 69, 71,
    75
Ward, General Orlando, 391
Warren, Joseph, 70, 71, 73, 75
Warrington, Commodore, 182
Warsaw Pact, 418, 422
Washington, George, 49, 61, 212–213,
    217, 335, 380
  general, 75, 76, 77, 78, 79–81, 82,
    83–84, 86, 87, 88–91, 93, 152
  and Ohio Valley, 26–28, 75
  president, 94, 97–98, 102, 103, 136,
    165
  surveyor, 25, 26, 75
Washington, Lawrence, 25, 26
Waters, Colonel John, 392, 393
Wayne, General Anthony (Mad An-
    thony), 83, 98–100
Webster-Ashburton Treaty, 195
Webster, Daniel, 211, 230
Wedemeyer, General Albert C., 414–
    415
Weinberger, Caspar, 485
Welles, Sumner, 362
Wellington, Arthur Wellesley, Duke
    of, 139, 150, 155, 158
Wells, William, 99
West, expansion in, 229, 232, 247
    (See also Northwest; Southwest)
West Point, 86, 156, 237, 451
Westmoreland, General William C.,
    470–471, 499

Whaling business, 183, 207–208, 209,
    215, 217–218, 261
Wheeler, Burton K., 380
Whipple, Captain Abraham, 78
"White man's burden," the, 291, 310
White Oak Swamp, 240
White, Sailing Master, 147
Whitney, William C., 263
Whittlesay, Major Charles, 348
Wild Cat, 195–196
Wilderness, the, 242, 244
Wilhelm I, Kaiser, 261, 281
Wilkes, Lieutenant Charles, 185
Wilkinson, General James, 149, 151
William (see King William's War)
Williams, John, 18
Wilson, Henry Lane, 326
Wilson, Woodrow; Wilson administra-
    tion, xiii, 319, 322, 323, 325, 326,
    327, 328, 330, 331, 332, 333–335,
    339, 350, 351, 354, 355, 356, 358–
    359, 360, 362, 379
Winchester, battle of, 240, 242
Winder, General William H., 153–
    154, 155, 156
Winslow, Colonel John, 29
Winthrop, Major Theodore, 236
Wolfe, General James, 33, 34–36
Wood, General, 201
Wood, General Leonard, 306, 331
Wool, General John E., 223
Wooldridge, Captain, 345
Woollcott, Alexander, 337
World War I, xiii, xv, 180, 323, 329,
    330–350, 351, 353, 379, 410, 416,
    435n, 446, 447, 462, 474, 487
  air, 338, 346
  casualties, 336
  gas, 340, 343, 345
  and food for the Allies, 337–338
  naval action, 331, 338
    submarines, xiii, xv, 332, 333,
      334, 335, 337–338
  and occupation of Russia, 351–360,
    364
  and the press, 462
  trenches, trench warfare, 340, 348
  weapons, 340, 343
  (See also entries for specific battles
    and campaigns)
World War II, ix, xv, 172, 180, 208,

World War II *(cont.)*:
    284, 296, 304, 337, 352, 377, 378–
    408, 409, 411, 412, 415–416, 417,
    422, 427, 428, 430, 437, 441, 447,
    457, 474, 487, 489
  air, xv–xvi, 385, 386, 389, 392, 402–
    404, 406–407
    kamikaze, 404, 405, 407
  artillery, 389, 392
  and atrocities, 400–401, 406–407, 472
  China, 380, 385, 401, 404, 413, 450
  Europe, 384, 386, 389, 394–399,
    404, 407–408
  and Japan *(see* Japan)
  lend-lease, 381, 383
  naval action, 378, 381–382, 385,
    386–387, 396, 401–404, 405–406
    submarines, xv, 379, 381–382,
      384, 389, 396, 400, 401, 463,
      479
  and Nisei, 395
  North Africa, 384, 386, 387, 389,
    390–394, 395, 396
  Pacific, 384–388, 390, 400–408, 411,
    450, 497
  and the press, 462–463
  (See also entries for specific battles
    and campaigns)

Worth, General William Jenkins, 204,
    206, 220
Wounded Knee massacre, ix, 258
Wyden, Peter, 461

Yale University Naval Aviation Unit,
    338
Yalta Agreement, 410–411, 412, 418,
    424, 436, 450
Yamamoto, Admiral Isoroku, 373,
    375, 386–387, 402
Yangtze, opening of, 369–377
Yank magazine, 395
Yankee Doodle, 75–76
Yarnell, Admiral Henry, 376–377
Yhuryev, Comrade, 356
York, Sergeant Alvin, 349
Yorktown, 88–91, 239
Young, Lieutenant Bennett H., 245

Zamora, Mario, 493
Zapata, Emiliano, 326
Zelaya *(see* Santos Zelaya)
Zimmermann telegram, 330, 333

Hoyt, Edwin Palmer.
  America's wars and military
excursions / Edwin P. Hoyt. - New York

DATE DUE

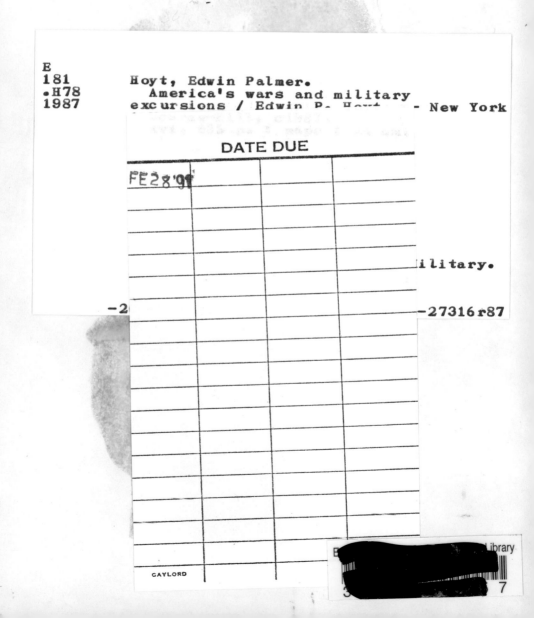

DATE DUE		
FE 28 '91		
GAYLORD		

military.

-2   -27316 r87